OUR GLORIOUS CENTURY

READER'S DIGEST

OUR GLORIOUS CENTURY

GRAEME DECARIE, Ph.D.
CONSULTANT

Reader's Digest

THE READER'S DIGEST ASSOCIATION, INC.   MONTREAL / PLEASANTVILLE, NEW YORK

OUR GLORIOUS CENTURY

CANADIAN STAFF

Editorial

Editors
Sandy Shepherd
Deirdre Gilbert

Copy Editors
Joseph Marchetti
Gilles Humbert

Editorial Assistant
Elizabeth Eastman

Research

Research Supervisor
Wadad Bashour

Picture Researcher
Rachel Irwin

Art

Art Supervisor
John McGuffie

Designer
Andrée Payette

Production

Production Manager
Holger Lorenzen

Production Coordinator
Susan Wong

CANADIAN CONTRIBUTORS

Principal Consultant
Graeme Decarie, Ph.D.
Professor of History,
Concordia University

Researchers
Enza Micheletti
Caroline Solomon

Indexer
Judy Yelon

Graphics
Jacques Perrault
Pierre Rousseau

U.S. STAFF

Editorial

Editor
Edmund H. Harvey, Jr.

Senior Editor
David G. Rattray

Senior Associate Editors
Kathryn Bonomi
Thomas A. Ranieri

Associate Editor
Audrey Peterson

Art

Group Art Editor
Joel Musler

Project Art Editor
Sandra Berinstein

Senior Art Associate
Nancy Mace

Art Associate
Bruce R. McKillip

Research

Research Editors
Sandra Streepey
Susan Biederman

Research Associate
Kathleen Derzipilski

Research Librarian
Nettie Seaberry

The credits and acknowledgments that appear on pages 502–504 are hereby made a part of this copyright page.

Canadian Cataloguing in Publication Data
Main entry under title:
Our glorious century
   Includes index.
   ISBN 0-88850-525-6
   1. Canada — History — 20th century. 2. Canada — Civilization — 20th century. 3. United States — History — 20th century.
   4. United States — Civilization — 20th century.
   I. Reader's Digest Association (Canada).

E741.096 1996   973.92   C95-900928-0

Printed in Canada, by Imprimeries Transcontinental Inc.
First Printing, March 1996

U.S. CONTRIBUTORS

Editor-Writers
Bryce Walker (Chief)
John L. Cobbs
Anne Moffat
George Walsh
Henry Wiencek

Writers
Robert Brown
Terry Brown
Tom Callahan
Rita Christopher
Justin Cronin
Joseph Durso
Martha Fay
Thomas J. Fleming
Marjorie Flory
Annette Foglino
Mark Gasper
Kevin Gillespie
Roger E. Hernandez
Eileen Hughes
William C. Nowels
Josh Ozersky
Donald Pfarrer
Karla K. Powell
Curtis W. Prendergast
Susan Harrington Preston
Carl Proujan
Thomas L. Robinson
Gerry Schremp
Charles A. Silliman
Jozefa Stuart
Evelyn Toynton
Daniel Weiss

Designers
Richard Boddy
Ed Jacobus (Maps)
Design Five (Charts)
Steve Karp
    (Computer Graphics)

Copy Editor
Joan Wilkinson

Researchers
Mary Hart (Chief)
Pamela Kladzyk
Willard Lubka
Marlene McCampbell
Joan Walsh

Picture Researchers
Mary Leverty (Chief)
Mary Burns
Romy Charlesworth
Richard Fox
Sue Israel
Jerry Kearns
Sybille Millard
Sabra Moore
Marion Paone
Richard Seidel
Yvonne Silver

Indexer
Sydney Wolfe Cohen

U.S. CONSULTANTS

Principal Consultants
Col. John R. Elting
    U. S. Army (Retired)
Irwin Unger, Ph.D.
    Professor of American History, New York University

Consultants
Alan C. Aimone
    Assistant Librarian for Special Collections, U.S. Military Academy Library
Claudia Anderson
    Senior Archivist, Lyndon Baines Johnson Library
Frank Aucella
    Assistant Director, Woodrow Wilson House, A Museum Property of the National Trust for Historic Preservation
David Bafumo
    Researcher, National Archives
Paul Boyer
    Merle Curtis Professor of History, University of Wisconsin – Madison
Bruce Conforth, Ph.D.
    Curator, Rock and Roll Hall of Fame and Museum
Vincent Demma
    Historian, U. S. Army Center of Military History
Amy Devone
    Curator, Sagamore Hill National Historic Site
John A. Gable, Ph.D.
    Executive Director, Theodore Roosevelt Association
Ron Grantz
    Curator, National Automotive History Collection of the Detroit Public Library
Henry Guzda
    Industrial Relations Specialist, U.S. Department of Labor
Elaine Tyler May
    Professor of American Studies and History, University of Minnesota
J. Kenneth McDonald
    Chief Historian, Central Intelligence Agency
Valerie Neal
    Space History Curator, National Air and Space Museum
Mary Nolan
    Professor of History, New York University
Sam Tanenhaus
    Author and Editor
Bernard Weisberger
    Historian
Warren W. Wrenn
    Supervisory Park Ranger, Wright Brothers National Monument

Foreword

YOU'RE AN AMERICAN, AREN'T YOU?" It's a question that sets the travelling Canadian's teeth on edge. "No," is the answer. No, Canadians are not Americans. The difference shows most powerfully in the two best-known symbols of the pioneer days in the west of each country. For the American, it's the cowboy with the only law he knows slung at his side in a holster. For the Canadian, it's the mountie, the ultimate symbol of law and order who went out ahead of settlement. Canadians and Americans are very different, and yet...

Mary Pickford, the actress Americans called "America's Sweetheart," was really a Canadian. For generations of Americans, the imagined face of Abraham Lincoln was that of another Canadian film star, Raymond Massey. To this day, there are U.S. cities whose names betray the Canadian origins of their founders, cities with French names like Detroit and Baton Rouge. Nor was the traffic one way. Canada's greatest engineering accomplishment of the nineteenth century, the Canadian Pacific Railway, was directed by William Cornelius Van Horne — of Illinois. Canada's minister of munitions and supply in World War II was Clarence Decatur Howe — of Massachusetts. And, it might be added, one of the great engineering triumphs of the postwar world, the St. Lawrence Seaway, was built by Canadians and Americans together.

In this century we have fought as allies in three major wars, and as allies in all but name through virtually every other conflict and period of tension. Both nations, in much the same way and at the same times, have also suffered the prosperity and pain of industrialization — the dust bowl years and the Great Depression of the 1930's, and the heady prosperity of the 1950's, 1960's, and 1980's. Our closeness was perhaps best illustrated in 1979, when the U.S. Embassy in Tehran was stormed, and the Canadian ambassador and his wife hid and then spirited six Americans to safety.

Our Glorious Century is a look at the twentieth century as it was shared by two nations, perhaps in more ways than either has realized. For a century, Canadians and Americans have driven the same cars, watched the same movies, and rejoiced in the same fads. If, as some say, Canadians have been more moderate in their politics, they have still reflected the swings from right to left and back again that have marked the United States, and they have done so almost in time. Growing aware of the power of advertising and the media in the 1950's and 1960's, people of both nations turned to Herbert Marshall McLuhan for understanding: that he was born in Edmonton and taught at the University of Toronto seemed irrelevant.

There are times when we eye each other across our border suspiciously — for example, when U.S. business reaches out for Canadian resources or when Canada reacts viscerally against American culture. But, we might remember our common histories and reflect, even as we criticize each other, that the fruit has not fallen far from our common tree.

CONTENTS

Chapter 1 ∻ *1900–1913*

Dawn of the 20ᵗʰ Century

**Immigrants bound for Canada
pp. 12–13**

Chapter 2 ✠ *1914–1919*

WORLD WAR I: THE WAR TO END ALL WARS

**Infantry in no-man's-land
pp. 62–63**

Chapter 3 ◆ *1919–1929*

THE UNRULY DECADE

Jazz and the blues
pp. 100–101

Chapter 4 ● *1930–1939*

The Down-and-Up 1930's

Surviving the bad times
pp. 146–147

Chapter 5 ★ 1939–1945

WORLD WAR II: HOME FRONT & BATTLEFIELD

D-Day in Europe
pp. 188–189

Chapter 6 ● 1945–1959

POSTWAR CHALLENGE AND CHANGE

Peace, promise, and peril
pp. 244–245

Chapter 7 ❧ 1960–1969

The Clamorous 1960's

Dreamers and marchers
pp. 302–303

Chapter 8 ♥ 1970–1979

THE SEESAW 1970's

The United States turns 200
pp. 352–353

Chapter 9 ☯ *1980–1990's*

THE CLOSING YEARS

Prelude to 2001
pp. 386-387

FACTS AT YOUR FINGERTIPS

Chapter 1

Dawn of the 20th Century

Bristling with energy fuelled by natural resources and new industries, Canada and the United States vault onto the world stage, led by a host of dreamers, explorers, crusaders, inventors, and tycoons.

Immigrants from Russia crowd the deck of the S.S. Lake Champlain in 1900, bound for Quebec City, then the Manitoban prairies, and a new life.

ROARING INTO A NEW ERA

North Americans launched into the 20th century confident, vigorous and eager

to assert themselves. Prosperous at home, they stood poised in the wings to play

a prominent role in world affairs.

"The twentieth century belongs to Canada," exulted Canadian Prime Minister Sir Wilfrid Laurier. In an editorial of December 31, 1899, *The New York Times* was equally confident. "We step upon the threshold of 1900 . . . facing a still brighter dawn for human civilization." The outlook shone for people right across North America. Factories were humming and incomes were on the rise. Remarkable new inventions — the automobile, the electric light bulb, the telephone, to name just three — were transforming the way people lived. "Laws are becoming more just, rulers humane," declared a pastor; "music is becoming sweeter and books wiser." It seemed obvious to everyone.

▲ *Prosperous and secure, a family of 1900 poses for a photograph in its Sunday best.*

Already the United States was the world's largest industrial power. After a severe economic slump in the early 1890's, its annual output of goods and services was pushing toward a record $19 billion. The nation had nearly half the world's railway mileage, shipped half its freight, pumped half its oil, forged a third of its steel, and mined a third of its gold. In just 30 years the number of Americans had doubled and now stood at 76 million. Canada, beginning the century at 5 million, would spurt ahead to almost 7.5 million within a decade as industrial development, railway building and the promise of wheat exports attracted immigrants.

Many aspects of the old century lingered on, to be sure. A majority of people lived in rural communities and small towns. The largest occupation was farming. Church attendance was high — half the population attended church at least once each Sunday. Almost nobody got

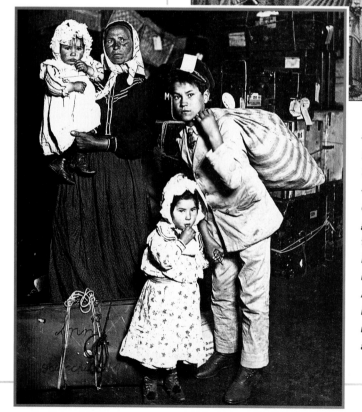

◄ *Newcomers to the United States from Italy — weary, apprehensive, determined to make good — move through the reception area at Ellis Island. By 1910 nearly one out of seven Americans was foreign-born. In Canada the number was even higher, at more than one in five.*

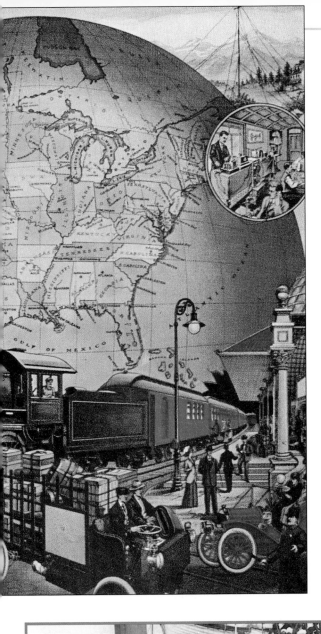

◄
A 1909 railway poster celebrates progress and material wealth. The map of the U.S. shows 48 states. Oklahoma, the newest state, was added in 1907.

▼ *By 1900 most of Canada's Indians had been relocated on reserves — mostly for the benefit of the new white settlers. The largest reserve was inhabited by the Blood Indians, in Alberta.*

divorced. Many used a horse and buggy for transportation. Sugar cost 4 cents a pound, corned beef 8 cents, and $2.50 bought a handsome pair of men's shoes. The term *radio* did not exist in 1900, nor did *vacuum cleaner* or *electric toaster*. Hollywood was still an orange grove. There was not a single traffic light, and no one had to pay an income tax.

Massive changes were under way, however. The great American frontier — the vast stretch of untamed land that ever since colonial days had been a source of both lurking dread and unbounded opportunity — had largely disappeared. The Canadian West, too, rich in farming potential and recently opened by railway, swarmed with settlers drawn from eastern Canada, from Europe, and even from the United States. Gold, discovered in Canada's Yukon just before the close of the century, added a touch of romance and adventure to the opening of the new century.

For all their agricultural wealth and promise, both Canada and the United States were becoming increasingly

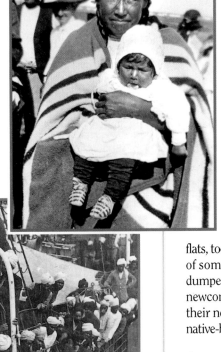

urbanized. New York, Chicago, and Philadelphia had reached a population of a million or more. In Canada, Montreal was nearing a half million. Southern farmers, many of them Blacks, moved to northern cities in the United States in search of jobs. In Canada, the drift was from the Maritimes as well as from rural Quebec and Ontario. At the same time, a massive influx of foreign immigrants arrived, mostly from Europe.

More than 10 million newcomers arrived in North America between 1900 and 1910, landing with their bundled belongings, foreign garb and hopeful, bewildered faces. Most came from southern or eastern Europe — Italy, Russia's western regions, the multiethnic lands of the Austro-Hungarian Empire — and very few spoke English. Many were Jewish or Eastern Orthodox, at a time when almost all North Americans were Protestant or Roman Catholic. The immigrants braved prairie sod-busting or crowded into cold-water flats, took what work they could find, and endured the scorn of some native-born. ("The scum of creation has been dumped on us," lamented one such irate citizen.) Yet the newcomers hung on, caught up in the golden promise of their new homelands, and as exuberantly confident as the native-born that things would surely get better.

◄
Sikhs on board the Komataga Maru *arrived in Vancouver in May 1914, to find that Canada's immigration policy at the time was distinctly racist. They were refused entry, and were held on the ship for two months until ordered to turn back.*

NORTH AMERICA FLEXES ITS MUSCLES

A deadly explosion in Havana Harbour, Cuba, and a British invasion of tiny republics on the African continent drew Canadians as well as Americans into imperial wars, and moved them both onto the world stage for the first time.

The 7,112-tonne U.S.S. *Maine,* the navy's newest battleship, rode quietly at anchor in Havana, Cuba, on February 15, 1898, its white hull gleaming in the tropical night. It had come to pay a courtesy call on the island's Spanish colonial government. Suddenly a deafening explosion tore through the vessel. The hull lifted, split into two sections, and then settled to the bottom; 250 U.S. sailors lost their lives. The cause of the blast was never fully determined, but most Americans took a quick guess. "Spanish Treachery," screamed William Randolph Hearst's New York *Journal,* and the country agreed.

Trouble with Spain had been brewing for more than a decade. A guerrilla insurrection was devastating Cuba, and some $50 million of U.S. investment in Cuban sugar and tobacco lay at peril. Press reports of atrocities by Spanish soldiers further inflamed public opinion. And now this. President William McKinley, elected to office in 1896, had promised "no jingo nonsense," such as sending U.S. troops overseas. His position quickly changed. "Remember the *Maine* and the hell with Spain!" became the national battle cry, and on April 25 the Congress declared war.

The first guns sounded halfway round the world in the Spanish-controlled Philippines. A naval task force under Commodore George Dewey steamed into Manila Bay on May 1, swung broadside, and trained its formidable big guns on the local Spanish squadron. "You may fire when ready, Gridley," Dewey told the commander of his flagship. The Spanish fleet, undergunned and badly trained, stood little chance; all 10 ships were captured or destroyed. Total U.S. casualties: eight men wounded.

In Cuba a U.S. invasion force arrived from Tampa with orders to knock out the harbor defences guarding Santiago, a seaport on

A gruesome lithograph (top, left) of the Maine *disaster helped fuel the outcry for war with Spain.*

▼ *The U.S. Navy's mighty Asiatic Squadron — four cruisers and two gunboats led by Commodore George Dewey (inset) — sweeps toward a decisive victory at the Battle of Manila Bay.*

U.S. marines raise the Stars and Stripes on Cuban soil near Santiago (below). In the Philippines (right), U.S. troops fought on through 1902 to subdue a revolt by local guerrillas.

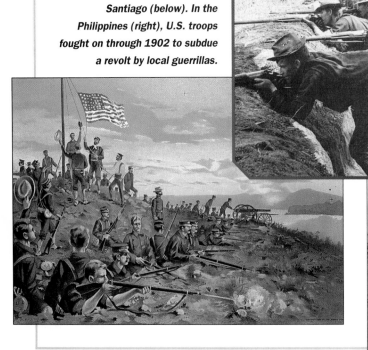

Sir Wilfrid Laurier

Graceful, charming, and a compelling speaker in French and English, Laurier was also blessed with luck. He came to power in 1896 just as improved strains of wheat and the building of railways made opening the Canadian West possible, and British capital and European immigrants were pouring into Canada, drawn by her natural resources and industrial potential. Laurier, the man of "sunny ways," governed until 1911, during a time when the sun shone bright for Canada.

But he also had to contend with rivalries between the French and the English, Catholics and Protestants, imperialists and nationalists; and his many compromises between them made more enemies than friends. In the end, he mourned the difficulty of governing a country in which the English were more British than the Queen, and the French more Catholic than the Pope.

▶ *A U.S. relief force sent to help quell China's Boxer Rebellion battles insurgents at the gates of Peking.*

the south coast. It was soon over and, in December of 1898, Spain ceded Cuba, Puerto Rico, the Philippines, and Guam. In the same year, the United States also acquired Hawaii. It had become an imperial power.

Canada was still a British colony in the 1890's, but like the Americans many Canadians, too, had yearnings for recognition of their own on the world stage. Britain, knowing it might soon face a war with Germany, was equally eager to encourage Canada to flex its muscles. Legally, this did not pose a problem, since if Britain declared war all British colonies were at war. However, the colonies did not normally contribute troops. But if Britain could establish a precedent for colonies doing so, this might serve to warn Germany that it faced a united empire.

In 1898, when Britain declared war against two republics in South Africa — Transvaal and Orange Free State — Canada was invited to participate. Prime Minister Wilfrid Laurier faced a divided country on the issue. Francophones, and a substantial number of anglophones, were opposed to a war that they saw as none of Canada's business. But a majority, especially of anglophones, clamored for battle glory and recognition in the world.

Laurier tried to compromise with a force of 1,000 Canadians who were to be paid for by the British. Later, they were supplemented by an additional 6,000 men, plus a full

regiment, Lord Strathcona's Horse. The regiment was financed by Lord Strathcona who had made a fortune from ventures that included the Canadian Pacific Railway.

Though the Canadians served with distinction — 244 died in the Boer War and 4 won the Victoria Cross — Laurier's compromise left a legacy of bitterness in Canada. Pro-British imperialists felt that Canada had not done enough. Their opponents worried that Laurier had set a precedent which might lead to grievous cost in future wars.

Hawaii's last monarch, Queen Liliuokalani (left), stepped down in 1893 to make way for a republic. Five years later the United States took possession in a flag-raising ceremony at the royal palace.

THE WORLD'S CONSTABLE.

For all his bluster, Roosevelt pursued a foreign policy of sober arbitration, backed up by a strong navy. So great was his reputation for solid dealing that nations from Latin America to the Far East turned to him, as this 1904 cartoon suggests.

TEDDY WIELDS THE BIG STICK

Teddy Roosevelt plunged into the U.S. presidency with a foreign policy of brash, high-pitched activism that thrilled Americans. Canadians were sometimes less enthusiastic.

It was over in seconds. On the afternoon of September 6, 1901, President William McKinley stood shaking hands in an ornate pavilion at the Pan-American Exposition, an international fair in Buffalo, New York. Up to the receiving line stepped a nervous young man, Leon Czolgosz, an avowed anarchist. Czolgosz raised a pistol and pumped off two quick shots. One bullet glanced harmlessly off a presidential vest button; the other pierced McKinley's stomach. Eight days later the president lay dead, his body ravaged by internal infection. Just a few houses away, in the formal library of a Buffalo mansion, Vice President Theodore Roosevelt was sworn in as the new president.

Roosevelt spoke the oath of office in a rapid-fire, high-pitched bark that gathered strength as he went along. The final "And so I swear!" rang out like an artillery salvo, an observer noted. He promised to follow McKinley's policies for prosperity at home and honor abroad. Then the new president rolled up his sleeves and went to work .

"Speak softly and carry a big stick; you will go far" was his political motto. And while he seldom spoke softly, he wielded the stick like a master. In 1902, when Germany blockaded Venezuela to collect unpaid debts, Roosevelt called in the German ambassador and suggested the matter go to arbitration. When the ambassador demurred, Roosevelt threatened to send in U.S. battleships. Germany agreed to arbitration. Two years later, when European governments moved against the Dominican Republic, also for overdue debts, the president unilaterally announced the Roosevelt Corollary to the Monroe Doctrine. Henceforth, he said, the United States alone would police all such disputes in the Western Hemisphere.

With similar directness, the president launched a project many people deemed impossible: a canal across the Isthmus of Panama. Everybody wanted one, for a canal would trim travel between New York and San Francisco by 12,800 kilometres and drastically shorten other world trade routes.

Remote and undisturbed until gold was struck in the Yukon, Lynn Canal became a major water route for transporting supplies from the Pacific Coast to the goldfields.

Roosevelt persisted. When Colombia, which governed Panama, refused to allow in U.S. engineers, despite a $10-million offer for digging rights, the Panamanians declared their independence. They then signed with Roosevelt, and in 1904 the United States started digging.

Roosevelt next sent 16 white-hulled battleships and their supporting craft around the world in a show of American naval strength. The Great White Fleet, as it was called, was a publicity triumph for his exuberant policies.

Living next door to that exuberance was often trying for Canadians. When the United States bought Alaska from Russia in 1867, maps showing the Alaskan boundary with British Columbia proved to be inaccurate. The discovery of gold in the Yukon in 1897 made those inaccuracies a serious matter because Canada's closest coastal access to the Yukon, the Lynn Canal, lay in the disputed zone.

Since Canada, still a colony, had no authority to negotiate with foreign countries, a British-American commission was appointed in 1903 to settle the matter, with Canadians as two of the three British commissioners. Predictably, the three American commissioners voted for the claim that placed the Lynn Canal in U.S. territory. The two Canadians voted for the Canadian claim. That left the deciding vote for the British commissioner, Lord Alverstone. His vote was never in doubt. Roosevelt, bellicose as always, had made it clear he would take the disputed area no matter what the decision. So the British commissioner, knowing that Britain had no wish to confront the United States over a matter of no importance to Britain, voted with the Americans.

Canada had lost its only possible port to serve the goldfields, and Canadians were furious. But, against such a powerful neighbor, there was little they could do. Some raged at British treachery, and the Canadian Club proposed that *O Canada* be adopted as an anthem in place of *God Save the Queen*. More practically, the International Boundary Commission was established in 1908 so that future disputes could be settled without British help. The Alaska Boundary Dispute had taught Canadians that they were on their own in dealing with the might of the United States.

In 1903, Lord Alverstone arbitrated in the Alaska Boundary Dispute. His vote in the U.S.'s favor lost Canada the Lynn Canal.

Teddy rides in the cab of a giant steam shovel on an inspection tour of construction at the Panama Canal.

Topsides gleaming, the Great White Fleet steams out of Hampton Roads, Virginia, on its 70,400-kilometre voyage to proclaim the United States a world power.

THAT COWBOY IN THE WHITE HOUSE

"I am only an average man, by George," he liked to say, but most people knew better. The new president was a bundle of nonstop energy and intellect who charmed some, alarmed others, and fascinated everyone.

Teddy Roosevelt moved into the White House at age 42, the youngest president ever, bringing a pretty young wife, six rambunctious children, and boundless self-confidence and zest. "In life, as in a football game," he once advised, "the principle to follow is: Hit the line hard." He was everywhere at once — meeting voters, shaping policy, writing books, galloping horses, rough-housing with his children — all the while barking orders and delivering opinions on every imaginable topic. He loved the spotlight. "Whenever he is in the neighborhood," said a friend, "the public can no more look the other way than a small boy can turn his head from a circus parade."

◄

TR's work clothes at Maltese Cross Ranch, in the Dakota Badlands, included a Western sombrero and chaps.

▶

Always firm in the saddle, the president smoothly clears a fence at a country club outside Washington.

▼

Outdoorsman and aristocrat both, the president goes over papers wearing white tie and riding puttees.

From Sickly Child to National Hero

All his life Roosevelt surprised people. Son of a patrician New York family, he had been a timid, nearsighted youth plagued by asthma attacks. To build his strength, he took up boxing. Later, entering politics as a crusading Republican, he applied the same fierce energy to cleaning up political abuses. As the New York City police commissioner, he strapped on a pistol and led his policemen on street patrols. When the Spanish-American War broke out, Roosevelt was in Washington as assistant secretary of the navy. He quit his desk and headed for Cuba. Organizing a volunteer cavalry regiment, the self-styled Rough Riders, he led a gallant, and highly publicized, charge under fire against enemy positions flanking San Juan Hill.

Teddy came home a hero, his toothy grin and steel-rimmed spectacles splashed across the nation's press. From San Juan Hill it was a quick gallop to the governorship of New York, and from there to the 1900 Republican national ticket as McKinley's running mate. Some old-guard party

3 a day, and he wrote 30 himself, on an astonishing range of subjects: history, biography, personal accounts of cattle ranching and wilderness travel, political writings, and scholarly works on natural science. He was such an authority on American wildlife that the Smithsonian, unable to name a rare species of mammal in its collection, called the White House to obtain positive identification.

Above all, he was a wonderful father. After his first wife's death, he married a childhood sweetheart, Edith Carow, who gave him five more children. They swarmed into the White House with a menagerie of pets — dogs, horses, birds, flying squirrels, a badger, a small black bear — and an abundance of high spirits. There were baseball games on the front lawn, tag in the front hall, and sledding competitions down the grand front staircase. Alice, the oldest daughter, stayed aloof from these frolics; the press corps dubbed her Princess Alice. But the president loved it all. "A household of children," he declared, "certainly makes all other forms of success and achievement lose their importance by comparison."

All spiffed up for the photographer, the Roosevelts sit still for a First Family portrait in 1903. Along with the president and Mrs. Roosevelt, they are (from left) Ethel, 11; young Ted, 15; Archie, 9; Alice, 19; Kermit, 13; and Quentin, 5.

leaders questioned the choice. "Don't any of you realize," cautioned Ohio's powerful Senator Mark Hanna, "that there's only one life between that madman and the presidency?" No matter: Teddy would win votes, and as vice-president he would be relatively powerless. Then, with McKinley's assassination in 1901, everything changed. "Now look," Hanna exclaimed, "that damned cowboy is president of the United States."

And cowboy he truly was, for he had ridden the range with the best of them. Years earlier, as a young man not long out of Harvard, he had gone west to recover from the deaths, on a single devastating day in 1884, of both his mother and his wife, Alice. (His mother died of typhoid, Alice after giving birth to his oldest daughter.) The grieving Roosevelt took refuge at a ranch he had purchased in the Dakota Territory. For two years he roped cattle, hunted buffalo, and tracked outlaws, often spending 14 to 16 hours a day in the saddle. Ever after he would preach the recuperative joys of "the strenuous life." As president, he would lead perspiring diplomats on hikes through Washington's Rock Creek Park, and more than once he swam the Potomac River in winter, through chunks of floating ice.

For all his physical vigor, the president was also a man of prodigious intellect. He devoured books at the rate of 2 or

TEDDY OUR HERO

Two Step and Song

RESPECTFULLY DEDICATED TO
COL. THEODORE ROOSEVELT
AND
THE BRAVE ROUGH RIDERS

BALLAD

Teddy's military exploits and his reputation for gallantry inspired a number of admiring popular songs, like these.

Decked out in his Rough Riders uniform, Teddy wears the battered campaign hat and crossed-sabers insignia of the 1st U.S. Volunteer Cavalry Regiment, which he helped organize. Even in the White House he held periodic reunions with his old troopers, who called him Colonel.

VOL. LXII. No. 1592. PUCK BUILDING, New York, September 4th, 1907. PRICE TEN CENTS.

"What Fools these Mortals be!"

Puck

Copyright, 1907, by Keppler & Schwarzmann. Entered at N. Y. P. O. as Second-class Mail Matter.

FLIM-FLAM FINANCE

HONEST SOAP

"YOU DIRTY BOY!"

▲ *In his role as trustbuster, a matronly TR gives a no-nonsense scrubbing to a shady financier in this cover cartoon from the magazine* Puck.

A SQUARE DEAL — FOR SOME

A born crusader, Roosevelt cut away at the corruption and greed of big business. Laurier was, to say the least, more prudent.

Through the 19th century, governments in both Canada and the United States had been closely allied to business. By 1900, critics in both countries were charging that the alliance was too close and that business was abusing its power. Roosevelt responded with characteristic vigor, Laurier with characteristic caution.

Roosevelt's first target was the growing wealth and power of big business. Giant holding companies, which enjoyed an almost unlimited power to set prices and squelch competition, had come to dominate the United States' basic industries. Tobacco, sugar, petroleum, copper — all were virtual monopolies. So, too, were many of the nation's railways, and here it was that Roosevelt stepped in. In 1902 he brought legal action against the Northern Securities Company, a railway trust that had gained a hammerlock on rail transportation from Chicago west to Seattle.

The young William Lyon Mackenzie King entered the political arena as Laurier's draughtsman of labor laws.

In attacking Northern Securities, TR took on four of the world's most powerful men: oilman John D. Rockefeller, railway tycoons James J. Hill and E. H. Harriman, and investment banker J. Pierpont Morgan. As Wall Street's leading financier, Morgan was used to settling differences quietly. "If we have done anything wrong," he told Roosevelt, "send your man to my man and they can fix it up." "That can't be done," the president replied. The attorney general, Philander C. Knox, explained further: "We don't want to fix it up; we want to stop it."

Roosevelt forced the break-up of Northern Securities. He then went gunning for Rockefeller's Standard Oil monopoly, American Tobacco, Du Pont, the Chicago meat packers, and some 40 other major trusts. He won every case.

The public loved it. That same year, 1902, a strike broke out in the coal fields. Supplies ran short, schools had to close, and prices shot from $5 to $35 a tonne. Roosevelt summoned the coal producers and the head of the United Mine Workers of America (UMW) to Washington and told them to negotiate. The union was willing, but the producers refused. Most people sided with the miners (who were laboring in deplorable conditions for wages of $2 a day), and eventually the producers gave in. Roosevelt came out glowing. He had given the miners, he boasted, "a square deal."

In Canada, despite charges of rampant price-fixing, monopolies, and combines (particularly on the part of banks and railways), Laurier's attention focused on working conditions. With a high accident rate due to unsafe machinery, employers who simply fired injured workers, and children working for 25 cents a day or less, there was plenty to focus on. But it was not the conditions that concerned him so much as the reaction to them in the form of union growth.

◄

On a campaign speaking tour, Roosevelt drives home his point with characteristic vehemence. He liked to refer to the White House as "a bully pulpit."

In 1901, the Trades and Labour Congress had 8,000 members; by 1911, it had 57,000. That growth, combined with obstinate owners, meant strikes.

In 1901, 5,000 CPR maintenance workers went on a strike that lasted five months. Strikes were common in the mining, shoe-making and textile industries, but they were most worrisome to Laurier in railways because these were the key to Canadian development.

Laurier found his answer in a young man who had studied industrial relations at university. William Lyon Mackenzie King prepared the Industrial Disputes Investigation Act (1907) which prohibited strikes in public utilities and mines until the government had time to arbitrate. Though useful to workers, the Act benefitted business at least as much by avoiding strikes. And complaints continued that Laurier was doing far less than Roosevelt in tackling abuses by business. Again, he turned to Mackenzie King. The result was the Combines Investigation Act (1910). Designed to crack down on abuses, it proved to be virtually unenforceable. Many said that was what it was meant to be.

At the end of the century's first decade, Roosevelt had established his government as the guardian of public as well as business interest. The Canadian government was on its way there.

▲ *Roosevelt's 1912 Bull Moose reelection bid as seen by Puck: a super patriotic Teddy blusters while Republicans and Democrats run for cover.*

▼ *The B.C. government chose confrontation rather than arbitration during the Vancouver Island Coal Strike in 1913.*

ECONOMIC COLOSSI

With vast natural resources and a huge supply of cheap labor, Canada and America grew to become two of the wealthiest nations in history.

A locomotive puffs around the bend toward a trestle bridge on the Canadian Pacific Railway. Rail unified Canada and made the exploitation of its vast natural resources more feasible.

For Americans, the yearly quantities seemed almost unimaginable. Fourteen million tonnes of steel. More than two million tonnes of coal. Nine and a half million bales of cotton. Plus enough finished lumber to build a small summer cottage for every family in the United States.

In 1904, Canada produced two million tonnes of wheat. Within less than a decade, it would be almost eight million. Most of it was carried on the CPR, the railway Canadians had built across the continent in the 1880's. In the first decade of the 20th century, they built two more railways across Canada, then still more in South America, Africa and China. Observers commented that while Americans built railways for development, Canadians seemed to build them just for the fun of it.

Much of the billions of dollars produced in the two countries poured into the hands of a few top industrialists, who simply could not build enough marble palaces or steam yachts to spend it all. Far less filtered down to the industrial rank and file: to the mill hands, mine workers, roustabouts, and office clerks, who helped make it happen.

A Golden Age for Tycoons

"I eat all I can, I drink all I can, I smoke all I can and I don't give a damn for anything." In those words, Sir William Van Horne summed up the brutal energy of the tycoon of the new century. From his start as the hard-driving general manager of the CPR in its construction, he became president in 1888, launching Canada's biggest company into passenger shipping with the Empress line and founding CP hotels like Banff Springs and the Chateau Frontenac. When he retired in 1899, he promptly began building yet another railway — in Cuba.

In the United States, John Pierpont Morgan, Sr., the Napoleon of Wall Street, bought out the steel empire of Andrew Carnegie for $480 million. He combined it with his own and others, and created the United States Steel Corporation. Its assets, valued at $1.4 billion, exceeded the entire

North America's natural resources seemed limitless in 1900, along with the muscle and enterprise to exploit them. In Butte, Montana, workers' houses nestle against the mines of the Anaconda Company (above), in the gritty shadow of its ore smelters. Butte yielded lead, zinc, and half the U.S.'s copper in 1900. Farther west, in Oregon (top), loggers attack a hefty Douglas fir, wielding only axes and a two-man saw.

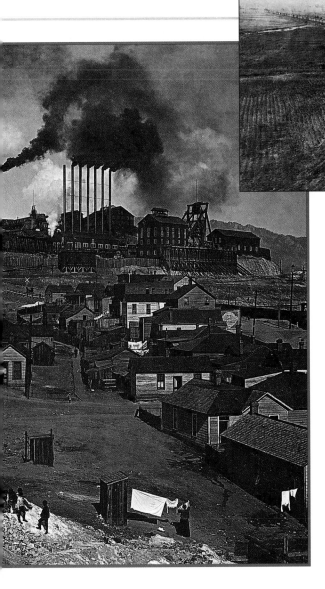

On the Illinois Central line, one of America's 65,000 locomotives hauls a freight train so long its cars vanish on the horizon.

drilling was causing overproduction and bankruptcies, and saw the answer. John D. Rockefeller built his own, highly efficient refinery and urged his competitors to join him. If they refused, he slashed prices and bought them out. His methods were often brutal, and some would later be deemed illegal. But as Rockefeller's domain expanded, the oil market stabilized. Profits soared. Then in 1882 he delivered his master stroke: a giant compendium of former rivals whom he cajoled into forming the Standard Oil Trust, with himself as chairman. As far back as 1879 Standard Oil Company had controlled 90 percent of America's refining capacity and most of the world's oil trade. Not even oil strikes in Texas, in 1901, and in Oklahoma, in 1905, could topple the trust's preeminence. Every one of its officers grew rich.

In each major industry, similar corporate Goliaths appeared. National Biscuit, Bank of Montreal, American Tobacco, United States Rubber, Ogilvie Flour Mills, American Can, United Fruit, International Harvester — the list grew

U.S. national debt. The new company owned iron mines, ore smelters, shipping lines, and fabricating plants, and it dominated fully 60 percent of the national steel market. This degree of economic clout made some people extremely nervous. "The world has ceased to be ruled by statesmen," fretted *Cosmopolitan Magazine*, and some observers prophesied dangerous social upheavals.

Vast concentrations of power and capital are the hallmark of an industrial age, however. The trend had been building since the 1870's. In Canada, an obscure foundry making farm machinery mushroomed into the giant Massey Manufacturing Company. In 1891, it merged with its chief competitor to become Massey-Harris, the largest producer of farm machinery in the British Empire.

In the United States, a young commodity broker surveyed the chaos of the Pennsylvania oil fields where wildcat

San Francisco Rises From Its Ashes

First came the earthquake: a bone-jarring convulsion that roared through San Francisco shortly before sunrise on April 18, 1906, smashing buildings, heaving up streets, shattering gas lines and water mains. Then came the fire. It blazed up south of Market Street, the main business thoroughfare, and swept across the city. Banks, skyscrapers, the magnificent opera house, the teeming immigrant districts of North Beach and Chinatown, the mansions on Nob Hill — all were consumed. Three days later, when the flames died out, some 500 people had lost their lives and 225,000 more were left homeless. But the city refused to die.

Even before the embers stopped glowing, orders went out for steel to rebuild. The entire nation pitched in. Washington sent $2.5 million in aid. Rockefeller donated $100,000, and press lord William Randolph Hearst arrived in person with $200,000. Los Angeles bakers contributed free bread, and the Philadelphia Athletics handed over a day's gate receipts. But no one did more to speed the city's recovery than A. P. Giannini, president of the local Bank of Italy. As the flames engulfed his offices, Giannini carted off the bank's assets — $80,000 in gold — under orange crates in a fruit wagon. Days later he was back in business, handing out construction loans from a makeshift desk on the waterfront. This display of civic confidence did wonders to restore San Francisco's natural energy and optimism. And Giannini's company, renamed the Bank of America, would grow into one of the world's largest financial institutions.

Refugees on Russian Hill watch the city burn while soldiers (inset) patrol a devastated Market Street.

In the era of giant trusts and the first billion-dollar deals, capitalists loomed larger than life. Immensely rich, ruthlessly ambitious, and mostly free from government regulation, they made decisions that affected the pocketbook of every citizen. Yet many started out poor.

Andrew Carnegie began working at age 13 in a Pittsburgh cotton mill for $1.20 a week. John D. Rockefeller's first job earned him $25 per month. Sir Donald Mann began his working life in lumber camps but, with partner Sir William Mackenzie (who began his working life as a teacher), built railways in the United States, South America, China and, across Canada, the Canadian Northern Railway.

To be sure, some of the period's plutocrats were born rich. J. Pierpont Morgan, Sr., as the scion of a well-established banking family, had his air of patrician grandeur from the cradle. With his imposing presence and piercing hazel eyes — likened by an associate to "the lights of an oncoming express train" — he seemed the living embodiment of power and purpose. Through a system of interlocking directorships, he controlled the destiny of 112 major corporations, and he commanded more respect than the president. During the economic depression of 1895, he bailed out the U.S. government with a timely loan of $60 million in gold. And when a financial panic hit Wall Street in 1907, he saved the nation once again by calling New York's top money men to a meeting in his sumptuous private library on Madison Avenue and forcing them to ante up the needed capital.

J. Pierpont Morgan ruled over American finance.

Donald Mann built railways on 3 continents.

John D. Rockefeller was the world's richest man.

Andrew Carnegie made $23 million tax free in 1900.

Making his bid to join the growing middle class, an African-American jeweler plies his trade, in about 1900.

steadily. And much as these giants alarmed their critics, there was no going back. For where the trusts took over, markets steadied and prosperity tended to follow. Even Teddy Roosevelt, for all his trust-busting zeal (see pp.22–23), had no objection to size alone. Only "bad" trusts — those engaged in price-fixing, for example — aroused his ire.

Railways were among the largest enterprises, with transcontinentals and regional systems sprawling across North America. In 1900, the United States had 308,800 kilometres of track. Canada, with only one-tenth the population but spurred by British investment and lavish government aid, had almost 28,800 kilometres and was averaging anoth-

These bright young office workers belonged to an army of "lady typewriters" who had joined the labor force by 1900. A female threshing crew (far right) helps tend a steam tractor on a prairie farm.

Japanese field hands cultivate a carrot crop on a fertile farm in the San Joaquin Valley of California, fast becoming the United States' truck garden.

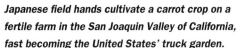

Proud and tough, lignite coal workers pose before a mine shaft in which they work. Productivity in mining rose dramatically during the century's first decade.

er 2,400 a year. As more railway lines were built, new towns sprang up in their wake, and new tracts of prairie land were laid open to farming. Railways gave access to the mines of Nevada, Montana, British Columbia and northern Ontario. They joined the forests and fisheries of the Pacific Northwest to the East. By 1910, more North Americans worked for railways than for any other employer.

Even in agriculture, changes were occurring on a massive scale. Mechanized farming brought wonders of efficiency to the business of growing food, but large capital investments were required. No longer could a farmer get by with 16 hectares; he needed chemical fertilizers, barbed-wire fencing, a reaper-thresher combine, perhaps a steam-driven tractor, and a broad sweep of land to work them on. As a result, traditional family farms gave way to large commercial spreads funded by eastern bankers and run by professional managers. One so-called bonanza farm in Minnesota's Red River valley covered 14 million hectares, employed thousands of workers, and had a wheat field larger than Manhattan. And in the Canadian West at harvest time, special trains carried armies of workers from eastern cities to bring in the grain.

Long Hours, Low Pay

The revenues generated by these giant enterprises went mostly to the owners and their bankers. Lucky workers might earn as much as $575 a year, but the average was $250 to $400 — much less for women and children. With an average wage, a worker earned only half of what was needed for basic survival for a family of five. Canadian workers had the added problem of thick winter ice that might close ports like Montreal for months, putting thousands out of work. In exchange for low pay, workers put in a work day of 10 hours or more, 6 days a week, often in punishing heat or cold, or in airless, ill-lighted factories. And no thought was given to worker safety around whirling machines.

GOOD-BYE HORSES, HELLO MODEL T

"The horse will continue indispensable for a long time," wrote a reporter after viewing the battery-, steam-, and gas-powered cars at the National Auto Show of 1900 (background photo). Then along came Henry Ford.

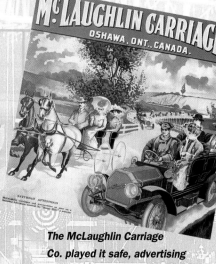

In storage at the Château de Ramezay in Montreal is a 1903 de Dion Bouton, the oldest surviving automobile in Montreal. It was the third car of a flamboyant real estate developer who, in 1898 and 1899, brought U.S.-built Locomobiles to Canada's city streets. By the time the de Dion Bouton appeared, there were already more than 40 companies in the United States building horseless carriages for 8,000 owners. In the same year, Henry Ford built a factory in Ontario, and his low prices spread cars over Canada as quickly as they had done in the United States. By 1913, Canada alone had 13,000 cars buzzing and clattering over its roads.

Autos were so new that no one quite knew what to call them. Suggestions ranged from "autobat" to "viamote," from "mocle" to "motorfly." Most resembled tricycles or horse carts, and a few came complete with a socket for a buggy whip. Steering was by tiller. Maximum speed seldom topped 48 kilometres per hour.

Even that was enough to terrorize most bystanders. Minneapolis car owner T. H. Shevlin received the city's first speeding ticket, in 1902: a $10 fine for driving at a breakneck speed of 16 kilometres per hour. A 1902 Vermont law required that autos be preceded by an attendant waving a red flag.

As engines grew more efficient and control devices improved, these strictures gave way. Car manufacturers continued to test power systems. The early favorites were electric automobiles, such as Woods and Bakers, which proved easy to start, smooth driving, and free of the sputtering noise and fumes of gasoline buggies. If slow compared to gas-driven autos, the electrics also seemed safer. As one manufacturer of electrics, Albert Pope, pointed out, "You can't get people to sit over an explosion." Steam-driven cars were the era's true speedsters. But steamers were a rich man's toy.

Any automobile meant a substantial cash outlay, to be sure. Millionaires paid $4,000 and more for Pierce Arrows and Panhards fitted with brass ornamentation and padded leather seats. The average list price of a 1900 vehicle topped $1,000, far too much for the typical family.

But that was about to change. In 1901 a small Detroit automobile factory burned down with all its inventory, except for a single car, a one-cylinder runabout with a rakishly turned-up front end. It seemed little enough to restart the business, but once back in production, the Olds Motor Works could scarcely meet the demand. So popular was the trim $650 runabout that it inspired one of the decade's biggest song hits: "Come away with me Lucille/ In my merry Oldsmobile...."

Detroit was a city of machine shops and skilled mechanics, and it attracted other automakers like Packard, David Buick

The McLaughlin Carriage Co. played it safe, advertising carriages as well as cars. Both, it suggested, would make for a pleasant outing. Shown here is the old stage road between Toronto and Montreal at a popular point near the "Rouge Hill," then 19 kilometres east of Toronto.

Fred Marriot (left) rocketed his Stanley Steamer to a 1906 record of 204.25 kph (127.66 mph) on the hard sands at Daytona Beach, Florida.

For protection from insects, dirt, and noxious fumes, the well-dressed motorist swathed herself in a duster, a bonnet, gloves, and, customarily, goggles and a mask.

and the Dodge brothers. Across the river, a Canadian bicycle manufacturer, CCM, began producing its Russell car. Among other Canadian cars were the McLaughlin, the Thomas, and the Comet. At $5,000, the Montreal-made Comet was pricey, but it offered an engine with the power of 24 horses pulling in step.

Mechanical Whiz, National Hero

Detroit's true pioneer — and the man who would transform the automobile from a passing fancy into one of life's necessities — was Henry Ford. A farmer's son with a genius for making things work, Ford built his first car, a gas-powered quadricycle with no brakes, in 1896. A parade of improved models followed, each designated by a letter of the alphabet. By 1907 Ford had reached *T*. "I will build a motor car for the great multitude . . . so low in price that no man making a good salary will be unable to own one."

The Model T was all that and much more. Wonderfully rugged, it bounded along dirt roads at speeds up to 56 kilometres per hour. Repairs were easy. And each year the price dropped, from $850 in 1908 to $490 in 1914 and then lower. Soon more than half the cars in the United States were Model T's, identical down to the color. "They can have any color they want," explained Ford, "so long as it's black." The cars rattled, spat oil, and were generally so uncomfortable that people joked about them. (Question: What shock absorbers does your Ford use?

Auto industry pioneer Henry Ford poses in his first motor vehicle, the 2-cylinder, 4-horsepower quadricycle, Model A. On June 4, 1896, he took the 226-kilogram car for a spin.

Answer: The passengers.) Even so, everyone loved the Tin Lizzie. "Your car lifted us out of the mud," said one owner.

So great was the demand for the Model T that to boost output, Ford began tinkering with the production process. The world's first automobile assembly line rolled into action in 1914 at his new Detroit plant. Quickly adopted by other carmakers, assembly-line production revolutionized the industry. A second innovation was equally far-reaching. Ford doubled his workers' salaries, to an unheard-of $5 a day, and initiated a profit-sharing plan, moves that made him a hero to just about all of the United States.

▼ *Mom looks on as Dad and the kids hop aboard the Model T for an outing. In 1914, a year after this photo was shot, every other new car bought was a Tin Lizzie.*

ORVILLE AND WILBUR GET UP FIRST

Europeans had flown airships and gliders, but powered heavier-than-air flight had eluded them. Then, the combined vision of two persevering brothers from Dayton, Ohio, changed the world with a new form of travel.

An eager crowd of reporters and government officials gathered in boats on Washington's Potomac River to witness a science spectacular: the launch of Samuel P. Langley's flying machine. For more than a decade, inventors had attempted to break the barrier to manned mechanized air travel. Finally, on October 7, 1903, it looked as though someone might actually do it.

As secretary of the Smithsonian Institution, Langley had spent five years and $50,000 to develop his tandem-winged "aerodromes." One of them now perched above the river atop a houseboat. The twin propellers whirred, the pilot braced himself, and then fiasco. "There was a roaring, grinding noise," reported *The Washington Post*, "and the Langley airship tumbled . . . into the water like a handful of mortar." Two months later Langley tried again, with the same result. Astronomer Simon Newcomb, Langley's contemporary, commented: "Aerial flight is one of that class of problems with which man can never cope."

Yet, at that moment, on a remote North Carolina beachfront, two lone geniuses were rapidly approaching that goal. For the past several years, brothers Orville and Wilbur Wright, young bicycle manufacturers from Dayton, Ohio, had been testing kites and gliders at Kitty Hawk. They had studied the dynamics of wind forces on airfoils, tried more than 200 wing shapes in their own wind tunnel, and

Poised on the brink, Otto Lilienthal surveys the land below before taking off in one of his bat-winged gliders.

Orville Wright

Wilbur Wright

developed just what Langley's aerodromes could have used: a system for maintaining stability in flight. Now they were ready to fly their first true airplane, a biplane of spruce and muslin, powered by a lightweight gasoline engine built in their shop. It was christened the *Flyer*. On the chilly morning of December 17, 1903, nine days after Langley's second attempt, they hauled the *Flyer* to its launching rail.

The toss of a coin three days earlier put Orville at the controls. As Wilbur trotted alongside, the *Flyer* rose from its track, wobbled briefly forward, and then settled back on the sand. The next flight went better, and the longest lasted 59 seconds and extended 260 metres. "SUCCESS FOUR FLIGHTS . . ." Orville telegraphed, "INFORM PRESS HOME CHRISTMAS."

Only six papers carried the news; *The New York Tribune* ran it on the sports page. Indeed, even as, in 1904 and 1905, the Wrights were clocking ever-longer flights, only buffs paid much attention. The U.S. War Department, invited on numerous occasions to watch a demonstration, twice sent nearly identical letters of refusal.

With the order "Let go the lines," Prussian Count Ferdinand von Zeppelin sent the first of his giant hydrogen-filled airships on its maiden voyage, over a lake in southern Germany.

Across the Atlantic, however, people had begun to take notice. Since the 1780's Europeans had sailed aloft in balloons; German aeronautical engineer Otto Lilienthal completed over 2,000 glider flights before crashing to his death in 1896; and, in 1900, Count Ferdinand von Zeppelin, a retired cavalry officer, ascended in the first of his giant dirigibles. Surely, in the race to propel a machine into the air, the Europeans should have come in first. But not until 1906 did Europe accomplish true mechanized flight. The pilot was a dapper expatriate Brazilian named Alberto Santos-Dumont, who that year skimmed over Paris in a gawky aircraft dubbed *Canard* for its resemblance to a duck. Frenchmen Henri Farman and Gabriel Voisin took to the air next, followed by their countryman Louis Bleriot, who became the first to fly across the English Channel, in 1909. By then the excitement of airborne travel had filtered across the ocean. On July 4, 1908, Glenn Curtiss, a motorcycle designer from upstate New York, flew his first airplane, *June Bug,* in a competition sponsored by *Scientific American*. As a crowd of dignitaries looked on, Curtiss lifted into the air. "We all lost our heads," recalled his daughter, "and everyone cheered . . . and engines tooted." Her husband chimed in: "Man flies!"

Curtiss never looked back. He designed the first successful seaplane and the first aircraft to take off from a warship. And, in a clash of geniuses, he lost a patent suit to the Wrights involving a wing design.

One of the eager young men who flocked to take part in pioneer flights in the United States was J.A.D. McCurdy of Nova Scotia. In 1909, with the experience of some 200 flights behind him, he returned to Nova Scotia to fly his own design, *Silver Dart*, at Baddeck in February 1909. It was the first controlled flight by a British subject in the British Empire. Though now almost forgotten, McCurdy was also the first to make an ocean flight — from Florida to Cuba. Flying machines — for sport, for travel, for defence — had flown in to stay.

Aviatrix Harriet Quimby's 1912 hop across the English Channel made her the first lady of the air.

J.A.D. McCurdy lifts his **Silver Dart** *about 9 metres above the frozen surface of Baddeck Bay, Nova Scotia, the first British flight in the British Empire.*

The first American air meet attracted a daily crowd of more than 20,000 spectators, who cheered intrepid French pilot Louis Paulhan on to collect some $19,000 in winnings.

With Orville Wright lying prone on the lower wing and his brother Wilbur running alongside, the Flyer rises half a metre above the track on its 30-metre-long initial flight, the first by a power-driven, man-carrying machine. The Wrights chose Kitty Hawk, a lonely stretch of sand on North Carolina's Outer Banks, as the site of their experiments because of the strong winds that prevail there.

"HELLO CENTRAL" AND THE WONDROUS WIRELESS

Suddenly telephones were in demand: businessmen traded stocks and farmers got prices by phone, the party line provided entertainment, and Central became a trusted friend. Meanwhile, radio waves were about to be news.

Back in 1877, the Canadian government considered cancelling a frivolous expense — something called a telephone that connected government offices to the governor general's residence. The telephone was saved only at the insistence of the governor general's wife, who loved listening to a talented civil servant sing over it to her guests. By 1900, that frivolous expense had spread to more than 40,000 homes in Canada and 1.3 million in America — figures that would increase fivefold by 1907.

When first shown to the public at the Philadelphia Centennial Exposition of 1876, the telephone had seemed little more than an ingenious toy. The following year Massachusetts resident Charles Williams installed the country's first private home phone. He put another set in his Boston office in order to have some place to call. The device spread rapidly, however, with energetic promotion by its inventor, Alexander Graham Bell, a Canadian who invented the device while at work in Boston and on holiday at his home in On-

Alexander Graham Bell makes the first long-distance phone call, from Paris, Ontario, to Brantford, 13 kilometres away.

A popular 1901 tune has a tearful child phone her prayers into Central: "Hello Central, Give me Heaven, for my mama's there!"

This demure young lady pays a "telephone visit" over her candlestick-style desk set.

HELLO CENTRAL GIVE ME HEAVEN

BY CHAS·K·HARRIS
AUTHOR of
"AFTER THE BALL"
SUNG WITH GREAT SUCCESS
ROBBINS & TRENAMAN

At a busy telephone exchange two operators work the switchboard while their supervisors look on. "Hello girls" followed strict rules: enter chairs from the left, place feet on the floor, and look straight ahead.

Marconi's Marvel

tario. The first central exchange started up in New Haven, Connecticut, in 1878. And while the Bell System controlled the lion's share of the service — it had a near-monopoly of cities and large towns in central Canada and controlled two-thirds of all telephones in the United States — it was rivalled by more than 6,000 independents.

In rural areas, farmers would cut wood for poles, string wire, and set up a switchboard, perhaps in someone's kitchen. Often the entire community shared a single circuit, with all the hazards of party-line calling. One farm wife, asked what she thought of her new phone, replied: "Well, we liked it a lot at first . . . only spring work is coming on so heavy that we don't hardly have time to listen now."

As phone lines proliferated, instruments took on a wonderful variety of sizes and styles. Besides the ordinary table phones and wall phones, there were elaborately carved cabinet phones and carpeted, oak-panelled phone booths. Callers lacking home telephones could walk to a nearby pay phone; some 81,000 were in service in the U.S. by 1902.

The key figure in these largely pre-dial days was the central exchange operator. Soft-spoken young women were employed to be "The Voice With a Smile," as the New York Telephone Company described its operators in 1912. They could be counted on to perform all kinds of tasks. A typical request, according to a 1905 magazine story, ran: "Oh, Central! Ring me up in 15 minutes so I won't forget to take the bread out of the oven." Small-town operators were known to babysit by wire: a busy parent would leave the receiver off the hook at cradle side. Railway baron E. H. Harriman depended on the telephone to an extraordinary extent: his country estate alone boasted 100 sets. Accused of being a slave to the instrument, he replied for all heavy phone users, "Nonsense. It is a slave to me."

While the telephone wove itself into the fabric of North American culture, radio, or "wireless," was still an exotic device used mainly by ships at sea and a few ham operators. It made its first public U.S. appearance in 1899 at the America's Cup yacht race. Sailing alongside to report the outcome was none other than Guglielmo Marconi, age 25, radio's most notable pioneer. Four years earlier, in his native Italy, Marconi had invented the first practical system for wireless transmission. He had come to peddle the device in the United States.

Marconi's reports, in Morse code, came in garbled, but the spark caught fire. Two years later Marconi sent the first transatlantic wireless signal, the letter *S*. It was a Canadian, Reginald Fessenden, who sent the first two-way, spoken message across the Atlantic — between Massachusetts and Scotland — in 1906. In that same year, on Christmas Eve, he made the world's first public broadcast of voice and music.

During crises on the high seas, the wireless proved itself a thousand times over. Some 300 vessels were equipped with wireless devices by 1909. That year an operator on the *Republic* coordinated the rescue of 1,700 survivors of a collision between his ship and the *Florida*. In 1910 radio would be used for the first time in the apprehension of a criminal. Aboard the liner *Montrose* as it steamed from Belgium to Canada were wife-murderer Hawley Harvey Crippen and his mistress, disguised as father and son. The sharp-eyed captain spotted the pair partway into the journey and wired the police, who arrested them as they disembarked.

The capture of Crippen, along with a growing number of radioed rescues at sea, secured the place of wireless in the world of communications.

Greeting cards promoted the new vogue for telephony, but the magazine Lippincott's Monthly *cautioned readers that "telephoning from habit finally becomes a vice."*

HERE COME THE CONSUMERS

A thrilling new sound, music to merchants' ears,

echoed through the land: the jingle of cash registers.

Almost everyone, it seemed, wanted to spend money on

something, and retailers were all too happy to oblige.

Every era has its folktales, but the story of a turn-of-the-century farm boy stands out as particularly apt. Asked by his Sunday school teacher where the Ten Commandments came from, the lad did not hesitate: "Why, from Sears, Roebuck, where else?" Indeed. At a time of ever-increasing prosperity, the giant Chicago mail-order house stood ready to supply every need, from age-old words of wisdom to the latest gadgets for home and workplace. In the United States, the giants were Sears and Montgomery Ward; in Canada, they were Eaton's and Simpsons. In cities shoppers flocked to the local department stores, which by 1900 had grown into glorious cathedrals of commerce, complete with art galleries, fashion shows, and retail areas offering everything from Parisian dresses to Persian rugs. Across the continent, people were awakening to an age of breathless mass consumption, when it seemed that everything, even happiness itself, was up for sale.

Happiness may have been the only item not listed in the great retail wish books. Running many hundreds of pages, they reached over 10 million households by 1910, and were almost as thick as the Bible that was a standard item in their book sections. For readers in remote farm country, they opened the door to the latest styles of the cities. On a more practical note, prairie farmers could find in the pages of the Eaton's catalogue everything from harness and buggies to complete, prefabricated houses.

Ladies learned about the latest fashions in dresses, kitchenware, and home furnishings; a section on patent nostrums touted "La Dore's famous bust food" for building "a plump, full, rounded bosom." Men browsed through ads for guns, farm tools, haberdashery, and grooming aids.

Out of young Frank W. Woolworth's idea of cutting prices on slow-selling merchandise grew a chain for thrifty shoppers.

The T. Eaton Co. Ltd.'s summer catalogue offered necessities and even some luxuries for outdoor leisure.

A housewife shows she needs just one hand to operate a washing machine bought from a catalogue. It was still manual labor, but less work than a scrub board.

Children, now a distinct consumer group, were bedazzled by pictures of Daisy air rifles, doll houses, stereopticons, and even live pets. More than one lonely farmer wrote the retailers to ask about buying a wife.

Urban husbands, meanwhile, were losing their wives to Wanamaker's in Philadelphia, Marshall Field's in Chicago, Macy's in New York City, and Morgan's in Montreal. When shoppers crossed the threshold to one of these magnificent iron-and-plate-glass emporiums, they entered a consumer's fantasyland. And once inside, they had little reason to leave. Some stores offered amenities ranging from libraries to nurseries, and entertainments from tearooms to theatres, from botanical gardens to miniature zoos. Who could possibly resist them?

Bargain Prices and Electrical Appliances

What department stores provided in luxury and comfort, cash-and-carry vendors, such as the Hudson's Bay Company, F. W. Woolworth, and The Great Atlantic and Pacific Tea Company (better known as the A&P), delivered in savings. Woolworth's five-and-tens peddled tin cookware, sewing notions, and other inexpensive items; by 1910 Woolworth had more than 200 stores. Discount grocers, forerunners of today's supermarkets, lined their shelves with low-cost staples.

The upsurge in consumer goods worked a miraculous transformation on the home. As North Ameri-

▲ *As electrification spread, demand rose for appliances like the General Electric range (1913) and the Model C Hoover cleaner (1908). The Kodak Brownie camera sold for $1.00.*

ca became wired for electricity, a steady flow of labor-saving appliances came on the market. Housewives no longer had to stand over the heat of a coal-burning stove; an electric range with automatic timer promised to "do oven watching" for them. Hoover vacuum cleaners made short work of the soot from open fireplaces. Electric irons appeared in 1908, followed by toasters, coffee percolators, and hot plates. For men, the Gillette safety razor, patented in 1895, meant no further need for daily trips to the barbershop at 30 minutes per shave. Now a man could be "master of his own time and appearance," just as the ads suggested.

Fanning the rage for consumer goods, advertising and packaging gained unprecedented importance in the plans of businessmen. The signature label of the Campbell's tomato soup can made its debut in 1899. Eastman Kodak plugged the Brownie in 1900 as a camera "so simple a child can use it." The Woodbury soap ads of 1911 pictured a man and a woman locked in an embrace, together with the words "the skin you love to touch." Though the Woodbury advertising scandalized readers of *The Ladies' Home Journal*, causing some to cancel their subscriptions, even more subscribers signed on because of the ads. And the admen discovered a fundamental lesson for the new consumer age: sex can sell a lot of soap.

Crammed to overflowing, a Montgomery Ward truck delivers a load of mail-order goods. For decades "Monty Ward" and Sears, Roebuck vied for mail-order customers, and both opened retail outlets. For city dwellers, department stores, like R. H. Macy's in New York City (right), offered all the delights that catalogues could only picture.

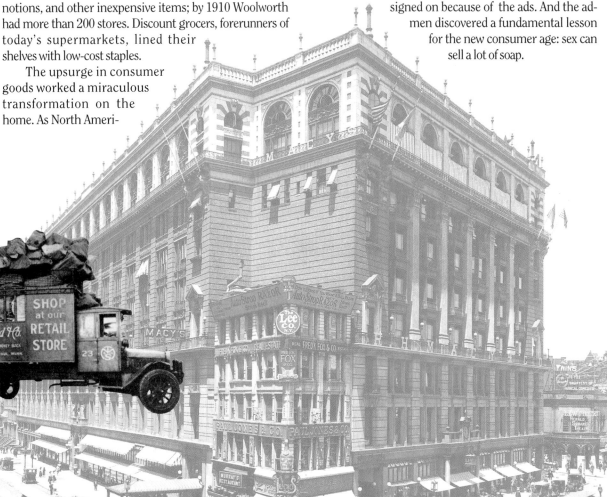

An Age of Artful Advertising

His Master's Voice 🐾 1904
A loyal if somewhat baffled dog vouches for the audio fidelity of the Victor Talking Machine, or Victrola.

Flexible Flyer 🐾 1905
Kids sped downhill on the sturdy, steel-runnered wooden sleds that bore an inflexibly patriotic eagle.

Gold Medal 🐾 1906
Until 1928 America's Washburn Crosby Company made Gold Medal flour, then the company merged with several others to form General Mills. But the Gold Medal emblem has endured to this day.

Morton Salt 🐾 1933
The girl has been "modernized" over the years, but the basic image and "When It Rains It Pours" date from 1914.

About the time we discovered we were an economic powerhouse, capable of producing a vast volume and variety of almost everything, advertising became a surging growth industry. By 1900 companies regularly used talented artists and writers to create pitches for their wares. Some companies had their own creative advertising teams; others hired one of a swelling number of ad agencies to create the words and pictures that would sell their products, services, or ideas. By 1950 advertising expenditure in America was $5.7 billion a year; in the 1990's the annual figure for Canada and America was more than $100 billion. On these two pages are 20 ad images that caught our attention in this century.

Breck 🐾 1937
Idealized "Breck girls" sold a lot of shampoo. This painting of 17-year-old Roma Whitney later became a Breck trademark.

Beautiful Hair **BRECK**

Bon Ami 🐾 1918
A chick and the slogan "Hasn't Scratched Yet" pitched the gentler scouring power of Bon Ami.

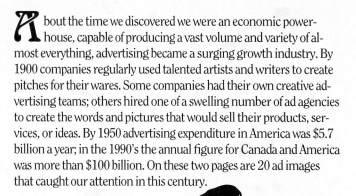

Fisk Tires 🐾 1914
A memorable ad for replacement tires, the idea hit 18-year-old advertising artist Burr E. Giffen as he lay abed one night in 1907. He leaped up and illustrated the pun "Time to Re-Tire?" with a tyke, a candle, and a Fisk.

Bon Ami

Bright as Silver—

Cracker Jack 🐾 late 1920's
Immortalized in the 1908 song "Take me out to the ball game," the crunchy confection added in-box prizes in 1912.

Wabasso 🐾 1955
Associated with durability and quality, Wabasso Cottons appealed to the 1950's homemaking ethos many women lived by at that time.

Traditionally the Home Maker's Choice

Always ask for Trademarked **WABASSO COTTONS**

Howard Johnson's Restaurants ❧ 1942

By the 1940's, this "Simple Simon Met a Pieman" logo was becoming a familiar sight up and down the East Coast.

Motorola TV ❧ 1950

When TV was new, consumers wondered how the sets would fit in their homes. Makers responded with stylish cabinets.

Coca-Cola ❧ 1953

Ads for the soft drink have long linked it to good feelings and happy times.

Coppertone ❧ 1960's

"Little Miss Coppertone," in magazines and on billboards, was such a hit in the 1960's that 9 out of 10 Americans recognized her suntan lotion's name.

Clairol ❧ 1968

The ambiguity of "Does she or doesn't she [use hair coloring]?" offended some but did wonders for Clairol sales.

Revlon ❧ 1980's

The ads left no doubt that Charlie fragrance was for confident career women.

Xerox ❧ 1977

The leader in office copiers in the 1960's, Xerox used inspired advertising to try to hold its market share.

Air Canada ❧ 1992

The enormous carrying power of the pelican's bill and pouch made a humorous and effective symbol for Air Canada Cargo, and won this Cossette Communication-Marketing ad high acclaim and awards.

Fruit of the Loom ❧ 1987

Until their retirement in 1992 after years of service, these happy fellows in fruit costumes promoted the goods of "America's No. 1 manufacturer of men's underwear."

Smokey Bear ❧ 1987

Forest-fire prevention and Smokey teamed up in the 1940's, when the Foot, Cone & Belding ad agency paired them for the U.S. Forest Service.

Energizer ❧ 1992

One brand of battery looks much like another, but the tireless bunny gave Energizer batteries a winning personality all their own.

HIGH SOCIETY HIGHS AND LOWS

▼ *Newspaper baron and future lord of San Simeon castle in California, William Randolph Hearst, with his wife and son.*

The Potter Palmer château in Chicago.

In the days before movie stars, the nobs and swells of high society were our celebrities, and their every move, from the staging of silly costume balls to wilder misadventures, riveted the public.

Every year society parties got curiouser and curiouser. In 1899 Rudolf Guggenheimer feted 40 guests at the Waldorf-Astoria, its Myrtle Room transformed for the occasion into a lush garden overgrown with roses, hyacinths, and tulips, and populated by a chorus of blackbirds, canaries, and nightingales. In 1902 the Cornelius Vanderbilts transported the cast of the Broadway musical *The Wild Rose* to their Newport estate for an evening's diversion. Mrs. Stuyvesant Fish once coaxed a baby elephant to pass out peanuts to the company gathered at her home, and Harry Lehr served a bone-and-biscuit feast to 100 dogs. Mrs. Fish and Mr. Lehr teamed up to honor mystery guest Prince del Drago of Corsica, who turned out to be a monkey dressed in formal evening wear.

Wealthy Canadians were usually more restrained — perhaps because, like the Eatons, their strong religious beliefs kept them in check. But against that they had the advantage of access to British aristocracy in the form of the

▼ *Echo Camp, the Adirondack "lodge" of Phineas C. Lounsbury, Connecticut governor and president of the Merchants Bank, was typical of the mountain hideaways favored by America's Eastern elite.*

During the summer and winter seasons wealthy enclaves from Newport, Rhode Island, to Palm Beach, Florida, saw the rich participate in a dizzying rush of activities including debuts, balls, and fetes such as this garden party.

William Massey Birks and family, photographed in 1903. He and his two brothers were partners in their father's firm, Henry Birks & Sons, the world's fourth-largest jewellery-maker.

governors general. Those who served from 1900 to 1910 were earls, no less. With their aides and attendants, they were the centrepieces of lavish skating parties to which millionaires and aristocrats came garbed as native hunters and coureurs de bois.

It was a great time to be rich. Maintaining a household staff was inexpensive, and no federal income tax would be imposed until 1913 in the United States, and 1917 in Canada. American nob James Hazen Hyde, heir to the vast Equitable Life Insurance fortune, threw a fancy dress ball in 1905 at which guests dressed as courtiers of Louis XV. The wife of a Chicago department store magnate scintillated in a diamond dog collar and a tiara. With orchestra, a corps de ballet and sumptuous dining, the bill for the evening came to a reported $200,000.

Pursuing Comfort, Nobility, and Virtue

The wealthy spared no expense in the pursuit of leisure. Their second homes, which they called "cottages," were lavish estates in resorts from St. Andrews, New Brunswick, to Pebble Beach, California. In Newport, Rhode Island, playground of the great New York families, William K. Vanderbilt's Marble House, an $11-million edifice in Louis XIV style, came complete with a portrait of the Sun King gazing regally over the dining room. Willie K.'s brother, Cornelius, summered at The Breakers, a 70-room villa staffed with 33 servants and 16 bewigged footmen. The opulence of Newport proved overwhelming for one French visitor: "There are too many tapestries, too many paintings on the walls . . . too many plants, too much crystal, too much silver."

Newport days and nights were filled with horseback riding, yachting, tennis and polo matches, soirées, and balls. But though they lived the lives of kings, the doyens of high society aspired to something more: a noble title. Even that could be bought. It wasn't hard to find a European noble willing to exchange his title for a handsome dowry and a carefree existence. John Graham Hope Horsley-Beresford (fifth lord Decies and major of His Majesty's 7th Hussars) made Vivien Gould a lady and, with the wedding, got the first taste of his own newly acquired status. More than 200 seamstresses assembled the bride's trousseau, and the wedding cake was a $1,000 confection topped by cupids bearing the groom's coat of arms.

While the Canadian press rarely had anything but polite praise for the rich, the press in the United States used the antics of the well-heeled for gossip fodder. A prime target was Harry K. Thaw, scion of a Pittsburgh steel and mining family. Thaw's escapades — he tore apart cafés and once rode horseback up the stairs of the Union League Club — turned deadly on June 25, 1906, the evening he and his wife, Evelyn Nesbit, attended opening night of a musical at Madison Square Garden. Just as the final strains of "I Could Love a Million Girls" lilted from the stage, Thaw rose from his chair, walked up to architect Stanford White, seated nearby, and muttering, "You ruined my wife," shot him. It seems White had carried on an affair with Evelyn when she was 16. Two murder trials ensued, and Thaw, found "not guilty because insane," was institutionalized. His defence team had portrayed their client as a man who had "struck for the purity of the wives and homes of America."

Chorus girl and artist's model Evelyn Nesbit formed one corner of the love triangle conjoining her hot-tempered husband, Harry K. Thaw, and her lover, the eminent architect Stanford White. White designed Madison Square Garden, New York City, the site of his murder at the hands of Thaw.

A Grim Night on the North Atlantic

The *Titanic,* "the world's safest liner," had a pool, a Parisian café, luxury rooms for its first-class passengers — and too few lifeboats: only 1,178 lifeboat spaces for 2,207 passengers and crew. When the ship hit an iceberg, the captain, Edward Smith, ordered "women and children first" into the lifeboats, but many first-class male passengers got into the boats anyway. Meanwhile, women and children farther below in second and third classes failed to reach the boats in the confusion, and were doomed. Some of the wealthy men who survived were branded cowards, but high society had its heroes too. Financier John Jacob Astor put his new bride in a lifeboat and went down with the ship.

A large number of the dead lie buried in a churchyard in Halifax. For many, they represent the price of a decade of overreaching pride. Just two years later, that pride took another blow when the *Empress of Ireland* went down in the Gulf of St. Lawrence. It sank in just 14 minutes, taking 1,015 with her.

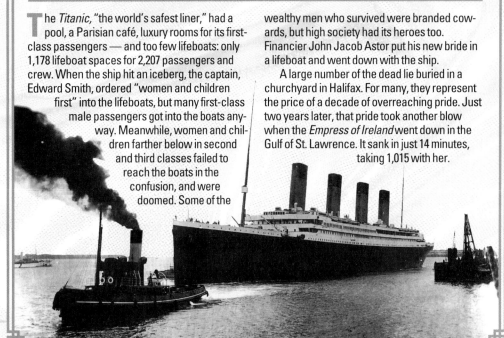

We DISCOVER OUR NERVES

Nervous conditions certainly existed before 1900, but when psychologists theorized that overuse of the intellect was the cause, neurosis took on a certain glamor. Sigmund Freud proposed a radically different source of neurological disorders: the unconscious mind.

As North America entered the 20th century, across the entire continent its populations suffered attacks of nerves. The bustle and strain of the modern industrial era, according to medical experts of the time, had jangled our nerves — so much so that the very word *nerves* took on a new meaning. Formerly, having "nerves" meant that a person was blessed with coolness under pressure, but by the turn of the century, *nerves* had become synonymous with *jittery*, *jumpy*, and *irritable*. Annoyances were things that "got on one's nerves." Doctors theorized that each person had a limited reservoir of "nerve force" and that when the supply was used up, mental illness resulted. Some doctors, with a fine disregard of Canadian participation, called the new malady American nervousness.

One of the most prominent neurologists of the era, George M. Beard, attributed these mental woes to the ever-accelerating pace of life brought on by the steam engine, the telegraph, the printing press, and other modern contrivances. Cities, in which such baleful influences multiplied, were portrayed as modern versions of the primeval jungle, where the workingman used "nerve power" instead of physical strength in the struggle to survive. Fitness experts worried that the shift from rural to city jobs represented an unnatural trend. "Is it not shameful," wrote one doctor, "to think of a

▲ **The Toronto Hospital for the Insane (above) was the first Canadian setting for the practice of Freud's theories. His disciple Ernest Jones (inset) scandalized the public by living with a mistress, and by exploring the sexual problems of his patients. Jones's career at the hospital lasted all of five years.**

◄

An illustration from an advertisement depicts a man in the throes of an attack by vicious demons representing catarrh (sinusitis), neuralgia, headache, toothache, and "weak nerves." The recommended cure? Wolcott's Instant Pain Annihilator, of course.

big, well-built man, brought up on the farm . . . spending his days . . . whispering into a Dictaphone?"

To describe the malady he diagnosed with increasing frequency, Dr. Beard used the word *neurasthenia*, meaning weakness of the nerves. Oddly enough, it was chic to be diagnosed as neurasthenic. The intelligent were considered especially prone to the condition, their brains being susceptible to exhaustion from thinking too much. Before long, *neurasthenia* became a catchall term for any inexplicable ailment. Complaints as varied as insomnia, asthma, headache, skin rash, hay fever, and even baldness were all attributed to nervousness.

Charlatans promoted all manner of nerve medications, guaranteed to bring relief from "brain fatigue."

In newspapers across Canada and the United States, tucked among the ads for bicycles and sewing machines, one could find the electric belt, an apparatus that, when strapped about the waist, sent electric impulses coursing through the body. The official cure called for treatments that differed according to gender: men were advised to head out west for a dose of fresh air and exercise; women were told to stay indoors and avoid all stimulation.

The United States Welcomes Freud

The U.S.'s penchant for looking at itself made that country fertile ground for the revolutionary theories of Viennese neurologist Sigmund Freud. Using dream interpretation to delve into the unconscious mind, Freud theorized that the repression of impulses and experiences, including those of a sexual nature, underlay many mental abnormalities. In 1909 Freud made a triumphant visit to the United States, giving a series of lectures at Clark University, in Worcester, Massachusetts. He was surprised and delighted at his warm reception. Freud's host in Worcester, having heard of his guest's fondness for cigars, placed a box in every room of the house.

Canadians were less receptive to his ideas. When Ernest Jones, one of Freud's most brilliant disciples, was appointed to the Toronto Hospital for the Insane in 1908, he shocked staid colleagues both by having a mistress and by his practice of looking for sexual problems in his patients. After several years of scandals, he left in 1913. Canadians might accept electric belts, but they were not yet ready for Freud.

Russian physiologist Ivan P. Pavlov used dogs in a series of experiments to prove his conditioned-reflex theory by demonstrating that neurotic behavior can be learned.

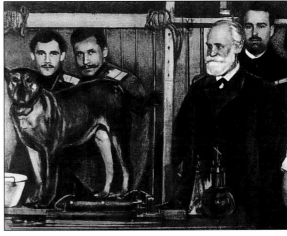

MEDICINE GETS A DOSE OF SCIENCE

The patent-medicine industry was exposed as a hoax, and health officials, armed with scientific know-how and training, waged a winning battle against illness and filth.

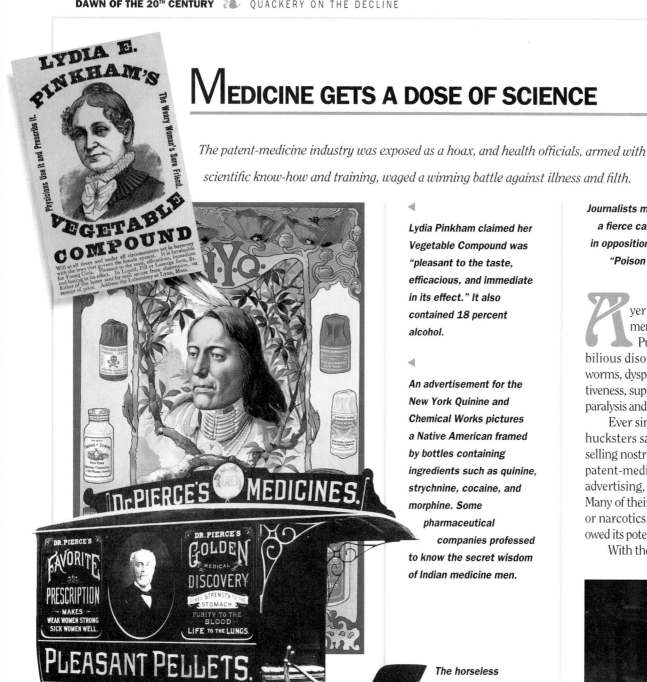

Lydia Pinkham claimed her Vegetable Compound was "pleasant to the taste, efficacious, and immediate in its effect." It also contained 18 percent alcohol.

An advertisement for the New York Quinine and Chemical Works pictures a Native American framed by bottles containing ingredients such as quinine, strychnine, cocaine, and morphine. Some pharmaceutical companies professed to know the secret wisdom of Indian medicine men.

Journalists mounted a fierce campaign in opposition to the "Poison Trust."

yer's Cathartic Pills, according to the advertisement in Canadian newspapers, were the "Prince of Purges," a sure cure for headache, foul stomach, bilious disorders, liver complaints, dysentry, diarrhea, worms, dyspepsia, impurity of the blood, constipation, costiveness, suppression, rheumatism, gout, neuralgia, dropsy, paralysis and — just in case it had missed something — fits.

Ever since the days of the travelling medicine show, hucksters saw a way to make money by concocting and selling nostrums promising cure-all benefits. It didn't take patent-medicine hawkers long to discover that through advertising, their products reached a far wider audience. Many of their secret compounds consisted largely of liquor or narcotics. Dr. King's New Discovery for Consumption owed its potency to both opium and chloroform.

With the new century, the medical tide began to turn.

The horseless carriage replaced the old-time snake-oil peddler's painted wagon, but the pitch remained pretty much the same.

Crusading physicians and muckrakers in the United States challenged the leaders of the patent-medicine industry (the "Poison Trust") and, in 1906, forced passage of the Pure Food and Drug Act, requiring drug manufacturers to list contents on labels. As it had been in controlling the trusts, Canada was slow to act. Not until 1939 would it impose controls on the pharmaceutical industry.

The era of modern medicine had begun. Doctors and public health officials made inroads against the appalling urban squalor that bred diseases, including cholera, diphtheria, and typhoid. Sanitation and nutrition standards in late-19th-century New Orleans had been so poor that the life expectancy for a white person was 38.1 years and for a black person, 25.5 years. For infant mortality, the worst city in the western world was Montreal, with one of three babies dying in their first year. But by the turn of the century, cities, states, and provinces were establishing health departments, and the fight was on for proper sanitation, a reduction of air and water pollution, and a healthy food supply.

With each new advance, physicians pondered the many medical marvels that lay ahead. Under the headline "May Transplant the Human Heart," *The New York Times* reported in 1908 that pathologist Simon Flexner had predicted the transplanting of hearts, kidneys, and other organs in

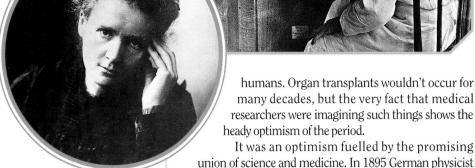

A French physician in 1895 examines his patient with an early X-ray device. X-rays were first used in diagnosis and later for therapy.

In 1903 Marie Curie, her husband Pierre, and Antoine Becquerel received a joint Nobel Prize for their research in radioactivity. To this day the Curies' notes are tainted by dangerous levels of radiation.

humans. Organ transplants wouldn't occur for many decades, but the very fact that medical researchers were imagining such things shows the heady optimism of the period.

It was an optimism fuelled by the promising union of science and medicine. In 1895 German physicist Wilhelm Röntgen had discovered the X ray, a form of radiation. Shortly thereafter, French scientist Antoine Henri Becquerel noted the phenomenon of naturally occurring radiation, and Marie and Pierre Curie embarked on research that would lead to the isolation of two radioactive elements. The uses for radiation in cancer treatment would become evident over time, but medical applications for the X ray were immediately apparent: for the first time doctors could look inside the human body without performing invasive surgery. During the Spanish-American War, U.S. military surgeons took X-ray machines into the field. By 1903 an American doctor was using X rays to treat leukemia.

But the era's most dramatic feat was the conquest of yellow fever. To test the theory that mosquitoes were the agents of the disease, American doctors and soldiers and Cuban civilians volunteered to subject themselves to the bites of mosquitoes that had already bitten yellow-fever victims. When several volunteers contracted the disease and died, the experts had the dreadful evidence they needed to prove that mosquitoes were indeed the culprits. Medical teams set about exterminating the insects in Cuba, Panama, and the American South. The mainland United States saw its last major epidemic in 1905.

A nurse for the Board of Health weighs a baby. By 1915 pediatrics would become a specialty.

Children play in an open gutter on New York's Lower East Side. Citizens' groups, largely made up of women, sought to clean city streets of litter, sewage, and spoiled produce.

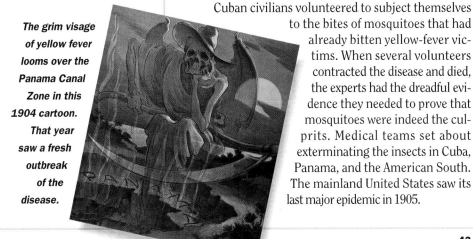

The grim visage of yellow fever looms over the Panama Canal Zone in this 1904 cartoon. That year saw a fresh outbreak of the disease.

CONQUERING EARTH'S FROZEN FRONTIERS

Most of the world's wild places — the jungles of Africa, the deserts of Arabia — had by now been explored. But the earth's two polar regions were still blanks on the map. The challenge of reaching them brought triumph to some, tragedy to others.

Hundreds of artifacts celebrated Robert Peary's Arctic achievements, including this portrait from a 1910 souvenir dinner menu. More than a decade earlier, artist F. W. Stokes had painted the explorer's ship (far left) under a shimmering aurora borealis on an expedition to Greenland. A 1909 photo (inset) shows a group of Peary's sled dogs and Inuit guides.

Dr. Frederick Cook, who claimed he reached the North Pole first, takes a breather during his 1908 Arctic venture. He delayed his announcement, he said, because he got lost on the way home.

ore than 640 kilometres beyond remotest Greenland, amid the constantly shifting pack ice of the Arctic Ocean, lies the planet's northernmost point. No landmark indicates the North Pole; only readings from a sextant or other navigational device will show its exact position. Yet by the turn of the century, the desire to reach it had become an obsession. For around it — and around the South Pole in Antarctica 180 degrees to the south — spread the last unexplored regions of planet Earth. To some their call was irresistible.

Robert E. Peary first journeyed to the Arctic in the 1880's as a surveyor for the U.S. Navy. He trekked through Greenland, mapped its north coast, and brought back valuable data for science. And all the while his attention drifted north toward the pole — "the goal of the world's desire," as he put it. He made his first attempt to reach the pole in 1893

but was forced back. In 1905–06 he came within 322 kilometres, farther north than anyone before him. And in 1908, at age 52, he ventured forth once again.

He took six companions, including a black assistant, Matthew Henson, who shared all his exploits. His ship, the *Roosevelt*, was a steamer he had designed himself. In Greenland they picked up dogs, sleds, Inuit guides, and, for food, 71 tonnes of whale meat and walrus blubber. Then, in the deepening twilight of Arctic summer, they ploughed through the ice floes to Cape Sheridan, on the north coast of Ellesmere Island. There Peary and his men hunkered down in the round-the-clock darkness of polar winter.

The pole lay 660 kilometres across the ice pack from Ellesmere. On February 28, 1909, they set out: 7 Americans, 17 Inuit, and 133 dogs pulling 19 sturdy sledges. Behind them the returning sun cast a pale yellow

This photograph of the doomed Capt. Scott (center) and his party at the South Pole was developed from film found with their bodies. Lt. Bowers (bottom, left) had snapped the shutter with a piece of string.

graciously penned a welcome note to Scott, and headed for home. The trip had run as smoothly as silk over glass.

With Scott, meanwhile, everything went wrong. Instead of sled dogs he used Mongolian ponies, a disastrous choice. The ponies died in the cold, and his men had to pull the sleds. Food ran low, and exhaustion set in. Grimly, Scott drove on with four companions. They reached the pole on January 17, 1912 — only to find Amundsen's note. The trip back was worse. Weakened by malnutrition and exposure, they perished in a blizzard only 17.5 kilometres from a food cache. Even so, Scott died a hero. A relief expedition found his diary, with a final entry that seemed to represent the ultimate triumph of grace over adversity. "We shall stick it out to the end . . ." it said, "and the end cannot be far." And then a postscript: "For God's sake, look after our people."

glow; temperatures hovered at 50 degrees below zero, cold enough to freeze a flask of brandy Peary carried under his parka. Ahead stretched a frozen, gale-swept chaos of ice ridges and flats cut by ominous black leads (channels) of open water. Advance teams, moving in relays, set up camps and food caches. Finally, Peary, Henson, and four Inuit made a final dash for the pole. They sped the last 213 kilometres in just four days, and on April 6, 1909, they were there. Crisscrossing the ice to make sure of his position, Peary chose a low ice mound and marked it with the American flag. Then, reaching Labrador on his return trip, he cabled his wife: "Have made good at last. I have the old Pole."

But had he? Only days earlier a rival explorer, Dr. Frederick A. Cook, had turned up in Denmark claiming to have reached the North Pole the previous summer. The newspapers labelled Cook a hero. Then over the next months it became clear that the doctor was lying; according to his Inuit guides, he had never gone beyond sight of land. But for a while, a cloud hung over Peary's triumph.

South in Antarctica, two nations were in a race to the planet's other pole. Capt. Robert Scott of the British Royal Navy landed at McMurdo Sound in early 1911 on his second trip to the frozen continent. At almost the same time, a rival expedition, led by Roald Amundsen of Norway, disembarked on the Ross Ice Shelf, some 640 kilometres to the east.

Amundsen had already scored some notable firsts in the Far North, including his discovery of the long-sought Northwest Passage between Greenland and Alaska. Relying on his years of Arctic experience, he equipped himself with skis, dog sleds, Inuit parkas, and seal meat to ward off scurvy. In mid-October he led his men across the ice shelf, then worked his way over the 3,658-metre-high glaciers of the Queen Maud Mountains. On December 15 he reached the world's basement. He raised the Norwegian flag,

▼ Roald Amundsen, clad in furs, scans the Antarctic horizon. Here the Norwegian carries snowshoes and an alpenstock, but usually he travelled on cross-country skis.

Staking Canada's Claim

In 1866, at the age of 14, he was a cabin boy. At 17, he was captain of a ship carrying timber across the North Atlantic to England. Joseph-Elzéar Bernier of L'Islet, Quebec, went on to command more than 100 ships during a lifetime at sea, but his greatest ambition was to reach the North Pole.

He taught himself navigation, became an authority on polar navigation, and bought a ship named *Arctic* in preparation for a voyage to the North Pole. In 1904 the Canadian government hired Bernier and his ship to establish a presence in the Arctic, to collect customs duties from whalers, to contact settlements and, when time permitted, to explore.

Spending winters locked into the ice while mapping a still unknown region, Capt. Bernier solidified a shaky claim and ensured that the Canadian Arctic would indeed belong to Canada.

CRUSADERS FOR A BETTER WORLD

Their consciences stung by reports of widespread poverty and corruption, North Americans embarked

on a series of needed reforms. Private charities, government legislatures, and individual citizens all pitched in.

In the fall of 1902 wealthy socialite J. G. Phelps Stokes made front-page headlines in *The New York Times* with a shocking announcement: he would leave the family mansion on Madison Avenue and live permanently at the University Settlement on Eldridge Street, in the heart of the slums, where he would spend the rest of his life working with the poor. His parents must have been astonished. Yet, from patrician drawing rooms to middle-class parlors, from church socials to the loftiest corridors of political power, an awareness was growing that large segments of society were in need of major repair. The result across the continent was a groundswell of social activism, which ranged from simple charity to business and labor reform to improved housing and health care to such radical programs as woman suffrage, socialism, birth control, and the prohibition of strong drink.

Champions of "the Other Half"

The most glaring social problem was poverty. In 1890, journalist Jacob Riis published a book of photographs of immigrant tenements on New York's Lower East Side. *How the Other Half Lives*, with its images of ragged children, decrepit rooming houses, and sweatshop working conditions, stung the American conscience. In Canada, Herbert Brown Ames published *The City Below the Hill* in 1897. Its account of filthy streets, crowded housing and outdoor privies in the centre of the city showed the problem in Montreal to be at least as bad as it was in New York.

At a time when most North Americans were enjoying the liveliest economic boom in decades, it was clear that

Upton Sinclair's savage indictment of America's meat- ▲ packing industry told of tubercular hogs, foul working conditions, and mistreatment of employees.

millions of others were leading lives of appalling deprivation. Boston, Chicago, Montreal, Toronto — almost every major city contained a ghetto neighborhood characterized by shoddy housing, poor sanitation, high unemployment, and rampant disease. In these dark precincts, crime flourished and drunkenness prevailed.

Some people were quick to blame the victims, many of whom were immigrants from eastern and southern Europe. "The vice and crime which they have planted in our midst are sickening and terrifying," lamented one observer. Others took a more reasoned look. In his 1908 study of Winnipeg, *The Strangers Within Our Gates*, clergyman J. S. Woodsworth examined the poverty of immigrants and pointed an accusing finger at exploitive businessmen and indifferent politicians.

Even as these alarms were sounded, individual citizens rolled up their sleeves to make things better. The remarkable Jane Addams, a former medical student, moved to the Chicago slums and opened Hull House as a centre of relief, comfort, education, and settlement for the city's needy. Saint Jane, as she was dubbed, taught sewing and reading, ran a kindergarten, organized boys' clubs, offered baths to families with no running water, and badgered municipal authorities for better schools, sewers, and other services. Similar settlement houses sprang up across Canada and the United States, and together they gave respectability to a newly developing profession: social work.

Mabel Peters of St. John, New Brunswick, was dismayed at the sight of children learning crime in the shabby streets that were their only playground. (City councillors, chosen largely from the wealthy, built most parks in their own districts.) Ms. Peters cajoled schools into opening their yards and converted vacant lots for supervised play. Her Playground Movement spread across Canada to become the basis of modern city parks and playgrounds.

Social reformer J. S. Woodsworth accused businessmen and politicians of increasing poverty among immigrants in Winnipeg.

Journalist Ida Tarbell set the era's muckraking style with her exposé of Standard Oil, which caused the monopoly's breakup.

Volunteer nurses report for duty at the Henry Street Settlement, on New York City's Lower East Side. Nearly 100 settlement houses were already ministering to immigrants' needs in the nation's slums when the century opened, and most of them took their cue from Chicago's Hull House, founded by social pioneer Jane Addams (inset) in 1889.

A crew of teenage "breaker" boys at a coal mine poses for the camera of muckraking journalist Lewis Hine. Miners' sons normally went full-time to the pits at age 10; they sorted coal from other rock as it emerged from a crushing machine, or breaker. Starting pay for children at the mines was 35 cents a day.

Immigrants in a New York City tenement building might have lived as many as seven to a room, as in this 1910 family portrait by Jacob Riis. There was no fire escape, no central heat, no hot water, and sanitation facilities were a privy in the backyard.

Ladies on the March

Suffragette campaign buttons promised a glorious new dawn in American politics, in which votes for women would end corruption, graft, and other evils.

In 1900, governments believed that women belonged at home tending the children. They had no business voting. In Canada, women who owned property in their own names could vote in most municipal elections, but not federally or provincially. In the United States, only Wyoming, Colorado, Idaho, and Utah permitted women to vote. For the rest, it was understood that God himself had worked out a social and political order with men on top. "Sensible and responsible women do not want to vote," declared former President Grover Cleveland. Astonishingly, millions of wives and daughters dutifully agreed.

But the reality was changing rapidly. In addition to working-class women who had

As women paraded for the vote draped in patriotic glory (left), men reacted first with scorn, then alarm. The male readers at right scan bulletins posted by a Washington, D.C., anti-suffragette lobby.

always worked outside the home, by 1900 hundreds of thousands of young ladies had left their kitchens to be teachers, salesclerks, or office assistants. In 1875, Mount Allison College in New Brunswick was the first in the British Empire to award a baccalaureate to a woman, and colleges across Canada and the United States soon followed. By the early 1900's, women

were learning to drive cars and run businesses. They were even invading such male preserves as swimming, golf and tennis.

In 1901, E. Cora Hind became agricultural editor of the *Winnipeg Free Press*. The sight of her inspecting crops and wearing a practical costume of breeches and a slouch hat shocked men. But they had to recognize her as the best agricultural analyst in the country. Alice Roosevelt, the American president's beautiful, high-stepping daughter, shocked her elders by playing poker and puffing cigarettes, and nonetheless became a national idol of liberated womanhood.

Terrible inequality still existed, to be sure. But the political clout of the ballot box would go far toward correcting the balance. Dr. Emily Howard Stowe, Canada's first woman doctor, had begun a woman's suffrage movement in Canada in 1876. American women had been led by Susan B. Anthony and Elizabeth Cady Stanton. But the movement languished until inspiration came from England. There, ardent campaigners like Emmeline Pankhurst were storming parliament and getting themselves jailed. In North America, women were less violent, but just as determined. By the 1890's, the Woman's Christian Temperance Union had entered the fray and, by 1910, Canada's influential National Council of Women offered its support.

Male opposition was strong at first; a suffragette, scoffed an unknown wit, was "one who has ceased to be a lady and not yet become a gentleman." But the momentum grew. Some 15,000 women and a brigade of male supporters, cheered on by an estimated 500,000 spectators, marched down Fifth Avenue in New York in May of 1912 in a parade that *The New York Tribune* called "the greatest demonstration of women in American history." By the time the First World War began, in 1914, it was obvious to all that the vote for women was just around the corner.

Francis Stephens Spence (1850–1917) was an Irish-born journalist, politician and social reformer. His father was a vocal temperance crusader, who even churned out pamphlets from a printing press in his home. Francis edited several prohibition journals, and in 1902 founded **The Pioneer,** *which became the official organ of the temperance movement in Ontario. He served in several offices for the city of Toronto as a Liberal reformist, favoring female suffrage, the playground movement, and unions, all of which he saw as essential to material and moral progress. But crucial to this progress was the destruction of the liquor traffic, to which he devoted most of his life. From 1886 to 1907 he was secretary of the Ontario branch of the Dominion Alliance, a militant Prohibition organization. And in 1908 he was made its honorary president.*

Some reformers sprang from the ranks of the victims themselves. Seamstresses in New York City sweatshops regularly worked 10-hour days, 6 days a week, and earned as little as 30 cents a day. In 1900 they banded together in the International Ladies' Garment Workers' Union (ILGWU) and pushed for higher pay. The American Federation of Labor (AFL), founded in 1886 and headed by New York cigar maker Samuel Gompers, already boasted more than 500,000 members in 1900, and it was growing. Slowly, wages and working conditions would begin to improve.

According to the 1900 census in the United States, more than 1.7 million children were "gainfully employed." Most worked on farms, but some 284,000 boys and girls toiled in coal mines, textile factories and the like. The Canadian census for 1901 shows a child labor force of 28,000 under the age of 16. But this figure does not take into account the tens of thousands working on farms, in home workshops, or in domestic service. The last suffered even longer working hours than the 10- or 12-hour day, 6 days a week, common in industry. One of the most poignant verses of the time did not exaggerate:

The golf links lie so near the mill
That almost every day
The laboring children can look out
And see the men at play.

Legislation to prohibit child labor did not pass the U.S. Congress until 1916, and even then the Supreme Court struck it down. Canada tackled the problem with legislation requiring children to attend at least primary school. By 1914, all provinces but Quebec had such a requirement. In other areas, government moved firmly to curtail abuses. New York City, responding to Riis's slum photos, passed a series of landmark housing laws. In Chicago, at Jane Addams's urging, officials opened the first juvenile court.

No sector of life was immune from the crusaders' zeal. J. S. Woodsworth followed his study of immigration with another of poverty in Winnipeg, *My Neighbour.* His indictment of big business brought him a step closer to the socialism he would soon espouse. In the United States, Upton Sinclair, researching a novel about the hard life of Chicago meat-packers, discovered that much of the nation's output of breakfast sausages contained tainted pork. Sinclair's *The Jungle* caused such a furor that it spurred passage of the 1906 Pure Food and Drug Act. No one was more astonished than the novelist himself. "I aimed at the public's heart," he said, "and by accident I hit in the stomach."

Some 2,000 journalistic exposés appeared during the decade in the popular magazines, and so strident did their tone become that even Teddy Roosevelt, surely one of the era's most outspoken crusaders (see pp. 22–23), grew tired of them. The authors were muckrakers, the president declared. But the muckrakers wore their title proudly and continued to attack social ills.

Roosevelt had another name for radical extremists in any reform movement: the lunatic fringe. The group included labor agitators and those who urged violence to bring about change. Also among its members were some Protestant clergymen attracted by the Social Gospel, a movement which condemned capitalism as anti-Christian because it was competitive. Rev. J. G. Shearer, through the Presbyterian Moral and Social Reform Council, put his church in the vanguard of social reform in Canada.

And there were the formidable ladies of the Woman's Christian Temperance Union (WCTU). Convinced that demon rum was the cause of society's ills, these advocates of Prohibition joined the militant Anti-Saloon League in the United States and the Dominion Alliance for the total Suppression of the Liquor Traffic in Canada, to take arms against the liquor dealers. With rallies, revival meetings, and marches as their weapons, they forced county after county to close bars and liquor stores. In 1901, they scored a major victory when Prince Edward Island became Canada's first province to enact a prohibition law.

The prohibitionists did not stop at the attack on liquor. By 1900, some alcohol reformers were also demanding pensions for the elderly, domestic training for working-class girls and a few were even talking of something they called Christian socialism. But whatever the secondary issues, they remained united in their demand for prohibition. By 1910, it was clear in both Canada and the United States that Prohibition would soon become the law of the land.

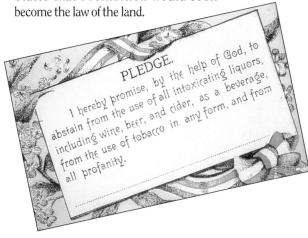

PLEDGE.

I hereby promise, by the help of God, to abstain from the use of all intoxicating liquors, including wine, beer, and cider, as a beverage, and from the use of tobacco in any form, and from all profanity.

The pledge of the Woman's Christian Temperance Union forswore not only drinking, but also smoking and swearing.

Loving the Great Outdoors

"Thousands of tired, nerve-shaken, over-civilized people are beginning to find out that . . . wildness is a necessity," observed American naturalist John Muir, a tireless battler for unspoiled areas.

As cities became more crowded, places like Yosemite Valley (above left) and the Canadian Rockies (left), drew increasing public attention.

Most North Americans of the early 19th century detested the wilderness. To them, it was an obstacle to progress, a place of danger, discomfort, and hard work, crammed with trees that had to be chopped down and then chopped up. But as the countryside filled with cities noisier, dirtier, and more dangerous than the forests had ever been, the wilderness took on a new appeal. In contrast to the city, it came to be regarded as a place of physical and spiritual cleanliness, where one could return to the natural state. The Canadian Pacific Railway capitalized on that feeling to attract tourists to the Canadian West. In 1887, it encouraged government to protect a wilderness region for tourism with the creation of Rocky Mountain Parks Reserve (now Banff National Park). In the United States, support for the wilderness movement came from Theodore Roosevelt who, in turn, was inspired by his hiking guide, John Muir.

Then 65, John Muir had long called for the preservation of the wilderness. At last the country had begun to heed his pleas and respond to the lyrical prose of naturalist John Burroughs of New York, whose writings on life in the Catskills were among the most popular of the era. Facing staunch opposition from would-be developers, Muir helped set the stage for Roosevelt's campaign to save as much wilderness as he could. "I hate the man who would skin the land!" Roosevelt thundered, and during his term of office he set aside some 93 million hectares of land for preservation.

Roosevelt signed laws to withdraw important watersheds from settlement and to protect Alaskan fisheries; he appointed the National Conservation Commission to undertake a survey of natural resources, established the first federal wildlife refuges, and doubled the number of national parks. Among his strongest supporters was the railway industry, one of the great engines of development. The railway barons recognized that the creation of national parks would give a tremendous boost to tourism and that the railways, in turn, would profit.

Legacy of the Lost Hetch Hetchy

John Muir crusaded valiantly to preserve a spectacular valley, called Hetch Hetchy, to the north of Yosemite. He praised it as "one of Nature's rarest and most precious mountain temples." The city of San Francisco wanted to dam the waters of the valley and turn it into a reservoir system. "Dam Hetch Hetchy?" Muir spluttered. "As well dam for water-tanks the people's cathedrals and churches, for no holier temple has ever been consecrated by the heart of man." He was able to hold off the dam builders for several years, but in 1913 Woodrow Wilson's secretary of the interior engineered the removal of the valley from federal protection. Muir died the next year, defeated in his last major battle. A fresh army was forming to fight for future Hetch Hetchys, however, an army of youngsters who would learn first-hand a reverence for nature.

Nowhere was the yearning for the outdoor life more evident than in the explosive growth of the Boy Scout movement. Scouting had been founded in Great Britain in 1908 by Lt.-Gen. Robert Baden-Powell, who

Robert Baden-Powell in the "practical, cheap, and comfortable" uniform he designed for the Boy Scouts.

Half Dome rises above John Muir and Theodore Roosevelt on their 1903 Yosemite trip. When Muir (inset left) and John Burroughs (inset far left) visited the park together in 1909, Burroughs quietly contemplated its wonders as Muir exuberantly hailed waterfalls and rock formations.

Ruffling Some Feathers

In the early years of the 20th century, millinery fashions reached their height — literally. Hatmakers piled their creations high with ostrich and egret plumes and jaunty sprays of bird-of-paradise and parrot feathers. Some hats were taxidermic still lifes that featured a stuffed oriole, wren, skylark, even a sea gull or owl, as the centrepiece.

But such fashions came at a price: the loss of native birds by the thousands each year. In 1903 Roosevelt took steps to end the devastation by establishing the first federal wildlife refuge, on Pelican Island, Florida, a nesting place for the besieged waterfowl of the area. This action, along with a shift in taste toward smaller, less downy headdress, marked the beginning of a comeback for many birds.

had won international fame and the admiration of young boys for his exploits in the Boer War. Spontaneously, these boys formed neighborhood groups calling themselves "Scouts" in emulation of Baden-Powell's ideas of roving military units. By 1908, Baden-Powell found himself, almost accidentally, the leader of a world movement which he organized along the lines of British public schools. The school master became the scout master and the prefects patrol leaders. The movement was designed to make obedient and trustworthy workers out of young boys, an aim that won wide support among business leaders. It came to Canada in 1908 and spread to the United States in 1909 where, within two years, more than 125,000 boys joined.

The lack of a similar outdoor group for girls led quickly to the formation of the Camp Fire Girls in the United States and the Girl Guides in Canada. Not everyone was pleased at that development. The editor of Canada's *Saturday Night* feared that that movement would create wild "cowgirls" rather than young ladies.

Both nations were gripped by an immense enthusiasm for the outdoors early in the century. As they moved headlong to becoming urban societies, many of their citizens came to recognize the value of wilderness lands as places of sanctuary and moral uplift. "It is blessed to lean fully and trustfully on Nature," wrote Muir, "to experience the infinite tenderness and power of her love."

From 1907 to 1919, Ty Cobb (right) of the Detroit Tigers led the American League in batting 12 times, won 4 RBI titles, and stole the most bases 6 times.

THE CENTURY'S GAMES BEGIN

Modern sports took the field in the century's opening decade. Firsts included baseball's World

Series, college football's Rose Bowl, tennis's Davis Cup, and Olympic Games held in America.

In the 19th century, Canadians were world leaders in organized sport. They had invented modern lacrosse, ice hockey, North American football, and basketball. Only the rich could play in those days. But by 1900, betting and growing audiences were providing salaries that made it possible for working-class athletes to play. The rich, annoyed at this invasion of their sporting clubs, indignantly retreated to polo, yachting and golf, leaving the athletic spotlight to the professionals.

And what professionals they were! Joe Malone, who joined the Quebec Bulldogs hockey team in 1909, once averaged more than two goals a game for a full season, and even scored nine goals in just one game. Newsy Lalonde, who played for the Montreal Canadiens in their first season in 1909–10, was a star in both hockey and lacrosse. It was a combination that earned him 30 times the income of a working man. Professional sport had truly come to Canada.

Baseball, though long popular among working-class and rural Canadians, did not catch on quickly as a professional sport in Canada. The game was looked down on by the wealthy as both lower class and tainted by Americanism, which left Canadian baseball players no option but to drift to professional teams in the United States, where the World Series had been played since 1903. One of those Canadians, from Ontario, achieved such fame that an American father named his son after him. The son never became a baseball player, but he did become Speaker of the House of Representatives. His name was Tip O'Neil.

Professional boxing, though frowned on in Canada and outlawed in many American states, captured the headlines

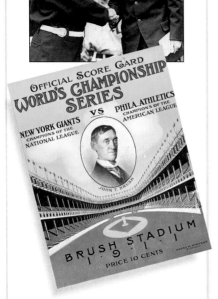

New York Giants' manager John McGraw (left) greets the Philadelphia Athletics' Connie Mack before the 1911 World Series. McGraw managed for 33 years, Mack for 53.

OFFICIAL SCORE CARD
WORLD'S CHAMPIONSHIP SERIES
NEW YORK GIANTS
CHAMPIONS OF THE NATIONAL LEAGUE
VS
PHILA. ATHLETICS
CHAMPIONS OF THE AMERICAN LEAGUE

JOHN T. BRUSH

BRUSH STADIUM 1911
PRICE 10 CENTS

The Shamrock Lacrosse Team, "Champions of the World, 1899–1900," were symbolic of how prominent Canada was becoming in sport.

Shamrock Lacrosse Team.
CHAMPIONS OF THE WORLD, 1899-1900.

Miss Lillian B. Hyde tees off at a women's amateur match in New Jersey, 1914, when golf was starting to surge in popularity with both men and women.

in 1910. Undefeated heavyweight champion Jim Jeffries, after six years of retirement, was coaxed back into the ring in Reno, Nevada, to dethrone Jack Johnson, a Texan who in 1908 had become the first black champion. Johnson's marriages to white women and his defiant attitude had released a torrent of racism; Jeffries was billed as the Great White Hope. Instead, Johnson toyed with his opponent, and dispatched him in the 15th round. Three years later, a dubious morals charge forced the champion to flee the country.

College football, which had originated at Canada's McGill University in the 1860's, flourished. The first Rose bowl contest took place in the United States on January 1, 1902. But it was a violent game. In the 1905 season in the United States, 18 players died from injuries received in the game. That same year President Theodore Roosevelt, an ardent fan, called together officials from Yale, Harvard, and Princeton to demand that they take the lead in reducing the mayhem. They created the forerunner of the National Collegiate Athletic Association (NCAA) to monitor competition, and wrote rules to make football safer. Coaches added innovative offences: at the University of Chicago, Amos Alonzo Stagg dreamed up the backfield shift, and at the Carlisle Indian School, Pop Warner introduced the single wing. By 1913 a little-known school named Notre Dame, with a sticky-fingered end named Knute Rockne, came east with a forward-passing game and upset mighty Army 35–13.

In the first Davis Cup match, Malcolm Whitman, Dwight Davis, and Holcombe Ward beat the British 5–0.

Even country-club tennis and golf were producing world-class athletes. In 1900 Harvard student Dwight Davis initiated the Davis Cup to spur competition with England and stimulate U.S. interest in tennis. The U.S. Open golf tournament, begun in 1895, finally crowned its first American champion in 1911, when New Jersey's Johnny McDermott turned the trick.

Lacrosse was at the height of its popularity, and Canadian teams dominated the game, winning Olympic gold medals in 1904 and 1908. In 1910, railway magnate Sir Donald Mann donated a cup for the amateur championship. Made of gold, the Mann cup was the most expensive sporting cup of the day.

Although 1904 saw the first Olympics ever held in North America, in St. Louis, the 1912 Stockholm Olympics capped the era. It spotlighted the triumph, and tragedy, of Jim Thorpe, an Oklahoma-born American Indian whose athletic feats had helped tiny Carlisle Indian School reach top status in football and track. Thorpe's incredible versatility enabled him to take gold medals in the pentathlon and the decathlon (setting a record for total points). Everyone from kings to presidents toasted him. Then tragedy struck: when the Olympic panjandrums learned that Thorpe had earned $60 a month to play minor league baseball, they stripped him of his medals. Thorpe's medals were not returned until 1982, nearly 30 years after his death.

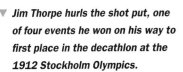

Jim Thorpe hurls the shot put, one of four events he won on his way to first place in the decathlon at the 1912 Stockholm Olympics.

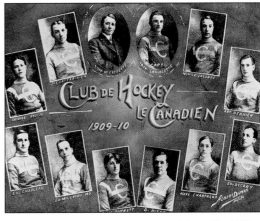

The first Canadiens hockey team debuted in 1909 and immediately made the grade thanks to their star player Newsy Lalonde (top right).

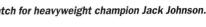

On July 4, 1910, Jim Jeffries (left) proved no match for heavyweight champion Jack Johnson.

▲ *This 1894 kinetoscope of the mighty sneeze of Edison lab worker Fred Ott was a runaway hit.*

FRED'S SNEEZE, NICKELODEONS, AND HOLLYWOOD

Within 15 years what had begun as turn-of-the-century tinkering with awkwardly moving images evolved into a multimillion-dollar industry that shed glamor on a patch of California sagebrush.

For years photographers and inventors had demonstrated to fascinated Victorians that images could seem to move in "trick" machines with weird names like Projecting Phenakistiscope and the Wheel of Life. In 1891 Thomas A. Edison, already world famous for the light bulb and the phonograph, exhibited the kinetoscope, a box with a peephole and a crank that rolled a few seconds of "moving" images past a viewer (above, left). Soon kinetoscope parlors with rows of boxes enthralled viewers, who paid pennies to see "Fred Ott's Sneeze" or a clown juggle.

Across the Atlantic, pioneer French filmmakers had thrown a kinetoscope image onto a large screen for a Paris audience, creating arguably the first picture show. (Edison's attempts to project kinetoscope images onto a larger screen were not so successful.) Another Parisian, the magician Georges Méliès, discovered something else when his camera jammed shooting a Paris street scene: a hearse "magically" replaced a bus, and special effects were born. Méliès pushed on with "magic" films, like *Christ Walking on the Waters* (1899), *The India Rubber Head* (1901), *A Trip to the Moon* (1902) with frilly "moon girls" and a rocket ship, and, later, *Conquest of the Pole* (1912).

Edison, too, was busy. Creating interior scenes on a Manhattan rooftop set and outdoor scenes on location in New Jersey, he produced the first western. Filmed by Edwin S. Porter, *The Great Train Robbery* (1903) electrified viewers. Into 12 minutes it packed a train robbery, a horseback chase, a running gunfight, and the villains' deaths. The public clamored for more movies, and for places to see them.

The first permanent movie theatre in Canada, the Ouimetoscope, opened in Montreal on New Year's Day, 1906. Patrons watched melodramas of maidens in distress and leering scoundrels, many of them made by the propri-

Filmmaker Georges Méliès works on a painting of a rocket rammed into the moon's right eye for A Trip to the Moon.

▲ *At Edison's New Jersey "Black Maria" studio (above), some 300 movies were shot from 1893 to 1903. The building rotated on a centre pivot and was pushed to follow the sun. In* The Great Train Robbery, *Justus T. Barnes (top) fires his six-gun directly at the audience. Many nickelodeon owners used this sensational scene both to begin and to end a showing.*

etor, Léo-Ernest Ouimet. Within a year there were 1,000 nickelodeons, and the number reached 10,000 by the decade's end, when people were spending nearly $100 million in nickelodeons and more than 25 percent of the population of New York City went to a nickelodeon once a week. By 1914 the first "picture palace" opened on Broadway, with crystal chandeliers and a live orchestra.

Early films made no claim to sophistication. Sometimes called Democracy's Theatre, nickelodeons coupled movies with sing-alongs, vaudeville comics, dog acts, and illustrated lectures. The audiences contained mainly workingmen (a blue-collar city like Pittsburgh had a hundred theatres).

Most movies came from three producers: Edison, Biograph, and Vitagraph. Using natural light, they filmed in open-air studios on rooftops in New York City, across the river in New Jersey, and in Philadelphia. There, as in Canadian cities, rain and cold often interrupted production. Los Angeles sunshine, coupled with cheap actors and a lack of unions, drew movie makers to California. That, and the larger U.S. market, drew Canadian performers south, too. Mack Sennett left his home in Richmond, Ontario, to become one of the most successful Hollywood directors. Mary Pickford, of Toronto, went to Hollywood to become "America's Sweetheart."

In Hollywood the first studio was a roadhouse leased to movie people because local prohibition laws had doomed it to bankruptcy. Agnes de Mille, the great dancer and choreographer, later remembered "wild, wild hills. Sagebrush, and rattlesnakes, and coyotes. . . ." Sunset Boulevard, mostly dirt, followed an old cattle trail; early studios provided hitching rails; and a sign on the back of a streetcar warned, "Don't shoot rabbits from the rear platform."

Everywhere new directors and stars flourished. At Biograph, D. W. Griffith invented the language of film in one-reelers, developing techniques of pacing, editing, cross-cutting, and close-ups. After his first movie, *The Adventures of Dollie,* in 1908, Griffith directed some 400 movies over the next five years. He never abandoned the melodrama of cliffhangers like *Her Terrible Ordeal* (1910), a one-reel thriller about a secretary locked in the company safe. But his camera technique was an inspiration to other directors.

At Keystone Studios, Griffith's protégé Mack Sennett gave the frenetic Griffith chase scene a comic turn. In 1912 he directed the first of the rollercoaster Keystone Kops shorts. They were dazzling orgies of action, with actors racing, sliding, falling, and driving, always wildly out of control and endlessly colliding with cars, animals, pies, and each other.

Two years later Sennett's Keystone Kops romped in America's first feature-length comic film, *Tillie's Punctured Romance,* starring Marie Dressler (also Canadian-born) as a farm girl deceived into marriage by a dastardly smoothy. Her costar was a wispy British music hall comedian who had just joined Keystone Studios at $150 a week: Charlie Chaplin.

The Keystone Kops start the chase, in one of 500 shorts made by Canada's Mack Sennett from 1912 to 1917.

MODERNISM HITS THE ARTS

New ideas threatened some, but they stimulated others to rethink their views of what art could be. One critic wrote: "We are in the midst of . . . a new Renaissance in art — an epoch whose means and discoveries have opened . . . an infinitude of possibilities."

◀ **Marcel Duchamp's "Nude Descending a Staircase," dismissed by one critic as "an explosion in a shingle factory," created a stir at the New York Armory Show.**

United States: a display of 58 drawings by Auguste Rodin. He followed that exhibit with the first American showing of Henri Matisse, then with Toulouse-Lautrec, Rousseau, and a major exhibit of Picasso's works in 1911. Among the innovative U.S. painters Stieglitz introduced were Max Weber, Alfred Maurer, and Georgia O'Keeffe, who married Stieglitz in 1924.

The movement that began in Stieglitz's tiny studio burst into a larger American consciousness in 1913 with the New York Armory Show. There were an estimated 1,300 art works in the Armory Show, one-third by European artists and two-thirds by Americans. Europe was represented by some of

◀ **Innovative photographer Alfred Stieglitz (second from right) critiques artwork with other groundbreaking artists at his New York gallery "291."**

A farm house by a stream with a cow or two nearby were staples of Canadian painting in 1900 — so much so that it was said paintings were priced according to the number of cows in them. But an artistic revolution was bubbling under this bucolic surface. In Victoria, Emily Carr was studying native art whose scuptural forms she molded into her own powerful and colorful images (though Canadians did not immediately respond to them, and she had to make a living managing a small apartment house). Tom Thomson was painting in gale winds and rain to capture the savagery of the Ontario wilderness, but his fame, linked to the Group of Seven, still lay in the future. And James Wilson Morrice was recreating the cold colors and bleak light of Quebec's winter in broad brushstrokes, before retreating to Europe where the climate was kinder and the public more appreciative.

In New York, a bespectacled engineer named Alfred Stieglitz turned his attic into a photographic gallery he called "291." There, photography, still suspect in artistic circles, was displayed along with radically new paintings. In January 1908 he put up the first modern art exhibit in the

▶ **"Winter Scene, Quebec," c. 1900, by J. W. Morrice, portrays the emptiness and silence of winter using simple brushstrokes painted right onto panel, a technique favored by artists at the turn of the century.**

Vaslav Nijinsky, star of the Ballets Russes, dances the ballet Giselle.

Impresario Sergei Diaghilev woke up the world of ballet.

the reigning giants of modern art, among them Picasso, Matisse, Braque, and Cézanne. Traditional critics lost little time in skewering the Armory Show. *The New York Times* worried about modern artists being "cousins to the anarchists in politics," and former President Theodore Roosevelt labelled some of the Armory artists "the lunatic fringe."

Stirrings in the Staid World of Dance

The trend in the performing arts, too, was away from the forms of the past and toward more vitality of expression. The Ballets Russes, launched in 1909 in Paris by impresario Sergei Diaghilev, amazed and sometimes outraged audiences accustomed to the narrowly prescribed movements and conservative themes of traditional ballet. The sweep of Diaghilev's vision was matched only by the talent of his company, which included prima ballerinas Anna Pavlova and Tamara Karsavina, as well as the great Vaslav Nijinsky. As a dancer, Nijinsky brought to the stage a sexual magnetism and athletic ability that set new standards and exploded ballet goers' sense of what was possible.

Still, for creating sheer excitement, Nijinsky was surpassed by an American dancer, Isadora Duncan. Her dancing was something completely new. She had no formal training, for one thing, and danced alone, without the set steps or the tutus and box-toed shoes of the ballet. Dressed in a daring Greek-style tunic, her bare arms and legs visible to all, the dark-eyed melancholy beauty seemed to let the music itself control her, as if she weren't dancing to music but inside it.

Audiences were electrified. "Her body is as though bewitched by the music," wrote one reviewer of her first performance in St. Petersburg in 1904. "Here *everything*

As free-spirited in life as in her dancing, Isadora Duncan here strikes a classical pose.

dances: waist, arms, neck, head —*and* legs. Duncan's bare legs and bare feet are like those of a rustic vagabond; they are innocent. . . ."

North Americans were less enraptured. It was, after all, an age in which audiences were scandalized by a film less than a minute long because it showed a couple kissing. Like her dancing, Isadora's ideas on nearly every subject were ahead of her time, and her lifestyle was unorthodox. She kept many lovers, bore children out of wedlock, and finally married a man 17 years her junior, the Russian poet Sergei Esenin. Duncan scandalized audiences on an American tour in 1922, delivering revolutionary speeches between dances and baring her breasts to an audience of staid Bostonians. City after city cancelled her performances in the interests of public safety.

Finally, Isadora proved too much for North America. She returned to Europe, where she died in a freak accident in 1927. We were hungry for all things new — but not as new as Isadora Duncan.

"Animal dances," such as those featured in the song sheets above, exuberantly pronounced that formality was out, abandon was in.

► In 1912 Irene and Vernon Castle returned from Paris and sparked a nationwide ballroom dancing craze, especially for their Castle Walk.

RAGTIME AND RAZZLE-DAZZLE

Heralding the decades to come, a new breed of entertainers shook off fusty traditions and wowed us with their originality, innocence, confidence, and rebellion.

Dancers did the bunny hug. They also did the camel walk, the buzzard lope, the monkey glide, and the kangaroo dip. And if they looked a little silly bouncing on the balls of their feet like turkeys or scratching the dance floor like chickens, who cared? A new century called for a whole new rhythm.

The new rhythm was ragtime. From the start, rag was played mostly on the piano, and its origins were too many to count. In its syncopated rhythms and catchy melodies, there were echoes of everything from European marches to plantation spirituals. The original rag musicians drifted through the southern U.S. and along the eastern seaboard playing honky-tonks and saloons; most could not read music, so few of their rags were recorded, except as piano rolls.

The recognized king of ragtime was Scott Joplin, the son of a black railway laborer from Texarkana, Texas. As a teenager Joplin joined the itinerant ranks of piano thumpers in bawdy saloons up and down the Mississippi River. After a long sojourn in the tenderloin districts of St. Louis, he settled in Sedalia, Missouri, where in 1899 music publisher John Stark heard him playing at the Maple Leaf Club. Stark bought the piece then and there, and before long, sheet music sales had made Joplin and "The Maple Leaf Rag" household names.

Joplin created many of the classic rags of the decade, but there were others who were nearly as important: Eubie Blake, whose lightning-quick tempos and hard-rolling base lines made him the unofficial dean of the Eastern school of rag; New Orleans-based Ferdinand (Jelly Roll) Morton, who pioneered the music called jazz; and, of course, Irving Berlin, whose "Alexander's Ragtime Band" was on the lips of nearly every North American in 1911. The explosive growth of ragtime — as well as of blues, jazz, and dance steps — was part of a general freedom sweeping the popular arts.

"The Vaudeville Theatre is an American invention," wrote *Scribner's Magazine* in 1899. "There is nothing like it anywhere in the world." Some theatres ran almost non-stop: a dozen shows a day, each with 20 or more acts. Providing sheer unpretentious enjoyment, vaudeville had become respectable, and entertainers of every stripe — Broadway and classical artists, too — appeared to try out new acts or to earn what were sometimes huge appearance fees. Those artists included Will Rogers, the Marx Brothers, Anna Pavlova, Joe E. Brown, Sarah Bernhardt, and Ethel Barrymore.

The Canadian experience of vaudeville was exactly that of Americans. In fact, with U.S. syndicates such as Shubert Brothers and the New York Theatrical Syndicate controlling virtually all theatres in Canada, Canadian cities and towns were, for all practical purposes, simply stops on the American vaudeville circuit. For performers like Fanny Brice and Sophie Tucker, Winnipeg and Halifax were American cities that happened to be farther north and colder. The one exception was Quebec, which had a lively French-language theatre, though

Sophie Tucker (top) debuted in the 1909 Follies. Later, she sang the first tune by Noble Sissle (left) and Eubie Blake.

that, too, would soon succumb to the attraction of rag-time, blues, and movies.

Meanwhile, all of Broadway was thriving. In 1901 New York had more legitimate theatres, 33 to be exact, than any other city in the world. That same year George M. Cohan debuted in his play *The Governor's Son*. The talented Cohan — he sang, danced, acted, directed, produced, composed music and lyrics, and wrote plays and musicals — would light up Broadway for 40 years.

If Broadway produced little serious or innovative drama in the first decade of the new century, audiences were seldom bored. A flock of soon-to-be-major stars began their careers in this high-spirited era: the Barrymore family, Katharine Cornell, Helen Hayes, Peggy Wood, Eddie Foy, Al Jolson. Plays like *Peter Pan* (opening in 1905) were enchanting audiences, and everywhere there were signs of a new openness and vitality, a breaking free from the restrictive forms of the past.

▲ *Irving Berlin, born Israel Baline in Siberia, made ragtime more popular than ever with his 1911 hit; his career would span more than 50 years.*

▼ *In* **The Ziegfeld Follies of 1910***, Billy Reeves (left, as Jim Jeffries) and Bert Williams (as Jack Johnson) restage the era's most famous boxing fight.*

NEW LITERATURE, NEW LIBRARIES

The nascent century saw a widening of literary tastes. While romantic tales of virtue triumphant never really went out of style, publishers began to bring out books that probed darker aspects of the human experience.

The heroine of Lucy Maud Montgomery's *Anne of Green Gables* (1908) is a spunky, rebellious girl, but she never really goes beyond girlish stubbornness. Anne may kick against the traces, but in the end she is always thoroughly respectable. In *The Trail of 98: a Northland Romance* (1911), Robert Service's young goldminer falls in love with a girl, but he never marries her because she had been the mistress of another man. Even though she had been forced into the affair, that didn't matter — she was tainted. Canadians of the early 1900's liked a strong dose of moral propriety in their reading.

Americans, too, looked for morality in their literature and, if possible, a happy ending. The first bestseller of the century was *To Have and To Hold,* about an English noblewoman who escapes the lustful clutches of Lord Carnal and finds bliss in the arms of a hardworking American. Other successes in the romantic genre

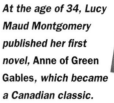

At the age of 34, Lucy Maud Montgomery published her first novel, Anne of Green Gables, *which became a Canadian classic.*

included *Mrs. Wiggs of the Cabbage Patch* (1902), *Rebecca of Sunnybrook Farm* (1904), and *Pollyanna* (1913).

Of course, some people were reading more than just sentimental romanticism. From the "Editor's Study" at *Harper's Monthly,* William Dean Howells championed the work of his friends Mark Twain and Henry James. By 1900 Twain was world famous, but at 65 he had his best work behind him. He continued to write for magazines (at the princely sum of 20 cents a word) and to lecture extensively until his death in 1910. Henry James, who had forsaken America for England, published *The Wings of the Dove, The Ambassadors,* and *The Golden Bowl* in the first four years of the century. He returned to the U.S. for a visit in 1904 and met President Roosevelt, who thought him "effete" and "a miserable little snob." James referred to TR as "the mere monstrous embodiment of unprecedented resounding Noise."

The finely tuned sensibilities of Henry James's upper-middle-class world contrasted with that of a group of young writers who called themselves naturalists. Characters in their novels battled to survive in a cruel environment — in the slums, mills, and jails of industrial North America or in the untamed, savage wilderness. The most popular naturalist was Jack London, the rugged, flamboyant author of two-fisted tales about men and beasts driven by elemental forces. London was an apostle of social Darwinism — the idea of survival of the fittest applied

This caricature of U.S. expatriate Henry James, who lived most of his life in England, conveys the novelist's elitism, which antagonized Teddy Roosevelt when he met James in 1904.

▶

James Montgomery Flagg's sketch of Jack London captured the tough, adventurous spirit of the author, whose first bestseller, The Call of the Wild, *featured a dog named Buck and stressed London's view that one needed to adapt to survive.*

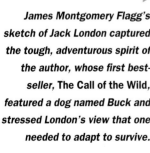

to human society — and his titles reflected his themes: *The Son of the Wolf* (1900), *The Call of the Wild* (1903), *The Sea Wolf* (1904), *The Strength of the Strong* (1911).

There was room for both naturalism and romanticism in the growing literary market. By 1910 more than 90 percent of adults were literate, and books had never been so cheap and plentiful. Public libraries were sprouting all over the country; steel magnate and philanthropist Andrew Carnegie alone spent millions building them. Magazines such as *The Ladies' Home Journal, The Busy Man's Magazine* (later *Maclean's*), and *Cosmopolitan* published great quantities of fiction, reaching a diverse audience, from housewives to mechanics. In Quebec, *Le Samedi* published writers like Emile Nelligan who challenged the ideas of a dominant church.

Poetry reached a vast, new audience with Robert Service's *Songs of a Sourdough* (1907). Tales like "The Shooting of Dan McGrew" and "The Cremation of Sam McGee" thrilled Canadians and Americans alike with the adventure of life in the Yukon gold fields. His earthy, rugged rhymes of common people and hard work made him a wealthy man. Those themes were being picked up by other poets, too, though in quite a different style. In 1912, American Harriet Monroe launched *Poetry* magazine — not in New York, the traditional literary centre, but in Chicago. She "discovered" a Midwestern poet named Vachel Lindsay in 1913, and just a year later *Poetry* published a rough, muscular ode

called "Chicago" by young Carl Sandburg. It opened:

> Hog Butcher for the World,
> Tool Maker, Stacker of Wheat,
> Player with Railroads and the
> Nation's Freight Handler;
> Stormy, husky, brawling,
> City of the Big Shoulders. . . .

"Chicago" shocked many people. The subject seemed crude, commonplace, even unpoetic; but the poem caught the spirit of a literature moving out of the parlor and becoming raw, democratic, undignified — but alive. It was a long way from the "respectable" *Anne of Green Gables*.

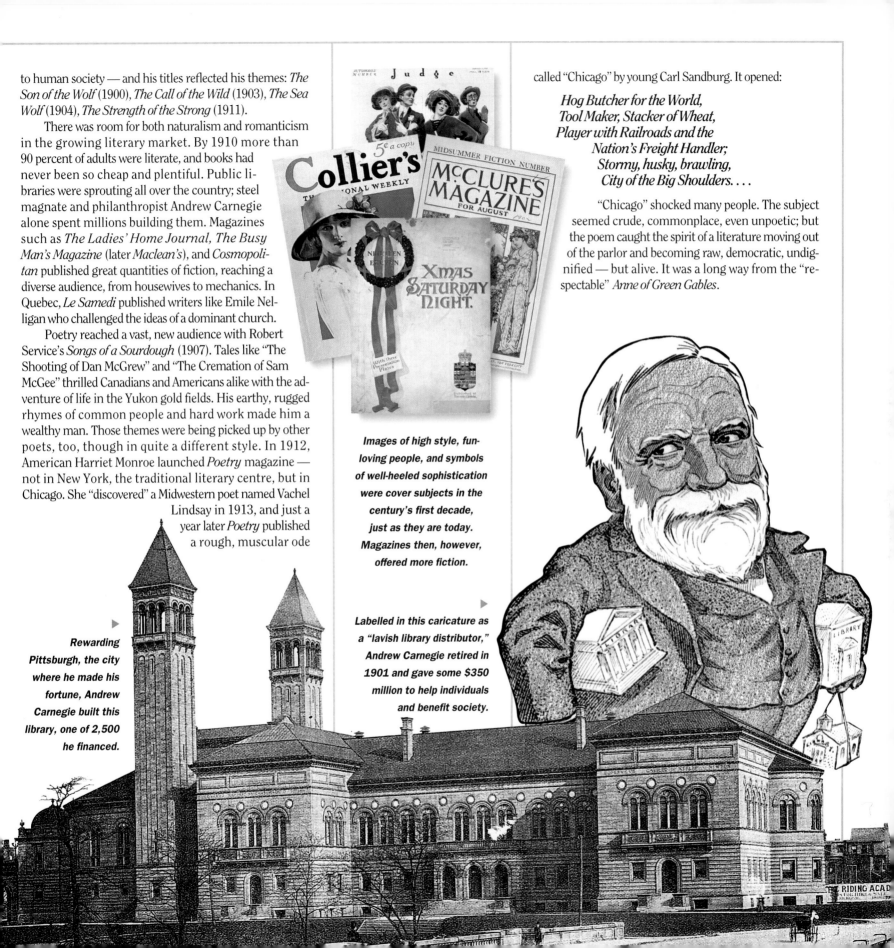

Images of high style, fun-loving people, and symbols of well-heeled sophistication were cover subjects in the century's first decade, just as they are today. Magazines then, however, offered more fiction.

Labelled in this caricature as a "lavish library distributor," Andrew Carnegie retired in 1901 and gave some $350 million to help individuals and benefit society.

Rewarding Pittsburgh, the city where he made his fortune, Andrew Carnegie built this library, one of 2,500 he financed.

Chapter 2

WORLD WAR I
THE WAR TO END ALL WARS

It begins with hopes of quick victory on

both sides, descends into the hell of barbed wire, machine

guns and trench warfare, and ends with more than a

hundred thousand Canadians and Americans dead.

The thunder of shells exploding above them, barbed wire ripping through the sucking mud beneath them, the 29th Infantry Battalion struggles across no-man's-land to take Vimy Ridge, April 1917.

On the eve of World War I, Britain led the world's powers with heavily armored, big-gunned battleships like Dreadnought (below), launched in 1906, and Iron Duke (above), in 1912.

Storm Clouds Gather

Oddly, national anxieties about who would control the seas were a major theme in the prelude to the most devastating land battles in history. Neither Germany nor Great Britain was inclined to play peacemaker.

In 1914, Canada was a colony. That meant it was automatically at war whenever Britain was. Canada was under no obligation to commit troops to a war, but Britain was Canada's only major ally; it was also Canada's major source of investment capital. These two factors made it certain that if a major war broke out in Europe, Canada would have to take part, both legally and militarily.

As just such a war loomed through the summer of 1914, most Americans saw it differently. The American Revolution had ended any legal or emotional obligation to Britain and, since it had no powerful neighbor to threaten it, the United States didn't need an ally. But if its public was unconcerned, American policymakers were nervous about the possibility of a war that might leave Germany the master of Europe, poised to expand its influence across the oceans.

▲ *Canada's Prime Minister Robert Borden visited London in 1912 to discuss naval defence in the light of Germany's naval build-up.*

Great Britain's policy was to keep the European nations divided so that no one nation could control the balance of power. That delicate balance was threatened by rising German power. Since the late 1800's Germany had enjoyed a steady growth in population, foreign trade, and industrial might. Many Germans believed that they had reached a pivotal point in their history. It was time, they thought, for their country to assume a more active role in world affairs. "In the coming century," one of them said, "the German nation will be either the hammer or the anvil."

Great Britain feared that Germany's increasing share of world trade would inevitably hurt British interests. The British home islands depended on overseas colonies as sources of raw materials and as markets for manufactured goods. When Germany began to build up its navy to protect its own foreign trade, many British leaders were thoroughly alarmed. They saw a more powerful German navy as a serious threat to Britain's economic lifelines.

As early as 1907, American diplomat Henry White expressed dismay at the offhand way that Arthur James Balfour, then the British Conservative Party leader, talked of going to war with Germany to preserve Britain's commercial and naval supremacy. White told Balfour it would be immoral for England to sacrifice human lives to fight a nation "which has as good a right to a navy as you have." The American further suggested, with annoying righteousness for a man whose country had just fought Spain for less reason: "If you wish to compete with German trade, work harder."

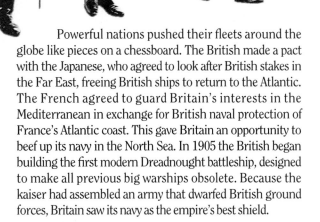

To that remark Balfour replied: "It would be simpler for us to have a war." Balfour was not alone in contemplating the benefit of a war. In Germany, the writer Thomas Mann wondered if war might be good for humankind: might it not sweep away the cobwebs of the old order and prove to be "a purification, a liberation, an enormous hope"?

A fragile web of pacts and understandings held Europe together. The English and the French had put aside their long-standing enmity — their "snarling and scratching," as one diplomat put it — and signed a treaty of friendship. On the other side of Europe, Russia bristled at the growth of German ambition, especially because Russian pride and power had suffered a grievous blow in the Russo-Japanese War. With a jaundiced eye on the Germans, Russia entered into alliances with England and France, and offered its protection to Serbia, which was in danger of being swallowed up by Germany's ally, the Austro-Hungarian Empire.

▲ The future Lord Balfour of Great Britain believed that German ambitions had to be checked, by war if necessary.

Powerful nations pushed their fleets around the globe like pieces on a chessboard. The British made a pact with the Japanese, who agreed to look after British stakes in the Far East, freeing British ships to return to the Atlantic. The French agreed to guard Britain's interests in the Mediterranean in exchange for British naval protection of France's Atlantic coast. This gave Britain an opportunity to beef up its navy in the North Sea. In 1905 the British began building the first modern Dreadnought battleship, designed to make all previous big warships obsolete. Because the kaiser had assembled an army that dwarfed British ground forces, Britain saw its navy as the empire's best shield.

Hot Air Feeds the Flames

Against the backdrop of these grand strategic ploys, politicians in both England and Germany whipped up public hysteria over the threat of imminent attacks. Bedevilled by England, France, and Russia, Germany felt a naval and diplomatic noose tightening around its neck. Kaiser Wilhelm II, a master at sabre-rattling, let loose a stream of threats, hoping to frighten Europe into granting him greater power, prestige, and influence, but he did not really want to fight. In the words of one historian: "He wanted the gladiator's rewards without the battle." The kaiser may well have believed that war was avoidable, that the ambassadors in their dapper clothing and the monarchs in their impressive uniforms were mere actors in a diplomatic drama. But as the threats and counterthreats multiplied, the atmosphere grew ever more heated, and not much was needed to ignite it.

▲ Flanked by his six sons, all resplendent in military finery, Kaiser Wilhelm II of Germany (top) parades in Berlin, in a photo dated circa 1914. Though much of the world blamed "Kaiser Bill" for plunging Europe into chaos, most Germans backed his bellicose actions. Germany's first and second battleship squadrons (above), at Kiel before the war, showed the kaiser's resolve to make his navy second to none.

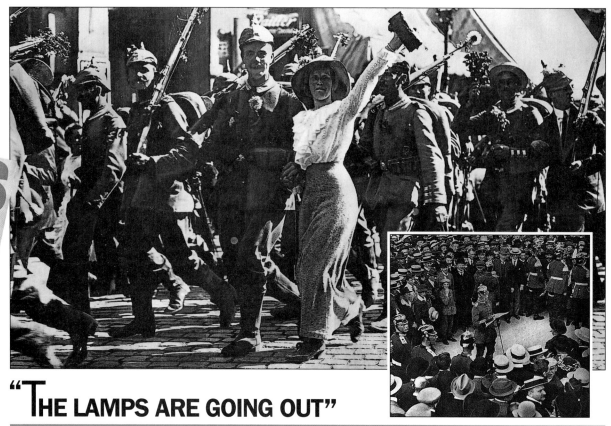

▶

Berliners cheer their soldiers marching off "on the first mile to Paris" after the kaiser's order for mobilization, here being read by a German officer (inset) on August 1, 1914.

BRITONS

"WANTS"

YOU

JOIN YOUR COUNTRY'S ARMY!

GOD SAVE THE KING

Reproduced by permission of LONDON OPINION

▲

Lord Kitchener calls Britons to arms in the poster that inspired America's famous Uncle Sam recruiting image.

▼ *Archduke Francis Ferdinand and his wife, Sophie (both seated at right), set out on the fateful ride in Sarajevo.*

"THE LAMPS ARE GOING OUT"

When Austria-Hungary picked a fight with Serbia after Archduke Ferdinand's assassination, it all seemed too irrational to lead very far, but then Russia and Germany jumped in, and Europe began tumbling into chaos.

It was a narrow escape. As their motorcade wound through the town of Sarajevo, Archduke Francis Ferdinand and his wife, Sophie, watched in horror as a man emerged from the crowd and tossed a bomb at their car. The bomb thudded onto the hood, skidded off, and detonated on the street, injuring a number of bystanders.

Ferdinand, the heir apparent of the Austro-Hungarian Empire, had been warned not to go to Sarajevo, capital of the provinces of Bosnia-Herzegovina. These provinces, once part of the Ottoman Empire, had been formally annexed in 1908 by Austria-Hungary, a power grab that deeply rankled neighboring Serbia. Serbian extremists were known to be plotting Ferdinand's assassination, perhaps with the aid of Russian agents intent upon weakening Austria-Hungary and its ally, Germany.

Leaving Sarajevo, Ferdinand and Sophie abruptly ordered their driver to take them to see the victims of the bomb attack, an act of both charity and bravery. As the car came to a halt, a young Serbian named Gavrilo Princip stepped from the curb and fired several pistol shots point-blank at the royal couple. Both were dead within minutes. No one realized it at the time, but those shots of June 28, 1914, would ignite all Europe.

Although the Serbian government disclaimed involvement in the assassination, Austria-Hungary used the murders to demand powers over Serbia's internal affairs. To everyone's surprise, on July 25 Serbia agreed to many of the demands, but to everyone's greater surprise, Austria-Hungary began bombarding Serbia anyway. Dominoes began to fall. Germany's kaiser, Russia's czar, and diplomats on both sides sought to defuse the situation, but Germany and Russia ordered full mobilization of their armies. The military machines of the Continent began to roll into action, and the delicate web of defensive alliances became an iron net that dragged nations into war.

In the first days of August, Germany declared war on Russia, France, and Belgium; Britain declared war on Germany, after the German Army surged into Belgium in the first offensive of the war. Eventually the belligerents would arrange themselves into the Central Powers (Austria-Hungary, Germany, Turkey, and Bulgaria in 1915) fighting the Allies (Britain, France, Russia, Belgium, and Italy in 1915, joined by the United States in 1917).

President Wilson proclaimed on August 4, 1914, that America would be neutral. He envisioned a great role for the United States: to serve humanity as the arbiter of conflict. He decided to allow loans and shipments of food and war supplies to both sides. He admitted that American interests might best be served by an Allied victory, but he was careful not to offend Germany.

Canada had only a tiny army of 3,000, but 33,000 volunteers eagerly added themselves to it. Untrained as yet, and ill-equipped but brimming with confidence, they sailed for Europe in October of 1914, just two months after war was declared.

The Germans were also optimistic. More than a decade earlier Germany had devised a strategy to achieve a quick, decisive victory over France. The plan called for a massive semicircular manoeuvre through Belgium to outflank French defences. Called the Schlieffen Plan after its author, Count Alfred von Schlieffen, chief of the general staff, it depended upon speed of execution to knock out France before the Russians and British could finish mobilizing.

But the Schlieffen Plan worked better on paper than it did in the field. Scheduled to take just 42 days, the plan called for advances of 32 to 40 kilometres a day, a timetable that was just too ambitious for the soldiers and their supply lines to sustain.

The British Expeditionary Force (BEF) crossed the Channel and met the Germans at the town of Mons, Belgium. The Battle of Mons, hailed as a British victory, in fact ended with a British retreat. Though slowed briefly, the German war machine pushed relentlessly onward. In some minds there arose the ugly thought that this war might not be the short and glorious outing that the generals had promised. That possibility haunted Sir Edward Grey, the British foreign secretary, who had written on the night before war erupted: "The lamps are going out all over Europe; we shall not see them lit again in our lifetime."

▶

Outgunned by the Germans, Belgian soldiers and their dog-drawn machine guns retreat to Antwerp, August 20, 1914.

▼ **Britain expected its far-flung colonials to join its fight in Europe, as this Australian recruiting poster makes very clear.**

The British historian John Keegan, seeking later to understand how the world fell into the first "total war," noted that no group of countries in history had ever fielded so many soldiers, as a percentage of population, as did Europe in August 1914. In the first two weeks of the war, the belligerent nations put some 20 million men in uniform, or nearly 10 percent of the total population.

As the soldiers marched away, their leaders said they would be home before the leaves fell, or by Christmas at the latest. The trouble was that though the nations knew how to raise armies, they no longer knew how to use them. Machine guns, massed artillery, and other new tactics and weapons had changed the realities of battle. Never before had head-on assaults faced such devastating firepower.

A GHASTLY KIND OF WARFARE

After the Allies halted the German push into France,

it looked as if the war might soon wind down. What

followed, however, was a three-and-a-half-year

deadlock, which reached new depths of agony and slaughter.

In the final days of August 1914, seven German armies were driving like knives toward the heart of France. Their plan was to take Paris, demoralizing the French, and bring all of Western Europe to its knees. Along a 480-kilometre front, from northeastern France to central Belgium, the French and their allies in the Belgian Army and the British Expeditionary Force were fighting valiantly, but they were giving ground almost everywhere.

As the Germans surged southwest, the commander of the French armies, Gen. Joseph-Jacques-Césaire Joffre, was doing everything he could to halt the German advance. He had ordered the military governor of Paris, Gen. Joseph-Simon Gallieni, to forge the French Sixth Army into a force that could join in an effective counterattack. Gallieni, a renowned old soldier called out of retirement in his country's hour of peril, threw himself into the task while at the same

Rushing troops to stop the German thrust at Paris, General Gallieni (above) drafted 1,200 taxis (above). Six months later, an ugly war got uglier when the Germans used poison gas, making gas masks (top) vital for survival.

The French foot soldier, or poilu (right), was Verdun's real hero.

time solidifying plans for the defence of Paris. Short of men, he appealed to the French high command: "What do we have in troops to defend this heart and brain of France? A drop in the bucket." Joffre responded by calling up more reservists and daringly transferring troops from sectors where the German offensive had slowed.

But almost everywhere the Germans kept coming. Early in September, their advance scouts were less than 40 kilometres from Paris. By then the French government had fled the city, but Gallieni and his men stayed. On September 5, near Monthyon, about 48 kilometres from Paris, a German corps pounced on a unit of the French

"THEY SHALL NOT PASS!"

On February 21, 1916, in the gray light of a winter's dawn, the kaiser's artillery opened up the most intensive barrage of the war so far: as many as 1,400 heavy guns, including 13 giant 420-mm howitzers, lobbing 100,000 shells an hour for 12 excruciating hours. "We were lifted and tossed about," recalled a French survivor. "Our blinded, wounded, crawling, and shouting soldiers kept falling on top of us and died while splashing us with their blood...." It seemed that nothing could live.

Finally the savage pounding stopped, but the French had little time to enjoy the silence. Toward them came the forward battalions of the German Fifth Army, 140,000 strong.

The German objective was to draw the French into an all-out defence of the city of Verdun, which the French high command regarded as a key strategic link in protecting France's interior. The French would attempt to hold Verdun at any cost, the Germans reasoned. And if forced out, they would pay any price to win it back. "If we plan properly at Verdun," declared Gen.

Sixth Army that was moving up to counterattack. It was the start of the First Battle of the Marne, the "miracle on the Marne" that shattered the kaiser's hope of quick conquest.

To strengthen the Sixth Army, Gallieni commandeered 1,200 Paris taxicabs. Each cab, carrying up to five soldiers per trip, made one or more trips to the front, bringing a total of 6,000 fresh troops to fight the Germans.

Meanwhile, in an unaccountable blunder, the attacking German First and Second Armies had split too far apart, opening a gap between them. As the French Fifth Army hit the flank of the German Second Army, the BEF crept slowly into the gap. Hundreds of fierce little engagements led to

For holding Verdun, Henri Pétain won France's adoration, but his World War II collaboration with Germany disgraced him.

British Field Marshal Haig kept pouring men into the hell of German guns.

Erich von Falkenhayn, the German chief of staff, "we can bleed the enemy white."

In the months that followed, it seemed that Germany would do just that. When the Germans quickly took Fort Douaumont, one of Verdun's protective bastions, France began pouring in men to save the city. Gen. Henri-Philippe Pétain, summoned to assume command, demanded nothing less than his men's utmost heroism. With casualties running at some 16,000 men a week, he established a roadway, La Voie Sacrée, over which shuttled a continuous stream of fresh troops and munitions. And an order rang out — *"Ils ne passeront pas!"* ("They shall not pass!") — that became the rallying cry of the French defence of Verdun.

And hold the French soldiers did, through explosive hailstorms of enemy artillery, against repeated German infantry assaults, amid clouds of choking phosgene gas, and in defiance of a terrifying new weapon, the flamethrower (painting below). By the year's end the French had retaken some of the ground they had lost, and stood poised to gain a bit more. But at what cost! France had lost more than half a million men at Verdun in dead, wounded, and missing. The Germans, in their effort to "bleed the enemy white," had depleted their own forces by more than 400,000 troops.

widespread confusion, but gradually there came a realization that the Allies had at last halted the German advance.

The Germans withdrew 64 to 80 kilometres north and dug deeply into positions north of the Aisne River. Hoping to outflank the Allies, they sent some of their forces westward toward the English Channel. In a series of battles called the Race to the Sea — along the Aisne and Yser rivers, through Flanders, Picardy, and Artois — the Allies fought the Germans to a draw and kept them from taking key ports.

In the first three weeks of the war, as later calculated, each side had lost half a million men to death, wounds, or capture. But worse was to come. The fall of 1914 marked the beginning of a three-and-a-half-year standoff that made the word *trenches* a synonym for the horrors of war.

Hundreds of kilometres of battlefront in Western Europe stabilized into two opposing and roughly parallel trench networks with a belt of no-man's-land in between. Beneath the surface trenches often lay elaborate subterranean shelters, sometimes connected by minirailways, to protect troops and supplies against artillery bombardments. And beneath no-man's-land, sappers from each side tried to

Heeding Britain's call, Canadians soon had some tough battles under their belt (poster, right); West Indian (inset) and Anzac (Australian–New Zealand) forces (below) fought at the Somme.

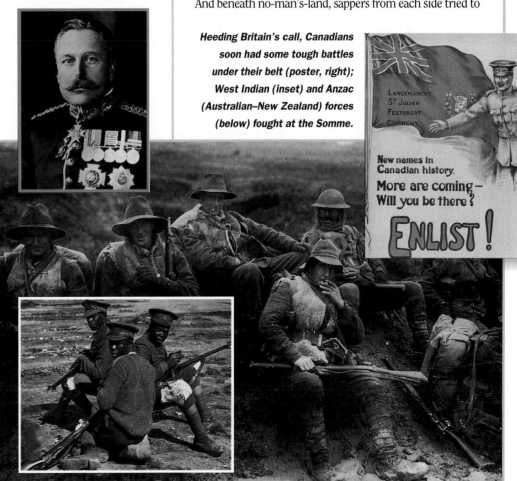

burrow under the other's positions to set off huge explosions that sometimes lifted whole fields into the air. No-man's-land became a nightmare landscape of blasted trees, sucking mud, water-filled shell craters where men drowned, and flesh-and-bone-ripping shrapnel and bullets.

Heaps of the dead were buried in vast cemeteries that spread behind the trenches. The endless rows of crosses moved a Canadian surgeon, Col. John McRae of Guelph, Ontario, in 1915, to write the lines that became a memorial to the millions who died in the mud of France and Belgium:

> *In Flanders fields the poppies blow*
> *Between the crosses, row on row,*
> *That mark our place; and in the sky*
> *The larks, still bravely singing, fly*
> *Scarce heard amid the guns below.*

When enemy shells cut the wires connecting field telephones, carrier pigeons, and sometimes dogs, carried messages along the front lines.

Soldiers of the 2nd Canadian Division (bottom of page) trudge across a rain-soaked landscape beaten to muddy mush by artillery in the Allies' Passchendaele offensive near Ypres, Flanders, in the summer and fall of 1917.

> *We are the Dead. Short days ago*
> *We lived, felt dawn, saw sunset glow,*
> *Loved, and were loved, and now we lie*
> *In Flanders fields.*
>
> *Take up our quarrel with the foe:*
> *To you from failing hands we throw*
> *The torch; be yours to hold it high.*
> *If ye break faith with us who die*
> *We shall not sleep, though poppies grow*
> *In Flanders fields.*

In 1918, Colonel McCrae, too, was buried in Flanders fields. He lies in the cemetery at Wimereux in France.

At the First Battle of the Somme, in the summer of 1916, British big guns blasted the German trenches for a solid week, sending some 1.5 million artillery shells into the enemy positions. On the morning of July 1, the bombardment ceased, giving way to an eerie silence. One British soldier heard a lark singing; another, music from a German gramophone. Then came the attack. Seventeen British divisions and five French divisions went over the top and into no-man's-land. The Germans, in dugouts 9 to 12 metres deep, waited out the rolling barrage. As it stopped, they emerged from their shelters. When the Allied infantry reached the barbed wire in front of the German trenches, the machine guns mowed them down by the thousands. In four months at the Somme, the British suffered 410,000 casualties, the French 195,000, and the Germans 500,000.

British medics tend to a wounded, thirsty Tommy in a trench near Thiepval, on the Somme battlefield, in September 1916.

A German machine-gun crew awaits an Allied infantry attack on the western front.

In his sixties and famous, American artist John Singer Sargent went to the front and witnessed a gas attack's grim aftermath.

Facing such carnage, each side desperately sought any advantage. Thus the Great War became the proving ground for tanks and flamethrowers. The same was true of airplanes, which quickly evolved from flying observation posts into offensive weapons (see p. 95). And it was where one of the most terrifying weapons of all, lethal gas, was first used. Around dawn on April 22, 1915, near Ypres, Belgium, French colonial troops heard a hissing from the German lines and saw a strange, some said an almost beautiful, green cloud wafting toward them. It was chlorine gas, and it soon settled into the trenches, bringing terror and death. In fact both sides used gas, which, if it did not kill, destroyed eyes, lungs, skin, and other tissues, leaving its victims blinded, crippled, and scarred.

A year after the terrible losses at the Somme, the British commander Field Marshal Douglas Haig launched a new offensive, in Flanders. Starting on July 31, 1917, he headed for the heavily fortified 45.5-metre height of Passchendaele Ridge. Massive artillery barrages were followed by waves of infantry. Haig's artillery so demolished the marshy region's drainage system that Flanders's fields became a virtual lake — "a porrage of mud," as one observer put it. It took four months, and 300,000 British casualties, to advance eight kilometres to the top of Passchendaele. The campaign's only real success occurred at the town of Cambrai, where a force of 324 British tanks gained more ground in six hours than had been won by all the bloodshed in Flanders. But even this was an exercise in futility, for the Germans soon won back the lost ground.

Late in 1914 the front lines ran a ragged arc from Flanders to the Swiss border. Three years later, when American troops began to arrive in force, the lines had shifted by no more than a few dozen kilometres. More than 2 million men had given up their lives to maintain this stalemate.

British and French tanks became attack weapons.

HUMOR FROM HELL

What Bill Mauldin would do for the American GI in World War II (see p. 211), Bruce Bairnsfather (below) did for British Tommies in World War I. A 27-year-old British officer on combat duty in France, Bairnsfather began publishing cartoons of life at the front in July 1915. They were a hit with soldiers and civilians. His anything-but-professional soldiers are fed up, but they will never give up, and they can laugh at trench life. Two of his regulars were Old Bill, a middle-aged cockney with a walrus moustache and a pipe, and his buddy Bert, a callow youth with a cigarette dangling from his lips. Below is his famous 1916 cartoon, whose caustic caption became one of the most quoted phrases of the Great War.

Well, if you knows of a better 'ole, go to it!

Travellers packed the Lusitania (below) on her fateful voyage despite warnings by the German Embassy published with Cunard schedules (right).

On PERILOUS SEAS

The sinking of the British luxury liner Lusitania *showed the world the horrifying work that submarines could do. But Germany exulted in a weapon that undercut Britain's naval superiority.*

The great Cunard liner *Lusitania*, queen of the British passenger fleet, steamed majestically eastward past the Irish coast en route to Liverpool from New York. It was May 7, 1915, and so far the crossing had been as smooth as anyone could have wished. But now, as the vessel entered British waters, a certain tension gripped her nearly 2,000 passengers and crew. German submarines had been reported lurking nearby. Shortly after 2 P.M., as the first-class ticket holders were stepping onto the promenade deck for an after-luncheon stroll, a U-boat's periscope broke the ocean's surface. One passenger, leaning against the starboard rail, noticed "a long, white streak of foam," a "frothy fizzing," moving rapidly toward him. Then came a heavy thud, followed by a thunderous explosion. The unthinkable had happened. A German torpedo had struck the *Lusitania*.

The liner heeled violently to starboard, then began to settle. Another torpedo hit the listing ship, shattering the hull and sending up a gush of flame and hot metal. Passengers crowded into lifeboats, but the stricken liner's steeply pitching decks prevented many boats from being lowered. Within just 18 minutes the great vessel slid under, leaving a ghastly flotsam of overloaded boats, thrashing swimmers, and charred and mangled bodies. Of the 1,198 souls lost, 128 were Americans.

Losses like that of the cruiser Blücher (below), sunk by the British in 1915, led Germany to rely on its submarines. But U-boats could not break the blockade that, with poor harvests, eventually reduced Germans to eating potato peels (right).

The United States was outraged. President Woodrow Wilson threatened to sever relations with Germany and even to intervene on the Allied side. The Germans replied that they had done no wrong and in fact had issued a warning, a notice in *The New York Times* that the *Lusitania* risked attack. They claimed, with justification, that passenger ships could also carry ammunition and war goods.

Why the Kaiser Liked His U-boats

Until the submarine demonstrated its lethal effectiveness, military strategists had measured naval might by the firepower of large surface ships: battleships and battle cruisers, which could range far and wide and pummel the enemy with their batteries of guns that fired shells 28 to 46 centimetres in diameter. To the British, who chose to use their subs mostly for shore patrol, the submarine seemed a marginal weapon, even a bit unsportsmanlike: "underhanded, unfair, and un-English."

But the Germans disagreed. At the war's outset, the kaiser had 33 U-boats — short for German *Unterseeboots* — of which 28 were fitted for long-range missions. Packed with a dozen torpedoes each, they could harass enemy warships and merchant vessels alike. And as a naval underdog, the kaiser saw his U-boats as critical to victory. His surface fleet was only half the size of Britain's Grand Fleet. With increasing German U-boat activity, certain broad conventions governing naval attacks, designed to protect the lives of civilians and the rights of neutral nations, began to fray.

To attack an unarmed merchant ship, a U-boat could surface and launch a torpedo, but armed prey required a submerged approach.

Customarily, for example, a merchant ship suspected of carrying military supplies to the enemy could be stopped and searched, and its goods confiscated. But even if the suspect ship flew an enemy flag, its seamen were given a chance to escape. German surface raiders in the Pacific followed these rules to the letter. One famous marauder, the cruiser *Emden*, managed to bag 24 Allied ships with virtually no loss of life.

But such chivalrous niceties did not survive in the North Atlantic. Any U-boat that surfaced to capture a potential prize might have found itself rammed or sent to the bottom in a hail of fire. To combat the submarine menace, the British launched decoy vessels, Q-ships, which looked like tramp steamers but carried hidden guns. Furthermore, many British ships disguised themselves by flying the flags of neutral nations. So the U-boats continued to attack in stealth, though the kaiser, fearful of pushing the United States too far, ordered his commanders to spare all American ships.

In the first month of the war, British cruisers had swept Germany's North Sea coast and sunk four ships in the Battle of Heligoland Bight. Less than four weeks later, a lone U-boat retaliated by sinking three British cruisers within an hour. Sharp, bloody exchanges flared up when enemy squadrons met in the Southern Hemisphere, off Chile and the Falkland Islands. But only once did the world's two great navies — Britain's Grand Fleet and Germany's High Seas Fleet — slug it out ship to ship: at the Battle of Jutland in May of 1916. Both sides suffered heavy losses of ships and men, but the result was a tactical draw.

After the stand-off at Jutland, the kaiser did not choose to risk his surface fleet again in battle on the high seas. Most of Germany's ships stayed in port, safe from British guns. And so Great Britain won control of the North Sea. It then proceeded to cut off supplies to Germany from the outside world. As Britain tightened its blockade, poor harvests compounded Germany's predicament. Thousands of Germans died of starvation and disease in the "Turnip Winter" of 1916–17.

However, German submarines could slip through the blockade, and their attacks, particularly on ships carrying Canadian wheat, brought British food supplies perilously low, in return. But that wasn't enough. American supplies had to be stopped, too; so Germany ordered the sinking of all ships, including American ones. In the first four months of 1917, German subs sank an average of 10 ships a day. At that rate England, too, would starve. England's answer was to gather its ships in convoys so that attacking subs would have to face armed escorts as well. It worked. Sinkings dropped off, and the lifeline of food and munitions to the Allies remained open.

On their flimsy perch attached to a bomb-carrying dirigible, British airmen search for U-boats in the North Sea below them. The Lewis machine gun gave some defence against attacking German fighters while other crewmen looked for signs of subs lurking along convoy routes.

A PAINFUL LESSON LEARNED

▲ *Thousands of volunteers answered the call to fight (inset) in 1915, and set off from Quebec for Nova Scotia and England.*

By 1917, Canadian soldiers were closely acquainted with gas warfare (below) and death in the thick mud of northern Europe (bottom). ▼

Undertrained, ill equipped, and incompetently led in 1914, Canada's military quickly recovered to become the elite of the Allied armies.

As a colony, Canada was not required to participate in any war declared by Britain. But in 1914, Canadians were deeply enthusiastic about playing the greatest role possible. Within weeks after the government called for 25,000 army volunteers, 33,000 men had assembled at Camp Valcartier in Quebec.

Their enthusiasm would soon wane. The core of regular soldiers was only 3,000. Many of the volunteers had come from the militia, which had provided only scanty training. And they were led by often incompetent men, cronies of Minister of Militia Sam Hughes, appointed by him to high military rank. Hughes had also equipped the troops with Ross rifles (produced by yet another crony). Soldiers detested these unreliable weapons and often threw them away on the battlefield, replacing them with Lee-Enfields picked up from the bodies of fallen British soldiers.

The Price of Unpreparedness

Few of the Canadian soldiers who sailed to England in October of 1914 had the slightest idea of what it would mean to face machine guns that fired at almost 500 shots per minute, to become entangled in barbed wire that pinned men in place until the machine guns could

Lieut. Gordon Flowerdew

Lieut. Jean Brillant

"FOR VALOUR"

The Victoria Cross, the British Empire's highest award for valor, was won by 69 Canadians between 1914 and 1918. This figure represents more than two-thirds of the Victoria Crosses that Canada has received in all its wars since 1854.

Though Canada had no air force until after the war, by 1918 it provided one-quarter of all pilots in British service, and three of them won the Victoria Cross. Flying ace Billy Bishop (see p. 95) of Owen Sound had a deadly aim that brought down 72 enemy aircraft. Nineteen-year-old Alan McLeod of Manitoba, flying a slow reconnaissance plane, was wounded five times by German fighters and his plane set afire. But McLeod managed to clamber out onto a wing and control the plane so that his gunner could destroy three of their attackers. Major William Barker, also of Manitoba, won his Victoria Cross for a single-handed fight against some 40 to 60 German fighters. Wounded three times, he shot down three opponents before crash-landing his battered plane.

Victoria Crosses were also won by a number of valiant Canadian soldiers. In August 1918, near Amiens, Lieut. Jean Brillant of Quebec's Royal 22nd Regiment went forward alone to capture a German machine gun. He was wounded, but insisted on leading another attack that captured 150 enemy soldiers and took 15 machine guns. Despite a second wound, he led yet another attack on a field gun, but collapsed from loss of blood before he could reach it. He died the next day.

A few months earlier, Lieut. Gordon Flowerdew of Lord Strathcona's Light Horse had led his troopers in a suicidal charge against infantry and machine guns to prevent them from being deployed against retreating British troops. The attack was so unexpected and so fierce that the Germans scattered in retreat. Flowerdew's men, though, suffered a horrifically high rate of casualties — 70 percent of them were wounded. Among them was Flowerdew, who died.

Lt.-Gen. Arthur Currie

The 43rd Canadian Battalion marches through the streets of Mons, following their liberation of the town, which marked the end of the war.

Canadian soldiers escort prisoners taken during the Battle of Amiens, August 1918.

find them, or to hear the crump of high explosive shells that turned the battlefield into a swamp through which men could advance at barely a kilometre an hour.

Over the next two years, Canadian soldiers paid dearly for their deficiencies. Thousands lost lives and limbs in the mud of northern France, falling at places rarely mentioned in their school geography books — Ypres, St.-Eloi, and Beaumont-Hamel, where the First Newfoundland Regiment was annihilated with almost no chance to fire a shot in return. They paid, but they learned. By 1916, the army had discarded the Ross rifle. Hughes was fired from the cabinet, and his officer-cronies were posted to jobs where they could do no more harm. Better officers replaced them who, significantly, often had little or no military experience. Lacking the burden of old ideas, they adjusted to this modern war far quicker than the career soldiers did. After a shaky start, by 1916 the Canadian Corps was a solidly professional army.

From Amateurs to Professionals

Near Arras, France, was a ridge that overlooked Allied trenches on the plain below and provided a base for German artillery. Years of battle for control of Vimy Ridge had filled vast cemeteries with tens of thousands of crosses — British, Canadian, French, and German. Vimy had to be taken, and the task was given to the Canadian Corps. Commanded by British Lt.-Gen. Sir Julian

Byng, the Canadians approached the battle after weeks of training and careful planning. On April 9, 1917, they attacked. Five days later, Vimy Ridge was in Canadian hands, the greatest victory the Allies had won to that point.

Shortly after, a Canadian, Lt.-Gen. Sir Arthur Currie, was given command of the Corps. A brilliant choice, he has often been ranked as the best general on either side. Certainly, he was one of the few who understood how meticulous planning could win battles. When the Canadians were ordered to take Lens, Currie discarded the old method of simply using his soldiers as cannon fodder, and took nearby Hill 70 so he could use his artillery to make cannon fodder of the enemy instead.

On August 8, 1918, with the Allied armies reeling from a massive German assault that destroyed Britain's Fifth Army and threatened to end the war, the Australians and the Canadians were ordered to ease pressure with an attack near Amiens. Currie skilfully shifted his attacks from point to point, always seeking out the weakest one. In 100 days, he shattered the Germans' recovery, driving them back all the way to Mons, Belgium. On November 11, the day the Canadian Corps took Mons, the war ended.

Once past the early years of the war, the Canadian army performed magnificently. But the cost had been terrible, with 60,000 dead and many times that number wounded.

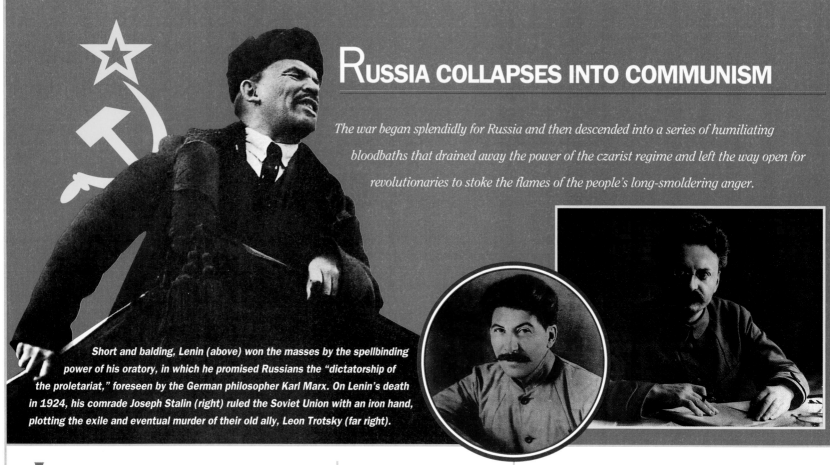

RUSSIA COLLAPSES INTO COMMUNISM

The war began splendidly for Russia and then descended into a series of humiliating bloodbaths that drained away the power of the czarist regime and left the way open for revolutionaries to stoke the flames of the people's long-smoldering anger.

Short and balding, Lenin (above) won the masses by the spellbinding power of his oratory, in which he promised Russians the "dictatorship of the proletariat," foreseen by the German philosopher Karl Marx. On Lenin's death in 1924, his comrade Joseph Stalin (right) ruled the Soviet Union with an iron hand, plotting the exile and eventual murder of their old ally, Leon Trotsky (far right).

If the war had continued to go as well for Russia as it did in the first three weeks, there might never have been a Communist revolution. The Russians pushed the Germans back in East Prussia, trouncing them at the Battle of Gumbinnen on August 20, 1914.

That was enough for Kaiser Wilhelm. He quickly gave responsibility for the war against Russia, the so-called eastern front, to two generals whose names would soon inspire their whole nation: Paul von Hindenburg and Erich Ludendorff. Within days the Germans had lured the Russians into an inferno called the Battle of Tannenberg.

Less a battle than a systematic slaughter of encircled Russians trying to flee the German troops, Tannenberg cost the Russian Army 125,000 men and 500 guns. And it set the pattern of Russia's military fortunes in World War I. A poorly armed and badly led army, ill-clothed and hungry, would gain a victory by sheer guts, then suffer a strategic defeat with appalling casualties. By the end of 1915, the Russians had given up all the land they had taken from the Germans and had lost 2 million men killed, wounded, or captured.

▼ **Canadian guns, sent to support "White" Russians, take part in an Allied march-past at Murmansk.**

▶ **Captured at Tannenberg, columns of Russian soldiers await their captors' orders.**

Then in his spectacular offensive of June 1916, the Russian general Alexei Brusilov thrashed the Austro-Hungarian Army and recovered considerable territory, but lost a million men. Such a drain of blood washed through Russia, weakening the pillars of traditional society and eroding loyalties to the czarist regime.

December 1916 began one of the worst winters in Russian memory. With no coal or bread, hunger and disease stalked the cities. More than two years

President Wilson first hailed the czar's overthrow, then sent U.S. troops to Archangel in northern Russia (above) to help an Allied army keep Russian war materials out of German hands. Meanwhile, in Moscow, American journalist John Reed (above, right) championed the Reds' cause.

of war had left over 300,000 dead, and the wounded and the starving choked the streets. The people cried for relief.

But "the people" terrified Czar Nicholas II, who had stood by the shattered body of his dying grandfather Alexander II, victim of a bomb hurled by "the people." His wife, Alexandra, German-born granddaughter of Queen Victoria, was autocratic to the core: "Russia loves to feel the whip," she wrote. "We have been placed on the throne by God." The royal couple were politically, and spiritually, guided by the "holy man" Rasputin, an unkempt, semiliterate peasant and debauchee (the meaning of the name Rasputin). He was also a mystic who used hypnosis to control the hemophilia of the czarina's son. His hold over the royal family ended when he was murdered in 1916, but his poor advice had weakened their rule and contributed to their downfall.

In Petrograd angry mobs sang "The Internationale," the anthem of world revolution. After the city's army garrison joined the protests, Nicholas, who had taken command of the troops at the front in 1915, finally gave up his throne on March 15, 1917. A provisional government, led by Alexander Kerensky, took over. He called for moderate socialist reform and continuation of the war.

But what the Russian people really wanted was "Peace, Land, and Bread." That was the cry of the radical Communists — the Bol-

sheviks, led by Vladimir Ilyich Lenin, Leon Trotsky, and Joseph Stalin. Outside the Petrograd railway station on April 16, 1917, Lenin proclaimed: "I greet you as the vanguard of the worldwide proletarian army." Arriving at Bolshevik headquarters, he demanded a second revolution to overthrow Kerensky's government and end the war.

Four months later, the "Kerensky offensive" on the eastern front floundered, the death knell for the provisional government. By mid-November, 1917, Lenin and the Bolsheviks had engineered and won their second revolution, known as the October Revolution. The new Soviet leadership ordered troops on the eastern front to stop fighting and opened peace talks with Germany.

The Allies, though they had disliked czarist tyranny, became alarmed at the Soviets' quick peace-dealing with the Germans. Fearing that German troops would now be free to move to the western front, they sent troops to support "White" Russian armies against Lenin's "Red" forces in the bloody civil war that convulsed Russia until 1920. At the urging of Britain, Canada contributed 6,000 troops. Though relatively few lives were lost, the Allied intervention was a blunder. It achieved little militarily, and it gave Soviet leaders a grudge against the western Allies for most of the rest of the century.

◄

In December 1915 Nicholas II, son Alexei, and daughter Tatyana pause in a snowy field. Two and a half years later, Lenin ordered the czar, his wife, and their five children shot.

▼ *Rebellious soldiers fire on police in Petrograd in February 1917.*

Distant Guns

With Britain, France, and Germany all possessing colonies around the globe, the war could hardly be contained on European soil. Then Turkey got into the act, spreading the conflict to vast reaches east of the Mediterranean. And a third front in Europe became inevitable when Italy joined the Allies.

Indian Lewis gunners, part of the British force in Mesopotamia (present-day Iraq), fire at attacking aircraft, which Turkey used skillfully to harass Allied movements.

As the world focused on the collision of mighty armies on Europe's eastern and western fronts, fighting broke out in the Italian Alps and along the Aegean's sunny coast. It spilled across the deserts of Egypt and Arabia, erupted on the sands of today's Iraq, and rolled through the plains and jungles of Africa.

In the Pacific, Japan joined the Allies and plucked off German holdings on the coast of China and in the Marianas, the Marshalls, and the Carolines. Western Samoa fell to a New Zealand force without a single casualty. Australians took just a week to subdue German New Guinea.

In Africa the Allies seized chunks of Germany's colonial empire. French and British troops overran Togo in the first month of war, then moved into the Cameroons. But in East Africa, a wily Prussian, Col. Paul von Lettow-Vorbeck, and his 12,000 askaris resisted an Allied army 10 times their size. Lettow-Vorbeck's depleted forces finally gave up on November 25, 1918, two weeks after the armistice.

Mauled by murderous Turkish fire on the beaches of the Gallipoli Peninsula, Anzac and British units held on valiantly for over eight months, but finally evacuated in January 1916.

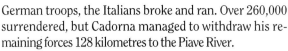

Winching light artillery over icy passes was picturesque (left), but ambulance driver Ernest Hemingway (above) later wrote of the despair and hardship on the Italian front in A Farewell to Arms. The Italian Crown Medal (left) recognized valor in the bitter campaign.

In the Palestine campaign, T. E. Lawrence (below, left) gave the British some successes against the hard-fighting Turks. With him is American journalist Lowell Thomas, whose reports helped create the legend of Lawrence of Arabia.

From the outset of the war, Serbia's small army had held off assaults by Austria-Hungary. Then in October 1915, the armies of Germany and Austria, joined by their new ally, Bulgaria, swooped down 300,000 strong. Outnumbered two to one, the Serbs retreated toward the Adriatic coast, battling enemy shells, winter snows, raids by Albanian tribesmen, and a raging typhus epidemic. Entire families joined the exodus: wives, grandfathers, 12-year-olds carrying rifles and ammunition belts. Tens of thousands died.

By this time Austria-Hungary had another enemy: Italy. The two nations faced off on a 960-kilometre front snaking from the Swiss Alps to the Adriatic Sea. The Italian chief of staff, Gen. Luigi Cadorna, planned to advance his 875,000-man army through the Isonzo River valley and on to Vienna. Italy's morale sagged when Cadorna's first four assaults cost 170,000 Italian casualties (to his enemy's 117,000). Yet by September 1917, it was the Austrians, being battered simultaneously on the Russian front, who seemed about to crack.

That possibility alarmed Kaiser Wilhelm, and he sent six German divisions to the Italian front. The Germans joined nine Austrian divisions in a drive toward the town of Caporetto, a weak point in Cadorna's lines. Under devastating artillery bombardment and gas attacks, climaxed by the appearance of fearsome

German troops, the Italians broke and ran. Over 260,000 surrendered, but Cadorna managed to withdraw his remaining forces 128 kilometres to the Piave River.

A year later, under the popular Gen. Armando Diaz, the Italians revenged their defeat at Caporetto. On October 24, 1918, seven Italian armies, spearheaded by British and French units and joined by an American infantry regiment, stormed Austrian positions north of the Piave, around the resort town of Vittorio Veneto. In just over a week, Austrian resistance collapsed, and on November 3 a truce ended the fighting on the Italian front.

When the Turks, keepers of the declining but still formidable Ottoman Empire, entered World War I on the side of the Central Powers in October 1914, the geographical scope of the war vastly enlarged. One key Turkish possession was the Dardanelles, the strait connecting the Black Sea with the Mediterranean, which was the sole warm-water supply route to the armies of Russia. Aiming to control this vital passage, the British sent a large force to the Gallipoli Peninsula, at the head of the strait. On April 25, 1915, some 7,000 troops waded ashore. But the main body of Anzacs — Australians and New Zealanders — met murderous Turkish fire from the cliffs above their narrow beachhead. Further landings brought only more carnage. Finally, devastated by fighting, sunstroke, and dysentery, the Allies withdrew. Of 480,000 Allied soldiers who served at Gallipoli, more than half fell victim to disease and enemy guns.

In Mesopotamia, too, Britain faltered. Early in the war the British seized Basra, Turkey's Persian Gulf oil port. Then a 9,000-man British division advanced up the Tigris River toward Baghdad, outran its supplies, and had to surrender.

The British did better in Egypt. Gen. Edmund Allenby, a cavalryman with a genius for speed and deception, pushed through Gaza and on December 9, 1917, took Jerusalem, calling it a Christmas present for England. From there he marched north toward Damascus.

If the victories went to Allenby, world attention came to focus on a young British intelligence officer T. E. Lawrence. In Arabia, where the Turks maintained garrisons in important cities, he helped incite an Arab revolt. He and other Allied officers led daring guerrilla actions against the Turks.

After the war Lawrence chose to serve quietly in the Royal Air Force and drop into obscurity. But Lawrence of Arabia lived on in all his lustre and romance. Of him, Winston Churchill said: "One of the greatest beings alive in our time; I do not see his like elsewhere."

PARLOR GAMES FAVORITE

Lotto
Bingo, housy-housy, keno, and screeno (played in U.S. movie theatres during the Depression) are names for variants of this ever popular game of chance.

Dominoes
Millennia ago, the Chinese played a game using pieces much like today's "bones."

Nancy Drew
Fans of the popular young fictional detective, created in 1930, applied their own sleuthing powers to solve mysteries in this 1958 game.

It has a quaint ring — parlor games. It calls up tree-lined streets with comfortable houses, in which the parlor was the room for entertaining guests and playing games around a table. Later it became the room where the radio went, and then the television set. Whist and bridge, pinochle and rummy, cribbage and checkers, backgammon and chess, Parcheesi, lotto, and dominoes were old standbys in the parlor. Then, reflecting the country's surging entrepreneurial spirit, manufacturers began turning out board games with topical tie-ins and dressing up old games of luck and skill in fancy new packages, often adding clever twists. It was only a matter of time before games and electronics teamed up. And despite the tube and all the other enticements and distractions at the end of the 20th century, kids of all ages keep sitting down to play parlor games, with or without a parlor.

Train for Boston
Steam locomotives were glamorous in the early 1900's, when parlor travellers twirled a spinner to try to reach Beantown by rail from one of four cities.

Monopoly
The classic real estate game, with property names derived from Atlantic City, took off after Parker Brothers issued an edition in 1935.

Jackie Gleason's TV Fun Game
In 1956 the comic's popularity spawned a game in which the most "Laffs" won.

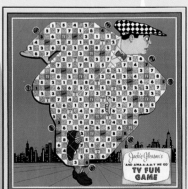

Tabletop Hockey
In the Days of a Six-Team NHL, children dressed in the colors of their favorite Maple Leafs or Canadiens (or, in parts of the Maritimes, the Boston Bruins) thrilled to the action of tabletop hockey. They still do, though now with the added realism of electronic scoreboards.

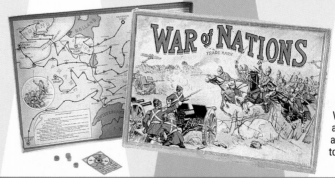

War of Nations
The tactics and the uniforms on the cover of this 1918 game are a far cry from the reality of World War I, but the airplane and the artillery get closer to the truth.

Sorry!

Getting home is not easy when a roll of the dice can mean forward or backward moves, slides, or picking a card that sends you back to Start — Sorry!

Chutes and Ladders

Preschoolers often graduate from Candy Land to this slightly more difficult game. A lucky spin sends a player up a ladder; an unlucky one, down a chute.

Trivial Pursuit

Riding the information wave of the 1980's, several Canadians invented a game that tested factual knowledge and caught on with a generation better educated than before.

Candy Land

The first board game many children play, it requires neither reading nor number skills, just a knowledge of basic colors to move gingerbread men around the board to the Candy Castle.

Scrabble

Crossword puzzlers and anagram buffs find this game right up their alley. Each letter used in a word builds up points.

Simon

Computer-varied sequences of color and sound challenge players to remember and repeat as many sequences as they can exactly.

Clue

A murder has been committed and players vie to solve it with the clues provided as they move around the board. Who did it? Where? With what weapon?

Nintendo

A prince of video games in the 1990's was Nintendo's little plumber with the moustache, Mario (below). In 1993 a third of U.S. homes had Nintendo ware (left), which hooks into TV sets.

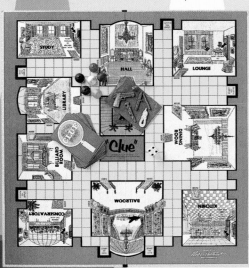

Battle at Sarlaac's Pit

Return of the Jedi, last in the *Star Wars* trilogy, inspired this 1980's cliff hanger.

"WE'RE COMING . . . OVER THERE"

After Germany launched unrestricted U-boat warfare and its diplomats plotted with Mexico against the United States, neutrality was dead. Most Americans were eager to join the battle, and a number of Yanks were already fighting under Allied flags.

Pvt. T. P. Loughlin, Rainbow Division, bids good-bye to his family before shipping out.

Congress (below) hears President Wilson ask for war, and four days later, April 6, 1917, he signed the formal declaration. Arthur Zimmermann (inset) and his infamous telegram had outraged Americans.

President Wilson was still valiantly trying to negotiate peace in Europe when the German ambassador, late on the afternoon of January 31, 1917, delivered a note to him. With a look of blank amazement, as the president's secretary later recalled, Wilson read Germany's total rebuff of his mediation efforts. Far from pursuing peace, Germany was about to escalate the war, according to the note. Starting February 1, only eight hours away, Germany would attack all shipping to Britain "with every available weapon and without further notice"; in other words, the dreaded U-boats aimed to take control of the North Atlantic and would no longer spare American ships. Three days later the United States broke

THE CHICAGO DAILY NEWS.

FRIDAY, APRIL 6, 1917.

WILSON SIGNS; WAR IS ON

GOVERNMENT SEIZES
GERMAN TRADE SHIPS

ILLINOIS TROOPS RUSH
PLANS, AWAIT ORDERS

LATE NEWS BULLETINS
EXTRA

YOUNG WOMAN SLAIN
IN SOUTH SIDE ALLEY

WASHINGTON RUSHES
MILITARY MEASU

At a National Guard tent camp in a New York City park, recruits get their first lesson in saluting.

J. M. Flagg's Uncle Sam is famous, but other World War I recruiting posters were just as pointed.

▼ A phonograph cranks out state-of-the-art French lessons to officers who may soon be on their way to France.

relations with Berlin. On March 12 the renewed U-boat fury took its first American victims: two women passengers who died aboard the torpedoed Cunard liner *Laconia*. On a single day, March 18, German subs sank three U.S. ships.

The German high command was gambling, and the stakes were ultimate victory or defeat. Although the kaiser and his top brass knew that winning the trench war on the western front was at best uncertain, they believed that if their U-boats were successful in stopping the flow of aid to Britain, Germany could concentrate on polishing off its enemies on the eastern front. Then the Germans could throw almost all their forces at Britain and the Allies on the western front, before America could mobilize. It was clear that the United States was many months away from mounting a serious military threat; and the Germans took heart from their reading of U.S. public opinion, which seemed to be running strongly against mobilization, a step many Americans felt would inevitably plunge their country into war.

But then German diplomats committed a blunder that would turn U.S. public opinion against Germany and bring America roaring into the war.

At Camp Bowie, Texas, recruits learn how to use the bayonet.

Arthur Zimmermann, the kaiser's foreign minister, was caught red-handed trying to foment trouble between the United States and Mexico.

Lacking transatlantic telegraph links (since the British had cut Germany's undersea cables in 1914), Zimmermann, in Berlin, was communicating with the German ambassador in Washington over U.S. State Department wires, a privilege granted to Germany to aid Wilson's peace efforts. But the American circuit from Europe came through England, and there, in mid-January 1917, British intelligence picked up a message being relayed via Washington to the German ambassador in Mexico. Zimmermann had sent it in the mistaken belief that Germany's diplomatic code was unbreakable. British agents quickly deciphered the message, but delayed divulging their coup to avoid alerting Berlin that they had broken the German code.

Then, in early March, the British slipped the Zimmermann telegram to the American embassy in London, and within hours its contents exploded in Washington. The telegram said that the kaiser welcomed an alliance with Mexico if the U.S. went to war against Germany. In return, Germany would condone Mexico's retaking of the land in Texas, New Mexico, and Arizona that Mexico had lost following the Mex-

At the end of June 1917, large detachments of U.S. troops began landing in France at ports like St.-Nazaire (below), but it would be months before they reached the front in force.

George M. Cohan, Broadway's "Yankee-Doodle Dandy," gave AEF doughboys their unofficial marching song.

Gen. John J. Pershing (front) pays a visit to the port of Boulogne, France, on June 13, 1917, to check preparations for the arrival of the American Expeditionary Forces.

ican War of 1846–48. Clearly this was more than a threat to America's right to freedom of the seas. The Zimmermann telegram raised the spectre of renewed warfare on the Mexican frontier and brought the war to the heart of America.

It was a cheering, foot-stamping, flag-waving Congress that heard Wilson, on April 2, excoriate the Imperial German Government for its submarine "warfare against mankind" and for its attempts "to stir up enemies against us at our very doors." After Wilson's ringing call, "the world must be made safe for democracy," the Senate voted 86 to 2, the House 373 to 50, for war on Germany. The formal declaration of war came on April 6.

"Fighting for Liberty, Justice, Civilization"

In June the first military draft since the Civil War began, and nearly 10 million men registered almost festively. "Thanks for drawing 258 — that's me," a young Mississippian wired the secretary of war, who had reached blindfolded into a fishbowl to draw the first draft number. Patriotism soared. A navy recruiting poster showed a young woman in a sailor uniform sighing, "Gee! I Wish I Were a Man." Songs like "Johnny Get Your Gun" and "Over There" — the latter promising "the Yanks are coming. . . . And we won't come back till it's over, over there" — whipped up the nation's fighting spirit.

In fact, thousands of Americans were already "over there," and many had been wounded or killed. Ever since the war broke out in the summer of 1914, Americans had volunteered for the Allied cause. Some had relatives or friends in Canada, the British Isles, or France and went out of loyalty. Others went because they believed the Central Powers had to be defeated; still others, because they thought the war would be a grand adventure. Volunteer ambulance groups, like the American Ambulance Field Service, drew hundreds of idealistic Americans to war-torn Europe, where they risked their lives to save the wounded. One volunteer was a Philadelphian named Dillwyn Starr, who began driving an ambulance on the western front in October 1914. Then, as his father later wrote, Starr found that he "disliked the idea of being protected by a red cross on his sleeve. . . . the conviction grew strong within him that the place for a free man was on the side of the Allies fighting for liberty, justice, civilization — the world's cause." Starr joined a British motorized unit, fought in France, and went to Gallipoli on the ill-fated Dardanelles expedition. He returned to France as an officer in the Coldstream Guards and was killed on September 15, 1916, leading a charge at Ginchy during the Battle of the Somme, in the same assault in which British tanks made their clanking debut in World War I.

Like Starr, many young Americans died fighting under foreign flags. The French Foreign Legion had a sizable contingent of Yanks, as did Canadian combat units. Perhaps the most famous American volunteers were the airmen who flew with the French in the Lafayette Escadrille. Among them were the future authors of *Mutiny on the Bounty*, Charles Nordhoff and James Hall.

▼ **A lot of wishful thinking inspired this song, which saw Parisian revelries awaiting American soldiers in France.**

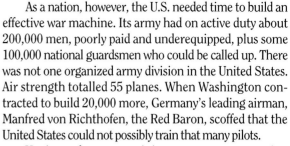

As a nation, however, the U.S. needed time to build an effective war machine. Its army had on active duty about 200,000 men, poorly paid and underequipped, plus some 100,000 national guardsmen who could be called up. There was not one organized army division in the United States. Air strength totalled 55 planes. When Washington contracted to build 20,000 more, Germany's leading airman, Manfred von Richthofen, the Red Baron, scoffed that the United States could not possibly train that many pilots.

Yet in weeks, army training camps were sprouting up across the country. On Wilson's orders, Gen. John J. Pershing hurried back from the Mexican border to get the American Expeditionary Forces (AEF), ready to ship out for Europe. The first draft swept half a million men into uniform; by war's end, more than 4 million would serve.

The U.S. Navy, while augmenting its antisubmarine patrols with converted yachts and revenue cutters, had destroyers in the British Isles for convoy duty by May 1917, and on July 4, advance troops of Pershing's AEF paraded through Paris to ecstatic cheers. That day, at the tomb of the Marquis de Lafayette, the French hero of America's Revolutionary War, an aide to Pershing, Col. Charles E. Stanton, spoke the words that gave a weary France, and all the Allies, new hope: "Lafayette, we are here."

◀

In London, crowds cheer an AEF column on August 15, 1917. By midsummer of 1917, convoys of troopships holding up to 15,000 Yanks each were landing in France and England.

▼ *At Lafayette's tomb in Paris, three of Pershing's officers pay their respects to the gallant Frenchman who helped America win independence. The date was July 4, 1917.*

FIGHTING ON THREE CONTINENTS

The terrible battles on the western front — such as the Marne, the Somme, Ypres, Meuse-Argonne — were only

part of the conflagration that consumed most of Europe and set off secondary explosions in Africa and Asia.

Rivalrous tyrants had made Europe and the Middle East a battleground for thousands of years, but nothing had prepared the people of these lands for the wholesale devastation and carnage of World War I. From Arabia and Africa to Scandinavia, armies using new weapons and tactics squared off, and always both sides paid dearly in blood. Nowhere was the fighting more vicious, or the opposing forces more stubbornly heroic, than on the western front, where hundreds of thousands died. At war's end, the map of Europe was redrawn to suit the victors, but many of the new boundaries would last less than a generation. World War II was just over the horizon.

▶

EUROPE AFTER WORLD WAR I:
Nine new nations (right) sprang
from prewar empires (below).
Gone was Austria-Hungary, most
of it split into Austria, Hungary,
Czechoslovakia, and Yugoslavia.
And Russia, which had left the
Allied cause after the czar
abdicated, lost vast western
borderlands, which became
independent Poland, Lithuania,
Estonia, Latvia, and Finland.
Parts of Germany went to
France, Belgium, and Poland.

MAJOR BATTLEFIELDS, EUROPE AND THE MIDDLE EAST

Key
- Allied Powers
- Central Powers
- Neutral countries

Areas where fighting occurred are shown in contrasting shades within red lines.

Allied land ——
Central Powers land ——

IMPORTANT MILITARY ACTIONS OF WORLD WAR I

1914
Austria-Hungary attacks Serbia, July 29.
Germany invades Belgium, Aug. 4.
Battle of Tannenberg (Stebark), eastern front, Germans defeat Russians, Aug. 26–30.
Battle of Lemberg (Gnila Lipa), eastern front, Russians defeat Austrians, Aug. 26–Sept.1.
First Battle of the Marne, western front, Allies block German advance, Sept. 6–9.

1915
German U-boats and surface ships start attempt to blockade Britain, Feb.
Second Battle of Ypres, Allies beat back Germans, who use poison gas, from which Canadian troops suffer almost 7,000 casualties, Apr. 22–May 25.
Battle of Gallipoli, Dardanelles campaign, Turks repel Allied force, Apr. 25, 1915–Jan. 9, 1916.
German U-boat sinks British passenger liner *Lusitania*, May 7.

1916
Battle of Verdun, western front, French block repeated German attacks, Feb.–Dec.
Siege of Kut, Mesopotamia campaign, Turks capture 10,000 British after nearly a 4-month siege, Apr. 29.
Battle of Jutland, North Sea, British and German fleets fight to a costly draw, May 31–June 1.
First Battle of the Somme, western front, Allies gain little against dug-in Germans, more than 1 million casualties on all sides, July 1–Nov. 18.

1917
German U-boats, after more than 16 months of restraint, resume unrestricted attacks, Feb. 1.
Battle of Arras, western front, Apr. 9 – May 3; British score only limited gains after heroic Canadian capture of Vimy Ridge, Apr. 9.
French offensive, western front, Germans yield little ground north of Aisne River, Apr.–May.
Russian offensive, eastern front, after Nicholas II abdicates, armies under Russia's new government stopped by Germans, June–Sept.
Third Battle of Ypres, Germans stop large Allied offensive, which gains only a few kilometres to Passchendaele, Belgium, July–Nov.
Passchendaele offensive completed by Canadians, over Gen. Currie's objections that human cost would be too high. Of 20,000 Canadian troops, almost 16,000 are dead or wounded, Oct.
Fall of Jerusalem, Palestine campaign, British enter the holy city as Turks retreat, Dec. 9.

1918
German offensives, western front, three attacks — at the Somme River (beginning Mar. 21), at the Lys River near Ypres (beginning Apr. 9), and at the Aisne River (May 27) — have early success, then stall as Allies stiffen.
Battle of Cantigny, western front, in their first major engagement, U.S. troops help French advance against Germans' Somme offensive, May 28.
Battle of Château-Thierry, western front, U.S. troops help French stop Germans' Aisne offensive, June–July.
Near Amiens, Allied spearhead formed by Canadians and Australians break German line for final offensive, Aug. 8.
Second Battle of the Marne, in the turning point of World War I, Allies halt last major German offensive on western front, July 15–Aug. 6.
Battle of Amiens, western front, British and French launch successful offensive, Aug. 8.
Battle of St.-Mihiel, western front, first major American offensive succeeds, Sept. 12–14.
Canadian troops capture Mons, Belgium, where British and German troops first met in 1914. Fighting ends, Nov. 11.

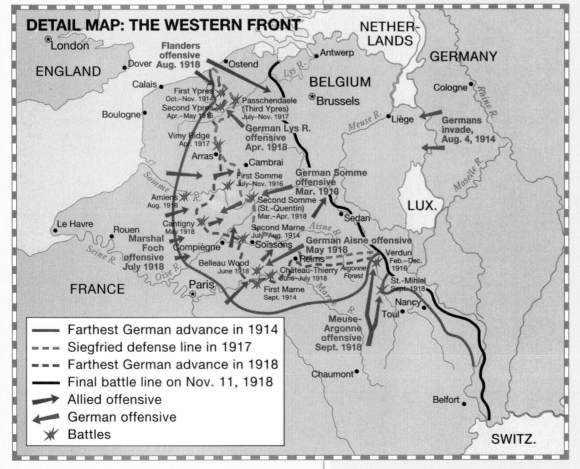

DETAIL MAP: THE WESTERN FRONT

Legend:
— Farthest German advance in 1914
--- Siegfried defense line in 1917
--- Farthest German advance in 1918
— Final battle line on Nov. 11, 1918
➜ Allied offensive
◄ German offensive
✳ Battles

THE FIDDLERS
BY
ARTHUR MEE

3D HOW LONG
FIDDLING

Prime Minister Sir Robert Borden (right) implemented the War Measures Act in 1914, which allowed his government to ban publications that criticized the war effort, such as **The Fiddlers** *(above), written early in the war by British author Arthur Mee.*

Canada's Home Front

If Canada's army was unprepared in 1914, the government was even less ready. While the army learned quickly how to survive, the government allowed the issue of conscription to split the country.

When it went to war in 1914, the Canadian army was enthusiastic but had no realistic view of the challenges it faced. The Canadian government, too, had never thought of what was involved in a large-scale war. As a nation of barely 8 million people, should Canada's major contribution be in troops? Or would it be wiser to contribute food and manufactured goods instead? Was it a fight until both sides decided that no further sacrifice could be made? Or was it a fight to the last man and the last bullet? How much would it cost, and where would the money come from? These were questions that few asked.

But it would not have mattered if they had. The Canadian government tended to manage the economy by tinkering with the tariff and by giving subsidies to business friends. Nor was the civil service — small, poorly skilled, and filled with political appointees — in any position to provide guidance. It was to be

the fate of the Canadian government to blunder its way through the war.

Prime Minister Borden's first move was to proclaim the War Measures Act, which allowed his government to place more than 8,000 "enemy aliens" (nationals of Germany and of the Austro-Hungarian and Turkish empires, 3,000 of them Canadian citizens) in internment camps without charge or trial. Newspapers and books written in "enemy" languages or even hinting at criticism of the war effort were banned. The reading material banned to Canadians included major U.S. newspapers and *The Fiddlers*, an anti-alcohol tract that called for prohibition as a patriotic measure.

To gear industry for war, the government simply raised the lending limit for banks so that farmers and businessmen could borrow to increase productivity. In the short run, it worked. Farmers borrowed to buy agricultural machinery, which pushed production to new highs. Businesses built factories that made everything from

◄ *Women, recruited to work in munitions factories during the war, helped to make this the biggest industry in Canada at that time.*

◄ *A procession of "enemy aliens" tramps through the snow in an internment camp, one of 24 set up in Canada during World War I for the nationals of enemy nations.*

Their needles clicking furiously, many women formed knitting bees to make socks and sweaters for the men on the front.

uniforms to trucks for the front. When British industry could not keep up with the war's enormous appetite for artillery shells, the Imperial Munitions Board was established to manufacture them in Canada. By the end of the war, 250,000 Canadians were employed in making munitions, and the industry had become Canada's biggest single business enterprise. Some of those employees, as in other industries, were women brought in to replace men who had been recruited to the war, but their numbers were not great and their wages, as ever, were well below those of the men they replaced.

The Price of Mismanagement

Production was impressive, but so was its cost. Putting so much borrowed money into circulation drove up prices to create severe inflation. And converting to war production created consumer shortages, despite efforts by Canadians to have a meatless and fuelless day every week. Then there was the problem of finding the money to pay for all that production. Lacking income tax, the federal government could pay only by borrowing. Traditionally, Canada had borrowed on the London market. But now London needed all the money it had. So, for the first time, Canada turned to New York. Spending far more money than it collected, the government raised Canada's debt from $463 million in 1914 to almost $2.5 billion in 1918.

Desperate for still more finances, the government went to a source once considered impossible. In 1915, it offered bonds to the public. To everyone's amazement, the strategy raised $100 million, twice what the government had hoped for. But there was an ominous sign in that success. Some 80 percent of the bonds were sold to corporations and wealthy individuals. Crushed by inflation that wages could not match, most Canadians had

BUY FRESH FISH

A GOOD BUTCHER

SAVE the MEAT *for* **our Soldiers and Allies**

OUR EXPORT TRADE IS VITAL BUY VICTORY BONDS

little to spare for bonds. Only the wealthy, fattened by profitable government contracts and untroubled by taxes, could afford bonds — bonds which all would have to repay, with interest, after the war. Ordinary Canadians, thinking of the price they were paying in blood and money, began muttering an ugly, new label for their business leaders — "war profiteers."

'Knit or Fight'

Despite their growing anger, Canadians volunteered for dozens of tasks in the war effort. When men joined the army, they often left behind families in serious hardship, for whom the Canadian Patriotic Fund raised money. Women's groups knitted clothing and made bandages for soldiers, obeying a popular slogan "Knit or Fight." And the Military Hospitals Commission did all it could to improve the condition of the wounded.

Some volunteer activities were less commendable. Anti-foreigner sentiment made itself felt in the firing of workers of German and Austrian descent. Patriotic young ladies patrolled the streets, looking for young men not in uniform and handing each a white feather — the badge of cowardice. Anxious to distance themselves from their German heritage, the people of Berlin, Ontario, changed their city's name to Kitchener in honor of Lord Horatio Kitchener, a respected British field marshal.

◄ *With food and finances in short supply, the Canadian government issued posters appealing to Canadians at home to help relieve food shortages and to donate funds. The Victory Bonds campaign raised $100 million for the war effort.*

The Gazette.

WEATHER FORECAST:
FAIR; NOT SO COLD

TEMPERATURE YESTERDAY
Max. 3 above; min. 10 below

MONTREAL, TUESDAY, DECEMBER 18, 1917.—TWENTY PAGES

VOL. CXLVI. NO. 302

PRICE TWO CENTS.

Unionist Government Has Won Decisive Victory Without Aid of Soldiers' Vote; Standing is 138 to 91

CANADA'S REPLY TO MEN'S APPEAL WAS DECISIVE

Unionist Government Policy Given Emphatic Endorsation

MAJORITY MORE THAN 45

Every English-Speaking Minister Elected—Solid Quebec ... West

Standing By Provinces

	Un.	Op.
P. E. I.	0	4
Nova Scotia	9	7
New Brunswick	7	4
Quebec	3	62
Ontario	71	11
Manitoba	11	0
Saskatchewan	16	0
Alberta	11	0
British Columbia	13	0

Unionist Majority ...
Returns are inco...
one Alberta and on...
Columbia constitu...
elections are de...
Halifax (2) Ne...
and Yukon until ...

SPECIAL WIRE BORE RETURNS TO SIR ROBERT

Prime Minister Received Results in Senate Chamber

LAURIER SPENT ELECTION DAY EN ROUTE EAST

Learned Result at 10 p.m. on Reaching Fort William

...IFICATION CONTINUED HIS JOURNEY

ISLAND OF MONTREAL

Seat	Elected	Party	Maj.
St. Antoine	Sir Herbert Ames	Union	1,596
St. Law-St. Geo.	Hon. C. C. Ballantyne	Union	1,446
St. Anns	Hon. C. J. Doherty	Union	1,761
Geo. E. Cartier	S. W. Jacobs,K.C.	Liberal	4,832
St. Denis	Alph. Verville	Liberal	8,400
Westm't-St.Henry	Alf. Leduc	Liberal	1,807
Maisonneuve	Hon. R. Lemieux	Liberal	4,460
Laurier-Outremont	Dr. J. E. Lesage	Liberal	2,317
Hochelaga		Liberal	8,752

ANTI-QUE... FEELING... OVER...

Only Ten La... of ...

SOME F...

Six Owe...
Germ...

LIEUT. PEAT TALKS IN SAMMIES' CAMPS

Canadians Now Crack Shock Troops of British Army, Returned Soldier Says

40,000 HUNS BACKED BY 2,000 GUNS FAIL

Vainly Hurled Themselves on Italians in Continuous Waves Along the Brenta

◀ On December 18th, 1917, *The Gazette announced the victory of the Unionist government in the national elections. In the run-up to the election, Liberals had sensed defeat, and so abandoned their leader Laurier (left) to join Borden's Conservatives.*

◀ *The call for volunteer soldiers was answered by many men, but it was still not enough. So Canada's Conservatives voted to conscript men into the war, a policy that helped them win the election.*

Bitterness and Crisis

A federal general election was due in 1916, but both Borden's Conservatives and Laurier's Liberals agreed to extend the government's life for at least a year. Most Canadians believed that to divert effort to an election while men were dying at the front would be unpatriotic.

By 1917, public frustration was focussed on two demands — conscription of men and conscription of wealth. Newspaper pages were filled daily with the names of men killed and wounded. But the daily list of volunteer replacements dwindled as the unemployed were soaked up by war industries. In fact, Canada was very close to the practical military maximum — 10 percent of the population in

◀ *A Toronto newspaper boy announces the Liberals' defeat.*

uniform — that any nation can sustain. But Canadian pride demanded that its country's commitment of four divisions in Europe be maintained. And since there were not enough volunteers, the obvious solution was to conscript men, forcing them to join.

As English-speaking Canadians scanned the casualty lists and noted the scarcity of French names, they had no doubt it was Quebeckers who had to be conscripted. Their prejudice was confirmed by Quebec spokesmen like Henri Bourassa who advised Quebeckers that their real enemies were the "boches of Ontario," who had closed French schools in that province. Through the years of war, charges and countercharges in a jingoistic press inflamed linguistic antagonisms.

In fact, whatever spokesmen like Bourassa might say, French-speaking Quebeckers had served with distinction in the war. True enough, the proportion of volunteers from Quebec was low. But few noticed that it was also below average in provinces like Prince Edward Island and Nova Scotia. The large numbers came from Ontario and the West, where there were high proportions of newly arrived British-born residents. Anyone studying the figures carefully would have concluded that enthusiasm for volunteering tapered off with the length of a person's stay in Canada. But few were in the mood for careful study.

The cry for conscription of wealth in the form of taxes had great appeal for the hundreds of thousands of Canadians who had lost friends and relatives in the war while business made enormous profits. But it was not at all appealing to the businessmen who were the core of Borden's government. When Sir Thomas White, Minister of Finance, bowed to the inevitable in 1917, he imposed very modest income taxes on individuals and corporations. He cushioned even that demand by making bond purchases exempt from tax.

▲ *On December 6, 1917, two munitions ships collided in Halifax Harbor, causing an explosion that flattened the north end of Halifax. Almost 2,000 people were killed and thousands more were made homeless (right).*

A Rigged Election

Such a small effort to conscript wealth was scarcely enough to impress voters. To do that, Borden decided to make military conscription the issue. He knew this would divide Canada, but by uniting English against French, conscription might just win his Conservatives the election.

To make sure of the Conservatives' success, Secretary of State Arthur Meighen introduced new rules for the election. The vote was taken away from all Canadians of enemy origin who had become citizens since 1902. It was given for the first time to women — but only to those who were wives, mothers, or sisters of servicemen. It was also given to all soldiers, regardless of age. Since many soldiers had no permanent residence in Canada, the Chief Returning Officer (a Conservative appointee) was empowered to place their votes wherever he chose. At a stroke, Meighen disenfranchised hundreds of thousands of Liberal voters, and added hundreds of thousands who would be almost certain to vote for the Conservatives' conscription policy.

Liberal candidates in English ridings, sensing sure defeat, abandoned Laurier to join Borden in what was called a Union government. On December 17, 1917, the Liberals maintained their seats only in Quebec and the Maritimes. From the Ottawa River to the Pacific Ocean the Unionists ruled.

The result of that election was a deep and lasting wound to the nation. Its gain was a conscription law that scraped together barely 25,000 men, far short of what was needed. The reality, as everyone involved should have realized, was not that Canada was full of slackers but that there were few men left to spare. And so a year of bitterness closed, made all the more terrible as, just days before the election, a munitions ship blew up in Halifax Harbor, killing more than 1,600 people.

More than four years of economic hardship in the face of profiteering, of economic mismanagement, and of devastating loss of life proportionately ten times as great as that of the United States, had strained Canada's social fabric to the breaking point. The strain would continue to be felt decades after the guns fell silent.

"We thought then of those men who will never again see their good old Canadian home." How right the words of this song, written in 1915, would prove to be.

WARTIME ENTERTAINMENT

As the clouds of war grew ever more ominous and finally broke in fury over the world, entertainers did their utmost to banish glumness.

Theodosia Goodman (far left) renamed herself Theda Bara (an anagram for "Arab death") and made more than 40 silent films before her vamp appeal waned after the war. Elsie Janis (left) cheered the boys with her songs of hope and love.

On the frontline, Canada's own Dumbells (below) entertained soldiers with cross-dressing cabaret.

George M. Cohan reached his peak in World War I. Here he acts in The Little Millionaire, which he also wrote, directed, and produced.

anadian troops on the western front quickly picked up the songs of their British counterparts, and the muddy roads of Flanders echoed to choruses of the tongue-twisting "Sister Susie's sewing shirts for soldiers. What skill at sewing shirts our dear young sister Susie shows . . ." Then there were "It's a Long Way to Tipperary," and the hit of the London stage, "The Whole World Is Waiting for the Sunrise." Frontline entertainers, often with one soldier playing the part of a woman, were drawn from serving regiments. For one such group, the 3rd Division's Dumbells, the music went on until 1932, with tours in Canada and the United States.

Nobody gave America more songs than the outstanding composer Irving Berlin, who never learned to write music and could play the piano only in the key of F. Russian immigrant at 4, teenage singing waiter in Chinatown, Berlin was not yet 25 when "Alexander's Ragtime Band" made him famous. Drafted in 1917, he put together a show called *Yip, Yip Yaphank* at Camp Upton. In it he sang his theme song of the common soldier: "Oh, How I Hate to Get Up in the Morning." The show was light, so Berlin pulled out the song "God Bless America" as "too patriotic," and it sat on his shelf for 20 years.

On Broadway, the Barrymores — John, Ethel, and Lionel — were already big and starred in several dramas during the war years, but the musical reigned supreme. In 1916 only three of the dozens of show openings were serious dramas. Musicals, comedies, and revues made up the rest.

A self-proclaimed Yankee-Doodle optimist whose only regret was being born a day too soon, on the third of July, George M. Cohan, a one-and-a-half-metre-high bundle of Irish energy, touched America's heart again and again. In a dozen musical comedies and revues before 1917, he wrote and performed unforgettable numbers, like "Give My Regards to Broadway" and "You're a Grand Old Flag." Then three bugle notes inspired him to write "Over There." It became the American anthem of the war.

Cohan knew America's heart, but impresario Florenz (Flo) Ziegfeld knew its libido. He kept right on producing his annual *Follies* during the war. Ziegfeld interviewed 15,000 chorus-line hopefuls a year to find a hundred or so who fit his ideal: "36, 26, 38, with the emphasis on the hips." He then had 50 at a time gambol on ornate ladders, spring up as flowers from trap doors, and perform scores of other such show-stoppers. For comic relief, the highest-paid jokesters in the world spun their patter: Will Rogers, W. C. Fields, Eddie Cantor, and Fanny Brice were all Ziegfeld regulars.

The master of ragtime, Scott Joplin, died in 1917, but his music lived on everywhere. There was another new sound, too, something between ragtime and blues. It travelled up the Mississippi from New Orleans with musicians like W. C. Handy, who wrote the immortal "St. Louis Blues" in 1914, Jelly Roll Morton, and Blind Lemon Jefferson. "Spell it Jass, Jas, Jaz, or Jazz," announced the bulletin of the Victor Talking Machine Company when it released the world's first jazz recording in 1917.

By 1915 more than five million people a day went to the movies. The public's thirst for vicarious adventure made stars of swashbuckling Douglas Fairbanks and strong and silent cowboy W. S. Hart. A middle-class girl from Cincinnati, Theodosia Goodman, renamed herself Theda Bara, told fan magazines she was an Arab born in the Sahara, and with sultry stares, raven hair, and fleecy bras, created the screen's

Enrico Caruso sings the Don José role in Carmen. **A hugely popular entertainer, Caruso visited troops and led War Bond drives.**

first sex symbol. As the "vampire of love" (shortened to "vamp"), Theda was a far cry from Toronto-born Mary Pickford, who became America's Sweetheart. She made her American debut as a $5-a-day extra, but after a string of lucrative tearjerkers, like *Tess of the Storm Country,* bargained herself up to $2 million a year before the armistice.

Although controversial even then for its stereotyping of black people, director D. W. Griffith's 1915 *Birth of a Nation* proved once and for all the power of film to tell a story and move an audience. After it became the first movie shown in the White House, President Woodrow Wilson said, "It is like writing history with lightning."

Opera stars Madame Ernestine Schumann-Heink and Enrico Caruso split their time between paid performances, entertaining troops, and selling War Bonds. But the most heroic star may have been actress Sarah Bernhardt, dubbed the Divine Sarah by Oscar Wilde. She wowed Americans on several farewell tours, playing roles from Cleopatra to Juliet; she was past 70 and had a wooden leg.

The Ziegfeld Follies of 1915 *perfectly illustrates Flo Ziegfeld's recipe for show-business success: attractive women in expensive costumes.*

▲ **Comedians Eddie Cantor and Fanny Brice ham it up in** **The Ziegfeld Follies of 1917,** *the show that also starred W. C. Fields and Will Rogers.*

Up FROM THE TRENCHES AT LAST

In the spring of 1918, the German high command believed they had every chance of executing a plan of mighty multiple offensives that would force the Allies to seek peace on Germany's terms. But rebounding Allied spirit turned the war around.

Germany's moment had arrived, the general staff's chief strategist, Gen. Erich Ludendorff, told the kaiser in late 1917. The Allies' failed offensives in Italy and on the western front, the collapse of Romanian resistance, and revolution in Russia, ending the threat on the eastern front, "make it possible to deliver a blow on the western front," Ludendorff wrote. "We should strike . . . before the Americans can throw strong forces into the scale." For the Allies, dispirited by three years of warfare, the Americans were arriving too slowly — "in dribbling fashion," Britain's prime minister, David Lloyd George, complained. Of the million men Gen. John J. Pershing had requested, only 175,000 were in France by January 1918.

From the Hindenburg Line — the Allies' name for the German defences angling southeast from Belgium across France — five German armies emerged on March 21, 1918. It was the start of the Germans' Somme offensive, aimed at splitting the British and French armies, then pushing the British to the sea. Simultaneously German guns with 35.5-metre barrels and a 120-kilometre range began shelling Paris. Damage was light, but the shock was great.

▲ *Backed by a 37-mm gun, men of the U.S. 23rd Infantry, 2nd Division (of Belleau Wood fame), move forward. Side by side (above, left) are a German leather helmet, used until 1916, and a U.S. metal helmet.*

▶

In 1917, Canadian soldiers were making their way across a quagmire that had once been Flemish fields, on their way to victory at Passchendaele.

In France in 1918, artillery captain Harry S. Truman (right) had a reputation for cussing. Future general George S. Patton (below) became a tank advocate.

In this emergency, and to preserve the shaky Allied coalition, Britain's Field Marshal Douglas Haig agreed to subordinate his forces to French command, under Marshal Ferdinand Foch. Pershing, now with eight American divisions, declared it would be a "great honor" to do likewise.

The bloodletting was frightful — 340,000 British and French casualties — but Ludendorff's Somme offensive was checked in April after initial gains. U.S. troops did not see action. But on April 20, two companies of the 26th (Yankee) Division, got a thrashing in the St.-Mihiel sector when German raiders captured and held the village of Seicheprey for 12 hours, then pulled back. It was a bitter blow to the Americans, who suffered 482 casualties. The Germans captured 179 men and 24 machine guns.

Ludendorff kept pushing. In late May he swept across the Aisne River. In three days his forces advanced 72 kilometres, reaching the Marne River at Château-Thierry, 48 kilometres from Paris. Now the Yanks were in the thick of it, and at Château-Thierry the U.S. 3rd Division repelled German attempts to cross the Marne.

With the U.S. 3rd Division holding fast, the Allied command trucked the U.S. 2nd Division, under cover of darkness, to help block a German advance toward Paris. Then the Yanks were ready to counterattack. They struck at Belleau Wood, a 1.6-kilometre-square boulder-strewn patch of trees. Attacking through machine-gun fire, pausing in shallow foxholes dug with bayonets and mess kits, a marine brigade led the way. On June 14 two army regiments joined the battle, and by June 25 Belleau Wood was secure.

ACES, PORTENTS, AND A SHORT LIFE EXPECTANCY

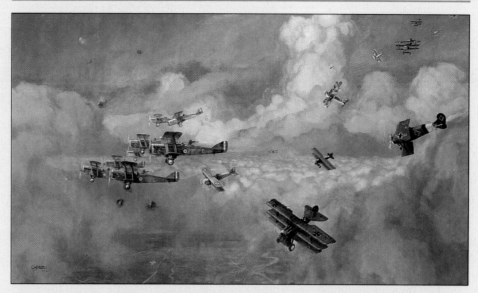

"Closing Up," by G. H. Davis, shows British DH-9A bombers (left) pulling into tight formation to focus a hail of gunfire on a Jagdstaffel ("hunting pack") of German Fokker triplanes and D-VII's.

World War I broke out less than 11 years after the Wright brothers made their historic flight. Before hostilities ended, airplanes added a new dimension to warfare and created a new species of hero, the air ace. At first, both sides used aircraft for reconnaissance and scouting only. Then a British pilot aimed his revolver at a German plane, and fired. The German landed, the first pilot ever forced down in such a way.

In 1915 a French pilot, Roland Garros, mounted a gun in his cockpit, and firing through his whirling

Billy Bishop

prop, felled five enemy planes. Then, working for Germany, the Dutch aviation pioneer Anthony Fokker invented a device that timed a machine gun to fire between prop strokes. The fighter plane was born.

A fighter pilot's life, however gallant and thrilling, had exhaustion and death as constant companions. One-third — 50,000 — of the war's airmen died. Their average life span at the front was three weeks. Against such odds, it is surprising that any pilot survived long enough to down the five enemy aircraft that made him an ace. But Germany's "Red Baron" (below) got 80; Frenchman René Fonck, 75; Edward Mannock of Britain, 73; Canadian Billy Bishop (left), 72; and American Eddie Rickenbacker, 26. Of these six aces, only Fonck, Bishop, and Rickenbacker lived to see the armistice. More than 22,000 Canadians served in the Royal Flying Corps and the Royal Naval Air Service. One of them, Col. Billy Barker, won the Victoria Cross for a single-handed battle against 60 German aircraft.

As the war progressed, fighters improved dramatically — they had to. The Germans' Zeppelin airships, which flew well above the ceiling of the defenders' fighters, dropped 223 tonnes of bombs on England before 1916, when the British built fighters that could reach them. The airship raids stopped. But the Germans then briefly sent twin-engine Gotha bombers over England. The Gotha and its Allied counterparts did relatively little damage, but they portended the massive bombing assaults of World War II.

The Red Baron, Manfred von Richthofen

More than 1 million American troops were now in France, arriving at the rate of 300,000 a month. A vast supply network, manned by black stevedore and construction units, backed the AEF. More than 1500 kilometres of railway had been laid. Ordnance, however, remained a problem. Lacking their own artillery, U.S. troops used French and British guns; and of 4,400 tanks the U.S. War Department had ordered, only 15 reached France — after the war ended.

Ludendorff kept pressing, but in a series of attacks and counterattacks known as the Second Battle of the Marne, the Germans finally had to abandon their threat to Paris. Then, on August 8, 1918, a date that Ludendorff called "the black day of the German Army," British, French, Canadian, and Anzac divisions, behind more than 450 tanks, hit along the Somme near Amiens, catching Ludendorff off guard and panicking his troops. By September 2 the Germans were back to the Hindenburg Line and Ludendorff's resolve had cracked. "The war must be ended," he wrote the kaiser.

Canadians Spearhead Allied Offensive

In comparison to the European powers, most of whom had large, standing armies with career officers of long service, Canada began the war with an army that was untrained and, for the most part, led by officers whose only service had been as part-time soldiers. They paid heavily to learn the craft of war but they did learn. By 1916, Canadians had won recognition as the best fighting unit in the Allied armies.

They were led by 1.8-metre, 136-kilogram Arthur Currie. Born in Strathroy, Ontario, he was, like his men, a novice at war. Unlike more experienced officers, though, he soon learned the folly of throwing bodies against machine guns. By 1916, he had so mastered the arts of meticulous planning and surprise that his battles were notable for spectacular success at minimum cost. When he was appointed commander of the Canadian Corps in 1917, his reputation for military genius stood so high that British Prime Minister Lloyd George actually considered replacing Field Marshal Haig with Currie as commander of the British forces.

On August 8, 1918, the start of the final Allied offensive, it was only logical that the Canadians under Currie should be the spearhead. In that one day, they broke through the German line that had held for four years, and spilled across the open land behind it for the final hundred days of unbroken success. The Canadians were very much on German Field Marshal Ludendorff's mind when he referred to August 8 as "the black day of the German army."

While the Allies were battering Germany's defences, that country was crumbling from within. In the fall of 1917, a small group of sailors had begun agitating for peace negotiations; two of them were executed. Metalworkers went on

DULCE ET DECORUM EST . . .

Col. John McCrae, physician and poet, author of "In Flanders Fields."

In the voices of the poets and writers of the Great War echo all the complex passions aroused by the worst man-made catastrophe known up to that time. No war has inspired so large, so distinctive, and so fine a body of literary work.

Rupert Brooke caught his fellow Englishmen's swelling patriotism in 1914 with the lines: "If I should die, think only this of me:/ That there's

Rupert Brooke

some corner of a foreign field/ That is forever England." The next year, on a troopship bound for Gallipoli, Brooke died of disease. The war killed many other soldier-poets, including Britain's Wilfred Owen, Isaac Rosenberg, and Edward Thomas, Canada's Col. John McCrae ("In

Flanders Fields") who died of pneumonia in 1918, and Joyce Kilmer, author of the familiar "Trees." One of the greatest modern French poets, Guillaume Apollinaire, died of influenza in 1918 after suffering a head wound.

Owen began the war with the patriotic zeal of Brooke, but the bloodshed soon changed him. In 1918, the year he fell in action, in a poem about a gassed comrade, he used the Latin epitaph *Dulce et decorum est pro patria mori* ("Sweet and fitting it is to die for one's country") and called it "the old Lie." His friend, the twice-wounded Siegfried Sassoon, turned more savagely bitter; in one poem he calls staff officers "incompetent swine."

Of the many novels by soldiers, two that have stood the test of time are *All Quiet on the Western Front*, by the German writer Erich Maria Remarque, and the openly antiwar *Under Fire*, by Henri Barbusse, a French poet who, past 40, volunteered for the infantry and was discharged in 1917 after being badly wounded.

Wilfred Owen

His fighting done, Sgt. Alvin C. York poses for a portrait after the war. A religious conscientious objector at the war's start, York, as a private in October 1918, singlehandedly overcame a machine-gun unit, killing 15 Germans and capturing 132.

strike in January 1918. In that month President Wilson announced his Fourteen Points, a peace plan calling on Germany to withdraw from occupied lands; it also supported self-determination for the peoples of Europe. The plan was noteworthy for what it did not demand: the partition of Germany.

By October the Germans had accepted Wilson's Fourteen Points, but sought better terms for an armistice. Then the pace of events quickened. Austria-Hungary gave up. German sailors mutinied, refusing to fight. On November 9, as the Meuse-Argonne offensive forged ahead, rebels seized Berlin. The kaiser, having taken refuge with his army in Belgium, had little choice. He abdicated his throne and fled to Holland. With him went the last obstacle to peace.

Soldiers of Company M, 6th Infantry, at Remoiville, France, cheer the armistice. Enemies meet (inset) to sign the cease-fire in a railcar in a forest near Compiègne.

At about 5:00 A.M. on November 11, 1918, German and Allied representatives, meeting in a railway carriage at Compiègne, France, signed an armistice agreement that would take effect six hours later, at the 11th hour of the 11th day of the 11th month of the year.

It was the middle of the night in Canada and the United States. At 3:00 A.M. the Associated Press wires flashed news of the armistice and, in the harbors of New York City and Halifax, ships' horns split the night air. Most people heard the news by rumor, and not until the morning papers would they realize that this time the rumor was true. Cities exploded in spontaneous parades of relief.

But in a thousand city streets and in small towns and villages, the end also came as a numbing reminder of the husbands, sons and fathers who would never come back. It was, if anything, worse in Canada, whose loss of 60,000 from a smaller population represented 10 times what the United States had lost.

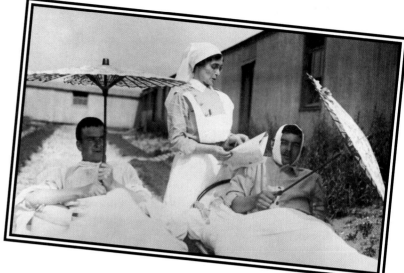

With a concertina, the tricolor, and the Stars and Stripes, four happy Allies in France salute the war's end. Two wounded Canadian soldiers (above, right) recuperate in the French sunshine with some style before being allowed to return home.

▶ *A soldier stands guard near the Rhine River in the sector of Germany occupied by Americans after the armistice. By the fall of 1919, most American troops had left Europe.*

WHO WON THE WAR?

Of course, the Allies lost less than the Central

Powers. But even the victors were badly hurt,

and they failed to fashion a durable

peace. Medicine advanced, but influenza

had the last word in causing human misery.

C anada and the United States emerged from the war economically stronger. But Europe was broken in economic and human terms. Four empires had collapsed: Germany, Austria, Russia, and Turkey. A fifth and sixth, Britain and France, emerged from the conflict spiritually and materially exhausted. Though the sheer size of combat forces — 65 million — foiled attempts at precise accounting, as many as 10 million soldiers had perished in battle, and twice as many had been wounded. Four million civilians had lost their lives.

In the face of these almost unbearable losses, it was comforting for some to believe that the Allies had won, at least, a victory for democracy and liberal thinking. Gone were the pampered princes and archdukes of imperial Europe, the Ottoman sultans, the Romanovs and Hapsburgs, and in their stead stood the new indepen-

dent nations of central Europe: Austria, Hungary, Czechoslovakia, Poland, Finland, Estonia, Latvia, and Lithuania, all vaguely democratic, all fiercely nationalistic. Turkey surrendered its Arab lands to the British and French, and colonial peoples the world over saw reason to hope that the new egalitarian spirit sweeping the globe would include them too. For a time it seemed that the Wilsonian principles of national sovereignty and political self-determination would create a just and lasting peace and a new age of international cooperation. But such was not to be.

Many have said that the Allies won the war but lost the peace, and it is true that the peace conference at Versailles created as many problems as it solved. Forced to admit responsibility for the conflict and pay billions in war reparations, Germany's infant democracy was hamstrung from the start, but the terms were not so severe as to prevent a resurgence of German militarism. Worse, because Germany had sued for peace before the Allies invaded, many Germans believed that they had not really lost the war but had been stabbed in the back by Jews, Bolsheviks, and Socialists.

Underestimating the depth of German resentment may have been the costliest mistake of the century. Ten months after the armistice, a corporal named Adolf Hitler attended his first meeting of an anti-Semitic group that would later name itself the National Socialist German Workers' Party. Though no one knew it yet, the winds of tyranny were blowing again in Europe. By the end of the 1920's, totalitarian regimes had subverted parliamentary democracy in Italy and Russia; Poland, Hungary, Turkey, and Yugoslavia had all reverted to one-man rule.

Not all the war's legacies were so ruinous. Spurred by

▲ *In London, on his way to Versailles, President Woodrow Wilson (above, left) rides with King George V of England. As peace talks began, influenza engulfed the world. A Massachusetts tent camp (above) offered fresh air to cure flu.*

wartime needs, technological advances came quickly and then just as quickly found peacetime applications. Lessons learned from tanks made better tractors. Lightweight alloys developed for aviation proved a boon to automotive engineers, and in Germany economic isolation gave birth to flourishing chemical and plastics industries. Out of the war came airplanes that flew faster, farther, and higher and captured worldwide fascination. By war's end, the warring nations had built some 200,000 aircraft, and the armistice freed hundreds of trained pilots to fly passengers and mail.

Medical Advances From the Battlefield

New weapons, the abominable conditions of trench warfare, and the millions of wounded added up to an unprecedented medical challenge. High-velocity bullets and artillery shrapnel inflicted massive tissue damage, and wounded soldiers lying in the manure-rich fields of France were at great risk of contracting gas gangrene and tetanus. Poison gas caused nearly 185,000 Allied casualties. In the trenches, waterborne diseases such as cholera and dysentery were always a threat. Crowded, unsanitary conditions permitted the breeding and spread of lice and fleas, carriers of the bacterium that causes typhus.

Doctors, nurses, and medics struggled heroically to save lives. Chlorine in the drinking supply cut disease rates, and immunization not only reduced typhus deaths but laid the basis for better understanding of the body's immune system. For the first time motorized ambulances saw wide use, as did X-rays and the restoration of blood volume by transfusion. French army surgeon Alexis Carrel and British chemist Henry Dakin joined forces and developed a surgical

therapy to irrigate and sterilize wounds without harming adjacent tissues. Psychiatry, still in its infancy, gained respect by treating shell shock, a post-battlefield mental illness characterized by hysteria, disorientation, and paralysis. Similarly, the ravages of war hastened advances in physical therapy, plastic surgery, prosthetics, orthopedics, anesthesiology, and the treatment of respiratory trauma.

Still, nothing could have prepared medicine for the influenza that raged across the globe in 1918. The loss of life was staggering. Worldwide, as many as 27 million people perished, half a million in the United States and 50,000 in Canada. For Canada, the death toll almost equalled that of the war.

Coffins became valuable, and when Washington, D.C., health officials learned that a shipment, bound for Pittsburgh, lay at the railroad station, they arranged to have it go no farther. All found use in the nation's capital.

In the United States the epidemic peaked in the last week of October 1918, when 21,000 died — the highest domestic one-week mortality rate on record. Then, unaccountably, it faded. By the spring, the virus had ceased its rampage. It has never been identified, although other flu viruses, ball-shaped organisms so small that 30 million can fit on the head of a pin, have since been isolated and studied. To this day no one knows why the 1918 virus turned so deadly. Perhaps, as many have suggested, influenza was nature's way of showing humanity who was still boss.

Instituted by Queen Victoria in 1856, the Victoria Cross is the Commonwealth's highest military decoration, awarded for exceptional bravery in the face of the enemy.

Chapter 3

THE UNRULY DECADE

Prohibition uncorks a spirit of exuberance.

Flappers, fast cars, and faster airplanes.

Jazz and tabloids. Scandals and fads.

Valentino and the Babe. Then . . . Crash!

Thomas Hart Benton's 1930 mural "City Activities and Dance Hall" portrayed the passions of the 1920's.

Mustered out of the army in 1918 at the end of World War I, these soldiers celebrate their departure from Camp (later Fort) Dix, New Jersey.

SIDESTEPPING A WORLD ROLE

Canada and the United States each took a major part in the most devastating war humanity had yet seen.

But were they ready to continue playing lead roles on the world stage?

When the guns fell silent over Europe, the victorious Allies reacted with joy and bewilderment. Frontline soldiers stayed in their trenches, scarcely daring to believe an end had come. One hundred and sixty kilometres or so to the west, a multitude of delirious Frenchmen sang "La Marseillaise" against the backdrop of the dazzlingly illuminated Paris Opéra.

Back home in Canada and the United States, ecstatic throngs turned out with parades and other celebrations to welcome home the returning soldiers. The fuzzy-cheeked lads who had gone overseas to fight were coming back heroes, and they carried themselves with a newfound sense of worldly self-assurance. "How ya gonna keep 'em down on the farm (after they've seen Paree)?" asked a popular song lyric. It was a good question. And like those returning heroes, the two nations themselves appeared to have grown up, ready to assume their rightful places in world affairs.

It was in this upbeat atmosphere that President Woodrow Wilson sailed to France for peace negotiations in December of 1918. Canada, too, was represented. As a colony, it would not normally have been entitled to a role in the negotiations, but Canadians assumed that their 60,000 dead would inspire both gratitude and recognition.

The American president brought with him a peace plan based on his famous Fourteen Points, the visionary precepts for international accord he had announced earlier

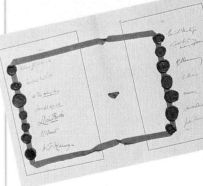

Allowed to sign the Treaty of Versailles only as a member of the British Empire delegation, Canada shared this page with delegates from Australia, South Africa and India.

that year. The plan included self-determination for European nationalities, an end to secret diplomacy, and even more ambitiously, a League of Nations to settle future international disputes. It was a sublimely idealistic document.

But Wilson's plan met with the grim realities of European politics. France, invaded twice in 48 years by Germany, intended to cripple its hated neighbor; Ukrainians, Poles, Slavs, Magyars and others demanded homelands, in many cases from each other; Italy wanted a piece of the Balkans. Canada was humiliated to find that its immense sacrifice won it the privilege to attend the conference, but it did not have a voice in any major decisions. Though Prime Minister Sir Robert Borden demanded the right to sign the treaty for Canada as an equal signatory, the British insisted that they would sign for the whole empire — the Canadian signature was a mere indent.

For Germans the Treaty of Versailles was a humbling document. Germany saw its once mighty army dismantled and its Rhineland region declared a demilitarized zone. The treaty exacted reparations, later set at $32 billion, and required Germany and Austria to accept full blame for the war. American delegates were horrified. Herbert Hoover predicted that the harsh terms

▲ **U.S. President Wilson arrived in England in December 1918 as part of his European tour, bearing a peace plan, and was thronged by rose-throwing crowds.**

Flawed Peace

On June 28, 1919, after months of hard negotiating, President Wilson signed a peace treaty at the palace of Versailles, near Paris. But the U.S. Senate failed to ratify the treaty, and the United States remained technically at war with Germany until 1921. Many Germans considered the Versailles treaty unfair, and Adolf Hitler was later to take full advantage of their bitterness. Although France's Premier Georges Clemenceau and Britain's Prime Minister David Lloyd George sat at Wilson's side at the signing, both had snubbed the ailing Wilson during the negotiations and had even come to blows with each other. (Clemenceau actually challenged Lloyd George to a duel!) On the day of the signing, the French delegates, who had won most of their objectives, could not conceal their glee, while the Germans behaved like chastened offenders. It was not an auspicious day for world peace.

▶ **Henry Cabot Lodge, powerful Republican senator from Massachusetts, offered to stop opposing "Wilson's treaty" if the president dropped the provision that would send U.S. troops to help defend League of Nations members. Wilson refused, and Lodge continued to prevent the treaty's ratification.**

would "ultimately bring destruction." Wilson himself was inclined to believe the treaty was too punitive, but he signed it in exchange for Allied support of his precious League.

Back home, when he submitted the Versailles treaty for Senate approval, Wilson faced an even tougher fight. Isolationist Republicans, who wanted no more of Europe's nasty squabbles, objected in particular to U.S. membership in the League of Nations and sponsored an amended treaty. The president rejected their modifications and took his case to the people, crossing the country aboard the presidential train, *The Mayflower*. It was a punishing ordeal. At 62 years of age, against the advice of doctors, Wilson travelled a gruelling 12,800 kilometres and made more than 30 prepared speeches. Three weeks into the trip, his strength gave out entirely. *The Mayflower*, blinds drawn, sped back to Washington.

A few days later the President suffered a massive stroke. For weeks he could not sit up or even sign his name. Without his influence, the Senate vote was short of the two-thirds majority required to ratify the treaty.

Canada did apply for admittance into the League of Nations and was accepted, a major step to its international recognition as a nation. But Canadian delegates to the league consistently opposed the collective security provisions of its charter, provisions that would have required Canada to go to the aid of any threatened league member. It was a sign that Canada, like the United States, was unwilling to become further embroiled in European affairs.

PROHIBITION SETS OFF A SPREE

Hoping to promote sobriety, morality, and good health, legislators passed a sheaf of laws banning the sale of liquor. The result was years of illicit drinking.

"Monster Demonstration", said the ribbons, "March 8th, 1916: Ontario Dry." Through the streets of Toronto marched 15,000 people wearing those ribbons, followed by three truckloads of petitions. It was the biggest demonstration of a campaign that had begun in Canada almost a century ago. Canada was going dry.

Prince Edward Island led the way with a prohibition law in 1901. Most of the other provinces followed during the war, with Quebec joining in — though only partially and only briefly — in 1919.

The law obviously had majority support. From 1870 to 1900, Canadian consumption of wine and distilled liquor had steadily gone down. However, the consumption of beer had risen just as steadily, a worrying sign that working-class Canadians had no intention of converting, as their middle-class compatriots had done, to water. Their resistance was what made Prohibition necessary, and the wartime mood for sacrifice swept opposition aside.

It wasn't as sweeping a prohibition as it was in the United States. In most provinces, home-made beer and wine

▲ **Three thirsty ladies at a brewery stand ready to hoist their beer steins the moment Prohibition ends.**

Amendment XVIII

1. After one year from the ratification of this article the manufacture, sale, or transportation of intoxicating liquors within, the importation thereof into, or the exportation thereof from the United States and all territory subject to the jurisdiction thereof for beverage purposes is hereby prohibited.

2. The Congress and the several States shall have concurrent power to enforce this article by appropriate legislation.

▲ **In the United States, Prohibition was imposed by the 18th Amendment to the Constitution, approved by Congress in 1917. Two years later, three-fourths of the states had ratified the amendment, making it the law of the land.**

▲ **In March 1916, a line of bartenders almost three-quarters of a kilometre long tramped through the snow on Toronto's Yonge Street to protest against Prohibition.**

were legal, as was medicinal liquor. Even so, Canadian Prohibition was shortlived, and most provinces abandoned it in the 1920's. The exception was Prince Edward Island, where it lingered until 1948.

The rise of illegal sales and crime helped to end Prohibition. But two other factors were as important. From 1900, sales of wine and distilled liquor began to increase — a sign that the Canadian middle class was changing its tastes. In addition, the number of cars and trucks on the roads was growing. Provincial governments needed more money to build those roads, and what better way to raise it than through government sale of liquor? So, as Canadians rejected Prohibition, the provincial government liquor store was born.

Americans were just a little slower than Canadians in adopting the "noble experiment." At 12:01 in the morning of January 16, 1920, from the smallest towns to the largest cities in the United States, tavern doors closed and Prohibition lay hard on the land. Only a few hours later, officials seized four stills, a taste of things to come. Within the year liquor was pouring over the borders from Canada and Mexico.

Many of the bootleggers were Canadians. With liquor bought in Ontario for $18 a case and sold in the U.S. for

$120, Rocco Perri of Hamilton made his grocery store the centre of a bootlegging empire whose profits bought him a 19-room mansion. Labatt's Brewery of London, Ontario, delivered its beer to New York by railway. The Bronfmans smuggled liquor across the prairie border. Nova Scotia fishermen found a use for their outdated schooners in smuggling liquor along the American coast.

As saloons closed in the United States, speakeasies sprang up in their place. By 1926 officials estimated there were 100,000 speakeasies operating in New York City alone. Breweries, restricted by the Volstead Act to the manufacture of low-alcohol near beer, simply ignored these legal niceties. In California the hectares devoted to growing wine grapes ballooned from 39,000 in 1919 to 276,000 in 1926. Moonshine stills, once limited to the backwoods, sprang up everywhere: in tenement basements, in the kitchens and bathrooms of private homes, in the darkest reaches of abandoned coal mines.

Drinkers carried and smuggled hooch in every conceivable container, from hip flasks to life preservers. "In time," noted a German tourist in 1927, "I learned that not everything in America was what it seemed to be. I discovered, for instance, that a spare tire could be filled with substances other than air, that one must not look too deeply into certain binoculars, and that teddy bears, which suddenly acquired tremendous popularity among the ladies, very often had hollow metal stomachs."

To the dismay of some, criminalizing liquor increased its appeal. What's more, since all drinkers became tacit partners in crime, Prohibition had a democratizing effect. Cultural and class barriers fell with a resounding thud. Once a habit more widespread among laborers, who drank beer, and the wealthy, who drank wine and spirits, the use of intoxicating beverages now found a multitude of enthusiastic converts among the traditionally sober middle class.

Enforcing Prohibition proved hopeless. Though many members of Congress were willing to vote "dry" in principle, and thus protect themselves from the wrath of Anti-Saloon Leaguers and other drys, they were less eager about appropriating funds to police the nation's drinking habits. Toward the end of "the noble experiment," Herbert Hoover himself estimated that a police force of 250,000 men would be needed to make it work, further demonstrating, as he remarked, "the futility of the whole business." The prohibition laws, too, were full of holes, voted into the statute books in many cases by men who went on tippling with the rest of America. Federal Prohibition officials and local police, undermanned and underfunded, were hard pressed to withstand the considerable temptations of the liquor trade and the pressures of organized crime. One Prohibition official called his bureau "a training school for bootleggers."

For most bootleggers, the chance of big money ended with the American repeal of Prohibition in 1933. But others, like the Bronfmans, profited. They had had the foresight to buy a legitimate distillery in Montreal where they then built a fortune based on a new taste the Americans had developed under Prohibition — Canadian rye.

A painting by New York artist Ben Shahn shows some ingenious ways a gentleman tippler might hide his whiskey.

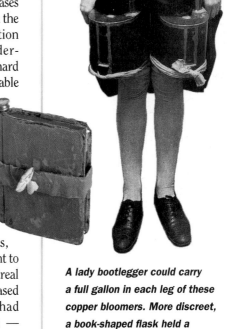

A lady bootlegger could carry a full gallon in each leg of these copper bloomers. More discreet, a book-shaped flask held a generous nip.

▲ Federal agents proudly display a moonshiner's captured backyard still. But for every still raided, hundreds more continued to operate undetected.

SPEAKEASIES AND BOOTLEGGERS

"Mother makes brandy from cherries;
Pop distills whiskey and gin;
Sister sells wine from the grapes on our vine —
Good grief, how the money rolls in!"

No sooner had the 18th Amendment taken effect than many Americans' ideas about good citizenship seemed to evaporate. The production, sale, or transporting for sale of alcoholic beverages was illegal, but breaking the law — bootlegging — was widely winked at. Formerly law-abiding families fired up kitchen stills and filled their bathtubs with homemade gin. Not nearly so innocent were the big-time bootleggers who claimed they purveyed real whiskey and were lauded as public benefactors. Yet these same sellers often cut their supplies with industrial alcohol and other toxic substances, then sold the adulterated stuff at immense profit.

The handiest outlet for bootlegged hooch was the speakeasy, the illicit reincarnation of the corner tavern. No doubt the atmosphere of romance, danger, and secrecy that surrounded speakeasies contributed to their popularity. Adding to the allure was the assortment of colorful types who ran the leading speaks. Few other hostesses could project such brazen good cheer as Mary Louise (Texas) Guinan, former cowgirl, vaudevillian, and silent-movie actress who became queen of the New York nightclub scene. Drinking in Miss Guinan's establishments was not cheap — the cover charge alone was between $5 and $25, depending

▲ *With "Hello, Sucker!" and a big smile, Texas Guinan (seated, in dark dress) greets a customer at one of her speakeasies.*

Clip joint, bathtub gin, cement overshoes, the one-way ride — never has a decade so enriched our vocabulary with memorable idioms of lawlessness and vice.

The speakeasy (known as a roadhouse or a blind pig in Canada) served up concoctions that offered kicks, if nothing else. Newfoundlanders traded salt cod for a powerful rum that became known as Screech. Maritimers sloshed water in old rum barrels to produce a brew called Swish, while Quebeckers opted for Caribou — hot wine mixed with dilute alcohol.

The American South liked Squirrel Whiskey, a moonshine so strong it made men climb trees. Chicago's Yack Yack Bourbon, laced with burnt sugar and iodine, was also a favorite. Discriminating tipplers looked for the Real McCoy, smuggled in pure and unadulterated from the Bahamas by legendary rumrunner Bill McCoy.

Any of these potions could get a drinker lit, lubricated, fried, canned, or corked. More would make him stinko or spiflicated. The morning after would bring the jumps, the shakes, or — worse yet — the screaming meemies.

When a thirsty motorist tried to smuggle in booze from Mexico, customs officers from Marfa, Texas, seized all 110 bottles.

on the night — but for nearly a decade Texas packed them in.

Prohibition enforcement produced its own share of colorful characters. In Canada there was Rev. J. O. Spracklin, a Methodist clergyman of Windsor, Ontario. An ardent prohibitionist, he had signed on as an Ontario liquor licence inspector in July 1920. In four spectacular months he made headlines with his tough handling of illegal liquor dealers. But on the morning of November 8 he went looking for Beverly "Babe" Trumble, wearing a pair of six-guns. Spracklin broke into Trumble's office, and Trumble went for his gun — too slowly. Spracklin was acquitted of manslaughter, but the Ontario government took away his badge. Two years later, Spracklin moved to the United States.

There, bootleggers were becoming organized criminals. Scarface Al Capone, hardly the decade's only crime boss, was certainly the most ruthless. "I call myself a businessman," the Chicago gangster explained, then added ruefully that many did not. "When I sell liquor it's bootlegging. When my patrons serve it on silver trays on Lake Shore Drive, it's hospitality." With his private army of 700 gunslingers, Capone seized control of all the Windy City's 10,000 speakeasies, and edged into gambling, prostitution, and racketeering operations throughout the Midwest. Scores of policemen and politicians were on his payroll. Conservative estimates place his gross take at $100 million a year. The drys looked upon him as evil incarnate, but to Chicago's many tipplers he was a savior.

Capone's climb to the top left a trail of bullet-riddled corpses. As rival gangs battled for a piece of the action, Cook County suffered nearly 400 mob slayings a year. The vio-

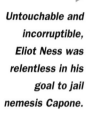

Public Enemy Number One, crime boss Al Capone, kept the good times flowing — at the point of a gun.

Untouchable and incorruptible, Eliot Ness was relentless in his goal to jail nemesis Capone.

lence culminated on February 14, 1929 — St. Valentine's Day — when Capone ordered the death of North Side boss Bugs Moran. Seven North Side gang members were waiting at a garage for a shipment of hijacked liquor. Pretending to be policemen, Capone's men disarmed their victims, lined them up against a wall, and cut them down with machine-gun fire. Moran escaped, but his crime career was over.

As the body count rose, Capone's popularity sank. A vigorous public relations campaign by the Chicago Crime Commission, and the invention of the Public Enemies List, helped speed his downfall. In October 1931 he was arrested for income tax evasion and sentenced to 11 years in prison.

Nobody was more pleased than Eliot Ness, of the U.S. Justice Department's Prohibition Bureau, who had battled for years to put Capone away. The crime czar himself was unrepentant. "All I ever did was supply a demand," he reminisced.

Elegantly dressed patrons sip bootleg drinks at a speakeasy, as seen by painter Ben Shahn's unsentimental eye.

THE SEARCH FOR NORMALCY

When the war ended, Canadians and Americans yearned for a return to normalcy — the times before the war.

But in both nations the society and its needs had changed, and normalcy proved elusive.

The American mood in 1920 was not good. Like Canadians, Americans began the decade suffering unemployment and high prices. But unlike Canadians, who voted in Mackenzie King on the basis of his promised social programs, the Americans readily voted for a leader who promised nothing much.

Warren G. Harding was an ex-newspaperman and politician whose amiable nature compensated for the lack of anything that might be called wisdom. Once Harding won the Republican nomination, it was an easy step to win the presidency in 1920, so soured were Americans by President Wilson's visions of world leadership. Harding didn't even promise a new age. "Our supreme task," he told them, "is the resumption of our onward normal way."

Despite Harding's quiet virtue and honesty, some of the old political friends who came with him to Washington were unprincipled characters. At the notorious Little Green

When the Harding oil scandals came to light, cartoonists had a field day at the Grand Old Party's expense.

TEAPOT DOME NAVAL OIL RESERVES

House on H Street, the president met Attorney General Harry Daugherty and other cronies of his "poker cabinet" for late-night sessions of cards, bootleg liquor, and off-color stories. Fortunately, Harding had also named to his Cabinet a few supremely competent men. With Herbert Hoover as commerce secretary and Andrew Mellon as treasury secretary, the Harding administration paved the way for the economic expansion of the later 1920's.

But Harding and the presidency were soon in trouble. "I never find myself done," he complained. "I don't believe there is a human being who can do all the work there is to be done in the president's office." To compound his troubles, Mrs. Harding became gravely ill with a kidney

After Harding died, his name was linked to several women other than Florence Harding (bottom). One was Carrie Phillips (top), wife of a Marion store owner. Another, unwed mother Nan Britton (middle), claimed her daughter's daddy was the president himself.

Campaigning from his front porch in Ohio, Harding (front row, left) plays host to Broadway star Blanche Ring and singer Al Jolson; Mrs. Harding holds a scroll. An ornate medal (right) served as a memento of Harding's nomination.

COMMITTEE ON NOTIFICATION

REPUBLICAN NATIONAL CONVENTION NOTIFICATION OF THE HONORABLE WARREN G. HARDING MARION OHIO JULY 4, 1920

Women Get the Vote

Women had neither the intellectual nor the emotional capacity to make political decisions. So said men who wanted to keep the vote to themselves. But there were women who thought otherwise.

In 1876, Dr. Emily Howard Stowe, Canada's first woman doctor, formed the Toronto Women's Literary Club with a circle of friends — but it was the vote they discussed, not literature. On the prairies, persuasive voices like that of Nellie McClung rallied women and not a few men to the cause. Across Canada the Woman's Christian Temperance Union mounted a polite but persistent campaign for woman's suffrage. In 1916 and 1917 they won victories as all provinces from Ontario west to British Columbia gave the vote to women.

In 1917, Ottawa gave the federal vote to women who were relatives of servicemen, but for one election only. It was a political trick to win that election for the government. But it broke the ice, and in 1919 the federal government recognized that all women had the right to vote in all federal elections. The remaining provinces soon fell into line — with the exception of Quebec. There, women led by the courageous and determined Thérèse Casgrain finally gained the provincial franchise in 1940.

---

infection. The handsome Harding, who had long suffered digestive and heart ailments, began to look wan and exhausted. In mid-January 1923 he caught a severe case of the flu, which sent him into visible decline.

Skulduggery Too Vast to Ignore

Ill health was only the beginning of Harding's troubles, however. Rumors of financial double-dealing on the part of his Ohio cronies had begun to circulate. The easygoing Harding at first paid no attention; he was a man for whom trust in others came all too naturally. But the evil was real, and it would soon explode in an avalanche of corruption. The first hints emerged early in 1923 from the unlikely quarter of the Veterans Bureau. It seems that bureau director Charles R. Forbes, a member of the so-called Ohio Gang, was peddling government medical supplies on the open market. There was also a matter of kickbacks on hospital construction contracts.

President Harding (seated at centre) relaxes with (seated from left) Henry Ford, Thomas Edison, Harvey Firestone, and Protestant churchman William Anderson. Said Edison of Harding: "Any man who chews tobacco is all right."

Harding, deeply shaken, angrily confronted Forbes, grabbing him by the throat, said a witness, "as a dog would a rat." Forbes left Washington on a timely trip to Europe, where he mailed in his resignation. The spotlight turned next to the Veterans Bureau legal counsel, Charles F. Cramer, who chose a grimmer method of escape. Fearing a formal Senate investigation, Cramer shot himself.

Rumors of crimes and corruption reverberated around the Harding administration. One target of suspicion was Jesse Smith, an unofficial aide to Daugherty, who allegedly could fix any problem for a price. Smith, too, shot himself. "What's a fellow to do," Harding was overheard saying, "when his own friends double-cross him?"

Worse was yet to come. In 1922 two oil executives had secretly won exclusive drilling rights at naval oil reserve sites at Elk Hills, California, and Teapot Dome, Wyoming. These oil interests had been major backers of Harding's campaign. Furthermore, the rights had been awarded not through competitive bidding but in exchange for a pay-off to Interior Secretary Albert B. Fall. Teapot Dome, like Watergate 50 years later, became synonymous with corruption, cover-up, and scandal at the highest levels of government. The beleaguered president sought the counsel of Herbert Hoover. "Mr. Secretary, there's a bad scandal brewing," he lamented. "What do you think I ought to do?" The upright Hoover advised his boss to come clean; but Harding could not implicate his friends. His distress deepened. In the summer of 1923, while vacationing in Alaska, the president fell ill. Returning to California, he checked into San Francisco's Palace Hotel on July 29. Four days later, with his wife at his bedside reading aloud from *The Saturday Evening Post*, Harding suffered a cerebral hemorrhage and died.

Change in Canada

In the summer of 1919, some Canadians thought the Russian Revolution had come as 30,000 Winnipeg workers walked off their jobs in a city-wide strike. Antistrikers hung a huge banner in downtown Winnipeg that read "Down with Bolshevism." In fact, the Winnipeg General Strike had nothing to do with Bolshevism. The war had made a handful of profiteers rich at the expense of everyone else. Seething resentments were made worse by unemployment or dreadful working conditions. Then there were the veterans, many unemployed and all bitter at their treatment by a Canada that seemed already to be forgetting them.

On June 21, the strikers gathered for a peaceful demonstration. When they ignored an order to disperse, constables of the North-West Mounted Police rode into the crowd, killing one person and injuring 30. That day — "Bloody Saturday" — ended the strike. But notice had been served that there could be no return to the Canada of 1914. Two months later, with the meaning of the strike on their minds, federal Liberals met to choose a new leader.

Their choice fell on William Lyon Mackenzie King, whose background, significantly, had been in settling strikes

Antistrikers on the steps of Winnipeg's City Hall make plain their views of the city-wide strike in June 1919.

A celebrated hunter of Reds, U.S. Attorney General A. Mitchell Palmer (right, with young admirer) aspired to the White House but never made it. Neither did Socialist Eugene V. Debs (below), who launched his 1920 presidential campaign from a jail cell.

FOR PRESIDENT · CONVICT NO. 9653

Radicals Left and Right

Profound social stresses affected the U.S. in the first two decades of the 20th century. Unrestricted immigration up to World War I had opened the gates to a surge of foreigners — many of them from southern and eastern Europe, poor, illiterate, and often Catholic or Jewish. Clinging to their native languages and old ways, they were often targets of scorn and prejudice. Moreover, many immigrants were drawn to labor unions, which in turn were mainly blamed for an epidemic of strikes — some 3,000 in 1919. Americans often found it difficult to distinguish between union activity for better working conditions and conspiracies by foreign-born anarchists, Communists, and Socialists.

Radical leftists were in fact on the rise. Some joined the American Communist Party, formed in 1919 after the Bolshevik revolution in Russia. The Bolsheviks advocated the overthrow of existing governments and promised more revolutions. Was any nation now safe?

One evening in June 1919 U.S. Attorney General A. Mitchell Palmer was preparing for bed when a powerful blast rocked his house. On Palmer's front porch lay the corpse of the man who had delivered the bomb, and alongside him was an anarchist pamphlet. Palmer, to that point restrained in his dealings with radicals, now took drastic action.

On November 7, 1919 — the second anniversary of the Russian Revolution — federal agents, under orders from Palmer, set upon alleged radical centres in 18 U.S. cities and arrested hundreds of immigrants for

Anonymous in all but their regalia and beliefs, the Ku Klux Klan meets in Kingston, Ontario. Organized in the 1920's, it attacked Jews, Roman Catholics, and immigrants.

deportation. Palmer's men cast a wider net the next year, rounding up some 10,000 leftists. Americans who found Palmer's methods excessive were told that the Red conspiracy must be stopped at any cost.

An array of reactionary groups took up the cry, denouncing and persecuting persons whom they deemed un-American. No group was more savage than the Ku Klux Klan. This white supremacist organization, born after the Civil War, had died out in the early 1870's only to be resurrected in 1915. By mid-1920's it claimed 2 million members in the United States and more than 40,000 in Canada, mostly in Saskatchewan. The Canadian wing appealed mainly to anti-Jewish and anti-Catholic sentiment. However, KKK lynchings and floggings in the United States discredited the movement in

Marcus Garvey dressed as "provisional president" of the African nation he yearned to create.

the eyes of Canadians, and in Canada it declined rapidly.

At the same time, many blacks in Canada and the United States rallied behind the charismatic Marcus Garvey, who argued that they could find justice only in their original homeland. His "Back to Africa" message attracted some 2 million followers, few of whom actually made the journey to Africa. After Garvey was jailed for mail fraud in 1925, his movement fell apart.

By the end of the decade, the appeal of radical voices, whether from the left or the right, had declined, partly because of the prolonged boom in industry. Troubling currents of bigotry and labor-management antagonism remained, but the American mainstream would prove deep and wide enough to assimilate all but the most alienated.

through negotiation. Of equal significance, the platform the Liberals drafted for the coming, postwar election seemed to recognize that Canada had changed since 1914. For the first time, a federal Liberal platform promoted social legislation for an industrialized, urbanized Canada.

King's Liberals won the election of 1921. This was no surprise as the Conservatives were still suffering from wartime unpopularity across Canada and from having imposed conscription in Quebec. But what was astonishing was that the Conservatives came third, behind a new party, the Progressives, formed out of farmer and labor discontent in Ontario and the West. Whatever normalcy might mean, in Canada it would never again mean a two-party system.

Urban poverty and unemployment cried out for the social programs the Liberals had outlined. Then there was the constitution. Designed to create a strong central government for the age of railway building, by 1921 it was outdated. Now, nation building rested on roads and hydro power, but responsibility for these fell under the provincial governments. With so much to be done, what would the new government do? The answer was — almost nothing. Taxes for social programs would alienate the business leaders who contributed to Liberal campaign funds. Besides, Quebec's Roman Catholic church was adamant that social aid was a church responsibility in which government had no business. And the Liberals depended on the Quebec vote.

Constitutional reform would have been even riskier. Quebec would lead the way in opposing any shift of power back to Ottawa. There, priest-historian Lionel Groulx was beginning to have an influence with his romanticized histories of the Quebecois as a people who needed a strong provincial government to keep out alien threats. As well, Quebec would certainly be joined by Ontario and British Columbia in rejecting any change that might mean sharing their wealth with the poorer provinces.

Unwilling to risk action at home, the government turned to the one area most Canadians agreed on. They wanted nothing more to do with close imperial ties that might take them into another world war. So the Liberals began loosening their ties with Britain, a policy that would lead to Canadian independence. It was a policy that ignored Canada's major problems. But it offended few and it cost nothing. In effect, it was remarkably like American isolationism.

THE ODD COUPLE

Though he said little and appeared to do even less, Calvin Coolidge was loved by most Americans. Across the border, more Canadians voted for Mackenzie King than for any other leader in Canada's history, but few ever loved him.

Sober and taciturn, Coolidge stayed calm in any crisis, a quality that inspired the "Keep Cool" slogan used on stickers (bottom of this column) during his 1924 campaign. Big business was positively exuberant about his hands-off economic policies, as a 1920's cartoon (below) illustrates.

At a time when Puritanism . . . is at its lowest ebb," wrote columnist Walter Lippmann, "the people are delighted with a Puritan." The sobersided individual in question was Calvin Coolidge, the nation's 30th president, known to almost everyone as Silent Cal. Dour, taciturn, with pale blue eyes and a tight-lipped smile, he appeared, said one wit, to have been "weaned on a pickle." Yet Coolidge possessed a flinty integrity that seemed just right.

What pushed Governor Coolidge into national prominence was his forceful handling of the 1919 Boston police strike. When the city's patrolmen walked off the job with demands for higher pay and the right to join a union, Coolidge called in the National Guard. "There is no right to strike against the public safety by anybody, anywhere, any time," he declared. The next year, as delegates to the Repub-

lican National Convention cast about for a vice presidential nominee, their glance fell upon Coolidge.

The news of President Harding's sudden death in 1923 found Coolidge vacationing at his father's farm in Vermont. It was shortly after midnight. Coolidge senior, a notary public, swore in the new president by the light of a kerosene lamp. Then both men went back to sleep.

As he took office, the scandals of the Harding administration were just bursting into full public view. Moving with deliberate speed, he fired Attorney General Harry Daugherty and ordered a special investigation that sent Harding's secretary of the interior, Albert Fall, to jail for taking bribes. Coolidge then cut taxes, trimmed costs, and managed to lop $3 billion off the national debt. After this feverish spring-cleaning, he took pains to avoid any unnecessary action. "Many times, if you let a situation alone," he liked to say, "it takes care of it-

▲ Harking back to his boyhood on a Vermont farm, Coolidge strikes a rustic pose.

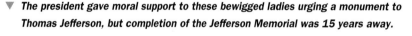

▼ The president gave moral support to these bewigged ladies urging a monument to Thomas Jefferson, but completion of the Jefferson Memorial was 15 years away.

With what looks like bemused dignity, Silent Cal plays cowboy at a 1927 Fourth of July gala in South Dakota.

▶

A bachelor for all his life, Mackenzie King sought company rarely. Perhaps his closest companion was his dog Pat (right), who slept next to King's brass bed, and who accompanied King as he wandered the grounds of his Gatineau estate, Kingsmere. King's mother remained a strong influence on his life even after her death. He prayed every day before her lamplit portrait, and even tried to communicate with her through mediums.

self." In dealing with Congress, he would study new legislation and then find reasons for dismissing it. In all, he vetoed 50 bills. His do-nothing approach did not amuse everyone. But with the nation prospering and at peace, most people agreed with Supreme Court Justice Oliver Wendell Holmes, Jr.: "While I don't expect anything astonishing from [Coolidge], I don't want anything astonishing." Coolidge did not run for president in 1928, and died five years later.

In contrast, Canada did expect astonishing things from its prime minister, Mackenzie King, but nothing like what was revealed after his death. To all appearances he was an extraordinarily religious man. When he sang hymns in church, tears rolled down his cheeks. He said morning prayers every day, kneeling before a picture of his mother. He had been a prominent campaigner for many church-related causes, including Prohibition. But there was more to King, much more, than appearances revealed. A desperately lonely man, he spent every evening writing thousands of self-pitying, self-justifying words in his diary. They frequently lamented

▼ *The Rt. Hon. W. L. Mackenzie King campaining at Cobourg, Ontario, for the Federal Election of September 26, 1926.*

WELCOME TO
RT. HON. W.L.
McKENZIE KING

yet another excursion to Ottawa's brothels. He also, in a personal amendment to Ontario's Prohibition laws, kept a private stock of liquor.

The grandson of William Lyon Mackenzie, who had led a rebellion against the government of Upper Canada in 1837, he wrote of himself as a rebel too, fighting for the poor against the rich and privileged. He also wrote of the need for social legislation, but he was remarkably slow in delivering it. In all the years he was prime minister in the 1920's the pressure for social change came not from him, but from the Progressives. It was they who forced King, in 1926, to adopt Canada's first Old Age Pension legislation.

Yet King, who would be Canada's prime minister longer than any leader before or since, had a remarkable instinct for political success. As an observer noted, he talked in the currency of big denominations but dealt in small change. Nevertheless, King's strategy worked, as Canadians voted for his Liberal party in election after election.

FROM ACES TO AIR TRAVEL

Suddenly pilots were no longer war heroes but merely stuntmen. But by the decade's end, the airplane had spawned national mail services and a plethora of fledgling airlines.

One of the crazier barnstorming stunts was aerial tennis, which required hidden cables to tie the players to the wing. No feat was thought too daring or too silly if it drew a crowd of paying customers.

AIR MAIL
is Socially Correct
the First Ounce *10* for each additional Ounce

6

The Canadian Post Office first allowed air delivery in 1927, to areas cut off from land transport in winter. Ten years later (above) airmail was being promoted as affordably stylish.

After the glory and excitement of World War I, pilots who had honed their skills dogfighting German air aces faced a bumpy landing. In America, most of them returned to workaday jobs that offered no glamor. Eddie Rickenbacker, America's most famous ace, became a car salesman. But a few diehards tried to parlay their experience into civilian flying careers.

Some became barnstormers, flying from town to town and executing breathtaking routines of aerial acrobatics for admiring crowds. And some were wing walkers who actually swaggered across the aircraft in flight, hung by their fingers from fuselages, and climbed from one plane to another on rope ladders. Inevitably, some crashed. Yet despite the dangers and the terrible pay — World War I ace Dick Depew

said the greatest danger was "the risk of starving to death" — the barnstormers wanted only to fly. After each performance spectators would pay $5 to $15 for a three-minute "joy hop." Some 10 million people took rides.

The U.S. Post Office transformed airplane flight from a carnival curiosity into a serious endeavor in 1918, when it began airmail service. Flying the mail was not for the fainthearted. Hours in cramped, noisy cockpits tortured mind and body, and bad weather added to the discomfort with bone-chilling wet and cold. With no radios and few navigational instruments, pilots relied heavily on landmarks. "If a farmer painted his barn a different color, we'd be lost," one recalled. Another judged his speed by listening to the air stream past his open cockpit: "If it's whistling pretty loud and shrill, you're going too fast. If it's barely whispering, then you're near a stall." Little wonder that 31 of the first 40 mail pilots on the New York–Chicago run died in crashes. But with salaries ranging from $800 to $1,000 a month, others stepped eagerly forward to take the risk.

When war ended in 1918, Canada found itself with new resources in the form of 20,000 pilots and hundreds of surplus aircraft. Some returning fighter pilots became bush pilots, flying people and goods to remote settlements and camps. Some worked for companies such as Price Brothers, a Quebec lumber company which, in 1920, began using aircraft to survey its holdings and to spot forest fires.

In 1919 the Canadian government set up an Air Board to regulate flying and, over the next few years, established the Royal Canadian Air Force. Aided by private companies, the air force carried out forest and soil surveys, pioneered airline routes, and experimented with crop spraying. It monitored forest fires, and even fought them, often flying through dense smoke and landing on the shores of northern lakes to join firefighters.

In 1920, the air force began a massive task it still performs, mapping Canada from the air, using cameras developed to photograph German trenches. Within a few years, its work proved invaluable in designing Canada's highways. In 1927, it took on the fearsome task of mapping ice conditions in Hudson Bay so that Churchill, Manitoba, could be developed as an ocean port.

In that same year, Charles A. Lindbergh, Jr., a mail pilot, flew *The Spirit of St. Louis* from New York to Paris. His triumph sparked an upsurge of enthusiasm for air travel. Within a year the number of air passengers quadrupled. Companies like Boeing and National Air Transport, both airmail carriers, began flying regular passenger routes. By the

▼ *In the late 1920's, much of Canada's airmail was carried along the north shore of the St. Lawrence, from Quebec City to Sept-Îles and Anticosti Island, using Fairchild monoplanes fitted with skis (in winter).*

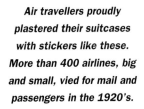

Air travellers proudly plastered their suitcases with stickers like these. More than 400 airlines, big and small, vied for mail and passengers in the 1920's.

Lindbergh poses with The Spirit of St. Louis before taking off on his solo transatlantic flight. His success inspired millions, including songwriters (right).

end of the decade there were 44 scheduled U.S. airlines and many nonscheduled ones. Transcontinental Air Transport joined with Pennsylvania Railroad to provide a cross-country service from Los Angeles to New York. Passengers flew during daylight, then transferred to sleeper cars at night. The trip took 48 hours.

As more people flew, plane travel became increasingly safe and comfortable. Adventurous travellers in the early 1920's would hop mail flights and ride among the letter sacks. Then came wicker chairs in heated cabins, where the passengers munched sandwiches handed out by flight attendants. As often as not the plane they boarded was a Ford Tri-Motor, which made its debut in 1925 as the nation's first metal-skinned commercial aircraft. The Ford aircraft was dubbed the Tin Goose. Ford Tri-Motors remained in service in some parts of the world for the next 30 years.

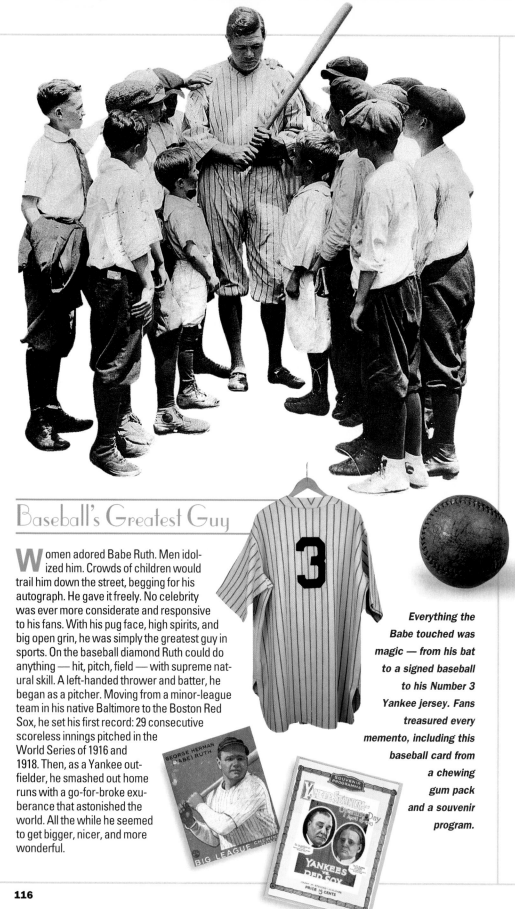

GIANTS OF SPORT

It was a golden age of sport with batters like Babe Ruth and boxers like Jack Dempsey. Hockey was made hugely popular by stars such as Howie Morenz, who brought the major league to the U.S.

When George Herman Ruth (known as Babe or the Bambino) arrived in New York in 1920 to play for the Yankees, baseball was in trouble. The year before, eight players of the Chicago White Sox were accused of taking bribes. "Say it ain't so, Joe," a young fan pleaded with one of them, Shoeless Joe Jackson. But a remorseful Jackson had to nod yes, it was true. The game of baseball, and professional sports in general, seemed permanently tainted.

Then came Ruth. He stepped up to the plate, a big paunchy man with a remarkably dainty grace, and whacked balls out of the park with amazing consistency. He hit 54 home runs his first season as a Yankee. The next year he hit 59. He became the Sultan of Swat, and he restored the lustre to America's national game.

What the Babe did for baseball, another extraordinary athlete did for the ancient sport of boxing. Jack Dempsey, the Manassa Mauler, crashed into the national consciousness on July 4, 1919, when he demolished champion Jess Willard in just three rounds. There seemed to be no stopping him. In 1921 he knocked out Frenchman Georges Carpentier before more than 80,000 fans, drawing boxing's first million-dollar gate. He demonstrated his fierce courage in 1923, when he kayoed Luis

Ethel Catherwood scissors over the high jump at the Amsterdam Olympics in 1928 and wins a gold for Canada.

Baseball's Greatest Guy

Women adored Babe Ruth. Men idolized him. Crowds of children would trail him down the street, begging for his autograph. He gave it freely. No celebrity was ever more considerate and responsive to his fans. With his pug face, high spirits, and big open grin, he was simply the greatest guy in sports. On the baseball diamond Ruth could do anything — hit, pitch, field — with supreme natural skill. A left-handed thrower and batter, he began as a pitcher. Moving from a minor-league team in his native Baltimore to the Boston Red Sox, he set his first record: 29 consecutive scoreless innings pitched in the World Series of 1916 and 1918. Then, as a Yankee outfielder, he smashed out home runs with a go-for-broke exuberance that astonished the world. All the while he seemed to get bigger, nicer, and more wonderful.

Everything the Babe touched was magic — from his bat to a signed baseball to his Number 3 Yankee jersey. Fans treasured every memento, including this baseball card from a chewing gum pack and a souvenir program.

Howie Morenz, star of the Montreal Canadiens, poses for the inaugural issue of Hockey Magazine, in 1927, at the peak of his career. He was to score a total of 270 goals in his lifetime.

Tennis aces for the ages, Helen Wills (far left) and Bill Tilden were the first Americans to win at Britain's Wimbledon. Tilden took six U.S. titles, while Wills won every match she played between 1927 and 1932.

Firpo, of Argentina, in the second round, after Firpo had knocked him out of the ring in the first round. He made his exit in 1927 after he lost the fight to Gene Tunney, light-heavyweight champ of the World War I AEF.

In football the nation lavished its applause on Notre Dame coach Knute Rockne, who almost always found a way to win. After Notre Dame beat Army in football in 1924, the sportswriter Grantland Rice conferred immortality on four of its student athletes when he wrote of them as " the Four Horsemen . . . Famine, Pestilence, Destruction, and Death."

In Canada, hockey grew in popularity as lacrosse declined, a casualty of its own violence. Stars like Howie Morenz of the Montreal Canadiens spread the major league game to America. Boston Bruins joined the National Hock-

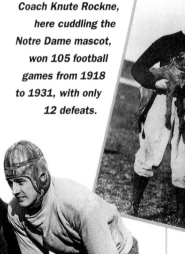

Coach Knute Rockne, here cuddling the Notre Dame mascot, won 105 football games from 1918 to 1931, with only 12 defeats.

ey League in 1924 and, within two more years, 6 of the 10 teams in the league were American.

Canadian football was taking on characteristics that would mark it for the rest of the century. In 1921, Edmonton Eskimos were the first western team to challenge for the Grey Cup. They lost, but the cup has been a symbol of east-west rivalry ever since. Four years later, Frank Shaugnessy of McGill, the first professional coach in Canadian football, introduced the huddle. The 1920's also saw the beginning of imported American players, especially by western teams to whom the game was still new.

At the same time, women were making up for their exclusion from sport. The Edmonton Grads, a women's basketball team, dominated world play from 1915 to 1940, winning four world championships and setting a record mark of 502 wins in 522 games.

In the 1928 Amsterdam Olympics, Ethel Catherwood of Saskatchewan romped to a gold in the high jump. Nicknamed the Saskatoon Lily for her beauty, she was offered a Hollywood contract. But she was unimpressed. Of the Hollywood contract, she said, "I'd sooner gulp poison." And as for her Olympic victory, "It was no big thing. I went, I did it, and quite frankly I'm sick and tired of the whole thing."

Notre Dame's Four Horsemen, lauded by Grantland Rice, made up in speed what they lacked in weight.

Columnist Damon Runyon
earned acclaim for his colorful
stories of low-life guys and dolls.

JOURNALISM, WICKED AND WISE

Never had there been such a varied or attention-grabbing diet of reading matter. Tabloid newspapers dished up titillating sagas of sex and crime. At the same time, some lively new magazines offered more uplifting fare.

On The New Yorker's first cover, a dandified Eustace Tilley squints through his monocle at the world.

Drawing by Rea Irvin; © 1925, 1953, The New Yorker Magazine, Inc.

The first tabloid to hit the United States was the illustrated *Daily News*. The premier issue appeared on June 26, 1919, in a format designed for easy reading on crowded New York subways. Since then, the sensational headlines of the tabloid press have screamed for our attention: "Brooklyn Vice Barons Lure Innocent Girls to Sin Dens!" "Boys Foil Death Chair!" "Mate Gives Cheating Wife to White Slave Torturers!" By 1924 the *News* had the largest circulation of all the dailies in the United States, and its competitors were not far behind.

The strongest challenge came from William Randolph Hearst, titan of American journalism, who in 1924 brought out the look-alike *Daily Mirror*. Hearst promised his readers "90 percent entertainment and 10 percent information — and the information without boring you." Close behind came physical culture guru Bernarr MacFadden and his sensation-packed *Daily Graphic*.

Sex and violence were the essentials, with a large dose of celebrity scandal — as the tabloid imitations created on these two pages suggest. The disappearance of Hollywood evangelist Aimee Semple McPherson (who was born and grew up in Ingersoll, Ontario) was splashed across front pages in May 1926. A month later, when McPherson stumbled out of the California desert claiming to have been kidnapped, the tabloids covered her ordeal in heartrending detail. Then came the kicker: evidence that McPherson may have made up the whole story to disguise a lovers' tryst.

A good murder did wonders to boost circulation, and when fresh bodies were lacking, the editors simply dug up old ones. In 1926 the *Daily Mirror* revived the four-year-old Hall-Mills case, in which the corpses of Episcopal minister Edward W. Hall and a comely parishioner, Mrs. Eleanor Mills, had been discovered together on an abandoned New Jersey farm. The killer had never been found, so the *Mirror*

Where was Aimee?

Was She Abducted? Or Did She Just Pretend?

HELD AGAINST MY WILL!

HOLLYWOOD – "Sister Aimee" Semple McPherson, the famous revivalist preacher whose thousands of devoted followers have anxiously _____ each new revelation in the ____ ____ disappear____

Family Herald and Weekly Star.

Specially for Women

MONTREAL, CANADA, WEDNESDAY, MAY 7, 1924.

NO GENERAL RULE FOR SUCCESSFUL MARRIAGE

"Marriage Is a Problem That Is Never Completely Solved and Settled, Once and For All, Until Both Parties Are Dead and Buried,

(By Dorothy Canfield.)

proposed a conspiracy by Hall's socialite wife. The accused were acquitted, but the story made juicy reading for weeks.

But not all was sensationalism. Rural Canada was still important enough to sustain Montreal's *Family Herald and Weekly Star*. Church publications remained popular, and the women's market surfaced spectacularly when *Chatelaine* gained almost 60,000 subscribers in 1928, its first year. Also popular, for francophone women, was *La revue moderne*, which in 1960 would merge with a French version of *Chatelaine*.

Saturday Night was still the magazine of intellectual readers, but more challenging ideas were coming from a western journal, *Grain Growers' Guide*. Championing western farmers, it argued for cooperative marketing, educational change and social programs, both for rural families and for industrial Canada. With writers like Nellie McClung and Violet McNaughton, it also offered effective leadership in improving the status of women.

The 1920's signalled that more was to come. DeWitt Wallace, a young war veteran, borrowed $5,000 and started *The Reader's Digest* in a basement in New York City's Greenwich Village. Within a decade its circulation reached half a million. Two other newcomers, Britton Haddon and Henry Luce, rewrote the week's news in crisp prose, added photographs, and distributed the results nationwide in *Time* magazine.

Highbrow readers subscribed to such journals as *The American Mercury*, whose editor H. L. Mencken wrote witty diatribes against the booboisie of small-town America. There was also *The New Yorker*, an adroit concoction of fiction, humor, and thoughtful observation that was definitely not "for the old lady in Dubuque." But its readers loved it, and *The New Yorker* is still the model of urban literary sophistication.

A Study of Isabel MacDonald — and — So Women are Persons, by Jean Graham

A man for all genres, Ring Lardner wrote sports, humor, fiction, and a column on the American scene, all of which made him one of the decade's most widely read journalists.

The acerbic H. L. Mencken, cofounder of The American Mercury, lashed out at almost everybody.

THE READER'S DIGEST

THIRTY-ONE ARTICLES EACH MONTH
FROM LEADING MAGAZINES — EACH
ARTICLE OF ENDURING VALUE AND
INTEREST IN CONDENSED AND
COMPACT FORM

FEBRUARY 1922

The first issue of The Reader's Digest condensed stories from McClure's Magazine, House Beautiful, and Scientific American.

TENNESSEE MONKEY TRIAL:
Was It Adam or the Apes?

Attorneys Clarence Darrow (left) and William Jennings Bryan (right) heatedly debate the right of Tennessee schoolteacher John T. Scopes (inset) to teach evolution.

VERDICT IN SCOPES TRIAL AWAITED
FUTURE OF SCIENCE, EDUCATION, HANGS IN BALANCE

DAYTON, TENN. – Renowned attorneys Clarence Darrow and William Jennings Bryan today made their closing arguments in the trial here of John T. Scopes, the local schoolteacher charged with propounding the Darwinian theory of evolution in his science classes, in defiance of a court order.

The verdict, hoped for tomorrow, is expected to have far-reaching implications for American public school education. It will determine the extent to which local religious groups can dictate school policy.

The theory, developed by naturalist Charles Darwin some 50 years ago, holds that all life on earth, including mankind, has "evolved" over the eons from simpler creatures—implying that man's closest ancestors were apes. This notion is offensive to many fundamentalist Christians, as it contradicts the account of

Plain Lives, Simple Pleasures

The 1920's were the last time that cars, electric appliances, paid vacations, retail chains, and candy bars could be called newfangled. Some things stayed the way they had always been.

Beyond the glitter of the rich and famous, in the small towns and rural areas, life in the 1920's was in many ways closer to the 19th century than it was to the Jazz Age. Church membership grew right along with the population, and churches remained the best places for newcomers to get acquainted. Doctors made house calls, venturing out at all hours and in every weather to treat a fever or deliver a baby. Many children walked several kilometres to school; the standardized yellow school bus was nearly a decade away. And while more and more people were buying automobiles, the railroad was still the most dependable way to travel to the city. On the farms horses gave way very slowly to tractors.

Band concerts, family picnics, and sing-alongs around the parlor spinet were still the main entertainments. After church, many Americans would reach for the comics section of the Sunday paper — a pleasure denied to Canadians by the Lord's Day Act of 1907 which forbade Sunday papers as well as most commercial entertainments on Sunday. But both Canadians and Americans could enjoy a belt-stretching Sunday dinner, perhaps a roast with all the trimmings.

But even as the old ways persisted, both countries were undergoing profound and lasting changes. In the 1920's, for the first time, more than half of their citizens lived in urban areas. Suburbs, now made possible by automobiles rather than trains, rolled out beyond city limits. One of the most spectacular examples was in California, already becoming the automobile capital of North America, where Beverly Hills grew to 25 times its former size.

At the same time, most people found they had more money to spend and more time to spend it. By 1920, the average male wage earner in Canada could expect close to $1,200 a year, a rise of almost 50% since 1911. Professionals like doctors and lawyers were making more than $5,000. Women, however, though they had almost doubled their wages since 1911, still averaged only about half of male earnings. Farm incomes, too, remained low, and it never paid to be a farm laborer. But the majority of people could feel life was looking up.

While wages grew, the time spent earning them began to shrink. The norm of the 6-day work week contracted to 5½ days as more and more businesses granted a Saturday half-holiday. In 1923 the Gary, Indiana, steelworks changed from a 12-hour day to 8-hour shifts. Ford went on a 5-day week in 1926, and International Harvester presented its employees with what seemed like the ultimate in company largess: two weeks of paid vacation.

A quiet revolution was altering the home. Electrification came first in the cities, more slowly in the smaller towns, where the central

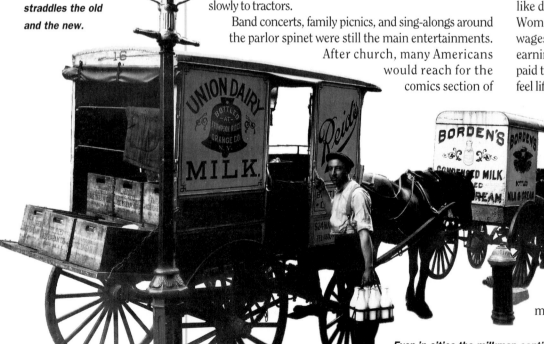

▲ **One hand milking, the other adjusting his radio receiver, this farmer comfortably straddles the old and the new.**

Even in cities the milkman continued to make deliveries by horse-drawn wagon. As long as their horses could do the job, many deliverymen stuck with animal power.

Little Orphan Annie (and Sandy) debuted in 1924 and won the hearts of comic-strip readers. Unlike most cartoons, her adventures followed a week-by-week story.

Ice cards in a window told the iceman how much ice to deliver, in cents or pounds, to refill the home icebox. Though sales of refrigerators soared, millions of households still did it the old-fashioned way.

Piggly Wiggly combined low prices with the trailblazing idea of self-service in its "grocerterias," forerunners of supermarkets. Sprouting across the southern United States, this chain grew from just over 500 stores in 1920 to 2,500 in 1929.

power plant might have shut down at night. Some rural areas had to wait another decade or two for public electricity. But as power lines began to stretch across the interior, and as the price of electricity went down, more and more families began reaping its conveniences. Edison's light bulbs replaced the smoky glow of kerosene lamps, radios blared, telephones jangled, refrigerators took the place of iceboxes. As a 1926 General Electric ad intoned: "Any woman who is doing any household task that a little electric motor can do is working for 3 cents an hour; human life is too precious to be sold at a price of 3 cents an hour."

The increasingly centralized populations, who were earning more money and spending fewer hours on the job, represented a new breed of consumers. For them, it was no longer necessary to make things at home. Almost everything, from cookies to suits, now came ready-made and conveniently packaged. National chain stores, selling prepackaged national brands, grew by leaps and bounds, spanning the continent. J. C. Penney added an average of 100 stores a year thoughout the 1920's, and The Great Atlantic & Pacific Tea Company averaged three new store openings every day during the decade.

It was a great time to launch national brands, and many of the newcomers became household names. For breakfast, Wheaties and Rice Krispies; for lunch, a can of Libby's tomato soup with a sandwich (using commercially baked, not homemade, bread) of Canada Packer's meat or Welch's grape jelly. For dessert, Hostess cakes and Eskimo Pies, and for snacking, Baby Ruth or Cadbury candy bars. Sanka to wash it down, and Brillo to help do the dishes.

Not everyone liked the changes, to be sure. "Radios and telephones make people farther apart," an invalided worker told the authors of *Middletown*, a 1929 study of a small Midwestern city. "Instead of going to see a person as folks used to, you just telephone nowadays."

But even in the large cities, some things stayed reassuringly the same. All through the 1920's milk still came in bottles. It would arrive on the doorstep before breakfast, brought by the local milkman, who would take away the empties left out the night before.

Mortimer in a silent cartoon, he became Mickey in the sound cartoon Steamboat Willie *(1928) and rose to be the most popular animated character.*

THE PHENOMENAL FLAPPER

Sassy, smart, and ready for anything, a new kind of rebel danced into view. In dress, manners, and morals, she kicked up her heels and led the way, much to her parents' everlasting dismay.

To some, she was a daring revolutionary. To H. L. Mencken, caustic critic of American manners and mores, she seemed "a somewhat foolish girl, full of wild surmises and inclined to revolt against the precepts and admonitions of her elders." What no one could deny was her breezy devil-may-care exuberance. The 1920's marked the appearance of the first youth culture, in which a generation of under-25-year-olds cut loose as never before and launched a whole new set of styles, attitudes, and ways of behaving. By far their most visible representative was the flapper.

Whatever she did — whether dancing the Charleston at a college fraternity party or joyriding in a roadster with one of her many beaux — she loved to be seen. To make sure she stood out, she dressed for shock

value. In her mother's time a woman's costume typically used some 17 metres of cloth and swathed the wearer from chin to toe. No longer. In 1920, in one exultant leap, hemlines rose from ankle to mid-calf. From then on, dresses got smaller, thinner, and lighter so fast they could almost be seen to shrink. Waistlines dropped; busts flattened. Sleeves became shorter or simply disappeared. Cotton stockings gave way to silk or rayon hose, rolled down at the top to allow a glimpse of bare kneecap. The idea was to look carefree and boyish — and ready to play.

Even as the public was reeling from the shock of the disappearing skirt, it was hit by another: bobbed hair. In what amounted to a rite of passage into flapperhood, girls

A high-stepping sheba shows plenty of thigh while her sheik dances attendance.

Helped by two perky young starlets, a dandy proudly shows off his extra-floppy oxford bags.

All dressed down for New Year's Eve, an exuberant flapper displays her high-voltage Charleston style.

▼ **The latest bathing suits of 1926 seem tame today, but back then, some women shrank at showing so much skin.**

Canada's artists of syncopation, and its lax liquor laws, drew revellers from near and far, even from across the border.

▼ Beads and bows give a coy distinction to this flapper's evening gown.

John Held, Jr.

No one captured the cheerful silliness of the flapper era more fully than cartoonist John Held, Jr. In drawings for *The New Yorker, College Humor,* and the covers of *Life* (top), he depicted a stylishly pert young creature with turned-up nose and turned-down hose who brazened her way through life's adventures with a wonderful combination of feckless innocence and worldly sophistication. Held himself had little taste for Jazz Age partying. Born in Utah, he arrived in New York at age 21 with $4 in his pocket. Soon he was earning $2,500 a week, a princely sum. He bought an estate in Connecticut staffed with its own golf pro.

began visiting men's barbershops to have their long tresses clipped into ultrashort cuts that barely grazed the ears. They rouged their cheeks and plucked their eyebrows. Still another change, if less visible, was just as significant. In a late-decade survey of 1,300 young women with jobs, fewer than 70 confessed that they still wore old-fashioned corsets. Release from constricting whalebone, hooks, laces, and attached garters went right along with other gestures of liberation and letting go.

In fact, flapper styles were a faithful barometer of social change, and as hemlines shortened and undergarments vanished, the country's flaming youth seemed bent on ever more outlandish behavior in the pursuit of pleasure. Much of the frivolity centred around college campuses. A flapper would arrive at a frat party and rush to the ladies' room to "park her girdle" (assuming her mother had insisted she wear one). Then, accompanied by a male escort in baggy pants

Swimwear models strike a daring classical pose as the Three Graces.

and with patent-leather hair, she would cut a rug on the dance floor, puff forbidden cigarettes, sip bootleg liquor (called by such names as hooch and giggle water), and gleefully offend propriety. The evening might continue with a fast ride in an open convertible and, perhaps, some more or less heavy petting. "None of the Victorian mothers . . ." wrote F. Scott Fitzgerald, the flapper's leading chronicler, "had any idea how casually their daughters were accustomed to be kissed."

Probably no Canadian city felt the impact of Jazz Age partying more than Montreal. In easy reach of New York and Boston, it was free of their ban on alcohol. What was more, it was governed by an indulgent city council which oversaw an even more indulgent police force. Montreal quickly developed a reputation as the night club capital of North America. Jazz musicians, gamblers and more questionable entrepreneurs flocked to the city. For almost 50 years, Montreal would be a mandatory stop for touring stars of stage and screen.

YES! NO SHORTAGE OF FADS

A giddy quest for the new and different spawned all kinds of odd diversions: mah-jong, crossword puzzles, flagpole sitting, dance marathons, a self-improvement craze, and much more.

Weary runners in the 1928 Bunion Derby, a 4,800-kilometre race from Los Angeles to New York, labor down the homestretch. Of 241 entrants only 55 finished.

One day in 1922 the bandleader Frank Silver was taking a stroll through the town of Lynbrook, New York. Feeling hungry, he stepped over to a sidewalk fruit vendor for something to eat. "Got any bananas?" he asked.

"Yes!" came the heavily accented response. "We have no bananas!"

A light bulb flashed in Silver's brain, and he began to think up some lyrics. His piano player, Irving Cohn, supplied a catchy tune. The song became a runaway smash hit. Perhaps that is not surprising, for a streak of nuttiness popped up in the 1920's, leading to a succession of wonderfully nonsensical fads and crazes.

They began with a retired French pharmacist named Émile Coué, who in 1921 came out with a seemingly sure-fire prescription for personal happiness. The key was to repeat a simple saying: "Day by day in every way I am getting better and better." The miraculous powers of autosuggestion, Coué declared, would then turn the saying into reality. "We are what we make ourselves and not what circumstances make us," he reasoned.

Drawn in by Coué's positive and encouraging message, some 40,000 clients a year flocked to his clinic in Nancy, France. By the time he visited North America in 1923, ballyhoo headlines were proclaiming his wonders: "Two Cripples Walk" and "Coué Makes Palsied Man Run." And folks everywhere were learning how to "Coué away" everything from a headache to a heartache.

Hard on Coué's heels came a heated love affair with anything exotic. Late in 1922 a British archeologist, Howard Carter, digging near Luxor, Egypt, stumbled upon the 3,000-year-old tomb of the pharaoh Tutankhamen. Inside was a dazzling trove of royal Egyptian treasure.

◀

Maestro of self-improvement Émile Coué (farthest right in photo) drills disciples in his method for making life better.

Suddenly a King Tut craze was sweeping the country. Clothes, jewellery, hairstyles, even furniture, took on a mysterious pharaonic glitter.

Another exotic fad swept in from China in the form of a game called mah-jong. With its carved bone tiles and their wonderfully inscrutable markings, mah-jong had caught the fancy of Joseph Babcock, an American oil executive in Soochow. Babcock simplified the rules, added roman numerals to the tiles, and in 1922 launched his version of the game on the market.

Propelled by a huge advertising campaign, Babcock's mah-jong took off. By 1923 more than 1,600,000 sets had been sold. Mah-jong clubs sprang up, where members entrusted their fortunes to the hazard of tiles marked "wind," "dragon," or the mythical "sparrow of a hundred intelligences." For authenticity, players decked themselves out in brocade robes and took refreshment from lacquered trays. As the frenzy grew, Chinese manufacturers ran out of calf shinbones, used to make the tiles, and had to order fresh supplies from Chicago slaughterhouses. Then, as suddenly as it had hit, the mah-jong mania evaporated. By mid-decade importers of the game were declaring bankruptcy, and cheap sets could be bought for a dime.

One fad that survived to become a permanent institution was the crossword puzzle. The *New York World* had pioneered the form in the previous decade, but it took two fledgling book publishers, Richard Simon and Max Schuster, to spread crosswords across the continent. Their very first venture, in 1924, was a collection of puzzles. To pro-

mote it they used an eye-catching gimmick: a No. 2 pencil attached to each volume. Everybody wanted this intriguing new book, and within a few months the public was crossword-puzzle crazy. One railway stocked its cars with dictionaries; ocean voyages became crossword orgies; a minister turned his sermon into a crossword puzzle; college teams duelled in crossword tournaments. One man became so absorbed in a puzzle that he was jailed for refusing to leave a restaurant. He welcomed his 10-day sentence because he could do puzzles in peace and quiet.

Toward the middle of the decade, the fads began to lose their giddy sparkle and took on a more earnest, muscular quality. An ex-sailor, boxer, and stuntman known as Shipwreck Kelly promoted himself by sitting on flagpoles for days on end. One year he spent 145 days on various masts and flagstaffs. Kelly had many imitators. In Baltimore 15-year-old Avon Foreman perched on a sapling in his backyard for 10 days. When Avon descended, the mayor of Baltimore wrote a tribute praising his "grit and stamina."

Endurance became everything. Most gruelling of all were the dance marathons, which became popular late in the decade. Couples shuffled through excruciating weeks in the hope of winning the often sizable prize money. Eventually exhaustion took over, and by then it was no longer fun.

◀

Perched high above a movie theatre in Union City, New Jersey, Shipwreck Kelly waves hello. His seat atop the flagpole is a small platform equipped with stirrups.

◀

Marathon dancers kept going until they dropped, like this brother-and-sister Chicago couple, who had danced 3,327 consecutive hours.

HOT, BLUE, AND AMERICAN

A typical living room in 1920 featured a piano stacked with sheet music and a windup phonograph with records of operatic and music-hall favorites. Something was missing. A whole new sound was about to burst onto the scene: jazz!

Chock-full of innuendo and nonsense words, such as boop-a-doop, up-tempo tunes provided fitting background music for those zany times when youth ran wild and made whoopee. The Sheik of Araby (top) may have sung of desert passion to his lady-love, yet even an ordinary swain could woo his girl with a song sheet and a little practice.

From the start jazz meant excitement, energy, pleasure. Jazz was alive — hot! It captured all that the wild young things of the 1920's wanted to be. No one knows the exact origin of the word, and its meanings were many, but above all it was a new musical style — marked by syncopation, improvisation, and blue notes — created by black people in the southern United States.

The primary birthplace of jazz was New Orleans, among the black Creole population, which had roots in both African and European musical traditions. After the Civil War, when the military bands stationed in New Orleans broke up, band instruments were often bought by the families of freedmen, who had long traditions of teaching music to their children. By 1900 there were scores of brass bands in New Orleans, playing for dances, parades, picnics, and funerals. They drew some of their tunes from popular white mainstream sources but developed them with the vivid harmonies and rhythms characteristic of African music. Flowing into this musical mix were other great streams of black music: ragtime and the blues. Some of the bands flourished in Storyville, the notorious red-light district of New Orleans. It was there, in the dozens of honky-tonks, that many of the early jazzmen, such as Kid Ory, Jelly Roll Morton, and Joe (King) Oliver, began to "play hot." This was musicians' slang for a sound replete with "bent" notes, growls, and plenty of vitality.

Louis Armstrong (left) created the Hot Five studio group (above) with his wife, Lil Hardin Armstrong, and with Johnny St. Cyr, Johnny Dodds, and Kid Ory. They rarely got radio play, still their restyled New Orleans sound reached appreciative ears.

The Incomparable Satchmo

The story of Louis (Satchmo) Armstrong began at the bottom of that hard and colorful world on July 4, 1900. He and his mother lived in the midst of a myriad of honky-tonks, including a music and dance emporium called Funky Butt Hall. "Before the dance," he remembered, "the band would play out front for about a half hour and us little kids would all do little dances. Then we'd look through the cracks in the wall of Funky Butt." When Louis was 12, he shot a pistol in the street celebrating New Year's Eve and was sent for more than a year to the Waifs' Home for Boys. It was in the home's brass band that he learned to play instruments, progressing from tambourine to lead cornet. Armstrong's musical gifts developed quickly, and after he was released, he was befriended by King Oliver, the top jazz cornet in New Orleans. The young Armstrong sold sacks of coal by day and played cornet in the honky-tonks at night while studying the horn with Oliver.

Paul Whiteman (top, right) led his orchestra to great heights of popularity by toning down the jarring elements of what a 1921 *Ladies' Home Journal* called "unspeakable jazz." Pianist Jelly Roll Morton and his band, the Red Hot Peppers (bottom, right), deliver up some spicy down-home jazz. Morton wrote his tunes in musical notation, making him the first jazz composer.

After the United States entered the world war in 1917, the U.S. Navy closed down Storyville. Many of the bands scattered. Oliver went north to Chicago and in 1920 formed the Creole Jazz Band. In 1922 he sent for Armstrong, who by that time was unsurpassed for his technique and his ability to improvise. Little of the music was written down. Lil Hardin, the band's classically trained pianist, who later wed Armstrong, recalled her amazement when Oliver told her the signal for the band to join in after his intro: "When you hear two knocks, just start playing." Oliver and Armstrong would plunge through their breaks at full tilt, never clashing a note. The astonished audiences loved it.

Jazz bands flourished in the nightclubs and speakeasies of Prohibition-era Chicago. The famous Jelly Roll Morton (who claimed to have invented jazz in 1902 by playing ragtime while stamping his foot in 4/4 time) came to Chicago with his Red Hot Peppers in 1926. The brassy sound fit perfectly into the gangster-controlled speakeasies.

Jazz Enters the Mainstream

Black musicians created jazz, but the popularity of the new music quickly attracted white imitators, who learned the black style and were playing the New Orleans sounds before World War I. The first major white group was the Original Dixieland Jazz Band, led by trumpeter Nick LaRocca.

Dubbed the Empress of the Blues, Bessie Smith sang an emotionally charged brand of country blues laced with jazz that made her famous among her mostly black audience.

No doubt the top talent among the white jazz soloists was Bix Beiderbecke, from Davenport, Iowa. Enthralled by the recordings of the Original Dixieland Jazz Band and the New Orleans Rhythm Kings, Beiderbecke learned the jazz cornet by playing along with records. He died at 28, but his style continued to be a major influence on jazz musicians.

Beiderbecke played for the most popular dance band of the 1920's, the "symphonic" jazz orchestra of Paul Whiteman. A classical violinist, Whiteman organized his orchestra in 1919 and hit pay dirt overnight in the record business. The orchestra's first recording, in 1920, sold 2 million copies. One record sold 3.5 million copies, which was amazing since there were only about 7 million phonographs in the United States at the time. His success enabled him to hire the best white jazz musicians, including Beiderbecke and both Tommy and Jimmy Dorsey.

While Whiteman played downtown New York, uptown the bands of Fletcher Henderson and Duke Ellington were riding the wave of the Harlem renaissance, presaging the big band era of the 1930's. All-black Broadway shows, such as Eubie Blake and Noble Sissle's *Shuffle Along,* of 1921, kept people begging for more right up to the end of the decade. White Manhattanites came north in droves for Harlem shows, which featured comedians, chorus girls, singers, such as Ethel Waters, and dancers, like Bill (Bojangles) Robinson. In 1927 the elegant and original Ellington began playing at the famous Cotton Club to a mostly white audience. People paid well for the thrill of being in such a colorful and exotic place as Harlem after midnight, and it flourished. And if they listened closely, underneath the gaiety and din they could hear the howl of jazz announcing it was here to stay.

George Gershwin's genius with symphonic jazz had musicians improvising, music lovers humming, and men and women "pulling and mauling each other" to get into the premiere of Rhapsody in Blue.

DREAM FACTORIES

The decade's brightest stars blazed in silent splendor in the fantasy world of the silver screen, bringing passion, laughter, and the spice of scandal to rapt audiences. Then they began to talk, a change that spelled disaster for some and even greater acclaim for others.

All the adventure, all the romance, all the excitement you lack in your daily life are in — Pictures." So trumpeted an advertisement in *The Saturday Evening Post,* and it was true. Movies brought people's dreams to life through the stars of the silver screen.

Canada's Mary Pickford already glittered in the Hollywood sky. So did Lillian Gish, famous since the days of D. W. Griffith's *Birth of a Nation* (1915). Other stars rose overnight to join them. One was the sultry Rudolph Valentino, whose 1921 film *The Sheik* made him North America's most sighed-over actor. Men were baffled; film mogul Adolph Zukor said Valentino's acting consisted of widening his eyes and flaring his nostrils. But so adept was Valentino at setting female hearts aflutter that when he died in 1926, grieving fans rioted at his funeral.

The role of Great Lover made great box office, but all that changed when in 1921 a 23-year-old actress named Virginia Rappe died after an alleged sexual assault in the hotel suite of the film comedian Fatty Arbuckle. (Arbuckle was later cleared, but his movie career was finished.) Fearing for their profits, studio heads hired an industry chaperone. He was Will Hays, a Presbyterian elder and high Republican official. Besides instituting such standards as the seven-foot rule (kisses could last no longer than seven feet, or two metres, of film), the Hays Office decreed that movies must show "compensating values," meaning that the bad guys had to lose in the end.

In practice, films could show five or six reels of sin as long as virtue eventually triumphed. In Cecil B. De Mille's 1923 film *The Ten Commandments*, worshippers revelled around the golden calf while Moses sought God on the high mountaintop, thus satisfying everybody. Other directors pushed good taste to its limits, particularly in films about liberated youth. Joan Crawford doing the Charleston in *Our Dancing Daughters* (1928) caught the very essence of exuberant Jazz Age hedonism.

Hollywood's firmament included "It" girl Clara Bow (draped across chaise at top), Douglas Fairbanks, and Mary Pickford (right).

In Safety Last (1923) comic Harold Lloyd scrambled up a skyscraper to impress his girlfriend.

The Gish sisters, Dorothy and Lillian (the younger by 2½ years), were silent film stars both individually and together.

The decade produced some of the funniest comedy scenes ever filmed. Acrobatic Harold Lloyd played a youthful Everyman who was constantly tripping up, but whose luck always carried the day. Charlie Chaplin won immortality as the soft-hearted little tramp. In movie after movie his gallantries toward the leading lady were thwarted by comic circumstance. Then there was the deadpan Buster Keaton, who battled technology at every turn. In *The General* (1926) Keaton captured a runaway train and won his dream girl almost in spite of himself.

Westerns galloped to new heights with a fresh crop of heroes who rode the range in the name of truth and justice. Such he-men as Tom Mix, Hoot Gibson, and Buck Jones thrilled the hearts of young boys. Adults, meantime, had their passions stirred by romantic dramas such as *Flesh and the Devil* (1927), in which Greta Garbo rocketed to stardom

Charlie Chaplin's little tramp (right) displayed a ragged elegance in The Gold Rush *(1925), while rescue dog Rin-Tin-Tin was voted the nation's favorite star in 1926.*

opposite John Gilbert. Or they delighted in the provocative ways of Clara Bow, dubbed the "It" girl in 1926. ("It" was sex appeal leavened with nonchalance.)

The decade also saw a small avalanche of Canadian films, many from Trenton, Ontario ("Hollywood of the North"). But they never seriously challenged the real Hollywood with its awesome publicity machine and glamorous stars. With the half-million dollar flop of *Carry on Sergeant!* and Hollywood studios controlling distribution, Canadian film-making sputtered out by the end of the decade, and Canadian performers continued the trek to the United States.

Everything changed in 1927, when sound came to the movies. "Wait a minute, you ain't heard nothin' yet," exclaimed Al Jolson in *The Jazz Singer*, and the Hollywood heavens shook. Clara Bow, it turned out, spoke with an accent few found pleasing. John Gilbert's flutelike tenor voice seemed positively unnatural for the romantic hero his fans knew. Yet, other stars gained. Despite her foreign accent, Garbo flourished as never before. So did a mouse called Mickey, who tootled his way into people's hearts when Walt Disney put a sound track on an animated cartoon called *Steamboat Willie* in 1928.

Gloria Swanson portrayed a modern woman in the silent melodrama Prodigal Daughters *(1923).*

▼ *This low-tech contraption filmed football action in* Brown of Harvard *(1926).*

An unflappable Buster Keaton took command in The General. *One of the era's great comics, Keaton never smiled on screen.*

Clad in a color later reserved for villains, good guy Hoot Gibson could shoot in any direction.

RADIO NETWORKS THE NATION

Born in a cacophony of static and squawks, radio matured into a clear-voiced adult that beamed news, comedy, music, sports, and, of course, commercials. People were all ears.

▼ *In the first scheduled commercial broadcast in the U.S., an announcer at KDKA relays the news of Warren G. Harding's election as president.*

The airwaves carried crooner Rudy Vallee to stardom.

▶ *An early classic, this 1923 Atwater Kent Model II receiver has a horn-of-plenty speaker and four tubes. It was battery-powered.*

Passengers on Canadian National Railways were abuzz in 1923. The railway had just provided radio, the newest delight, for its parlor car travellers. At $150 or more — almost two month's wages for a working man — for even a table set, radio was expensive, but a sensation.

Radio manufacturers fuelled sales by setting up their own stations, as Marconi did with Montreal's CFCF in 1922. (Marconi had established XVA, an experimental station, even earlier in 1919). By 1928, Canada had more than 60 stations, though even at that the airwaves were still uncrowded so that listeners could tune in to cities hundreds of kilometres away.

Radio was particularly important to isolated communities. In southern Saskatchewan, the radio was on 7½ hours a day on average by the end of the decade. In Alberta, a preacher named William (Bible Bill) Aberhart put his sermons on air in 1925, giving him celebrity status that would make him premier of the province within 10 years.

As stations proliferated, so did listeners. Thousands of amateur radio buffs built their own primitive receivers, using a fragment of germanium crystal, coiled copper wire, and headphones. Placing the headphones in a soup bowl created a loudspeaker effect, which allowed the whole family to listen in, but reception was far better on a factory-made set. By the middle of the decade people were buying brand name radios, such as

"He Shoots! He Scores!"

For more than 40 years, the name of Foster William Hewitt meant hockey night to Canadians. As a 21-year-old sports reporter for the *Toronto Daily Star* in 1923, he covered a senior league hockey game between Toronto and Kitchener, using a telephone to broadcast it over radio. Neither he nor radio ever looked back. When Maple Leaf Gardens in Toronto opened in 1931, Hewitt broadcast the first game. Then, in the 1950's, he repeated his success on the television screen. For generations of Canadian fans, the high point of any game was Foster Hewitt's shout, "He shoots! He scores!"

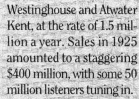

Westinghouse and Atwater Kent, at the rate of 1.5 million a year. Sales in 1925 amounted to a staggering $400 million, with some 50 million listeners tuning in.

Many manufacturers also owned stations. KDKA, for example, was founded by Westinghouse, which hoped to lure potential customers into purchasing its radios. But another source of revenue soon took command: paid commercials.

Even though not everyone approved of the invasion by hucksters of the new medium, it was not long before advertisers were not only buying air time, they were creating their own radio programs. The Ipana Troubadours serenaded toothpaste; the Cliquot Club Eskimos, soda pop; the A&P Gypsies, groceries. In 1928 the American Tobacco Company's flamboyant president, George Washington Hill, poured his advertising money into a broadcast campaign for Lucky Strike cigarettes, suggesting to women that they smoke to stay svelte. "Reach for a Lucky Instead of a Sweet," the slogan advised. Sales of Luckies jumped nearly 50 percent.

Comics, Crooners, and Competing Networks

For listeners everywhere, radio opened up an ether-borne treasure chest of comedy, drama, information, and wonder. As early as 1921 a listener within receiving range could catch stock market reports, newscasts, weather reports, and the World Series. The next year brought the New York Philharmonic's first broadcast. A machine-gun speaking style (217 words a minute) won celebrity for newscaster Floyd Gibbons. There was newfound fame for Broadway transplants like the cowboy-philosopher Will Rogers and the vaudeville comic Ed Wynn. Working in an empty studio disconcerted Wynn, however. One of the first studio audiences, a group of scrubwomen and others, was

assembled to laugh at his jokes. Music was the staple of early radio, and 80 percent of what Canadians listened to originated in the United States. Even so, in 1926 CNR scored a success with the first Canadian play written for radio, Marge Macbeth's *Superwoman*, heard on CNRO (Ottawa).

Some of radio's stars came from nowhere. Women seemed to melt at the nasal greeting, "Heigh-ho, everybody!" of a hitherto obscure bandleader named Rudy Vallee, who dubbed himself the Vagabond Lover. Two struggling performers from Chicago renamed their blackface act *Amos 'n' Andy* and created a hit for Pepsodent with a portrayal of blacks that would be unacceptable today.

By the decade's end the industry's revenues were edging up toward $1 billion. The dominant figure was David Sarnoff, who in 1926 had created the National Broadcasting Company (NBC). Sarnoff's radio experience went back to 1912, when, as a 21-year-old Marconi Wireless operator, he picked up distress signals from the S.S. *Titanic* and relayed the news of her sinking to a horrified nation. Now, with NBC, he set an industry pattern by using leased transcontinental telephone circuits to link affiliated local stations.

Within months competition arose from the 27-year-old son of a cigar manufacturer, William S. Paley. Taking over a nearly bankrupt chain of 16 radio stations, Paley launched the Columbia Broadcasting System (CBS). In two years CBS had 70 affiliates to NBC's 75. The ensuing battle for ears (and eyes) would last through the century.

In a trick photograph, radio comics Freeman Gosden and Charles Correll confer with their famous on-air characters, Amos and Andy.

Ed Wynn, dolled up for a radio audience that could never see him, wears his trademark vaudeville striped blazer.

CAN I HELP YOU?

ON THE ROAD

Some 23 million automobiles were using North America's roadways by 1929. With them came gas stations, trailer parks, road signs, traffic jams, and national highway systems.

The demands of war had made Canada the world's second largest producer of motor vehicles. But, by the 1920's, few Canadian manufacturers survived. Some, like McLaughlin which merged with GM, allied themselves to American producers who established branch plants in Canada. Others simply disappeared.

But, no matter where they were made, cars took the continent by storm in the 1920's. Every family that could afford a car bought one — so did many families that could not. Explained a motorist who owned a car but no indoor plumbing: "Why, you can't go to town in a bathtub!"

The point was to get moving — to town or any other place that was somewhere else. Farmers sped to market, city folk explored the countryside, vacationing factory workers took their families on week-long auto safaris to nature reserves and forests. Sunday driving became a national pastime, even for churchgoers. For young lovers, cars offered round-trip tickets to romance, far from the prying eyes of family and neighbors.

As the automobile worked its way into the fabric of everyday life, scores of new models came onto the market to fit every taste and budget. While only the very rich could summon up the $7,000 it took to buy a sporty Pierce-Arrow, almost any middle-class family could afford a $700 Chevrolet. The Model T Ford, which stayed in production until 1927, cost as little as $260, or only $5 a week on the installment plan. The price went up to $495 for the Model A, which replaced it, but the new Ford offered such state-of-the-art improvements as safety glass windshields, hydraulic shock absorbers, simpler gears, and self-starting ignitions. Who could resist?

A souvenir postcard (top) shows how a parked car could be as much fun as a moving one — particularly compared with the pace of Sunday traffic (left).

Eyes meet beneath the spread of an oak tree in a Nova Scotia field, a country tryst made possible by the car.

from the city limits, with Tudor cottages, Italian villas, and Spanish-style bungalows replacing what were once hayfields and apple orchards.

In 1920, Canadians in four provinces, and Newfoundlanders (who would not become Canadian until 1949), still drove as the British did, on the left side of the road. British Columbia, New Brunswick, Nova Scotia and Prince Edward Island finally accepted the North American imperative of driving on the right during the 1920's. But Newfoundland would hold out until 1947.

All across North America, adventuresome "car campers" were beginning to pitch tents in any available fields. And enterprising businessmen soon began constructing roadside tourist cabins. Then in California, in 1926, innkeeper Arthur Heineman opened the first motel, a term he coined because he could not fit the words *Milestone Motor Hotel* on his entrance sign. The age of the automobile had clearly arrived.

The newest look in urban transit was the Checker cab, which made its debut in 1922 when the Checker Motors Corporation of Chicago began manufacturing its own vehicles. Soon Checker franchise drivers were carrying riders in cities across America.

Whatever the vehicle, the decade's motorist set out with a sense of adventure. Almost 5 million kilometres of roadway crisscrossed the continent in 1920, most of it consisting of unpaved rural lanes intended for horses. Road signs, when present, tended to be an unreadable confusion of crude arrows, skulls and crossbones, and other strange icons. Some early routes were marked by daubs of colored paint on tree trunks and fence posts, a system that broke down entirely in the treeless, open spaces of the West.

Improvement came quickly, however. The world's first three-color traffic light went up in Detroit, in 1919. New York's Bronx River Parkway, the first limited-access auto route, opened in 1923, and the first cloverleaf interchange, at Woodbridge, New Jersey, opened in 1929.

The auto wrought other transformations on the landscape. Filling stations sprang up on vacant lots. Giant billboards crowded the highway panorama. A magnificent hodgepodge of roadside eateries appeared: wigwams, pagodas, giant milk bottles, all of them serving ice cream and hot dogs. Even more important, the ease of auto transport began to change living patterns. Suburbs rolled out

In the winter of 1926–27, inventor Joseph-Armand Bombardier built a snow vehicle with sleigh runners on the front and double wheels joined by a chain on the back. It was to be the prototype of the Snowmobile.

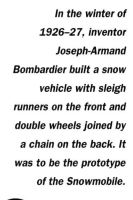

Filling stations doubled as grocery stores, sandwich shops, or, as here, a post office.

FOR THE LOVE OF CARS

1906 ◆ Stanley Steamer
The Stanley twins made their first steam-driven vehicle in 1897, and the last Stanley appeared in 1924, when gasoline-powered cars dominated.

1909 ◆ Waverly Electric
Despite running cleanly, quietly, and cheaply, electric cars could not go fast enough, nor far enough between recharges. In winter cold, they often couldn't go at all.

1927 ◆ Ford Model T Runabout
This sporty roadster appeared just before Chevrolet first topped Ford in annual car sales. Henry Ford responded by building the Model A.

1929 ◆ Duesenberg Dual Cowl Phaeton
The rich and famous owned Indiana-built Duesenbergs. Phaeton meant 4 doors, 2 cross seats, and a top that folded back.

1933 ◆ Packard Sport Phaeton Dietrich
Famous designer Ray Dietrich had a hand in custom-styling this majestic touring car.

1948 ◆ Studebaker Starlight
"First by far with a postwar car!" Studebaker crowed about its new look.

1930 ◆ Ford Model A
Sturdily built, and less than $500, it sold 1.3 million in 1930, but the Depression cut sales by half in 1931.

There came panting and chugging up that flat thoroughfare a thing . . . vaguely like a topless surrey, but cumbrous with unwholesome excrescences fore and aft, while underneath were spinning leather belts and something that whirred and howled and seemed to stagger. . . . 'Git a hoss!' the children shrieked, and gruffer voices joined them. 'Git a hoss! Git a hoss! Git a *hoss*!' " Thus, in *The Magnificent Ambersons*, did the novelist Booth Tarkington describe the coming of the automobile to an Indiana town. Since those days at about the turn of the century, Tarkington's mechanical monster has become part of the modern way, and it has changed our daily lives, our cities, our countryside. For all of this — or despite it — Canadians and Americans remain car lovers, perhaps because the car still represents personal freedom in a world that seems increasingly constricting. On these two pages, a few of the cars we have loved sit for portraits.

1951 ◆ Mercury Station Wagon
"Woodies," with real wood panelling, were popular before and after World War II.

1956 ◆ Ford Thunderbird Convertible Coupe
Ford made fewer than 16,000 of these T-Birds in 1956. Ageless good looks have made them collectors' pets.

1957 ◆ Volkswagen Beetle
Imported for the first time into Canada in 1952, this German gem cost $1200.

1978 ◆ Datsun 280Z
Then known widely as Datsun, the Japanese carmaker Nissan won praise for these Z-cars of 1970–78.

1992 ◆ Plymouth Voyager AWD
Like the truck-cars (right), roomy, boxy vans caught on with both Canadians and Americans starting in the 1980's.

1956 ◆ Lincoln Continental Mark II
At nearly $10,000, it cost too much for most Americans, but almost everyone agreed it was a classy classic. It was not sold in Canada, however.

1957 ◆ Chevrolet Corvette
Introduced in 1953, 'Vette sports cars, with fibreglass bodies, wowed car lovers, especially the elegant 1956 and 1957 models.

1958 ◆ Cadillac Coupe
Tail fins seemed to have a life of their own on General Motors' top-of-the-line cars, Cadillacs, in the mid-1950's.

1967 ◆ Oldsmobile Toronado
It reprised the 1966 model's front-wheel drive, great handling, and fastback styling.

1993 ◆ Ford Bronco
Trucklike personal vehicles were hot sellers in the 1990's, reflecting perhaps a nostalgia for rugged simplicity.

WRITERS WHO DAZZLED AND DARED

Some lived in Paris in self-imposed exile. Others stayed closer to their roots. Literary rebels, they brandished their pens with such exuberance and style that they created a new era in letters.

Ernest Hemingway poses with a marlin he caught off Key West in 1929. In approach and subject, his lean writing stressed courage and manly skill.

▲

Tennis-playing dramatist Eugene O'Neill drapes an arm around daughter Oona, the future Mrs. Charlie Chaplin.

In 1927, the Roche family of Ontario discovered it had a celebrity. Mazo (who wrote under the name of Mazo de la Roche) had just won a $10,000 prize for her novel, *Jalna*. It made her the world's best-known Canadian novelist. That same year, Manitoban Frederick Phillip Grove published an autobiographical novel, *A Search for America*, to establish himself as a writer. Not for years would Canadians learn that this self-styled son of Swedish aristocrats was, in fact, the son of a Hamburg streetcar conductor. No matter, Americans and Canadians alike were caught up in his vision of Canada as the spiritual heir to Europe and his condemnation of the materialism of the United States.

In fact, American writers of the decade seem to have come to much the same conclusion. Lashing out against everything from puritan morals to cultural boorishness to the consumer economy, they told the truth as they saw it. They dropped a bomb of prose so brilliant and new on America that they brought it to the fore of the international literary scene.

Some writers expressed their disenchantment by looking American society squarely in the face and calling it deficient. Sinclair Lewis burst into prominence with his novel *Main Street* (1920), in which he attempted to exorcise his childhood demons by creating a Midwestern town just like the one where he grew up. In a clear, unromantic, often biting voice, Lewis took aim at the narrow smugness of small-town life — "the village virus," as he termed it. Two years later he attacked the decade's business ethic with *Babbitt*, a novel about a bump-

Sinclair Lewis

tious Midwestern realtor who represented most of what Lewis found objectionable about America.

Astonishingly, both books were runaway best-sellers: popular tastes at the time leaned more often to Western adventure or sugary romance novels. But publishing was one of the decade's growth industries, with readership expanding and titles accelerating off the presses. American publishers brought out 10,187 new titles in 1929 (compared with about 100 in Canada), nearly double the number a decade earlier. There was room for every type of work, no matter how difficult, contrary, or experimental.

Much of what was new and exciting emerged from the bohemian byways of New York City's Greenwich Village.

Morality Rises from the Ashes

Of the Canadian and American writers in Paris who expressed dismay at the materialism of North American society, one was optimistic about its spiritual redemption — Morley Callaghan.

A law graduate, Callaghan struck out for Paris to find himself as a writer. There, his first published stories and novel (*Strange Fugitive*, 1928) brought him international attention. When he returned to Canada in the late 1920's, he found a ready market with leading magazines such as *Atlantic Monthly*.

Using material gathered from the poor and from stories of crime, he established the theme that would mark his finest novels, the struggle to reconcile materialism and physical drives with spiritual values. In later years, critics would name him one of the best writers to come out of the Paris days of the 1920's.

Playwright Eugene O'Neill went there to find himself. Son of a prominent actor, O'Neill by age 24 had dropped out of Princeton, gone to sea as a deckhand, sold sewing machines, prospected for gold, reported for a newspaper, been married and divorced. Washing up in the Village, he rubbed shoulders with thieves, hustlers, radicals, feminists, artists. And he began writing plays: *Anna Christie* (1921), *Desire Under the Elms* (1924), *Strange Interlude* (1928), and some 40 others, injecting a note of stark, brooding realism that utterly transformed the American theatre.

New York attracted scores of other young writers. John Dos Passos looked in but quickly left; his experimental *Manhattan Transfer* (1925) poured such contempt upon what he saw that one critic likened the book to "an explosion in a cesspool." But most writers settled in quite happily. Edna St. Vincent Millay, a Greenwich Village resident, thrived on the area's heady ideas and easygoing ways: "My candle burns at both ends;/ It will not last the night;/ But, ah, my foes, and, oh, my friends —/ It gives a lovely light!"

Edna St. Vincent Millay

To those writers who felt they could remain in North America not a moment longer, escape to foreign lands was the only solution: to Paris, London, the Riviera. Free-flowing liquor, cheap living, and more sophistication lured some of the most talented writers of the 20th century. F. Scott Fitzgerald breezed through France. T. S. Eliot settled in England to forge a brilliant new idiom of poetic expression.

Poet Ezra Pound moved to Italy, where he savaged modern life ("a botched civilization") in dense, cryptic verse that challenged traditional perceptions.

The brightest beacon was Paris, which enjoyed a boom of small publishing houses, such as Black Sun Press, and provocative literary magazines, such as *transatlantic review*. Newly arrived writers would head for the Café Dôme or the Dingo bar to see and be seen. Among them was John Glassco, a Montrealer who went to Paris at the age of 20. Though he later distinguished himself as a poet and translator, many feel his finest work was his remembrance of Paris, *Memoirs of Montparnasse*, published in 1970.

Beyond the gossip and aperitifs there was serious work to be done: new styles to be tested, new truths to be told. Urged on by friends, Ernest Hemingway quit his job as a journalist and devoted himself entirely to fiction. The result was his first novel, *The Sun Also Rises* (1926), which told of disillusioned American expatriates (much like the author and his pals) on a trip to Spain. Between the lines ran an undercurrent of discontent and shattered dreams. *A Farewell to Arms* (1929) followed next and then other novels and stories, all delivered in taut, stripped-down prose, which became the hallmark for a new kind of tough-guy American literature. It proclaimed in no uncertain terms that Hemingway, and his fellow writers both abroad and at home, were a force to be reckoned with.

The Algonquin Round Table

Not all American writers of the 1920's worked in Village garrets or Paris cafés. In Manhattan a group of wits enlivened the dining room of the Algonquin, a midtown hotel whose Round Table became a home away from home for a glittering set of literary luminaries. Their humor relied largely on rapid-fire delivery of the barbed insult. Dorothy Parker, a magazine editor and composer of light verse (e.g., "Men seldom make passes / At girls who wear glasses"), was a master. Nor were the others far behind.

This Al Hirschfeld cartoon of the Round Table shows (clockwise from bottom left) Parker, humorist Robert Benchley, journalist Alexander Woollcott, columnist Heywood Broun, playwright Marc Connelly, columnist Franklin P. Adams, novelist Edna Ferber, and playwrights George S. Kaufman and Robert Sherwood. At the smaller table (left rear) sit Broadway stars Alfred Lunt and Lynn Fontanne with *Vanity Fair* editor Frank Crowninshield hovering paternally nearby.

◄

T. S. Eliot moved to London in 1914 and wrote some of the century's most acclaimed poems in the English language, including "The Waste Land" (1922). He became a British subject in 1927. Here he explains some fine points of literary theory.

SCIENCE CAPTURES THE PUBLIC'S FANCY

From archeology to zoology, from outer space to the depths of the human psyche, a flood of astonishing discoveries shed light on some ancient mysteries while promising a better life for everyone.

Leonard Thompson was 14 years old, but he weighed barely 30 kilograms. A diabetic, he was suffering from the starvation that was the only treatment for his illness. But his suffering ended in 1922 when a medical team at the University of Toronto treated him with insulin. Soon, he was active and gaining weight. Diabetes, the dread affliction of millions of people worldwide, could now be controlled. Dr. Frederick Banting, a member of the team that treated Thompson, won a Nobel Prize to become one of the decade's many scientific celebrities.

Artificial silk. A cure for tetanus. Antiknock gasoline. A new hormone isolated. A giant star measured. The structure of atoms laid bare to mathematical scrutiny. Scarcely a week went by without the newspapers announcing some startling scientific achievement. Men with slide rules and laboratory coats became celebrities. As one editorialist noted, the words *science teaches us* were enough to settle any argument.

No area held such a grip on the public's attention as the rapidly developing field of psychology. With its batteries of tests and personality charts, psychology seemed able to solve any human problem, from crime to divorce to early morning blues. Businesses hired psychologists to run their personnel departments. Schools brought in testing agencies to determine students' IQ's. Parents debated the values of nature versus nurture and raised their children in accordance with Dr. John B. Watson's book *Behaviorism*.

Sex became a favorite topic of polite conversation, prompted in part by the writings of Sigmund Freud. When the Viennese doctor traced the cause of certain mental illnesses to sexual repression, an eager public took this finding as an excuse for almost anything. So heated was the sexual

Dr. Sigmund Freud, father of psychoanalysis, introduced the world to the id, the ego, and the dangers of a repressed libido.

Dr. Frederick Banting (right) and Charles Best (left) were co-discoverers of insulin, the lifesaving treatment for diabetes. Banting later shared his Nobel Prize money with Best.

George Washington Carver, to help black farmers in the American South, discovered how to make nearly 300 products from peanuts, including axle grease and shaving lotion.

The Wizard Who Folded Space

When Albert Einstein visited the United States in 1921, he was already a world celebrity. Two years earlier, astronomical observations had confirmed his general theory of relativity, which said that space is curved. The concept was beyond most news reporters, who mobbed his stateroom to ask him about everything else — from world politics to his thoughts on the New York City skyline to when the universe would end.

Scottish inventor J. L. Baird (left) displays his TV transmitter and the wooden dummy that was his star, while Vladimir Zworykin (right) shows his new cathode ray tube.

debate that Robert Benchley, then a drama critic at *Life*, wrote in exasperation: "Sex as a theatrical property is as tiresome as the Old Mortgage. . . . I am sick of rebellious youth and I'm sick of Victorian parents and I don't care if all the little girls in all sections of the United States get ruined. . . . "

Laboratories discovered or produced wondrous cures and treatments: vaccines against tetanus, whooping cough, and tuberculosis; vitamins B_1, which prevents beriberi, and C, the antiscurvy agent. A generation of youngsters dutifully choked down spoonfuls of cod-liver oil, which contains rickets-preventing vitamin D. In 1928 a British bacteriologist, Alexander Fleming, discovered penicillin, the first antibiotic. That same year George Papanicolaou invented the Pap test for detecting cervical cancer.

The research departments of mighty business corporations poured out a flood of inventions, swelling the number of patent applications during the 1920's. Among the new products were hand-held cameras, Kodak film, the Geiger counter, paint sprays, cigarette lighters, antifreeze, electric shavers, aluminum pots and pans, such plastics as vinyl and acetate, magnetic tape, hybrid corn, and the tommy gun.

Some achievements laid the groundwork for future marvels. For more than 40 years, inventors had searched for ways to transmit moving images over the airwaves. Then in 1926 a Scottish engineer, John Logie Baird, displayed the world's first television picture, a fuzzy image of a ventriloquist's dummy named Bill. Baird's equipment was crude, but a better system was at hand, based on Vladimir K. Zworykin's cathode ray iconoscope, the forerunner of modern TV technology.

Some branches of science pushed beyond the boundaries of earth itself. In Auburn, Massachusetts, physicist Robert H. Goddard sent the first liquid-fuelled rocket on a short flight in 1926, opening the way to space travel for future generations. Meanwhile, a 2.54-metre reflecting telescope, then the world's largest, went into operation at California's Mount Wilson Observatory. New stars came into view, and new galaxies were mapped. Astronomer Sir Arthur Eddington delved into the birth of stars, and America's E. P. Hubble found evidence that the universe was expanding outward. This information, coupled with the startling theories of a shy shaggy-locked physicist named Albert Einstein (who said that matter was energy and that space and time were both relative to how you viewed them), was heady material indeed. But to even the most befuddled observer, it was obvious that science had no limits.

Robert H. Goddard shows off his liquid-fuelled rocket. When it was launched in March of 1926, it covered a distance of 56 metres at an average 96 kph.

The Treasure Trove of Tutankhamen

For years archeologists had been frustrated in their search for treasures from the royal tombs of ancient Egyptian pharaohs. Most concluded that grave robbers had long since made off with anything of value. Howard Carter, an Englishman with little formal education, was an exception. Generously financed by the earl of Carnarvon, Carter spent 10 years digging in and around the Valley of the Kings, hoping to find something.

In October of 1922 Carnarvon reluctantly agreed to fund one more season. A month later Carter opened the 3,200-year-old tomb of the boy-pharaoh Tutankhamen. It was nearly intact: "Details of the room within emerged slowly from the mist, strange animals, statues, and gold — everywhere the glint of gold."

The world's press hailed the achievement, and by 1924, when Carter uncovered the polished funerary mask at left, King Tut had become a household name.

THE GREAT PROSPERITY ENGINE

Most North Americans, seeing corporate profits and personal incomes rise, came to think that business could sustain an expanding prosperity and provide everyone with steadily increasing wealth.

Behind all the hoopla and razzmatazz of the 1920's lay a single supremely vital fact: never before had Canada and the United States seemed so prosperous. After a sharp stumble in 1920–21, the economies took off. Factories hummed, jobs multiplied, and a seemingly endless gusher of consumer products poured out. The momentum continued, with a few minor pauses, until 1929. It was the swiftest expansion of national wealth that anyone could remember. When President Coolidge told a group of newspaper editors that "the chief business of the American people is business," most Americans wholeheartedly agreed.

Leading the parade was the auto industry. By 1926 a Model T Ford was rolling off the assembly line every 10 seconds of the working day. General Motors (GM) was catching up fast, with Chrysler not far behind. And that was only half the story, for the brisk pace of auto production spurred business in a score of related industries. Steel for bodies and frames, rubber for tires, plate glass for windshields — all were in greater demand. And the oil companies, once mainly purveyors of kerosene, began pumping out a new leaded gasoline said to quiet engine knock.

At the same time, giant utility companies were taking shape to supply the needs of manufacturers and to light the lamps and run the household gadgets of private consumers. Cheap electric power sparked further demand. So fierce was the appetite for Hoover vacuum cleaners that the company could not keep up. A specialist was brought in to streamline production, and output shot up to 1,000 new Hoovers a day.

Nowhere did electricity have a greater impact than in Canada. "White coal," as it was called, could be produced from the energy of waterfalls, and Canada had an abundance of those. The old limitations of direct current (it could be transmitted over only a few kilometres) were overcome with alternating current which made it possible for Niagara Falls to power the whole city of Toronto; Shawinigan Falls was able to supply Montreal at a distance of 135 kilometres.

But there was a double catch to hydro power in Canada. Only Quebec, Ontario, and British Columbia had enough water power to supply electricity in large quantities and attract power-hungry industries. With the coming of electricity, Canadian industrialization would be increasingly lopsided. The other catch was that hydro power fell under provincial jurisdiction, not federal. The growing importance of hydro-electricity meant that Ottawa became more a spectator and less a participant in the industrial boom.

Man and machine are one in Lewis Hine's 1920 photo of a mechanic adjusting the steam pump in an electric-power house.

In the early 1920's Raymond Hood won out over 300 architects with his soaring Neo-Gothic design for the 33-storey Chicago Tribune building.

A landscape of lumber spreads in front of the Powell River Paper Company mill in British Columbia. Canada's huge forests have supplied pulp and paper to export markets since the early 1900's.

Buying: A Sacred Mission

Such industrial capacity demanded more buying. Advertisers spread the gospel of material well-being with unabashed vigor on roadside billboards, in magazines and newspapers, and over the radio. Indeed, it was a duty to spend, and if people had to work a little harder to earn more dollars, all the better. "Looking at the ads makes me think I've GOT to succeed," declared a householder named Andy Consumer in a high-pressured magazine sales pitch that trumpeted the virtues of the advertising industry itself.

The industry had its own highly vocal prophet, Bruce Barton, who claimed his inspiration came from the very highest source. In *The Man Nobody Knows*, a best-seller in 1925 and 1926, Barton declared that the world's first marketing genius was none other than Jesus Christ. "He picked twelve men from the bottom ranks of business and forged them into an organization that conquered the world," the author wrote, and he went on to add that Christ's parables were "the most powerful advertisements of all time. . . . "

That the decade's hucksterism tended to aim at such non-Christian traits as greed, snobbery, and fear seemed not to matter to the advertising Philistines. An ad for a popular mouthwash asked, "Often a bridesmaid but never a bride?" then suggested that perhaps the problem was halitosis. The point was to sell.

If the customer lacked the ready cash for a new car or a washing machine, ads encouraged him to buy on the installment plan. Before World War I, most people's use of credit began and ended with a home mortgage. Ten years after the war, credit was the North American way to buy cars. Credit also propelled a boom in construction, which began in the decade's early years. Investment in new buildings, by both private and public sectors, nearly doubled.

Monolithic generators and turbines in the Ontario Power Company plant at Niagara Falls powered the city of Toronto.

Cities took on a new, more jagged profile as skyscrapers transformed the business centres. In Chicago, construction of the Neo-Gothic Tribune Tower, 33 storeys high, began in 1923. Other corporate spires soon followed — in Pittsburgh, Omaha, Memphis. Toronto's massive Royal York Hotel (1927–29) was the largest in the Commonwealth. The culmination came with New York's magnificent Art Deco Chrysler building. The piercing, energetic thrust of these mighty buildings seemed to echo the continent's highest aspirations and to promise that the good times would last forever. When, in 1928, Herbert Hoover declared that "we in America are nearer to the final triumph over poverty than ever before in the history of any land," the president was only repeating what many people throughout the world already believed.

◄

A delegation of visitors inspects the long line of cars rolling off the Ford assembly lines.

PROUD PEOPLE THAT GOOD TIMES FORGOT

The prosperity of the 1920's barely touched some people. Costly new machinery produced more than debt-ridden farmers could sell profitably; technology permitted factory and mine owners to hire fewer workers.

A lamp mounted in his cap was one of the few improvements in a Cape Breton miner's hard life in the 1920's.

Using mule or steam or gas power to harvest wheat, farmers tried to make up for falling prices by producing more, which only served to make matters worse. ▼

A Saskatchewan farmer, gazing out on rolling hectares of ripening wheat, saw nothing but trouble. Each year his land yielded its bounty in greater abundance. But prices were dropping, and each year crops brought in less money. During World War I, like many other farmers, he had taken out a mortgage in order to extend his holdings and buy the tractor and other equipment that made his record harvest possible. Now he couldn't meet his mortgage payments, and he had no idea where to find the cash.

The farmer was not alone in his misfortune. While many were enjoying an affluence they had scarcely dreamed possible, vast numbers found they had been left behind. Antiquated shoe factories and textile mills were

closing down. Coal mining, shipbuilding, lumbering, railways, the merchant marine — the building blocks of the old prewar economy — were also in trouble.

Agriculture had been by far the largest business at the decade's start, providing occupation for one-third of the citizens of Canada and the U.S. America produced more than

half the world's cotton and two-thirds of its corn. But even as the decade's rich harvests filled the storehouses, demand was falling. The Canadian government, which had encouraged its farmers to feed a world devastated by fighting, abandoned its purchasing in 1921, just as prices were dropping. The United States, as little concerned about protecting farmers as Canada was, raised stiff tariffs to protect domestic manufacturers against foreign imports — a practice that simply raised costs for farmers.

Canadian prairie farmers responded with successful co-operative ventures — wheat pools and buying "co-ops" — to market their produce and buy supplies. But the decade still took its toll, particularly on the prairies and in the Maritimes where thousands left the land every year. In the United States, there were 8,000 farm bankruptcies in 1925 with 1.5 million people leaving the land by the decade's end.

The Struggle for a Decent Living

Nowhere was the squeeze more painful than in America's rural South. Crops like cotton and tobacco were raised mostly by tenant farmers and sharecroppers, the latter of whom had to turn the bulk of their harvest over to the landowners. Often malnourished, always in debt, they fled the land in droves. Some found employment in the region's

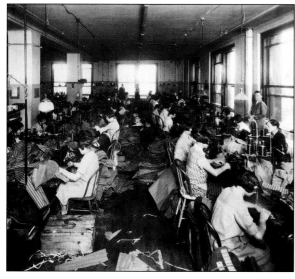

growing mill towns, which were taking over from those of New England as the nation's main textile producers.

But life as a wage earner in the mills was often no better. Revenues were falling in textiles as well; so to cut costs and maintain profits, the mill owners stretched shifts to 12 hours a day, 6 days a week. Weekly paycheques dwindled, by 1928, to as low as $18 for adult males, while women worked at half pay, and children for even less.

Logging in 1920's Canada was not mechanized, unlike many other industries at that time, and relied on the brawn of men and horses, and their endurance of winter's hardships.

In the 1920's John L. Lewis, dynamic head of the UMW, survived a series of cruel setbacks for labor.

◀

Although 2 million additional women joined the work force over the decade, they took mainly low-income jobs that men did not want, becoming teachers, nurses, office clerks, and garment workers, like those pictured at left.

Low wages, long hours, and deplorable working conditions set off a ground swell of labor unrest. The machinery of mass production was rapidly replacing workers, many of whom could not find other full-time employment. In 1920 strife broke out in the coal mines of Pennsylvania and West Virginia. The fiery, bushy-browed John L. Lewis, newly elected president of the United Mine Workers (UMW), set out to organize the work force at Matewan, West Virginia, where a day's labor in the coal mines paid as little as $2. The mine owners brought in "detectives," who began evicting union sympathizers from company housing. Violence spread throughout the state, with pitched battles between gun-toting miners and company guards. Eventually the National Guard restored order. But thousands of miners lost their jobs. And the UMW lost membership and prestige that it would not regain until well into the next decade.

Labor suffered similar reverses in other industries. When Cape Breton steelworkers tried to form a union in 1923, mounted provincial police beat them — and bystanders — in the streets of Sydney. The steelworkers' leader was arrested (supposedly for publishing false news) and sentenced to two years in Dorchester penitentiary.

In an era characterized by optimism and increased material well-being, such turmoil hardly seems possible. But while most people profited as the economies boomed — in the United States the number of people reporting assets of more than $1 million rose from 7,000 to 35,000 — others labored just to prevent their poverty from becoming even worse.

AND THEN CAME THE CRASH

In a decade of easy credit, frantic speculation, and rising fortunes, millions of people grabbed at almost any opportunity to win their pot of gold. It would prove shockingly illusory for most of them.

In the winter of 1933, one Canadian in five was surviving on relief rations provided by local governments and one worker in three was jobless. It was their own fault, according to Prime Minister Bennett, "The fibre of some of our people has grown softer and they are not willing to turn in and save themselves." Blaming the Great Depression on ordinary people was easy to do for one who was himself wealthy and had admired the get-rich-quick mania of the 1920's.

The mercenary madness of the time was epitomized by Charles A. Ponzi, a dapper, diminutive bank clerk who opened the Securities and Exchange Company in Boston in 1919. He claimed he could double investments every 90 days. It sounded too good to be true. But Ponzi paid out as promised, and he was soon taking in $1 million a week. Then the newspapers revealed that his business was a scam; he was simply paying off old customers with the money that flowed in from new ones. Ponzi was sent to jail. And for each customer who got rich, many more went broke.

Once out of jail, Ponzi turned up in Florida in 1925, at the height of a land boom seemingly tailor-made for him: both the swindlers and the "suckers" who resold their properties were making lots of money. (The hapless Ponzi was indicted for fraud in less than a year.) Beginning after World War I and continuing at a dizzying pace, developers had bought large stretches of beachfront and palmetto grove, carving out lots and selling them off at enormous profit. Miami's population swelled to 75,000 by 1925, more than doubling in just five years. Here was a place in the sun for all America, the sales pitch proclaimed. Tens of thousands of Americans arrived by auto and by railway to be feted with banquets, bused to a myriad of investment opportunities, and pried loose of their investment dollars. If a buyer found that his investment lay in a swamp or even under water, no matter: he could unload the deed on someone else for double or quadruple the purchase price. Properties worth a few thousand dollars a decade earlier were now fetching as high as $250,000. A lively and profitable market sprang up in slips of paper, called binders, that represented an option to buy a particular tract.

The Election of 1928

When Herbert Clark Hoover rose to deliver his inaugural address, in March 1929 (above), he had achieved a solid victory over his Democratic opponent, Alfred E. Smith. The differences between the presidential candidates could not have been more striking. Hoover was a dour Quaker and a public servant who shied away from the campaign trail and abhorred publicity. He had risen from humble beginnings in rural Iowa to become a wealthy mining engineer, and then applied his business skills to the organization of food relief in post–World War I Europe.

Al Smith was a cigar-chomping, back-slapping politician. His strong accent ("radd-ee-o" and "horspital") betrayed his origins on New York City's Lower East Side and alarmed many voters who saw cities as hotbeds of modern evils. Most damaging to his presidential aspirations was that he was Catholic. Smith worked hard to assure voters that his religious beliefs in no way influenced his official actions, but the rumor mill spun anyway: If you elect Al Smith, Protestant marriages will be annulled; he'll build a tunnel linking the Vatican to Manhattan.

Unfounded tales of drunken binges, fuelled by Smith's anti-Prohibition stance, quashed any hope he had of becoming president. Given the times, though, probably no Democrat could have won. As Will Rogers said, "You can't lick this prosperity thing."

The Democrats' donkey lacked the kick to help Smith overcome years of boom under the Republicans.

"My Government"

Dale jumped at a peculiar phrase Mr. Bennett used in a speech. He referred to "My Government," a phrase usually reserved for the reigning monarch.

The boom could not last. By early 1926 Florida had more house lots for sale than there were families in America. Then in mid-September a hurricane devastated much of south Florida. Four hundred people died, as did the dreams of quick riches in real estate.

Speculation Grips Wall Street

Incredible, but often true, tales of Wall Streeters making fast money in the stock market were luring millions of citizens, wealthy and not, to try their luck. The Great Bull Market saw volume on the New York Stock Exchange soar from 227 million shares in 1920 to an unprecedented 920 million in 1928. The volatility of the market gave everyone the chance to win, or lose, big bucks.

The Radio Corporation of America (RCA) launched in 1919, became a speculator's delight. Its stock traded in 1921 for $2.50 a share; by 1927 a share reached $85, and in the next two years, adjusted for stock splits, it rose to an astonishing $573.75. And it wasn't just RCA. The market seemed destined to move in only one direction: up.

Anyone with a few spare dollars could ride the Wall Street bull. Stories about the trained nurse who made $30,000 and the financier's valet who netted a quarter million travelled fast. And if a potential player lacked cash, he could buy on margin, permitting him to pay a small percent

Supremely confident in his own abilities, Bennett rarely delegated authority. Cabinet members did as he told them to, and it took a brave minister to make even a minor decision without his prior approval.

▲ *Early skepticism about the Florida land boom inspired this biting January 16, 1926, cover of* Judge.

▶ *Chalk-wielding stock clerks had trouble keeping up with the record-setting pace in 1929; brokers traded over a billion shares.*

Con man Charles Ponzi cashed in on America's get-rich-quick fantasies, only to die penniless in 1949.

of the stock's purchase price. His broker would put up the rest. If the stock's price dropped, the investor could be forced to sell all his holdings at a loss. But risk was the last thing on anyone's mind. The market dropped sharply in 1928, but quickly recovered and kept climbing. There were signs of trouble, such as banks closing and factories running at a loss, but almost everyone ignored them.

The top was reached in early September of 1929. Then prices started dropping, picked up speed, and on October 24 — Black Thursday — began a free-fall. At 1:30 P.M. a consortium of worried bankers sent Richard Whitney, an exchange vice president, to the floor with purchase orders totaling $20 million. Cheers went up from the traders. The market steadied. But on Tuesday, October 29, panic erupted again. Sell orders poured in, many driven by the forced liquidation of margin accounts. More than 16,400,000 shares traded hands, a record that would stand until 1968. The tape ran late, so nobody knew how much money he was losing.

Soon the damage was all too clear. At the day's end, close to $15 billion in market value had simply vanished; by mid-November the figure had risen to $30 billion, and an estimated 3 million people were out of work, versus 700,000 a month earlier. The bull market was over, and with it had crashed the high-flying hopes of an entire decade.

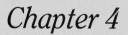
Chapter 4

The Down- and-Up 1930's

On the farms and in the cities, North Americans

manage to struggle through the Great Depression —

only to feel the ominous rumblings

of another world war.

Nature added to Depression woes with blinding, choking dust storms on the Prairies.

HOOVERVILLES AND BENNETT BUGGIES

In 1929, Herbert Hoover referred to economic woes as merely "a reduction in the consumption of luxuries and semi-necessities . . ." Mackenzie King refused to recognize that anything was wrong at all.

▲ **The stock market crash forced all kinds of people into situations they had never before imagined. To draw attention to his plight, a hard-hit businessman offers to sell his luxury automobile to passing pedestrians at a bargain price.**

The financial community picked itself up from the 1929 crash with the rueful humor of a man recovering from a wild night on the town. The New York Stock Exchange, determined to dispel gloom about the economy, rang in the new year with a whoop and a holler. A brass band played on the trading floor, confetti flew, and brokers jigged and pirouetted between the trading booths. For a while it seemed to have worked: stockprices actually rallied in the first four months of 1930. But in May the stock market began to wobble, and prices broke again, to continue their dismal trend downward.

High-Level Optimism, Mainstream Misery

A number of astute Wall Streeters had foreseen the crash and left the market in time. Bernard Baruch, adviser in

"I'm Awfully Cold Every Day"

Richard Bedford Bennett had the reputation of being a cold, hard man. Hard he certainly was. He ran his government like a dictatorship and he had no time for protestors or social reformers. But was he really as cold and unfeeling as he appeared to be?

Every day, he received a stream of letters like this one from Saskatchewan:

"Dear Sir, — I am a girl thirteen years old and I have to go to school every day its very cold now already and I haven't got a coat to put on. My parents can't afford to buy me anything for this winter. I have to walk to school four and a half mile every morning and night and I'm awfully cold every day. Would you be so kind to send me enough money so that I could get one.

My name is
Edwina Abbott"

There were many letters like that — from fathers watching their families die of cold and starvation, from mothers whose despair was past tears.

Bennett's wealth insulated him from the suffering of the Depression. But he had known poverty in his New Brunswick childhood, and he wasn't so cold that he had forgotten what it was to be poor. He sent Edwina Abbott $5 to buy a coat, as he sent money to many others who wrote to him. His problem may not have been coldness. It may have been that, like most politicians of the time, he could not understand that the economics of business had nothing to do with the economics of running a country.

WRAP YOUR TROUBLES
IN DREAMS
(And Dream Your Troubles Away)

Words by
TED KOEHLER
and
BILLY MOLL
Music by
HARRY BARRIS

Introduced by
BING CROSBY
"of Three Rhythm Boys"

financial matters to Presidents Harding and Coolidge, had shifted his assets into bonds, cash, and gold. Similar tactics had saved Joseph P. Kennedy, who remarked, "Only a fool holds out for the top dollar." In fact, Kennedy was among the many bears who made money by re-entering the market to take advantage of bargain stock prices.

But the collapse hurt many Americans badly, and the brunt of the disaster fell on those least able to afford it. In the three years following the crash, 9 million savings accounts were wiped out, and people stopped spending. All sorts of businesses — 86,000 of them — unable to sell their products or services, shut their doors. Millions of people were thrown out of work; no one was sure how many, but the total kept rising.

In Canada, it was even worse because Canadians relied so heavily on an export market that had all but vanished. By 1932, almost one-third of Canadian workers were unemployed, and one Canadian in five was dependent on government relief just to survive. Diseases of malnutrition, like scurvy, reappeared. When provincial governments desperately appealed for federal help, Mackenzie King's response was that he wouldn't give a penny to any province that was Tory. That unfeeling reaction helped to cost him the 1930 election and to bring Richard Bedford Bennett's Conservatives to power.

Bennett, a successful businessman, promised to blast his way into world markets, forcing other countries to reopen trade with Canada. But the only way to do so would have been to lower tariffs that protected Canadian industry from competition. Since Bennett wasn't prepared to do that, the Depression simply deepened. Soon, Canadian farmers with cars they couldn't afford to drive were hitching them up to horses. They called them "Bennett Buggies."

Herbert Hoover's optimistic pronouncements on the economy inspired a similar sardonic humor in the United States. Rural folk who had success hunting jackrabbits said they were dining on "Hoover hogs." Beggars with empty pockets pulled them inside out to fly their "Hoover flags." And groups of the homeless lived in makeshift villages dubbed Hoovervilles.

Like Hoover, both Bennett and King held the traditional view that balancing the budget and leaving the economy to the free market would solve the Depression. Others, perhaps closer to the sufferings of daily life, realized that it wasn't working, and it wouldn't work.

British Columbia premier Duff Pattullo launched public works to provide employment and to prime the

In May 1932, 20,000 World War I veterans met in Washington, D.C., and set up camp. Calling themselves the Bonus Expeditionary Force, they vowed to stay until they were advanced a bonus due them in 1945.

▼ *Planned in the 1920's, the Empire State Building was to be the very incarnation of American power and wealth. Instead, when it was opened in May of 1931 — thanks partly to the toil of brave riveters who worked 381 metres up — its 102 storeys remained largely empty throughout the Depression. The 24.4-metre steel dirigible-mooring mast that topped it was never used.*

economic pump. In Alberta, radio evangelist William (Bible Bill) Aberhart advocated inflation through his Social Credit Party. In Quebec, Roman Catholic clergyman-historian Lionel Groulx won government support for a "Back to the Land" movement which established unemployed urban families on farms. More a moral movement than an economic one (Groulx felt that rural life was spiritually superior), it was copied by Protestant churches with their Protestant Land Settlement Society. The federal government joined the movement with its Relief Land Settlement Agreement to place families on unsettled land. The experiences of most of those who took up the offers ranged from extremely hard to tragic.

Critics who saw the capitalist system itself as the cause of the Depression were less successful, partly because of repression. The Communist Party, for example, was effectively banned in 1931. But, in 1932, J. S. Woodsworth launched a serious challenge to free-market thinking with the Cooperative Commonwealth Federation. A social democratic party advocating a wide range of social programs and government ownership of key industries, its ideas would have a major impact on Canadian policies beginning in the 1940's.

Hoover's Late Efforts Fall Short

Whatever Canada might do, its recovery depended on the recovery of its export market in the United States — and that recovery depended on the man in the White House. President Hoover was probably the savviest person in Washington on economic matters, having served with distinction as secretary of commerce for his two predecessors. During World War I and its aftermath, he had headed a relief agency that sent millions of dollars in food and clothing to the devastated populations of a battle-scarred Europe. Surely he could and would do the same for America.

In his sober, methodical way, Hoover began to take the actions he felt the nation needed. In December of 1930, in an effort to create jobs, he launched a $100-million program of dam

Despite the fine location, sandwiched between a hotel and a restaurant, this barber seems to lack customers, who may have opted to spend 10 cents on a meal next door instead of a shave.

building, road construction, and other public works. He signed a relief bill for farmers, extending loans to purchase cattle feed. Hoping to stimulate trade, he gave foreign nations a one-year moratorium on repaying debts to the United States. Early in 1932 he created the Reconstruction Finance Corporation, with a potential funding of $2 billion, to prop up the nation's faltering banks, insurance companies, and other institutions and to prevent further job losses.

It was too little and too late. As the breadlines lengthened and the jobless lists multiplied, Hoover stood firm against direct federal relief for Americans. A government

On July 28, 1932, Hoover sent in the army, commanded by Gen. Douglas MacArthur (shown above left with aide Maj. Dwight D. Eisenhower), to remove the remaining veterans.

dole, he believed, would bankrupt the treasury and sap the nation's moral strength. And he was convinced that the crisis would eventually correct itself. "Prosperity," he declared, "is just around the corner." But as time went on, that corner continued to recede into a cloudy future.

Despair and Repression Breed Violence

In 1932, the Canadian government opened relief camps which offered work in wilderness areas to single, unemployed men. It was significant that the camps were administered by the Department of National Defence because they were only partly intended to provide work. Governments feared that young men congregated in cities would be infected by radical and, perhaps, revolutionary ideas. Better, then, to remove them far from trouble.

But gathering them in camps (an average of 20,000 at any time from 1933 to 1936) and paying them slave labor wages of 20 cents a day did nothing to discourage their discontent. In 1935, a thousand relief workers in British Columbia resolved to take their demands for better conditions in the camps to Ottawa, travelling by freight trains.

The "On To Ottawa Trek," as it was called, faltered when it reached Regina as it became clear that Prime Minister Bennett would not meet their demands. Though the protest was clearly dissipating, Bennett chose that time to order the arrest of the leaders. In the riot that followed, a policeman was killed and dozens of people were injured.

Considering the misery of the Depression years and the unresponsiveness of governments, the wonder is not that such violence occurred but that there wasn't more of it.

Readers and Writers Confront the Depression

In their time of economic trouble, the public looked to writers for solace, advice, and hope. Not surprisingly, escapist literature fared well in the 1930's. One of the biggest successes was James Hilton's *Lost Horizon*, which set millions of readers to dreaming of life in mythical, carefree Shangri-La. The most popular fiction book of 1931 and 1932 was *The Good Earth*, Pearl Buck's family saga set in faraway China. In the following year the adventure yarn *Anthony Adverse* transported its readers to Napoleon's world and made author Hervey Allen rich when it sold 300,000 copies in just six months.

Pearl S. Buck

Historical novels with heroic themes showing readers that the nation had undergone trials in the past and had triumphed were also successful. But the one that most captured the popular imagination was Margaret Mitchell's epic, *Gone With the Wind*, which topped the best-seller list for fiction in 1936 and 1937. Its spunky heroine, Scarlett O'Hara, saw her genteel society destroyed, lost her fortune, starved, and emerged tougher from the ordeal, proclaiming at the end of the book that "tomorrow is another day."

Books offering down-to-earth advice also climbed the best-seller lists. The best of the genre was Dale Carnegie's *How to Win Friends and Influence People* (1936), which told

Dale Carnegie

readers how, by following a few simple rules, they could become popular and respected.

Some of America's greatest writers did their finest work during the Depression. William Faulkner published four major books in the 1930's, including *Light in August* and *Absalom, Absalom!* In such books, wrote critic Malcolm Cowley, this "poet in prose, a creator of myths" wove "a legend of the South." Near the end of the decade, John Steinbeck focused on a small segment of the rural population and captured the turmoil and tragedy of the Depression. His great novel, *The Grapes of Wrath*, depicts the ordeal of the Dust Bowl farmers and their harrowing exodus to California. In the sufferings of the Joad family, readers found echoes of their own misfortunes, and the book became a best-seller.

William Faulkner

Few Canadian writers were optimistic. Ringuet (Phillipe Panneton) wrote of a disappearing rural Quebec in *Trente Arpents*. Newfoundland's E. J. Pratt turned his poetry to the social and economic problems of the 1930's, culminating in his antiwar poem *The Fable of the Goats* (1937). Irene Baird's *Waste Heritage*, set in Vancouver, raised social consciousness with its portrayal of class conflict. In contrast to this pessimism, however, were Morley Callaghan's stories of the seamy side of life in Toronto and Montreal (*Such Is My Beloved, More Joy in Heaven*) which always held out hope of redemption through religious faith.

John Steinbeck

Faith was not enough of an answer for F. R. Scott. A McGill law professor and member of the "McGill Group" of poets, he took his anger at a failed economic system into poetry and then into the political arena as a founder of the CCF (Cooperative Commonwealth Federation) party.

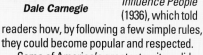

BLACK CLOUDS OVER THE FARMS

Far across the plains, the worst drought known in North America burned crops. Then came

plagues of grasshoppers, and the lowest prices ever recorded for grain.

Central and eastern Canadians, already battered by the Depression, listened to a radio broadcast from the Prairies where conditions were even worse. "With the increasing wind, the whole surface of the field is gently sifting along . . . a heavy black cloud is forming between sky and earth. It sweeps toward us rapidly at 40, 50, 60 miles an hour. . . A minute, and with a blast like a thousand lions it is upon us. We are alone in a stinging mass of hurtling soil, stinging sand . . . we can only drift helpless, choking, blinded." After the storm, the once-tilled land was smooth as glass and the crops destroyed.

Swarms of grasshoppers completed the destruction of prairie grain. As if that weren't enough, the price of a bushel of grain dropped from $1.63 in 1928 to 35 cents in 1932. Net farm income on the Prairies fell from $363 million in 1928 to minus $10 million in 1931. Desperate farmers used unsold grain to heat their stoves and to make a vile coffee.

Teachers that school boards couldn't afford to pay taught in schoolrooms that couldn't be heated. They faced rows of hungry children, many of whom walked kilometres to school in prairie winters wearing only the summer clothes that were all they had. Government bought up supplies of salt fish from the Maritimes for emergency relief. Though dry and tasteless, it was the difference between life and death for many prairie families. Still, in the midst of the Depression's most terrible suffering, some managed to find the strength for humor. When a farmer asked a banker for a loan, the banker asked to see his property. Just then a wind came up, and the farmer said, "Well, open up your window, cuz here she comes."

Grim Devastation in the American West

The same disaster struck the Great Plains of the United States, including much of Colorado, New Mexico, Nebraska, Kansas, Oklahoma, and Texas. A single immense dust storm, on May 11, 1934, blew away more than 300 million tonnes of topsoil, roughly the amount of earth dredged from the Panama Canal. It tossed the equivalent of 3,000 forty-hectare farms into the air.

The dust clouds struck with deadly speed. Farmers caught in their fields, or just a few steps from shelter, could be engulfed by dust and die of suffocation. Repeated exposure to the fine powder caused pneumonia and other respiratory ailments. To protect themselves, some people slept with wet cloths on their faces. Farmers and ranchers strung guide wires so they could find their way from house to barn in order to feed the livestock when a storm blew in. In the hardest-hit regions, agriculture ceased altogether and cattle died from eating dust-covered grass.

The devastation in the Dust Bowl touched off an enormous migration of farm families, lasting for years. Perhaps as many as 350,000 people loaded their belongings onto rickety vehicles and headed west in search of a promised land. Most travelled to California's San Joaquin Valley, where large orchards and cattle ranches offered seasonal work. But there were never enough jobs for the thousands who arrived monthly during the worst times.

Many of the migrants crowded into ramshackle settlements built of tent canvas and packing crates. Some found places at one of more than a dozen camps run by the Farm Security Administration (FSA), which offered washrooms and recreational facilities. A lucky few scraped together the $3 a month required to buy a tiny plot on which they could build their own house. All faced the scorn of Californians, who resented the influx of impoverished newcomers. They became known as Okies, the derogatory term applied to all migrants whether or not they came from Oklahoma.

The migrants just hunkered down and took it. After the privations of the Dust Bowl, they felt lucky to have food in their bellies and occasional work at $3 a day. With their eyes on the future and hope in their hearts, inch by inch they struggled to get ahead. "Jest like the cat eatin' grindstone," one man said, "a little bit at a time."

Dust Bowl Troubadour

The decade's most lyric spokesman for the downtrodden was folksinger Woody Guthrie (above), who hopped a freight train at age 15 to play his guitar in hobo encampments. When the dust storms hit, the Oklahoma-born Guthrie moved on to California, where he became a union organizer. His favorite audiences were the poor, the dispossessed, and children.

Guthrie poured the rueful humor and wounded pride of the Dust Bowl experience into songs that stand as American classics: "Hard Traveling," "So Long (It's Been Good to Know Yuh)," and many others. After the Depression he continued to champion the underdog. His "This Land Is Your Land" was a theme song of the 1960's civil rights movement.

Whipped along by 80-kph winds, a giant "black blizzard" — all dust, no rain — boils across the prairie. ▶

Shoeless and destitute, a Saskatchewan family returns home to drought and a life on welfare after they failed at making a better life for themselves farther north.

Staying put in Indiana, this farm couple took a federal loan to tide them through the dry years.

FDR PLEDGES A NEW DEAL

Rejecting advice that he wage a safe, stay-at-home campaign, Roosevelt toured the country talking about a wide range of issues. He was vague about solutions, but there was no question that he meant to take action.

This cast-metal electric clock, a popular premium from the 1930's, leaves little doubt as to who was the pilot of the U.S.'s ship of state.

▼ **Written for the 1929 movie, Chasing Rainbows, "Happy Days Are Here Again" was FDR's unofficial victory song in 1932.**

In June 1932 Democrats convened in Chicago to nominate a candidate for president. Since nearly everyone assumed that any Democrat could defeat Herbert Hoover, there was a fierce contest for the nomination. Not until the fourth ballot did the governor of New York, Franklin D. Roosevelt, emerge the winner. He then broke all precedent by flying to Chicago to accept the honor in person and to address the troubled country: "I pledge you, I pledge myself, to a new deal for the American people." That card player's phrase, new deal, would become the name for President Roosevelt's programs.

Years before, the young Roosevelt had been his opponent's effusive admirer, saying of Hoover, "I wish we could make him president of the United States. There couldn't be a better one." Yet Hoover appeared dour and bitter during the campaign, while Roosevelt exuded confidence and energy. His promises were not so different from Hoover's, but he seemed less hesitant about using government intervention to solve the economic crisis. To the tune of "Happy Days Are Here Again," he toured the country, shaking hands, chatting with local officials, making speeches from the rear of his train. To no one's surprise, FDR won the popular vote by 7 million, carried 42 states, and received 472 out of 531 electoral votes.

On the night of Election Day, as his son James helped Roosevelt into bed, the president-elect spoke the fears he had hidden in the campaign. "I'm just afraid that I may not have the strength to

▶

Because of the assassination attempt on FDR, this specially prepared New Yorker cover never saw print.

Holding on to son Franklin Jr.'s arm, a confident, jubilant candidate Roosevelt gives a cheerful wave to supporters at a campaign stop in 1932.

do this job. After you leave me tonight, Jimmy, I am going to pray. I am going to pray that God will help me, that He will give me the strength and the guidance to do this job and to do it right. I hope you will pray for me, too, Jimmy."

Bullets in the Night

In early February, with his inauguration still a month away, Roosevelt went on a 12-day fishing trip in the Bahamas. Upon his return he addressed a large crowd gathered in Miami's Bay Front Park. As FDR was leaving, shots rang out. Several people were hit, including Chicago's Mayor Anton J. Cermak, who was standing near the president-elect.

Later, at the hospital, the mortally wounded Cermak told Roosevelt, "I'm mighty glad it was me instead of you. I wish you'd be careful. The country needs you." The dying

▶ **With his arm around vice presidential candidate John Nance Garner, FDR leaves Topeka, Kansas, for the beginning of what would be thousands of miles of rail campaigning.**

The Bennett New Deal

On January 2, 1935, Canadians were stunned when Prime Minister R. B. Bennett went on the radio for a series of talks outlining a list of reforms he proposed to grapple with the Depression. They included minimum-wage and maximum-workhour laws, medical insurance, heavier taxes for the rich, and a Trade and Industry Commission to regulate competition.

Conservative business leaders were aghast. Surely, this was socialism, the communist revolution brought to Canada by the man they least expected would do such a thing. Everyone, mindful of Roosevelt's legislation, dubbed Bennett's program the Bennett New Deal.

Certainly, Bennett's language sounded radical enough for alarm. He said in the broadcasts, "... when capitalism controlled the modern state, the result was fascism. And there is no place for fascism in Canada." But the language was stronger than the program. There was nothing socialist about it and, though Roosevelt provided some inspiration, the Bennett New Deal had roots that went back long before Roosevelt.

With an election coming in 1935, pressure had been growing on Bennett to propose some economic reforms. That pressure had mounted with a report from a Royal Commission, which revealed examples of scandalous exploitation by big business. Essentially, the report echoed the complaints of small businessmen and farmers that they could not compete with big business. There was nothing new about such complaints. They had begun in the 19th century, when chain stores squeezed out local merchants and large factories displaced craftsmen.

What the Commission demanded — regulation of marketing and manufacturing — would preserve a bigger piece of the pie for those who already had a piece. But it would do nothing to restore markets or create jobs. If anything, it might make matters worse by sustaining inefficient producers. But in the confusion of the 1930's, it looked like radical reform. Bennett's New Deal simply extended a measure of protection against competition to the small businessman and the worker. The purpose was not to attack capitalism, but to protect small capitalists against big ones. No matter. Big business, traditionally a supporter of the Conservative Party, was alarmed because anything that limited it was socialist so far as it was concerned. As for most other Canadians, Bennett was still the morning-coated, arrogant, dictatorial millionaire. They didn't like him and they didn't trust him. In the election of 1935, Bennett led Conservatives into their worst defeat since Confederation, and Mackenzie King's Liberals returned to power with a huge majority.

R. B. Bennett

---

mayor's sentiments were echoed by millions of Americans, many of whom had learned of the assassination attempt immediately after it happened, because of the ever-widening reach of radio. The gunman, Giuseppe Zangara, was an Italian immigrant and unemployed bricklayer who harbored a hatred of "all officials and everybody who is rich." He was speedily tried and executed.

Many felt that the assassin's target had been not only FDR but America's hope for the future. It was widely noted that the president-elect had stayed calm in the face of mortal danger. From this baptism by fire both Roosevelt and the country's faith in him emerged newly strengthened.

"The Only Thing We Have to Fear"

On March 4, 1933, Roosevelt rode in the open presidential car to his inauguration. Seated beside Herbert Hoover, who barely spoke throughout the ride, FDR saw a sombre crowd, under tight security because of the assassination attempt. Then, in the blustery March wind, he assured his listeners that "the only thing we have to fear is fear itself." He closed the address by asserting: "The people of the United States have not failed. . . . They want direct, vigorous action."

Some months earlier, a friend had assured Roosevelt that he would be remembered as the greatest American president if he succeeded and as the worst if he failed. Confiding his understanding of the seriousness of the crisis, FDR answered, "If I fail, I shall be the last one." Now that he was in the White House, Roosevelt could no longer simply talk about America's problems and his proposed solutions. The time had come to act — to take the direct, vigorous measures he had promised. The nation held its breath.

The New Deal: 100-Day Scorecard

During his first 100 days in office, FDR guided over a dozen major laws to enactment, including:

Date	Act	
3/9/33	Emergency Banking Act	✔
3/20/33	Economy Act	✔
3/31/33	CCC established	✔
4/19/33	End of gold standard	✔
5/12/33	Federal Emergency Relief Act	✔
5/12/33	Emergency Farm Mortgage Act	✔
5/18/33	TVA established	✔
5/27/33	Truth in Securities Act	✔
6/13/33	Home Owners' Loan Act	✔
6/16/33	National Industrial Recovery Act	✔
6/16/33	Farm Credit Act	✔

ONE HUNDRED DAYS OF CHANGE

"At the end of February," wrote the columnist Walter Lippmann, "we were a congeries of disorderly panic-stricken mobs and factions. In the hundred days from March to June we became again an organized nation confident of our power . . . to control our own destiny."

Franklin D. Roosevelt, who had pledged action the day before in his inaugural address, proclaimed on March 5, 1933, a national bank holiday. The week before, millions of panicky citizens had withdrawn their assets in cash. The nation's banking system was on the verge of collapse; Roosevelt was determined to save it. The Treasury buzzed as new appointees put their heads together with old officials to create a program that would work. The new president's top priority was to calm fears — the public's fear of losing their hard-earned savings and the bankers' fear of being put out of business.

Within four days Congress, summoned by Roosevelt to an emergency session, had passed a new banking act. On Sunday evening, March 12, FDR broadcast the first of his famous fireside chats, to announce the reopening of the banks: "I can assure you that it is safer to keep your money in a reopened bank than under the mattress. . . . Let us unite in banishing fear. It is your problem no less than it is mine. Together we cannot fail."

FDR's blend of serenity and confidence touched off an enthusiastic response. All over America long lines of people queued up to redeposit their money in the banks. As the humorist Will Rogers put it, "The whole country is with him, just so he does something."

This was only the beginning. FDR had much more up his sleeve. Major programs were coming to restore purchasing power by correcting the worst imbalances in the economy, to enact reforms that would prevent another stock market crash, and finally, to launch a vast public works program creating new jobs.

To help formulate these programs, FDR had brought with him to Washington a group of college professors, called by his secretary Louis Howe, somewhat sarcastically, the Brain Trust. FDR had chosen some Brain Trusters for key Cabinet posts; others remained unofficial advisers. They in turn attracted more New Dealers, as they came to be known, and overnight Washington was revitalized. Seldom has such

Louis Howe (far right), FDR's trusted adviser, chairs a White House meeting with Brain Trust professors (from left) Adolf Berle, Jr., Rexford Tugwell, and Raymond Moley.

a high concentration of idealists, colorful personalities, hard-working intellectuals, and monumental egos assembled at the seat of power.

Coming from a wide variety of backgrounds, the Brain Trusters represented many conflicting points of view and approaches. FDR saw himself as a man of action, not a philosopher. He was brilliant at getting the best from this very diverse group. He explained his presidential role as similar to that of a quarterback: "If the play makes ten yards, the succeeding play will be different from what it would have been if they had been thrown for a loss." The president would not know until the next play was completed what would be his call on the play after next. To a young man who asked him what his philosophy was, Roosevelt responded, "Philosophy? I am a Christian and a Democrat — that's all."

▼ *In 1933 NRA supporters mounted a huge parade in New York City: 250,000 marchers and 2 million spectators.*

Fireside Chats

Many presidents have wished to conduct the real business of government behind closed doors. Not Franklin Delano Roosevelt. Instead, he tried to give people the feeling that they were participating in the decision-making process. More than once, both friends and enemies complained about

FDR's indirection and even deviousness, but no one could ever accuse him of not taking his program to the people.

This he did via the fireside chats, broadcasts he made often, starting the week he took office. "My friends," FDR began, and then he seemed to open his heart to the millions who backed him.

The reaction was overwhelmingly positive. A Brooklyn man wrote, "I felt that he walked into my home, sat down, and in plain and forceful language explained to me how he was tackling the job I and my fellow citizens gave him." Republicans could complain and call FDR a mealy-mouthed demagogue. But to many people eager to believe his soothing voice, FDR was a savior.

FDR kept up a dizzying pace. In all, 15 major bills were introduced and passed during those euphoric first 100 days, ranging from refinancing farm and home mortgages to guaranteeing bank deposits. The National Industrial Recovery Act set up the National Recovery Administration (NRA) and created the Public Works Administration (PWA), designed to provide jobs through a $3.3-billion program of construction projects. Other bold strokes included the establishment of the Civilian Conservation Corps (CCC) and the Tennessee Valley Authority (TVA), providing for a vast system of dams and hydroelectric plants to produce power for rural folk in the South who had never had it before. To critics it seemed an ill-sorted package; some called it creeping socialism. But its positive impact was profound.

A New Role for Government

The NRA, with its Blue Eagle thunderbird emblem bearing the words "We Do Our Part," seemed the most revolutionary of all the New Deal measures. It sought to check the downward spiral of output and prices and established government regulation of wages, hours, and working conditions. Some 2 million employers were persuaded, coerced, or stampeded into signing an NRA agreement, or else they could not display the high-flying Blue Eagle. NRA parades were staged in cities and towns across the country to encourage more converts. For millions, the NRA represented the best hope of the New Deal. For many conservatives, it became a hated symbol of government regulation. For everyone, the national political scene had been transformed.

Ladies raise their mugs in a toast after Congress passed a bill legalizing 3.2-percent beer and wine in March 1933.

GETTING PEOPLE BACK TO WORK

New Deal employment programs inspired confidence in government and support for FDR. "It's the first time in my recollection," a workman remarked, "that a president ever got up and said, 'I'm interested in and aim to do something for the workingman.' "

From 1935 to 1943, when it disbanded, the WPA put a total of 8.5 million people to work on 1.4 million separate projects.

Speaking of baseball, Roosevelt once said, "I am the kind of fan who wants to get plenty of action for his money." He might just as well have been describing his program for saving the country.

Millions were out of work when FDR took office, and so many had hit rock bottom that emergency relief programs were a top priority in the early days of the New Deal. FDR's choice to head up a Federal Emergency Relief Administration (FERA) was the veteran social worker Harry L. Hopkins, whose philosophy was outspokenly radical: "I believe people are poor because we don't know how to distribute the wealth properly." The cornerstone of FERA's action was work relief. Criticism was at first muted. As one politician put it, no one was going to shoot Santa Claus just before Christmas. ("The hell they won't," Hopkins retorted. "Santa Claus really needs a bulletproof vest.")

The New Deal proposed much more than a bit of leaf raking and ditch digging to put suppers on the table. With the Public Works Administration, Roosevelt had launched federal construction projects on a scale hitherto unimaginable. Ground for new highways, subways, bridges, schools, hospitals, and other public works was broken everywhere under the auspices of the Department of the Interior and its head, Harold L. Ickes, a reformer who had served as a campaign worker for Theodore Roosevelt a generation earlier.

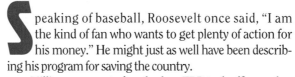

Harry L. Hopkins (left) and Harold L. Ickes share a rare companionable moment in 1938. Shrewd, intelligent, and rivalrous, both men held top government positions throughout FDR's long presidency.

Soon FDR saw the need to create another giant agency, which would complement the PWA with short-term projects: the Works Progress Administration (WPA). At the head of this new enterprise Roosevelt placed Harry Hopkins. Ickes and Hopkins became bitter rivals. Ickes favored grants to states and cities to pay for projects. Hopkins called for spending on labor itself: "We're for labor — first, last, and all the time. WPA is labor — don't forget that." Hopkins's philosophy and programs led to charges that the government was throwing money out the window on boondoggles, or useless make-work projects. The critics were not only Republicans. The administration itself was divided, with Ickes leading the opposition to Hopkins and the WPA. He wrote in his private diary at the time: "I am for substantial, worthwhile and socially desirable public works, while Hopkins is for what has come to be known as boondoggling."

Controversial Projects, Lasting Legacies

Despite the controversy, the WPA's achievements were considerable. Included under the WPA umbrella was a vast federal arts program. Thousands of murals and sculptures were commissioned. To this day WPA art can be seen on the walls of many post offices, courthouses, and other federal buildings. In addition, WPA money brought symphony orchestras and theatre to people who had never in their lives seen anything of the sort. A federal writers' program for unemployed writers led to the creation of a state guidebook series so excellent that several of the guides have remained in print ever since. To charges that taxpayers' money was being misspent, supporters could reply with a quote from George Washington's address to Congress in 1790: ". . . there is nothing which can better deserve your patronage than the promotion of science and literature."

The WPA put thousands of painters, sculptors, and designers to work across America. Artist James M. Newell created this study for a post office mural in Dolgeville, New York.

The Federal Theatre Project brought 1,000 shows to cities and small towns and entertained some 25 million people, many of whom had never before seen a live production. These actors perform The Swing Mikado.

Canada's Relief Camps and the "On To Ottawa Trek"

To R. B. Bennett and his fellow millionaires the ability to make a great deal of money was part of the Canadian way of life. In their view, the greatest danger of the Depression was that it might give rise to radicalism that would threaten this way of life.

Bennett especially feared that revolutionary ideas might spread among single, unemployed men congregating in cities. His solution was to move them away from the cities.

In 1932, he established Unemployment Relief Camps. Administered by the Department of National Defence, they provided barracks accommodation in remote areas where the unemployed could clear bush and build roads in exchange for room and board and 20 cents a day. Moving to a camp was officially voluntary, but those who refused might well be refused relief. Some 20,000 men were in the camps at any one time — a total of 170,000 from 1932 to 1936.

A Relief Camp Workers' Union was formed in defiance of regulations. In 1935, the union called a strike in British Columbia. At the end of May, 1935, camp workers decided to go to Ottawa to present their demands to the prime minister.

The strikers, peaceful and very well disciplined by their communist leaders, got as far as Regina. The Calgary relief commissioner wrote to warn Bennett of "a dangerous revolutionary army" that was on the way. But Bennett needed no warning. When he met strike leaders who had gone ahead to Ottawa, he accused them of trying to "break down the forces that represent law and order."

Discouraged strikers back in Regina organized a rally to raise money for the return home. Bennett, still convinced he was facing a revolution, sent mounted police into the crowd to arrest the leaders. The resulting riot killed one policeman and injured dozens of other people. It also contributed heavily to Bennett's election defeat later in the year. The succeeding King government closed the relief camps in 1936.

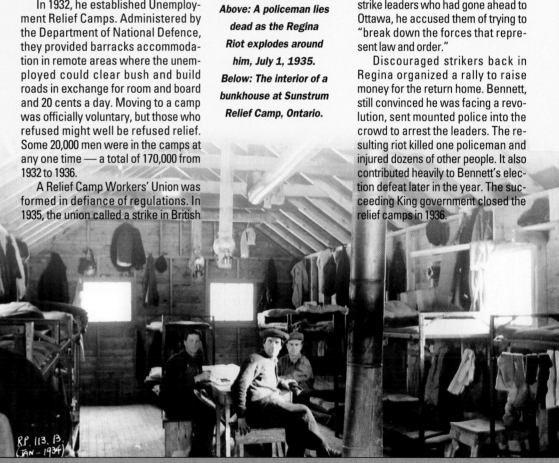

Above: A policeman lies dead as the Regina Riot explodes around him, July 1, 1935. Below: The interior of a bunkhouse at Sunstrum Relief Camp, Ontario.

THE SPLENDID SILVER SCREEN

Mickey Mouse and Shirley Temple, Groucho Marx and Greta Garbo, Busby Berkeley and Fred Astaire —

Hollywood kept people chuckling, gasping, and applauding all through the bad times.

When the spirit of the people is lower than at any other time, during this Depression," President Roosevelt said, "it is a splendid thing that for just fifteen cents an American can go to a movie . . . and forget his troubles." It was 1936. Most people had money only for necessities, and for the movies.

By the end of the decade, North Americans were buying more than 80 million movie tickets every week for as little as 10 to 15 cents each. That ticket bought a lot, too: a newsreel, a cartoon, a short subject, previews of coming attractions, and a double feature.

Of course, little had to do with reality, but that was the point. Production code censors banned words like *hell* and *damn,* along with brutal murders and the horizontal position in love scenes. In the movies people died without bleeding and bred without mating. And some of the most popular characters were not even people.

Hollywood called Walt Disney's studio the Mouse Factory, and the mouse was Mickey. In the dark days of 1933, Disney had set the country singing "Who's Afraid of the Big Bad Wolf?" from *The Three Little Pigs,* but cartoons about mice appealed even more. Among Mickey's early devotees were Italian dictator Mussolini and Queen Mary of England. Only Adolf Hitler was immune, and German propaganda declared the animated rodent "the most miserable ideal ever revealed . . . mice are dirty."

Across town from the Mouse Factory, the world's best-paid moppet ($100,000 a picture in 1938, more than Gable or Garbo) single-handedly kept 20th Century-Fox afloat. Shirley Temple sang, danced, giggled, and melted stony hearts in *Dimples, Curly Top*, and *Little Miss Marker* while

Elegance in motion, Ginger Rogers and Fred Astaire danced through 10 hit movies and spun a new ideal of American glamor.

Busby Berkeley's Footlight Parade (background, this page) and Born to Dance with Eleanor Powell (background, next page) formed fantasy backdrops to Hollywood's golden age of musicals.

▲

The pluckiest heroine of 1939 was Dorothy, played by Judy Garland, in The Wizard of Oz. She closed her eyes, clicked her ruby slippers, and whirled off to stardom.

Winsome Shirley Temple started acting at age three and made 27 films by the decade's end.

▶

Veteran Hollywood comic Stan Laurel hits his partner, Oliver Hardy, with a well-placed sight gag.

her mother stood by during filming shouting, "Sparkle, Shirley! Sparkle!"

Just as upbeat were the kaleidoscopic productions of choreographer Busby Berkeley, with dozens of long-legged beauties. Also, Fred Astaire and Ginger Rogers twirled with magical grace. Astaire's first screen test read: "Can't act. Slightly bald. Can dance a little." But the grand success of *The Gay Divorcée* in 1934 saved RKO Pictures Corporation, and the studio insured Astaire's legs for $1 million. His debonair charm played off Rogers's glamorous sex appeal, and both could dance the spots off a leopard.

A raft of brilliant comedies perked up weary audiences. Comedy ranged from Mae West's sensuous innuendo ("When women go wrong, men go right after them") to the inspired mayhem of the Marx Brothers in *Duck Soup, Animal Crackers,* and *A Night at the Opera*. There were working-girl comedies, like *She Married Her Boss*, family comedies, such as the Andy Hardy series, and screwball comedies, like Howard Hawks's *Bringing Up Baby*. All had happy endings.

The biggest movie year of all, 1939, saw two all-time masterpieces. One was *The Wizard of Oz*. The other, *Gone With the Wind,* should have been a disaster. The producer, David O. Selznick, auditioned 1,400 actresses for the role of Confederate belle Scarlett O'Hara including such notables as Joan Crawford and Tallulah Bankhead, then chose virtually unknown Vivien Leigh, who was British. Production gobbled up three directors, a stable of screenwriters, and a colossal $4,250,000. Nobody knew if audiences would sit through a film lasting nearly four hours, more than twice the usual length. Nor could anyone predict the reaction when Clark Gable, as dashing Rhett Butler, delivered his censorship-defying line, "Frankly, my dear, I don't give a damn!" Some 300,000 people turned out for the Atlanta premiere, and everybody loved it. Like Scarlett herself, the audience seemed to feel that no adversity was painful enough to break one's spirit.

Swedish-born Greta Garbo starred in Queen Christina, about Sweden's 17th-century monarch.

Walt Disney's 1937 Snow White and the Seven Dwarfs *(above) was the first full-length animated film ever. In* Bringing Up Baby *(right), Cary Grant and Katharine Hepburn played nursemaids to a pet leopard.*

▶

Clark Gable and Vivien Leigh burned up the screen in Gone With the Wind, *the decade's most talked-about film.*

The Shadow, which made its radio debut in 1930 and ran for 24 years, inspired many fan clubs and this pulp magazine.

LISTENING IN

ON THE AIR

Imagine, in the depths of the Depression, the magic of live radio shows starring Fred Allen, Bing Crosby, Lily Pons, Orson Welles, Kate Smith, Edgar Bergen, Duke Ellington, Gracie Allen, Arturo Toscanini, and many more.

Their pocketbooks may have been hurting, but North Americans had never enjoyed a more richly varied fare of entertainment than they did in the 1930's. It was the golden age of radio. By the end of the decade, 85 percent of the U.S. population and around 78 percent of Canadians owned a radio and thrilled to the news, sports, and entertainment that came "free" to their living rooms. The industry had become the most pervasive medium of communications ever.

Daytime listeners found companionship and vicarious romance in the serials — later known as soap operas because of their sponsors — that dominated early afternoon hours five days a week. One of the longest lasting, *The Romance of Helen Trent,* for 27 years posed the same question: "Can a woman over 35 find romance?"

Youngsters hurried home from school to tune in to their favorite adventure shows, such as *Buck Rogers in the 25th Century, Jack Armstrong, the All-American Boy,* and *Tom Mix and the Ralston Straightshooters.* Audiences not only listened, they also bought sponsors' products and mailed off the proof-of-purchase to collect the freebies offered to boost sales: a Green Hornet ring or a Captain Midnight code-o-graph.

Westerns, like *The Lone Ranger,* and mysteries, like *The Shadow,* were among the not-to-be-missed evening radio dramas. And listeners of all ages sat transfixed waiting for the masked rider's stirring shout of "Hi-yo, Silver!" and the phantom avenger's spine-tingling question, "Who knows what evil lurks in the hearts of men?"

The phenomenal success of *Amos 'n' Andy* had demonstrated to network executives, and to advertisers, that tickling the funny bone could be as profitable for them as it was pleasing to the public. In just three years after its debut in 1928, the show had become an institution, with some 42 million listeners tuning in for a ritual 15-minute dose of belly laughs from 7:00 to 7:15 P.M. every weekday. The show's white creators, Freeman Gosden and Charles Correll, might be drummed off the air today for portraying offensive racial stereotypes, but in the 1930's they were national icons.

The show's success inspired a proliferation of comedies starring former vaudevillians. Raspy-voiced George Burns smoked a cigar and played the straight man to scatterbrained Gracie Allen as she searched for an imaginary lost brother. Jack Benny parlayed his reputation as the stingiest man in the world into an enormously successful radio career, to the accompaniment of "Love in Bloom" squeaked out on his violin. Ventriloquist Edgar Bergen and his devilishly feisty dummy Charlie McCarthy exchanged caustic

On CBS, "Doctor" George Burns says to Gracie Allen: "This won't hurt because there's no sense. There's no feeling."

Jack Benny (left) and Fred Allen spent years hilariously feigning a fierce on-the-air feud.

Edgar Bergen and his dummy Charlie McCarthy appeared on NBC's Chase and Sanborn Hour on Sunday evenings.

banter with each other and a parade of celebrity guest performers.

Almost as popular as the comedy shows were musical programs featuring an incredible variety of styles and stars. Bing Crosby, Kate Smith, Lawrence Tibbett, and Lily Pons all sang. Bandleaders Paul Whiteman and Guy Lombardo conducted their pop orchestras. Weekly broadcasts of grand opera emanated from the Metropolitan Opera House in New York, where such eminent symphonic conductors as Arturo Toscanini wielded their batons.

All these programs were as popular in Canada as in the United States — so much so that attendance at Sunday evening church services wavered. But their popularity posed two questions. The first concerned commercialization. Were the airwaves — a valuable resource — simply to be handed over to advertisers as a sort of giant billboard? The second question arose from Canada's geography. Most Canadians lived within 150 kilometres of the border, within easy reach of major American centres, but distant from each other. American networks — which meant American news, perspectives and values — were smothering Canadian interests on the radio. But Canadians were too thinly spread to make a domestic commercial network viable.

The answer came in 1932 when the Bennett government established the Canadian Radio Broadcasting Commission to regulate a mix of private and public broadcasting. In 1936, Mackenzie King's Liberals added a public network, the Canadian Broadcasting Corporation, to be supported by licence fees for home radios. The CBC was especially important in saving both French and English theatre in Canada. Serious drama became available to Canadian listeners with

Surrender, Earthlings!

The Mercury Theatre had been on the air only a few months and had no sponsor. Orson Welles, the show's talented 23-year-old producer, was hardly a household name. But the show he planned for the evening of October 30, 1938, would change that forever. Welles announced that it was an adaptation of a book, *The War of the Worlds,* by H. G. Wells. But many people were listening to Edgar Bergen and Charlie McCarthy and tuned in late. All they heard was dance music interrupted by "news flashes" reporting the invasion of armed Martians. The fantasy became reality to Americans made jumpy by daily broadcasts of the crisis in Europe. Orson Welles's prank set off a panic. People called the police, packed their bags, or simply huddled at home, terror-stricken. Welles issued an apology, WCBS announced repeatedly that it had been a hoax, and by the next day nearly all that remained was a recognition of the stunning power of radio.

as many as 17 plays a week, starting with Merrill Dennison's historical *Romance of Canada* series, and CKAC's serial novel *Les Chercheurs d'Or*. With the creation of the CBC, Canadians would share, as they always had, the American experience, but they would also continue to blend and balance it with their own.

Glenn Miller kept his fans coming back for more with hits such as "Little Brown Jug," "In the Mood," and his signature song "Moonlight Serenade."

Bandleader Kay Kyser combined music and quiz show formats on his Kollege of Musical Knowledge.

◄ Duke Ellington's extraordinary musical abilities first attracted widespread acclaim in Harlem's Cotton Club from 1927 to 1932.

▼ Benny Goodman's virtuoso clarinet and crowd-pleasing renditions of familiar tunes earned him the title "King of Swing."

CHAMPIONS IN BODY AND SPIRIT

Big changes were in the air, and many of the era's most-gifted athletes faced challenges that had nothing to do with how well they played their game.

Every decade has its harbingers of things to come, but in sports the 1930's had more than their share of portentous events and significant beginnings. Increasingly, professional athletes caught the scent of more money to be made. The odious "color line" was still in place — even (if in a more subtle way) in Canada where black athletes had been squeezed out of most major sports in the 1910's. A rare exception was Sam Richardson of Toronto, who ran for the Canadian relay team in the 1936 Olympics.

Mildred Ella (Babe) Didrikson, perhaps the greatest woman athlete ever, outperformed most men in baseball, basketball, billiards, diving, swimming, and tennis. She electrified women's track and field (right). Then, still in her early twenties, she turned to golf. She was the dominant woman player for 20 years, courageously winning the 1954 U.S. Women's Open just a year after surgery for the cancer that killed her two years later. Along the way, she married a genial giant of a wrestler named George Zaharias.

Meanwhile, the other phenomenal Babe, from whom Didrikson's fans had borrowed her nickname, was

◄ Sam Richardson, of Toronto, one of Canada's first black athletes, crouches ready for the starter pistol and a 60-yard (55-metre) dash, in 1937.

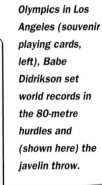

At the 1932 Olympics in Los Angeles (souvenir playing cards, left), Babe Didrikson set world records in the 80-metre hurdles and (shown here) the javelin throw.

pushing his employers to pay him what he thought he was worth. When the Yankee owners grudgingly gave Ruth a 1931 salary of $80,000, more than President Hoover made, the Babe tried to defuse accusations of ungentlemanly avarice by pointing out, "I had a better year than the president." True. When Hoover threw out the first ball in the 1931 World Series, fans booed the man most blamed for the Depression.

In other sports, too, there were hints of the big money to come for athletes. Playing more than 80 tennis matches on a 1938 tour, Fred Perry and Ellsworth Vines earned $34,000 each, a princely sum in those days.

Salaries were much lower in hockey where the National Hockey League took advantage of its monopoly to keep them low. Even Lionel Conacher, who starred at football, hockey, baseball and lacrosse, and who boxed three rounds with Jack Dempsey, had to suffer the league's parsimony. Salaries in Canadian football, with its mixture of college and amateur teams, also remained low; but change was on the way. In 1931, Montreal's "amateur" team hired an American quarterback. Warren Stevens threw the first forward passes in Canadian football and won the Grey Cup for Montreal. Winnipeg responded in 1935 by hiring nine

The Commercial Graduates Basketball Club (or the Edmonton Grads), photographed here in 1936, reigned supreme in women's basketball from 1915 to 1940. They won more than 90 percent of the games they played internationally as well as at home in Canada.

▶ Hank Luisetti's one-handed shot helped him score 50 points in a 1937 game for Stanford.

Lionel Conacher (1902–54) was Canada's greatest all-round athlete. The Big Train could run 90 metres in 10 seconds, and in 1921 scored 15 points for the Toronto Argonauts in a 23–0 win over Edmonton.

▼ Olympic gold medals in 1928, 1932, and 1936 propelled Norwegian skater Sonja Henie to Hollywood stardom.

▲ Avenging an earlier defeat, Joe Louis leaves a down-and-out Max Schmeling on the mat after only 2 minutes and 4 seconds of the first round in their second fight, in 1938.

Americans for a total of $7,500 to win its own Grey cup, the first for the West.

Boxer Lefty Gwynne, who won an Olympic gold medal in 1932, was among the few successful Canadian amateur athletes of the 1930's (the other exceptions were the Edmonton Grads and various hockey players). In boxing, however, as in most other sports, centre stage belonged to the professionals, particularly an Alabama native, Joe Louis. The Brown Bomber turned professional in 1934 at the age of 20. In 1937 he won the world heavyweight championship by knocking out James J. Braddock in eight rounds.

The year before, Max Schmeling had knocked out Louis in the 12th round. After that bout Schmeling sneered: "He fought like an amateur. This is no man who could ever be champion." But in 1938 Louis devastated the German heavyweight and humiliated Nazi Germany, which had made Schmeling a symbol of Aryan superiority.

A similar scenario had unfolded at the 1936 Olympics in Berlin, where Nazi sympathizers disparaged the black superathlete Jesse Owens. He burst their balloon of racist hot air by taking four gold medals.

▶ Fans loved the David-and-Goliath script when upstart Don Budge (left) beat old pros Fred Perry (middle) and Ellsworth Vines (right) in 1939.

ON STAGE: ROMP AND REALISM

Dorothy Stickney and Howard Lindsay starred in Life With Father, which set a Broadway record of 3,224 performances.

Luther Adler plays the boxer, and Art Smith, his manager, in Odets's Golden Boy (1937), about a prizefighter who wants to be a concert violinist.

When the sun went down, New York City's Times Square theatre district lit up the Depression-era sky, offering high-stepping musicals, sharp-edged comedy, and deep social relevance.

Broadway spoofed the classics in this musical based on Shakespeare's Comedy of Errors.

S atire," quipped playwright George S. Kaufman, "is what closes Saturday night." But for the worldly-wise audiences of the 1930's, satire played just fine. *Of Thee I Sing*, with songs by George and Ira Gershwin, was an uproarious musical parody of American politics, which opened in December 1931. A year later it was still running strong.

Even the most upbeat comic turns did not hesitate to touch on the issues of the day. Irving Berlin's revue *As Thousands Cheer* (1933) lampooned everyone from John D. Rockefeller to Paris sensation Josephine Baker. Increasingly, Broadway musicals reached toward the higher arts for inspiration. George Gershwin's *Porgy and Bess* (1935), a poignant story of poor blacks in the South, was a synthesis of folk, jazz, and operatic forms. Richard Rodgers and Lorenz Hart's *On Your Toes* (1936) featured dance sequences choreographed by ballet master George Balanchine. Another Rodgers and Hart show, *The Boys From Syracuse* (1938), took its plot right out of Shakespeare's *Comedy of Errors*.

Dramatic theatre addressed volatile topics. Maxwell Anderson's verse play *Winterset* (1935), based on the Sacco and Vanzetti case, took a hard look at the American justice system. The Southern sharecroppers portrayed in Erskine Caldwell's *Tobacco Road* (1933) were so true to life that one reviewer swore he detected the "smell of hot dust . . . and dried food leavings" wafting from the stage.

Some of the decade's most innovative stagings occurred beyond the glitter of Broadway. The Group Theatre, a privately funded repertory company, presented searching dramas, such as Clifford Odets's *Golden Boy* (1937). It also experimented with

A tap-dancing bevy of scantily clad chorines enlivens Cole Porter's Anything Goes, one of his best-remembered and most frequently staged musical confections.

audience participation. In Odets's *Waiting for Lefty* (1935), it transformed a Greenwich Village theatre into a meeting hall and the audience into taxi union members locked in a dispute with their bosses. Each performance closed with the taxi drivers chanting "Strike! Strike! Strike!"

But even in an age of confrontation, it was still possible to find old-fashioned escape. Clarence Day's *Life With Father* (1939) returned to simpler turn-of-the-century times. The essence of the period's escapist fare was Cole Porter's *Anything Goes* (1934), whose stellar cast, led by Ethel Merman, belted out such Porter gems as "You're the Top," "I Get a Kick Out of You," and the peerless title song. For a couple of hours, the show helped audiences to forget the Depression.

During the decade Broadway was home to three Canadian stars. Raymond Massey enjoyed the triumph of his career as

The cast of Tobacco Road brought the rural South to Broadway in controversial scenes that dealt frankly with issues of poverty, ignorance, and degradation.

Abe Lincoln in Illinois (1938), written by Robert Sherwood. Walter Huston played the dramatic lead in the stage version of Sinclair Lewis's *Dodsworth* (1934), and then took to the musical stage in Kurt Weill's *Knickerbocker Holiday* (1938), in which he sang "September Song." Brightest of all Broadway stars, Toronto-born Beatrice Lillie, enlivened glittering revues with her outrageous antics.

In Canada, bad times and the movies had curtailed theatrical activity by the 1930's. New York shows still played prominent theatres, such as Toronto's Royal Alexandra. Otherwise, Canadian theatre was dominated by well-established amateur groups, like the Montreal Repertory Theatre.

In the musical On Your Toes, George Balanchine's violent, erotic production number "Slaughter on Tenth Avenue," starring Ray Bolger, set a new standard of choreography for the Broadway stage.

On Your Toes

Todd Duncan and Anne Brown played the title roles in the tragic story of Porgy and Bess, hailed as "an American Folk Opera."

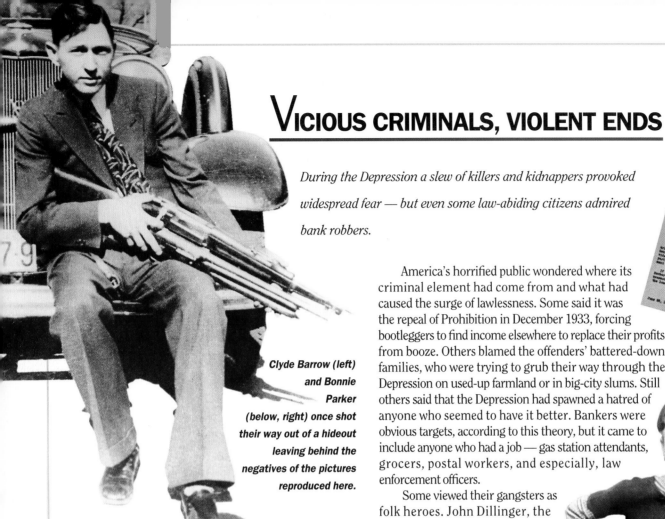

Vicious Criminals, Violent Ends

During the Depression a slew of killers and kidnappers provoked widespread fear — but even some law-abiding citizens admired bank robbers.

Clyde Barrow (left) and Bonnie Parker (below, right) once shot their way out of a hideout leaving behind the negatives of the pictures reproduced here.

WANTED

JOHN HERBERT DILLINGER

$10,000.00
$5,000.00

▲ **Murders, bank robberies, and jailbreaks made John Dillinger Public Enemy Number One in the United States, with both state and federal governments offering rewards.**

America's horrified public wondered where its criminal element had come from and what had caused the surge of lawlessness. Some said it was the repeal of Prohibition in December 1933, forcing bootleggers to find income elsewhere to replace their profits from booze. Others blamed the offenders' battered-down families, who were trying to grub their way through the Depression on used-up farmland or in big-city slums. Still others said that the Depression had spawned a hatred of anyone who seemed to have it better. Bankers were obvious targets, according to this theory, but it came to include anyone who had a job — gas station attendants, grocers, postal workers, and especially, law enforcement officers.

Some viewed their gangsters as folk heroes. John Dillinger, the most notorious of the bank thieves, was to many a modern-day Robin Hood. Dillinger's flair for the dramatic made some people forget that he had killed at least 10 people. His gang once posed as a movie company on location in front of a Sioux Falls bank. While thousands milled around hoping to catch a glimpse of a real star, real criminals, posing as movie actors, robbed the bank. After a nationwide manhunt, federal agents, tipped off by the madam of a brothel, shot down Public Enemy Number One in July 1934 outside a Chicago movie theatre.

Most of the big-name criminals from those years died as violently and as publicly as John Dillinger had. The lives of the infamous Bonnie and Clyde ended when they drove into an ambush. Going 135 kilometres an hour, the car careened out of control as their bodies absorbed more

As if the Depression were not misery enough, many Americans felt that their nation had become a hotbed of heinous criminal acts. Early in the decade came the repugnant kidnapping and death of little Charles Lindbergh, Jr. (see box, next page), and there seemed to be no stopping the epidemic of kidnappings, bank robberies, and gruesome murders all over the country. Measured by murders per size of population, the United States led the world in homicide.

In Canada murder actually declined, from 182 murders in 1929 to 124 a decade later. Nonetheless, the size of the prison population increased spectacularly at the depth of the Depression, in 1932 and 1933. Much of this increase was due to the detainment of more than 550 radical Doukhobors, whose potential for violence was feared by Canadian authorities. The only other increase in crime of note was in robbery without violence, which rose by some 20 percent. But on the whole, there was nothing like the crime that swept the United States.

This mug shot of Pretty Boy Floyd was taken when police arrested him for vagrancy in 1929.

Ma Barker — thief, kidnapper, and murderer — enjoys a peaceful moment with lover Arthur Dunlop. Insets: The sons she raised in her image, Dock (left) and Freddie (right).

than 50 bullets. Bonnie Parker, a 23-year-old tough-talking, cigar-smoking, quick-shooting former waitress from Kansas City, and her 24-year-old Texas-born lover, Clyde Barrow, had sped through the Southwest knocking off small-town banks, grocery stores, and gas stations. The lawless pair made a lark of their crimes, snapping souvenir photos of themselves and murdering passersby and law officers indiscriminately. Some 12 firearms, including 3 submachine guns were found in Bonnie and Clyde's car after they were killed.

Charles (Pretty Boy) Floyd succeeded John Dillinger as Public Enemy Number One. He robbed so many banks that the insurance rates doubled in just one year. The machine gun was his weapon of choice; for a while he even had one mounted on his car. His nickname, which he thoroughly

detested, was said to have been supplied by an admiring Kansas City bordello madam. Floyd met his demise in October 1934 when he was chased down by a 100-man posse.

Baby Face Nelson, who wanted to be known as Big George and who had always resented the fact that he never got as much media attention as his onetime partner, John Dillinger, became the next Public Enemy Number One. When federal agents finally cornered him, Nelson killed two of them, staggered back to the G-men's car with 17 slugs in his body, and made a getaway with his wife and another gangster. That evening, they tossed his dead, naked body into a ditch, where it was found the next day.

For matrimonial devotion, however, George Barker is unsurpassed in gangster lore. The 55-year-old Ma Barker left her plodding husband, George, so that she could wheel and deal to get her remaining two sons out of prison. (One had already committed suicide.) Once out, sons Freddie and Dock moved in with Ma and her new lover and took to robbing banks and kidnapping wealthy men. They were fabulously successful at both ventures: one bank job netted $250,000, and the ransom for a banker came in at $200,000. In January 1935 Ma and her son Freddie were killed in a six-hour machine-gun battle with federal agents. Her spurned husband had their bodies — and those of his other sons — returned to Welch, Oklahoma, and buried each of them within sight of his gas station there.

The Crime of the Century

Kidnappings increased at a frightening rate as the Depression deepened; in Chicago alone police logged some 200 in 1930 and 1931. But the abduction of the 20-month-old son of Anne and Charles Lindbergh (right) in March 1932 shocked the nation and aroused Congress to make kidnapping a federal offence. The press swooped down in droves, and the carnival atmosphere added to the Lindberghs' suffering. After the baby was taken from his home in New Jersey, investigators found a ransom note with Germanic misspellings. Two weeks later a retired Bronx teacher claimed to have contacted the kidnapper and agreed to pass along the $50,000 in demanded ransom. Lindbergh paid, but the baby was not returned. Police questioned suspects all over the country, to no avail. Every so often a ransom bill turned up, but no one could trace the source. In May truckers found the baby dead in the woods near the Lindbergh estate. More than two years passed before police arrested Bruno Richard Hauptmann (left), a Bronx carpenter with a record of petty crime in Germany. Hauptmann claimed he was innocent; when some of the ransom money was found in his garage, he said a friend had left it there. Hauptmann was tried in Flemington, New Jersey, a small town overrun by souvenir hawkers, curiosity seekers, and the press. The macabre circus ended when the jury of eight men and four women found him guilty. Hauptmann, still swearing his innocence, went to the electric chair on April 3, 1936, even though a confession would have saved him.

▶

J. Edgar Hoover's campaign to make the FBI America's premier crime-fighting force included these 1935 publicity shots. A G-man tests a submachine gun in the bureau's soundproof underground shooting range, and scientific sleuths inspect evidence in the FBI crime laboratory.

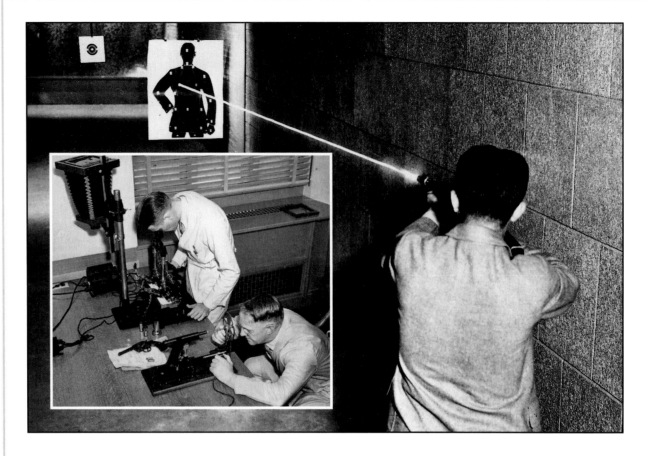

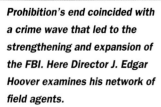

Prohibition's end coincided with a crime wave that led to the strengthening and expansion of the FBI. Here Director J. Edgar Hoover examines his network of field agents.

LAW AND ORDER

Canada spruced up its Royal Canadian Mounted Police, making it bigger, more effective, and more modern, while J. Edgar Hoover turned the FBI into a national crime-busting force with muscle.

In 1920, the Royal Canadian Mounted Police was created from a merger of the North West Mounted Police with the smaller Dominion Police. At that time, it was still a force that maintained order in mining camps and solved disputes in remote trading posts. But in the years that followed, on the instructions of governments fearful of a communist revolution in Canada, it was kept busy investigating suspected subversives. Then, in 1931, Brig. Gen. Sir James H. MacBrien was appointed commissioner to rebuild the force so that it could take on a range of more conventional police duties.

He established a crime laboratory and upgraded the scientific training of officers. Starting with 1,350 men, he enlarged the force by a thousand. Then, he contracted with Alberta, Manitoba, New Brunswick, Nova Scotia and Prince Edward Island to take on the policing of the provinces and many of their smaller towns. By the end of the decade, the RCMP had more to do with highway patrols and laboratories than it did with the frontier.

In the United States, there was no such thing as a national police force, but the dramatic crime wave sweeping the nation demanded action. It came — with all guns firing — from the little-known Bureau of Investigation within the Department of Justice. The bureau was headed by J. Edgar Hoover, who had been appointed in 1924 at the age of 29. He brought the management style of a martinet to the bureau — and he introduced tools of modern detection. By

1930 he had a file of 3 million fingerprints and had established a crime laboratory to evaluate evidence. But the bureau's jurisdiction was still limited to glamorless investigative donkeywork, such as tracking down perpetrators of federal bank frauds or violators of the act that prohibited transporting women across state or national boundaries for immoral purposes. Agents were not even authorized to make arrests or to carry firearms.

Then, Congress passed a law making kidnapping across state lines a federal crime. In addition, robberies of national banks, assaults on federal officers, and many other crimes involving interstate felonies became federal offences. Federal agents finally got permission to carry guns and make arrests. Hoover, once admiringly described by a reporter as a "sledgehammer in search of an anvil," had created a department ready for its new responsibilities.

Moving fast, Hoover's bureau compiled a list of 6,000 gangsters and suspicious persons, and it elevated a few to a new and highly publicized Public Enemies List. The bureau's agents were in on the capture or killing of the era's most notorious criminals: John Dillinger, Pretty Boy Floyd, Baby Face Nelson, Ma Barker and one of her boys, and more. By early 1935 Hoover and his agents — now known as G-men; the G for *government* — were very much admired. By the end of that year the bureau had been renamed the Federal Bureau of Investigation (FBI), and its members had become folk heroes.

How a Legend Grew and Grew

Hollywood is what made the difference. Its mythmakers zoomed in on gangster cases, and on the FBI, and turned them into popular entertainment. The first movie, *G-Men,* starred James Cagney, and it was a box office knockout. Quickly absorbing this lesson in the value of publicity, Hoover involved himself in the launching of a new comic strip, a radio show, and pulp magazines like *G-Men* and *The Feds.* All pushed the bureau as the model of clean-cut virtue and scientific efficiency, and Hoover as a model director. FBI communications with the media emphasized that the director was in personal charge of every important investigation. To publicize his starring role, Hoover began showing up at the capture of high-profile criminals and talking to the press afterward.

As success piled upon success, the FBI gained more muscle. In 1935 Hoover started the National Police Academy, a training school for local police officers from across the country. In 1936 FDR gave Hoover a mandate to seek out subversives deemed to be threatening national security.

As the bureau grew dramatically in size and prestige, more and more people saw the director as a man who could do no wrong. Tracking down a bank robber and his wife in New York City, Hoover shooed away city police while he and a squad of 25 G-men poured gunfire, then tear gas, into the fugitive's apartment. He defended his actions by saying, "The taxpayers got what they paid for, the apprehension of criminals." By the end of the decade, some were complaining that Hoover's dictatorial methods had become a serious problem — but Hoover's skilful use of publicity had already made him untouchable.

Melvin Purvis led the team of agents that killed John Dillinger. After a falling-out with Hoover, he left the FBI and did promotional work, like this how-to-fight-crime manual for Post Toasties.

▼ **The Boys Clubs of America presented "Public Hero Number One" their Distinguished Service Medal in 1936.**

Thousands of Junior G-Men (Melvin Purvis's club for kids) aspired to become the topflight, clean-cut professionally trained crime buster this photo publicized.

TOUGH BOSSES, TOUGH WORKERS

After years of unrest marked by more than 20,000 strikes, bloodshed, and seemingly endless setbacks, the labor movement rebounded in North America.

Organized labor suffered a near fatal blow during the Depression. High unemployment decimated membership ranks and permitted employers to fire workers with impunity. In the United States, unions, organized by craft and skill in the American Federation of Labor (AFL), had begun to lose the confidence of many of their rank-and-file members.

A number of laborers actually worked at gunpoint. Richard B. Mellon, chairman of the Pittsburgh Coal Company, told Congress in 1928 why he kept machine guns in the coal pits: "You cannot run the mines without them." Congress apparently agreed. Many employers spent huge sums hiring spies and goons to weed out union troublemakers. And organized protests were routinely squelched by local authorities.

New Weapon: The Sit-down Strike

Championing the workers' cause in the United States was a 1.8-metre mountain of a man of Welsh descent, John L.

A toddler is among the children of autoworkers who staged a parade calling for improved working conditions in 1937.

In May 1937, police attack protesters near the Republic Steel plant in South Chicago. Inset: In April 1937, 4,000 workers at General Motors in Oshawa went on strike for two weeks, demanding improved working conditions and union recognition.

Lewis. Lewis drove a Cadillac and wore custom-made underwear, but he used his booming voice and biblical oratory to fight uncompromisingly for the United Mine Workers (UMW). He saw to it that he was always photographed scowling; to be seen smiling might indicate softness.

Toughness paid off. Lewis won for the UMW "all the things deputy sheriffs usually shot people for demanding," a magazine wrote. In late 1935 Lewis, along with such progressive union leaders as David Dubinsky and Sidney Hillman, united skilled and unskilled workers on an industry-wide basis in the Congress of Industrial Organizations (CIO).

The CIO's big test came at the end of 1936. Newly organized autoworkers in a General Motors plant simply stopped working and sat down. It was the first sit-down strike in the United States, and its leaders included Walter P. Reuther, who would remain a force in the labor movement until his death in 1970, and his brother Victor, who later outlined the conditions that faced the Flint strikers: "Flint's mayor, chief of police, clergy, newspapers, and even its judges were under the thumb of General Motors." The strike spread: 60 plants in 14 states were affected. The strikers in Flint hung on for 44 days. Victory came when GM agreed to recognize and bargain with the United Automobile Workers (UAW) in all 60 plants.

New Target: The Steel Industry

Lewis's next target was United States Steel. The average steelworker earned $369 per year, and most steelworkers were part-time. Safety conditions were deplorable: in a single year more than 200 workers were killed, more than 1,000 permanently disabled, and more than 21,000 temporarily laid up. Lewis believed that if he won over U.S. Steel, other steel companies would follow. "If the crouching lion can be routed, it is a safe bet that the hyenas in the adjacent bush may be scattered along the plain." Surprisingly the chairman of U.S. Steel agreed, without a fight, to sign a contract with the CIO.

Other steel companies were not so easily won over. On Memorial Day, 1937, some 1,500 workers, with their wives and children, gathered for a demonstration outside the Republic Steel plant. A doctor described it as "simply a family picnic sort of thing: little kids, people dressed up in their Sunday shirts." But the picnic ended when 150 cops attacked the

▼ *After a bitter and debilitating power struggle, which lasted for nearly 20 years, the AFL and the CIO would merge in 1955.*

crowd with tear gas, nightsticks, and guns. Within 15 minutes, 10 demonstrators lay dead and more than 100 were wounded.

Trouble had already been brewing in Canada where workers lacked any legal right to collective bargaining, and employers preferred to deal with powerless worker committees. Ontario Premier Mitch Hepburn intended to keep it that way — by force if necessary. When foundry workers in Sarnia staged a sit-down strike in 1937, some people took the law into their own hands, beating up strikers with baseball bats. Premier Hepburn said, "My sympathies are with those who beat the strikers."

In that same year, GM announced that, despite a rise in profits, it would cut wages and speed up the assembly line. Four thousand employees promptly signed up with the CIO and, when GM refused to recognize the union, they walked out.

Premier Hepburn was as determined as the company to break the union, partly because he feared unionism would spread to the province's mines. In a series of inflammatory statements, he branded the union leaders radical foreigners who took money from Canadian boys. Then, he asked the federal government to send in RCMP officers. But there had been no violence to justify such a mustering of strength, and Ottawa was nervous at Hepburn's eagerness for violence. When they refused to send as many police as Hepburn wanted, he formed his own squad of 400 "specials." Strikers called them "Sons of Mitches." No thanks to Hepburn, the strike was settled when GM capitulated to all the workers' requests except recognition of their union. But his strong-arm tactics had polarized the province.

Public opinion across the continent was turning against government- and management-sponsored violence. In the United States, union membership more than doubled in the decade, as it would in Canada through the 1940's and 1950's. Politicians at all levels had to take notice of the power of organized labor.

◄

Jailed in Russian Poland for union activity, David Dubinsky escaped to America in 1911. As head of the International Ladies' Garment Workers' Union (1932–66), he helped launch the CIO but left it and rejoined the AFL in 1940.

LANDSLIDE FOR THE NEW DEAL

Roosevelt's opponents in 1936 ranged from financiers to communists, but he still won 60 percent of the popular vote. In Canada, the right did better politically — if not economically.

FDR and Eleanor stump together in Kansas City (top); often in 1936 they campaigned separately. The opposition, meanwhile, struck back hard, as in the cartoon above, which appeared on the cover of a satiric anti–New Deal pamphlet.

The American presidential election of 1936 was bitterly fought, and its lopsided result marked a smashing personal triumph for the Democratic incumbent. From the beginning President Roosevelt knew the campaign would hinge on how people felt about him: "There is only one issue in this campaign," he told an adviser. "It's myself, and the people must be either for me or against me."

The people against FDR were easy enough to spot. The millionaire John Pierpont Morgan, Jr. absolutely prohibited FDR's name from being mentioned in his house. When FDR visited Harvard, his (and Morgan's) alma mater, the president was booed by students and alumni who believed he had turned his back on his social class.

On the far right, Father Charles E. Coughlin, a Roman Catholic priest who had launched his own political party, railed against communists, Jews, capitalists, and "Franklin Double-Crossing Roosevelt" on national radio. On the left,

Financier J. P. Morgan epitomized the upper-class enmity toward Roosevelt and his programs.

Social Security

When in June 1934 President Roosevelt set up a committee, chaired by Secretary of Labor Frances Perkins, to study economic security, he told her that "there's no reason why everybody in the United States should not be covered . . . from the cradle to the grave." Perkins didn't think politicians would pass something so comprehensive, even though most European countries had done so a generation earlier. The Social Security Act authorized welfare payments and set up insurance for the aged, unemployed, and disabled. It was meant to supplement personal savings and private pension plans and covered about half the work force. Businessmen fought hard against a bill they felt would destroy initiative and discourage thrift. The left condemned it as too conservative and charged FDR with selling out to big business. In August 1935 the bill passed — and passed overwhelmingly. Few congressmen wanted to go on record as being against the interests of older people. The law signalled acknowledgment by the federal government that it had a responsibility for the everyday well-being of senior citizens. FDR had insisted that the program be funded by equal worker and employer contributions because he thought that future administrations would thus have a harder time taking away benefits. The initial payroll deduction was 1 percent of a worker's wages up to $3,000 per year.

In Canada, political change was not nearly as innovative as in the U.S. Bible Bill Aberhart's Social Credit Party won power in Alberta in 1935 but, instead of implementing its economic theories, it governed in the same conservative fashion as most Canadian governments. Similarly, Ontario's Mitch Hepburn and Quebec's Maurice Duplessis (whose Union Nationale won power in 1936) did little but attack "foreign" unionists and communists. In 1937, Duplessis introduced the Padlock Law which empowered the Attorney-General to close buildings used for communist purposes and to destroy communist literature. Since the law didn't define what "communist" meant, this gave the government wide powers of censorship over anything it didn't like.

In Ottawa, Mackenzie King's Liberals undertook two studies. A National Employment Commission report of 1938 recommended unemployment insurance to ease suffering. Two years later, the Royal Commission on Dominion-Provincial Relations recommended that Ottawa act much more forcefully in economic and social planning. Those reports came too late for the Depression, but they set the tone for decades to come.

▼ *Quebec Premier Maurice Duplessis (left) and Ontario Premier Mitch Hepburn (right) share an informal moment. Politically, they also shared an intense dislike of unionists and communists.*

Norman Thomas, the socialist candidate, told voters that only he could lead a revolution.

While many raised their voices to criticize Roosevelt, few could get excited about his Republican opponent, Alfred M. (Alf) Landon. A two-term governor of Kansas, Landon was described on the campaign trail as having "the unhappy look of a man who has just taken his seat in the dental chair for what is certain to be a long and painful ordeal."

But polls suggested that the contest was close, and Roosevelt remarked: "Never before in all our history have these forces been so united against one candidate as they stand today." When the real test came on election day, FDR won with 60 percent of the vote. He had put together a new coalition of voters: the urban working class, organized labor, farmers, and Southerners. For the first time in more than 40 years, the largest bloc of voters in the country considered themselves Democrats, not Republicans.

CLIPPING A PRESIDENT'S WINGS

With the New Deal flying high and his popularity soaring, FDR may have thought he was invincible. Then the Supreme Court nullified a key program, and the president responded with an audacious scheme to reshape the Court more to his liking.

Outraged
Democrats balked at FDR's
"innocent" Court-packing proposal.

▼ **Franklin D. Roosevelt, talking to reporters from his hand-controlled Ford, is brimming with confidence after some six years as president.**

For a while in 1935 it seemed as though the mighty Blue Eagle of Franklin D. Roosevelt's National Recovery Administration (NRA), the New Deal agency set up to regulate business and labor, would be brought down by a sick kosher chicken.

It all started with four brothers who ran a kosher poultry business in Brooklyn. After the NRA was passed, the Schechter brothers signed its Live Poultry Code, agreeing to pay a minimum wage, limit the number of hours for workers, and maintain a certain quality of chicken. In no time the brothers were indicted and convicted on 17 violations of the code, including selling a sick chicken for human consumption. Protesting their innocence, the Schechters carried their fight all the way to the Supreme Court.

A little after noon on a warm spring Monday, May 27, 1935, the white-whiskered 73-year-old Chief Justice Charles Evans Hughes read the high court's unanimous decision striking down the NRA as an unconstitutional infringement on the power of Congress by the president. "This is the end of this business of centralization, and I want you to go back and tell the president that we're not going to let this government centralize everything. It's come to an end," Justice Louis Brandeis told a Roosevelt aide.

President Roosevelt was livid. The Supreme Court had undercut a major program. Furthermore, upcoming decisions threatened the whole New Deal,

including Social Security and the Wagner labor law. He asked Attorney General Homer Cummings to prepare some alternative courses of action but waited until he was reelected in 1936 to do anything.

At his second inauguration he indicated that the New Deal was far from over: "I see one-third of a nation ill housed, ill clad, ill nourished," he said in his inaugural address. "The test of our progress . . . is whether we provide

▶

Two of the triumphant Schechter brothers hoist their lawyer, Joseph Heller, to celebrate their defeat of the NRA in the Supreme Court.

enough for those who have so little." Most people thought he meant to launch another attack on economic royalists. But Roosevelt had a different target in mind.

Just two weeks later FDR held his annual dinner for the federal judiciary at the White House. It was a pleasant evening, without a hint that he had big plans for changing the Court. Two days later Roosevelt presented his plan to key members of Congress: for every Supreme Court justice who failed to retire after 70, the president wanted to appoint a new justice, up to a total of six. With the addition of six new liberal justices, the conservative anti–New Deal majority on the Court would be smashed. FDR presented this as an "efficiency" measure to help the aged justices with their heavy work load. But it was immediately obvious that the measure was actually aimed at packing the Court in his favor. After winning the greatest landslide in U.S. history, FDR figured he was unstoppable. But he soon learned otherwise.

His New Deal coalition began to crumble. Vice President John Nance Garner came out against the plan; 79-year-old Senator Carter Glass of Virginia resented the implication that a man was washed up at 70. Chief Justice Hughes took the extraordinary step of writing a letter to Congress stating that more justices would actually increase their work load: "There would be more judges to hear, more judges to confer, more judges to discuss, more judges to be convinced and to decide."

FDR continued pushing the plan even as it lost popular support. But as Hugh Johnson, former head of the NRA, noted: "The old Roosevelt magic has lost its kick. . . . The diverse elements in his Falstaffian army can no longer be

Her Song Is Heard

They came from all walks of life: young and old, black and white, rich and poor. On that Easter Sunday, April 9, 1939, they gathered 75,000 strong around the steps of the Lincoln Memorial to hear the African-American contralto Marian Anderson. For many in the crowd, her concert represented a triumph for racial tolerance. Earlier that year, she had been denied the use of Constitution Hall, a building owned by the Daughters of the American Revolution (DAR), for a performance. Suspecting bigotry, some members of the DAR, most notably Eleanor Roosevelt, resigned. Then Anderson's backers had a brilliant idea: let her sing at the Lincoln Memorial. And there, from the moment she began to sing "My country! 'tis of thee!" Marian Anderson became a symbol of racial justice.

kept together and led by a melodious whinny and a winning smile." It wasn't that the president had lost popularity; he hadn't. But Congress and the public resented what appeared to be a power-grabbing scheme by the president.

Ironically, the justices themselves reversed course and upheld other key elements of the New Deal, such as Social Security, the Wagner Act, and a state minimum wage law. Later the president liked to say that he had lost the battle but won the war since he got what he wanted from the Court. But never again would Congress support him without question. And his next years were marked by a recession and high unemployment, which topped 19 percent in 1938.

The national debate shifted, focusing increasingly on tensions in Europe and Asia and on what, if anything, the United States should do. Roosevelt surprised much of the nation when he decided to try for an unprecedented third term in 1940. The threat of war and Roosevelt's desire to be succeeded by a liberal Democrat (the major contenders for the nomination were conservative) influenced his decision. His Republican opponent, Wendell Willkie, a utility executive with no political experience, attacked the New Deal. He charged that interfering with business had not returned the nation to prosperity. Toward the end of the campaign, Willkie even labelled FDR a warmonger. But the president assured the country: "Your boys are not going to be sent into any foreign wars." Although the New Deal had been floundering, FDR was still personally popular, and perhaps the country wanted someone they knew for the troubled times ahead. When the ballots were counted, Roosevelt had won convincingly, 27 million votes to Willkie's 22 million.

Wendell Willkie, here campaigning in Jersey City, attacked FDR's bid for a third term with slogans like "No man is good three times" and "No crown for Franklin."

GOING PLACES AS NEVER BEFORE

In spite of the Depression — some said because of it — the adventurous, rich and poor, expanded their travel

horizons in ways that were almost always faster, sometimes cheaper, and often riskier.

Charles Lindbergh had become an emblem of optimism and adventure in the late 1920's. If he could hop in an airplane and fly from New York to Paris all by himself, then there was nothing that couldn't be done. The Depression dealt this optimistic outlook a body blow, but a few gallant, and well-heeled, aerial pioneers continued to push the limits of how far we could go and how fast — and became instant heroes.

Wiley Post, a one-eyed ex-oilman and parachute jumper, be-came a hero when he and his navigator circled the globe in the record time of 8 days, 15 hours, and 51 minutes in 1931. Two years later, equipped with a radio navigational device and an autopilot to help him fly the plane, Post became the first person to fly around the world alone. And this time he did it in less than eight days. A shocked nation mourned in 1935 when he and his friend Will Rogers died in a plane crash in Alaska. The quest for records cost a number of aviators their lives. Amelia Earhart, or Lady Lindy as she was known to her adoring public, became the first woman to fly solo across the Atlantic, in 1932; but she disappeared five

When completed in 1931, the George Washington Bridge, here being built, joined New Jersey and New York City. The economical 1939 Crosley (left) promised 4 litres per 100 kilometres (60 miles per gallon).

Airship Tragedy

For wealthy travellers in the 1930's, nothing rivalled the luxurious airships built by Germany's Zeppelin Company. The *Hindenburg*, flagship of the new "average traveller's" fleet, could reach about 120 kph and had 25 passenger cabins, complete with hot and cold running water. Leaving Frankfurt on May 3, 1937, it had 36 passengers and 61 crew members. Due at Lakehurst, New Jersey, at 6 A.M. on May 6, the *Hindenburg* was delayed by head winds and was just passing over Times Square at 3:07 P.M. By 7 P.M. a ground crew of more than 200 and a large crowd eagerly awaited the arrival. Passengers first knew something was wrong when they saw people on the ground freeze and then run from the ship. Only 32 seconds elapsed from the first flame appearing in the stern to the bow hitting the earth. Miraculously, 62 people survived. But the horrifying photos, films, and radio broadcasts helped to doom passenger airships.

In 1937 a jaunty and very confident Amelia Earhart poses with her classic Cord convertible and the ill-fated twin-engine Lockheed Electra she planned to fly around the world.

Hoboes rode the rails for free in the 1930's. The postcard below touts a precursor of today's high-speed roads.

years later in the Pacific while attempting to circle the world at the Equator. A search by the navy — involving 4,000 men in 10 ships and 65 airplanes over 16 days — found nothing.

These kinds of tragedies led some to call for curbing risky flights; such grandstanding was senseless and discouraging to would-be passengers on the young domestic airlines. Discouraging, too, was the tiny, cramped space for passengers in most airliners. But in 1932 Trans World Airlines (TWA) engaged the Douglas Aircraft Company to design a plane more suitable for passengers than for cargo. The result was the Douglas Commercial-1 (DC-1). Its innovative wing flaps made landing slower, safer, and much smoother. Its design was further refined in the quicker, more comfortable DC-2. The DC-3, completed in 1935, became the most widely used plane of all time. By then, the airplane had become a national necessity. In 1937, Canada's parliament created Trans-Canada Airlines.

The ultimate in luxury liners was the Queen Mary, shown here in 1936. It was owned by Cunard–White Star, founded by Nova Scotian Samuel Cunard.

Of course, not many people were ready to try plane travel. Nor could many afford cruises on luxurious ocean liners like Canada's *Empress* ships, France's *Normandie*, and Britain's *Queen Mary,* which came into service in 1936 with carved wood interiors, hand-woven carpets, and silver fixtures. Even as the rich and famous patronized these "floating palaces," most folks travelled by train and car.

The cheapest way to travel was to steal a ride on a freight train: you didn't have to pay a thing, as long as the railroad bulls (police) didn't catch you. Almost anyone, of course, would have preferred to ride in an automobile.

Though car production fell 75 percent from 1929 to 1932, car registrations dropped just 10 percent. Manufacturers either adapted to lower demand or went bust. Particularly hard hit were makers of luxury cars, such as the Deusenberg, Stutz Bearcat, Pierce-Arrow, and air-cooled Franklin, none of which survived the Depression. By 1939 General Motors, Chrysler, and Ford made 90 percent of the cars in North America.

By the end of the decade, the continent had its first express tollway, running 256 kilometres from Harrisburg to Pittsburgh. It was distinguished, as were the many roads that followed, by two Canadian contributions. Highway numbering had already begun in 1920 in Manitoba. And in 1930, Ontario added the dotted lines that divide lanes. New as the automobile was, it had already started to change the North American landscape.

THE WORLD OF TOMORROW

The New York World's Fair glowed with visions of plenty, beauty, and social harmony, all brought within grasp by the wondrous alchemy of science and technology.

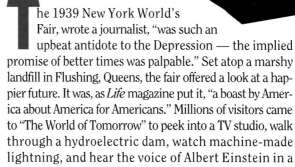

▲ **In 1939 New York's bold planner Robert Moses proposed a bridge connecting Manhattan's southern tip and Brooklyn. The project never got off the ground.**

The 1939 New York World's Fair, wrote a journalist, "was such an upbeat antidote to the Depression — the implied promise of better times was palpable." Set atop a marshy landfill in Flushing, Queens, the fair offered a look at a happier future. It was, as *Life* magazine put it, "a boast by America about America for Americans." Millions of visitors came to "The World of Tomorrow" to peek into a TV studio, walk through a hydroelectric dam, watch machine-made lightning, and hear the voice of Albert Einstein in a vivid sound-and-light show.

Sixty nations and more than 100 corporations participated in this monument to democracy and technology. Grover Whalen, the fair's president, dismissed mounting tensions in Europe and assured potential investors there would be no war: "Why, the king of Egypt told me positively that there'll be no war. . . . A wave of enthusiasm for our New York World's Fair is sweeping Europe. That's what Europe is thinking about, not war." Visitors came away believing in a not-too-distant future of 14-lane highways, air-conditioned high-rises towering over slum-free cities, a TV in every home, and a cancer cure. Many wore an "I Have Seen the Future" button after eyeballing General Motors's Futurama, Norman Bel Geddes's stunning conception of the landscape in 1960.

Industrial designers like Norman Bel Geddes (top) and Raymond Loewy (right) streamlined the look of the future. Above: Geddes applied the concept of aerodynamic streamlining to his models of buses and cars. Loewy came up with this design for a Pennsylvania Railroad train.

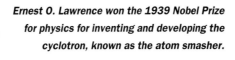

Even household objects took on the new sleek look. Walter Dorwin Teague designed this 1933 table radio; the clock's Art Deco style was enormously popular in the 1930's.

Frank Lloyd Wright (below), a genius who called his work organic architecture, was nearly 70 when he designed this innovative weekend retreat, called Fallingwater, for Pittsburgh department store owner Edgar Kaufmann in 1936.

▶

Ernest O. Lawrence won the 1939 Nobel Prize for physics for inventing and developing the cyclotron, known as the atom smasher.

Not far away, in midtown Manhattan, a project that would change the New York City landscape was nearing completion. Begun in 1931, Rockefeller Center was a complex of skyscrapers and shops, offices and services — a city within a city. Mayor Fiorello La Guardia's ambitious planner, Robert Moses, meanwhile, supervised the construction of a dozen new bridges and tunnels and several major highways, so that a motorist could drive nearly all around the congested city without stopping for a traffic light.

On the West Coast, engineer Joseph B. Strauss coordinated the construction of the remarkable Golden Gate Bridge in San Francisco, opened in 1937. Premier Duff Pattullo of British Columbia began work on Vancouver's spectacular Lions Gate Bridge, partly as a project to stimulate the economy. Meanwhile, in the stifling heat of the Nevada desert, thousands of men had worked to pour more than 6 million tonnes of concrete into Hoover Dam, the largest masonry structure built up to that time: 201 metres thick at its base, and nearly two-thirds as high as the Empire State

Building. In the Northwest, giant projects such as the enormous Grand Coulee Dam tamed the Columbia River.

Not only were dams and highways technological marvels, they also embodied the new sense of visual design that was sweeping the continent. The apostle of the futuristic look was a voluble industrial designer named Raymond Loewy, who preached the gospel of streamlining. Loewy smoothed the lines of the chunky Coldspot refrigerator for Sears, Roebuck, and sales quadrupled. He pioneered the shape of Studebaker cars, of Greyhound buses, of Pennsylvania Railroad trains, of ballpoint pens, and ocean liners.

Only a few of those who came to the World's Fair could see technology's full implications, however. One man who saw into the future was Albert Einstein. In the summer of 1939, after the World's Fair opened, he sent a letter to President Roosevelt urging the development of atomic energy, a pursuit that would soon give human beings a fearsome new force to reckon with.

▼ *A Union steamship sails beneath a section of the Lions Gate Bridge, Vancouver, under construction in 1938.*

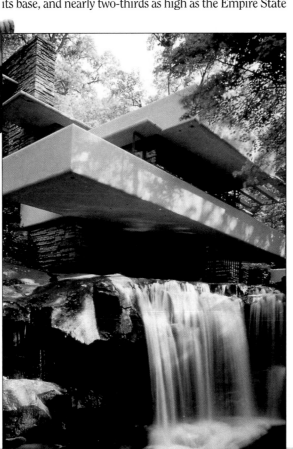

Buffalo ● 1901

The Lackawanna Railroad promoted its scenic route, along the Delaware River through the "gap" between New Jersey and Pennsylvania, to the Pan-American Exposition, whose aim was to further the prosperity of the Western Hemisphere.

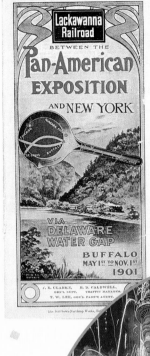

St. Louis ● 1904

Officially named the Louisiana Purchase Exposition in honor of President Thomas Jefferson's 1803 acquisition of 2,144,486 square kilometres of North America from France, the St. Louis world's fair spread over 502 hectares. Its theme was education.

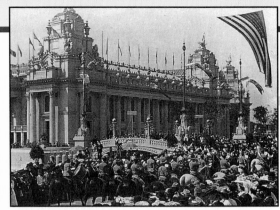

Every Year ● The 4th of July

Every American has a favorite way to celebrate America's birthday. These boys re-create the famous *Spirit of '76* by American painter Archibald Willard. Others go to a baseball game, have their annual extended family picnic, watch fireworks, and just enjoy being American.

GREAT CELEBRATIONS OF THE CENTURY

Just as nations seek world recognition, so do their cities — often in the form of festivities like fairs. More than just a show, the international fair is a sort of coming-of-age for a city, an announcement that it is now an adult. In the United States, this coming-of-age rite began with Buffalo's Pan-American Exposition in 1901. In Canada, it was Montreal that led the way with Expo 67. But wherever they were and whenever they were, they were memorable wingdings.

Tragedy clouded the first of the century's great fairs, when President McKinley was shot at the Buffalo exposition. But the United States bounced back three years later with a spectacle that convinced one wide-eyed New Yorker that St. Louis was no longer a backward prairie town. "The cascades and fountains were leaping in the still lagoon," 21-year-old Harper Silliman wrote his bride-to-be back in Massachusetts, and "I could almost imagine myself to be present at some great festival in Athens two or three thousand years ago." Such transcendent fantasies, whether of a glorious past or a fabulous future, are the common thread of the grand fairs and extravagant expositions remembered on these two pages.

San Francisco ● 1915

The Panama-Pacific International Exposition paid tribute to Balboa's reaching the Pacific in 1513, the Panama Canal's opening (1914), and San Francisco's recovery from the 1906 quake.

San Francisco World's Fair ● 1939
Visitors to the Golden Gate International Exposition could stroll the 304-metre-long Court of the Seven Seas (above), one of several avenues radiating from the 122-metre-tall Tower of the Sun in the background. This "Pageant of the Pacific" dedicated itself to world peace and brotherhood.

Chicago World's Fair ● 1933
The Windy City gave itself a 100th-birthday bash, celebrating "A Century of Progress" since the city's founding in 1833. In the depths of the Depression, the fair's upbeat themes drew 38.6 million people.

New York World's Fair ● 1964
"Peace Through Understanding" (souvenir button, left) was its theme, and its symbol, the Unisphere (below, seen through illuminated fountains).

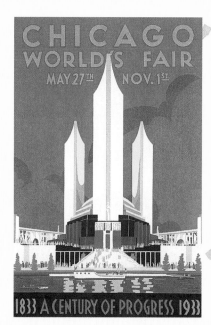

Montreal Expo ● 1967
Linked hands in the sinuous sculpture by Mario Armengol symbolized the theme of Canada's first world fair, Man and His World, and reflected the search for peace and love at that time. Expo 67 marked Canada's 100th birthday, and Montreal's debut as a city of international stature.

New York's World Fair ● 1939
The Perisphere, a huge white globe, and the Trylon, a tapering 222-metre-tall column, took centre stage in "The World of Tomorrow," a Utopian vision of marvels to come. But what came first was the horror of world war.

Vancouver ● 1986
Vancouver signalled its centenary with Expo 86,. the largest fair ever to have a single theme — transport and communication. The concept is continued in Canada Place, built for the fair, with its sail-like roof. The building is now a terminal for cruise ships.

A GREEDY GANG OF DICTATORS

Ironfisted strongmen emerged from the chaos following World War I, each intent on

grabbing absolute power, restoring national pride and prosperity, and humbling all enemies.

The dictators who emerged following World War I came in all sizes, shapes, and philosophies, but each one sought total control of his country.

After V. I. Lenin died in Russia in 1924, Joseph Stalin won a vicious power struggle and assumed leadership of the ruling Communist Party. He purged the government of potential rivals, including Lenin's heir apparent, Leon Trotsky, and launched the first of his five-year plans to industrialize the economy. Seeking to improve farm productivity, Stalin ordered all landowning peasants to give up their land or face exile, forced labor, or execution. By 1933 he had collectivized more than 80 percent of Soviet farms, but millions of kulaks, peasants who opposed collectivization,

were murdered or died of man-made famine. Stalin then set his secret police on his enemies within the party and the army; he killed or exiled roughly half the officer corps, some 35,000 men. He then turned on the secret police who had carried out his murderous schemes and replaced them with henchmen he deemed even more loyal. All this was done, Stalin explained, to ensure the U.S.S.R.'s security and to advance communism.

The threat of communism promoted the standing of dictators in other countries. The stridently anti-Communist Benito Mussolini postured and blustered as Il Duce (The Leader) for more than a decade, promising "peace, work, and calm . . . with love if possible, with force if necessary." Then in 1935, hoping to resurrect the imperial splendors of ancient Rome, he set his sights overseas — on Ethiopia.

Ethiopia's army carried muskets, swords, and spears; its barefooted cavalrymen wore lion skins. In October of 1935, 250,000 Italian troops swarmed across the border against an Ethiopian army a tenth that size. Ethiopia's Emperor Haile Selassie asked the League of Nations for help. He got none. Less than a year later, a defeated emperor

A month before this photo was taken in August 1936, Francisco Franco vowed to lead a fascist revolt against his government.

Joseph Stalin's smile at the party congress in 1934 masks plans for a brutal purge.

Ever the pompous posturer, Benito Mussolini (left, centre) struts before supporters in 1939. Ethiopia's Haile Selassie (below) had no hope of beating the Italian air force (bottom) but his forces put up a brave fight for seven months.

warned the League: "It is us today. It will be you tomorrow."

Halfway around the world, another League display of impotence cost 2 million Chinese lives. In September 1931 Japan had invaded Manchuria and conquered it within four months. The League condemned the aggression, but did nothing else. Six years later Japan took advantage of an ongoing civil war between Communists and Nationalists and invaded northern China, with massive destruction, looting, and killing in city after city. The worst was Nanking, where 20,000 girls and women were mutilated, raped, or killed and 20,000 young men were used for bayonet practice, gunned down, or doused with gas and set afire.

Adolf Hitler, meanwhile, planned a German empire. Defeated, angry over the humiliating losses in the Treaty of Versailles, mired in economic chaos, and torn by violent politics, Germany was ripe for Hitler's spellbinding oratory, which hypnotized millions with promises of glory, power, and vengeance. A decorated World War I corporal who was unemployed in the lean years after the war, Hitler spoke for the "little people" of Germany and had support in the army and big business. His National Socialist Party got one-third of the votes, and he was appointed chancellor. Then, during the same hundred days that opened FDR's first term, Hitler abolished the German republic, banned rival political parties, outlawed trade unions, and eliminated free speech. Gangs of Nazi Brownshirts beat up Jews, communists, and intellectuals.

◀

In October 1938, Japanese soldiers celebrate in Hankow — named the capital of China after the fall of Nanking — captured after an 89-day siege.

The government burned books and declared modern art degenerate. In 1936 Hitler sent troops into the Rhineland, German territory that had been demilitarized by the Treaty of Versailles. He expected Britain and France to resist, but they did nothing, which served only to encourage him to carry out further acts of aggression.

In Spain the fall of the monarchy in 1930 gave rise to a weak republic, which struggled against extremists of both the right and the left. Street violence, political assassination, and rumors of revolution peaked in July 1936, when most of the Spanish Army, under Gen. Francisco Franco, rebelled.

Franco and the Fascists Win Spain

From the start it was ugly. Franco called his Fascist cause a holy war to defend the church, the exiled monarchy, and Spain itself. Atrocities multiplied: a Madrid cathedral gutted by a mob, priests lynched, thousands of civilians killed by German bombs in the town of Guernica. Germany and Italy aided Franco, sending large shipments of arms and then troops. The republic's support came from the Soviet Union and from volunteers, including some 3,000 Americans and 1,300 Canadians (the Mackenzie-Papineau Battalion). Only half the Canadians survived, to return to a Canada which seemed embarrassed by their stand against fascism.

Finally, early in 1939, Franco took Barcelona and Madrid. Italian and German troops went home as heroes; Loyalists slipped over the French border in defeat. Ernest Hemingway, a Loyalist sympathizer in Spain while a reporter, immortalized the preview to World War II in *For Whom the Bell Tolls*. George Orwell, wounded fighting against Franco, returned to find his country "sleeping the deep, deep sleep of England, from which I fear . . . we shall never wake till we are jerked out of it by the roar of bombs."

▶

Hitler, his chief aide Hermann Göring, and Propaganda Minister Joseph Göbbels acknowledge cheers in Berlin a few days after the annexation of Austria, on March 12, 1938.

EUROPE BOWS TO A BULLY

"Britain and France had to choose between war and dishonor. They chose dishonor. They will have war." That view of the 1938 Munich accord, attributed to Winston Churchill, proved terribly right.

For years Winston Churchill had warned that dictators were pushing the world into war, and he urged England to rearm. When the Nazis militarized the Rhineland in 1936, Churchill cried out against it both in Parliament and in a syndicated newspaper column. The Reich, he wrote, "is arming more strenuously, more scientifically and upon a larger scale, than any nation has ever armed before." Outraged subscribers protested the "nationalistic" articles by Britain's "number one warmonger."

In early 1938 Churchill predicted that Hitler would move next into Austria, but on March 2 Prime Minister Neville Chamberlain assured Parliament that Austria was safe. Ten days later German troops goose-stepped across the border, uniting the two countries. Churchill urged an alliance of nations to stop Hitler's aggressions. While Parliament debated Churchill's proposal, Hitler paraded in Vienna before cheering crowds, proclaimed the end of the "Shame of Versailles," and declared that 6 million Austrians were now citizens of his Greater Reich.

Next, he turned to the Sudetenland, where a largely German population chafed under Czech rule. All summer Hitler ranted about the "oppression" of the Sudeten Germans; in August, Germany mobilized. Chamberlain flew to Munich to reason with the Führer. He bargained for hours with Hitler, Mussolini, and French Premier Edouard Daladier — but no Czechs — then agreed that a third of Czechoslovakia would be ceded to Germany. Chamberlain returned to England, confident that he had secured "Peace with honor . . . peace for our time." Churchill was undeceived. "We have sustained a total and unmitigated defeat!" he thundered. "This is only the beginning of the reckoning!"

Meanwhile, in Germany, Jews were forbidden to worship, hold most jobs, or own property. On November 7, 1938, a teenage Polish Jew killed a member of Germany's Paris embassy to avenge Nazi treatment of Jews. An enraged Hitler ordered retaliation, and a wave of sanctioned vandalism struck German Jews. So many shops and synagogues were destroyed that the night of November 9–10 was called Kristallnacht ("Crystal Night") for the shards of glass that littered the streets. The Nazis further humiliated the Jews by fining them to pay for the cleanup.

In March 1939 Hitler annexed more of Czechoslovakia and created a puppet state of the rest. Britain and France pledged "total and unqualified support" for Poland. In May Hitler and Mussolini signed the Pact of Steel, agreeing to come to each other's defence in case of war. Hitler called the

*All newlyweds received a copy of **Mein Kampf** (above), in which Hitler predicted Germany's rise to "lord of the universe." At Bad Godesberg on September 22, 1938 (top), Neville Chamberlain seemed unalarmed by Hitler's shocking demands.*

◀

German cavalry entering Düsseldorf signalled Hitler's remilitarization of the Rhineland in March 1936. The expected opposition from France never came.

Jugend dient dem Führer

Nothing pleased the Führer more than a show of loyalty from Germany's young men, seen marching below at a propaganda rally. As Hitler's power became more absolute, the headline on the recruiting poster at left, "Youth Serves the Führer," became more like an order.

This woman in Cheb (inset), a Sudeten border town, weeps openly as she and other residents salute the advancing Wehrmacht.

plight of Germans living in western Poland intolerable. Only fear of the Soviet Union kept him from attacking.

Then on August 23 Germany and the U.S.S.R. stunned the world by announcing a joint treaty of nonaggression. It openly assured mutual neutrality in case of war and secretly divided up Poland. Hitler was free to attack.

In later years, both Canadians and Americans would be critical of Britain and France for not acting more quickly against Germany. But where were they at the time?

As a member of the League of Nations, Canada had never supported action against aggressors. The United States hadn't even joined the league. As peace in Europe slipped away before everyone's eyes Britain had asked Mackenzie King's government to plan for the possibility of war. But, far from planning, King wouldn't even discuss it. In the United States, prominent Americans supported the America First Committee whose members, like Charles Lindbergh, opposed any American involvement in European affairs. But the war that threatened was one which could result in a world dominated either by Nazi Germany or the communist Soviet Union. Both King and Roosevelt knew that if such a war came their countries would not be able to stand by.

1 9 3 9 ★ 1 9 4 5

Chapter 5

WORLD WAR II

HOME FRONT & BATTLEFIELD

The bleak days just before and after Pearl

Harbor slowly give way to a dawning realization

that the Allies can and will win on land,

on the sea, and in the air.

Loaded down with bicycles and weapons, up to their necks in water, Canadian troops wade ashore at
Bernières-sur-Mer, Normandy, on D-Day, part of the Allied advance on German positions.

BLITZKRIEG, SITZKRIEG, AND FALL

A victory parade through Paris sends Wehrmacht regiments strutting past the city's majestic Arc de Triomphe. While German troops occupied northern France, the south became an independent pro-Nazi state with its capital at Vichy. What was left of the French Army fled to Africa, bringing tears to the eyes of patriots at home (above, right).

With swift and overwhelming fury, Hitler's armies swarmed into Poland, Scandinavia, and France. Then they turned on the U.S.S.R., badly underestimating the ferocity of "General Winter."

After months of diplomatic negotiation which attempted to prevent it, the worst finally happened. On September 1, 1939, Germany invaded Poland, moving with the speed and precision of an irate cobra. England and France immediately declared war on Germany. A week later, in a delay that was simply to underline its independence, Canada, too, declared war. World War II had begun. It would claim 50 million lives, destroy industry and commerce from the Urals to the Irish Sea, and leave much of Asia devastated.

The conflict ushered in a new dimension in military terror: blitzkrieg, or "lightning war." Hitler's Wehrmacht struck with massive force, moving into Poland 1.5 million strong. Panzer divisions with some 1,700 tanks led the way, racing ahead to cut supply lines, sever communications, and isolate defensive positions. Overhead swept an armada of 2,000 Luftwaffe aircraft: Heinkel bombers, Messerschmitt fighters, and Junkers dive bombers, the fearsome Stukas. By the end of September, Poland had been wiped from the map. Germany annexed its western half, while in the east the Russians took over, as previously agreed in a secret deal between Hitler and Soviet Premier Joseph Stalin.

After smothering Poland, Hitler paused to take stock. Western Europe experienced several months of eerie calm — the so-called sitzkrieg, or "sitting war." Then, in the spring of 1940, Hitler struck again, hitting Denmark and Norway. His next targets were France and the Low Countries. As the German armies penetrated deep into France in mid-May, panzer commander Gen. Erwin Rommel brimmed with elation. "It was not just a beautiful dream," he recalled. "It was reality."

Britain sent 10 divisions to head off the German advance, but by May 26 Hitler's panzers had sped across Belgium and reached the English Channel near Dunkirk. The British Expeditionary Force found itself cut off, along with almost half the French First Army and the entire Belgian Army. The Belgians would soon surrender. Only a massive rescue operation led by the Royal Navy prevented a total disaster. The Germans barely stopped to take notice. On June 14 they entered Paris. A week later an exultant Hitler laid down his terms to the French at Compiègne, in the same railroad car that was used for the German surrender in 1918.

The news for the Allies grew steadily worse. On June 10 Benito Mussolini, fascist premier of Italy, had joined the war on Hitler's side and ordered an attack on France by way of the Alps. President Franklin D. Roosevelt voiced the world's scorn: "The hand that held the dagger has struck it into the back of its neighbor." Romania, Bulgaria, Yugoslavia, and Greece fell quickly to the Germans.

But in the summer of 1941 Hitler made a fatal miscalculation. Despite his secret agreement with Stalin, Hitler

had long cast an envious eye on the fertile expanses of the U.S.S.R. Against the advice of his generals, Hitler decided to invade. "We have only to kick in the front door," he declared, "and the whole rotten edifice will come tumbling down."

So on June 22, 1941, Hitler sent the largest invasion force the world had yet seen, 162 divisions with a total of 3 million men, to conquer the largest country on earth. In the first months the Germans thrust northward along the Baltic coast to the outskirts of Leningrad. They captured Kiev to the south and pushed past Odessa to the Crimea. They struck east toward Moscow. Their successes were all but incredible. Hundreds of thousands of Soviet troops were captured or killed, and vast agricultural and mineral resources were brought under German control.

Then autumn arrived. Roads turned to mud in the October rains, slowing the panzer formations to a walking pace. A mid-November freeze solidified the roads, allowing a successful dash to Moscow. But by early December, when the Germans reached the city's suburbs, the nights had turned bitter cold. "General Winter" was in command.

Temperatures sank as low as 40 degrees below zero. The deep chill bit through the Wehrmacht's uniforms and up through the hobnails of boots. Thousands of frostbitten feet turned gangrenous and had to be amputated. Gun oil congealed, and machine guns jammed. Tank and truck batteries went dead. At the same time, Stalin's troops, reinforced by fresh divisions from Siberia, began to counterattack. "We have seriously underestimated the Russians, the extent of the country, and the treachery of the climate," a German commander observed. By Christmas the Germans had begun to fall back.

"THEIR FINEST HOUR"

As German bombers rained fire on Britain, and RAF fighter pilots

rose to meet them, a dauntless leader emerged who made survival

heroic, victory attainable, for his beleaguered people.

On a London rooftop an aircraft spotter scans the sky. St. Paul's Cathedral, in the background, endured heavy bombing.

With France gone, Britain stood alone with only limited help yet available from the Commonwealth. Canada so far had one division of troops in Britain, and it placed its few destroyers in the English Channel between the German armies and Britain's invasion beaches. Hitler now offered an astonishing proposal: recognize his conquests on the Continent, and he would leave England alone. If not, he would invade.

When England, predictably, refused to deal, Hitler drew up plans for Operation Sea Lion, a massive cross-channel assault by 250,000 combat troops. He first had to gain air superiority over the landing sites, a job left to Field Marshal Hermann Göring's Luftwaffe.

In July of 1940 German attack planes began testing the British defences, bombing and strafing coastal towns and Channel shipping. Small flights of Royal Air Force (RAF) fighter planes — Hurricanes and Spitfires — including Canada's squadron 1 (later renamed 401), mounted the skies to engage the German aircraft in swift, spiralling dogfights. Though outnumbered, the British often won.

Next Göring prepared a massive raid on RAF ground installations: airstrips, hangars, communications posts, radar warning towers, airplane factories. More than 2,000 German fighters and bombers stood ready at airfields in occupied France, Belgium, and Holland, awaiting his takeoff signal. Against them, the British defenders could loft only 700 first-line fighters, plus a number of older craft.

The first squadrons attacked in bright sunshine on August 13 — Eagle Day, in the German code designation — launching an aerial siege of brutal intensity, which came to be known as the Battle of Britain. Week after week, month upon month, multiple waves of Luftwaffe bombers, accompanied by their Messerschmitt fighter escorts, swept overhead to lay down patterns of fiery destruction.

The RAF pilots scrambled to intercept them. Sometimes they flew as many as six or seven missions a day and returned so tired they would drop to sleep the moment their wheels touched the runway. On one extraordinary day, August 15, the Germans launched nearly 1,800 sorties, and the British nearly 1,000. The RAF lost 34 fighters, but it sent 75 German planes spinning down in flames, a two-to-one ratio that British pilots would maintain overall in the months ahead.

A few days afterward Britain's new prime minister, the gruff, indomitable Winston Churchill, arose in the House of Commons to pay them tribute. "Never in the field of human conflict," he rumbled, his bulldog jaw thrust defiantly forward, "was so much owed by so many to so few."

On August 24, German pilots strayed off course and accidentally dropped bombs on London. An angry Churchill responded by ordering raids on Berlin. After four such hits, Hitler, stamping in fury, vowed: "We will raze their cities to the ground."

CHURCHILL THE MAGNIFICENT

Soldier, war correspondent, master politician, orator, author, national leader, world statesman — in more than half a dozen roles, Winston Churchill made a mark on history. But his finest hours came in the dark war years, stepping jauntily through the smoking rubble of London, his hand raised in his V-for-victory salute. "I have nothing to offer but blood, toil, tears, and sweat," he said on becoming prime minister at the age of 66, in May 1940. A month later, in the House of Commons, he proclaimed: "We shall not flag or fail . . . we shall defend our island . . . we shall never surrender." He was lovingly caricatured as a toy bulldog (above) with the words "Hitler terror" written on his steel helmet.

Above: Hurricanes flown by RCAF fighter squadron No. 1 shoot down a German plane in the Battle of Britain. Above, right: Spitfires prepare for takeoff.

R. THISTLE

government and industry. Some of them stayed under their own roofs to brave nightly raids. Others would gather their bedding and march to the relative safety of a shelter or the Underground, the city's deep-dug subway system. When Buckingham Palace took a hit on September 11, Londoners were gratified to learn that the royal family, too, was resolved to stick it out.

Over the months, as the Luftwaffe shifted its bombsights to England's civilians, the RAF was given breathing space to rebuild its shattered airfields and to equip its depleted squadrons with new planes and pilots. Eventually Hitler, realizing he would never achieve air superiority over England, had Operation Sea Lion quietly put to rest.

The London Blitz continued into 1941, with a final holocaust on the night of May 10–11, which took 1,212 lives. The raids then ceased entirely. They had spanned eight months, turned 250,000 Londoners out of their homes, and taken the lives of 40,553 men, women, and children. But London, and all England with it, had endured.

Nearly a year before the first German attack, Churchill had stood before Commons to proclaim his country's determination. "Let us . . . so bear ourselves," he said, "that if the British Empire and its Commonwealth last for a thousand years, men will still say: 'This was their finest hour.'" And so it was.

As a precaution against the Germans' possible use of gas, these English children wear masks for an air raid drill.

So began the Blitz, a sustained attack on Britain's great cities. London was hit again, on September 7, by a force of 320 bombers and 600 fighter escorts, and for the next 57 nights running. Liverpool, Manchester, Bristol, and Birmingham also felt the fury of Nazi raids. The bombs took such a toll on Coventry, on November 14, that when Churchill visited the wreckage, he broke down and wept.

But London suffered the worst. The Luftwaffe was dropping high explosives and incendiary bombs, and floating 2½-tonne land mines down by parachute. The resulting fires consumed whole blocks. The glow from the burning dockyards in the city's East End, which were hit repeatedly, could be seen from 48 kilometres away. "It was like a lake in Hell," said a survivor. Streetcar wheels welded themselves to the melting tracks. "Send all the pumps you've got," one firefighter called, "the whole bloody world's on fire."

Thousands of Londoners fled to the countryside. But millions more remained behind to operate the machinery of

▶

Londoners share tea, chat, and play darts in an underground shelter as German bombers pay a visit to the city above.

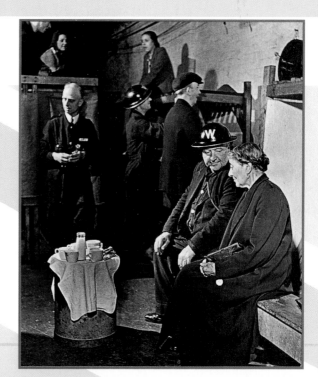

Headed for duty at Fort McClellan, Alabama, in October 1940, a soldier kisses his girl good-bye as his train leaves the Delaware, Lackawanna, and Western terminal in Hoboken, New Jersey.

▶

Bound for Britain laden to the gunwales with Lend-Lease war matériel, and on constant watch for U-boats, a convoy of freighters churns through the heavy seas of a North Atlantic storm. The United States gave $50 billion in aid by the war's end.

TWO PATHS TO THE SAME DESTINY

Canada and the United States prepare for war. The first, with desperate urgency, and the second, reluctantly. However, FDR met Churchill and agreed to lend vital war aid to the hard-pressed Allies.

Most Canadians accepted the necessity for war, but the country was woefully unprepared. The one army division it could send overseas in 1939 was far from battle ready, and Canada had only just begun to convert its cavalry to tanks. The navy had barely 3,000 men and only a handful of ships. The air force was small and had little equipment, almost all of it obsolete. Noting this, and remembering the bloodbath of World War I, Mackenzie King hoped to play only a minor role this time. But the fall of France ended those hopes.

In short order, Canada raised an army of nearly three-quarters of a million men and women, with three infantry and two armored divisions overseas, and three more divisions for home defence. Workers essential to home front tasks were assigned to them. Others were marked down for military service. The navy mushroomed to 100,000 men and women with 365 warships, the third largest of the Allied navies. The North Atlantic became the only theatre of war in which Canadians exercised supreme command, and this de-spite their outdated submarine detection equipment, and ships, particularly corvettes, made from inferior steel.

The RCAF grew to 250,000 men and women. Most air crew served with RAF squadrons, but 48 Canadian squadrons served in Europe, North Africa and the Far East, as well as closer to home in Alaska and over Atlantic convoy routes. By 1941, squadron 405 was operational in Britain and preparing to fly the difficult and dangerous "Pathfinder" missions that led bombers to their targets. Under the British Commonwealth Air Training Plan, Canada also trained more than 130,000 aircrew, including 6,000 Americans.

Mackenzie King was distrustful of American designs on Canadian territory, but he was personally close to Roosevelt and he needed American help in the war effort. In 1940, at Ogdensburg, New York, the two leaders agreed to set up a permanent board to discuss mutual defence problems. In 1941, with the Hyde Park Declaration, the two entered into close cooperation on defence production, too. Though one country was at war and the other at peace, it was clear that they would soon be working together.

The United States offers some help

To Americans of 1940 the war overseas seemed a world away. Although sympathetic with the embattled democracies, most people balked at the idea of being directly involved. In the United States it took all of President Franklin D. Roosevelt's considerable political skills to prod the country into action.

A vocal isolationist minority resisted the change. Many isolationists were bitter over what they saw as futile sacrifices in the war of 1914–18. "The People Say NO War!" proclaimed posters of the isolationist America First Committee. Senator Burton K. Wheeler, with bitter anti-New Deal sarcasm, denounced a proposal to aid

Britain as "a plan to plow under every fourth American boy." And some citizens were actively pro-German. Members of the German-American Bund adopted the Nazi salute and held military exercises in support of Hitler's Reich.

Ranged against the antiwar crusaders were those who advocated intervention on the side of the democracies. The Committee to Defend America by Aiding the Allies was organized by the newspaperman William Allen White. Leading supporters included *Time-Life* publisher Henry Luce and the playwright Robert Sherwood, who pointed out that even two broad oceans could no longer guarantee safety from dictators' warplanes, ships, and submarines.

Most North Americans, even isolationists, saw the Allies as the good guys and the Axis as the bad guys. Edward R. Murrow's riveting radio broadcasts from blitz-torn London during the Battle of Britain contributed to people's admiration for the plucky English. Meanwhile, the United States took practical steps to help. In an ingenious swap designed to silence antiwar critics, Roosevelt gave the British 50 "obsolete" destroyers in exchange for long-term leases on eight British naval and air bases in the Caribbean and North Atlantic.

Much more was needed. By December 1940 Britain had nearly run out of funds to buy urgently needed war supplies. In a press conference Roosevelt revealed what was on his mind: "Suppose my neighbor's home catches fire, and I have a length of garden hose. . . . I don't say to him . . . 'Neighbor, my garden hose cost me $15; you have to pay me $15 for it!' . . . I don't want $15 — I want my garden hose back after the fire is over." After two months of debate, Congress gave in to this folksy argument and to British Prime Minister Winston Churchill's appeal, "Give us the tools and we will finish the job." The act that became known as Lend-Lease allowed Britain — and, later, 37 other nations — to borrow or lease any equipment the president deemed vital to the defence interests of the United States.

▼ *Ice 30 centimetres thick coated the upper works of convoy ships in winter, threatening to capsize the vessels.*

▲ *A convoy of merchant ships gathers in Bedford Basin, Halifax (formally known by its cryptic description as "a port on the east coast"). Canadian destroyers and corvettes escorted many convoys across the North Atlantic to the United Kingdom, protecting the sea lanes along which they carried their cargoes of war supplies.*

THREAT FROM BELOW

Both sides used submarines with deadly effect, but it was the German U-boat campaign that almost changed the course of World War II. Part of Hitler's grand strategy called for U-boats to blockade the British Isles and starve Britain into submission.

Groups of U-boats, known as wolf packs, prowled the Atlantic and the Caribbean for convoys. While the United States was still officially neutral, American radio direction finders were warning British and Canadian convoys of the locations of wolf packs. Even with that help, by 1942 Allied ships were being sunk at the rate of one every four hours.

The turning point came in May 1943, with improved sub-detection devices and more warships and airplanes to shield the convoys. The next month just six ships fell victim to U-boat torpedoes. The Battle of the North Atlantic took a grim toll in lives and ships. Altogether the Allies lost 2,778 ships, 2,603 of them merchantmen. The Germans lost some 780 of the 1,162 U-boats they put to sea.

"A DATE WHICH WILL LIVE IN INFAMY"

On Sunday, December 7, 1941, at 7:49 in the morning, Japanese attack planes swooped down without warning and dropped their bombs on the U.S. naval base at Pearl Harbor, on the Hawaiian island of Oahu. A stunned and horrified America suddenly found itself at war.

Commander Mitsuo Fuchida, leading 183 carrier-based fighters and bombers of the Japanese Navy, scanned the target area with binoculars. Below, at the huge Pearl Harbor naval base, lay 8 battleships, 9 cruisers, 29 destroyers, and 39 lesser craft — the bulk of the United States Pacific Fleet.

Fuchida ordered his radioman to send out the signal to strike: *"To, To, To."* Then he dropped a wing and rolled in for the attack. Moments later he broadcast a second message: *"Tora, Tora, Tora"* ("surprise achieved").

Though the raid on Pearl Harbor was planned in utmost secrecy, anti-Western feeling among the Japanese was well known. For more than a decade Japan had aggressively expanded its power in the Pacific. Then, in September 1940, in an act of defiance addressed to the entire free world, Japan signed an alliance with Germany and Italy. America was horrified. President Franklin D. Roosevelt froze Japanese assets and placed an embargo on oil and steel shipments to Japan. Diplomats from both countries met in Washington in late 1941 to defuse the crisis.

But even as the diplomats parleyed, the Japanese strike force — 6 carriers and 14 escort vessels — was steaming toward Pearl Harbor. U.S. naval intelligence, which had broken the Japanese code, knew that the fleet had gone to sea, but since the Japanese sailed under radio silence, their whereabouts remained a mystery. On December 6, 1941, President Roosevelt appealed directly to Emperor Hirohito for peace. That same day, the strike force approached its launch point.

On Sunday morning, December 7, a sailor named Dick Fiske was just coming off watch on the battleship *West Virginia*, which was moored at Ford Island, in Pearl Harbor. "We saw the dive bombers coming in," Fiske said, "and we

Above, left: Days before the Pearl Harbor attack, U.S. Secretary of State Cordell Hull (centre) talked peace with diplomats from Tokyo.

Addressing a joint session of Congress — and, through radio, the entire nation — President Roosevelt calls for a declaration of war against Japan. Three days later, on December 11, 1941, Germany and Italy declared war on the United States.

thought they were army planes. Just another exercise. A friend of mine said, 'Let's go over to the port side and watch them dropping torpedoes on us.'" The next thing Fiske remembered "was a hellacious loud noise, and a wall of water that looked like a 15-foot wave came across the deck and washed us both to the other side of the ship."

Doris Miller, heavyweight boxing champ of the *West Virginia*, was a mess attendant and was not trained in gunnery. But he sprinted to a machine gun. "It wasn't hard," he said. "I just pulled the trigger and she worked fine." Miller became the first black man to win the Navy Cross, that service's second-highest decoration for gallantry.

Marine private James Cory, aboard the battleship *Arizona*, was opening the window of his battle station to get a clear view. "The bombs struck forward — forward of us," he said. "The bridge shielded us from flames coming aft. . . . But still, around the edges in these open windows came the heat and the sensation of the blast. We cringed there." An 800-kilogram bomb had pierced the bow and ignited the ship's huge forward magazine. A sailor on the nearby *Nevada* saw the *Arizona* "jump at least 15 or 20 feet upward in the water and sort of break in two." More than 1,000 American sailors and marines perished in the fireball.

Private Cory and a buddy jumped overboard and swam for their lives. "There were bomb splashes nearby," he said. "There was strafing in the water. You could feel the impact of the bullets. There was a tremendous amount of confusion and noise and all this sort of thing. Our own oil was bubbling up and congealing. . . . It was catching fire slowly and incinerating toward us." The two men struggled ashore. They were then "lifted up into the air and flung down" as a bomb detonated somewhere near them. Both men survived.

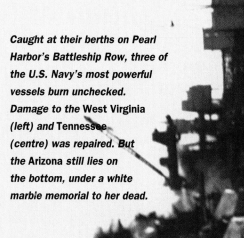

Caught at their berths on Pearl Harbor's Battleship Row, three of the U.S. Navy's most powerful vessels burn unchecked. Damage to the West Virginia (left) and Tennessee (centre) was repaired. But the Arizona still lies on the bottom, under a white marble memorial to her dead.

By 8:12 A.M. seven battleships lay heavily damaged or sunk, some resting on the harbor bottom with their twisted wreckage breaking the water. The second wave, of 170 Japanese attackers, arriving just before 9 A.M., kept pounding the battleships and scored major hits on other, smaller ships. The Japanese also destroyed 188 aircraft, most of them on the ground. They killed 2,403 Americans and wounded 1,178.

Returning to their carriers, the Japanese pilots urged their commander, Vice Admiral Chuichi Nagumo, to send a new wave against the American fleet's docking and fuelling facilities. Nagumo refused. The operation had already succeeded beyond anyone's hopes. He took his fleet to the safety of the Central Pacific.

In fact, the Pearl Harbor attack was a major strategic blunder. Most of the ships sunk or damaged there were repaired, some within a few weeks. The U.S. Pacific Fleet's three aircraft carriers, major targets, were not present and thus escaped damage. They would soon inflict terrible vengeance on the Japanese Navy. Even more significant, Pearl Harbor united the American people in a crusading zeal that sustained them throughout the war.

Calling upon Congress to declare war, President Roosevelt began solemnly: "Yesterday, December 7, 1941, a date which will live in infamy. . . ." Then he rallied the nation with these words: "With confidence in our armed forces, with the unbounding determination of our people, we will gain the inevitable triumph. So help us God."

Millions of Americans wore enamelled lapel pins proclaiming that they would "Remember Pearl Harbor."

HONG KONG

The British government understood well that Hong Kong could not be defended, and that if the Japanese should attack, the garrison would certainly be lost. Even so, in September of 1941 the British asked Canada to send reinforcements to the colony — and strangely Canada agreed. On November 16, 1941, almost 2,000 soldiers of the Winnipeg Grenadiers and the Royal Rifles of Canada arrived in Hong Kong. Three weeks later, the Japanese attacked.

The Canadians were far from ready for battle. Most lacked adequate training; some had no training at all. They faced elite Japanese assault troops, and the main attack was made right at the Canadian positions. When the surrender came on Christmas Day, 290 Canadians were dead — either killed in battle or murdered after surrendering. Almost as many would die in captivity. To that point, the Hong Kong battle was a story of cynicism and bungling by two governments. But there is more to it.

Though poorly trained, the Canadians fought with such doggedness that a Japanese colonel had to apologize to his superiors for the losses the Canadians had inflicted on him. The word he used for them was "heroic." He may well have been thinking of Sgt. John Osborne of the grenadiers who won the Victoria Cross for flinging himself on a hand grenade to save his comrades — or of the hundreds of others who fought hand to hand along the length of the Wong Nai Chong Gap.

If there can be nothing but shame for the people who sent them, there must be nothing but praise for the soldiers who fought the most courageous action in the history of the Canadian army.

JAPAN THRUSTS OUTWARD

In the wake of its Pearl Harbor strike, and of similarly devastating air attacks that same day on U.S. forces in the Philippines and British forces at Singapore, Japan moved with practised precision to carve out a vast realm in the Pacific.

By December 1941 the Japanese were masters of an empire on the western rim of the Pacific. They controlled Manchuria, Korea, much of Indochina, eastern China and its ports, Taiwan (then called Formosa), and a few smaller islands.

It was not enough. Japan's leaders hated the Western presence in their part of the world and craved to replace it with their own imperial system. In their Greater East Asia Co-Prosperity Sphere, the banner of the Rising Sun would fly over an area that spanned some 8,000 kilometres, from the Kurile Islands in the north through vast stretches of the South Pacific. It would include Burma, the Dutch East Indies, the Philippines, the British colonies of Hong Kong and Malaya, plus Thailand and New Guinea.

Between the Japanese and the fulfillment of their dream lay what seemed to be a disorganized and dispirited foe. Australia and New Zealand needed time to reach full fighting strength. In the East Indies and the Philippines, valiant Dutch and Filipino units were plainly outmatched; so for the time being were British imperial forces in Burma and India. As for the Americans, the U.S. Navy was apparently in bad shape after Pearl Harbor; and Japanese strategists doubted the will of

◄

Near victory in the Philippines, Japanese soldiers raise flags and swords on Bataan. Assured of the glory of their conquests, Japan's forces fought courageously and often pitilessly.

American boys to fight a long and bloody war thousands of kilometres from home.

The Japanese underestimated the Allies' fighting spirit. In New York City alone, hours after the Pearl Harbor attack, hundreds of young men waited all night outside army and navy recruiting stations, hoping to be among the first in their neighborhood to enlist.

But it would take months to train and equip the new recruits and to deploy them in combat. In the interim the Japanese taught the armed forces of the United States a terrible lesson. Just 10 hours after striking Pearl Harbor, the Japanese attacked Clark Field in the Philippines, the principal U.S. air base in the Far East. The American pilots had just returned from morning patrols and were relaxing in the mess hall. Suddenly, enemy bombers began unloading on the B-17 Flying Fortresses. Unforgivably, General MacArthur had his bombers parked wingtip to wingtip as if for a country fair. Within a matter of hours, more than a third of his air force was destroyed.

Hong Kong fell on Christmas Day. Then Japanese infantry advanced through Thailand and down the Malay Peninsula toward Singapore. The British fortress there had been bombed the same morning as Pearl Harbor. Incompetently defended, it fell to the Japanese on February 15, 1942. Far more than the Philippines, Singapore was the symbol of western power in Asia. News of its fall to an Asian army sickened Churchill, who sensed that the consequences would be felt for decades. Next came the Dutch East Indies and the Solomon Islands.

Meanwhile, a Japanese expeditionary force had landed in the Philippines and swept southward. By January 7, 1942, a combined force of U.S. and Filipino defenders, under Gen. Douglas MacArthur, had withdrawn onto the rugged Bataan Peninsula. Then began a campaign that

The Canadian contingent of almost 2,000 troops marches through the streets of Hong Kong on November 16, 1941, having just arrived to reinforce the garrison defending the colony from the Japanese.

horrified and transfixed the American people — and hardened their resolve to beat the Japanese into submission.

The defenders were sick, starving, short of munitions, and just about out of luck. Unrelenting attacks by the Japanese pressed them into a shrinking perimeter of land. Still, they held on. Early in March, when MacArthur left for Australia on President Roosevelt's orders, he announced with supreme confidence, "I shall return."

His return would take years. On April 9 the exhausted defenders of Bataan were forced to surrender. Then began the infamous Death March, on which the surviving Filipinos and Americans, now prisoners, were brutally herded through choking dust and sweltering heat to Camp O'Donnell, some 95 kilometres to the north. Along the way their captors systematically killed anyone too weak or too sick to keep up. "If you fell," said an American survivor, "you were dead. They bayoneted you right away."

Acts of brutality became routine. Once, a group of prisoners, parched with thirst, was ordered at gunpoint to wade a stream, but forbidden to drink from it. One man, in desperation, tried to dip his hands into the water. "He was 12 feet from me," a soldier related. "They shot him. Some guards on the bridge just popped him off."

The Filipinos fared worse than the Americans. During the march, according to some estimates, they died at some 10 times the rate of their American comrades. And those who withstood the march were subjected to equally rough treatment when they reached Camp O'Donnell. Of nearly 70,000 Americans and Filipinos captured at Bataan, some 23,000 perished before the war's end.

Some U.S. forces retreated from Bataan to the nearby island of Corregidor, at the entrance to Manila Bay. There, in a network of tunnels, they hung on for another month. When they finally surrendered — on May 6, 1942, five months less one day after Pearl Harbor — the entire Western Pacific belonged to Japan.

With a total length of 96.5 centimetres and a 73-centimetre single-edge blade, this Japanese Army katana was a sword meant for killing, not for ceremony.

TRADITION OF EMPERORS

When Shomu (top) reigned in the 8th century, Japanese emperors had vast power and the status of gods. As time passed, they lost their earthly power, but continued to be seen as divine. Real power lay with the feudal lords and, by the 20th century, with

the army and navy. Military leaders like Hideki Tojo backed Japanese aggression in the 1930's. Tojo and his cadre knew they had to appear subservient to the emperor to win popular support. Thus, at a military review in 1940 (above), Tojo bowed humbly to Emperor Hirohito. At the war's end, most Japanese still revered Hirohito. A new constitution made the will of the people paramount while retaining the emperor and his line as a national symbol. Tojo was hanged as a war criminal in 1948.

OUTFLANKING THE DESERT FOX

For Gen. Erwin Rommel, Germany's master tactician, North Africa was the best of times and the worst of times. His stunning victory at Tobruk elevated him to field marshal, but when he was forced to retreat from Kasserine, he was relieved of his command.

GI's assisted by British sailors lower themselves into an assault craft headed for Algeria's shore. Operation Torch, involving more than 500 ships, was the largest amphibious invasion thus far.

For most of the 107,000 or so American and British soldiers who clambered down the landing nets of troopships in early November 1942, North Africa was a land known only from books and movies, if at all. But long before the next six months were over, these men would have the names of Bizerte, Kasserine Pass, Maknassy, and dozens of other sun-scorched places between Casablanca and Cairo etched in their memories. On such battlegrounds GI's and Tommies would fight the best troops Germany and Italy could muster against them.

Operation Torch, the code name for the combined U.S.-British landings, struck at Oran, Algiers, and Casablanca. Its overall commander, Lt. Gen. Dwight D. Eisenhower, directed the invasion from his headquarters within the Rock of Gibraltar, on the other side of the Mediterranean.

Before Torch, Seesaw Battles

For more than two years before Operation Torch, Italian forces, aided by their German allies, had been trying to dislodge the British from East and North Africa. The prize was control of the entire Mediterranean area, including the Suez Canal. In June 1940 Italy's dictator, Benito Mussolini, launched the first of thousands of air attacks against the British-held island of Malta. In September he invaded Egypt. By February of the following year, British troops, under the command of Lt. Gen. Sir Archibald Wavell, had routed the Italians in Libya and Egypt. The hard-fighting British, it seemed, could be stopped only by their afternoon tea; so Hitler sent one of his best commanders to rescue his floundering allies.

The general was Erwin Rommel. Rommel took charge of the Afrika Korps, his main attack force, on February 12, 1941. For the next 15 months, the fighting seesawed. Rommel launched his first offensive on March 24 but failed to take Tobruk, a strategic garrison on the coast of Libya. By year's end the British, now led by Gen. Sir Claude Auchinleck, pushed Rommel back halfway across Libya.

On May 26, 1942, Axis forces counterattacked, with Rommel commanding some 760 tanks, 240 of which were virtually useless. On June 21 he seized Tobruk in a lightning one-day assault, and Hitler promoted him to field marshal. Next, Rommel pursued the retreating British Eighth Army eastward but was stopped at the coastal village of El Alamein, a scant 240 kilometres northwest of Cairo, Egypt's capital. The Axis seemed certain to take Cairo, but the newly appointed British commander in the Middle East, Gen. Sir Harold Alexander, and commander of the Eighth Army, Lt. Gen. Bernard L. Montgomery, had other ideas. Patiently Alexander built up the army at El Alamein with fresh troops and supplies. On October 23 nearly 900 of his big guns began a barrage on enemy positions. Two days later the revitalized Eighth Army had knocked out 90 percent of the tanks Rommel had deployed at El Alamein, and on November 4 a badly battered panzer army, with Montgomery in pursuit, began to draw back toward Tunisia.

For the British, El Alamein was a desperately needed success. Winston Churchill later wrote: "It may almost be said that before Alamein we never had a victory. After Alamein, we never had a defeat." To celebrate this turning point, Churchill asked that church bells be sounded all over Britain. (The bells had been silenced since 1940 and were to have been rung as a signal that England had been invaded.)

Four days after the Germans began their retreat, Eisenhower's Operation Torch invaded North Africa. Now Rommel faced one big army to the west and another to the east. Meanwhile, Hitler had fortified German forces holding on to northern Tunisia, and in late February 1943 they joined

◄

Shielding himself from the scorching Egyptian sun with a parasol, British Prime Minister Winston Churchill tours the desert near El Alamein in August 1942.

Rommel in a thrust toward the Kasserine Pass. American troops were savaged. But reinforcements poured in and, after his initial victory, Rommel had to retreat. On March 6 Montgomery's Eighth Army dealt him a brutal defeat, and three days later Rommel flew to Berlin to advise Hitler to give up North Africa. He was relieved of his command. In the spring of 1943 an estimated 275,000 German and Italian troops trudged into waiting Allied prisoner-of-war camps.

▲ *The North African campaign stretched from the coast of Morocco to the shores of the Nile, some 4,800 kilometres away.*

DUEL IN THE DESERT

The battle for North Africa pitted two masters of warfare against each other: Lt. Gen. Bernard Law Montgomery and Field Marshal Erwin Rommel.

Montgomery was so meticulous that his painstaking tactics often exasperated impatient superiors. His cautiousness, however, was born not of fear of the enemy but of love for his fellow soldiers. He had witnessed the horrors of World War I, and it made him forever determined to protect the lives of his men, who affectionately nicknamed him Monty.

If Montgomery relied on method, Rommel relied on instinct, boasting, "I sniff through the country like a fox." The Desert Fox, as he was called, took personal command of each battle, often eluding setbacks with swift improvisation. So great was his ability that even Winston Churchill declared, "We have a very daring and skilful opponent against us . . . a great general."

Bernard Montgomery

Erwin Rommel

Carefully concealed behind a makeshift shelter, a German soldier uses a range finder to spot the next target. The Afrika Korps, which was shifted from Europe to Africa with little preparation, underestimated the hostile climate.

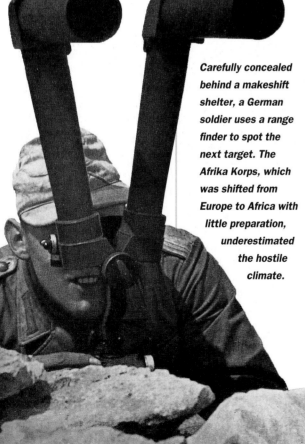

▼ *Trapped in his immobilized tank, a panzer crewman has little choice but to surrender to British infantrymen at El Alamein, where the Germans finally met their match.*

THE END BEGINS FOR HITLER

By 1942 Adolf Hitler had set his sights on the Russian city of Stalingrad, which he considered the ultimate test of his country's iron will. Meanwhile, Allied bombers began hammering at a strategic target of their own: Germany.

The Air Force Cross was awarded to officers and warrant officers for courage or devotion to duty while flying. RCAF Squadron Leader Victor Wentworth was awarded this cross in 1944.

The rosewood-panelled dining car of Adolf Hitler was the pride of the German railway system. On the evening of November 7, 1942, the train carrying that car stopped at a small station outside Munich. Inside, at a table adorned with polished silverware and fresh flowers, sat the Führer himself. Unexpectedly, a train of cattle cars pulled alongside and stopped. Hitler peered through his window. Staring back at him through the slatted sides of the cars were what appeared to be human scarecrows, held together by tattered uniforms and blood-stained bandages. They were wounded German soldiers returning from the Battle of Stalingrad, the Russian city that Hitler had ordered taken against the advice of most of his staff. For an instant Hitler looked into the eyes of those who had been part of the 300,000-strong force he had sent to conquer Stalingrad. Then he turned away abruptly from the window, ordered the shades to be drawn, and went on with his dinner.

If Hitler had chosen to take a clear-eyed look at his nation's fortunes, he might have seen the high tide of Germany's invincibility beginning to ebb. The unsuccessful siege of Stalingrad, then in its third bloody month, hinted strongly that the mighty German ground armies that had swept victoriously from one end of Europe to the other were not unstoppable after all.

To Hitler the news from Stalingrad must have seemed unbelievable. How could the ill-equipped defenders of that drab city on the west bank of the Volga continue to hold out after an artillery pounding so brutal that it turned most of the city into rubble? The answer was that Germany had failed to recognize the incredible resourcefulness and steely resolve of the enemy. "Before you die, kill a German," the Soviet high command ordered its soldiers, "with your teeth if necessary!"

At one point in the five-month-long fight for control of the city, the Germans occupied nine-tenths of Stalingrad, but it was a nightmare to hold such gains. "It is hard, often impossible, to distinguish between night and day, for vast clouds of smoke blot out the light," one German soldier wrote. "A street is no longer measured in metres," an officer noted, "but in corpses."

On November 19 the Soviet forces, strengthened by fresh soldiers, tanks, and artillery, began their counterat-

▼ *At Stalingrad the Red Army's cavalry played a key role in thwarting Hitler's Sixth Army. Siberian ponies not only manoeuvred through rough terrain, they outlasted panzers rendered immobile in subzero temperatures.*

The staggering death toll at Stalingrad began with heavy casualties on the very first day of battle, when a raid by 600 German bombers left 40,000 dead.

▼ "Forward! Toward Victory!" proclaims a Soviet poster. In the winter of 1942–43 the Soviets thwarted further gains by the Nazis, who, by then, had seized almost as much of the U.S.S.R. as the Mongol hordes did in the 13th century.

tack. They cut off and surrounded the German forces. On January 31, 1943 after 100,000 of his men were killed over the course of three weeks, the German commander gave up. Fighting ceased on February 2. To the Germans' devastating losses in battle were added thousands of deaths by starvation and exposure to disease in Soviet prisons. In all, only about 6,000 Axis soldiers of the original attack force of 300,000 are known to have survived to see the end of World War II.

Even before Stalingrad, the Soviets had demanded an Allied invasion of Europe to ease pressure on their front. The British knew such an invasion was not yet possible, but saw a need for some offensive display . The result was

Shortly after, U.S. bombers joined the Allied air offensive by hitting the Wilhelmshaven naval base. And in December 1943 help arrived in the form of U.S. P-51 Mustangs, whose 3,680-kilometre range enabled them to escort bombers all the way into and out of Germany. By March 1944 combined forces of 1,000 Allied bombers would roar daily into Germany. American B-17's, with their heavy armor and gun power to ward off fighters, flew by day. RAF and RCAF Lancasters, which sacrificed defensive power for a heavier bomb load, flew by night.

Dieppe. Badly planned and executed, the raid sent almost 5,000 Canadian troops and 200 British commandos against a German-occupied port on the French coast. Within hours, 900 were dead and more than 1,800 taken prisoner. After the disaster, the official alibi was that valuable lessons had been learned for the future. The alibi would have been more convincing if it had been the purpose of the raid in the first place.

The human cost was heavy — nearly 10,000 Canadian airmen of Bomber Command were killed. But the cost to Germany was even heavier both on the ground and among aircrew as Allied planes inflicted terrible damage inside the Third Reich.

In early 1944 Germany was losing more than 2,000 planes per month. By June, when Allied troops were poised for the D-Day landings on the beaches of northern France, their supreme commander, Gen. Dwight D. Eisenhower, offered words of comfort: "If you see fighter aircraft over you, they will be ours."

THE TIDE TURNS IN THE PACIFIC

At Midway the agile and accurate Douglas Dauntless dive bomber was the navy's most effective offensive weapon.

In the uncertain months after Pearl Harbor, Japan seemed all but unstoppable. But then came four key events that changed the course of the war: a raid on Tokyo and the Battles of Midway, Guadalcanal, and the Coral Sea.

On a fine spring morning in 1942, Tokyo residents had every reason to feel good about themselves and their country. Since their nation's surprise attack on Pearl Harbor, the war had been going Japan's way, with mainland and island conquests throughout the Pacific, and U.S. resistance in the Philippines crumbling fast. Tokyo itself sat safe from harm — or so its citizens believed that Saturday morning, April 18. Meanwhile 16 heavily fuelled U.S. Army Air Forces B-25 bombers fought their way aloft from the aircraft carrier *Hornet* amid gale-force winds and waves.

Their leader was Lt. Col. James H. Doolittle, a feisty doctor of science who had set a number of aviation speed records, and their main target was Tokyo, some 1,280 risk-filled kilometres away. So confident were the Japanese that their land was invulnerable that some waved cheerfully upward as the U.S. planes flew over

Each important U.S. Navy ship had an official insignia, such as this one belonging to the Yorktown.

Lt. Col. James H. Doolittle's B-25, headed for Tokyo, lifts off the U.S.S. Hornet. After the raid President Roosevelt told reporters that the planes came from "our secret base at Shangri-la" in order to maintain security. Doolittle, left, won the Medal of Honor for his heroism.

Tokyo and other cities. After releasing their bombs, the planes headed west: 13 of the original 16 reached China and 1 the U.S.S.R. Two other crews were captured in Japanese territory, and three of the fliers were executed.

Even though Doolittle's bombers did little damage, the incursion was a stinging blow to Japan's pride. Smarting from the insult, the Japanese Navy sent a large attack force toward Port Moresby, in New Guinea, thus posing a serious threat to Australia. But timely code-breaking had already alerted the Americans that the Japanese ships were on their way. A three-part naval force with two big carriers, the *Yorktown* and the *Lexington*, headed out to surprise the Japanese.

The Battle of the Coral Sea was about to begin. At first, neither naval force could pinpoint the location of the other's main fleet. Then, on May 7, 1942, American warplanes hit the carrier *Shoho*, sending her to the ocean floor. The next day one U.S. dive bomber pilot, Lt. John James Powers, who

Under towering coconut trees, four marines stroll through their headquarters on Guadalcanal. In addition to the enemy and torrential rains, GI's had to contend with leeches, rats, bats, and crocodiles.

had earlier made a vow to sink an enemy carrier, dived on the carrier *Shokaku*. The bomb he dropped from 91 metres put the ship out of action, but the force of explosions from the stricken vessel sent Powers and his plane crashing into the sea, killing him. His astonishing bravery was honored with a posthumous award of the Medal of Honor.

The U.S. fleet did not come through unscathed, either. One enemy bomb ripped through four decks of the *Yorktown*. The *Lexington* took two torpedoes and several bombs, but was still afloat. Then, two hours after the Japanese broke off action, she exploded when a generator caught fire. Almost 3,000 crew members arranged their shoes in neat rows on the flight deck, then dropped over the side to waiting rescue ships. Thus ended the first sea engagement ever fought in which ships of the opposing fleets never caught sight of each other. Airmen carried all the attacks.

Only a month after the Battle of the Coral Sea came the most decisive sea confrontation of the war, when the balance of power in the Pacific began tilting unmistakably toward the United States. This was the Battle of Midway. It took place some 2,400 kilometres off Hawaii when Japan's navy joined in air battles with the U.S. fleet, which was then about 640 kilometres away.

Airmen, flying both singly and in formation, attempted, starting June 4, to bomb each other's ships into oblivion. The U.S. side sustained a major loss, the *Yorktown*, but Japan's losses at Midway were staggering. At least 300 of its planes were shot down, and 4 of its great carriers went to the bottom, 3 knocked out within less than 10 minutes. The captain of the doomed carrier *Soryu* went under while still singing the Japanese national anthem.

The battles of the Coral Sea and of Midway showed the Japanese that U.S. forces were more than a match both on the sea and in the air. But Americans had yet to prove themselves on land. That chance came in the bloody battle for the island of Guadalcanal. Few memories of combat in World War II are more searing than those of the marines who invaded Guadalcanal or of the Japanese who defended it. Guadalcanal was the first of many such invasions in the Pacific by U.S. forces, with devastating losses suffered by Americans and Japanese alike.

At dawn on August 7, 1942, members of the 1st Marine Division waded ashore on the island, which had assumed strategic importance because of the airfield the Japanese were building there. Over the next six months, in rotting jungles filled with disease, intense heat, and Japanese ready to die for their emperor, U.S. troops engaged in some of the most savage fighting of the entire war. Approximately 1,600 Americans and nearly 24,000 Japanese died on the island, but on February 8, 1943, Maj. Gen. Alexander M. Patch could finally report that "the Tokyo Express no longer has a terminal on Guadalcanal."

TOKYO ROSE

Hello, you fighting orphans of the Pacific. How's tricks?" Thus began a radio show hosted by Iva Ikuko Toguri D'Aquino, one of the numerous female radio announcers collectively dubbed Tokyo Rose by the GI's. A nisei (second-generation Japanese-American), she acquired her English growing up in the United States. Though her teasing broadcasts were designed to make servicemen so homesick that they would lose the will to fight, her propaganda, with its blend of corniness and nostalgia, actually raised morale by giving GI's both entertainment and a target for sarcastic humor. In 1949 D'Aquino, then 33, was convicted of treason in a trial held in the United States. She spent six years in a federal prison in West Virginia and was granted a pardon by President Gerald Ford in 1977.

ARCTIC OCEAN

Germans attack Allied convoys
bound for U.S.S.R.
1941–45

Reykjavik
ICELAND

Murmansk

Battle of the Atlantic
Sept 1939–mid-1943

Archangel

FINLAND

NORWAY

Russo-Finnish Wars
Nov. 1939–Mar. 1940
June 1941–Sept. 1944

Oslo

Helsinki

Leningrad
German siege
Sept. 1941–Jan. 1944

SWEDEN

Baltic
Sea

Stockholm

Tallinn
ESTONIA

Riga
LATVIA

Moscow

Dublin

IRELAND

North
Sea

DENMARK

Copenhagen

Peenemünde

DANZIG

LITHUANIA

Vilnius

EAST
PRUSSIA

GREAT
BRITAIN

Battle of Britain/Blitz
July 1940–May 1941
London

Wilhelmshaven

Hamburg

NETH.
Arnhem
Sept. 1944

Hague
BELG.

Bergen-Belsen
Hanover
Berlin

Treblinka

Kursk
July 1943

UKRAINE

Channel
Islands

Allies evacuate
Dunkirk
May–June 1940

RUHR

Cologne

Buchenwald

GERMANY

Dresden

Warsaw
Jewish ghetto uprising,
Aug.–Oct. 1944

Kharkov
Feb.–Mar. 1943

Kiev

Brussels

Battle of
the Bulge
Dec. 1944
–Jan. 1945

Allies cross the
Rhine at Remagen
Mar. 7, 1945

RHINELAND

SUDETENLAND

POLAND

Auschwitz
-Birkenau

Sept. 1941,
Aug.–Dec. 1943

ATLANTIC
OCEAN

NORMANDY
D-Day
Jun. 6,1944

Rouen

Paris

LUX.

Stuttgart

Dachau

Prague

CZECHOSLOVAKIA

SLOVAKIA

FRANCE

Vichy
capital of
unoccupied
France

Bern

SWITZ.

Vienna

AUSTRIA

Budapest

HUNGARY

Odessa

CRIMEA

Sevastopol

Black Se

VICHY

Marseilles

Allies land
Aug. 15, 1944

ITALY

Belgrade

YUGOSLAVIA

ROMANIA

Ploiesti
Bucharest

PORT.
Lisbon

Madrid

SPAIN

Corsica

Sardinia

Rome
Allies liberate
June 4, 1944

Anzio
Allies land
Jan. 22, 1944

Salerno
Allies land
Sept. 9, 1943

Monte Cassino
Jan.–May 1944

Sofia

BULGARIA

Tirana
ALB.

Istanbul

GREECE

TURKEY

SPANISH
MOROCCO

Palermo

Sicily

July 9–10, 1943

Athens

Cyprus

Crete

MOROCCO

ALGERIA

TUNISIA

Malta
Axis bombing raids
Dec. 1941–July 1942

Mediterranean Sea

PALESTINE
TRANS-
JORDAN

FOR NORTH AFRICAN
CAMPAIGN, SEE P. 201.

LIBYA

El Alamein
July 1942;
Oct.–Nov. 1942

EGYPT

p. 192

p. 226

p. 190

p. 240

p. 222

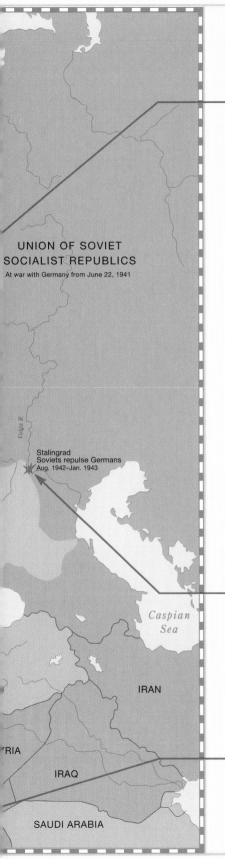

p. 191

THE WAR IN EUROPE

The map tells the story: Without going to war, Germany expanded west, south, and east. When it loosed its armies, the Allies staggered, then swept to victory.

Key

Germany up to Sept. 1, 1939

Axis powers and Axis-aligned nations, Sept. 1939–42

Areas conquered by Axis, Sept. 1939–42

Neutral nations

Allied nations and Allied-aligned nations, Sept. 1939–42

⊛ Capitals

✶ Battles

↟ Allied invasions

⬇ Important Allied bombings

⬇ Important Axis bombings

▪ Concentration/extermination camps

-→ Convoy routes

Long before German armies smashed into Poland on September 1, 1939, Hitler, by fair means or foul, had been acquiring territory, building his military strength, and forging alliances in Europe. The German expansion of the 1930's began in January 1935, when the people of the Saar, a region bordering France and Germany, voted to return to German rule after more than 15 years of administration by the League of Nations. Emboldened, Hitler the next year flagrantly ignored the Treaty of Versailles and remilitarized the Rhineland (see map), which included the Saar. Exactly two years later, taking advantage of Austrian economic and sociopolitical disorder, he brought Austria under German rule in the notorious *Anschluss* (union). A little more than six months later, Hitler began absorbing Czechoslovakia piece by piece into his Third Reich. Jumping north, Hitler then gobbled up the Baltic seaport territory of Memel in Lithuania. In less than five years, Germany had enlarged itself by thousands of square kilometres; and it counted among its European partners Italy, Bulgaria, Romania, and Hungary.

Bursting the Axis Bubble at Last

Threats, deceit, and Machiavellian alliances had served Hitler well. For almost three years after he attacked Poland, it seemed that armed aggression would serve him even better. By the fall of 1942, as the map shows, Germany and its Axis friends ruled an empire that stretched from the gates of Moscow to the shores of the Atlantic, from the deserts of Africa to the Arctic Ocean. But then came the British victory at El Alamein in North Africa and the heroic Soviet stand at Stalingrad. Momentum swung to the Allies. Amphibious invasions struck Axis-held Europe from the south and west; the Soviets rolled in from the east. Allied bombers rained destruction on the heart of Germany. East and west, Germany itself was breached, and the Allied armies poured in. Increasingly desperate, the Nazis accelerated mass slayings at concentration camps. Then Hitler killed himself in his Berlin bunker. On May 8, 1945, the war in Europe was over, five years eight months and seven days after it began.

p. 202

p. 201

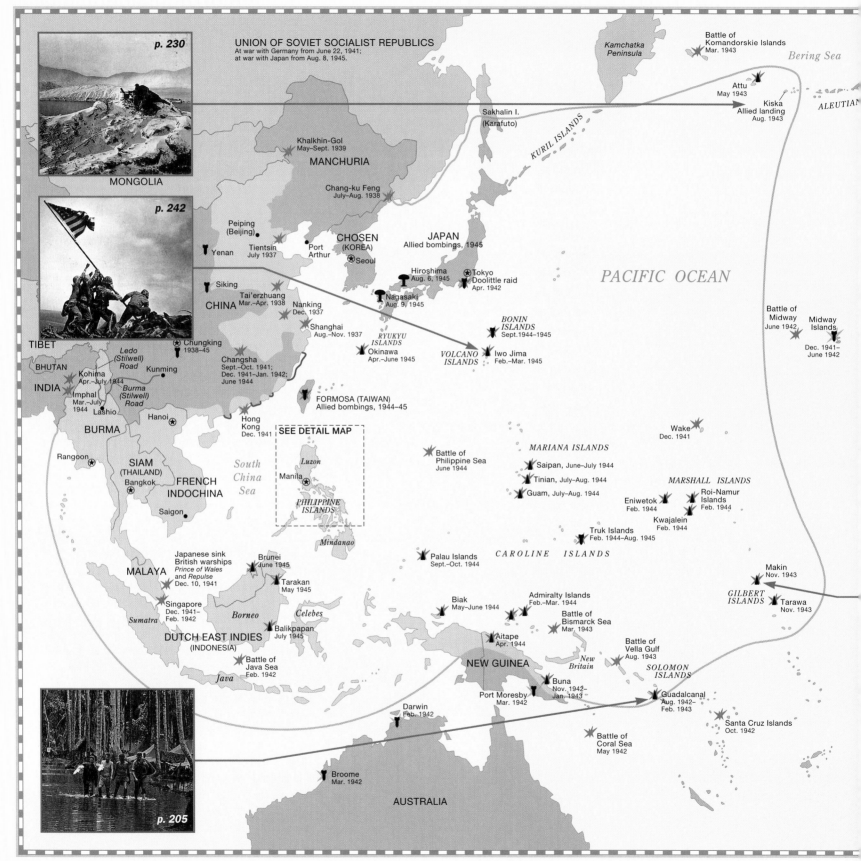

p. 230

MONGOLIA

p. 242

UNION OF SOVIET SOCIALIST REPUBLICS
At war with Germany from June 22, 1941;
at war with Japan from Aug. 8, 1945.

Kamchatka
Peninsula

Bering Sea

Battle of
Komandorskie Islands
Mar. 1943

Attu
May 1943

Kiska
Allied landing
Aug. 1943

ALEUTIAN

Sakhalin I.
(Karafuto)

KURIL ISLANDS

Khalkhin-Gol
May–Sept. 1939

MANCHURIA

Chang-ku Feng
July–Aug. 1938

PACIFIC OCEAN

Peiping
(Beijing)

Yenan

Tientsin
July 1937

Port
Arthur

Seoul

CHOSEN
(KOREA)

JAPAN
Allied bombings, 1945

Hiroshima
Aug. 6, 1945

Tokyo
Doolittle raid
Apr. 1942

Siking

CHINA

Tai'erzhuang
Mar.–Apr. 1938

Nanking
Dec. 1937

Nagasaki
Aug. 9, 1945

Battle of
Midway
June 1942

Midway
Islands

TIBET

Chungking
1938–45

Shanghai
Aug.–Nov. 1937

*RYUKYU
ISLANDS*

Okinawa
Apr.–June 1945

*BONIN
ISLANDS*
Sept. 1944–1945

Iwo Jima
Feb.–Mar. 1945

Dec. 1941–
June 1942

BHUTAN

Kohima
Apr.–July 1944

Ledo
(Stilwell)
Road

Kunming

Changsha
Sept.–Oct. 1941;
Dec. 1941–Jan. 1942;
June 1944

*VOLCANO
ISLANDS*

INDIA

Imphal
Mar.–July
1944

Burma
(Stilwell)
Road

Lashio

Hanoi

BURMA

Rangoon

FORMOSA (TAIWAN)
Allied bombings, 1944–45

Wake
Dec. 1941

MARIANA ISLANDS

SIAM
(THAILAND)

Bangkok

FRENCH
INDOCHINA

Hong
Kong
Dec. 1941

South
China
Sea

SEE DETAIL MAP

Luzon

Manila

Battle of
Philippine Sea
June 1944

Saipan, June–July 1944

Tinian, July–Aug. 1944

MARSHALL ISLANDS

Roi-Namur
Islands
Feb. 1944

Saigon

*PHILIPPINE
ISLANDS*

Guam, July–Aug. 1944

Eniwetok
Feb. 1944

Kwajalein
Feb. 1944

Mindanao

Truk Islands
Feb. 1944–Aug. 1945

CAROLINE   ISLANDS

Makin
Nov. 1943

Japanese sink
British warships
Prince of Wales
and *Repulse*
Dec. 10, 1941

Brunei
June 1945

MALAYA

Tarakan
May 1945

Palau Islands
Sept.–Oct. 1944

*GILBERT
ISLANDS*

Tarawa
Nov. 1943

Singapore
Dec. 1941–
Feb. 1942

Sumatra

Borneo

Celebes

Balikpapan
July 1945

DUTCH EAST INDIES
(INDONESIA)

Biak
May–June 1944

Admiralty Islands
Feb.–Mar. 1944

Battle of
Bismarck Sea
Mar. 1943

Aitape
Apr. 1944

Battle of
Vella Gulf
Aug. 1943

Battle of
Java Sea
Feb. 1942

Java

NEW GUINEA

*New
Britain*

*SOLOMON
ISLANDS*

Buna
Nov. 1942–
Jan. 1943

Port Moresby
Mar. 1942

Guadalcanal
Aug. 1942–
Feb. 1943

Darwin
Feb. 1942

Santa Cruz Islands
Oct. 1942

Battle of
Coral Sea
May 1942

Broome
Mar. 1942

AUSTRALIA

p. 205

THE WAR IN THE PACIFIC

p. 197

p. 224

p. 224

Key

- Japanese empire as of 1933
- Occupied by Japan before Dec. 7, 1941
- Occupied by Japan after Dec. 7, 1941
- Neutral versus Japan for all or part of war
- Allied-held throughout war
- ---- Limit of Japanese advance
- —— Japanese naval blockade
- ⊛ Capitals
- ✳ Battles
- ⚔ Allied invasions
- ⚓ Allied air and naval strikes
- ▼ Japanese invasions
- ⚑ Japanese air strike outside occupied area
- ⚐ Atomic bomb
- —— Roads

THE WAR IN THE PHILIPPINES

Aparri
Dec. 1941

Vigan
Dec. 1941

Luzon

Lingayen Gulf
Dec. 1941
Jan. 1945

Camp O'Donnell
Clark Field

PHILIPPINE
ISLANDS

Bataan and
Corregidor
Jan. 1941–
May 1942,
Feb. 1945

Manila

Lamon Bay
Dec. 1941

Mindoro

Legaspi
Dec. 1941

Samar

Panay

Leyte

Battle for
Leyte Gulf
Oct. 1944

Cebu

Leyte
Oct. 1944

Palawan

Negros   *Bohol*

Japan held sway over approximately 25 percent of the Earth's surface before the Allies rallied and began to push the tenacious Japanese back toward their home islands, the Land of the Rising Sun.

Like its Axis partner Germany, on the other side of the globe, Japan had already won large chunks of territory before it attacked any Western power in World War II. As the Germans were claiming regions that they considered rightfully theirs in Europe (see map, pp. 206–07), Japan was doing the same on the Asian mainland (map at left). At the same time, in a curious twist of history, Japan, which had been on the Allied side in World War I, was busy building military bases on some of the Pacific island groups, such as Truk and Palau, that Germany had lost to Japan as a result of that earlier war.

Japan, the Land of the Rising Sun, aspired to nothing less than domination of Eastern Asia and the Western Pacific. To achieve this grand design, Japan knew it would have to take on the Western powers sooner or later. Secretly it chose the place and time: the U.S. naval base at Pearl Harbor in the Hawaiian Islands, December 7, 1941. The attack on Pearl Harbor was essential to knock out the American fleet and give Japanese invasion forces free passage to Pacific strongholds and islands.

As the smoke cleared over Pearl Harbor — and for many months thereafter — it looked as if Japan's daring move had succeeded. Victory followed victory for Japan, until by mid-1942 fully a quarter of the world fell under its rule. But the attack on Pearl Harbor had missed the aircraft carriers, which were not in port at the time. At the Battle of Midway, those carriers signalled the end of Japanese naval dominance. Meanwhile, American submarines virtually destroyed the Japanese merchant fleet.

Within a year, the Japanese found themselves in retreat under severe pressure from the British, Indians, Australians and New Zealanders in Southeast Asia and the Americans in the Pacific — and with even more of their army tied up facing the Chinese. Japan's defeat was now inevitable, though the terrible toll in human lives would keep mounting as the Allies fought their way across Southeast Asia and the Pacific.

(above left map)
Aleutian Is.
1942

ALASKA
(U.S.)

ISLANDS

HAWAIIAN ISLANDS
(U.S.)

Pearl Harbor
Dec. 7, 1941

THE MUD-RAIN-WIND-AND-FROST BOYS

Kilroy was here!

Tough, sassy, grudgingly good-humored, they saw the war from the level of a foxhole. And while they griped about the food, the officers, and the absence of women, they fought with a dogged courage that changed the world.

Ernie Pyle, shown here on Okinawa just days before a Japanese bullet killed him, wrote unforgettable columns that made the folks back home feel the hardship and danger of army life.

There is a story that a general approached a Canadian base where a sentry in rumpled uniform with buttons undone lounged at the gate. The general saluted stiffly; the sentry idly gazed back at him without moving.

"Look here, private," said the general, "See this uniform? Doesn't this make you think of something?"

"Yeah," said the private admiringly. "You got a great outfit. Look at the lousy stuff they gave me."

▲ *Mail call on Espíritu Santo, a South Pacific island, means news from home.*

Leggy starlet Chili Williams, one of the soldiers' most popular pinups, radiates enthusiasm for tools of war.

Whatever the army, Canadian, American or British, that sentry spoke for the enlisted men, the common soldiers. American correspondent Ernie Pyle wrote of them, "They were the underdogs. They were the mud-rain-wind-and-frost boys . . . they were the guys without whom the Battle of Africa could not have been won." Even the enemy respected them, particularly those officers who had served in World War I and remembered those black days of the German army when the Canadian spearhead drove them all the way back to their starting point of 1914.

But the soldier thought less of compliments than he did of home, humor and the love of a sweetheart. He decorated his tent or barracks with pictures of his wife or girlfriend, or with pinups of Betty Grable, Rita Hayworth, and lesser-known beauties, like Hollywood hopeful Chili Williams, whom *Life* magazine first presented in a two-piece polka-dot bathing suit. Soldiers painted whimsical names, slogans, and cartoon characters on their tanks, airplanes, ships, trucks, and even guns and bombs.

SNAFU, Kilroy, and Joe and Willie

The overseas soldier was endlessly resourceful. He turned tin cans into pots or skillets and supplemented his woefully unappetizing (if virtually unspoilable) diet of canned rations with fresh vegetables, eggs, and wine bought or bartered from locals he met as he slogged through the mud according to some grand strategic plan of which he had little knowledge. An oil drum with holes punched in the bottom made a serviceable field shower. One marine unit in the South Pacific rigged up a wind-powered washing machine using an old airplane propeller. The

◄ *A soldier's mess-hall diet often came out of cans: powdered eggs, dried milk, baked beans.*

CARTOONISTS VIEW THE WAR

As Bruce Bairnsfather had in the First World War, cartoonists expressed the viewpoint of the soldier in the second. "Herbie" was drawn by Sergeant "Bing" Coughlin for the Canadian army daily *The Maple Leaf.* Sometimes brave, sometimes scared, usually on the lookout for easy money, and always in trouble with officers, soldiers recognized Herbie instantly as one of them. One his comments, as he crouched behind shelter, summed up the feelings of all of them, "What I want to git most out of this war . . . is me!"

Bill Mauldin's Willy and Joe were Herbie for American troops. Some officers, like General Patton, were offended at the two cartoon soldiers who looked like bums and ridiculed their officers. But General Eisenhower and hundreds of thousands of ordinary soldiers loved them. After the war, Mauldin became a syndicated political cartoonist.

"Hang on to the cat, we'll test this one next." Coughlin's Herbie always got the best out of life, even during a war.

▲ *Bill Mauldin's characters Willie and Joe were grubby, unshaven, and bleary-eyed, but Mauldin himself was just a kid. A writer who met him at Anzio in 1944 wrote, "When he is tired, he looks all of sixteen."*

◄ *Mauldin's own favorite cartoon shows a cavalry sergeant putting his broken-down "iron pony" out of its misery.*

soldier spiced his language with terms like SNAFU (Situation Normal, All Fouled Up) and Mae West (the flier's life vest, whose girth reminded him of the voluptuous entertainer). Perhaps his most famous creation was the elusive Kilroy, who always seemed to arrive at any particular place before anybody else, leaving the message "Kilroy was here" scrawled on walls from Paris to Polynesia.

Soldiers raced to mail call, and the lucky ones pored over letters from home, each with a name and serial number. When they wrote back, their letters passed through censors who cut out any parts that might reveal information useful to the enemy, leaving some letters to reach home looking like a string of paper doll cutouts. For reading material, soldiers had special armed forces editions of books and magazines. There were even daily newspapers published by and for soldiers. Canadians had *The Maple Leaf* and Ameri-

▲ *The U.S. Army weekly,* Yank, *appeared worldwide from April 1942 through 1945.*

     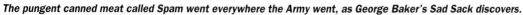

The pungent canned meat called Spam went everywhere the Army went, as George Baker's Sad Sack discovers.

WAR WORDS

Hundreds of expressions sprang up to accommodate the facts of wartime life. Much of this lingo covered things that no one had ever dreamed of before, but it was all wonderfully descriptive.

ashcan - an explosive charge (that looked like an ash can) dropped from a ship onto a U boat — and which sometimes provided fresh fish for the mess.

bazooka - an antitank rocket launcher; named after a novelty musical instrument it resembles.

blackout - the extinguishing or hiding of lights in case of an air raid. Also, momentary loss of consciousness in an accelerating plane.

blitz - a heavy air raid; from the German word for "lightning."

buzz - to fly over low in an airplane. Buzzing bathing beaches was a favorite stunt.

Dear John letter - a letter from your wife or sweetheart telling you it is all over between you.

flak - antiaircraft fire; from German *Fliegerabwehrkanone*, an antiaircraft gun.

flap - confusion, usually associated with a sudden retreat.

flattop - an aircraft carrier.

gremlin - an air force term referring to invisible creatures that made engines sputter, caused tires to go flat and guns to jam — or just generally made things go wrong.

gung ho - dedicated and enthusiastic; from the Chinese slogan meaning "Work together!"

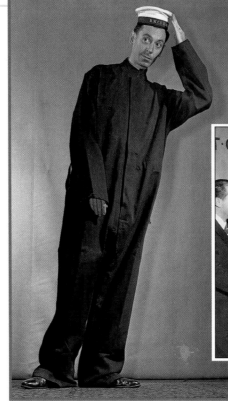

▶ *Petty Officer and comedian John Pratt entertains Canadian sailors in his "Meet the Navy Show," listing in his customary baggy uniform.*

▼ *Somewhere in France, Berlin-born anti-Nazi film star Marlene Dietrich belts out a ballad for GI's. Her theme song, "Lili Marlene," expressed a whole world of wartime loneliness.*

cans the *Stars and Stripes*. Americans also had the weekly *Yank*, featuring cartoonist George Baker's forever unlucky private, Sad Sack.

Among American correspondents, the most loved was Ernie Pyle who always tried to make his readers see what the common soldier saw and felt. When he was killed by a Japanese machine gun, soldiers erected a marker on his grave: "At This Spot the 77th Infantry Division Lost a Buddy, Ernie Pyle, 18 April, 1945."

One of the finest war correspondents was Canada's Ross Munro who, like Pyle, travelled with advancing troops. World War I veteran Greg Clark returned to his old battlefields to send back simple but touching stories of everyday happenings at the front. And none who heard him will ever forget the voice of Matthew Halton bringing the war to every living room in Canada. René Lévesque, too, served as a war correspondent — but for the American forces. He refused to join Canadian forces to fight for the British.

In War, Winds of Social Change

War brought stunning changes for women, as they did just about everything short of fighting, from nursing to truck driving. Some 300,000 women served in the U.S. armed forces. In Canada, with its smaller population, the number was proportionately even higher at 45,000. For the first time, women served as CWAC's (Canadian Women's Army Corps), WAAF's (Women's Auxiliary Air Force) and WREN's (Women's Royal Canadian Naval Services). As well, Canada enlisted more than 4,000 nursing sisters. Though deskbound Colonel Blimps snorted indignation at the thought of women in the forces, men at the front appreciated their skill and courage. Their strong performance challenged stereotypes and pointed the way for more change ahead.

Black servicemen, too, set social change in motion — though acceptance was even more grudging. In the United States, heavyweight boxing champion Joe Lewis won admiring headlines by enlisting in the army. In combat uniform with rifle and bayonet, he became one of the first black Americans to be featured on a patriotic poster. But black officers and men still served, for the most part, in segregated units, were commonly assigned noncombat duties such as grave-digging and road repairing, and were barred from many off-duty recreational facilities.

Canada had no official segregation, but the unofficial version was quite effective. Unlike the First World War, blacks had a place in the Canadian army — though their chances of reaching officer rank were slim. In the navy and air force, though, few were even accepted. Japanese-Canadians, despite their strenuous efforts to enlist, were flatly rejected by Canadian authorities. Not until the closing

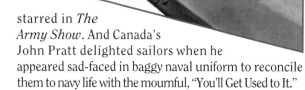

▶ *The Women's Auxiliary Ferrying Squadron (WAFS) flew planes from factory to airfield, sometimes shuttling them as far as England; here WAFS chief Nancy Love takes the controls of an army trainer. Unlike army Wacs and navy Waves (right), the women in WAFS were technically civilians.*

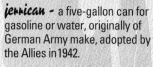

months of the war — and then in response to a British request for translators — would Canada ease its restrictions. For the most part, Canada and the United States would not give military equality to their racial minorities until after the war.

Common Bonds

Entertainers such as Vera Lynn, Bob Hope and Marlene Dietrich followed punishing schedules and endured no-frills military travel to bring serving men live shows. In the United States, the USO (United Services Organizations) became a kind of super impresario, sending scores of performers to entertain soldiers in every theatre of war where audiences could range from thousands to a mere 25 or so at the most lonely outposts.

Comedians Johnny Wayne and Frank Shuster came to Canadian attention when they enlisted in the army and were starred in *The Army Show*. And Canada's John Pratt delighted sailors when he appeared sad-faced in baggy naval uniform to reconcile them to navy life with the mournful, "You'll Get Used to It."

Between Allied servicemen of various nations there was much respect and a lot of good-natured rivalry. With waves of GI's arriving in England, the British were soon wryly describing the Yanks as "overpaid, oversexed, and over here." The Americans replied that the Brits were "underpaid, undersexed, and under Eisenhower." The Americans were amazed by stories of Scottish commandos proudly wearing their regimental kilts on daring raids into France. And like their U.S. counterparts, the Tommies loved poking fun at their officers and at military life in general. ENSA (Entertainments National Services Association), the British equivalent of the USO, was affectionately mocked as showing "Every Night Something Awful."

◀ *Late in the war a GI hands out caramels to a cluster of children in the bomb-blasted railway station in Caserta, Italy.*

Kilroy was here!

jerrican - a five-gallon can for gasoline or water, originally of German Army make, adopted by the Allies in 1942.

jungle juice - home-brewed booze concocted in the Pacific. In northern Europe, it might be called "rocket fuel."

liberate - to loot, commandeer, appropriate.

milk run - an easy or routine air force mission.

Newfie John - The port of St. John's, Newfoundland, a major base for convoy escort ships.

pusser - official issue naval uniform. Also anything done strictly according to the rules.

snow job - deliberately confusing, flattering speech.

socked in - prevented by weather from taking off in an airplane.

task force - a grouping of units for a given tactical operation.

wavy navy - The Royal Canadian Navy Volunteer Reserve, so called because of its officers' wavy stripes of rank.

zombie - a soldier who had been conscripted, but had not volunteered for overseas service.

COURAGE UNDER TYRANTS' HEELS

As the Axis cracked down hard, both at home in Germany and Japan and in the conquered lands, small groups behind the front lines strove valiantly to resist the new order. Meanwhile, Allied bombers wreaked another form of terror.

◄ *A poster by U.S. artist Ben Shahn decried Nazi atrocities in Czechoslovakia.*

G ive me five years," Adolf Hitler promised the German people during his rise to power, "and you will not recognize Germany." Such boastful rhetoric played a vital role in the Führer's master plan. "Hitler promised everybody something," explains one historian, "and a lot of people almost everything." He knew that there was only one way to achieve his imperial dream of a "thousand-year Reich," and that was to make all Germans share it.

The declaration of war troubled most Germans, but each new victory in Europe and the U.S.S.R. boosted their sense of national pride. Military success also brought Germans something more tangible. After two decades of economic privation following World War I, relief came in the form of long-scarce goods. Daily necessities as well as luxuries, such as Norwegian furs, French perfume, and Dutch dairy products, began to flow in from countries conquered by the Germans.

By late 1942, however, as thousands of wounded soldiers returned from the eastern front, Germany's short-lived halcyon days were over. Hoping to hasten Hitler's demise by breaking the spirit of his people, the Allies adopted a strategy of around-the-clock attacks, which some U.S. journalists dubbed terror bombing and which reached their height of fury in raids like the one on Dresden in February 1945. U.S. and British air squadrons dropped so many incendiary bombs on the splendid old city that it burned for a week. "Never would I have thought," mourned one eyewitness, "that death could come to so many people in so many different ways."

THE PLOT THAT FAILED

F ew Germans would voice their opposition to Adolf Hitler for fear of retribution, but some were willing to risk their lives to bring down the Third Reich. One group came close to succeeding. In June 1944, when Germany's ultimate defeat seemed assured, a number of prominent Germans, including both high-ranking army officers and influential civilians, began making plans to take over the government. Hoping to stop further bloodshed and to salvage some vestige of their country's honor, the plotters intended to outlaw the Nazi Party and the Gestapo, halt the extermination programs, negotiate peace with the Allies, and withdraw from all occupied territories. But they knew that first they would have to kill Adolf Hitler.

The man who volunteered for that mission was Col. Claus Schenk, count von Stauffenberg, a staff officer with direct access to the Führer. A war hero and intellectual who represented the

Stauffenberg

German aristocratic tradition, Stauffenberg had for years detested the Nazi regime. "I feel I must do something now," he confided to his wife, "to save Germany."

On July 20, 1944, at a meeting in Hitler's supreme command headquarters, in East Prussia, Stauffenberg placed a briefcase containing a time bomb near the Führer's feet, then excused himself to make a phone call. Another officer not involved in the plot accidentally kicked the briefcase, then moved it a few feet away. When the bomb exploded, Hitler escaped with only slight injuries. The Gestapo swung into action. Over the remaining months of the war, about 5,000 anti-Nazi Germans, including Stauffenberg, were executed for their complicity in the plot, or merely for their association with the plotters.

◄

Flanked by storm troopers, who used strong-arm tactics to intimidate foes of nazism, Hitler leads his retinue of jackbooted Nazi officers past rows of swastikas at a rally in northern Germany.

To keep Germans loyal, the Nazi Party employed every tool imaginable, from propaganda to terror. Hitler's dreaded secret police, the Gestapo, was ruthless in ferreting out and crushing even the slightest hint of opposition. People were urged to spy on family members for any sign of disloyalty. Listening to a foreign radio station was an act of treason, punishable by death.

Nazi Crackdown, Anti-Nazi Intrigue

The notorious chief of Hitler's "evil guardian angels," as the SS (short for Schutzstaffel, the Nazi police unit) was once described, was Heinrich Himmler, who in the early days boasted that his corps was so elite that even a filled tooth was enough to disqualify a candidate. Under Himmler's leadership, SS men became masters in the art of interrogation by torture. One concentration camp guard was fond of greeting new arrivals with the chilling welcome: "This is hell, and I am the devil." As the war widened, the SD (short for Sicherheitsdienst, the Nazi security service) and the Gestapo (secret police) extended their control to the occupied countries of Europe. Under Hitler's Night and Fog decree, enemies of the Reich were to be disposed of by being made to disappear into "night and fog," that is, without a trace.

Most conquered peoples succumbed to the terror. Some, in fact, enthusiastically cooperated. But there were those who resisted — even in Germany. In 1941, a Munich student named Hans Scholl founded the underground White Rose movement to resist the Nazis. He and his sister were guillotined in 1943. Others plotted to kill Hitler, but none succeeded. He even survived the explosion of a bomb that was placed near him in a briefcase on July 20, 1944 (see box at left).

But Hitler's megalomania could not stop the Allied bombing raids that were tearing apart his country and its people. In July and August 1943, for example, the Allies launched a massive assault on Hamburg, Germany's largest port and second-largest city. For nine days U.S. and British bombers unleashed their fury on Hamburg. The city and its population were devastated: 26 square kilometres lay in ruins and an estimated 50,000 civilians lost their lives. Across the country, people feared that what happened to Hamburg could happen to them — and in many cases it did. By the end of the war, most of Germany's large towns and cities were so ravaged that, true to Hitler's promise, they were unrecognizable.

WARRIORS OF THE SPIRIT

Most who warred against Nazism on its own territory were unarmed civilians. Some took direct action, such as hiding people wanted by the Gestapo. Others, like Protestant theologian Dietrich Bonhöffer, led double lives. While ostensibly working for Germany's intelligence service, Bonhöffer was at the same time transmitting messages to the British from anti-Nazi resistance leaders. The Nazis eventually caught and executed him.

Others served by keeping a record. The most celebrated of these witnesses was Anne Frank (below), a German-Jewish teenager. The Frank family had fled Germany for Amsterdam in 1933 to get away from nazism. When the Nazis marched into Holland, Otto Frank hid his family for two years in a secret annex in his office building. Upon learning of the hideout, the Gestapo took the Franks away to concentration camps in August 1944. All died except for Mr. Frank. When he returned to Amsterdam in 1945, his faithful employee, Miep Gies, gave him Anne's writings, which she had retrieved from the annex floor after the family's hasty departure. *The Diary of a Young Girl* remains the most vivid, warmly human document of the entire war.

One who resisted simply by living to tell the tale was Elie Wiesel (above). A gifted child of Jewish parents in Romania, young Elie had already written a book-length Bible commentary when, at age 15, he was taken to Auschwitz. Survival in a death camp was a matter of luck. Elie's parents and sister perished. Convinced that Providence had chosen him to bear witness to the Holocaust, the term he applied to the wholesale murder of Jews by the Nazis, Wiesel wrote his first book, *Night*, which appeared in English in 1960. A citizen of the United States since 1957, he was awarded the Nobel Peace Prize in 1986.

Bonhöffer, Wiesel, and Anne Frank were exceptional, but they were not alone. There were many warriors of the spirit. Most belonged to that unsung multitude who braved the Nazi terror and perished without leaving a trace.

BRAVE RESISTANCE ACROSS EUROPE

TOOLS OF A TRICKY TRADE

Routine searches and draconian punishments made the arts of disguise and concealment vital to resistance operatives. This inspired the invention of such ingenious low-tech espionage gadgetry as a real poison-pen (left) and a book hollowed out to conceal a handgun (below). Resisters hid items such as coded messages in the heels of their boots, and built radio receivers in a myriad of deceptive shapes.

Under the heel of German occupation, most people in the vanquished countries of Europe were simply glad to stay alive. The governments of France and Denmark, hoping to make the best of a bad situation, urged compliance with the enemy. Leaders of other defeated countries — Belgium, Luxembourg, the Netherlands, Norway, Poland, Czechoslovakia, Greece, Yugoslavia — fled to London, where they set up governments in exile. In BBC broadcasts they urged compatriots to sit tight and await liberation by the Allies.

Inevitably, small acts of resistance began to occur. Brave individuals hid persons sought by the Nazis. Young Danes wore red, white, and blue in solidarity with the British. Clandestine pamphlets and newspapers appeared. Factory workers staged job slowdowns when the product was intended for the Germans. Others, working with Allied intelligence services, ferreted out military secrets and radioed them to London and Moscow. Ham operators in Holland and Czechoslovakia were conspicuously active, and many paid with their lives. Sabotage became a key resistance tactic. In 1943 Norwegian underground fighters destroyed a heavy-water plant, effectively halting Germany's A-bomb program.

As the resistance increased, Germany's occupation troops began to crack down. On June 4, 1942, Czechoslovakia's notorious

A propaganda photo extols the courage of Yugoslav women partisans under the command of resistance leader Josip Broz (Tito). They are shown undergoing training before assignment to combat.

Nazi governor, Reinhard (Hangman) Heydrich, died of injuries sustained during an attempt on his life by British-trained agents. In a frenzy of reprisals the Germans killed more than 1,000 Czechs and later slaughtered 3,000 inmates of a local concentration camp.

In many occupied lands citizens banded together to wage guerrilla war. Soon after Hitler's battalions marched into the U.S.S.R., Soviet resistance fighters began attacking German supply lines, blowing up trains and bridges, and harassing rear-guard area military posts. By 1944 the Soviet partisans numbered as many as 300,000 men and women, controlled 518,000 square kilometres of territory, and effectively tied down 25 German field divisions. In both Greece and Yugoslavia, rival partisan factions armed variously by Moscow or London battled the German occupiers, and sometimes each other. In Italy anti-Fascist guerrillas resisted sweeps by German divisions. When fallen dic-

▲ *Two Greek freedom fighters wear pickup uniforms but carry no-nonsense carbines supplied by the Allies.*

A marksman with the French Resistance, shod in homemade straw boots, guards a road in Brittany.

tator Benito Mussolini was captured and executed, in 1945, Italian partisans carried out the deed.

Some resistance efforts backfired, with dire consequences. In 1944, as Soviet troops approached Warsaw, the local Polish underground revolted against their German occupiers. When the smoke cleared, 85 percent of Warsaw was smoldering rubble and 250,000 Poles lay dead. Soon after, the Soviets moved in and set up a Communist government.

But for every failure, resistance fighters scored a dozen victories. One of the most notable was achieved by the French, who in 1942 relayed Germany's coastal defence plans to London, thus helping Eisenhower plan the Normandy invasion two years later.

TERROR AND TRAGEDY IN ASIA

When news of the victory at Pearl Harbor reached the Japanese people, the prospect of plunging into a global war drew mixed reactions. "I never thought I should live to see . . . such a thrilling day, such an auspicious day," one citizen declared. "The good ship Japan has just been sunk," another lamented, fearing what lay beyond the glow of early triumph. In the short term Japan would extend its rule to more than 2.5 million square kilometres of territory and more than 150 million people, but as a result of the war, at least 2.5 million Japanese would be counted dead or missing and more than 10 million would lose their homes.

As the Japanese took over Southeast Asia, they Nipponized vanquished countries. They replaced the Roman calendar with the Japanese one. Western languages, one order decreed, "have ceased to exist." When a native happened to meet up with a Japanese, the native either bowed or received a slap in the face.

Secret Police and Phony Co-Prosperity

Japan did not accept Western ideas about humane treatment of prisoners or civilians. Japan's secret police, the Kempei Tai, were notorious for pulling out their victims' fingernails during interrogations. After the Japanese conquered Singapore in 1942, they massacred more than 5,000 Chinese residents. At the fall of Hong Kong, in December 1941, 56 hospitalized Canadian and British soldiers were bayoneted. Five doctors and two nurses who tried to stop the slaughter were shot. After the surrender, Canadian soldiers were subjected to years of heavy labor, inadequate food or medical care, and frequent beatings. Then they were shipped as slave labor to Japan. When the war ended, 557 of the almost 2,000 Canadian soldiers who had sailed to defend Hong Kong were dead, and most of the rest forever broken in health.

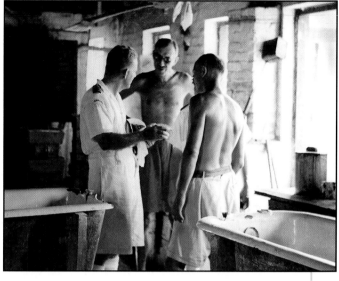

A naval officer from H.M.C.S. Prince Robert inspects the ablution facilities in Shamshuipo prison camp, Kowloon, after the release of Canadian POW's there in September 1945.

Since Japan had been at war with China for more than four years before Pearl Harbor, the Japanese people had grown accustomed to hardship and sacrifice, but their fortitude faced even harsher tests after 1941. "To live at all," recalled Foreign Minister Mamoru Shigemitsu, "the people reverted to a primitive existence." Rice imports fell to almost nothing as the Americans took command of the seas, and hardy, fast-growing pumpkin replaced rice as the national staple. Buddhist monks were conscripted to work in factories. Faced with shortages of both manpower and clothing, many women forsook centuries-old traditions. They traded their kimonos for baggy trousers and did what had to be done to keep family and society together.

No amount of sacrifice, however, could triumph over the lethal rain of bombs that fell on Japan beginning in 1944, and that would culminate a year later in the atomic devastation of the cities Hiroshima and Nagasaki. As one Japanese civilian said after a raid on Tokyo: "We finally began to realize . . . that the government had lied when it said we were invulnerable. We then started to doubt that we were also invincible."

THE FIGHTING FILIPINOS
WE WILL ALWAYS FIGHT FOR FREEDOM!

A U.S. poster rallied support for the Filipino resistance movement, which was secretly led by U.S. advisers.

INDUSTRY GOES TO WAR

While fighting men stood ready to make the ultimate sacrifice, home-front citizens kept them well armed and fully equipped by making some sacrifices of their own.

In the 1930's, Canadian shipyards built a total of only 14 steamers. But between 1939 and 1945, they built 398 merchant ships and 393 naval vessels, everything from patrol vessels to 10,000 tonners. There were Fairmiles for coastal and river patrols; cramped, rolling, and ugly but invaluable corvettes for ocean convoys; frigates for anti-submarine work; speedy destroyers; and ponderous freighters of the Park class.

Canada's aircraft industry, struggling before the war, produced 15,000 military airplanes from 1939 to 1945. Two-thirds were trainers; the rest were mostly front-line aircraft: Canso flying boats, Mosquito fighter-bombers, Lancaster bombers and Hurricane fighters.

But the automobile industry outdid them all, producing so many motor vehicles that one-quarter of all Commonwealth military vehicles of the Second World War began their lives in Canadian factories. Additionally, thousands more were delivered to the beleaguered Soviet armies. In proportion to its population, Canada came second to none in wartime production.

As industry in both Canada and the United States hummed into high gear, it needed hundreds of thousands and then millions of new workers, and women answered the call. The popular song "Rosie the Riveter" celebrated the women who took over factory jobs, especially traditionally male tasks, such as riveting and welding. Norman Rockwell painted Rosie as a mus-

cular Amazon for the cover of *The Saturday Evening Post* magazine. The inspiration for the Rosie legend may have been one Rosie Bonavita, who, with the help of another woman, pounded 3,345 rivets into the wing of a fighter plane in a record six hours.

New factories sprouted in cornfields and cow pastures. Near Detroit, at a creek named Willow Run, Henry Ford built a 28-hectare aircraft plant, which was called the "most enormous room in the history of man." Aviation pioneer Charles Lindbergh referred to it as "a sort of Grand Canyon of a mechanized world."

Factories alone could not work miracles, however. In the past airplanes and ships had been put together one at a time. Now plant managers had to figure out by trial and error how to assemble them on a mass-production basis. J. D. Kindelberger, North American Aviation president, commented: "You cannot expect black-

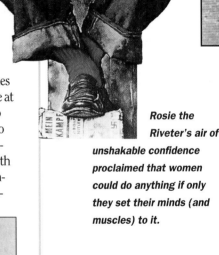

Rosie the Riveter's air of unshakable confidence proclaimed that women could do anything if only they set their minds (and muscles) to it.

Spurred on by posters like the one rallying all Canadians to do their bit for the war (upper left), workers across North America assembled planes, such as the B-17F (circle inset), at record speeds and completed an entire Liberty ship (left) in only 10 days.

▲ *North Americans across the continent held scrap drives to fight shortages. Above, U.S. Boy Scouts collected more than 80 tonnes of rubber.*

HERES OUR ANSWER PRESIDENT ROOSEVELT

We're in the army now

YOUR AID IS VITAL!
Save METALS RAGS PAPER
BONES RUBBER GLASS
THEY ARE USED IN WAR SUPPLIES

▼ *Champions of the Allied armored forces, these M-4 Sherman tanks receive finishing touches from Ford mechanics, 1942.*

smiths to learn how to make watches overnight." Nevertheless, industry rose to the occasion. By 1944 bombers were coming off Henry Ford's assembly line at the rate of one every 63 minutes.

In Canada, the genius presiding over industry was Clarence Decatur Howe, minister of munitions and supply. Tough and efficient, he won the support of business leaders as he proved he could ensure delivery of the materials they needed to meet his demanding quotas.

In the United States, the War Production Board (WPB) quickly took control of supplies and stopped the production of all materials nonessential for the war, a list that included refrigerators, beer cans, toothpaste tubes and wire clothes hangers.

North Americans launched scavenger hunts for reusable rubber and metal. Boy Scouts and Girl Guides scoured attics, basements, and garages for old automobile and bicycle tires, overshoes, aluminum pans, rubber mats, and hot-water bottles. Hollywood and Broadway pitched in too, as when the actress Merle Oberon lent her beauty to orchestrating an aluminum drive at the Stork Club, a stylish New York night spot.

With organization and dedication like that, the Axis powers were beaten on the two fronts that mattered most — in the field, by fighting men, and in production, largely due to the overwhelming manufacturing capacity of the United States and Canada.

Make DO OR DO WITHOUT

Whether it meant cutting down on cigarettes, driving less, eating less meat, turning the front lawn into a cabbage patch, or resisting the blandishments of black marketeers, folks at home strove to do all they could for the war effort.

When you ride ALONE you ride with Hitler!

Join a Car-Sharing Club TODAY!

As Canadians had done in 1939, Americans learned a new refrain as 1942 began: "Use it up, wear it out, make it do, or do without." If tempers frayed because of the long workdays and limited goods, complainers were stopped short with an impatient, "Hey! Don't you know there's a war going on?"

Many companies were quick to discover that a patriotic image was good for business. "Lucky Strike Green Has Gone to War," proclaimed the American Tobacco Company to explain the switch from green to white packages; supposedly, green dye contained precious metals that were vital to the war effort. Whatever the package color, home-front smokers frequently waited in block-long lines to purchase their favorite brands, since most cigarettes went to the servicemen.

In both countries, gasoline became scarce early in the war and many filling stations closed. The Wartime Prices and Trade Board (in Canada) and the Office of Price Administration (in the United States) issued windshield stickers to indicate how much gas drivers were entitled to. For most drivers, it might be only a few litres a week, rising for drivers whose cars were necessary for defence work or other essential services.

Pleasure driving all but stopped. Montrealers were treated to the sight of tramway inspectors doing their rounds in horse-drawn buggies. Retail stores eliminated home deliveries; milkmen rediscovered horses and wagons. Home-front workers made car pooling a North American institution, while departing servicemen tenderly put their

DO YOUR BIT! SKATE TO WORK SAVE GAS

A poster lashed out at solo driving (above, left), while in a promo stunt for the 1942 Broadway musical Roller Vanities these girls show off an alternative.

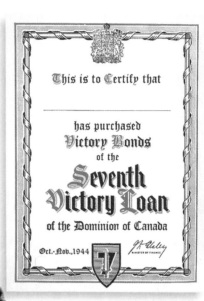

This is to Certify that

_____

has purchased
Victory Bonds
of the
Seventh Victory Loan
of the Dominion of Canada

Oct.-Nov., 1944

Raising money for the war effort in World War II, Canada issued nine Victory Loans in which ordinary citizens could participate and lend their money to their country.

cars up on blocks in the garage. At the same time, express buses suspended service, plane tickets were unavailable for ordinary civilian travel, and the government took over steamships.

Inevitably, black marketeers appeared on the scene. Some forged gas coupons; others stole real ones. But, despite the criminals, gas rationing worked with remarkable effectiveness.

Travel restrictions were an inconvenience, but food restrictions cut closer to the bone. Coffee was added to the list of rationed goods, and so was sugar. Sugar imports from the Philippines had been cut off, and ships that normally transported sugar from Cuba and Puerto Rico, and coffee from South America, were appropriated for defence. It was not that food was in short supply (North Americans produced enough of most foods to feed themselves as well as needy Allies); it was rather a question of ensuring that food be fairly distributed, that prices be kept down, and that there be no wastage. Both countries, therefore, instituted systems of rationing, with each person issued coupons which had to be exchanged, along with money, for any food purchase. Even restaurant meals called for ration stamps.

By July 1943 the Allies began to win the battle against U-boats, and more cargo space became available for nonmilitary shipments. Coffee rationing ended, and the weekly civilian allotment of sugar rose. Meanwhile, by February 1943 the military's need to send food overseas had brought rationing to canned meat and fish. In March other canned foods were added, followed by fresh meats, butter, and cheese.

People found a number of ways to stretch their coupons. One called for ingenuity in the kitchen (see box at right). But the best and most patriotic coupon-stretcher was the victory garden. With feverish enthusiasm, people spaded up everything from a few square metres of land to hectares. Flower beds became cabbage patches, and grass surrendered to lettuce. What wasn't eaten fresh went into mason jars as homemakers returned in droves to the old-fashioned art of putting up their harvest.

From the beginning of the war, the Canadian and American governments managed production and their economies masterfully. Wage and price controls kept costs within reason. Heavy taxes on profits soaked up excess money to ease inflation and help pay for the war. So did war bonds which were made available in small donations and on the instalment plan. Even children contributed by buying mini-war bonds from their allowances. Called war savings stamps, they sold for 25 cents each in Canada, 10 cents each in the United States, and yielded 5% interest at the end of the war. In Canada, mandatory saving from pay cheques also kept inflation down and provided pent-up buying power for the postwar period.

In short, both governments did what economists had urged them to do during the Depression — but what governments and business in both Canada and the United States had said was impossible. They intervened forcefully to create economic growth by creating jobs through government spending, and they kept that growth healthy through extensive systems of controls. Many North Americans, remembering the harshness of the Depression, had no desire ever to return to the laissez-faire days of the 1930's.

EATING TO WIN THE WAR

Although it isn't / Our usual habit
This year we're eating / The Easter Rabbit.

So went a poem in a 1943 issue of *Gourmet* magazine, when World War II made sugar, dairy products, meat, and coffee scarce or unavailable. With rationing in effect from early 1942 through 1946, preparing meals became an experiment in creativity. Women stretched everything to the limit and substituted foods they could get for ones they couldn't. Pork, fish, chicken, or even horse meat replaced beef. Casseroles and stews were made from whatever icebox leftovers the family would tolerate. And meatless meals meant families sitting down to supper and facing Cottage Cheese Loaf as the "meat dish." For dessert they might have had a sugarless Yankee Doodle Prune Pie with a low-shortening Victory Pie Crust. Not enough java to serve with it? Then chicory was added to the brew, or coffee drinkers took President Roosevelt's wry advice and rebrewed their grounds. Even the White House went on an austerity plan: reduced portions for the help. Homemakers cut down on baking, and restaurants put less sugar in their sugar bowls to help "build final and complete victory." Most North Americans regarded the lack of sugar — and of almost everything else they most loved — with a resigned acceptance that was usually more wistful than grumbling. The popular columnist Walter Winchell summed it up best:

Roses are red, violets are blue.
Sugar is sweet. Remember?

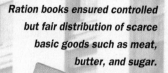

Ration books ensured controlled but fair distribution of scarce basic goods such as meat, butter, and sugar.

One of 20 million or so North Americans to grow a victory garden, this parking lot owner spaded up enough asphalt to grow 13.5 kilograms of tomatoes, 100 ears of corn, and 75 fine heads of cabbage.

Hard Fighting in the Soft Underbelly

Striking directly into Europe, Allied troops battled their way up the Italian peninsula — to the noisy delight of most Italians. Unfamiliar place-names dominated the morning headlines: Salerno, Anzio, Monte Cassino.

Lashed by a summer gale, the armada of 3,000 ships rolled and pitched in heavy seas off Malta. Crammed in troop carriers, some 160,000 U.S., Canadian, and British soldiers fought varying degrees of seasickness and prebattle jitters. Their destination: the island of Sicily. Above the invasion fleet an airborne force of some 4,000 men — glider troops and paratroopers — droned ahead to open the assault behind the beaches. It was July 9, 1943, and Operation Husky had begun.

Next morning, the troops stormed ashore. Lt. Gen. George S. Patton, Jr., sporting his ivory-handled revolvers, led the U.S. Seventh Army onto Sicily's south coast. The British Eighth Army, commanded by Gen. Bernard L. Montgomery, landed to the east. The island's defenders, 350,000 Germans and Italians, under Field Marshal Albert (Smiling Albert) Kesselring, fell back to regroup.

Operation Husky was the first Allied thrust into Western Europe, and it aimed at the "soft underbelly" of Axis power, as Winston Churchill put it. And despite a few major blunders — Allied antiaircraft fire downed a number of Allied planes, for example — the campaign was a success. Italian units, never eager to march for Hitler's generals, surrendered in droves. The island's civilians greeted the Allies as liberators, embracing them and plying them with wine

Allied troops roll into Palermo, capital of Sicily (top), while jubilant residents wave flags and shout welcoming slogans, such as "Down with Mussolini!" Keeping a sharp lookout for snipers (circle inset) a Canadian patrol advances cautiously up a narrow lane in Agira, central Sicily, in July 1943.

and fruit. The harsher experiences of war were never far away, however. As the Allies pushed Kesselring's remaining 60,000 Germans into a corner in the northeast, heavy fighting took many casualties. For the Canadian soldiers of the 1st Division and 1st Armoured Brigade, it was their first extended action of the war, and a foretaste of what was to come. More than 1,600 were wounded and 564 killed in the Sicily fighting.

In mid-August Kesselring withdrew his surviving forces across the Strait of Messina to the Italian mainland. Enemy resistance appeared to be dissolving. Benito Mussolini, Italy's Fascist head of state, had been replaced, and the new government was conducting secret armistice negotiations. All that was needed to take Italy out of the war, it seemed, was to land a few troops on the mainland.

Fierce German Counterattacks

But no one had reckoned with the strength of German determination. Hitler poured in men and weapons. Montgomery's Eighth Army landed first, on September 3, at Reggio di Calabria, on the Italian toe. Then, six days later and 320 kilometres up the Italian boot, Lt. Gen. Mark W. Clark's U.S. Fifth Army splashed ashore at Salerno, a day's march south of Naples.

Both armies immediately discovered that the narrowness of Italy, combined with difficult terrain gave a tremendous advantage to the seasoned German troops under Kesselring. The Germans gave ground slowly and expensively in Allied lives, falling back to the Gustav Line that ran south of Rome from Ortona on the east coast to Cassino on the west. Both were natural fortresses, with defences stoutly reinforced by German engineers.

Warned of a pending attack by Allied bombers, two Benedictine monks at Monte Cassino pack treasured books and parchments, including an 11th-century Latin grammar, for emergency shipment to the Vatican. After the monastery had been obliterated, German soldiers set up gun nests in the ruins, slowing the Allied advance.

The U.S. Fifth Army attempted to go around the Gustav Line, landing at Anazio to the north of Rome. But German armor and artillery pinned it to the beaches. Meanwhile, the British Eighth Army headed for Cassino, while the Canadians were assigned to Ortona.

With every farmhouse booby-trapped, with roads mined and German artillery ranged over them, every inch came at human cost. When Capt. Paul Triquet of the Royal 22nd Regiment led his company through 17 hours of combat to capture a vital crossroads, only 10 men survived of the original 81. Captain Triquet became Canada's first winner of the Victoria Cross in Italy.

There followed days of house-to-house fighting through the town of Ortona, defended by elite German parachutists. Ortona fell on December 27, 1943. The Gustav Line was broken, but at a cost to the Canadian 1st Division of 1,372 dead. On the east, Cassino fell to the British in May, leaving only the Hitler Line to block the road to Rome.

With Ortona, the Canadians were recognized once more as crack shock troops, just as they were in the First World War. That made them the natural choice to break the Hitler Line. In May of 1943, they broke through, letting in the tanks of the 5th Canadian Armoured Division. This eased the pressure on the U.S. Fifth Army at Anzio and opened the way for it to liberate Rome.

In Italy, the Canadian army which had waited so long in Britain was at last put to the test. To the dismay of the Germans, it proved to be every bit as good as the Canadian army of 1914–18. But the cost was high. When Canadians were transferred from the Italian front to Holland in 1945, they left behind more than 5,764 dead, with another 20,000 either wounded or missing.

IRON PONIES OF THE WAR

One day in 1941 a flying wedge of 18 odd-looking box-like vehicles charged onto a German airfield in North Africa with their specially fitted Vickers machine guns blazing. Within minutes they destroyed or damaged 37 planes, then bounced off into the desert before Rommel's people had time to figure out what had hit them. Manned by British soldiers, the American jeep had just made its combat debut. First developed in 1940, this olive-drab box on wheels weighed a quarter-tonne, had four-wheel drive, got 8.5 kilometres to the litre, and could go just about anyplace. The word *jeep* came both from the designation GP (general purpose) and from the name of a cartoon character, Popeye's pal Eugene the Jeep.

Canadian troops also used the Bren gun carrier. From towing guns to evacuating the wounded, this mini-tank did much the same work as the jeep. However, it ran on treads, making it slower but more suited to difficult terrain. And its light armor gave passengers some protection from rifle and machine gun fire.

The Bren gun carrier was purely a creature of war, with few peace-time applications. But the jeep survives long after the guns have fallen silent.

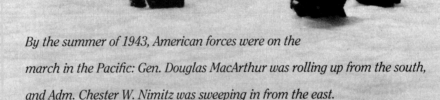

ISLAND BY ISLAND TOWARD TOKYO

Adm. Chester W. Nimitz

▶

American infantrymen wade ashore at Makin, an atoll near Tarawa, following an intense bombardment by navy guns.

With majestic aplomb, General MacArthur leads his aides to the beach at Leyte in the Philippines, shortly after U.S. Sixth Army assault troops had cleared the way. "I have returned," the general declared, keeping a promise he had made back in 1942. It took four months of bitter fighting to complete the island's capture.

By the summer of 1943, American forces were on the march in the Pacific: Gen. Douglas MacArthur was rolling up from the south, and Adm. Chester W. Nimitz was sweeping in from the east.

For Japanese garrisons in the far-flung outposts of the South Pacific, the reports were not good. In early March 1943, Allied bombers swooped down on a Japanese troop convoy in the Bismarck Sea, northeast of New Guinea, and all but demolished it. The pilots used a new, lethally effective technique called skip bombing, and it sent 12 of the convoy's 16 vessels plunging to the bottom. Some 3,000 Japanese soldiers and seamen lost their lives.

Allied airmen soon delivered a second sharp blow. Adm. Isoroku Yamamoto, Japan's top naval commander,

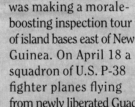

was making a morale-boosting inspection tour of island bases east of New Guinea. On April 18 a squadron of U.S. P-38 fighter planes flying from newly liberated Guadalcanal pounced on Yamamoto's plane over the island of Bougainville. Japan's most brilliant military leader, the strategist of Pearl Harbor, spun earthward to a fiery death.

In every sector Allied forces were swinging over to the offensive. On the ground in New Guinea, U.S. and Australian troops, under Gen. Douglas MacArthur, pushed through malaria-ridden jungles to clean out Japanese strongholds. On MacArthur's right flank Adm. William Halsey, nicknamed Bull, led a series of amphibious assaults on the 1,126-kilometre-long Solomon Islands.

Meanwhile, in the vast reaches of the Central Pacific, the Pacific Fleet, under Adm. Chester W. Nimitz, struck Japanese bases on widely scattered mid-ocean islets and coral reefs. The first target was Tarawa, a heavily fortified atoll in the Gilbert Islands. On November 20, after intensive naval bombardment, a division of marines hit the beach.

The navy's guns had pounded Tarawa's defences with about 3,000 tonnes of high explosives — enough, presumably, to obliterate all resistance. Not so: the Japanese, dug into the coral in steel-lined bunkers, withstood the shelling.

As the marines rushed ashore, they faced withering fire from Japanese shore batteries and automatic weapons.

Individual acts of heroism propelled them forward. Lt. William D. (Hawk) Hawkins, a 29-year-old Texan, single-handedly assaulted a cluster of machine-gun nests, running from one to the next to toss hand grenades through the firing slits. Wounded, he kept going — "I came here to kill . . . not to be evacuated," he shouted — until an explosive shell claimed his life.

Adm. Isoroku Yamamoto

Gradually the firing sputtered out. "The Americans," one Japanese commander had predicted, "could not take Tarawa with a million men in a hundred years." Four days were all they needed. But four days of hell! The marines lost 1,115 dead and 2,234 wounded. Of 5,000 Japanese defenders, only 17 men survived.

Adm. William Halsey

The U.S. fleet moved on through the Pacific, landing troops on the Admiralty Islands, the Marshalls, the Carolines. New tactics and equipment — including amtracs (amphibious tractors) to get ashore and flame throwers to wipe out enemy bunkers — helped reduce casualties. Even so, the advances came at a terrible cost in lives.

American strategy called for taking a trio of islands in the Marianas: Saipan, Tinian, and Guam. The U.S. fleet, 535 vessels strong, approached in mid-June 1944 and quickly scored a remarkable victory. The Japanese moved up a carrier force, much smaller in size, and a four-day battle ensued in which U.S. Navy pilots sank three Japanese carriers and shot down hundreds of enemy planes, a rout the Americans dubbed The Great Marianas Turkey Shoot.

Capturing the islands was another matter. The Japanese defenders on Saipan, ordered to die for their emperor, hurled themselves against the Americans in repeated banzai attacks. Both sides took heavy losses. The Japanese, running out of ammunition, charged with bayonets tied to sticks. The corpses piled so high that U.S. machine gunners had to keep moving their weapons just to clear their firing lanes. The Americans suffered 16,525 casualties, while the Japanese lost some 29,000, many of them in the largest suicide attack of the war.

▶

Mission accomplished, the U.S.S. Langley leads a task force of Pacific Fleet carriers and battleships back to base after pounding enemy positions in the Philippines.

While U.S. pilots blasted the enemy from the sky, submarine skippers struck from below, like this one peering through his periscope (bottom, right). Crews boasted of their kills with homemade battle flags (below). A cartoonlike fish figure identified the submarine, while each Japanese flag represented a merchantman or warship either maimed or destroyed by the sub.

The Allies' two lines of assault — MacArthur moving up from New Guinea and Nimitz's armada of ships sweeping in from the east — began to converge. In late October 1944, 132,000 of MacArthur's men stormed a beach at Leyte in the Philippines. A few hours later the general himself waded in. Already Japan's last great carriers and battleships were steaming toward Leyte for a final do-or-die confrontation with the U.S. Third and Seventh fleets.

The Battle for Leyte Gulf lasted three days, spread over hundreds of kilometres of ocean, and saw no fewer than 282 warships engage in combat. It was the largest armed struggle in naval history. When the smoke cleared, the Japanese Navy lay crippled beyond repair. But in its death throes it launched a horrifying new weapon: the kamikaze attack. A Japanese pilot crashed his plane onto the U.S. escort carrier *St. Lo,* killing himself and irreparably damaging the ship. Attacks by kamikazes ("divine wind," in Japanese legend) would terrorize American sailors until the war's end.

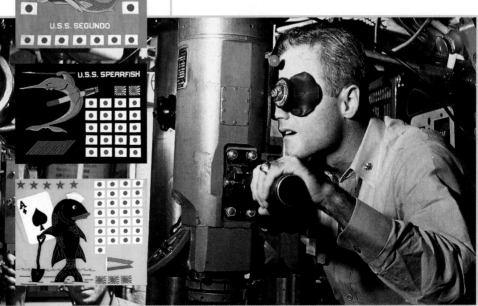
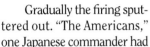

TIGHTENING THE NOOSE

At an airfield in England, General Eisenhower tells D-Day airborne troops, "Nothing less than full victory!" Dropped north of St.-Lô, they faced snipers, mine-tipped sticks, and flooded landing zones.

In retrospect, Hitler's fate was sealed when the Western Allies stormed and held the Normandy beaches and Red armies smashed into Poland. But the Germans had other ideas.

"Y ou are about to embark upon a great crusade!" With these forceful, inspiring words Gen. Dwight D. Eisenhower launched Operation Overlord against the Atlantic wall of German-occupied Europe. Beginning in the small hours of June 6, 1944, Operation Overlord eventually sent almost a million Allied troops across the English Channel to land on the coast of France. It was a massive logistical undertaking put together piece by piece in deepest secrecy over the previous 13 months.

Up to the last possible moment, the Allies tried to confuse the Germans with a blizzard of feints and fake plans, to conceal their true objective: the broad beaches of

Normandy. As zero hour approached, Allied warships began a thunderous bombardment, 2,000 planes dumped bombs on German seacoast defences, and three divisions of paratroopers leapt from the dark skies.

Canadian Third Division and an armored brigade landed at Juno Beach, aiming for Carpiquet Airport, near Caen. Counter-attacks from German tanks provided stiff opposition, and by the morning of June 7, 358 Canadians were dead and more than 700 wounded. But the Canadians had reached their goal within a day, the only Allied force to do so.

Meanwhile, some 2,400 kilometres to the east in northern Europe, the Soviets were headed for a climactic showdown. Since their victory at Stalingrad early in 1943, they had barely survived a German counteroffensive. Then, on July 5, 1943, Soviet and German tanks clashed at Kursk, in

southwestern Russia, igniting the greatest tank battle in history and shattering the myth that German tank units, the panzers, were invincible. In June 1944, about two weeks after D-Day, Soviet Field Marshal Georgi Zhukov launched 166 divisions, more than a million men, in a major westward offensive into Poland.

The Breakout from Normandy

Normandy was a brutal countryside for tanks and infantry. Hedgerows — tall banks of dirt topped with thornbushes and trees — hid German machine guns, mortars and tanks. At the core of Normandy was the city of Caen, defended by elite troops of the 12th SS Division. The Canadian and British role was to pull most of the German armor to the defence of Caen, allowing the American army to pour through weakened positions. The strategy worked, and after more than a month of bitter fighting, Canadian and British troops took Caen, and Gen. Patton's U.S. Third Army broke through at Avranches for a spectacular advance.

The German armies, confused and broken, fled through an escape corridor near the town of Falaise. Canadians and British pursued them relentlessly, aiming to link up with the Americans and encircle their fleeing enemies. Canada's Lt.-Gen. Guy Simonds put his infantry in "Kangaroo" armored transports (converted from tanks), and

bounced searchlights off the clouds to provide artificial moonlight for an attack that brought his troops within five kilometres of Falaise against desperate German resistance.

Overhead, massive Allied air power had all but driven the outnumbered Luftwaffe from the skies. Wave after wave of planes bombed and strafed the German defences with devastating results. A bitter joke circulated through the German ranks: "If you see a white plane, it's an American. If you see a black plane, it's the RAF. If you see no plane at all, it's the Luftwaffe."

Just past midnight on August 7, 1944, Hitler ordered four panzer divisions to unite for a counterattack. But the Allies, having broken the German codes, knew what was coming. Canadian and British forces, striking from the north, joined Patton's forces, moving up from the south, and trapped many of the Germans in a pocket near Falaise, where planes and artillery inflicted heavy casualties. By August 19 the battle for Normandy was over. German losses in the pocket fight alone were 10,000 killed, 50,000 captured, and 500 tanks destroyed.

The invasion of Germany was next on the Allied agenda. On September 17 the Allies on the

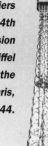

Tourists for a moment, soldiers of the U.S. 4th Infantry Division gawk at the Eiffel Tower after the liberation of Paris, August 1944.

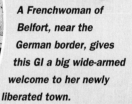

A Frenchwoman of Belfort, near the German border, gives this GI a big wide-armed welcome to her newly liberated town.

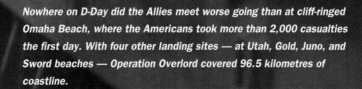

Nowhere on D-Day did the Allies meet worse going than at cliff-ringed Omaha Beach, where the Americans took more than 2,000 casualties the first day. With four other landing sites — at Utah, Gold, Juno, and Sword beaches — Operation Overlord covered 96.5 kilometres of coastline.

LETTER FROM A WOUNDED SOLDIER

When Charles dictated this letter for a Red Cross nurse to send to his mother, a month had passed since he received his combat wounds (for which the United States confers the Purple Heart, above). One eye gone and the other virtually sightless, he wanted to reassure his family about his injuries. Later, sight came back in his right eye as he had faith it would, although his doctors at first had been pessimistic. In the half century after shrapnel felled the infantry second lieutenant as his unit advanced into Germany near Aachen, Charles fulfilled his prewar dream of becoming a professional writer. Married to his wife, Betty, since 1947, he has a son, a daughter, and two granddaughters. He considers himself a lucky man.

My dearest Mother,

I have been informed that now since a certain period of time has elapsed since my injury it will be O.K. to tell you about it. I'll begin with my head and work down. . . . As you probably guessed, my eyes have been my chief worry lately. I lost my left eye and my right eye was sympathetically affected but the doc has been working hard on it and he says it is going to be O.K. So far though I can't see too well with it. They are making me a very handsome artificial eye for the left side. The eyes are made of the same material they make false teeth of, so, I go to the dentist to have it fitted which seems quite funny. Speaking of the dentist, remember . . . all those damn fillings I got and how I fought . . . to keep them from pulling teeth. Well, I'll be damned if a piece of shrapnel didn't come along and knock out all my front teeth and some of the back ones. It also broke my jaw. . . . This hasn't bothered me much except for the fact that I have to be on a liquid diet all the time and you know my appetite. The rest are getting peanut butter, hash, potatoes and all those things while my mouth waters, but the time is almost up now and they'll be able to take the wiring out of my jaw.

Charles in 1943 . . .

Then I got two shrapnel wounds in my chest which went rather deep and penetrated my lungs, but they patched them up and tapped my lungs for excess fluid so that now I can breathe O.K. . . . But at first it was my most serious wound. Then I got a big wound in the back of my left shoulder which broke the shoulder and most of my ribs on the left side. These are all healing up. . . . The main thing lately has been my eye but as I said I am getting an artificial one for the left side and the right one will be O.K. The army doctors are doing a wonderful job over here. Some of them are the best in the world in their particular specialty, so, don't worry. I know that you will feel much better now that you know what is wrong with me. . . . My mind is O.K., it is not shell shocked and I don't have the jitters. I'll look a little different but I'll still be the same old guy. There is no more news as to how long I'll be here or where I'll go next but I'll let you know as soon as I find out.

. . . and 50 years later

Give my love to all the family and I'm really looking forward to seeing you and father. . . . Won't we have a lot to talk about. All my love to you both,

Your devoted son,
Charles

◄ *These U.S. paratroops were to thrust north toward British forces dropped near Arnhem in the Netherlands. But the linkup failed, and the Germans held Arnhem and its bridge.*

Private E. A. "Smoky" Smith, of the Seaforth Highlanders of Canada, fully deserved his Victoria Cross. While crossing the Savio River in northern Italy, on October 21, 1944, he and his fellow riflemen came under German attack. He blew up a tank, fought ten Germans and killed four of them, drove off another attack, and carried a wounded rifleman to safety.

In the eerie quiet of a fresh snowfall, U.S. soldiers guard their forest position north of the Meuse River in Belgium, early January 1945. Three weeks earlier German armies had launched the desperate counterattack now known as the Battle of the Bulge, which threw the entire Allied advance into a confused, if temporary, turmoil.

northern flank tried to break through into the Reich in a daring but ill-fated assault by way of the "back door" from the Netherlands. Paratroopers planned to seize key bridges over the Lower Rhine, but a counterattack kept Allied units from reaching the Red Devils of the British 1st Airborne Division, isolated at Arnhem. Trapped without hope of victory or escape, many of the British were forced to surrender.

From Antwerp to the Rhine

Though Normandy was firmly in Allied hands and the way clear for a rapid American advance to Paris and beyond, German troops still held crucial ports along the English Channel and the North Sea from Antwerp in Belgium through Holland and into Germany. The channel ports were vitally important because without them the Allied advances would stall for lack of supplies. Then there were the German rocket launching sites along the channel coast, which rained high explosive on British cities. Clearing that coast was a task assigned to the Canadian army. It would prove one of the most difficult it had ever had to face.

On September 8, 1944, 2nd Canadian Division took Dieppe, the port that had cost them so many lives just over two years before. Le Havre had fallen earlier, then Boulogne and Calais. Dunkirk, another port of painful memory, also fell. By October, 1st Canadian Army was at Antwerp, clearing the banks of the Scheldt that lay between the port and the sea so that Allied supply ships could enter.

As 1945 dawned, Canadian troops fought through the flooded lands of the Hochwald and Reichswald forests all the way to the banks of the Rhine. They stormed across the river, Germany's last natural line of defence, on March 23. Then, they turned north to liberate Holland, then west again into the north German plain, taking the city of Oldenburg and driving for the great naval base at Wilhelmshaven. They were preparing for their final push on Wilhelmshaven when the war ended in May.

It had been a brutal campaign, fought through rain and mud that bogged down tanks and chilled the bone. But all the spectacular victories farther south hung on the ability of the Canadian soldiers to clear the supply lines. The second-highest casualties of all Allied divisions in Europe were suffered by 2nd Canadian Division; 3rd Canadian Division took the third highest. Canada's army in Europe suffered almost 45,000 casualties, and of them, more than 11,000 died.

Guarding an ice-rimmed passage in the Aleutian Islands, U.S. marines hunker down in the snow with their machine gun.

Chugging across the wide Irrawaddy River on a makeshift barge in December 1944, a British unit joins the southward push that eventually broke the Japanese stranglehold on Burma.

FORGOTTEN ARMIES: BURMA AND THE ALEUTIANS

From the steaming forests of Southeast Asia to China to ice-bound Alaskan islands, the war spanned a

35,400-kilometre front and touched some of the world's most remote and punishing climates.

Some of the most vicious, and heroic, fighting of World War II erupted on the far reaches of Japanese expansion. One short, bitter action occurred on American territory in the northern Pacific: the Aleutian Islands, off Alaska. Another bloody campaign — involving British, Chinese, Indian, Australian, New Zealand and many other Allied nationalities — ground on for years in Southeast Asia, with Burma as its epicentre.

During the Battle of Midway, in June 1942, the Japanese had put troops on Attu and Kiska, two small, deso-late islands of the Aleutian chain. In the grand military strategy of the war, this had little significance, but it allowed the Japanese to boast that they occupied American soil. Determined to reclaim its territory, the United States sent 11,000 troops to Attu on May 11, 1943. Waiting for them were more than 2,300 Japanese soldiers, battle-ready despite heavy bombardment by American planes. In fact, many of the bombs had missed their targets because of the dense, ever-present fog that shrouded the region. After 18 days of bitter fighting in tundra mud, the Japanese commander,

Shoulder patches worn by U.S. troops include the blue-and-green shield of a behind-the-lines Burma unit (left) and the lotus-blossom triangle (right) of the army engineers who built the Ledo-Burma Road.

realizing that reinforcements would not arrive in time, ordered his remaining 1,000 men to make a desperate attack. When 100 were killed, the rest, determined to die on the battlefield , blew themselves up with hand grenades. Just 28 of the Japanese defenders survived to be taken prisoner. But the victory was costly for the Americans as well: some 600 U.S. soldiers lost their lives.

On August 15, 1943, the Allies invaded nearby Kiska with a combined force of more than 34,000 Americans and Canadians. Once again fog aided the enemy. Weeks earlier the Japanese, obscured by a white wall of mist, had evacuated their entire garrison of nearly 6,000 men, leaving three dogs behind. When the Allies landed, visibility was so poor that some soldiers mistook each other for the enemy. Twenty-five GI's were killed and 31 wounded by friendly fire.

Toughing It Out in Burma

When the Japanese occupied Burma in May 1942, they gained rich oil fields and mineral deposits and also cut the Burma Road, a main overland supply route into China. Without Allied aid sent over this lifeline, Chiang Kai-shek's Nationalist Chinese Army stood little chance against the determined Japanese. Adding to Chiang's worries was distrust of the Chinese forces loyal to the Communist leader Mao Tse-tung. For nearly three years Allied planes flew oil and munitions over the "hump" (the Himalayas) to help Chiang keep on fighting.

Meanwhile, aiming to wrest India from British control, the Japanese expanded its occupation, from Burma into the Indian state of Assam. The Chindits — a mélange of British,

Early in 1945 U.S. convoys again rolled into China from India and the south, using the Ledo and Burma roads and this 21-curve stretch on the last leg to Chungking.

Bound for China over the "hump" of the Himalayas, a U.S. C-46 Commando hauls four tons of cargo to help Chinese troops halt the Japanese invaders.

Burmese, and Gurkhas — under Brig. Orde C. Wingate responded by blowing up railways and bridges behind enemy lines in almost suicidal raids. Wingate, who was soon killed in a jungle plane crash, was regarded by Churchill in the same heroic light as he saw Lawrence of Arabia.

In its climate and terrain, Burma was unmatched for pure torment. It mingled sodden swamps, jagged mountains, and parched plains, where temperatures frequently soared well over 38°C. To make matters worse, soldiers had to contend with monsoons, ever-present leeches, and swarms of stinging insects. Tropical diseases claimed many lives, and festering wounds brought down equal numbers.

Only a major offensive could dislodge the tenacious Japanese from Burma, and that job fell to the brilliant British commander Lt. Gen. Sir William Slim. Displaying a mastery of both conventional and guerrilla warfare, Slim manoeuvred his Anglo-Indian troops to isolate large chunks of the Japanese Army. Near Rangoon, on April 27, 1945, Japanese armed with explosives mounted on poles led suicide attacks on British tanks. But the tide had already turned. In January 1945 the Burma Road, with extensions to Ledo, India, and Chungking, China, had reopened. It was one of the great engineering feats of any war and ensured that hundreds of thousands of Japanese troops would be kept busy in China, with even more being savaged by British Empire and Commonwealth troops in Southeast Asia. The latter claimed, with justice, that they were forgotten armies. But the defeats they inflicted on Japanese armies were crucial to American successes in the Pacific.

"ONE OF THE MOST IMPORTANT SINGLE CONTRIBUTIONS TO VICTORY": WINSTON CHURCHILL

In April of 1942, a Japanese invasion fleet was heading for the British naval base of Colombo, Ceylon (now Sri Lanka). Their plan was a surprise attack that would give them control of the Indian Ocean and pave the way for the assault on India. Suddenly, a tiny speck appeared in the sky above their ships. It was a Catalina flying boat on patrol.

They shot it down and took the crew prisoner; but it was too late. Pilot Officer Leonard J. Birchall of St. Catharines, Ontario, had managed to get off a warning to Colombo. When Japanese aircraft appeared over Colombo, they got such a savage reception that the invasion fleet turned back and Ceylon was saved.

Birchall survived years of captivity and beatings to receive the Order of the British Empire and praise from Winston Churchill for making it possible to inflict the first serious reverse on the Japanese.

BOOM AND UPHEAVAL AT HOME

The turmoil of war overseas reverberated across the home front, changing it in ways that were often unexpected, sometimes funny, occasionally shattering. Jobs beckoned, romance blossomed, neighborhoods shuddered, and teenagers felt their oats.

◀

Female factory workers prepare a locomotive for shipment in a Kingston, Ontario, plant during wartime, November 1943.

Going to war meant uncertainty, upheaval, and fear for loved ones in the service. But World War II also brought something that had been sorely missed for a decade or more: jobs. Month by month, war shook Canada out of the Depression as unemployment disappeared completely by 1943, and the average annual income rose from $975 in 1940 to $1,538 in 1945. As factories and shipyards frantically raised production and male workers left for the armed forces, hundreds of thousands of women replaced them — though at only two-thirds the wages of men. By 1944, more than one million women were working full-time in industry, with another 800,000 working on farms.

This expansion was soon repeated in the United States where an estimated 15.3 million people relocated to find war work. The South boomed. The population of Mobile, Alabama, jumped more than 60 percent; that of Norfolk, Virginia, almost 45 percent. Nearly 2 million people moved to California. And more than 7 million left rural areas, as farmhands became soldiers and defence workers. To compensate for the lost manpower, farmers upped their use of machines and fertilizers and grew some 30 percent more food in 1945 than in 1940.

Wherever the jobs were, housing was at a premium. Converted garages, attics, even chicken coops, rented for top dollar. Newcomers took whatever space they could afford, whether in trailers, tents, or shantytowns. Some workers lived in their cars. Others rented "hot beds," which cost 25 cents for eight hours: when the day shift left in the morning to go to work, the night shift crawled into the vacated beds for some sleep.

Though the Canadian government provided day-care services for the very young children of working mothers, many children in Canada, as in the United States, became "eight-hour orphans"

VICTORY SUITS VS. ZOOT SUITS

The armed forces' demand for textiles led to shortages of wool and rayon, causing fashion changes at home. The so-called Victory Suit saved fabric by being single-breasted and without vest, lapels, or cuffs. The U.S. War Production Board banned ruffles, pleats, and patch pockets (right) and restricted yardage in clothes. The result was a tailored look in women's fashions (upper right).

Women in factories gamely wore slacks and covered their hair with bandannas or woven-mesh snoods. Denied silk and nylon hosiery, women painted their legs with makeup and drew lines on the backs of their calves to simulate seams.

Bucking the fabric-saving trend were men sporting zoot suits (far left): long coats called drapes with 7.5 to 15 centimetres of padding at the shoulders, and baggy "peg leg" trousers fitted snugly at the ankles. A broad-brimmed hat completed the effect, proclaiming its wearer to be a jive-talking hepcat. Zoot-suiters' women friends also favored long jackets, worn with short skirts.

Perceived — usually correctly — as showing contempt for patriotism, the zoot suit was despised by servicemen. In Canada and the United States, clashes between zoot suiters and servicemen were frequent and bloody.

left to fend for themselves in new and sometimes dangerous neighborhoods. In some places the waves of arriving residents strained social-service facilities, crowded schools, overburdened hospitals, and all but swamped law-enforcement agencies.

In Canada, tensions sometimes led to street brawls between servicemen and young men not in uniform. In the United States, race added its own explosiveness to the tensions. One hot afternoon in June 1943 blacks and whites scuffled in a Detroit park. Rumors of gang killings swept the city. Mobs, armed with stones and clubs, rioted. Violence continued for more than 30 hours before federal troops restored peace; by then, the rioting had killed 34 people and injured more than 700. Two months later, a racial clash in the Harlem area of New York City left six dead and 543 injured.

Civil Rights, "Dear Johns," and Teens

In response to these and other race riots, more than 200 commissions on interracial understanding sprang up, and the government spurred enforcement of antidiscrimination rulings. Some blacks began to get better jobs, though segregation persisted. Nonetheless, gains that blacks made during the war laid the groundwork for desegregation and equal-opportunity legislation afterward.

Meanwhile, amid the uniforms, the marching, the sailings, and the furloughs, romances bloomed and the marriage rate jumped. Some hasty marriages succeeded, but a lot ended as abruptly as they began. Even stable marriages faced severe strains with husbands gone, and home-front families adapting to new ways of coping and living. For servicemen, mail call might bring a dreaded "Dear John" letter, breaking off an engagement.

Millions of teenagers, filling jobs in transportation, retailing, and construction, found they had more money and freedom than they had ever dreamed of having. With their new independence came an exuberance that many adults found appalling. For example, some 30,000 young fans — mostly teenage girls — showed up outside the Paramount Theatre in New York in October 1944 to hear silken-voiced Frank Sinatra. Though fewer than 4,000 got inside, their screams at times drowned out his singing. Outside, 700 riot police tried to keep order. Often dismissed as "just bobbysoxers" because of the anklets (bobby socks) girls wore with loafers or saddle shoes, these wartime adolescents were, for better or worse, the vanguard of the teen revolution of later decades.

Two U.S. Navy lieutenants use a dress sword to cut their wedding cake. Now grandparents, this couple made their wartime marriage work.

Mr. and Mrs. Gustav J. Nickel
announce the marriage of their daughter
Virginia Elizabeth
Lieutenant (jg) W.A.V.E.S.
to
Richard Charles Nehring
Lieutenant (jg) United States Naval Reserve
on Tuesday, the second of January
Nineteen hundred and forty-five
Winnetka, Illinois

The foot stamping and gyrations of the jitterbug became a popular antidote for wartime tensions.

Canadian troops enjoy the "Invasion Revue," in Danville, France.

"FOR THE BOYS"

Nothing was too good for servicemen on leave. Young ladies fêted them, starlets lionized them, and songwriters and bandleaders kept them dancing to the latest popular tunes.

Wherever they went in Canada, and often overseas as well, Canadian servicemen found a home away from home. In England, R. B. Bennett opened his estate to them. In Winnipeg, Mr. and Mrs. Augustus Cannell entertained some 350 airmen through the war years, a story that had its counterparts in Halifax and Moncton and every Canadian centre with servicemen based nearby. The Victoria Hostess Club provided nightly dancing. Eaton's department stores sponsored troupes of entertainers. C.B.C. broadcast *The Army Show,* featuring two army comics, John Wayne and Frank Schuster. Nor were the families of men at war forgotten, as neighbors pitched in to help out with house repairs and take children to the circus.

In the United States, more than 1 million Americans donated their time to help run 3,035 USO centres. Churches, museums, yacht clubs, barns, railway cars, and even log cabins housed USO facilities, where coffee and doughnuts were plentiful, jukeboxes blared, and invitations to home-cooked dinners were almost impossible to avoid.

USO hostesses were usually in their late teens or twenties. And while they were closely chaperoned, and dating was strictly forbidden, romance blossomed. Many girls married the soldiers or sailors they met at USO canteens.

Willie Gillis, Norman Rockwell's jug-eared GI, scarfs down all the goodies he can eat, and is rendered speechless by the attention.

Wartime songs ranged from sprightly and cute ("Mairzy Doats") to achingly poignant ("When the Lights Go On Again All Over the World").

◄ **At the grand opening of a lavish new USO club in Puerto Rico, servicemen on their best behavior dance with local girls in full formal evening dress.**

kept the GI's dancing — and all America with them. The big bands of Harry James, Artie Shaw, Tommy Dorsey, Benny Goodman, and dozens of others packed ballrooms and nightclubs. People jitterbugged and lindy-hopped to numbers like Glenn Miller's "Chattanooga Choo Choo," which sold 1 million records and was one of the period's biggest hits. (An appreciative RCA gave Miller a disc of the song sprayed with gold paint, making it the industry's first "gold" recording and launching a promotional gimmick that persists today.) Sentimental ballads, like "The Nearness of You" and "The White Cliffs of Dover," sent couples into slow, clinging fox-trots.

The bands and ballads were as popular in Canada as in the United States, but in Canada they had to share the limelight with radio's "Happy Gang," with singer Wally Koster, and with the down-home music of Don Messer. For the highest patriotism, nothing could match the emotion generated by Britain's Vera Lynn defiantly singing, "There'll Always Be an England." But the music that best summed up the wartime mood came from the concert hall. It was the opening four notes of Beethoven's Fifth Symphony, which echoed the *dot, dot, dot, dash* rhythm of the letter *V* in Morse code. *V* stood for *Victory*, and it was tapped on car horns and flashed in lights throughout the free world.

Points of embarkation — like San Francisco, San Diego, New York City, and Honolulu — were places to have a fling before shipping out to the war zones, and the port cities went all out to give GI's a great time. As one amazed soldier put it, "Even if you got money, they don't let you spend it." In New York soldiers and sailors were treated to free or half-price tickets to Broadway shows such as *Oklahoma!*, which opened in 1943. The composer Irving Berlin's smash musical *This Is the Army* opened with a cast of 300 soldiers. The showman Billy Rose put on a star-studded extravaganza at Madison Square Garden and raised $10 million to fund USO activities.

Radios and jukeboxes

▲ **Bing Crosby reprised his 1942 hit song "White Christmas" in a 1954 movie of the same name.**

Berlin's hit show, a spoof on life in boot camp, beat a rousing patriotic drum.

► **The gorgeous "Forces' Favourite" Vera Lynn entertained Allied troops around the world with her rousing ballads.**

IT'S OUR WAR

CANADIANS FIGHT TO GO TO WAR

Conscription, like a virus that had slumbered for two decades, struck at Canadian life again in World War II. But this time Canada had a prime minister who was a master physician, who stemmed the disease and kept the body of Canada whole.

General Crerar, speaking of the fighting on the Italian front, said, "This war is so much like the last one, it's not even funny." He could as well have been talking about the bickering back home in Canada, where politicians and civilians alike had revived the 1917 quarrel over conscription almost as soon as the Second World War began.

For Mackenzie King, Canada's cautious, tiptoeing prime minister, conscription was the issue he most feared since it could split the country and destroy the Liberal party, just as it had in 1917. To defuse the quarrel, he declared in 1939 that there would be no conscription. Military service would be voluntary.

Then, in the summer of 1940, France collapsed, and it became evident that the war was going to be longer and harder than anyone had realized. Canada would have to play a larger part in the war. Reluctantly, King's government passed the National Resources Mobilization Act which, among other things, provided for conscription for military service — but in North America only. It wasn't enough for opposition Conservatives. And as young men were conscripted, some anglophones angrily gossiped, contrary to fact, that most of the conscripts — those who had to be forced to defend their country, rather than those who honorably volunteered — were from Quebec. Unfortunately, a seeming confirmation of this prejudice came early.

War posters produced in Canada (above) encouraged Canadians to feel they had a part to play in the war. By 1942, most of Canada wanted to send conscripts overseas, and voted yes in the national plebiscite (left).

THE WAR AGAINST THE PREMIERS

Maurice Duplessis

Premiers Mitch Hepburn of Ontario and Maurice Duplessis of Quebec ruled their provinces like private fiefdoms, and neither had much respect for either the authority or the person of prime minister Mackenzie King. He gave both of them, however, a sharp lesson in politics.

In 1939, King took on broad powers under the War Measures Act to deal with the war emergency. Duplessis immediately complained that this infringed on provincial powers, and called a provincial election on the issue. King responded by sending in a team of his toughest campaigners, Ernest Lapointe, P.J.A. Cardin, and C. G. Power. After a rough election, Duplessis' Union Nationale party was defeated.

In 1940, Hepburn allied himself with the pro-conscription Conservatives, pushing a motion that denounced King's war policies. Once again, King turned the challenge to his own advantage. Using Hepburn's denunciation as an excuse, he called a federal election on conscription, in which his Liberal party soundly defeated the Conservatives.

Salvos in the Conscription War

Before the war, mayor Camillien Houde of Montreal had vigorously opposed conscription and even the very idea of going to war. When King introduced conscription, even though for North American duty only, Houde foolishly advised young men not to register. It was enough to stir the usually cautious King, and he acted before too many Quebec dissidents could rally behind Houde. Within hours, Camillien Houde found himself under arrest by RCMP officers and taken off to an internment camp where he remained for the rest of the war.

It's your baby, Mr. King

◀

John Collins's cartoon published on November 28, 1944 illustrates the position King found himself when, under pressure from his Cabinet, he had to break his vow not to send conscripts overseas.

The next gun in the conscription war was fired by Arthur Meighen, leader of the Ontario Conservatives and an acid-tongued debater who despised King. Though Canada had plenty of troops on hand, its anglophones wanted conscription immediately. Knowing that the issue could well destroy the King government, Meighen promptly led the call for sending conscripts overseas.

King's answer was a national plebiscite in which Canadians were asked whether they would allow him to abandon his promise not to conscript for overseas service. Most Canadians said yes. But within Quebec, 75 percent gave a resounding "No!" In a baffling response, King replied that there would be "conscription if necessary, but not necessarily conscription." It bought time for him but, as he acknowledged in his diary, "I am not at all sure that we are by any means out of the woods." The Liberals were not.

Conscription Wins the Day

In 1944, just months after D-Day, Connie Smythe, owner of the Toronto Maple Leafs hockey team and a major in the Ca-

The general service lapel pin given to conscripts.

▼ *Mayor Camillien Houde addresses a crowd at an anti-conscription rally, in 1939.*

nadian army, returned to Canada. He reported that the army was so desperately short of reinforcements that wounded soldiers were being sent back into action. Meighen pounced, renewing his demands for conscription. And anglophone Canada, convinced that French Quebec was not doing its share, roared its support.

The situation was not as severe as it seemed, since Canada still had ample numbers of troops who had volunteered for overseas service but who were yet to be sent to the front. King knew, however, that he could calm the storm only by sending over conscripts. Added to this, some of his cabinet ministers were talking of resigning if he did not send conscripts overseas. Reluctantly, fearing a mass walkout of his Quebec ministers and a resulting split across the nation, King gave in to the demand.

In the end, only one Quebec minister, C. G. Power, resigned. And he did so because he had given his word to his voters that he would never support conscription. The rest, led by Louis St.-Laurent, recognized that King had withstood the pressure as long as possible and that conscription was necessary for Canadian unity. In November 1944, 16,000 conscripts were ordered to Europe.

Conscription was of little military value. Of the conscripts sent overseas, barely 2,400 reached the front before the fighting ended. But the issue still had the power to tear Canada apart. When Borden manipulated the issue for short-term political gain in 1917, it did just that. King, by delaying until it was clear to all he could delay no more, defused the crisis.

▼ *Some 50,000 Montrealers welcomed Camillien Houde after his release from four years in detention for antiwar activities.*

MAKING W★A★R IN THE MOVIES

Charlie Chaplin prodded people into taking fascism seriously with *The Great Dictator*, a film that infuriated American conservatives who, even after the United States entered the war, vilified him as a "premature anti-fascist." During the war years, movies like Gary Cooper's *Sergeant York* and the National Film Board's *Canada Carries On* series kept up morale. After the war came escapist fantasies like *The Green Berets*, but also the hard questions posed by *Apocalypse Now* and Canada's even more controversial *The Valour and the Horror*.

Throughout the century, films have pampered, inspired, and challenged us — and none more so than those about war. Here, then, we take a nostalgic look at a few of the movies that helped define our feelings not only about World War II, but about ourselves and all wars.

WORLD WAR 1

All Quiet on the Western Front ★ 1930
This version of Erich Maria Remarque's searing novel relates the horrors of war in the trenches from the viewpoint of young German students who joined the kaiser's army.

Sergeant York ★ 1941
The eve of the U.S.'s entry into World War II was a perfect time for Gary Cooper to play a hillbilly who becomes a hero by single-handedly capturing more than 100 German soldiers in 1918.

THE SPANISH CIVIL WAR

For Whom the Bell Tolls ★ 1943
For moviegoers of 1943 the Spanish Civil War prefigured the Allied war on fascism. Ernest Hemingway's classic novel became a film starring Gary Cooper and Ingrid Bergman.

THE MEXICAN REVOLUTION

They Came to Cordura ★ 1959
Five soldiers and one woman trek to a remote outpost in the Mexico of 1916 during the U.S. expedition against revolutionary general Pancho Villa's forces, which nearly resulted in war. The movie played to U.S. audiences worried about the Communist threat next door in Cuba.

WORLD WAR II

The Great Dictator ★ 1940
Charlie Chaplin as The Great Dictator, Adenoid Hynkel (left), and Jack Oakie as Napoloni (right) hilariously lampoon the all-too-real rise of dictators Hitler and Mussolini.

Casablanca ★ 1942
Cynical loner Humphrey Bogart meets old flame Ingrid Bergman in a nest of spies and double agents in Axis-leaning French North Africa. He quickly decides to join the fight for freedom.

Bataan ★ 1943
Starring Robert Taylor, this saga of U.S. defeat in the Philippines appeared only a year after the actual events and reinforced the public mood of grim determination.

PT 109 ★ 1963
This rendering of John F. Kennedy's deeds as a PT boat commander in the Pacific was released the year of the presidential assassination.

Guadalcanal Diary ★ 1943
Audiences who had seen newsreel coverage of U.S. victories in the Solomon Islands only months earlier could now see Hollywood's dramatic re-creation of the events.

Patton ★ 1970
Filmed at the height of the Vietnam War, this blockbuster about Gen. George S. Patton, Jr., showed hawk and dove alike that in a popular war a tough-minded military man could attain the status of hero.

THE KOREAN WAR

The Sullivans ★ 1944
Many moviegoers wept when they saw this heartrending tale of five brothers who die bravely in action while serving in the U.S. Navy.

Pork Chop Hill ★ 1959
Starring Gregory Peck, this starkly realistic drama takes moviegoers back to the final bloody moments of the Korean War.

M*A*S*H ★ 1970
Audiences needing relief from daily Vietnam body counts found humor in this story of an army medical unit trying to stay sane in Korea.

The Gates of Italy ★ 1944
The National Film Board's first ever series, *Canada Carries On* (1940-1959) featured a number of wartime films such as this, narrated by Lorne Greene.

13 Rue Madeleine ★ 1946
James Cagney heads a group of agents in occupied France in this thriller, presented in the style of *The March of Time* documentaries.

REVISIONS

THE VIETNAM WAR

The Green Berets ★ 1968
John Wayne's blood-and-thunder epic of Special Forces operations in Vietnam met with mixed reactions from a public torn by debates about the war.

Stalag 17 ★ 1953
William Holden thrills audiences as a sergeant suspected of being a spy in this grimly humorous saga of life in a German prisoner-of-war camp.

Apocalypse Now ★ 1979
A powerful statement that the hell of war is rooted in the human heart, this nightmarish film played to a public still grappling with the lessons of Vietnam.

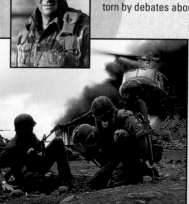

The Valour and the Horror ★ 1992
The McKenna brothers produced this highly controversial series about the Canadian role in World War II, using actors to dramatize personal accounts.

Victory in Europe

By the spring of 1945, Allied forces were racing through Germany on their way to Berlin. With Hitler's suicide in an underground bunker, the thousand-year Reich came crumbling down.

▲ **Amphibious assault boats known as Buffaloes rescue a Canadian division marooned in a flooded village east of Nijmegen, Holland. The Germans were blowing up dikes and river crossings on the Rhine to prevent the Allies advancing into Germany.**

Dodging machine-gun bullets, Sgt. Alex Drabik, of the U.S. First Army, sprinted across the Ludendorff Bridge, at Remagen, a town straddling the Rhine River. It was the afternoon of March 7, 1945, and for nearly a week the Germans had been blowing up Rhine crossings, hoping to stem the Allied advance. But at Remagen the dynamite charge had failed. Quickly Drabik's company carved out a bridgehead. Gen. Dwight D. Eisenhower had dreaded the logistical problems of bringing his armies across the Rhine. Now the river had been spanned.

Other units soon followed. Gen. George S. Patton's Third Army charged across the river some 130 kilometres to the south. The British and Canadians, under Field Marshal Montgomery, swept over to the north. In a pincer movement, the Allies trapped more than 300,000 enemy troops in the Ruhr, Germany's industrial core. Allied planes flew more than 42,000 sorties, smashing Luftwaffe bases and wiping out Germany's air power. On April 11 the U.S. Ninth Army reached the Elbe River, 85 kilometres west of Berlin.

There they stopped, on Eisenhower's orders. A month earlier, the three Allied leaders — Winston Churchill, Joseph Stalin, and an ailing Franklin D. Roosevelt — had met at Yalta, in the Crimea, where they agreed that Soviet troops should enter Berlin first. Indeed, the Soviets had marched through Poland, swept past the Oder River, and were poised for a final assault on the Nazi capital.

Death Camps and Nazis at Bay

As the Allies closed in, Adolf Hitler retreated to the Führerbunker, a 19-room underground command centre beneath the Reich Chancellery garden, in Berlin. He ordered movements for troops that had ceased to exist, and with members of his inner circle he studied astrological charts, searching for signs of a saving miracle. He ranted against his generals and the German people. Factories, railways, reservoirs, and food supplies should be destroyed, he commanded; if he was to perish, so must Germany.

Meanwhile, the Canadians, British and Americans were discovering a horror that made it difficult to show Germany any mercy: the death camps. On April 14 British soldiers

An exuberant camaraderie marked the meeting of GI's and their Red Army allies at Germany's Elbe River.

The grief of an entire nation at FDR's death from a cerebral hemorrhage on April 12, 1945, at Warm Springs, Georgia, seems to flow with the tears of this navy accordionist. With full military honors the president's body was put aboard a train to Washington, and his name appeared on the Pentagon's regular casualty list, along with the name of every serviceman who died that day.

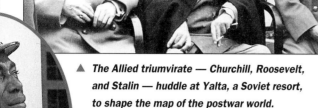

▲ *The Allied triumvirate — Churchill, Roosevelt, and Stalin — huddle at Yalta, a Soviet resort, to shape the map of the postwar world.*

Germany's top-secret security weapon, the Enigma Machine, put all messages typed on it into a supposedly unbreakable code. But early in the war British cryptologists decoded Enigma, an intelligence coup that helped speed the Allied victory.

entered the Bergen-Belsen concentration camp and gazed in appalled disbelief at "a precinct littered with corpses, people dying of starvation." In the next few weeks Americans encountered similar spectacles at Buchenwald. At Dachau the scenes were so awful that enraged GI's executed some of the SS guards on the spot. Eventually it was determined that Hitler had killed 6 million Jews along with 5 million Slavs, Gypsies, and other presumed undesirables.

On April 13 Joseph Göbbels, Hitler's minister of propaganda, had telephoned the Führerbunker in a state of wild excitement. The propaganda department's astrological studies had convinced Hitler and his advisers that the second half of April would bring a dramatic turning point. "My Führer," Göbbels exclaimed, "I congratulate you. Roosevelt is dead!" For once the Nazi propaganda master was telling the truth.

The day before, Vice President Harry S. Truman had taken the presidential oath of office in the White House Cabinet Room. He confirmed that the war would continue until Germany and Japan surrendered unconditionally.

In Italy, Allied armies broke through the last German defence line into the Po Valley, capturing Bologna as well as other cities. In Germany, Patton's Third Army rolled east toward the Czech border. Other units moved south into

Bavaria and Austria. On April 25 a U.S. patrol on the Elbe converged with a Soviet unit in a historic meeting that cut the Reich in two.

Soviet tanks and infantry moved into Berlin, destroying German resistance in savage hand-to-hand street fighting. Their opponents were mostly teenage boys and bewildered old men. But more than 5,000 Nazi defenders battled a fire raging through the parliament building. In the nearby Führerbunker, with the sounds of battle echoing all around, Hitler shot himself in the mouth with a pistol. His companion, Eva Braun, took cyanide. Their bodies were placed in a shell hole and burned.

Exactly one week later, on May 7, in a modest schoolhouse in Rheims that served as Ike's headquarters, the Germans signed a document of unconditional surrender. The news was announced May 8, the official V-E Day, and a grateful world went wild with celebration.

▶

Ottawa's ticker tape-strewn streets resounded with brass bands and joyful cries on Victory Day, May 8, 1945.

VICTORY OVER JAPAN

More than 1,500 kilometres, and months of potentially devastating combat, lay between the farthest Allied advances and Japan's home islands. Then came Hiroshima, and a flash of fire that ended the war in a matter of days and changed the world forever.

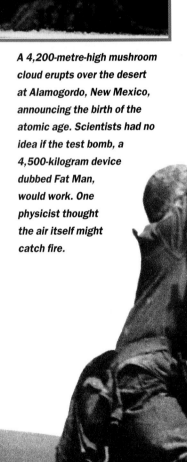

A 4,200-metre-high mushroom cloud erupts over the desert at Alamogordo, New Mexico, announcing the birth of the atomic age. Scientists had no idea if the test bomb, a 4,500-kilogram device dubbed Fat Man, would work. One physicist thought the air itself might catch fire.

President Harry S. Truman stared at a cable an aide had just handed him: DIAGNOSIS NOT YET COMPLETE BUT RESULTS SEEM SATISFACTORY. The cryptic wording concealed a fact of shattering significance. That morning, July 16, 1945, at a test site in the New Mexican desert, U.S. scientists had exploded the world's first atom bomb. Only a few top officials were allowed to know. Meanwhile, American forces continued their bloody island-by-island progress across the Pacific, and British Commonwealth troops were making rapid advances in Southeast Asia. The Japanese fought on, spurred by a national pride that allowed no room for surrender. The number of dead and wounded continued to mount relentlessly on both sides.

Five months earlier, on February 19, two entire marine divisions plus reserves had stormed ashore on tiny Iwo Jima, a desolate pile of volcanic rock and ash equipped with three airfields. It took them almost a month of hand-to-hand combat to clear out the defenders, who had dug themselves into a honeycomb of caves and tunnels in the rock. More than 6,800 marines lost their lives; it was the worst casualty rate in the corps's 168-year history. Of the island's 23,000 Japanese defenders, almost all were annihilated. And at Okinawa, the next major Allied target, the toll was even more alarming. More than 100,000 Japanese died, including large numbers of civilians.

It seems unbelievable that the Japanese could keep going. Army Air Forces Maj. Gen. Curtis E. LeMay was systematically bombing every military and industrial target on the home islands. Huge formations of B-29 Superfortresses hit factories, railways, and oil dumps. Japan became so starved for oil that its giant battleship *Yamato,* sailing to help defend Okinawa, could not return for lack of fuel.

Just as terrible was the toll on Japan's civilians. In one raid, on March 9, 300 B-29's showered Tokyo with incendiary bombs, igniting a fire storm so intense that otherwise unharmed people dropped dead from suffocation. More than

◄

In a formal ceremony aboard the U.S.S. Missouri, Foreign Minister Mamoru Shigemitsu signs the documents that ended history's most destructive war while Gen. Douglas MacArthur (at microphone) stands in full, imperious command.

Mass euphoria swept the world with the news of Japan's surrender, as this sailor embracing a nurse enthusiastically demonstrates.

80,000 residents were killed. As the spring wore on, LeMay was sending 500 planes on fire raids every other day.

But the end would come sooner than anyone knew. Ever since April 1943, nuclear scientists at Los Alamos, New Mexico, had been secretly working to develop the ultimate victory weapon. Brig. Gen. Leslie R. Groves, the army administrator in charge of the project, called the scientists "the largest collection of crackpots ever seen." But the "crackpots" included some of the world's greatest minds, such as physicists J. Robert Oppenheimer and Enrico Fermi. And with the benefit of two years time and $2 billion in government money, the bomb was now ready for testing.

The trial took place on a desolate stretch of sand called Alamogordo, 320 kilometres south of Los Alamos. A fireball with a core heat three times greater than the sun's roared up from the desert floor, casting a glow so intense it could have been seen from Mars. The vibrations rattled windows more than 320 kilometres away. The only journalist present, William Lawrence of *The New York Times*, wrote: "One felt as though one were present at the moment of creation when God said, 'Let there be light.'"

President Truman, at a summit conference in the Berlin suburb of Potsdam, passed the news to Winston Churchill and Joseph Stalin. The three Allied leaders issued a stern ultimatum to Tokyo: surrender or suffer "complete and utter destruction." The Japanese made no reply.

So early on August 6, 1945, Col. Paul W. Tibbets, Jr., lifted off the island of Tinian in *Enola Gay*, a B-29 bomber he had named for his mother. He headed for Hiroshima, a Japanese seaport of 240,000 inhabitants. In the plane's belly rode a 4,000-kilogram atomic device nicknamed Little Boy. At 8:17 A.M. Little Boy dropped toward its target, Hiroshima's Aioi Bridge. Moments later a fireball incinerated everybody and everything within three kilometres of the bridge. Outside that radius the wounded lay writhing and screaming. Entire trains were flung off their tracks like toys. The remains of factories sailed skyward in a whirlwind of air. Three days later a second atom bomb fell upon Nagasaki. Japan was finished. A sorrowing Emperor Hirohito told his war council, "I cannot bear to see my innocent people suffer any longer," and announced his decision to surrender.

The official ceremony, on Sunday, September 2, 1945, had the formal pomp of a scene from grand opera. Eleven tight-lipped Japanese emissaries climbed aboard the battleship *Missouri*, anchored in Tokyo Bay, and signed the instruments of surrender while thousands of Allied servicemen looked on. Then the Japanese departed as silently as they had arrived. World War II was history.

◄ *The image of five marines raising the Stars and Stripes atop Iwo Jima's Mount Suribachi came to symbolize the indomitable courage of the Allied forces that would bring ultimate victory.*

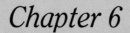
Chapter 6

POSTWAR CHALLENGE AND CHANGE

Emerging from the war stronger than ever,

North America gets a rude shock as

the Soviet sphere becomes its dedicated adversary

in every aspect of world affairs.

A pair of baby boomers and their parents face the future: a new house on a new lot in a postwar suburb.

A PEACE TO BE BUILT

"Today we are faced with the pre-eminent fact," wrote FDR, *"that, if civilization is to survive, we must cultivate the science of human relationships — the ability of all peoples, of all kinds, to live together and work together in the same world, at peace."*

Clement Attlee (Britain), Harry S. Truman (U.S.), and Joseph Stalin (U.S.S.R.) pose for posterity at Potsdam, Germany.

Building a lasting peace meant first putting Europe back together again. The cityscape on these pages is viewed from the cathedral in Cologne, Germany, which, miraculously, suffered little damage. Below, Berliners return home in July 1945 after evacuating their besieged city.

In July 1945 Harry S. Truman, president of the United States for just three months, had written to his mother and sister: "I am getting ready to go see Stalin and Churchill. I have to take my tuxedo, tails . . . high hat, low hat, hard hat. . . . I have a briefcase filled with information on past conferences and suggestions on what I'm to do and say. Wish I didn't have to go. . . ." Truman was preparing to leave for Potsdam, a suburb of Berlin, for his first major international conference and his first meeting with Winston Churchill and Joseph Stalin. Following up on the tenuous postwar alliance forged at Yalta, the Big Three were convening to decide how to shape the peace. Before the conference began, Truman wrote in his diary: "I hope for some sort of peace — but I fear that machines are ahead of morals by some centuries and when morals catch up there'll be no reason for any of it." That very afternoon he received word of the successful atom bomb test in New Mexico.

The leaders had to decide how to administer a defeated Germany, already portioned into four zones of military occupation (France having the fourth zone). At Potsdam, Germany was divided into Eastern and Western zones, and everyone agreed to its demilitarization. Other borders had to be established in Europe. East Prussia was divided between Russia and Poland. Poland was moved 322 kilometres west, into what had been Germany. In fact, the Big Three altered the entire map of Eastern Europe. No timetable was set for democratic elections in Eastern European countries, so Soviet occupation meant they would fall within the Soviet sphere of influence. (The Soviets would soon force totalitarian regimes on Bulgaria, Hungary, Poland, Romania, and, in 1948, Czechoslovakia.)

The Big Three took one other important action. They issued an ultimatum, the Potsdam Proclamation, demanding Japan's unconditional surrender. Not only had Truman secured Stalin's agreement to enter the war against Japan, but he decided while at Potsdam to use the atom bomb if Japan failed to respond to the Potsdam Proclamation, which only hinted at the bomb's existence and power.

But Potsdam left many questions unanswered. And the Big Three themselves changed in mid-conference: Winston Churchill lost his bid for reelection, and Clement Attlee of the Labor Party replaced him as Britain's representative at Potsdam. Like Roosevelt before him, Truman had a tendency to distrust the British. Stalin surprised him as "a little bit of a squirt" (1.65 metres) and he was certainly a brutal dictator but, again like Roosevelt, Truman came away with the mistaken impression that Stalin could be trusted. The feeling was not mutual. Stalin later told Nikita Khrushchev that he thought Truman worthless.

Forums to Punish War and Promote Peace

The Potsdam conferees agreed that surviving Nazi leaders should be prosecuted for "crimes against humanity." The Nuremberg trials began in November 1945 and lasted for nearly a year. Of the 22 Nazis tried by the international tribunal, 12 received death sentences, 3 life imprisonment, 4 shorter prison terms, and 3 were acquitted. Trials against accused Japanese war criminals, begun in May 1946, ended with prison terms for 16 and death sentences for 7.

The best hope for the resolution of future disputes lay in the United Nations. At a conference in San Francisco, delegates from 50 nations, including Lester Pearson for Canada, had agreed on a charter for the body. The preamble expressed lofty goals: " . . . to save succeeding generations from the scourge of war . . . to reaffirm faith in fundamental human rights . . . to establish conditions under which justice and respect for . . . international law can be maintained, and to promote social progress and better standards of life."

◀ *Adm. Karl Dönitz, who was to receive 10 years in prison, addresses the war crimes court in Nuremberg in October 1946. Seated in front of him, from left to right, are Hermann Göring (death), Rudolf Hess (life in prison), Joachim von Ribbentrop (death), Wilhelm Keitel (death), Ernst Kaltenbrunner (death), and Alfred Rosenberg (death).*

▼ *Lester Pearson adds his signature to the U.N. charter at the San Francisco Opera House on June 26, 1945.*

In 1946, John Peters Humphrey of McGill University's Law Faculty led the drafting of the U.N.'s Universal Declaration of Human Rights, a document that has been called the "Magna Carta of mankind."

The new organization appeared to have advantages over the League of Nations: all the major nations that had emerged victorious from the war belonged; the Security Council, especially its five permanent members (the United States, the Soviet Union, Britain, France, and China), had vital decision-making powers; although smaller nations had argued against granting the five nations veto rights, the balance of power between the Security Council and the larger General Assembly at least reflected the real relationships among members; and the U.N. was more committed than the League to addressing social and economic issues globally.

The war had left a drastically changed world. Western Europe lay in ruins. World War I veteran Truman remarked after seeing Berlin: "I never saw such destruction." Churchill, whose own country was bankrupt, called Europe "a rubble heap, a charnel house, a breeding ground of pestilence and hate." Old nations had been swallowed up, new ones created. Eastern Europe was falling increasingly under the influence of the Soviet Union. Japan's empire had crumbled, along with the European colonial empires in the Far East. And across the world, the Russians and the Americans eyed one another warily.

On May 12, 1945, soldiers at Fort Dix, New Jersey, learned that they were about to become civilians. The army's demobilization system gave credits for each of the following: months of service, months overseas, battle stars, combat decorations, and each child under 18.

COMING HOME

"The guys who came out of World War II were idealistic," recalled wounded veteran Harold Russell. *"They sincerely believed that this time they were coming home to build a new world."*

▲ Sam Macchia, wounded in both legs in Normandy, greets his mother and father back home.

When discharged, U.S. veterans received an emblem for honorable service, the Golden Eagle lapel pin (above, left, twice actual size), popularly known as the "ruptured duck."

When news of Japan's surrender swept across the continent, joy was mixed with apprehension. War, for all its horrors, had brought jobs and prosperity to people whose last memory of a peacetime economy was the Depression of the 1930's. Now, with the war over, would industries close once again? Would we plunge back into joblessness and despair?

For Canadians, there was no need for concern. Compulsory wartime savings by both civilians and service people were now released to fuel a consumer demand that converted factories from the manufacture of weapons to that of peacetime machinery almost overnight. Further spending power came as a result of the Family Allowances Act of 1944, under which mothers of children under 16 received $5 to $8 a month. The bottled-up hunger for cars and other peace-

time goods might have created inflation and a black market, but the Canadian government wisely kept many of its wartime controls in place until 1949. As a final spur to continued productivity, Canadian factories were included in the Marshall Plan to resupply devastated Europe. For Canadians, the transition from war to peace was remarkably smooth. For Americans, it was more difficult.

Within a year of V-J Day, 9 million American service personnel had been sent home and demobilized. No vet would ever forget what it meant to come out of the terrifying, destructive war alive and feel the warm embrace of loved ones. But, for many, the return to civilian life would prove difficult. The sudden influx of millions of GI's into the ranks of those seeking work strained an economy that was shifting from wartime to peacetime production. Ten days af-

Veterans parade through Montreal in 1947, in protest against the lack of housing for them and their families.

ter V-J Day, 1.8 million workers received pink slips; six months later 2.7 million were out of a job. Labor union leaders, angered that wages and salaries remained flat as corporate profits mounted, staged loud and frequent strikes. Problems were compounded when the U.S. government, bowing to business pressures to end wartime economic restrictions, lifted price controls almost immediately after V-J Day. The result was soaring costs and a black market in such items as clothing, beef, and lumber.

Veterans in both countries were treated far better than their predecessors in World War I, partly because those of the earlier war were now in government and were determined to do it better this time. Canada's veteran rehabilitation programs included university training — taken advantage of by 50,000 former servicemen. Another 96,000 received help to establish themselves in farming, fishing, and business. There were also pensions for war disabilities and for widows, orphans and for veterans in need or in poor health. Despite some omissions (former prisoners of war, for example, were neglected), the Canadian program was generally regarded as the best in the world.

In the United States, returning servicemen who were unemployed received a disbursement of $20 weekly for 52 weeks (they were dubbed the 52-20 club). But the capstone of postwar aid for U.S. veterans was the GI Bill of Rights, passed in 1944. The $14.5 billion it provided (until it was phased out in 1956) enabled more than half of the veterans of World War II to attend college or technical school. Classrooms bulged with new students, schools expanded their facilities, and in 1949 and 1950 more than twice the number of degrees were conferred than had been granted 10 years earlier. A long-running boom in education had begun.

THE BABY DOCTOR

Almost from the moment it was published in 1945, *The Common Sense Book of Baby and Child Care* became the child-rearing bible for hundreds of thousands of parents. Dr. Benjamin Spock, a pediatrician with a background in psychology, wrote his guide for a receptive audience: young newly-weds who wanted to put the war behind them and start a family. The book sold some 750,000 copies in its first year and has become a perennial best-seller. *Baby and Child Care* revolutionized people's ideas about raising children. Whereas a popular behaviorist in the first half of the century, John B. Watson, had advised parents not to hug and kiss children, or "let them sit on your lap," Dr. Spock insisted that love, reason, and parental example were essential elements in the healthy development of the child. He encouraged parents to use their common sense and assured them that "there's a happy medium between adapting to the baby's individual needs and maintaining a sensible control over him." He felt strongly that a mother's place was in the home, particularly during the first three years of a child's life. He opposed excessive rigidity, leading some detractors to accuse him of fostering permissiveness. Through his gentle counsel, this "father" to the millions of baby boomers, born between 1946 and 1964, reshaped North America's concept of child care.

Veterans in search of affordable housing were greeted by a shortage, as illustrated in the cartoon at left. The family below had to settle for a Quonset hut resting on bare earth, but they took every step to make their home comfortable.

FASHION STATEMENTS, TRENDY LOOKS

The postwar fashion era reflected an odd mix of seemingly contradictory attitudes: a devil-may-care, let's-try-anything sentiment and a yearning to return to a normal way of life and simply follow the leader.

World War II had been over for just 18 months when an obscure dress designer named Christian Dior sent a file of models down a Paris runway wearing what seemed like a thousand excess metres of fabric. Waists were tiny, hips and bosoms rounded, skirts flared to within 30 centimetres of the ground. With its voluptuous curves and ample skirts, the New Look harked back some 50 years to the Victorian period. "God help the buyers who bought before they saw this," gasped one store rep. Women who had been forced to make do with skimpy this and skimpier that — because wartime clothing regulations limited the amount of fabric manufacturers could use — revelled in the folds, tucks, and swishing sounds that came along with skirts big enough to topple over a set of tenpins. Within a year, stores were selling knockoffs of the $450 originals for $20 or less. The New Look had its dissenters, of course, such as the 300,000 members of the Little Below the Knee Club.

A Touch of Zaniness

Daily life during the postwar years was shaped by a longing for conformity. Very few men, women, or children wished to be left out or left behind. For the average middle-class person, the urge to keep up with the Joneses turned into a way of life. Extravagantly endowed with new opportunities and obligations and deeply awed by the certainty that technological advances would soon transform ordinary life almost beyond recognition, the public was at once giddy and anxious. "Let's try something new!" was the prevailing impulse. "Let's do it together" was its ever-cautious companion.

Even though the sack dress enjoyed wide popularity at the end of the decade, its nightgown variety never caught on. Outlandish dark glasses, such as the ones shown at the upper left, were all the rage, particularly when worn with a bikini.

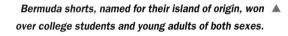

Bermuda shorts, named for their island of origin, won ▲ over college students and young adults of both sexes.

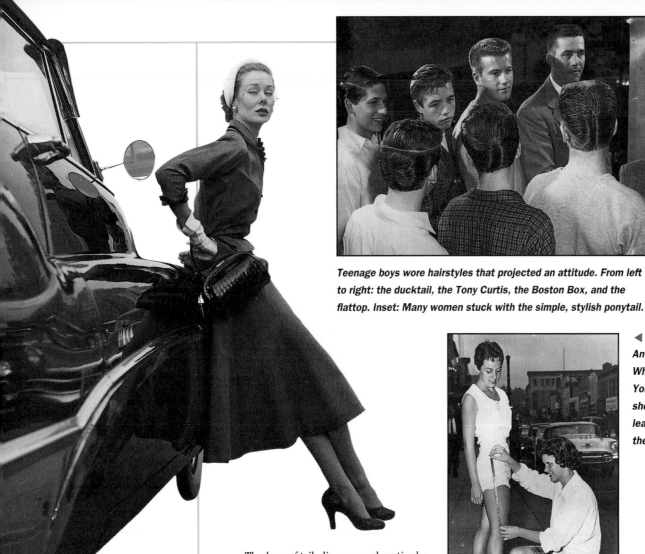

Teenage boys wore hairstyles that projected an attitude. From left to right: the ducktail, the Tony Curtis, the Boston Box, and the flattop. Inset: Many women stuck with the simple, stylish ponytail.

◄ **Designer Christian Dior dominated the world of high fashion throughout the decade. This model sports his look from head to toe.**

◄

For the woman who aspired to reach the top of the fashion ladder, a complete outfit demanded the very latest in accessories, from sophisticated millinery styles to tasteful jewellery and hand wear.

◄ **An ordinance for White Plains, New York, provided that shorts must reach at least halfway down the thigh.**

► **This teenager spent some time perfecting her outfit: rolled-up jeans, a man's flannel shirt, scuffed and dirty saddle shoes, and bobby sox.**

The lure of tribalism proved particularly strong among teenagers. Now that the lean war years had ended, parents indulged their children, leaving more money at their disposal than any earlier generation had enjoyed. Poodle skirts, sweater sets, motorcycle jackets, white bucks or saddle shoes were some of the pricier spoils of parental indulgence. And the kids purchased their fair share of flash-in-the-pan items as well. Extra earnings from babysitting and lawn-mowing jobs went to buy ankle bracelets, golf-ball-size cuff links, garrison belts, and crinoline petticoats. But the most conspicuous display of youthful mass lunacy, a succession of *de rigueur* hairstyles, cost the wearer very little: for the girls, poodle cuts, beehives, pageboys, and pixies; for the boys, crew cuts, flattops, Apaches, pompadours, and the infamous ducktail, which foreshadowed the next decade's hair rebellions.

Even middle-class adults succumbed to trendy fashion statements. Women donned tube dresses, short shorts, pop-it necklaces, and a new line of at-home wear, featuring lounging pants and velveteen pyjamas. The designer of the bikini — named for postwar nuclear bomb tests at Bikini atoll in the Pacific — touted the swimwear's "explosive potential." A few bold men ventured beyond the staid male fashions of the time and put aside gray flannel suits to sport pink dress shirts, string ties, and Bermuda shorts — even at the office.

In an odd bit of symmetry, the postwar era closed as it had begun, with an out-of-left-field style. The inelegant sack dress appeared just as veterans of Dior's New Look were wondering where their tiny waists had gone. Amid howls of protest, the shapeless chemise ruled for a season, then quickly was thrown aside.

"AN IRON CURTAIN HAS DESCENDED"

▶

Gen. George C. Marshall, army chief of staff during World War II, later served as secretary of state (1947–49) and secretary of defence (1950–51). He won the Nobel Peace Prize in 1953 for the European Recovery Program, which put a stricken Europe back on its feet.

Amid fears of Soviet expansion in Europe, the Truman administration decided that the containment of communism would be the linchpin of American foreign policy.

Europe lay destitute in the spring of 1947. Severe shortages of food and fuel, rampant disease, and faltering economies had left the Continent in shambles. Ominously, the Soviet Union was holding the peoples of eastern Europe under dictatorial rule, isolating them from the rest of Europe. This prompted Winston Churchill (above), when he spoke at Westminster College in Fulton, Missouri, on March 5, 1946, to warn of Soviet expansion, declaring: "From Stettin in the Baltic to Trieste in the Adriatic an iron curtain has descended across the Continent." The British fear was that the nations behind the iron curtain would exploit an economically weak Europe to encourage Communist uprisings, as was already happening in Greece. Economic aid would help western Europe to contain the threat, but Britain, itself shattered by the war, could not continue the aid it had been giving. It urged the United States to take up the task of containing communism.

Truman Gets Tough on Communism

In 1947, Truman discussed such a task with key members of Congress. Said Senator Arthur Vandenburg, "Mr. President, if that's what you want, there's only one way to get it. That is to make a personal appearance before Congress and scare the hell out of the country."

On March 12, 1947, Truman did just that, asking for $400 million in economic and military assistance for Greece and Turkey. "I believe that it must be the policy of the United States," he said, "to support free peoples who are resisting attempted subjugation by armed minorities or by outside pressures." That policy of containment came to be called the Truman Doctrine. A month later the dawning era got its name from a speech delivered by financier Bernard Baruch: "Let us not be deceived — today we are in the midst of a cold war." Veteran American diplomat and Russian scholar George Kennan published a forceful argument that communism could be contained with strength. The battle lines of the Cold War were drawn.

In late spring of 1947, the lengthening Soviet shadow loomed ominously over Eastern Europe. The French Communist Party was flexing its muscles, and Italian voters seemed poised to choose a communist majority. Against this backdrop, Secretary of State George C. Marshall outlined a bold plan to aid European recovery. In a commencement address at Harvard University on June 5, 1947, he offered economic assistance to Europe. Britain, to its heavy cost, was excluded. The Soviet Union, though it was

CARVING OUT A NEW NATION

An issue that demanded prompt attention after the war was how to compensate the Jewish survivors of the Holocaust. Since the late 19th century, Jewish Zionist leaders had been pressing for a homeland for their people in Palestine, site of the ancient kingdom of Israel. Beginning in the 1920's, great numbers of Jews emigrated from around the world to the largely Arab region. As the Nazis rose to power in Germany, Jewish refugees poured into Palestine. When World War II ended, Britain, which had controlled Palestine since 1918, referred the question of the Jewish state to the United Nations.

In November 1947 the U.N. voted to divide Palestine into two states, Arab and Jewish, responsibility for which would be turned over to the U.N. within six months. Jews around the world celebrated the decision, and Arabs condemned it as a declaration of war. Canadians and Americans generally supported the Zionist cause. Secretary of State George C. Marshall argued for a U.N. trusteeship until the differences between Palestinians and Jews could be resolved. He called attention to the growing value of Middle East oil reserves and asserted that partition

could lead to war, possibly involving the Soviets. Great Britain thought partition unworkable. Dr. Chaim Weizmann, who would become Israel's first president, wrote Truman a letter urging: "The choice for our people, Mr. President, is between statehood and extermination. History and providence have placed this issue in your hands and I am confident that you will yet decide in the spirit of moral law."

Israel was proclaimed a state on May 14, 1948, to the approval of all of North America. The next day five Arab states invaded Israel. For the first time in more than 2,000 years, the Jews had an independent homeland, but at the price of unending turmoil in the Middle East.

included, rejected the assistance. In April Congress approved initial outlays of money for the plan. The impact of the Marshall Plan on a Europe still devastated by war was dramatic. Needy citizens received food and clothing; new trains hauled goods along freshly laid tracks; dikes were erected in the Netherlands; mines hummed to life, and factories geared up. "Ordinary thanks are inadequate," wrote the editor of a British newspaper. "Here is one of the most brilliant successes in the history of international relations." It was not pure charity. For Canada, which was a donor together with the United States, the plan boosted exports and averted a balance of trade crisis. And as distrust toward the Soviets mounted, the plan forged new bonds of friendship between North America and Western Europe.

In June 1948, the U.S.S.R. showed that fears about its intentions were not exaggerated. Their target was West Berlin, occupied by British, American, and French troops, but lying 176 kilometres within East Germany. Their aim was to force out the allies by blocking all roads connecting the city to West Germany. Within a week, bread and meat supplies dwindled to one month's worth. Gen. Lucius D. Clay, U.S. commander in Berlin, warned: "If we mean . . . to hold Europe against communism, we must not budge . . . the future of democracy requires us to stay." Some officers proposed ramming through the railway blockade with an armored locomotive, but Clay called Gen. Curtis E. LeMay, U.S. Air Force chief in Europe, and asked: "Curt, can you transport coal by air?" The Berlin Airlift was born.

The airlift depended on clockwork precision: as soon as a plane touched down, crews worked feverishly to unload it and send it back aloft within 30 minutes. For 321 days, medicine, food, coal, and other vital goods were flown into Berlin, to the outrage of the Soviets. By the fall of 1948, some 5,000 tonnes of supplies

were arriving daily. The Berlin crisis proved the need for an alliance that would protect Western Europe against Soviet aggression. Escott Reid, of Canada's Department of External Affairs, feared the United States would return to isolationism, so he proposed the alliance that became a reality on April 4, 1949. The North Atlantic Treaty Organization (NATO) joined Canada, the United States, and 10 European countries to coordinate military assistance. Finally, in May 1949, the Soviets lifted the blockade in Berlin, handing the West its first real Cold War victory.

Young airlift spotters watch a four-engine C-54, carrying 10 tonnes of supplies, as it nears West Berlin from Frankfurt. "The sound of the engines is like music to our ears," wrote one victim of the Soviet blockade.

THE NEW CANADIANS

Some 40,000 war brides (mainly British) and their 20,000 children, most under the age of three, arrived in Canada at the end of the war.

Canada accepted massive immigration after the war, hoping the newcomers would add to Canadian prosperity without making any changes. They did make Canada more prosperous, but they also changed it — for the better.

From 1945 through the 1950's, they poured into the harbors and railway stations of Canada. First it was the young brides of Canadian servicemen, then it was the British and Dutch and Germans, followed by the Italians and Poles and Hungarians and Greeks. These were the immigrants of the postwar years, and they flooded into Canadian cities, towns, and farms at an average of 10,000 a month — more than 350 a day — for almost 200 months. Two-thirds of them found homes in Canada's largest cities — Toronto, Montreal, and Vancouver.

Not all Canadians welcomed them, especially in the early years when so many immigrants were those who had been penned up in camps and robbed by war of homes and even countries. "Displaced Persons" was their official title, and "DP" was often said with a sneer.

This advertisement, posted by the Canadian Department of Citizenship and Immigration in about 1950, encouraged English-speaking Europeans to emigrate to Canada.

Il Corriere Italiano, the most widely read Italian newspaper in Canada, was first published in 1954 and is still going strong.

A Stimulus to the Economy

Most of the newcomers, however, were far from the popular image of huddled masses. Professionals and skilled workers, they played critical roles in modernizing Canadian industry and enriching Canadian cultural life.

Even at the basic level of personal spending, the immigrants stimulated national prosperity. In 1953, immigration officials calculated that over 400 million dollars had been brought into the Canadian economy. As early as 1951, the Canadian census reported that one-third of immigrant families had purchased homes and, of those, almost a third were mortgage free. Immigrant households had also bought 52,000 radios and 43,000 kitchen stoves, and a third owned cars. To those figures, add the 350 million dollars annually spent on food and then the amount spent on clothing and furniture, and the economic stimulus to Canada is obvious.

Open Arms, But Not For Everyone

The welcome mat was out for the British and French first, then Dutch, Belgian, and German immigrants, people who, it was thought, would be absorbed immediately into Canada as it already was. But these groups, accustomed to labor unions and a regulated workplace, were not nearly so welcome to Canadian industry. British trade unionists in particular, fresh from the near-warfare between labor and management in Britain, proved disturbingly militant on the Canadian scene. To counter that militancy, industry demanded workers from low-wage southern and eastern Europe, a demand that was met as Italians, mostly from the agricultural south, became the largest single immigrant group by the late 1950's.

There were other people Canada did not welcome generously, because we did not want to, as Prime Minister Mackenzie King put it, "make any fundamental alteration in the character of our population." In plain language, Canada didn't want Jews, Orientals or blacks.

Anti-semitism was widespread in Canada through the 1930's and 1940's. Jews were discriminated against at every level from universities to jobs and

housing. Anti-semitism was so deeply rooted in both the government and civil service that fleeing Jews were denied sanctuary from Hitler's Germany, even during the war when it was known that they were being condemned to death camps. Then, for several years after the war, Canadian immigration agents were instructed to make it almost impossible for Jews to migrate to Canada. Only intense lobbying by the Canadian Jewish Congress, under its long-time president Sam Bronfman, brought an easing of restrictions in the late 1940's.

Orientals had been effectively banned since 1908, a ban that was lifted in 1947, partly because it was so obviously an act of racism directed at wartime ally China. However, Asian and black immigration remained effectively limited during the 1950's through education and skill requirements that gave a strong preference to north Europeans.

In spite of the difficulties, within a generation, the new Canadians were fully Canadian, adding to the country's economic power, and filling the nation's schools with promise for the future. But they didn't become as invisible within the old Canada as Mackenzie King had hoped. Rather, they measurably brightened and enlivened every place they settled, their restaurants, theatre, music and clothing bringing a new variety and richness to the Canadian scene. Only in one city did their presence create a cloud of apprehension.

In Montreal, the second city of choice for immigrants, the newcomers gravitated to the English-speaking community. This was partly because English was the language of economic opportunity in North America, and partly because French schools preferred not to have the new immigrants. The Quebec government, fearing that Montreal would soon become a predominantly English city, pressed the Canadian government to seek out immigrants from France or Belgium. But few French wished to emigrate, and those Belgians who did showed the European tendency to gravitate to English. So it was that in the immigration of the 1950's were planted the seeds of the hostility toward language differences that would burst over Quebec a decade later.

Thomas J. Bata (above), a Czech émigré, arrived in Canada in 1939 to build a shoe factory, and stayed. He is now chairman of Bata Ltd., which makes more than a million pairs of shoes a day. Sam Bronfman (right), a Russian immigrant, founded the Seagram Company Ltd., the largest distilling company in the world.

A five-year-old immigrant from Hong Kong, newly arrived in Edmonton, waits for her parents among a pile of luggage.

▼ *William Kurelek's painting* Hot Day in Kensington Market, *done in 1972, depicted the already cosmopolitan character of Toronto. Jewish, Hungarian, and Portuguese stores were well established and frequented by then.*

RISING FEARS OF COMMUNIST SUBVERSION

"Party labels don't mean anything anymore," said Hollywood's George Murphy. "You can draw a line right down the middle. On one side are the Americans; on the other are the Communists and Socialists."

◀ **Uncle Sam sifts the Truman administration for Communists in a Buffalo Courier Express *cartoon*.**

▼ **In March 1949 anti-Communist hysteria led protesters to picket outside a meeting of the Cultural and Scientific Conference for World Peace in New York. Composer Dimitri Shostakovich headed the Soviet delegation.**

"We have these fits of hysteria," President Truman observed. The hysteria — a rising suspicion that the continent was riddled with Communist spies — was all too apparent. Though it was not illegal to be a Communist in Canada, Communists and their sympathizers were harrassed by police, politicians, and news media. For Canada, the tempo increased in 1945 when Igor Gouzenko, a clerk at the Soviet Embassy in Ottawa, defected and produced evidence of Soviet espionage. Fred Rose, a Labour Progressive Party (Communist) member of Parliament, was jailed for being a spy. Communists in the union movement immediately became targets, even without evidence of spying, in a round of union smashing. In 1946, Madeleine Parent and Kent Rowley, organizers of textile workers in Valleyfield, Quebec, were imprisoned. Three years later, the Canadian government broke up the Canadian Seaman's Union, forcing members into the gangster-controlled Seafarer's International Union. Immigration authorities deported or rejected people on even a suspicion of radicalism, while loosening restrictions on Nazis so much that the RCMP complained Canada was becoming a haven for war criminals. But the hysteria in Canada was modest in comparison with that in the United States.

Under pressure from Congress and the Justice Department, Truman introduced some anti-Communist measures of his own. In 1947 he established a Federal Employee Loyalty program by executive order. Over the course of four years, more than 3 million Americans were screened and cleared; several thousand resigned, but only 212 were dismissed for misconduct or as security risks.

To those eager to find it, Communist influence was everywhere. Had Soviet agents penetrated the boardrooms of capitalism? A booklet put out by a conservative think tank contained the following advice on "how to spot a Communist in your own business": familiarize yourself with the Communist Party line as printed in left-wing publications and watch how workers respond to anti-Communist labor leaders. Suspicions of communism spread. Had it infiltrated the education system too? Fearful that left-wing professors might fill students' heads with Marxist propaganda, state legislatures and college administrations in the United States began to demand that educators sign loyalty oaths. Some 11,000 professors in the University of California system alone were required to take the pledge. Failure to do so

could end in a person being fired, as more than 120 recalcitrant professors at UCLA found out.

The anti-Communist fervor also invaded libraries, which emptied their shelves of everything suspect, from Communist organs, such as the *Daily Worker,* to mainstream publications, such as *National Geographic.* Even books on Robin Hood came into question. Didn't the bandit of Sherwood Forest steal from the rich and give to the poor? In the turbulent sea of suspicion, voices of moderation were all but lost.

Congress Seizes the Initiative

The noisiest, most persistent investigative body in the United States was the House Committee on Un-American Activities (HUAC), which had been set up in Congress in 1938 to investigate foreign subversion. Turning its sights from Nazis to Communists, HUAC aimed at a target sure to gain maximum attention: Hollywood.

As part of the war effort, several studios had made pro-Soviet films. Then a series of labor strikes hit the film industry — instigated, some studio heads suggested, by Communists. So in 1947 the committee held two weeks of hearings to expose the contamination. Scores of industry witnesses — from producers Walt Disney and Jack Warner to actors Robert Taylor, Gary Cooper, George Murphy, and Ronald Reagan — took the stand. Some decried Communist infiltration of the Screen Writers Guild and other unions. So-called unfriendly witnesses faced the obligatory question: "Are you now or have you ever been a member of the Communist Party?" Refusing to respond on the grounds that the question violated their First Amendment rights, 10 of those who were subpoenaed, including writers Ring Lardner, Jr., and Dalton Trumbo, headed off to jail on charges of contempt. But the Hollywood Ten were not the only casualties. Perhaps as many as 500 writers, directors, and actors were suspended from work when their names ended up on studio blacklists established to satisfy HUAC.

The next year, 1948, the committee turned its attention to the State Department. In the sweltering heat of a Washington August, a tall, handsomely tailored former State Department official named Alger Hiss strode into a

Stars who came to Washington to protest Red hunts in Hollywood included (from the bottom row, left to right) Richard Conte, Lauren Bacall, Humphrey Bogart; Paul Henreid, June Havoc, Geraldine Brooks; Marsha Hunt, Evelyn Keyes; Jane Wyatt, Danny Kaye; Mrs. Sterling Hayden, Gene Kelly; and, behind Kelly, Sterling Hayden.

congressional caucus room to refute allegations that he had been a Communist. With his upper-class bearing, good looks, and record of high achievement in a number of key government posts, Hiss seemed the embodiment of the public-spirited American. Now, in his early forties, he headed the prestigious Carnegie Endowment for International Peace. That such a man could betray his country seemed unimaginable. Yet this was the charge levelled against him.

His accuser, Whittaker Chambers, projected quite a different image. Dumpy and dishevelled — "a fat, sad-looking man in a baggy blue suit," according to one reporter — Chambers had joined the Communist Party in the 1920's. In 1938 he underwent a change of heart and, renouncing communism, became an ardent patriot. He later joined the staff of *Time* magazine, where he rose to the rank of a senior editor. Now, under subpoena, he began to identify associates in his old Communist cell. Hiss was the most prominent.

Hiss met the allegations with cool disdain. Did he know Chambers? At first he answered no, then at a second hearing conceded he had known Chambers, but under a different name. Had

he let Chambers stay in his Washington house? Yes. In fact, he had also given him a used car. A freshman congressman from California, Richard M. Nixon, doggedly pursued this line of questioning; and as Hiss and Chambers continued to offer conflicting versions of the same events, Hiss's story began to unravel. It became clear that Hiss had been more deeply involved with Chambers than he had let on.

The Plot Thickens

After Chambers repeated his charges against Hiss on radio's *Meet the Press,* Hiss sued him for libel. Chambers next produced an assortment of papers that he said Hiss had passed on to him and that he had hidden away after emerging from the Communist underground 11 years earlier. Some were notes in Hiss's handwriting; others were summaries of State Department documents, which experts attested had been typed on Hiss's old Woodstock typewriter. Chambers gave investigators as further evidence several rolls of microfilm, which he dramatically removed from a hollowed-out pumpkin on his Maryland farm. This proof led to Hiss's indictment. Because the statute of limitations on espionage had expired, Hiss was charged with two counts of perjury for having lied about his relationship with Chambers and about having transmitted confidential material to him.

The proceedings shifted from the caucus room to the federal courts, where distinguished public servants, including Supreme Court Justice Felix Frankfurter, testified to Hiss's good character, while Chambers was assailed as a self-confessed traitor. The jury failed to reach a verdict, and a second trial was set. This time the prosecutor hammered away at the documentary evidence, the "pumpkin papers." Hiss was found guilty and sentenced to five years in prison. His conviction was the most compelling evidence so far that Communist infiltration of the government had posed a threat to national security. Hiss staunchly maintained his innocence and repeatedly sought to have his conviction overturned on appeal.

Several weeks after the first Hiss trial had ended, the State Department released a white paper conceding that China had been lost to Mao Tse-tung and the Communists. "We picked a bad horse," muttered Harry Truman. Over the previous four years, America had provided $2 billion in support to the Nationalist forces of Chiang Kai-shek, but Chiang's government was corrupt, inefficient, and militarily inept. When the Communists won, forcing the Nationalists to retreat to Taiwan, Chiang's American supporters hinted darkly at a pro-Communist conspiracy within the U.S. government. Had America betrayed its wartime ally Chiang Kai-shek? Henry Luce, the conservative publisher of *Life* and *Time,* along with other members of the so-called China

Whittaker Chambers (inset), a confessed ex-Communist, seemed no match for the debonair Alger Hiss (above). Then Richard Nixon took on the case as a personal crusade. Robert Stripling, HUAC's chief investigator, said later: "Nixon had his hat set for Hiss. . . . He was no more concerned about whether or not Hiss was [a Communist] than a billy goat." At right are Stripling, Nixon, and the "pumpkin papers."

Chiang Kai-shek and his Wellesley-educated wife meet Gen. Joseph Stilwell in Burma in 1942. After the war $2 billion in U.S. aid did not save China for Chiang.

Assistant secretary of state under Roosevelt (1941–45), Truman's "top brain man," Dean G. Acheson, served him as undersecretary (1945–47) then as secretary of state (1949–53).

Lobby, apparently thought so. They accused the State Department of having Soviet leanings and of making a shambles of U.S. foreign policy. One Republican congressman even charged Truman's secretary of state, Dean Acheson, with being on the Kremlin payroll. Hard-liners began referring to Acheson as the Red Dean. In December 1949, Republicans passed a resolution urging Dean Acheson's firing; President Truman ripped it in two. But for years the hunt continued for the traitors who had "lost" China.

Since the end of World War II, the rising fear of communism had been tempered by the knowledge that the United States had the atom bomb and the belief that the U.S.S.R. could not develop one for years. But in September 1949, the unmistakable radioactive fingerprint of an atomic blast had been detected somewhere over the wasteland of Soviet Siberia. The four-year U.S. monopoly on atomic weapons vanished in a flash. How had the Soviets so quickly mastered the construction of the world's most destructive weapon? Few people understood the complexities of an atomic chain reaction, but it seemed plausible that Communist spies must have relayed the bomb's secret. Less than five months later, that suspicion was confirmed by the confession of British spy Klaus Fuchs (see pages 272–273). Never before had the West felt so vulnerable. In the United States, the stage was set for the dramatic charges of Sen. Joseph R. McCarthy.

Just a year after the Communists had proclaimed the People's Republic of China in October 1949, thousands of Chinese carrying likenesses of Mao Tse-tung parade to celebrate National Day. The decades-long struggle between the Communists and Nationalists for control of China effectively ended when Mao drove Chiang Kai-shek from the mainland.

EMBRACING SUBURBIA

While some social critics found the new suburban communities drably conformist, residents disagreed: "Levittown was like a godsend. . . . We all got along because we all started with a clean slate, we were all in the same situation."

A s veterans streamed home, many families had to double up in crowded apartments or occupy unused military barracks. Others moved in with in-laws.

Two years after the war ended, developer William J. Levitt purchased 2,430 hectares of potato fields in Nassau County, New York, and within a few months a whole prefabricated community stood where none had been before. A hundred houses appeared at a time: plain, boxy structures, all looking very much alike. They were not glamorous, but the price was right: the smallest house cost less than $8,000, and the government would help finance it with low-cost loans provided under the GI Bill. Couples camped out for days for the chance to buy. By 1951, 82,000 residents lived in Levittown's 17,447 homes. The Canadian government had anticipated the need for housing, and at the war's end could offer mass-produced prefabricated houses to veterans for prices as low as $3,000.

A Home of One's Own, at Last

The postwar suburbs were hardly posh, but neither could they be called slums. Individual houses might have been small and lacking in architectural grace notes, but what did it matter? They were still houses, and they filled an aching need. Men and women who had suffered the deprivations of the 1930's, and years of wartime separation, yearned for the opportunity to blossom: a patch of grass, a large and healthy family, the comfort and security of their very own home. Here was their chance. Thanks to a robust economy, veterans' benefits, and subsidized mortgages, homeownership blossomed. And so began the postwar move to the suburbs. Of almost 14 million homes constructed in the 1950's, more than 11 million sprang up on the fringes of city limits. While the population of Toronto remained stable, that of its suburbs quadrupled in 20 years. In the United States, the population of Orange County, south of Los Angeles, tripled.

Developments like Levittown, New York (right, about 1950), made possible the dream of marriage, homeownership, and parenthood (inset, above right) for thousands of young people who longed for wholesome stability.

Part of that surge was attributable to an explosion of births. Brides and grooms were younger than at any other time during the century; the average age of marrying men dropped to 22 and of women to just 20. From 20 births a year per thousand people in the 1930's, Canada's birth rate soared to almost 30 in 1947. Divorce, too, rose immediately after the war, but then dropped as quickly and stabilized through the 1950's across North America as population numbers soared. Then there were the immigrants: Canada received 1,800,000 from 1945 to 1961 — 282,000 in 1957 alone. The net result for Canada was a rise in population from 12 million in 1945 to more than 18 million in 1961.

Every migration leaves a vacancy, and the rush to the suburbs forever changed cities. They increasingly became places in which to work and shop only. A mass commuter culture evolved as office workers poured into downtown business districts each morning, and eagerly headed home at 5 P.M. Before long, many stores joined the urban exodus, and industrial parks sprouted along the expressways.

"YOUNG MEN IN GRAY FLANNEL SUITS"

The new suburbia was not without its critics. As early as 1950, sociologist David Riesman shook suburban complacencies with his best-selling book, *The Lonely Crowd,* which examined suburban conformity. Then Professor C. Wright Mills presented a detailed and often scathing portrait of middle-class life and values in *White Collar* (1951) and *The Power Elite* (1956). In *The Organization Man*, William H. Whyte wrote that people had become obsessed with "togetherness," "team work," and "group think," sacrificing individuality to get ahead in huge corporate conglomerates.

Criticism of suburbia was not confined to academia. Fiction writers joined the chorus, notably Sloan Wilson with his partly autobiographical novel, *The Man in the Gray Flannel Suit* (1955), which was made into a movie starring Gregory Peck (inset, centre) in 1956. It is the story of a young couple, Tom and Betsy Rath, who struggle against the pressures of middle-class conformity. Tom is a war veteran commuting to an ad agency job he doesn't much like, and which pays him not enough money. Their house is too small for their three children; the furniture is old and worn. What should have been an upwardly mobile couple enjoying the fruits of honest labor is shown instead to be a sorely discontented pair, deep in debt and scurrying to keep up with their neighbors, who, it turns out, are equally unhappy. The book's title comes from Tom's sudden realization that "all I could see was a lot of bright young men in gray flannel suits rushing around New York in a frantic parade to nowhere." Then Tom looks down and discovers, to his horror, that he, too, is wearing gray flannel. In the end, Tom and Betsy confront their problems and work them out; both their marriage and their principles remain intact. But the issues Wilson portrayed struck a resonant chord with millions struggling to make something of their lives.

High employment and rising wages swelled the ranks of the middle class, whose enormous buying power soon boosted the economy. Enticed by advertisers to buy more and ever-larger slices of the good life, North Americans took material consumption to new heights. With less than 7 percent of the world's population, they drove 80 percent of its automobiles, consumed nearly half its energy, and produced almost half of its manufactured products. And yet, despite so many outward signs of prosperity, anxieties lurked at the heart of suburban life. Many suburbanites were living beyond their means. Homeownership, the pride of the decade, floated largely on bank loans: the equity stake was often a mere $1,000. Most cars were bought on credit, and personal indebtedness ballooned as suburban dwellers struggled to "keep up with the Joneses." Real wages did rise by 30 percent during the decade, to be sure, but often what was bought with them did not fully belong to those who spent them. Perhaps the frenetic pace with which suburbanites gobbled up material goods stemmed, in part, from life's very precariousness, the fear that everything — houses, cars, swimming pools — could vanish in a second. The face of suburbia wore a smile, but a nervous one.

◀

The 1950's was a boom decade for real estate agents across North America, when whole communities of new houses sprang up in the suburbs and were sold quickly.

THE GOLDEN AGE OF TELEVISION

"Make no mistake about it," predicted Wayne Coy of the Federal Communications Commission in 1948,

"television is here to stay. It is a new force unloosed in the land."

The Canadian Broadcasting Corporation brought network television to Canada in 1952. Overnight, it made stars of Don Messer, Gordie Tapp and, on the French-language *Point de Mire*, of a young journalist named René Lévesque. NHL hockey became a fixture from the start, soon followed by the quiz show *Fighting Words* and the dramatic series *La Famille Plouffe*. *Front Page Challenge* began its long run in 1957. But despite these successes, audience demand forced the CBC to carry popular American programs. That appeal of American TV culture was also felt in Europe, where it was referred to as "the Canadian problem."

One of the most popular U.S. shows was *I Love Lucy*. Within six months of its debut in 1951, it hit the top spot in the ratings. When Lucille Ball became pregnant, she and her husband, Desi Arnaz, worked this happy condition into the script. They shot an episode celebrating the future arrival of Little Ricky, and CBS aired it Monday, January 19, 1953 — the very day Lucille Ball actually gave birth. More than 70 percent of all TV households in North America tuned in, far more than watched the televised broadcast of President Dwight Eisenhower's inauguration the next day.

Lucy's success was just one example of the explosive growth of television. In 1945 TV was an exotic toy. Three years later, in the United States, Milton Berle had an audience pushing 5 million. Berle, a popular nightclub comic noted for borrowing jokes, became the first big television star. Starting with a mixture of wacky costumes, old vaudeville routines, and a parade of wisecracking burlesque buddies, Uncle Miltie hosted *The Texaco Star Theater* and made Tuesday nights *his*.

Berle's closest rival was gossip columnist Ed Sullivan, who hosted a Sunday night variety show called *The Toast of the Town*. Sullivan — who, said comedian Fred Allen, "will be around as

Television reached 17 million living rooms by 1951, delighting viewers with the high jinks of "Uncle Miltie" Berle (above), with Kukla, Fran and Ollie (on screen), and with lots more.

◀ Lucy and Desi head for California on episode 110 of I Love Lucy, with their friends the Mertzes (Vivian Vance and William Frawley) riding in the back seat.

▼ Ed Sullivan gave dozens of top stars their first big break when he booked them on his show.

▼ Napoleon gives his mother an affectionate kiss in the highly popular La Famille Plouffe, a TV miniseries in the 1950's, set in urban, working-class Quebec.

long as somebody else has talent" — debuted in 1948 and remained on the air for 23 years. TV won new audiences for show biz veterans Jimmy Durante and Red Skelton and also for Groucho Marx, whose *You Bet Your Life* quiz program became a launching pad for his own outrageous one-liners. Sid Caesar and Imogene Coca brought viewers 90 minutes of sheer hilarity in *Your Show of Shows*.

Sitcoms, born on radio, learned to spread their wings on TV. *The Goldbergs* made the transition. Burns and Allen continued trading gags (George: "What do you think of TV?" Gracie: "Wonderful! I hardly ever watch radio anymore."). Jackie Gleason played Brooklyn bus driver Ralph Kramden in *The Honeymooners,* about a working-class family dreaming of, and scheming up, ways to get ahead in life.

As broadcast hours increased and more homes tuned in, television found a new role to play: electronic babysitter. Soon after *Howdy Doody* began in 1947, the tube's potential for influencing kids grew by gleeful leaps and bounds. Next came *Kukla, Fran, and Ollie,* which charmed adults as well as youngsters. *Ding Dong School,* a show for toddlers starring soft-voiced Miss Frances, and *The Mickey Mouse Club* both enjoyed enormous success. *Captain Kangaroo* debuted in 1953 and stayed on the air for three decades.

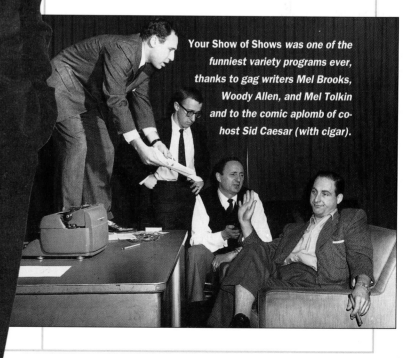

Bus driver Jackie Gleason of The Honeymooners warns TV wife Audrey Meadows — "One of these days, Alice . . . Bang, zoom!" — as Art Carney and Joyce Randolph look askance.

Your Show of Shows was one of the funniest variety programs ever, thanks to gag writers Mel Brooks, Woody Allen, and Mel Tolkin and to the comic aplomb of co-host Sid Caesar (with cigar).

263

The Lone Ranger (Clayton Moore) and his companion, Tonto (Canada's Jay Silverheels), get ready to ride. They galloped on screen in 1949 and stayed until 1957 in one of TV's most popular horse operas for kids.

Front Page Challenge, first aired in 1957, is the longest-running game show in North America. The panellist, above, had criticized the Liberal government in The Ottawa Journal. Her appearance in this show drew controversy to the CBC.

Flesh-and-blood image of the Man of Steel, George Reeves played Superman — intrepid defender of "truth, justice and the American way" — on TV from 1952 to 1957.

Jack Webb (left), director and star of Dragnet, just wants the facts. Ben Alexander plays his partner, Officer Frank Smith.

Westerns, too, were kids' favorites, beginning with *Hopalong Cassidy* (1949), starring William Boyd, and followed quickly by *The Roy Rogers Show*, *The Gene Autry Show*, and *The Lone Ranger*. By 1958, viewers could choose from more than 20 regularly scheduled westerns each week, many of them targeting an adult audience. James Arness spent 20 years playing the stalwart Marshal Matt Dillon in *Gunsmoke*. James Garner's *Maverick* was an affable poker-playing antihero just one step shy of a con man.

If such series seldom rose to real drama, viewers had only to spin their dials. In 1947 the *Kraft Television Theatre* broadcast TV's first live production, and soon TV was offering more than 10 live dramas every week. Prestigious showcases, such as *Playhouse 90* and *Studio One,* featured written-for-TV plays, like J. P. Miller's *Days of Wine and Roses.*

In Canada, CBC television stimulated an outburst of dramatic writing such as Patricia Joudry's *Teach Me How to Cry*, which went on to appear on New York and London stages. In Quebec, Radio-Canada produced a record 100 hours of television theatre in 1958.

Meanwhile, TV news departments emerged as powers within the networks. Coverage of political conventions and congressional hearings attracted huge audiences, loyal to particular anchormen, like NBC's Chet Huntley and David Brinkley. Canadians tuned in to René Lévesque on Radio-Canada's *Point de Mire* and to CBC's *Close-up* produced by Ross Munro. Perhaps the most Canadian TV star was not a news reporter at all. It was weatherman Percy Saltzman, who combined meteorological expertise with a light touch that captivated viewers, and who inspired a generation of young Canadians to practice flipping pieces of chalk into the air — just as he did at the end of each forecast.

With clean-cut friends like these — the original cast of Walt Disney's Mickey Mouse Club — what grade-schooler could resist becoming a Mouseketeer and wearing a pair of rodent ears? Premiering in 1955, the show delighted a generation of children with its clever mix of cartoons, songs, and skits.

▼ One of America's great investigative journalists, Edward R. Murrow, pioneered the TV documentary with See It Now on CBS, and brought the camera into newsmakers' living rooms with Person to Person.

▼ On the quiz show Twenty-One, emcee Jack Barry presides while Charles Van Doren (left) and Herb Stempel (who blew the whistle on Van Doren) ponder a question from isolation booths, which were supposed to ensure honesty.

From the beginning, television had its critics. Intellectuals mocked it as "the idiot box" or "the boob tube," and even defenders worried when, by the end of the decade, the average family spent some five hours a day in front of it. Edward Murrow, host of CBS's *See it Now,* called it "the real opiate of the people" and wondered if TV news coverage could ever "sort out the charlatan from the statesman."

The mania for quiz shows in the late 1950's certainly provided fertile ground for chicanery. Charles Van Doren, an earnest young Columbia instructor, became a TV star when, seeming to strain for answers, he won thousands of dollars on *Twenty-One*. Three years later he admitted that the producer had given him the answers. Columbia fired Van Doren and so did NBC, which had taken him on as a commentator at $50,000 a year. Even so, popular sympathy ran with Van Doren, and a poll suggested that most people, given the chance, would have done just the same thing.

▶ The Today Show on NBC — with affable host Dave Garroway and his more-or-less-silent partner, J. Fred Muggs — set the style for chatty morning news programs.

RELIGION RESURGENT

Most people in the 1950's considered themselves religious, though few Canadians supported the attitude expressed by a writer for The Christian Century *that it was unpatriotic to be unreligious.*

In the 1950's, the United States experienced a profound religious resurgence. People flocked to the nation's churches in growing numbers: by 1955 half the adult population, 49 million congregants, regularly attended services. Expenditures on church construction rose from $409 million to nearly $1 billion.

Increasingly prayer accompanied the events of daily life: on railways, where dining car menus came with a suggested grace; during radio programs, which scheduled breaks to allow time for private meditation; and before athletic contests. When New Yorkers found themselves at a loss for words in their moment of need, they turned to Dial-A-Prayer, a one-minute telephone service set up by the minister of a local church. Drivers along America's byways could find spiritual solace at roadside and drive-in churches and by turning to their own dashboards, which, peopled by images of holy figures, became moving altars.

In the years after World War II, urban Canadians too built more churches than they had in all their history. Most were in the suburbs where, for a decade or so, churches filled a gap as social centres. Even so, there was a profound difference between religious expression in Canada and that in the United States, where even the most ribald comics might end their acts with a "God bless you all" — a public intrusion of religion that was alien to most Canadians.

Piety Wins in Washington and in the Media

Among a growing number of Americans, belief in God became intertwined with patriotism. As one minister put it: "An atheistic American is a contradiction in terms." In 1954 Congress added the words "under God" to the Pledge of Allegiance. Two years later, the phrase "In God We Trust," made the nation's official motto not long before, was engraved on all U.S. currency. When the Supreme Court ruled that "released time" was constitutional, allowing students to leave public schools early one day a week for religious instruction, Justice William O. Douglas's opinion read: "We are a religious people whose institutions presuppose a Supreme Being." President Dwight D. Eisenhower stated his view of the place of God in government: "The Almighty takes a definite and direct interest day by day in the progress of this nation." And, in those Cold War times, many believers saw their faith as a bulwark against communism. FBI Director J. Edgar Hoover urged Americans: "Since communists are anti-God, encourage your children to be active in the church."

With polls indicating 9 out of 10 Americans believed in God, Hollywood produced religious blockbuster movies — *The Ten Commandments*, *Quo Vadis*, *The Robe* — and smaller films treating spiritual themes. "He was everybody's kind of guy. . . . He was God's kind of guy," ran the ad for *A Man Called Peter*, about a U.S. Senate chaplain.

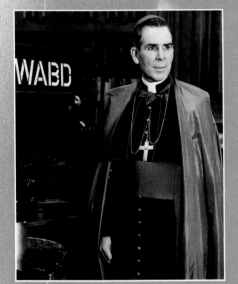

The dynamic, yet straightforward and humorous, style of Bishop Fulton J. Sheen (above) appealed to his television viewers. The Reverend Billy Graham (right) was at his best in spacious arenas, where he urged thousands to come forward for Christ.

A NEW POPE

On October 28, 1958, white smoke rose from a chimney above the Sistine Chapel in the Vatican to signal the election of a new pope. Angelo Giuseppe Roncalli, the aging cardinal and patriarch of Venice, seemed to be a "caretaker" choice by the College of Cardinals. Taking the name Pope John XXIII (shown above in his first official photograph), he moved swiftly to demonstrate that his reign would differ from that of his predecessor, Pope Pius XII. Within months, his evident compassion, humility, and sense of humor won over millions around the world. Then, in 1959, he stunned the church hierarchy by calling for an ecumenical council, the first in nearly 100 years. Finally convened in 1962, the council, called Vatican II, initiated numerous changes in Roman Catholic religious life and liturgy, among them that church officials could substitute the vernacular for Latin in the Mass, and that discrimination of any kind, and anti-Semitism in particular, was to be condemned. Pope John XXIII, who died in June 1963, won praise from church officials and the people alike for his reforms.

▲ *Rev. Norman Vincent Peale and his wife pose with his best-seller, which taught "a simple yet scientific system of practical techniques of successful living that works."*

◄

The pastor of a Bronx, New York, church, greets one of the 200 worshippers to arrive for the first of a series of services to be held at the Whitestone Bridge Drive-in.

A few clergymen, aware of the power of the media, reached out to audiences in print and through radio and television. The best-selling book *Peace of Mind* (1946) by the Radio Rabbi, Joshua Loth Liebman, inspired Bishop Fulton J. Sheen to write *Peace of Soul* (1948) and evangelist Billy Graham, *Peace With God* (1952). A 1952 edition of the Bible, the Revised Standard Version, sold 26.5 million copies in its first year. After the Bible, Rev. Norman Vincent Peale's *The Power of Positive Thinking* (1952), which remained on best-seller lists for 186 weeks, ranks as one of the best-selling works of spiritual literature in history. The pastor of New York's Marble Collegiate Church, Peale combined popular psychology with religion, advising readers to "cast out those old, dead, unhealthy thoughts" and trust in God. In 1953 his radio program reached 1.5 million listeners; his television show would ultimately attract 5 million viewers.

Fulton Sheen, the Roman Catholic auxiliary bishop of New York, went on the radio with *The Catholic Hour* in 1930, but he reached the pinnacle of his teaching ministry when his *Life Is Worth Living* ran on national TV weekly in the years 1952 to 1957. At its height the program was watched by 10 million people; in 1953 Sheen topped the popular Milton Berle program in the Nielsen ratings.

But the clergyman who acquired the greatest mastery over the media was Rev. Billy Graham. Through his best-selling books, his radio show (*Hour of Decision*), numerous TV appearances, and worldwide Crusades for Christ, Graham preached old-time religion, calling on sinners to repent and be saved. When accused of being more adman than preacher, Graham countered: "I am selling the greatest product in the world; why shouldn't it be promoted as well as soap?" Though critics found him overzealous, many Americans affirmed the urgency of Graham's message.

Popular TV shows reflected the nation's religious resurgence. Here, the Anderson family of Father Knows Best pauses to say grace before eating a humble turkeyless Thanksgiving dinner.

HOLDING THE LINE IN KOREA

In the aftermath of the North Korean invasion of South Korea, the whole of North America supported U.S.

President Harry Truman when he said, "If we are tough enough now, there won't be any next time."

It came like a bolt out of nowhere: at 4:00 in the morning of June 25, 1950, some 90,000 soldiers from North Korea stormed across the border into South Korea. The very next day, with most of South Korea's forces in headlong retreat, American fighter planes swept in from their bases in Japan. The U.S. Seventh Fleet steamed toward the area. And shortly thereafter the first U.S. ground troops were sent in. "We've got to stop those sons of bitches no matter what," Truman declared.

The United Nations Security Council (minus a boycotting U.S.S.R.) voted unanimously to send in troops. For the first time in history, a world organization was mobilizing to stop aggression. Some 16 nations sent troops. Canada, despite worries about the United States' conduct of the war, contributed more than 25,000 soldiers and sailors during the course of it. All Canadians, unlike Americans, were volunteers.

Brilliance, Miscalculation, Stalemate

At the end of World War II, U.S. troops had occupied the Korean peninsula south of the 38th parallel, while the U.S.S.R. took over in the north. The arrangement was meant to be temporary, but as in so many other theatres throughout the Cold War world, the lines hardened and froze. The result was two Koreas: a Soviet-sponsored Democratic People's Republic of Korea in the north and the U.S.-backed Republic of Korea in the south. No one knew what role the Soviets had played in the attack, but government leaders assumed that Russia had orchestrated it and believed that the United States had to stop the Communist aggressors.

Supplied with Soviet-made tanks and weapons, the North Korean Army pushed U.N. forces, using vintage equipment from World War II, down the length of Korea until by early August the defenders held a mere toehold of ground on the southeast coast. There, along a 120-kilometre perimeter enclosing a pocket around the port of Pusan, they dug in.

The man who broke the stalemate was Gen. Douglas MacArthur. Then age 70, and supreme U.S. commander in the Far East, MacArthur devised a plan of astonishing boldness: an amphibious assault at the west-coast port of Inchon, some 400 kilometres behind enemy lines. "I can almost hear the ticking of the second hand of destiny," the general declared. "We must act now or we will die."

So on September 15, after an air strike and naval bombardment, U.S. marines scrambled up 3.5-metre sea walls and sent the North Koreans reeling. It was the most brilliant stroke of MacArthur's long career. The troops holding Pusan linked up with the marines, and the U.N. forces sped inland, liberating Seoul. Then the forces turned north, reached the 38th parallel, and swept into North Korea.

It was a fateful step. What had begun as a U.N. police action to defend the south had now expanded into an offensive drive for all Korea. Truman approved the action, but with deep reservations: should the fighting spill over into

TRUMAN SACKS MACARTHUR

As the Chinese offensive in Korea continued, Gen. Douglas MacArthur began calling in public for an expansion of the war into China. Truman refused and asked MacArthur to clear any future statements with the White House. By March of 1951, U.S. troops had pushed the Chinese back to the 38th parallel. MacArthur proposed cutting them off at the Yalu River by seeding its banks with radioactive waste. Truman said no. Then on April 5, Minority Leader Joe Martin read a letter on the House floor that was written by MacArthur and condemned the limited war strategy. It asserted, "There is no substitute for victory." Truman resolved to fire his general because, as he said, "I could no longer tolerate his insubordination." Amid fears that the news might leak, the announcement was rushed out at 1:00 A.M. on April 11. Truman said that he did not want MacArthur "to be allowed to quit on me." Reaction was swift. Senator William Jenner claimed that the country lay "in the hands of a secret coterie" controlled by Soviet agents. Senator Richard Nixon charged Truman with giving "the Communists and their stooges . . . what they always wanted — MacArthur's scalp." In Worcester, Massachusetts, Truman was hanged in effigy. On April 19 MacArthur stood before Congress. "I address you with neither rancor nor bitterness in the fading twilight of life, with but one purpose in mind: to serve my country." A record audience watched his masterful performance on television. "I now close my military career and just fade away — an old soldier who tried to do his duty as God gave him the light to see that duty. Good-bye." The public acclaim that followed the speech was unprecedented. But as Truman had anticipated, the adulation did not translate into support for MacArthur's strategy. Eventually, MacArthur did fade away. Civilian control of the military was reaffirmed.

▶

On December 24, 1950, U.N. forces blew up the North Korean port of Hungnam before withdrawing to reinforce the Eighth Army in South Korea. The port was demolished to prevent the Communists from using it following the defeat of the U.S. forces at Chongjin Reservoir a few weeks earlier.

China, directly across the Yalu River to the north, it might precipitate World War III. MacArthur remained cocky. The Chinese were far too weak to pose a real danger, he assured Truman. The soldiers would be home by Thanksgiving.

It was not to be. As the U.N. armies neared the Yalu, they traded gunshots with Chinese units. Then, on November 27, China entered the war with some 360,000 troops swarming over U.N. positions. Wave after wave of Chinese reinforcements poured across the Yalu, sending U.N. forces into a headlong retreat that the Americans referred to, unconvincingly, as a "strategic withdrawal." Eventually the

Chinese advance was halted and a stalemate was reached near the 38th parallel, along a rim of low-lying peaks later dubbed Heartbreak Ridge and Pork Chop Hill. MacArthur proposed to break the stalemate by all-out war on China, perhaps using atomic weapons. This was precisely the sort of thinking that had worried the Canadian government when it committed troops. Worse, MacArthur's persistent lobbying for a war in China showed no respect for civilian control of the military.

The war sputtered on another two years while delegates from both sides met to negotiate an armistice. Finally, on July 27, 1953, they signed an accord at Panmunjom, in the no-man's-land between the two front lines. By then, almost 34,000 Americans and more than 300 Canadians had been killed in action. Casualties among North and South Koreans, military and civilian, numbered in the millions. And for all the slaughter, the boundary between North and South Korea had shifted by no more than a few dozen kilometres.

Men from the U.S. 7th Infantry Division eat turkey for Thanksgiving dinner near the Yalu River on November 23, 1950. Just a few days later, the Chinese entered the war, forcing the U.N. troops to retreat.

U.S. jet fighters, such as these Republic F-84's, gave U.N. forces dominance of the skies during the Korean War.

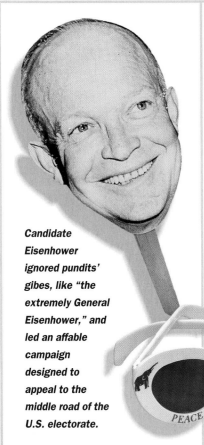

Candidate Eisenhower ignored pundits' gibes, like "the extremely General Eisenhower," and led an affable campaign designed to appeal to the middle road of the U.S. electorate.

GOVERNMENT BY A BOARD OF DIRECTORS

After the turmoil of the Depression and war, people seemed to want a period of calm in their lives. Politicians obliged, keeping to the middle of the road, but using a managerial style more suited to the boardroom.

The middle of the road is all of the usable surface." said Dwight D. Eisenhower, referring to his chosen path of government. "The extremes, right and left, are in the gutters." Canadian Prime Minister Mackenzie King had beaten him to that realization years earlier. Although King had introduced unemployment insurance in 1940 and family allowances in 1944, post-war prosperity eased demand for social legislation, and King was content to stay in the middle of the road he had created.

In 1948, he was persuaded to retire, and was succeeded as prime minister by Louis St. Laurent, who seemed less a politician than a chairman of the board. One of the "board" members was Lester Pearson of External Affairs, who won the Nobel Peace Prize for 1957 for proposing a United Nations peacekeeping force at the time of the Suez crisis. Such

expertise in the cabinet won the Liberals the vote in1949 and 1953, which seemed also to imply approval of their style of government. Management rather than political debate took Canada into NATO, brought Newfoundland into Confederation as the tenth province in 1949, and built the St. Lawrence Seaway in cooperation with the United States.

But by the mid-1950's there were warning signs that Canadians were not entirely happy with their government. In 1956, C. D. Howe introduced a bill to Parliament to build a natural gas pipeline across the country. The opposition was aghast at the prominence of American interests in the proposed company that would construct it, TransCanada PipeLines Limited. When the opposition tried to debate the issue, the Liberals put a limit on the debate and rammed the bill through. It was poor timing for a show of arrogance.

Candidates Richard Nixon and Dwight Eisenhower, alongside their wives, Patricia and Mamie, raise their arms in victory after being nominated at the 1952 Republican Convention.

Nor was concern about American influence in Canadian affairs limited to the pipeline. With the pervasiveness of American culture, particularly through movies and television, and with much of Canadian business under American ownership, Canada looked very much like an American colony. All the situation needed was someone who knew how to channel Canadian resentments and fears. That someone was the new leader of the Progressive Conservative Party. Half-lawyer, half-avenging angel, John George Diefenbaker flayed the Liberals for their arrogance and their subservience to American big money. In the federal election of 1957, the Liberal "board of directors" was ousted and John Diefenbaker became Canada's 13th prime minister.

Nonpartisan Politics in the United States

Americans, like Canadians, turned to a management style of politics in the early years of the decade. "I don't think he has any politics," wrote the county clerk in Abilene, Kansas, when a high official of the Republican Party inquired into Gen. Dwight D. Eisenhower's party affiliation. The assessment might have damaged any other presidential candidate; but Eisenhower's reputation as nonpartisan, a man above politics, was a key to his enormous popularity. The Democrats had been in office for 20 years. Rumors of corruption within the Truman administration were rife, and investigations into Communists in government, ongoing. The Korean conflict dragged on, and many Americans hoped that this war hero, supreme commander of the Allied forces during World War II, would end the stalemate. Ike was nominated to run for president on the first ballot at the 1952 Republican Convention.

But on September 18 scandal rocked the Eisenhower campaign. The *New York Post* headlined a story "Secret Nixon Fund" and reported that Ike's running mate, Richard M. Nixon, maintained a secret slush fund. Some Republicans suggested that

Lester B. Pearson, accompanied by his wife, displays the Nobel Peace Prize he has just received, in Oslo, December 10, 1957. The only Canadian ever to win this award, he earned it by setting up the United Nations Emergency Force that helped to defuse the Suez crisis in the previous year.

▼ *Countering slush fund charges, Richard Nixon spoke to TV viewers about his daughters, Julie and Tricia, and their puppy, Checkers. Nixon broke down in tears after the broadcast because he felt his appeal to voters had failed.*

Nixon withdraw, and Eisenhower himself called for a careful examination of the matter. Nixon decided to take his case directly to the American people via television.

As an audience of some 55 million watched, Nixon reviewed the fund and denied any misuse of its contents. In so doing, he laid out his own finances for public inspection. He was not a rich man, Nixon said. He owned a 1950 Oldsmobile and owed money on two houses; his wife wore "a respectable Republican cloth coat." He plucked listeners' heartstrings. Within hours of the telecast, supportive telegrams deluged Republican headquarters. By casting himself as the common man, Nixon had saved his candidacy and given the whole campaign a boost.

On October 24, Eisenhower made a dramatic announcement that likely clinched the election for him. He would "concentrate on the job of ending the Korean War." Ike won the popular vote by a margin of more than 6,500,000. While some Americans lamented the end of an era under the Democrats, most looked forward to what they felt would be the firm leadership of General, now President, Eisenhower.

LOYALTY ON TRIAL

For a while in the early 1950's, the U.S. was caught up in the idea that all problems could be solved by ferreting out and destroying Communists.

On February 3, 1950, the British government announced that physicist Klaus Fuchs, who had worked on the atom bomb project at Los Alamos, had confessed that he had passed atomic secrets to the Soviets. The revelation confirmed the U.S.'s worst fears. Indiana Senator Homer Capehart railed: "How much more are we going to have to take? Fuchs and Acheson and Hiss and hydrogen bombs threatening outside and New Dealism eat-

Separated by a screen, Ethel and Julius Rosenberg are transported in a police van to their jail cells after being found guilty of espionage and conspiracy.

Pickets outside the White House march in support of the death penalty for the treasonous Rosenbergs.

Klaus Fuchs, who passed atomic secrets to the Soviets for eight years, served nine years in prison before being deported to East Germany.

ing away at the vitals of the nation. In the name of Heaven, is this the best that America can do?"

Less than a week after the Fuchs confession, Senator Joseph R. McCarthy rose to provide an answer. At the McLure Hotel in Wheeling, West Virginia, he said the United States was in trouble. Foreign policy failures, such as allowing China to fall to the Communists, could be traced to Communist infiltration of the U.S. government and particularly of the State Department. "I have in my hand a list of 205," he declared, waving a paper, "a list of names known to the Secretary of State as being members of the Communist Party and who nevertheless are still working and shaping policy in the State Department."

A gasp rose from the audience, and within days, the charges echoed across the front pages of the nation's newspapers. The effect was just what McCarthy wanted. In four years as the Republican senator from Wisconsin, he had done little to capture wide attention. But with elections coming up, he was looking for a way to further his career, and he had found it.

Sophie Rosenberg, Julius's mother, leads a demonstration to stop the scheduled execution, less than a week away.

In speech after speech, McCarthy lashed out. He inveighed against "parlor pinks and parlor punks," against "egg-sucking phony liberals" and the "Communists and queers who sold China into atheistic slavery." McCarthy's diatribes were denounced by many, including Edward R. Murrow on TV, but the public at large supported him.

Some news reports seemed to lend credence to what McCarthy was saying. Four months after Klaus Fuchs's con-

fession, one of his accomplices, Philadelphia chemist Harry Gold, was arrested. Gold in turn implicated another Los Alamos employee, army machinist David Greenglass. From there the trail led to Greenglass's wife, Ruth, and sister Ethel Rosenberg and her husband, Julius. All were arrested, and all confessed, except for Ethel and Julius Rosenberg. The Rosenberg case dragged slowly through the courts, with each appeal upholding the original conviction and its terrible consequence: the death sentence. At any point the Rosenbergs could have saved themselves by pleading guilty and asking for clemency. They did not. "Always remember that we were innocent," they wrote in a letter to their sons, "and could not wrong our conscience." Amid great protest, they were put to death in the electric chair at Sing Sing, the state prison in Ossining, New York, on June 19, 1953.

Even after the Republicans swept into office in 1952, McCarthy, intoxicated by his newfound power, stepped up his attacks. At the end of 1953, the senator turned his attention to the U.S. Army. In his widening hunt for subversives, he challenged the routine promotion of a captain, Irving Peress, who held left-leaning beliefs. The army mounted a counterattack. It seemed that McCarthy's top aide, 27-year-old Roy Cohn, had made repeated attempts to arrange a commission for his friend Pvt. G. David Schine and had warned he would "wreck the Army" if it was not granted. In March 1954 the army charged McCarthy and Cohn with using the threat of investigation as a form of blackmail.

For 36 days, 20 million Americans watched the Army-McCarthy hearings unfold on television. At one table sat Army Secretary Robert Stevens and the army's special counsel, the courtly Massachusetts lawyer Joseph Welch. At the other was McCarthy, dishevelled and combative, and Cohn. No match for Welch's deft questioning, McCarthy resorted to smear and innuendo. He accused a junior member of Welch's own law firm of being a Communist. Welch listened in growing fury, and then he responded: "Until this moment, Senator, I think I never really gauged your cruelty or recklessness. . . ." "Point of order! Point of order!" McCarthy cried. But Welch continued: "Let us not assassinate this lad further, Senator. You have done enough. Have you no sense of decency, sir, at long last? Have you left no sense of decency?" The entire room broke into applause.

And so, then, did most Americans. The U.S. Senate formally condemned McCarthy in December 1954, after which he finished out two more years as senator and slid into rapid decline. He died in 1957, but the fears and ideas he exploited survived him.

▲ *Joseph R. McCarthy (left) and his top counsel, Roy M. Cohn, discuss strategy in 1953. That year the two men considered investigating the CIA before they set their sights on Communist infiltration of the U.S. Army.*

▲ *In April 1954 army counsel Joseph N. Welch, seated next to Army Secretary Robert Stevens, presents a memo denying that the army tried to impede McCarthy's inquiry.*

Emily Carr ●
Big Raven, c.1928
A native of Victoria, British Columbia, Carr brought to her art a unique vision of the Northwest Coast landscape and the sculptures of the Indians who lived there.

Mary Cassatt ●
After the Bath, 1901
Pennsylvania-born Cassatt focused on women's daily lives. An impressionist, she lived in France from 1874 until her death in 1926 at 82.

Charles Demuth ● ***The Circus, 1917***
Studies of nightclub and vaudeville entertainers, like this watercolor-and-pencil work on paper, occupied Demuth from 1917 to 1919. Then he turned to architectural and industrial subjects.

Georgia O'Keeffe ● ***Red Canna, c. 1924***
Lyrical evocations of the inner structure of flowers followed O'Keeffe's minimalist drawings and cityscapes and preceded the desert motifs of her New Mexico work.

George Luks ●
The Polka Dot Dress, 1927
A member of The Eight, the nucleus of the Ashcan School, Luks rejected New York's upper crust and turned his gaze on the city's common people.

Grant Wood ●
Daughters of Revolution, 1932
Resisting European modernism, Wood and fellow painter Thomas Hart Benton chose a realistic style that became known as regionalism. His prim "daughters" stand before Emanuel Leutze's *Washington Crossing the Delaware.*

PAINTING MAKES ITS MARK

To the typical art lover at the turn of the century, impressionism was modern art, and the postimpressionists Cézanne, Gauguin, and Van Gogh were just reaching respectability. Then in 1913 the Armory Show opened in New York City. It exhibited the freshest in American art, and work considered avant-garde in Europe — cubism and fauvism, for example. In the early 1920's, in Canada, two unique styles were developing, from The Group of Seven in the east, and from Emily Carr (see above left) in the west. By the late 1940's, North America, and in particular New York City, became the centre of Western art. Abstract expressionism, led by de Kooning and, in Canada, Riopelle (see next page), as well as by Mark Rothko and others, dominated Western art for several years, until such styles as pop art (see pp. 344–45), minimal art, and a rebirth of realism arose to fascinate artists and connoisseurs alike.

Jacob Lawrence ● *Migration Series*, 1940-41
On 60 masonite panels measuring 30 cm by 45 cm, Lawrence memorialized the U.S.'s ongoing exodus of blacks from the rural South to northern cities.

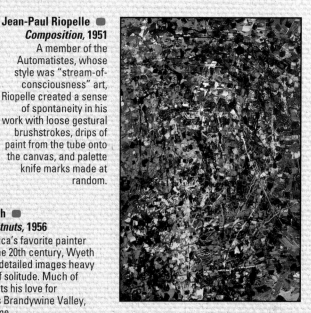

Jean-Paul Riopelle ●
Composition, 1951
A member of the Automatistes, whose style was "stream-of-consciousness" art, Riopelle created a sense of spontaneity in his work with loose gestural brushstrokes, drips of paint from the tube onto the canvas, and palette knife marks made at random.

Willem de Kooning ● *Composition*, 1955
After exhibiting his controversial series of wildly incongruous female figures, de Kooning then created a number of abstractions like this one.

Andrew Wyeth ●
Roasted Chestnuts, 1956
Perhaps America's favorite painter at the end of the 20th century, Wyeth created richly detailed images heavy with a sense of solitude. Much of his work reflects his love for Pennsylvania's Brandywine Valley, his lifelong home.

Stuart Davis ●
General Studies, 1962
Cubism, jazz, and the city's pulse infuse Davis's work, whose abstract forms, bold colors, random scrawls, and visual echoes of familiar objects are major elements of American modernism.

Alexander Colville ●
Church and Horse, 1964
Sharply realistic, Colville's works also have a visual poetry, created by cool colors contrasted with a disturbing element. His flat, crisp images are painted meticulously after careful measurement and proportioning.

Frank Stella ●
Sacramento Mall Proposal #4, 1978
In his teens Stella forsook representational painting for abstract expressionism. Then, taking a further step to concentrate on stripes and rectangles, he became known as a leader of minimal art.

Janet Fish ●
Gold Tea Set, 1986
Realism and conventional subjects continued to captivate many late-20th-century artists like Janet Fish, whose still lifes sparkle with light and color.

LEARNING TO LIVE WITH SUPERBOMBS

Comparing the atom bomb to the hydrogen bomb, Winston Churchill wrote: "The atomic bomb, with all its terrors, did not carry us outside the scope of human control . . . in thought or action in peace or war."

At the highest levels of government, debate raged over development of the so-called superbomb. Many scientists, led by J. Robert Oppenheimer, director of the Manhattan Project, objected to the undertaking on moral grounds. Hiroshima was bad enough; the prospect of working on stronger weapons, capable of eradicating whole populations, raised fundamental questions about the role of science. A few scientists hypothesized that the detonation of the hydrogen bomb might start a chain reaction and incinerate the globe itself. Others, notably Hungarian-born physicist Edward Teller, disagreed. Fusion weapons were possible, asserted Teller, and they were inevitable. And woe betide the nation that sat on its hands and let the Soviets build one first.

The question of the H-bomb was settled in early 1950, when British physicist Klaus Fuchs confessed to passing nuclear secrets on to the Soviets over an eight-year period. What else did the Kremlin know? In the U.S., President Truman elected to err on the side of caution, and on January 31, 1950, he announced that development of the hydrogen bomb would proceed under Teller's direction. Less than two weeks later, Albert Einstein appeared on television to warn

The first thermonuclear detonation, above, was photographed 2 minutes after zero hour, at about 3,600 metres some 80 kilometres away. Physicist Edward Teller (inset, left) championed the bomb's development. J. Robert Oppenheimer (inset, top), opposed it.

FALLOUT SHELTER

CAPACITY 1730

THERE IS NO SHELTER IN NUCLEAR WAR

I WANT TO GROW UP

that "radioactive poisoning of the atmosphere, and hence annihilation of any life on earth, has been brought within the range of technical possibilities...."

Thus the early 1950's became the age of nuclear anxiety. In manuals such as *You Can Survive an Atomic Attack*, U.S. civil defence officials advised Americans to stockpile food and water, purchase Geiger counters, plan escape routes, build backyard shelters and institute nuclear-attack drills. Fear of nuclear attack drove Canadians into a closer relationship with the United States. Three lines of radar stations (one of which was the Distant Early Warning line) to detect Soviet bombers were built across northern Canada. In 1957, air defence for both countries was placed under a single command called North American Air (later Aerospace) Defence Command — or NORAD. In theory, there was to be joint responsibility for the radar lines and the air command. In reality, Canada was a very junior partner.

Both Sides Get the Hydrogen Bomb

In the fall of 1952, Teller's H-bomb was detonated. A fireball 8 kilometres wide lit the Western Pacific sky, sending a mushroom cloud roiling 40 kilometres into the air. The heat at ground zero was estimated at five times that of the sun's interior. The closest observers — some 80 kilometres away — watched dumbstruck as Elugelab, a 1.6-kilometre-wide atoll in the Marshall Islands, disappeared.

A blast of such magnitude was impossible to hide. Newspapers reported that the bomb could have flattened San Francisco, Spokane, St. Louis, or Washington, D.C., and vaporized a large part of New York City. A congressional subcommittee estimated that in a thermonuclear confrontation, 20 million people would perish on the first day.

The development of the H-bomb — matched by Russia a mere nine months later — brought a fundamental change to military strategic planning; both sides had the bomb and the rocket technology to deliver it. The result was a nuclear stalemate lasting four decades. The H-bomb also seemed to deflate public interest in surviving, let alone winning, a nuclear confrontation. Evidence accumulated that fallout could prove lethal hundreds of kilometres downwind from ground zero, and that strontium 90, a by-product of nuclear testing, had made its way into the food chain, appearing in the milk people bought at the corner grocery. Against such awesome power, backyard shelters seemed insignificant; quickly they filled with bicycles, flowerpots, and old snow tires. Where once people had faced the prospect of nuclear confrontation with gritty optimism, a new fatalism emerged. When asked what he would do should war come, a New York City bank teller replied that he would "run under the bomb and get it over with quickly." Concerns about the growing Soviet arsenal of intercontinental ballistic missiles (ICBM's) further eroded confidence in the future.

Fears surfaced in books and movies, notably Nevil Shute's novel *On the Beach*. Published in 1957 and made into a movie two years later, Shute's tale of the last survivors of a nuclear holocaust, awaiting certain death as a radioactive cloud approaches them, put a human face on the grim abstraction of atomic annihilation.

THE COURT CANCELS "SEPARATE BUT EQUAL"

The U.S. Supreme Court's 1954 decision on public school segregation ruled separate educational facilities "inherently unequal" and set in motion a civil rights revolution that changed the nation forever.

In 1946, no blacks were accepted on major league baseball teams in the United States. The Brooklyn Dodgers intended to change that with a brilliant young player named Jackie Robinson, sending him to a farm team to prepare him. They chose the Montreal Royals because of Canada's reputation for racial tolerance.

Robinson was a success in Montreal, but Canada's lack of racism was exaggerated. Blacks were routinely denied access to restaurants, housing, and jobs across the country. Segregated schools didn't exist in law, but they existed in fact, especially in Nova Scotia. If Canada did not experience racial confrontation in the 1950's, it had more to do with the small numbers of blacks than with racial tolerance.

In the United States, though, the black middle class had begun to gain momentum. Its first objective was the right of all children to equality in education, a right being denied by the segregation of public schools. The test case was eight-year-old Linda Brown of Topeka, Kansas, who was forced to go to a school 25 blocks from home rather than a white school just four blocks away. Her father sued. *Brown* v. *Board of Education* became one of five lawsuits used by the National Association for the Advancement of Colored People (NAACP) to battle segregated schooling across the nation.

An Appeal for Justice

At the heart of the issue was the argument that "separate but equal" facilities — hospitals, public transportation, schools — fulfilled the U.S. Constitution's promise to uphold the rights of all citizens. In practice, black schools were poorly funded and black teachers were underpaid. In 1955 the Supreme Court unanimously directed the states to desegregate public schools "with all deliberate speed."

The South called for "massive resistance." In Virginia, officials closed public schools, some for up to two years. In Congress, 82 representatives and 19 senators signed a Southern Manifesto that accused the Supreme Court of

◀

On December 21, 1956, Rosa Parks at last rode legally in the front of a Montgomery bus (far left). Some nine months later, 15-year-old Elizabeth Eckford (left) was jeered as national guardsmen turned her away from Central High School, Little Rock.

▶

Before he became the United States' first black Supreme Court justice, in 1967, Thurgood Marshall won 29 of 32 cases he brought before that body.

abusing its powers. Six years after the Brown decision, four Southern states had not integrated a single public school.

Attempts to desegregate schools and other facilities were often followed by violence. But, under the charismatic leadership of Dr. Martin Luther King, Jr., pastor of a Montgomery, Alabama church, blacks met violence with non-violence: they turned the other cheek. In December 1955 a seamstress named Rosa Parks refused to surrender her seat on a crowded bus to a white man, and she was arrested. Montgomery blacks decided to boycott the bus company and asked the 27-year-old King to organize the campaign.

In a matter of days, 90 percent of black bus riders were walking, carpooling, or bicycling to their destinations. During the 381-day boycott, King's house was bombed and he was jailed twice: for conspiring to organize an illegal boycott and for a minor traffic violation. In November 1956 the Supreme Court ruled against the bus company.

Resistance to the growing civil rights movement did not end there. In 1957 a Senate filibuster, kept alive for 24 hours and 18 minutes by Strom Thurmond of South Carolina, nearly derailed a federal initiative, the Civil Rights Act of 1957. But it passed, in large part because of the efforts of the Senate Democratic majority leader, Lyndon B. Johnson.

Intervention by the President

President Eisenhower, who tried to avoid involvement in the civil rights fray, was compelled to act in 1957 when Orval Faubus, governor of Arkansas, pitted state law against federal law. The crisis began that September when Faubus ordered the Arkansas National Guard to surround Little Rock Central High School in order to stop nine blacks from enrolling. On September 3 the black students braved a white mob, only to be turned away at the school doors. When 15-year-old Elizabeth Eckford walked alone through the crowd, the scenes of whites screaming curses at her flashed across the country — indeed, around the world.

Under court order, Faubus sent the Guard home on Friday, September 20, leaving 150 city policemen to protect the black students the next week. On Monday more than 1,000 whites attacked blacks and sympathetic whites outside the school. Police made no move to protect them; one officer simply removed his badge and walked away. The next day, Eisenhower took control of the Arkansas National Guard and brought in 1,100 paratroopers. Central High was integrated, but troops had to remain there for the entire school year. The struggle for civil rights was far from won.

In the racially tense Montgomery of 1956, Reverend King, his wife, and daughter Yolanda share a family moment.

Earl Warren (inset) was in his first year as chief justice when the Court issued the historic school desegregation decision. On May 17, 1957, more than 15,000 people, including Dr. Martin Luther King, Jr., and Roy Wilkins, gathered in Washington to mark the third anniversary of the decision.

Barbara Ann Scott of Ottawa leaps to victory at the world figure skating championships in 1947. A year later, aged 19, she won the Olympic gold medal.

Maureen (Little Mo) Connolly was just 17 when she won her second U.S. women's singles title at Forest Hills in 1952.

Unforgettable Athletes, Legendary Games

Whether they pitched, fielded, hit, passed, sprinted, lobbed, rebounded, jabbed, or putted their way into the record books, sports figures captivated fans and gave television viewers hours of entertainment.

The National Hockey League entered its heroic age in the 1940's and 50's. The Toronto Maple Leafs, led by Syl Apps, dominated in the 1940's until they gave way to Gordie Howe's Detroit Red Wings in the early 1950's. The Montreal Canadiens replaced them as the most successful team in professional sport, winning five Stanley Cups in a row from 1955 to 1960. Their star forward, right-winger Maurice Richard, arguably the most exciting player in the game's history, scored 50 goals in 50 games in the 1944–45 season, then went on as the core of a sports dynasty that included "Toe" Blake, Doug Harvey, and Elmer Lach.

Canadian football, which had been edging toward professionalism before the war, continued in that direction when the war ended, with a massive importation of American players. The Grey Cup game was becoming a national event comparable to the Stanley Cup series. But the new prominence of football had a heavy price. Smaller teams,

like Toronto Balmy Beaches and university teams, were forced out of competition for the Grey Cup by the mid-50's. In 1958, the Canadian Football League was formed as a purely professional league, with the Grey Cup as its trophy.

With the coming of television in the 1950's, an old sport found a new popularity in Canada. Sports purists laughed, but fans were delighted when American wrestler Gorgeous George entered the ring and sprayed it with perfume. Within months, Canadians had a host of their own wrestling heroes, from Quebec's Johnny Rougeau to Ontario's "Whipper" Billy Watson — and a giant called Yukon Eric who entered the ring dressed as a lumberjack.

In 1951, people all across North America were gripped by the World Series, when the Dodgers and Giants played what many fans consider the most exciting baseball game of all time. From a 13½-game deficit, the Giants had steadily gained on the Dodgers. The regular season ended with the

The 1940's and 1950's were great years for the stars of sports. (Above left), Branch Rickey points with his cigar to the dotted line in Jackie Robinson's 1950 contract. Wilt the Stilt Chamberlain (above) leaps to block Bill Russell's shot at Boston Garden in 1959. Ben Hogan, winner of eight Grand Slam tournaments, tees off in Miami. Rocky Marciano lands a right to Jersey Joe Walcott for the heavyweight title in 1952; he was never defeated. A 25-year-old medical student, Roger Bannister, breaks the four-minute mile on May 6, 1954.

teams in a dead heat, forcing a three-game play-off. They split the first two games. In the ninth inning of the third game, the Dodgers led 4–2. With two men on base and one out, Bobby Thomson, the Giant third baseman, came to the plate. Reliever Ralph Branca threw a strike. Then he unwound another pitch that streaked in high and inside. Thomson swung and hit "the home run heard around the world." Pandemonium broke loose in the stadium; Thomson felt as though he were "living one of those middle-of-the-night dreams" of glory.

New York City's other baseball franchise, the Yankees, played the game as if they owned it in the 1950's. With superb pitching, the power hitting of sluggers like Mickey Mantle, and Casey Stengel's inspired managing, between 1949 and 1960 the Yankees won 10 pennants and 7 World Series, 5 of them in a row.

Thrilling Stories in Every Sport

Champions emerged in a wide variety of sports. Canadian figure skater Barbara Ann Scott won the Olympic gold at St. Moritz in 1948. In 1953 Maureen Connolly stroked and smashed her way to win the grand slam of tennis — the championships of Australia, France, Britain, and the United States — the first woman in history to do so. In 1957 and 1958, Althea Gibson, one of the first black tennis stars, won both the British and American national championships. In boxing, Joe Louis finally retired and Rocky Marciano took control of the heavyweight crown. Sugar Ray Robinson, called pound for pound the best fighter of all time, fought his way to the middleweight title five times.

Professional American football mesmerized the entire continent on a mild December day in 1958, when 50 million viewers tuned in to the National Football League championship game between the New York Giants and the Baltimore Colts, a contest many call the best football game ever played. The Colts tied the score seven seconds before the clock ran out, sending the game into sudden-death overtime. The Giants could do nothing on their first possession and punted. The Colts, with the incomparable Johnny Unitas at the helm, marched 80 yards up the gridiron in 13 plays, finally winning 23–17 when fullback Alan Ameche plunged over the goal line from the Giant one-yard line.

The story in professional basketball was the Boston Celtics, led by playmaker Bob Cousy and 1.85-metre defensive standout and centre Bill Russell. In 1959 the Celtics won their first of eight straight National Basketball Association championships.

Professional golf provided the drama of one of sport's greatest individual comebacks, that of the diminutive Bantam Ben Hogan. For 17 agonizing months after a near fatal automobile accident in 1949, Hogan wondered whether he could ever compete again in the sport he so dearly loved. But he won the U.S. Open in 1950 and the Open and the Masters in 1951. Seven years later Arnold Palmer's charge to victory in the televised 1958 Masters would attract a whole new generation to the sport.

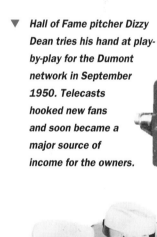

▼ *Hall of Fame pitcher Dizzy Dean tries his hand at play-by-play for the Dumont network in September 1950. Telecasts hooked new fans and soon became a major source of income for the owners.*

BRIDEY, DAVY, HOWDY, AND A LOT MORE

Emerging from two decades of depression and war, and riding the crest of a booming economy, people spent much of their leisure time lurching from one fad to another. Perhaps the most amazing aspect of all the craziness was its unrelenting variety.

The phone-booth-stuffing craze originated in South Africa and, in 1959, enjoyed a few months' popularity in the United States, primarily on the West Coast.

TELEPHONE

The Bomb had created an age of anxiety. Many people seemed to work, or play, harder as a way of coping with the thought that their world might vanish in an instant. Perhaps the perilous times made the idea of reincarnation especially attractive, for the story of a Colorado housewife who claimed to have lived a previous life in 19th-century Ireland touched a chord. The best-seller *The Search for Bridey Murphy* was serialized in more than 35 magazines and newspapers. Hostesses threw "come-as-you-were" parties and served "reincarnation cocktails."

The 1950's were also a time of unprecedented general prosperity. Not only was there a chicken in every pot but a car in every garage, a washing machine in every basement, a television set in every rec room, and, thanks to fluoride, a perfect set of teeth in every child's mouth.

The first toy that every kid had to own — the by-product of a marine engineer's research — practically leapt off the shelf when a Philadelphia store displayed it early in 1947. The Slinky, a springy coil of wire that, among other feats, "walked" downstairs, sold like hotcakes for several years before settling down to become a classic.

The Slinky was just the beginning of a feverish accumulation of goods. By 1948, when some 100,000 homes boasted TV sets, children were greeting one another with a bouncy "It's *Howdy Doody* time." Kids collected souvenirs of the show's characters: Howdy Doody hats, pyjamas, bathing suits, watches, and Clarabell horns; and they dressed up as Princess Summerfallwinterspring. North America turned into one big circus, thanks to Buffalo Bob Smith, the show's host, and to shrewd marketing.

Television brought children a series of heroes with product tie-ins. Few kids had heard of Davy Crockett be-

▶

At the height of the Davy Crockett hysteria in 1955, the opportunity to get a real coonskin cap caused near riots by youthful Crockett fanatics.

fore Walt Disney broadcast a three-part series on the Indian fighter beginning in December 1954. In Canada, the CBC responded with a sort of Canadian Crockett, the coureur de bois Pierre Radisson. But it was Davy Crockett whose product tie-ins captured both countries. By 1955, every child's ambition was to own a coonskin cap and to wear it even in 27-degree weather. Four million 45 r.p.m. records of Davy's theme song were sold, and an estimated $100 million worth of Davy T-shirts, lunch boxes, sheets, towels, and buckskins. It couldn't last and it didn't. Davy the man had lived for 50 years; Davy the fad barely made it to 11 months.

Among college students, a strange new rite of spring developed in 1952, the panty raid. The phenomenon began when male undergraduates at the University of Michigan swept across campus and descended on a

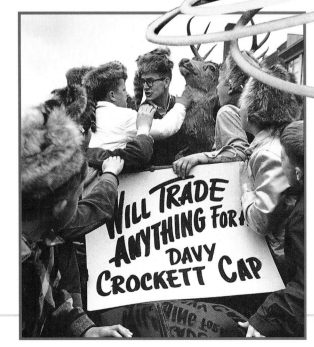

This 38-centimetre marionette was one of a series of puppets, based on Howdy Doody *show characters, in the early 1950's.*

▼ *Most people were happy to master one Hula-Hoop, but experts, young and old, delighted in seeing how many they could spin at once.*

women's dorm demanding tokens of esteem from residents. The coeds responded by tossing their undergarments from windows and balconies, and the rite was soon adopted on campuses across the continent. Adults everywhere shook their heads in dismay. Inevitably some raids resulted in minor injuries and property damage, and university officials were compelled to crack down on them.

While certain postwar fads incited generational distress, a handful seemed to reinforce notions of family togetherness. Scrabble and canasta, both of which had been around for years, were rediscovered in the 1950's and became wildly popular overnight.

Near the end of the decade, a passion for knockoffs of the bamboo hoops used in Australian gym classes seized North America with a grip mightier even than that of Davy Crockett himself. In 1958 everyone who was not bedridden seemed engaged in the struggle to keep a brightly colored, lightweight plastic hoop orbiting somewhere above his or her hips. By Halloween, when the fad petered out, 100 million had been sold. At $1.98 apiece, the Hula-Hoop may well have been one of the least expensive muscle toners ever to appear on the market.

NOVEL EVENTS

Two first novels published in the 1950's saw pockets of moral decay beneath the surface of life at that time. The books had several things in common. Both sought to expose hypocrisy and did so using strong, blunt language that shocked or titillated readers. Both were banned in some schools and libraries, and they were instant best-sellers, particularly among students. J. D. Salinger's *The Catcher in the Rye* (1951) chronicled two days in the life of 16-year-old Holden Caulfield, an articulate youth given to musings about phoniness and corruption who runs away from his prep school to New York City. *Peyton Place* (1956), by Grace Metalious, tells a sordid tale of lust, rape, incest, and adultery set in a picture-perfect New England town. *Peyton Place* sold 60,000 copies in its first 10 days, and the 1957 movie caused a new surge in paperback sales. Salinger won critical acclaim, but he became a recluse and published nothing after the mid-1960's. Although Metalious's future as a novelist looked promising, she subsequently published two unsuccessful novels. She died in 1964 at the age of 39.

▼ *In the spirit of togetherness that became an ideal in the 1950's, this family of five bounces its way through a fun-filled afternoon on pogo sticks.*

ROCK AND ROLL COMES TO STAY

Favored with unprecedented buying power, teenagers contributed to the spectacular success of rock and roll, a music largely written and performed by members of their own generation.

The year was 1956. The New York *Herald Tribune* called him "an unspeakably untalented and vulgar entertainer." Popular television emcee Ed Sullivan declared him "unfit for a family audience." But just weeks after he had condemned Elvis Presley, Sullivan bowed to public demand and booked him for three guest spots on his show, at $50,000 a performance. By Elvis's third appearance, Sullivan instructed his camera crew to shoot the rock and roller from the waist up, cutting off from view the gyrating hips that made Elvis a sensation at 21.

A poor truck driver from Memphis, Elvis was discovered when he dropped into Sun Records to cut a disc for his mother's birthday. The head of the studio, Sam Phillips, had been on the lookout for "a white boy who could sing colored" and signed Elvis up. RCA liked what they heard, bought his contract, and launched a publicity campaign that included national TV appearances.

Presley brought rock and roll into the mainstream, but he didn't invent it. Rock's origins go back to the early 1950's, when black gospel, blues, and jazz were melded into what was called rhythm and blues. Because of its association with blacks, this music was largely relegated to small, indepen-

"If I stand still while I'm singing, I'm dead, man," said Elvis Presley. "I might as well go back to driving a truck." His onstage gyrations thrilled teenagers, horrified their parents, and helped propel Elvis to the heights of musical royalty as the King of Rock and Roll.

▶

Rock and roll's greatest poet, Chuck Berry, is as much renowned for his athletic "duck walk" as for his personal sound on the electric guitar, displayed in classic songs such as "Johnny B. Goode."

On radio stations in Cleveland and New York City, disc jockey Alan Freed spun the records and promoted the rock music teenagers wanted to hear.

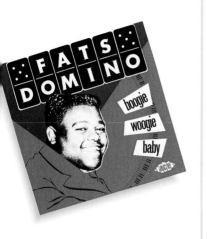

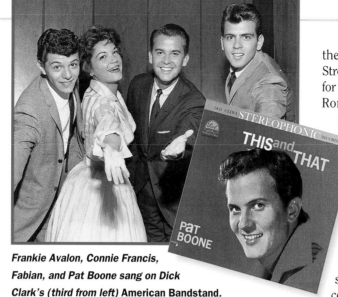

Frankie Avalon, Connie Francis, Fabian, and Pat Boone sang on Dick Clark's (third from left) American Bandstand.

▼ Texas country boy Buddy Holly and his backup group, the Crickets, made numerous rock and roll hits before Holly's untimely death at the age of 22 in an airplane crash, which also took the lives of Ritchie Valens ("La Bamba") and The Big Bopper ("Chantilly Lace").

the new steps, among them the Hand Jive, the Bop, the Stroll, and the Slop. Clark engaged every hit maker he could for the program, from girl groups, such as Ronnie and the Ronnettes and the Shirelles, to street-corner singing groups, such as The Platters and Dion, to clean-cut pop singers, such as Annette Funicello and Bobby Darin. The cleanest cut of all the young performers was Pat Boone, who frequently rerecorded songs by other artists, many of them black ("Tutti-Frutti," "Ain't That a Shame").

Even the likes of Pat Boone could do little to silence rock and roll's critics, one of whom cautioned that the music "inflames and excites youth like jungle tom-toms readying warriors for battle." Still, record sales tripled, and by 1958 teenagers were buying 70 percent of all the albums issued. The decade's end saw adult resistance to rock soften. "Just as hot jazz of the twenties (then anathema to our grandparents) did not destroy our parents, and swing (anathema to our parents) did not destroy us," wrote Arnold Shaw in the May 1959 *Harper's*, "it is quite unlikely that rock 'n' roll will destroy our children."

dent recording companies and black radio stations. But, attracted by the sexually charged imagery and driving beat of rhythm and blues, young white music fans began to listen as well. Disc jockey Alan Freed tapped into the burgeoning market and, in 1951, launched *Moondog Rock and Roll Party*. In doing so, Freed became the first to employ the term *rock and roll* to define a genre of music. In March 1952 he organized what is generally regarded as the first-ever rock and roll concert, featuring black performers and drawing an audience that was two-thirds white.

In 1953 a white country singer named Bill Haley recorded the rock song "Crazy, Man, Crazy," which became a minor hit. Haley and his group, the Comets, developed a hybrid of rock and roll, combining rhythm and blues, country and western, and swing. Filmgoers were electrified by his "Rock Around the Clock," in the movie *The Blackboard Jungle*, for some viewers their first taste of rock and roll.

Gradually black rock and roll stars became recognized nationwide. Chuck Berry — who recorded "Maybellene" in 1955, followed by dozens of hits, including "Rock and Roll Music" and "Sweet Little 16" — was arguably the most influential, but Little Richard ("Good Golly, Miss Molly") and Fats Domino ("Blueberry Hill") had great runs, and Bo Diddley made hits as well. White artists such as Buddy Holly ("That'll Be the Day," "Peggy Sue") and Jerry Lee Lewis ("Whole Lot of Shakin' Goin' On") took inspiration from black performers.

Attempts to bring rock to a wider audience continued, most notably on a new TV program hosted by the 27-year-old impresario Dick Clark. In 1957 the show hit viewers as *American Bandstand*. Every afternoon, for an audience that ultimately reached 40 million, rock stars lip-synched their songs while teens danced

Flamboyant Little Richard, seen here in a 1957 movie, claimed credit for being the architect of rock and roll.

Big Movies, Beloved Stars

After a record-setting year in 1946, movie revenues began a precipitous decline. Hollywood responded with new technologies, a spate of science fiction and horror flicks, big-screen blockbusters, and some outstanding performances by old and new stars.

◀

In Alfred Hitchcock's 1959 thriller North by Northwest, **Cary Grant is pursued by a murderous crop duster and winds up climbing down Mount Rushmore.**

Postwar Hollywood seemed the creation of a malicious screenwriter who harbored a grudge against the movies. While most industries were ready to savor prosperity, movieland languished in the doldrums. In 1947, 90 million Americans went to the movies every week; by 1950 it was half that, with 3,000 theatres closing by the summer of 1951. Television was the reason, and Hollywood fought back: Cinema-Scope, VistaVision, and Todd-AO expanded the screen to gargantuan proportions, each claiming a better image. Cinerama surrounded the audience, using broad, curved screens, three projectors, and stereophonic sound. In 1952 audiences peered through red-and-green Polaroid glasses at their first 3-D production, *Bwana Devil*. That film was quickly followed by other B-grade movies in which everything from spears to rockets seemed to leap from the screen. But Cinerama was limited to the few theatres that could afford the expensive equipment. And it didn't take long for people to joke that 3-D stood for "Dead, Dead, Dead."

Some 2,000 drive-ins opened in the late 1950's, though not in Quebec where Premier Maurice Duplessis banned them as threats to morality. Everywhere else, teenagers swarmed to these "passion pits," which also drew families seeking informality and a good bargain. From the comfort of their automobiles, moviegoers cringed as biological

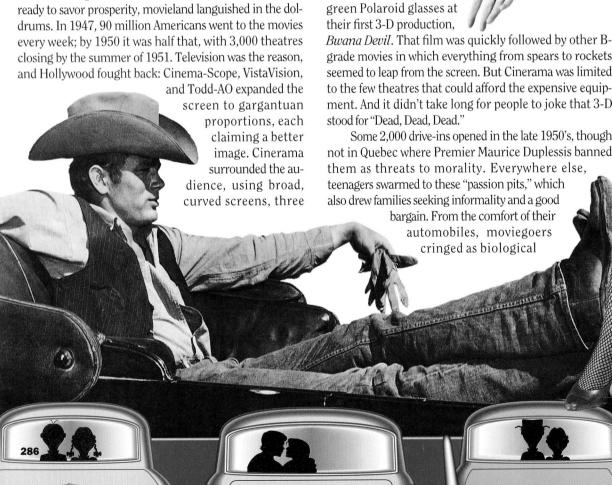

Playing a second-rate club singer, Marilyn Monroe sings "That Old Black Magic" in the 1956 adaptation of William Inge's play Bus Stop.

◀

James Dean was an icon of disaffected youth. This shot is from Giant (1955), which costarred Rock Hudson and Elizabeth Taylor, and was completed only a week before Dean's death.

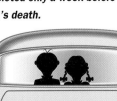

aberrations lurched and slithered across the screen in horror pictures, many of them inspired by the nuclear arms race: *The Fly, The Creature From the Black Lagoon, Them, The Thing, The Blob* (versus Steve McQueen). Some science fiction fantasies, such as *Forbidden Planet*, one of Leslie Nielsen's first movies, thrilled audiences with special effects; others, like *The Invasion of the Body Snatchers,* won critical praise and developed cult followings.

The studios unleashed big-budget extravaganzas as well. Henry Fonda, Audrey Hepburn, and an army of extras reenacted Napoleon's retreat from Russia in *War and Peace*. David Niven globe-trotted in *Around the World in 80 Days*. Charlton Heston, as Moses, led his people out of Egypt in Cecil B. DeMille's *The Ten Commandments*. Critics may have panned the epics, but audiences flocked to them.

A cluster of young movie actors, including Canada's Glenn Ford and Raymond Burr, as well as Kirk Douglas, Gregory Peck, William Holden and Paul Newman, joined Spencer Tracy, Humphrey Bogart, John Wayne, and other established stars in the Hollywood firmament. And a new breed of leading man, restless and tormented, came to the screen. Montgomery Clift made his acclaimed debut in *The Search* (1948). Marlon Brando reprised his Broadway role in *A Streetcar Named Desire* (1951), then turned in an Academy Award–winning performance in *On the Waterfront* (1954). James Dean established the archetype of the troubled teen in *East of Eden* and *Rebel Without a Cause,* both released in 1955, the year he died, at 24, in a car accident.

This scene between Burt Lancaster and Deborah Kerr broke Hollywood taboos. *From Here to Eternity* (1953) won the Academy Award as did the film's supporting actors, Frank Sinatra and Donna Reed.

While female stars of the 1930's and 1940's, such as Joan Crawford, Katharine Hepburn, and Myrna Loy, continued to make box office magic, younger actresses rose to stardom: 13-year-old Elizabeth Taylor in *National Velvet* (1945); Grace Kelly in *High Noon* (1952); Natalie Wood in *Rebel Without a Cause* (1955); Doris Day, an audience favorite, in *The Man Who Knew Too Much* (1956) and *Pillow Talk* (1959); Kim Novak in *Picnic* (1956); Audrey Hepburn in *Roman Holiday* (1953), for which she received an Academy Award; and the inimitable Marilyn Monroe in *The Asphalt Jungle* (1950), *Gentlemen Prefer Blondes (*1953), *How to Marry a Millionaire* (1953), and *Some Like It Hot* (1959). But, for sheer Hollywood, nothing could beat the fancy stepping of Gene Kelly, Debbie Reynolds, Donald O'Connor, and Cyd Charisse in *Singin' in the Rain* (1952).

Movies were not all glamor and glitter, however. The studios also made well-crafted films dealing with serious issues. Elia Kazan exposed anti-Semitism in the film version of Laura Z. Hobson's *Gentleman's Agreement* (1947). John Ford's western *The Searchers* (1956) examined bigotry, too. And a number of movies, among them *The Caine Mutiny* (1954) and *Bridge on the River Kwai* (1957), took a hard look at military ethics.

◄ Robert Mitchum starred as a psychopathic preacher in **The Night of the Hunter (1955)**, the only film directed by Charles Laughton.

▼ Clad in black leather and jeans, a brooding Marlon Brando plays Johnny, leader of a gang of motorcycle hoods, in Stanley Kramer's 1954 production **The Wild One.**

New Magic on Old Broadway

The stage was bursting with talent of every kind. Composers, lyricists, and choreographers created a fresh musical theatre, and gifted playwrights woke up Broadway with brilliant dramas.

The New Haven tryout looked like a disaster. "No Girls, No Gags, No Chance!" grumbled one critic. So much for quick judgments. At opening night on Broadway, as the soaring cadences of "Oh, What a Beautiful Mornin'" swept over the audience, everyone knew that *Oklahoma!* was something extraordinary. Richard Rodgers and Oscar Hammerstein II, two old pros now working together for the first time, had achieved an almost operatic fusion of song and story. Dances by newcomer Agnes de Mille flowed into the action with amazing grace. The result was pure, jubilant enchantment. *Oklahoma!*, which opened in 1943, was still lifting people's spirits more than 2,200 performances later.

The golden age of musical theatre had arrived. Rodgers and Hammerstein made magic again in 1945 with the musical drama *Carousel.* Then came *South Pacific,* with a dozen hit tunes and a provocative May-September pairing of Mary Martin and Metropolitan Opera star Ezio Pinza. Rodgers and Hammerstein went on to create *The King and I,* among other works, and in 1959 *The Sound of Music* opened, their final show together.

Other Broadway veterans picked up the new operettalike style. Irving Berlin wrote his most brilliant score for *Annie Get Your Gun* (1946), thus allowing Ethel Merman to blast her way to superstardom. Cole Porter, brushing up on his Shakespeare, chimed in with *Kiss Me, Kate* (1948). Some remarkable new talents caught fire. Alan Jay Lerner and Frederick Loewe unrolled their first Broadway hit in the Scottish mists of *Brigadoon* (1947), then soared into box office heaven with *My Fair Lady* (1956). Who could resist the courtly Rex Harrison, as speech professor Professor Henry Higgins, teaching Julie Andrews's cockney Eliza Doolittle to say "The Rain in Spain Falls Mainly in the Plain"? *My Fair Lady* charmed audiences through an astonishing run

Composer Richard Rodgers (above) and librettist Oscar Hammerstein (top) teamed up on nine Broadway musicals, including South Pacific *in 1949. Based on a book by James Michener, it starred Mary Martin as navy nurse Nellie Forbush, shown here romping through "Honey Bun" at a talent show.*

Demanding "Shall We Dance?" a puckish Yul Brynner, as ruler of old Siam, attempts a waltz with Gertrude Lawrence in The King and I *(1951). It was his first Broadway show and her last.*

of 2,717 performances. And composer Leonard Bernstein joined 27-year-old Stephen Sondheim to create the riveting music and lyrics for *West Side Story* (1957).

Serious drama flourished, too. A long-silent Eugene O'Neill — not a word since winning a Nobel Prize in 1936 — returned to the stage in 1946 with *The Iceman Cometh.* Set among the patrons of a seedy bar, the play heralded the last, strongest phase in the career of America's greatest playwright. Eleven years later, the posthumous production of O'Neill's *Long Day's Journey Into Night,* based on his own tormented family, would win a Pulitzer Prize.

Fresh dramatic voices gained attention. Arthur Miller made his Broadway debut in 1947 with *All My Sons,* then followed it in 1949 with *Death of a Salesman,* a work so powerful that the first-night audience refused to leave the theatre. Everyone seemed to know Willy Loman, a huckster down on his luck, and his fall from grace hit hard. Miller's harrowing look at the dark side of the American dream won a Pulitzer Prize. His next play, *The Crucible*

▼ Brutal and passionate, a 23-year-old Marlon Brando torments Jessica Tandy in A Streetcar Named Desire, an emotion-packed drama by Tennessee Williams (inset).

(1953), focused with the same gritty realism on the notorious witch trials of colonial Salem. No one missed the grim parallels with Senator Joe McCarthy's anti-Communist crusade (see pp. 272–273).

Another major new talent dealt in bittersweet flights of fantasy and pathos. Tennessee Williams burst into the limelight in 1945 with *The Glass Menagerie,* about a widowed mother thinking back to the "gentleman callers" of her Southern girlhood and about her crippled, withdrawn daughter. The narrator, Tom Wingfield, sets the tone: "Yes, I have tricks in my pocket, I have things up my sleeve. . . . I give you truth in the pleasant disguise of illusion."

Illusion dominated Williams's next triumph, *A Streetcar Named Desire* (1947). Marlon Brando, young and unknown, played the brutish Stanley Kowalski, who assaults and crushes the forlorn pretence of gentility indulged in by his sister-in-law, Blanche DuBois. Blanche's passionate credo might belong to all the defeated dreamers of Williams's plays: "I don't want realism. I want magic. Yes, yes, magic!" *Streetcar* won Tennessee Williams his first Pulitzer Prize; a second came in 1955 for *Cat on a Hot Tin Roof.*

The list of distinguished American dramatists was growing substantially. Carson McCullers won praise for the 1950 stage adaptation of her novel *The Member of the Wedding.* William Inge hit Broadway with *Come Back, Little Sheba* and earned a Pulitzer Prize for *Picnic.* And Archibald MacLeish, taking inspiration from the biblical Job, penned the 1958 verse drama *J.B.,* also winning a Pulitzer.

▲ In a balletic rumble in West Side Story, two street hoods fight over a woman. Jerome Robbins's choreography won high praise from critics.

▲ At a moment of crisis in Death of a Salesman, Lee J. Cobb, as despairing Willy Loman, confronts his wife (Mildred Dunnock) while sons Biff and Happy (Arthur Kennedy and Cameron Mitchell) look helplessly on.

SPUTNIK BEEPS A CHALLENGE

As the United States answered the Soviet success with its own satellite, Wernher von Braun promised that space travel would "free man from . . . the chains of gravity," opening to him "the gates of heaven."

After the Soviets launched the world's first artificial satellite (model at left), Premier Nikita Khrushchev crowed that in the near future the U.S.S.R. would be "turning out long-range missiles like sausages."

On Friday, October 4, 1957, at the Baikonur Cosmodrome in Kazakhstan, U.S.S.R., a rocket engine gave off a shattering roar. "And then suddenly came a bright light," reported an eyewitness. "Flames burst from the launch pedestal . . . and slowly and confidently the white body of the rocket moved upward."

Driven into the sky by 120,000 kilograms of thrust and trailing a fiery plume, the rocket penetrated the blackness. Within minutes, it had streaked to more than 800 kilometres above the earth's surface and was speeding around the planet at an average velocity of 28,795 kilometres an hour. Suddenly an aluminum sphere, just more than half a metre across and weighing slightly more than 295 kilograms, separated from the rocket's third and last stage. Four antennas whipped out from its surface. Two radios clicked on, emitting a steady beep . . . beep . . . beep. The sphere, dubbed *Sputnik* (Russian for "travelling companion"), began to circle the earth. The shiny Soviet "moon" had become our planet's first artificial satellite.

That evening, the event became real for millions of North Americans as the chirping of *Sputnik* interrupted their favorite radio and television programs. The first reaction was shock, and then anger and fear set in. U.S. Senator Stuart Symington sounded an alarm. "The recently announced launching of an earth satellite by the Soviets," he warned, "is but more proof of growing Communist superiority in the all-important missile field." If the Soviets could send a satellite whirling around the world, could they

not use the same technology to deliver a nuclear bomb to a Western city? Concern increased when, just a month later, the Russians launched a much larger satellite, *Sputnik II*, carrying a five-kilogram dog, Laika. Senator William Fulbright expressed his conviction that far more than the launch of satellites was at stake. "The real challenge we face," he said, "involves the very roots of our society. It involves our educational system, the source of our knowledge and cultural values."

Some observers, including President Eisenhower, downplayed the significance of Russia's achievement. "One small ball in the air," the president scoffed, "something that does not raise my apprehensions, not one iota." The chief of naval operations belittled *Sputnik* as "a hunk of iron almost anybody could launch."

But an anxious public sought answers to two simple questions: How did the Russians get ahead of us? How can we catch up?

Dr. Wernher von Braun, the former technical director of wartime Germany's rocket program, and now chief of development at the U.S. Army Ballistic Missile Agency at Huntsville, Alabama, provided some answers. He assured people that the problem had to do with timing, not lack of talent: "We

▲
Uncle Sam tries to recover his balance as Sputnik I whizzes overhead in The Detroit Free Press *cartoonist Frank Williams's depiction of the impact of the Russian satellite on American scientific pride.*

▼ **By sending a living mammal, the dog, Laika, into orbit, the Soviets gave a clear indication that they were getting close to manned space flight.**

Flying saucer sightings, which began in the late 1940's, fuelled interest in UFO's (unidentified flying objects). This comic book purports to give documented proof supporting claims of extraterrestrial visitations on Earth.

FLYING SAUCER ENCOUNTERS

On June 24, 1947, Kenneth Arnold, a businessman and trained pilot, spotted "saucerlike things … flying like geese in a diagonal chainlike line" as they approached Mount Rainier. By the end of the year, hundreds of sightings had been reported, marking the dawn of an era of "flying saucers." The U.S. Air Force, responsible for investigating each event, concluded that most of the phenomena were either man-made or of natural origin. But there were some that the air force could not explain. At various times during the summer of 1951, science professors at Texas Tech observed lights in the sky. A local teenager even managed to photograph some of them. In July 1952 an air traffic controller in Washington, D.C., saw mysterious blips on his radar screen coming from the sky over the White House and near Andrews Air Force Base, a report confirmed by at least one commercial pilot.

Books, movies, comic books, tabloids, and TV shows featured tales of alien encounters. An "abductee" named Buck Nelson, who claimed to have travelled to Mars, the moon, and Venus, sold $5 packets of hair taken from a 175-kilogram Venusian dog. In the California desert, George Adamski met a blond longhaired creature from Venus called Orthon, who made him "feel like a child in the presence of one with great vision and much love.…" Howard Menger told *Tonight Show* viewers he had been born on Saturn and later cut a record called "The Song From Saturn."

Believers gave various explanations as to why aliens would wish to visit Earth: the explosions of the atom and hydrogen bombs, Communists in league with extraterrestrials, and after 1957 the threatened invasion of the aliens' territory by space satellites. Many charged that the air force was covering up data that proved UFO's existed. With no hard, irrefutable physical evidence, the debate over the existence of UFO's continued as the 1950's drew to a close.

James Van Allen looks on (inset, below) as Wernher von Braun explains the workings of the Jupiter-C rocket, which got the U.S. space program on track with Explorer (right).

could have done what they did if we started in 1946 to integrate the space flight and missile programs." Sensing the country's impatience, President Eisenhower authorized the launching of a U.S. satellite as soon as possible.

Two efforts went full speed ahead, one by the U.S. navy's Vanguard team, a mission that failed when the rocket toppled over at lift-off, and the other by Von Braun and the army's Jupiter-C team. Von Braun's Jupiter-C rocket lifted the little *Explorer* satellite into orbit on January 31, 1958. Although it weighed in at just over 13.5 kilograms, *Explorer* delivered a hefty dividend. As it soared to a height of more than 2,400 kilometres, physicist James Van Allen monitored the number of electrically charged particles it encountered in outer space. Abruptly the signals stopped. The instrument had become overloaded as it passed through areas of space thick with charged atoms. No one had guessed that such bands, which came to be known as Van Allen belts in honor of their discoverer, existed.

By July, Congress had set up the National Aeronautics and Space Administration (NASA) to plan and execute space exploration, and within a year, NASA named seven men North America's first astronauts. Congress also passed the National Defense Education Act to enrich the United States' pool of quality scientists and teachers and to make the country, if not first in space, best in space. The beep, beep of *Sputnik I* had turned out to be a wake-up call.

Canada, too, was moving into space — on a smaller scale, but with international recognition in its specialized fields. Beginning with research at the University of Saskatchewan in the 1920's, by 1954 Canadians were extending space research with rockets developed by Bristol Aerospace at Winnipeg. In 1958, Canada expanded its research to include communications satellites, launching *Alouette I* in 1962.

In 1959 NASA named its first astronauts (clockwise from back row, left): Alan Shepard, Virgil Grissom, Gordon Cooper, Scott Carpenter, John Glenn, Donald Slayton, and Walter Schirra.

LIVING ON THE BRINK OF WAR

According to U.S. Secretary of State John Foster Dulles, Eisenhower's defence policy gave the United States "a bigger bang for a buck." In essence, it meant that the nation would risk war if an adversary refused to back down.

When this photo of Ho Chi Minh was taken in May 1954, he had defeated the French at Dien Bien Phu, ending an eight-year war that had cost 400,000 lives.

President Eisenhower welcomes President Ngo Dinh Diem of Vietnam for a state visit in May of 1957. The United States had helped install him and backed him for the next eight years.

After the defeat of Japan in World War II, the French were ready to reclaim their holdings in Southeast Asia. But they were not prepared for the redoubtable Ho Chi Minh, leader of the nationalists in French Indochina. Ho appealed to the United States for military support and aid, which were granted in 1945. But after China and the Soviet Union recognized Ho's government, U.S. support for him became impossible.

Instead, Presidents Truman and Eisenhower both provided military aid to the French forces fighting the Vietnamese rebels and found they had backed a loser when Ho won a decisive victory at Dien Bien Phu in 1954. That same year the Geneva Accords were signed. Laos and Cambodia were given their independence, and Vietnam was divided in half, with the Communists taking power in the north and Prime Minister Ngo Dinh Diem's non-Communist government controlling the south. Elections were scheduled for 1956 to decide who would govern a united Vietnam, but they were never held. Diem, fearing a Communist victory at the polls, cancelled the election and staged his own rigged balloting in its place. He laid claim to 98 percent of the vote.

In Saigon, his capital, Diem faced a chaotic situation, with various religious, political, and criminal factions plotting against him. He unleashed a repressive crackdown on his enemies, while local Communist sympathizers, known as Vietcong, launched a terrorist campaign to oust him. President Eisenhower refused to commit U.S. troops on a large scale, but he did send a number of military advisers to aid the Saigon government. Most people had never heard of Vietnam, but Washington policymakers saw it as a crucial piece in a geopolitical puzzle. Eisenhower's support was based on the domino theory, which he first described in a 1954 news conference. "You have a row of dominoes set up, you knock over the first one, and what will happen to the last one is the certainty that it will go over very quickly. So you have the beginning of a disintegration that would have the most profound consequences."

As Eisenhower wrestled with the tangled situation in Vietnam, another crisis flared up in Asia. In September 1954 Chinese Communist troops began to shell offshore islands held by Chiang Kai-shek's forces. Fearful that this provocation could escalate into full-scale war, Eisenhower, through diplomatic channels, made it clear to Mao Tse-tung that the United States stood ready to use nuclear weapons if necessary. The shelling stopped, and an uneasy peace settled over the troubled rim of the Far East.

Eisenhower's primary concern, of course, was the worldwide spread of communism. By the late 1950's the reins of power in the most powerful Communist country had passed to the hands of Nikita Khrushchev. Khrushchev was a tough, shrewd former coal miner who seemed to offer a refreshing change from the arctic chill of the Stalin era. In the summer of 1955, Khrushchev, then the head of the Communist Party, and President Eisenhower met for the first time when the first summit conference since World War II convened in Geneva. Khrushchev set the tone as he announced, "Things are different now," but it was Eisenhower who made a startling proposal. Saying "I have had enough of war," he offered to have the United States and the U.S.S.R. trade a "complete blueprint of our military establishments, from

U.S. Secretary of State John Foster Dulles had to balance his foreign policy act delicately, as shown in this 1954 cartoon from The Washington Star.

▼ Nikita Khrushchev, here addressing the National Press Club in 1959, was the first Soviet leader to visit North America.

The 1956 uprising in Hungary, led by civilians untrained in warfare (left) and some factions within the army (above), was doomed once the Soviet Union invaded with force.

Looking For a Way Out of the American Embrace

The telltale white dome of a radar station marks the DEW site at Hall Beach, in the Northwest Territories.

By 1945, Canada had became a very junior partner to the United States in its role in world affairs and even in the defence of its own territory. As the relationship continued after the war, many Canadians feared becoming as much colonials of their powerful neighbor as they had once been of Britain.

This fear partly lay behind Canada's encouragement of the creation of NATO in 1949. An alliance with European powers would give Canadians a counterweight to U.S. influence. But fears of Russian nuclear attacks still drew Canada ever closer to the United States, and made it ever more a prisoner of that country's foreign policy — a policy whose bellicosity, especially under John Foster Dulles, created terrible unease. That unease was heightened in 1957 when Herbert Norman, one of Canada's finest diplomats, was driven to suicide when a U.S. Senate committee spread Communist smears against him.

The noose tightened from 1950 to 1957 as the United States constructed with Canada a series of radar warning lines across Canada to detect nuclear bombers that might come from the U.S.S.R. The Pine Tree Line was established at the Canadian-U.S. border; the Mid-Canada Line followed the 55th parallel; and the DEW (Distant Early Warning) Line was built in the Arctic. These lines, though in Canada, were essentially for U.S. defence and under U.S. control. It gave few Canadians comfort to realize that downed bombers (and their nuclear cargoes) would crash into Canadian soil.

The next logical step was to place all air defences under a unified command which, given Canada's size, would in reality be U.S. command. That was accomplished with NORAD in 1957. Canada now seemed thoroughly subordinate to U.S. policies . James M. Minifie, deeply respected Washington correspondent for the CBC, was deeply concerned about U.S. dominance of foreign policy and indifference to Canadian opinion. In his book *Peace Maker or Powder Monkey*, published in 1960, he argued that Canada was so tied to American policy decisions that it was no more than a messenger boy for the United States.

The first sign of an escape route from that dominance appeared just a few years earlier when, in 1956, British, French and Israeli forces attacked Egypt. External Affairs Minister Lester B. Pearson proposed that the warring sides withdraw, and that peace be enforced by United Nations peacekeeping troops. Both sides accepted his proposal, although Egypt refused to accept Canadian troops on the grounds that they looked and sounded too much like the British. However, the U.N. did appoint a Canadian, Gen. E.L.M. Burns, to lead the force, and Canada supplied him with support staff.

The success of Pearson's proposal in ending the war won him a well-deserved Nobel Prize for peace, in 1957. More importantly, it showed Canadian leaders the way to a more independent role — not as powder monkeys for a dominant power, but as peacemakers through the United Nations.

one end of our countries to the other, as a prelude to disarmament." To police the agreement, he suggested that both the Soviet Union and the United States open their skies to aerial photography.

The Russians did not accept the "open skies" proposal, but the conference ended on a note of goodwill between the superpowers. Not every U.S. official, however, shared the optimistic spirit of Geneva. Just a few months after the summit conference, the hard-line Secretary of State, John Foster Dulles, gave an interview to *Life* magazine describing his strategy of creative confrontation with the Soviets. "You have to take chances for peace, just as you have to take chances in war," Dulles said. "The ability to get to the verge without getting into the war is the necessary art . . . if you are scared to go to the brink, you are lost." But in an era when war meant worldwide nuclear destruction, the concept of brinkmanship was a chilling one. Ignoring Dulles's bellicose stance, Khrushchev stunned the Soviet Union and the world by declaring that war between Communist and capitalist nations need not be inevitable; it was possible for the two sides to enjoy "peaceful coexistence."

Khrushchev had welcomed a warming of relations between the United States and Russia, but his speech had other, unintended results. His denunciation of Stalin caused hopes to soar in the Eastern European countries under Soviet domination; but when a more liberal regime gained power in Hungary, Khrushchev crushed it. The Western World, whose sympathies Khrushchev had so adroitly secured, was repelled by photographs of Red Army tanks rolling through the streets of Budapest. Thousands of Hungarian citizens were killed during three days of street fighting in November 1956. Eisenhower and Secretary of State Dulles backed off from giving the Hungarians U.S. military support once the Soviets invaded.

A Series of Crises in the Middle East

On October 29, 1956, Israel invaded the Sinai Peninsula in an effort to expand its security zone. Two days later, France and Great Britain bombed military targets in Egypt and sent in troops to regain control of the Suez Canal, which Egyptian leader Gamal Abdel Nasser had nationalized. President Eisenhower, who had not been contacted before the incidents, demanded that the forces be pulled out. Recognizing a rare opportunity to divide the North Atlantic Treaty Organization (NATO) allies, Khrushchev threatened to launch missiles against Britain and France if their troops were not withdrawn. Yielding to pressure from Eisenhower and the U.N., the British, French, and Israelis pulled out, but the diplomatic turmoil lasted for weeks, offering the world a nerve-racking demonstration of brinkmanship.

The next summer the Middle East flared into crisis again. Iraq's King Faisal II was assassinated by military officers who objected to their country's ties to the West. Neighboring Jordan and Lebanon feared similar coups. In a show of force, Eisenhower sent the Sixth Fleet to the Mediterranean. The marines landed in Lebanon, where they remained for a few months without major incident.

Communism Strikes Closer to Home

In Cuba, just 145 kilometres from the North American continent, a young nationalist named Fidel Castro formed a band of guerrillas and ousted the corrupt dictator Fulgencio Batista in January 1959. Many people viewed Castro's takeover with favor and elevated him to the status of folk hero. But the U.S. government rejected requests for support, and relations deteriorated rapidly as he stepped up his anti-American rhetoric and moved increasingly to the left.

The closing months of Eisenhower's presidency were haunted by a confrontation with the Soviets. Since 1956 the CIA had been flying reconnaissance missions over the Soviet Union. U-2 planes, capable of flying at altitudes over 22,000 metres, had gathered invaluable intelligence. But on May 1, 1960, the Soviets shot down a U-2 and captured its pilot, Francis Gary Powers. The incident, coming just weeks before a planned summit in Paris, ruined hopes for a productive meeting. A.J. Liebling described the administration's posturing in *The New Yorker:* "After denying we did it, admitting we did it, denying Ike knew we did it, admitting Ike knew we did it, saying we had a right to do it and denying we were still doing it, we dropped the subject." Khrushchev denounced American "banditry" and relished his propaganda triumph.

In his farewell address, Ike wearily confessed to feelings of disappointment. He had kept us out of war, the president said, but a lasting peace was not in sight. He issued a warning: " . . . we must guard against the acquisition of unwarranted influence . . . by the military-industrial complex. The potential for the disastrous rise of misplaced power exists and will persist."

Francis Gary Powers's ID card (below) told the Soviets who he was after they shot down his U-2 plane: a U.S. agent for the Defense Department. A Soviet trial (inset) found him guilty of spying and he was sentenced to 10 years in prison. The aircraft below is a later version of Powers's plane.

EPOCHAL FIRSTS IN SCIENCE AND MEDICINE

Who could have guessed in 1946 that the descendants of an electronic behemoth called ENIAC would change the world or that the dreaded poliomyelitis would be banished by a simple inoculation?

◀ *J. Presper Eckert, in the foreground, and John W. Mauchly, behind Eckert, work at ENIAC, the first fully electronic digital computer.*

On February 14, 1946, the U.S. War Department unveiled a top secret machine called ENIAC, an acronym for Electronic Numerical Integrator and Computer. Developed to calculate the trajectories of artillery shells, it consisted of 18,000 vacuum tubes and several kilometres of wiring, weighed 30 tonnes, and took up 84 cubic metres of space. J. Presper Eckert, one of the inventors, predicted, "The old era is going, the new one of electronic speed is on the way...." But the computer would have to be brought down to a manageable size.

The insignificant-looking transistor proved to be the first step in the shrinking process. Its invention was announced in 1948 by Bell Laboratories, and by 1954 nearly all hearing aids used the tiny transistor. Research at the University of Toronto, at Atomic Energy of Canada and, most of all, at IBM, led to the transistorized computer that was far smaller than ENIAC. By 1959 Jean Hoerni of Fairchild Semiconductor had devised a transistor that fit on a wafer of silicon crystal, which led to a critical invention for the nascent computer industry: the integrated circuit. The stage was set for the age of computers.

Electronics were also contributing to the arts. In Canada, research physicist Hugh Le Caine had built an electronic keyboard in his home studio, in 1945. Known as the sackbut, it was the first electronic synthesizer. Following his inventions of other electronic musical instruments, the University of Toronto opened the first electronic music studio in Canada in 1959. Le Caine's composition *Dripsody* (1955), based on the sound of a single drop of water transformed, has become a classic of electronic music.

While the electronics industry advanced apace, a series of stunning discoveries was transforming the world of medicine. Every summer, year after year, as the polio season dragged on, newspapers would print weekly tallies of new cases. In 1952 alone the crippling and sometimes fatal disease had struck almost 58,000 North Americans, most of them children. Scientists knew that poliomyelitis, also

▲ *By 1959, transistors had made a big impact on the consumer market, most notably inside small, powerful radios that could be carried almost anywhere.*

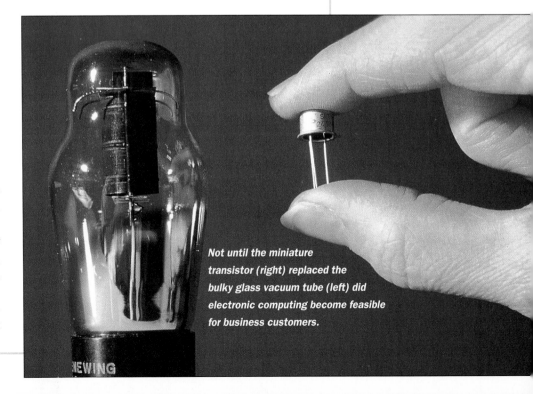

Not until the miniature transistor (right) replaced the bulky glass vacuum tube (left) did electronic computing become feasible for business customers.

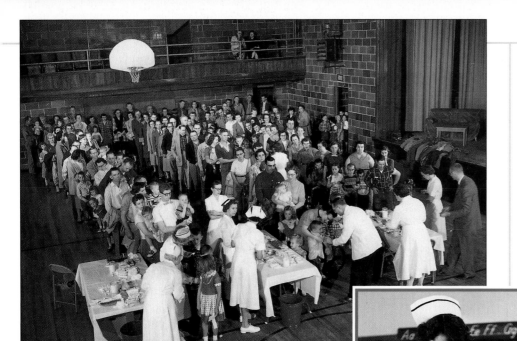

called infantile paralysis, was caused by a virus that attacked the nervous system. What they didn't know was how to prevent or cure it.

In 1954 a vaccine developed by Dr. Jonas Salk at the University of Pittsburgh was tested in a study involving more than 1,830,000 children. The experiment was rigorously scientific: 440,000 children received the vaccine, 210,000 were injected with a saltwater solution, and a control group of 1,180,000 was given neither injection. Scientists evaluated the test results and concluded, on April 12, 1955, that the vaccine worked. Three years later tests began on an oral form of the vaccine developed by Dr. Albert Sabin.

Important changes were taking place in the operating room too. On May 6, 1953, doctors employed a device during surgery that for the first time took over the work of the heart and lungs. The heart-lung machine would save many lives thereafter.

Medicine was also advancing in Canada. At the University of Saskatchewan, in 1951, Harold Johns discovered the cobalt-60 "bomb," and developed cobalt therapy units that revolutionized radiation treatment for cancer.

Studies in Human Traits and Behavior

On April 25, 1953, a team of scientists published the results of its research into the transfer of genetic traits. They had created a model for deoxyribonucleic acid (DNA), the molecular codifier in the chromosomes, at Cavendish Laboratory in Cambridge, England. The researchers, Francis H. C. Crick and Maurice H. F. Wilkins, both British, and an American, James D. Watson, were awarded the Nobel Prize for physiology or medicine in 1962.

While Crick and his colleagues investigated components of the cell, another biologist looked into a basic aspect of human behavior: sexuality. Whether Dr. Alfred Kinsey's books on the sex lives of men (1948) and women (1953) qualified as science or guides to depravity was a hotly debated topic of the times. In *Sexual Behavior in the Human Female*, Kinsey described his work as showing simply that no individuals or couples are identical in their sexual behavior. Congressman Louis B. Heller demanded that the books, which he condemned as obscene, be barred from the stores. Clyde Kluckhohn, a Harvard University professor, thought otherwise: "This book makes an enormous contribution . . . to our knowledge of sexual behavior . . . it is science, serious science." Though Kinsey originally intended his work to be read by physicians and other professionals, hundreds of thousands of ordinary people bought the books, making them bestsellers and opening the way for the frank discussion of human sexuality.

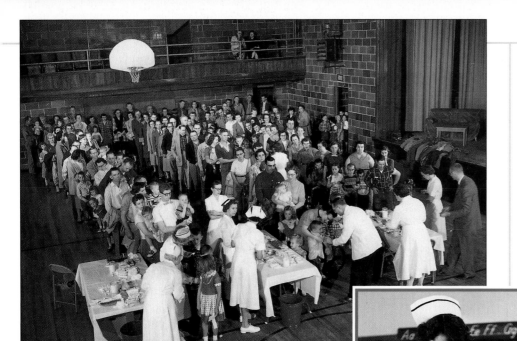

▲ Dr. Jonas Salk (above) administers polio vaccine to a young boy. Mass inoculations were sometimes given at high school gymnasiums, such as the one at top.

◄ In 1953 James D. Watson (left) and Francis H. C. Crick illustrate the double-helix structure of DNA with their model. Watson was 25; Crick, 12 years older.

Dr. Alfred Kinsey

▶ Flamboyant tail fins, enormously popular and certainly the most eye-catching feature of postwar car styling, served no functional purpose.

▼ Our love affair with the road led to a demand for convenient travellers' accommodations. In the 1950's motels more than doubled in number and size.

For '59...only Plymouth wagons gr

FOR THE MOTORIST, MORE OF EVERYTHING

Towering fins and sheets of gleaming chrome; the throaty purr of a 300-horsepower, high-compression V-8; the elegant lines and nimble cornering of a ragtop sports car — the automobile was the winged chariot of postwar prosperity, a one-way ride to the good life.

North America emerged from World War II in a deep state of vehicular withdrawal. Gas rationing had curtailed travel, and the conversion of the auto industry to war production had cut the manufacturing of cars from over 4 million in 1941 to under 100,000 in 1945.

But the good news was that at war's end people had money to spend — more than $100 billion in wartime savings — and much of it went on a car-buying spree. Spurred by urban flight, rapid population growth, advertising, and easy credit, the annual sales of passenger cars grew to over 8 million in 1955, the apogee of the postwar boom. North Americans were far ahead of the rest of the world, ranking first in car ownership per capita.

General Motors led the field, with Ford and Chrysler trailing. Car manufacture had become Canada's biggest industry, and few, in the excitement of producing ever more and newer models, were concerned that the business was almost entirely American-owned.

The new cars were longer, wider, and more powerful than ever before. They bristled with technical innovations, such as power steering and brakes, automatic transmis-

sions, high-compression engines, padded dashboards, and fibreglass construction. Radios and air-conditioning became standard features on many luxury cars. In spite of 5 million annual road accidents, safety did not seem to be an issue with buyers. Tail fins reached ludicrous dimensions, and designers piled on the chrome and air scoops. One industry official remarked that "a square foot of chrome sells 10 times more cars than the best safety door latch." Some models, such as the '53 Corvette and the '57 Chevy, set industry standards for design and engineering. Others did not fare so well.

Named after one of Henry Ford's sons and unveiled with great fanfare in September 1957, the 1958 Edsel was a hodgepodge of bewildering technology, bizarre looks, undistinguished performance, and pointless detail. It lasted a mere two years. The Edsel was the victim of its own hype, but it also represented, in the words of *Time,* "the classic case of the wrong car for the wrong market at the wrong time." By 1957 the economy had slid into recession, and the love affair with the gas-guzzling behemoth, which averaged just 5 kilometers per litre, had soured. Reluctantly, domes-

GRANT MOTEL
HOTEL SERVICE

UNITED MOTOR COURTS

AAA

RECOMMENDED BY DUNCAN HINES

so many luxury features...and low price,

▲ *Aimed squarely at the young family, an advertisement in the November 17, 1958, issue of Life magazine features the latest-model Plymouth station wagon. By the end of the decade, the major car companies directed the largest part of their advertising budget to spots on television.*

tic manufacturers turned to smaller models. In the meantime, imports had arrived. British cars, like the economical Austin, enjoyed a brief popularity until a German "people's car" swept all before it. The Volkswagen, a surprisingly efficient vehicle, established a loyal following, despite general moaning over its peculiar appearance. One thing the VW had going for it was price: $1,300, well below the average North American car price of $1,900.

In spite of record car sales, roads were in bad shape, making long-distance travel by car no journey for the frail or timid. Canadian drivers became accustomed to detour signs as frantic work began on building new roads and upgrading old ones. Most spectacular was the Trans-Canada Highway, though it was not completed until 1970. In the United States, the Interstate Highway Act of 1956 provided for the construction of 66,000 kilometres of divided expressways. Millions responded by loading up the family car and heading for the open road.

New facilities sprang up catering specially to the motorist. In place of the clusters of tiny cabins and roadside camps that had accommodated travellers in the past came sleeker, more comfortable motels, with swimming pools and roomside parking. Banks, restaurants, and dozens of other businesses instituted drive-through service. Milkshake-machine salesman Ray Kroc shook up the restaurant world when, having walked into a thriving hamburger joint owned by two brothers, Maurice and Richard McDonald, and being bowled over by their assembly-line cooking method, he persuaded them to let him franchise their products. In 1955 Kroc opened his first McDonald's, in Des Plaines, Illinois, and the rest is history.

The expansion of the automobile culture had wide-ranging effects. It changed the way people worked and played, closed the gap between city and country, and tamed, once and for all, the far reaches of the continent. Many debated the wisdom of these changes, but one thing is certain: by decade's end, the automobile had joined the beaver and the eagle as national symbols.

In January 1949 the first Volkswagen arrived for sale in North America (top). Nobody foresaw the car's impact on the auto industry, especially after only two were sold that year. The McDonald brothers opened their first restaurant in 1940. They sold out for $2.7 million to Ray Kroc, who built his first McDonald's in Des Plaines, Illinois (above, in 1955). This restaurant is now a McDonald's museum.

THE TIGHT HUG OF TOGETHERNESS

Alternately hailed as golden sanctuaries of family life, and scorned as the ultimate in 20th-century blandness, the suburbs of the 1950's have generated both rhapsodic nostalgia and widespread derision.

In a show of hospitality, the civic groups of Fullerton, California, posted the display at left. They hoped to attract clean-cut families, such as the one portrayed in television's **Leave It to Beaver** (above).

▼ *A perfect TV hostess demonstrates Admiral Corporation's Telebar, a 21-inch screen plus the means for entertaining.*

The TV sitcom *Leave It to Beaver* each week portrayed a suburban never-never land populated almost entirely by nurturing moms, wise and loving dads, and healthy, well-adjusted children. If this bucolic idyll did not exactly mirror reality, it accurately reflected most people's hopes for what life *should* be.

Surveys in the 1950's revealed that a large majority of North American adults considered themselves middle-class. Most of them had either just moved to suburbia or wanted to. Residents of the new suburbs tended to be white and between the ages of 25 and 35, with roughly equivalent incomes. They wore similar clothes, drove similar cars, and filled their kitchens with the same array of laborsaving gadgets. The houses on a given street were identical or slight variations on a theme. But in almost every way, suburban life far surpassed the dreams of young couples who had grown up during the hard times of previous eras. To most, conformity did not seem a problem; it was a relief.

McCall's said that adults could find their "deepest satisfaction" by marrying at an early age and rearing large families. Fewer than 1 in 10 Americans polled answered yes to the question of whether "an unmarried person could be happy." A book called *Modern Woman: The Lost Sex* traced every problem, including alcoholism, juvenile delinquency, and war, to neurotic career women. Instead, the media glorified something called togetherness, which seemed to consist of weekend barbecues, drives in the family car, and hours of fellowship in front of the TV set.

At the heart of suburban culture was a profound change in the ways families led their lives. The growing size of young families, and the close quarters of tract developments, established the idea of "the neighborhood" as an extended support group. But this support group was ever-shifting, since families were more transient than before: the average corporate manager relocated 14 times in his career. As a result, suburban mothers relied on one another for a sense of belonging, and suburbanites were relentlessly social; from Home and School or PTA to bridge groups to cocktail parties, there was always a reason to gather.

Trouble in Paradise

Although more husbands were helping out with chores and child rearing, by far the biggest change for men was the rise of huge corporations. During the decade, more than 3,000 smaller companies were swallowed up by 500 larger ones. By 1959, 200 corporations controlled 50 percent of U.S. business assets. (Apprehensive Canadians noted that they also controlled most of Canada's manufacturing and natural resources industries.) Junior executives disappeared daily into these impersonal monoliths to become nameless, interchangeable cogs in the wheels of progress. If the 1950's father no longer played the role of a woodshed disciplinarian, most likely he was either still at work or else just too plain tired.

The "keeper of the suburban dream" was the housewife. Closed out of the well-paying jobs they had held in wartime, and excluded from most professions, women turned their energies to the home, becoming the domestic engines of middle-class life. Throughout the 1950's, only about one-third of the college undergraduate population was female, and even those women who earned degrees hesitated to seek outside careers. At a college commencement, young women were reminded of their duty "to restore valid, meaningful purpose to life in the home" and to keep their husbands "truly purposeful."

Many women felt bored and isolated in what had been billed as paradise. Other cracks began to appear in the smooth countenance of suburban life. Juvenile delinquency was on the rise; even good kids seemed drawn to rebels like James Dean or Jerry Lee Lewis. Alcohol consumption was increasing. As the decade closed, there was a general restlessness among women, who felt stifled by their domestic lives. By the 1960's the suburban dream was no longer enough, and 40 percent of all women over 16 had decided to enter the labor force.

SUBTERRANEAN VOICES: THE BEAT GENERATION

While most of the continent pursued the suburban dream, a small group of non-conformists was busy running as fast as it could in the opposite direction. These bohemians saw no particular virtue in politics or current events; most did not bother to read the newspaper, and few owned TV sets. They shunned work and

scorned middle-class life, preferring to inhabit, as one of them insisted, a netherworld "of dingy backstairs 'pads,' cafeterias, bebop joints, night-long wanderings, meetings on street corners ... and the streets themselves." Poet Allen Ginsberg referred to them as "subterraneans."

Novelist Jack Kerouac

They were the Beat Generation, so-called by Jack Kerouac, one of their early spokesmen, who probably heard jazz musicians using the term "beat" to mean exhausted or down-and-out. The son of Quebecois parents, Kerouac was born in Little Canada, Massachusetts. He attracted a following in Montreal, Toronto, and Vancouver as much as New York where his disciples, dressed in shabby black, sipped endless cups of coffee.

Out of the Beats' opposition to convention emerged a gritty, experimental new literature. Beat authors liked to shock. They peppered their writings with references to drugs and sex, used

Young Beats filled clubs to hear a new sound called bebop, played by innovative jazzmen, like Charlie (Bird) Parker, seen here in 1946.

obscene language, and borrowed slang from black culture: "hip," "cat," "dig," "square," "bread." Inspired by the fast-paced bebop riffs of saxophonist Charlie Parker, trumpeter Dizzy Gillespie, and pianist Oscar Peterson, they cultivated a hard-hitting, improvisational writing style. "I saw the best minds of my generation destroyed by madness, starving/ hysterical naked,/ dragging themselves through the negro streets at dawn looking for an angry fix ..." began Allen Ginsberg's poem "Howl," which he recited at a San Francisco gallery on October 7, 1955.

Jack Kerouac tapped out "spontaneous prose" on a 36.5-metre roll of Teletype paper to create *On the Road*, a rambling narrative about "the raggledy madness and riot of our actual lives ... the senseless nightmare road." (As Truman Capote later remarked, "That's not writing, it's just ... typing.")

The 1957 publication of *On the Road* brought the Beats major public recognition: the book sold 500,000 copies. The press dubbed them beatniks and mocked their unkempt hair, their sandals and beards, their dark verse, and their seedy hangouts. But the Beats had something to say, unlike the silently smug suburbanites.

Publisher Barney Rosset confers with writers (from far right) Allen Ginsberg, Gregory Corso, and Peter Orlovsky at a Greenwich Village party.

Chapter 7

The Clamorous 1960's

A dizzying decade of highs and lows sees

triumph and tragedy in civil rights,

JFK slain, flower power, Quebec separatism explode into

violence, Expo 67, the ordeal of Vietnam, medicare in

Canada, and men on the moon.

An uncertain Alabama sky silhouettes the voting rights march from Selma to Montgomery in March 1965.

NEW AGE — OR FALSE START?

The 1960's began with the opening shots of the Diefenbaker-Pearson war, in Ottawa, and the election of a glamorous young president in Washington.

John George Diefenbaker could charge a room with electricity simply by walking into it. For 10 years, as leader of the Conservative party in Canada, his electricity crackled around Lester Bowles Pearson of the Liberal party, as the two fought out the most rivetting political duel in all Canadian history.

"Dief the Chief," who was raised in Saskatoon, sharpened his debating skills as a defence lawyer, and honed them further when he entered Parliament in 1940. By 1956, he was leader of a Conservative party that seemed forever mired in opposition to the Liberal dynasty. But Diefenbaker was fired by the almost messianic conviction that he was destined to lead the ordinary people of Canada to victory over the rich and powerful. The Liberals, become arrogant in power, were easy meat for Diefenbaker's rousing denunciations. In 1957, he humbled them by winning a narrow election victory. A year later, he won the biggest election majority to that time.

John F. Kennedy is sworn in as the 35th president by Chief Justice Earl Warren. Looking on are Jacqueline Bouvier Kennedy; exiting President Dwight D. Eisenhower; Kennedy's vice president, Lyndon B. Johnson; and Eisenhower's vice president, Richard M. Nixon.

Once in power, he increased old age pensions and boosted payments to the poorer regions of the country. Taking his moral stance abroad, he led the fight to expel South Africa from the Commonwealth because of its racial policies. But then came a descent as spectacular as his rise.

Diefenbaker's misfortune was to come to power just as the postwar boom was ending. Unemployment rose and the dollar fell 7½ cents, an inspiration to Liberals who printed mock Diefendollars worth 92½ cents "more or less." It was also his misfortune to govern when Canadians were distrustful of U.S. policies but, sharing the American fear of communism, had no alternative to them. Diefenbaker bridled at President Kennedy's brash assumption that Canada was to do as it was told in foreign affairs. And when a crisis developed over U.S. relations with Cuba, he refused an American request to put Canadian forces on alert. He accepted U.S. Bomarc missiles on Canadian soil, but then refused the atomic warheads without which they were useless. Canadian-U.S. relations plunged to their lowest level in decades as American politicians and the American media openly intervened in Canadian politics to defeat Diefenbaker's Conservatives in the election of 1963.

Political friends abandoned him, but Diefenbaker soldiered on, buoyed by his belief that "the people" were with

Cartoonist Duncan Macpherson, of the Toronto Star, makes fun of Diefenbaker, Pearson, and Douglas in the run-up to the June 1962 election.

Tens of millions of viewers tuned in to watch each of the four televised presidential debates pitting Nixon against Kennedy.

him in his struggle against "the big interests." Both gleeful and vicious in the heat of battle, defeat as prime minister simply freed him to be the stormiest leader of the Opposition Canada had ever seen.

It was a time when the United States seemed to be taking quite a different path to the future. On January 20, 1961, President Dwight D. Eisenhower, one of the oldest persons to hold that office in the U.S., stood bundled against the chill air while his successor, John F. Kennedy, took the oath. At age 43, Kennedy was the youngest man ever elected to the presidency and the first born in the 20th century. Tanned and coatless, he addressed the crowd gathered before the Capitol: "We observe today not a victory of party but a celebration of freedom . . . signifying renewal as well as change."

During the campaign Kennedy had promised to pioneer a New Frontier, conquering "uncharted areas of science and space, unsolved problems of peace and war, unconquered pockets of ignorance and prejudice, and unanswered questions of poverty and surplus." Now, in the same ringing tones, he sent a warning to the Cold War enemies of the United States: "We shall pay any price, bear any burden . . . to assure the survival and success of liberty." And he summoned all Americans to the cause: "Ask not what your country can do for you — ask what you can do for your country." The audience came to its feet in a standing ovation.

In 1946, Jack Kennedy ran for Congress in a Boston district and won handily, thanks to his father's financial backing and the energetic electioneering of the Kennedy clan. Then, in 1952, after three uneventful terms in the House of Representatives, he sought a seat in the U.S. Senate. He ran against the Republican incumbent, Henry Cabot

The Arrow that Ended a Dream

In 1950, A. V. Roe of Canada produced a successful, long-range jet interceptor, the CF-100 Canuck. Canada seemed poised to become an important manufacturer in the profitable market for military aircraft.

Then, in 1957, the CF-105, the Arrow, made its appearance. Supersonic, twin-engined and all-weather, it was capable of operating over long ranges in the far North and was faster than any aircraft of its type. The Arrow was a brilliant design — but expensive, at

$12.5 million. American and European buyers turned it down. They had also possibly lost interest in it because the threat of attacks by Soviet bombers was being superseded by that of ICBM missiles.

The Arrow's price tag was certainly too much for Canada. In 1959, Diefenbaker cancelled the project, and ordered its designs to be destroyed. The dream of Canada ever building its own military aircraft was effectively ended.

Lodge, Jr., and won by some 70,000 votes while the Republican Eisenhower was winning the presidency in a landslide. He narrowly lost the vice presidential spot on the 1956 Democratic ticket, but four years later he won his party's nomination for president of the United States.

Kennedy and his opponent, 47-year-old Vice President Richard M. Nixon, stood reasonably close on the issues in 1960, a year when the country enjoyed wide prosperity and faced no international crises. Both candidates took a hard line on communism, stressing the importance of economic and military superiority over the Soviet Union. Kennedy charged, however, that under Eisenhower and Nixon the United States had begun to lag behind its great adversary. Both candidates called for civil rights legislation, but Nixon made few overtures toward black voters, while Kennedy actively courted their vote and promised that, as president, he would be their strong advocate.

Narrow Victory, Ambitious Start

The two candidates were tireless, forceful campaigners, effective in their many stump speeches. But the election, close throughout, hinged on a few tense hours in the final weeks, when JFK and Nixon clashed in debates, the first presidential debates ever broadcast live on television and radio. The radio audience judged the debates a draw. But millions of TV viewers came away with a

Kennedy's attorney general and closest confidant was his brother Robert.

different impression: they saw a calm, confident Kennedy, whom pundits had labelled inexperienced, appear the equal of his seasoned opponent. Nixon, on the other hand, who had refused to wear makeup for the first debate, looked haggard, his face darkened by a five o'clock shadow. But as Election Day neared, many voters wavered: Kennedy's Catholicism left them uneasy. In the end, he won — but barely. His margin over Nixon was fewer than 120,000 votes: 49.7 percent of the popular vote to Nixon's 49.5.

Once in office, President Kennedy established his own style of leadership. He assembled a Cabinet drawn from the elite ranks of the academic and business worlds. He named Dean Rusk of the Rockefeller Foundation as secretary of state; Robert S. McNamara of the Ford Motor Company as secretary of defence; McGeorge Bundy of Harvard University as national security adviser; and as attorney general, his brother and campaign manager, Robert. "I don't see what's wrong with giving him a little experience before he goes out to practice law," said Kennedy on the appointment of the 35-year-old Bobby.

This team, skilled as it was, met with mixed results. Congress rejected a number of their domestic initiatives but supported other innovative programs: the Peace Corps sent thousands of volunteers to Third World countries (see box below); the Alliance for Progress sought to ease poverty in Latin America; and in the space race with the Soviets, Kennedy committed the United

The Peace Corps

In early 1960 Congress studied the idea of sending young Americans to developing nations to improve living standards. During a campaign speech in San Francisco that November, John Kennedy proposed a peace corps: "There is not enough money in all America to relieve the misery of the underdeveloped world in a giant and endless soup kitchen. But there is enough know-how and knowledgeable people to help those nations help themselves."

The corps would promote mutual understanding and world peace. The United States also hoped the presence of Americans in the Third World would counter Communist influence there.

On March 1, 1961, shortly after Kennedy took office, he signed the Peace Corps into existence by executive order. His brother-in-law Sargent Shriver was made director. But not everyone shared Kennedy's enthusiasm for the enterprise. Detractors renamed the corps Kennedy's Kiddie Korps; Eisenhower labelled it "a juvenile experiment."

Then, in September 1961, the first volunteers, who averaged 26 years of age, left for their host countries. Eighty men and women arrived in Ghana and Tanganyika, now Tanzania, 17 in St. Lucia, and 62 in Colombia. Hundreds of other volunteers were enrolled in eight-week training programs, in which they studied such subjects as Swahili and snakebite treatment.

Peace Corps volunteers Tom Livingston and Georgianna Shine taught in Ghanaian schools. John Arango was sent to Cutaru, Colombia, where he helped reconstruct river wharves, convert a local jail into a health clinic, drain a swamp, and build housing. In 1966 Peace Corps enrollment peaked at 15,550 volunteers serving 50 countries around the globe.

States to put the first man on the moon (see pp. 320–321).

Kennedy's socialite wife, Jacqueline Bouvier, added to the presidential glamor. Her elegantly coiffed hair and stylish outfits, from pillbox hats to A-line dresses, set the fashion for many women. On a June 1961 presidential trip to Paris, it was Jackie, fluent in the French language and at home in that country's culture, who starred. Clad in a stunning succession of couturier suits, dresses, and ball gowns, her hair done twice daily by France's leading stylist, she was simply "*ravissante!*" "I am the man who accompanied Jacqueline Kennedy to Paris," her husband remarked. As for the Kennedy children, photographers found them irresistible: Caroline toddling into the middle of a press conference in her mother's high heels and John-John hiding under daddy's desk.

Some Called It Camelot

Kennedy tastes gave rise to other trends. The clan's mania for sports stimulated a fitness craze. Jack's penchant for James Bond novels made them bestsellers. His partiality for rocking chairs boosted their sales. And when Jackie hosted a TV special, in which she gave a tour of the recently restored White House, more than 48 million viewers tuned in.

The Kennedys revived the tradition of White House musicales. Cellist Pablo Casals, violinist Isaac Stern, and others performed for the likes of Robert Frost and André Malraux. One Kennedy guest list included 49 Nobel Prize winners, prompting the president to observe that the event marked "the most extraordinary collection of talent . . . at the White House" since "Thomas Jefferson dined alone." In later years the Kennedy White House was dubbed Camelot.

But the fairy tale was not as perfect as it seemed. The United States faced troubled relations with some of its neighbors in the Western Hemisphere and also with its Cold War adversaries. The conflict in Vietnam was brewing. And there was talk of Jack's philandering ways. Still, for one brief shining moment — the "thousand days" of Kennedy's presidency — vitality, culture, and wit reigned in the White House.

▶

Spanish-born maestro Pablo Casals, age 86, takes a bow before the distinguished guests gathered in the East Room of the White House for his cello recital in 1961.

▲ *A photographer catches John-John playing hide-and-seek under his father's Victorian desk.*

▶

First Lady Jacqueline Kennedy, with children, Caroline and John, Jr., sits for a formal portrait.

Hot spots in the cold war

Nikita Khrushchev appeared more moderate than other Soviet leaders, but tensions around the globe just worsened. Everywhere Communists took a hard line: Eastern Europe, China, North Korea, Africa.

As the United Nations delegates looked on in astonishment, Soviet Premier Nikita Khrushchev took off his shoe and pounded it vigorously on the table. The gesture was the climax to weeks of theatrics by Khrushchev, from finger shaking to heckling and name-calling. The premier was protesting one delegate's charge that Eastern Europe had been "swallowed up by the Soviet Union," but few doubted that Khrushchev's real aim was to disrupt the proceedings whenever they failed to go his way.

By 1960 Communist right-wingers in the Politburo were pressuring the Soviet leader to reassert Soviet authority in global affairs. Khrushchev heeded the hard-liners in his policy toward Africa, where nations fighting for their independence from Western colonial powers seemed fertile ground for the spread of Soviet influence. The following January Khrushchev announced his "unlimited support" of Third World nations "fighting for their liberation."

But Khrushchev chose Berlin, in Soviet-controlled East Germany, as his flash point. In August of 1961 the Russians erected a concrete and barbed-wire barrier down the middle of the city, cutting the Western sector off from the Eastern zone and obstructing a major escape route for East Germans fleeing the repressive Communist regime. Democratic nations expressed outrage at so blatant an infringement of human rights. President Kennedy visited the wall on the West Berlin side in 1963 and to demonstrate U.S. support for the freedom seekers declared, "*Ich bin ein Berliner.*" But since he could tear down the wall only by declaring war, it stood as a symbol of the West's helplessness. Kennedy's assassination in the fall of that year (see pages 312–313) cast the United States into weeks of mourning and soul-searching. Meanwhile, the Communists kept up the pressure everywhere.

Outside the U.S.S.R., the Communist threat presented itself in another ominous form: a mushroom cloud billowing above Lop Nor in the desolate wastes of Sinkiang, China. It was 1964, and Red China had the atom bomb.

▲ The Soviets parade solid-fuel missiles through Red Square on November 7, 1963, during celebrations marking the 47th anniversary of the Bolshevik Revolution. A few months before, the United States, Great Britain, and the Soviet Union had signed the first nuclear test ban treaty.

Two years later dictator Mao Tse-tung incited a movement that would reignite the Communist revolutionary flame in China. Under the banner of the Cultural Revolution, Mao sent forth radicals, among them millions of young people called the Red Guards, to ruthlessly purge China of bourgeois tradition and "corrupt" Western influences. Weddings, funerals, modern art were outlawed. Even cosmetics and holding hands were banned. The young fanatics ransacked libraries, burned books, and shut down universities, driving professors into the countryside to perform manual labor and undergo "political reeducation." Most of the middle class was exiled or exterminated. Leaders of the Communist Party's moderate faction were paraded in dunce

◀ A leader of the paramilitary group the Red Guards rallies supporters in the port of Shanghai in February 1967. Mao Tse-tung's protégés laid siege to many of China's major cities in an effort to set up communes in place of local governments.

▼ Bloodied but defiant Czech students wave their nation's flag from atop a Soviet tank in August 1968. Over 500,000 troops invaded Prague, the Czechoslovakian capital, that summer to enforce Leonid Brezhnev's directive reversing the Prague Spring reforms.

caps before student courts and forced to renounce their deviation from the teachings of Mao. In the grim years of "purification," nearly 500,000 Chinese lost their lives.

The greatest humiliation to the United States in this Cold War decade came not from China but from China's close ally, North Korea. In 1968 the North Koreans seized the intelligence ship U.S.S. *Pueblo* as it cruised in international waters off their coast. For almost a year the North Koreans held Capt. Lloyd Bucher and his crew, brutally torturing the men to exact confessions of spying. Some U.S. senators called for military retaliation. Instead, the United States made futile appeals to the Soviet Union and the United Nations to intervene. But not until the U.S. government submitted an official admission of intrusion into North Korean waters and issued an apology were the captives released.

By this time Khrushchev had been unceremoniously removed and replaced by Stalinist hard-liner Leonid Brezhnev. Under the new leader, the Soviets cracked down on nations in the Eastern European bloc that had begun to test the limits imposed by their Soviet masters. Czechoslovakia, led by Alexander Dubcek, was enjoying an unheard-of measure of liberty in political and artistic activity. The new freedoms culminated in the Prague Spring of 1968, a brief interlude when the press went uncensored and students rallied openly for more reforms. In August, Soviet tanks rumbled into Czechoslovakia and silenced the voices of change.

The Six-Day War

In the 1960's hostilities between Israel and the neighboring Arab nations in the Middle East escalated. Commandos from Syria and Jordan mounted an unrelenting barrage of border raids on the Jewish state. Israel retaliated forcefully and, by early 1967, had won decisive victories in battles against the Arab aggressors. Egyptian president Gamal Abdel Nasser ordered United Nations troops to leave the Arab-Israeli border and sent Egyptian troops into the Sinai in preparation for all-out war.

Then, on June 5, 1967, Israel struck without warning. The Israelis wiped out or severely damaged four enemy airfields and annihilated the Egyptian army. They occupied the Sinai Peninsula and annexed the Gaza Strip (Egypt), East Jerusalem and the West Bank (Jordan), and the Golan Heights (Syria).

The Six-Day War dealt a crippling blow to the Arab states. Their ally, the Soviet Union, also suffered a serious embarrassment. But, thanks to Soviet Premier Aleksey Kosygin's first-time use of the hotline to the United States, a superpower confrontation was averted.

CONFRONTING CARIBBEAN TURMOIL

When Cuban rebel Fidel Castro overthrew Fulgencio Batista, many North Americans thought they had gained a friend in Latin America. But many soon changed their minds as Cuba turned to the Soviet Union for aid.

By 1960 the situation in Cuba had become deeply troubling. Denied U.S. support in modernizing Cuba, Premier Fidel Castro seized U.S.-owned oil refineries and businesses, and nationalized the country's major industries. He turned to the only other power able to support him — and Soviet loans, arms, and advisers arrived in a steady stream. Fidel Castro now headed a Communist state, right on the doorstep of the United States.

In response, President Dwight D. Eisenhower ordered CIA Director Allen Dulles to secretly train thousands of anti-Castro refugees living in Florida for an assault on Cuba. By March 1961, Dulles was urging the new president, John F. Kennedy, to set loose the clandestine force on the island nation, with the assurance that once the commandos landed, the Cuban people would rise up to throw off Castro's yoke. An uneasy Kennedy gave the go-ahead, but to maintain the

▶

At the height of tensions between Cuba and the United States — the 1962 missile crisis — Castro staged a display of Soviet weaponry in his capital, Havana.

illusion that it was a Cuban-sponsored operation, he ordered: "There will not be . . . any intervention in Cuba by the United States. . . . The basic issue . . . is between the Cubans themselves."

The Bay of Pigs invasion was a fiasco from the start. On April 15, eight B-26 bombers manned by Cuban exiles fired on Castro's airfields, knocking out some planes but leaving key aircraft unharmed and, worse, tipping Castro off to the coming invasion. The dictator swiftly rounded up thousands of suspected dissidents, dashing any hope of a civil uprising. On the night of April 17, 1,400 troops landed on the island. The CIA had led them to expect a smooth landing on a deserted beach. Instead, their boats ran aground on coral reefs within sight of a public park. Within 24 hours of the landing, Castro had sent 20,000 Cuban regulars to the area to block the drive inland. The next day four B-26's left Nicaragua for an attack on Castro's forces, but failing to take into account the difference in time zone, the pilots arrived at their targets an hour before their escorts. Castro's jets swatted them down like flies. By nightfall on the third day of the invasion, Castro had won.

"The Other Fellow Just Blinked"

The Soviet buildup in Cuba continued. On October 16, 1962, alarming news reached Kennedy: aerial photographs revealed that the Soviets were installing ballistic missiles on the western side of the island. The missiles could be fitted with nuclear warheads. Wider ranging missiles, spotted two days later, could reach targets as far west as Montana. Were the Soviets, through Castro, planning a secret attack? Thirteen days of crisis ensued. Kennedy called together his closest aides to decide on a course of action — the Soviet missiles had to be destroyed or removed, and promptly — but the president warned: "[Khrushchev] can't permit us to take out their missiles, kill a lot of Russians, and do nothing." Defence Secretary Robert McNamara advocated the use of a naval blockade to force Khrushchev's hand while enabling him to withdraw the missiles quietly.

On October 22 Kennedy apprised the nation of its danger: "The purpose of these bases," he said in a televised address, "can be none other than to provide a nuclear strike capability against the Western Hemisphere." All-out nuclear war suddenly seemed possible. The United States girded itself. The entire fleet of B-52's was sent aloft, the largest ground force since World War II was assembled, and scores

▼ *Determined to prevent "another Cuba," President Johnson sent 20,000 U.S. troops to the Dominican Republic during an outbreak of civil unrest in 1965.*

of warships and air squadrons swept the Caribbean. "I guess this is the week I earn my salary," Kennedy remarked. For four days while the nuclear clock ticked, Khrushchev remained silent. But at sea, Soviet freighters, confronted by the U.S. Navy, stopped dead in the water. "We're eyeball to eyeball," said Secretary of State Dean Rusk, "and I think the other fellow just blinked."

Then, late on October 26, a letter arrived from the Soviet leader: the weapons would be removed if the United States pledged not to invade Cuba. Hours later a second letter demanded the United States remove its own missiles from Turkey, which were within striking distance of the Soviet Union. Kennedy answered the first missive, agreeing to its condition, and ignored the second, and on October 28 Khrushchev promised to remove the missiles from Cuba. This time, Kennedy had won.

Although they were as uneasy as the Americans about a Communist presence so close to home, many Canadians were furious that the U.S. expected Canada to fall into line with it, without even consulting them on policy. They also felt that U.S. intransigence over Cuba stood in the way of a reasonable settlement. As the decade wore on, the United States maintained a hostile attitude to Cuba while Canada strove for more sympathetic relations.

NOVEMBER 22, 1963

People around the world would never forget where they were, what they were doing, when the news reached them that President Kennedy had been shot. Everyone mourned.

Just after noon on a sun-splashed Friday, President John F. Kennedy's motorcade made its way past cheering crowds along its 18-kilometre route through downtown Dallas, Texas. So balmy was the fall weather that Kennedy rode in an open limousine, without benefit of the usual protective bubble. Smiling and waving, the president sat in the back seat next to his wife, Jackie, who looked luminous in a pink suit and pillbox hat. Texas Gov. John B. Connally, Jr., and his wife greeted well-wishers from the fold-down jump seats in front.

The presidential caravan glided down Main Street and turned right then left onto a less populated side street. Suddenly, the sharp crack of gunshots shattered the air. Pandemonium set in. Governor Connally collapsed in his wife's lap. "My God, they are trying to kill us all!" he cried, critically wounded in the chest. Jackie reached out to help Secret Service agent Clint Hill clamber over the rear of the limousine as it sped toward the hospital. Police ran toward a nearby grassy knoll, thinking the shots had come from that direction. A bullet had pierced Kennedy's throat and another hit him in the head. Within minutes, a team of doctors at Parkland Hospital was working frantically to keep him alive. Miraculously the president showed vital signs — but to no avail. At 1 P.M. Central Standard Time on November 22, 1963, a half hour after the bullets had reached their mark, Kennedy, age 46, was pronounced dead.

Soon after the shooting, police had entered the Texas School Book Depository, a building less than 85 metres from the point where Kennedy and Connally had been hit. Eyewitnesses had spotted an armed man in a sixth-floor

On the day he turned three, John junior bade his father farewell at St. Matthew's Cathedral.

One of the last glimpses of John F. Kennedy shows the president, first lady, and Gov. John B. Connally settling into their open limousine for the ride through Dallas.

window of the building. A search turned up a bolt-action rifle fitted with a telescopic sight. One worker was missing: 24-year-old Lee Harvey Oswald, a clerk who filled book orders. Oswald was an ex-marine and a qualified sharpshooter. He had lived in the Soviet Union and championed pro-Castro causes. Within little more than an hour after JFK was shot, police arrested Oswald inside the Texas Theater. He had taken cover there after killing veteran police officer J. D. Tippit, who had stopped him for questioning.

A President Is Buried; Oswald Shot

John Kennedy's lifeless body was transferred to *Air Force One* for the flight back to the capital. Vice President Lyndon Johnson took the oath of office in the plane's cramped quarters before it left the tarmac. Then he turned and gently instructed the pilot, "Let's be airborne."

The plane landed, and the casket was transferred to Bethesda Naval Hospital and then to the White House. The Kennedy family gathered for a private ceremony in the East Room of the White House, where, almost 100 years before, the murdered Lincoln had lain. On Sunday afternoon, a horse-drawn caisson bore the flag-draped casket to the

◀

Citizens line Memorial Bridge to pay their last respects as the caisson bearing Kennedy's casket, followed by a five-kilometre-long funeral cortege, crosses the Potomac River.

towering Capitol rotunda. An honor guard representing all the armed services kept watch around the catafalque. The Navy Band sounded a heartrending dirge, a measured "Hail to the Chief." Then Senate Majority Leader Mike Mansfield delivered a eulogy, denouncing "the bigotry, the hatred, prejudice, and the arrogance which converged in that moment of horror" to bring the president down. Some 250,000 people waited in line for six or more hours to file past Kennedy's bier. Tens of millions more watched the ceremony unfold on television.

Even as Senator Mansfield spoke, Oswald lay dying of gunshot wounds sustained while in police custody. His killer was nightclub owner Jack Rubenstein, known as Jack Ruby, who claimed to be a fierce Kennedy admirer. When Ruby saw "a smirk on [Oswald's] face," he told his brother Earl, he decided to shoot. (Shortly after Lyndon Johnson took office, he named a special commission, under Chief Justice Earl Warren, to look into the Kennedy assassination. The 888-page Warren Report, issued after the commission had spent nearly a year collecting 26 volumes of testimony by 552 witnesses, concluded that Oswald had acted alone in killing Kennedy.)

On Monday morning, the funeral cortege departed from the Capitol rotunda and proceeded up Pennsylvania Avenue. In a gesture symbolic of the fallen chieftain, a riderless charger with boots reversed in the stirrups accompanied the caisson. Bagpipes wailed, muffled drums resounded. Delegates from 92 nations joined the retinue at the White House and, led on foot by Mrs. Kennedy together with the slain president's brothers, Attorney General Robert Kennedy and Senator Edward Kennedy, continued on to St. Matthew's Cathedral. Richard Cardinal Cushing celebrated the mass and prayed, "May the angels, dear Jack, lead you into Paradise." The procession resumed, passing the Lincoln Memorial toward Arlington National Cemetery. At the grave site, atop a hill overlooking the Potomac River, there were final prayers, the sound of taps, the crash of a rifle volley. The widow accepted the folded flag. She lit the eternal flame and departed. All was silent.

Less than 48 hours after the Dallas police arrested Lee Harvey Oswald (above), he was fatally shot by Jack Ruby. Numerous conspiracy theories have since arisen linking Oswald to an array of groups from the Soviet KGB to organized crime.

Vice President Lyndon Johnson, flanked by his wife and a grief-stricken Jacqueline Kennedy, takes the oath of office before Judge Sarah T. Hughes.

The architect of the Quiet Revolution, Jean Lesage.

QUEBEC'S QUIET REVOLUTION

The year 1960 began a decade of change in Quebec. And though changes were made, the desire for more became so overwhelming it led to an explosion of violence.

Premier Maurice Duplessis of Quebec appeared to be a political bully who governed the province by means of the yes-men who made up his Union Nationale party. He was, in fact, a political bully. But he was also a servant of the two groups that really directed the province. The wealthier anglophones, who controlled business, dictated decisions that affected English-speaking Quebec. The wealthier francophones, who dominated the professions and a very conservative Roman Catholic Church, dictated decisions that affected French-speaking Quebec. Both groups acted through Duplessis and his Union Nationale.

Eager to attract American investment, the two elites wanted to keep wages low. Duplessis satisfied their desire by bringing in his notoriously brutal provincial police to deal with strikers. Other than contracts, low taxes, and an occasional show of force, the two elites wanted nothing from government, so Duplessis had no need for a civil service that was anything but small, unskilled, and badly paid.

The Roman Catholic schools, largely francophone, were the hardest-hit victims of this system. Church control of the curriculum starved the schools of education in the sciences and business. The schools were also starved of funds. Prosperous francophones, who controlled school finances through the school boards, sent their own children to private schools. Accordingly, their only interest in public schools was to keep the tax rate down. For most French-speaking children, that meant education ended in grade school, providing almost no opportunity for the better-paying jobs in industry.

When Duplessis died suddenly in 1959, the discontent that had been simmering among the less wealthy francophones for more than a decade spurred them into action. Within less than a year, lawyer Jean Lesage led his Liberal Party to power and began six years of reform that came to be known as the Quiet Revolution.

The civil service, long a haven for political timeservers, mushroomed in size and skills. Its new employees came from the universities and even from the clergy, who realized that the days of church dominance were over. They staffed new departments, such as cultural affairs, and established a provincial pension plan that provided funds for massive government investment in the development of the province. A department of education established government control of schools, and French public education was raised to a standard comparable to the rest of North America. French high school and university education were revamped to prepare graduates for science and business as well as for law and theology. Provincial spending rose from $745 million in 1960–61 to $2.1 billion in 1966–67.

▶

The headquarters of Hydro-Québec, the newly nationalized hydroelectricity company, makes its mark on the Montreal skyline, a prominent symbol of Quebec's growing self-determination. The building was completed in 1962.

On the banks of the Carillon power dam, on the Ottawa River (below left), René Lévesque contemplates his brainchild, the nationalization of hydroelectric power and greater economic ◀ *control for Quebec.*

Thus far, the Quiet Revolution was no different from what governments had already been doing in much of the Western World. But a new dimension was added when private hydroelectric companies were nationalized in 1963. The idea came from a popular cabinet minister named René Lévesque. Putting all hydroelectric power into the hands of a government corporation would give the Quebec government control of the most influential area of economic development. It would, as Lévesque said, make Quebeckers "Maîtres chez nous" — "Masters in our own home." The phrase struck an emotional chord.

It was a popular myth in Quebec that most anglophones were rich and all francophones poor — a myth that ignored both the mansions of wealthy francophones and the slum districts of poverty-stricken anglophones. But the myth was reinforced by many industries that employed francophones on the shop floor and anglophones at management level. This apparent discrimination occurred partly because anglophone schooling was superior, and partly because Quebec business traded with an English-speaking North America. But there was also actual discrimination against francophones in those industries. So when Quebec's new power corporation, Hydro-Québec, was formed, it heeded Lévesque's call for greater francophone control and phased out senior anglophones, replacing them with French-speaking managers and technicians.

By the time Lesage left office in 1966, he had replaced the church with the state as the defender and leader of francophone Quebec. He had also brought francophones and anglophones together under the same bureaucracy. But there were some who were demanding that even more powers be transferred from Ottawa to Quebec and that it was not happening quickly enough.

As early as 1960, those who wanted to separate from Canada so that all power would be in the hands of Quebec's francophone majority formed Le Rassemblement pour l'Indépendance Nationale (RIN). In 1968, Lévesque left the Liberals to join a new, separatist party, the Parti Québécois. Anglophones who had supported the aims of the Quiet Revolution were now alarmed by the militantly anti-English tone of the RIN and the PQ. They feared that the modernization of Quebec was becoming an anti-English crusade.

Change created such a demand for more rapid and more radical change that violence came to Montreal. Bombs were set off in mailboxes, in federal buildings, and even in a college. In 1963, Sgt. Maj. Walter Leja was severely wounded while defusing a bomb in the English district of Westmount. The Quiet Revolution was no longer quiet.

Expo 67

Quebec's coming-of-age was celebrated in 1967 with great hoopla, by holding a world fair in its most cosmopolitan city, Montreal. In honor of the event, the theme of which was Man and his World, a new housing complex called Habitat 67 was built. Representatives of nations from all around the world came to share in Quebec's achievements and display their own. As a tourist attraction, Expo 67 was enormously successful, generating $480 million in tourist revenue.

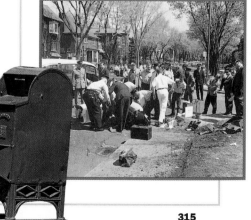

▼ *Montreal mailboxes were routinely searched for bombs in the 1960's (inset). A bomb discovered by Sgt. Maj. Walter Leja blew up while he was defusing it, and badly maimed him (below).*

"I HAVE A DREAM . . ."

A Bill of Rights is passed in Canada protecting racial equality, and sit-ins, Freedom Rides, black registration at all-white schools, and marches in the United States stir that nation's social conscience.

In 1963, Leonard Braithwaite was elected to the provincial legislature of Ontario. What made his election newsworthy was that he was the first black person in Canada to be elected at that level. Five years later, Lincoln Alexander of Hamilton, Ontario, became the first black to be elected a federal member of parliament. The federal Canadian Bill of Rights, which outlawed racial discrimination, was passed in 1960 and was followed by provincial Human Rights bills. And changes in the Immigration Act oiled the door for nonwhite immigrants to pass through into Canada. It seemed as though blacks enjoyed racial equality here, but appearances were a little misleading.

Blacks had lived in Canada since the earliest days of New France, in the 17th century, many of them fleeing slavery in the United States. A century later, however, they still suffered discrimination in employment, wages, housing, and education. Even so, there were few militant demands for change because, at far less than one percent of the population, Canadian blacks had no significant political influence.

By the reflecting pool of the Lincoln Memorial, on August 28, 1963, civil rights supporters assemble to hear Martin Luther King, Jr. (right) deliver his "I have a dream" address. In 1964, at 35, Dr. King became the youngest recipient of the Nobel Peace Prize.

"You can kill a man but you can't kill an idea"

KEEP THE IDEA OF FREEDOM ALIVE

JOIN NAACP

In the United States, where numbers were far higher, pressure for change intensified in the 1960's. In February 1960 four black college students seated themselves at the whites-only lunch counter of a Woolworth store in Greensboro, North Carolina. They ignored the hostile looks cast their way and waited all day for service they knew would never arrive. The next day 20 more students joined the 4 at the Woolworth's counter. Within two weeks, sit-ins were being staged in 15 other U.S. cities. In Nashville, Tennessee, protests came to a head when a bomb blast destroyed the home of a lawyer who defended sit-in participants. After an estimated 6,000 protesters marched on City Hall, Nashville mayor Ben West ordered the luncheonettes opened to all. By summer's end, blacks and whites ate side by side in restaurants across the southern United States.

In using nonviolent means to bring about change, the students had followed the teachings of Rev. Martin Luther King, Jr., leader of the civil rights movement. "Segregation is on its deathbed," King pronounced upon their success. Segregation was indeed in the throes of death, but it did not go quietly. The next major challenge facing civil rights workers was to desegregate interstate bus terminals. James Farmer, director of the Congress of Racial Equality, organized the Freedom Rides: a group of volunteers would travel on buses, and on the way deliberately disregard

▲ **Black students do schoolwork during a lunch counter sit-in. Inset: A poster pictures the widow of NAACP activist Medgar Evers, who was killed by a sniper in the doorway of his home in 1963.**

▼ **Len Braithwaite, Liberal MPP for Etobicoke, Ontario, and the first black person in Canada to be elected to the provincial legislature, says stop to pollution of the Humber Valley.**

signs designating segregated seating and whites-only bus terminal facilities. "We were counting on the bigots . . . to do our work for us," explained Farmer. "We figured that the government would have to respond." The Freedom Riders departed on May 4, 1961. As the journey progressed, antagonism toward them escalated. At first they were taunted, then threatened. In the Deep South violence broke out. An incendiary bomb was tossed into a bus in Anniston, Alabama. A gang of thugs attacked riders in Birmingham. And in Montgomery a mob numbering in the thousands fell on the riders as their bus pulled into the station. The initial Freedom Rides ended in Jackson, Mississippi, but they galvanized other campaigns. By the end of the year, integration came to interstate travel in the U.S.

Soon another barrier fell, the one barring blacks from entering traditionally white Southern universities. In 1962, James Meredith was blocked from enrolling at the University of Mississippi by Gov. Ross Barnett. After days of confrontation, U.S. marshals were summoned to escort Meredith to the campus. That night full-scale rioting broke out, resulting in two deaths. Only when President Kennedy ordered army troops to the scene did fighting cease.

The fight against segregation grew fiercer. In the spring of 1963, Rev. King initiated demonstrations in Birmingham, Alabama, which he dubbed "the most segregated city in the U.S." The infamous Birmingham police chief, T. Eugene

▼ **Demonstrators in Birmingham, Alabama, huddle in a doorway against the fierce blast of a fire hose. The water's force tore the clothes off some protesters' backs.**

Black Muslim leader Malcolm X

▼ On March 21, 1965, three thousand voting rights marchers cross the Edmund Pettus Bridge toward the Jefferson Davis Highway, leading from Selma to Montgomery. Inset: A young supporter at a California rally.

(Bull) Connor, ordered the arrests of hundreds of protesters, including children and King himself. When thousands of demonstrators thronged downtown Birmingham, Connor met them with attack dogs and fire hoses. As the media captured every nasty turn of the confrontation, the King forces gained leverage. Local officials and businessmen finally backed down and agreed to desegregate some public facilities and to hire blacks.

In August 1963 some 200,000 civil rights advocates, black and white, marched on Washington, D.C. "Civil Rights — Now!" "Integrated Schools — Now!" "Decent Housing — Now!" their placards read. King addressed them movingly: "I have a dream that one day on the red hills of Georgia the sons of former slaves and the sons of former slave-owners will be able to sit down together at the table of brotherhood . . . that my four little children will one day live in a nation where they will not be judged by the color of their skin, but by the content of their character."

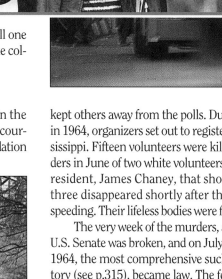

The Right To Vote Is Won

Black voters had long been discriminated against in the Southern U.S., where literacy tests and poll taxes discouraged most of them from registering and racist intimidation

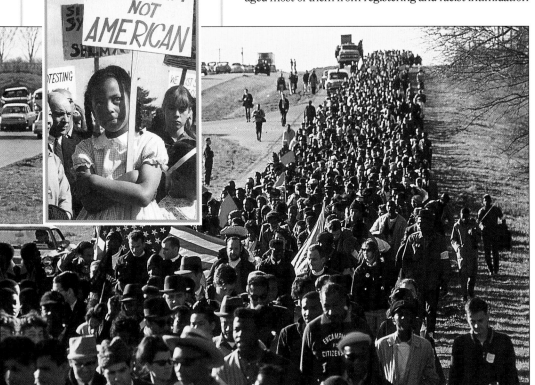

kept others away from the polls. During Freedom Summer in 1964, organizers set out to register all black voters in Mississippi. Fifteen volunteers were killed. But it was the murders in June of two white volunteers, and a black Mississippi resident, James Chaney, that shocked people most. The three disappeared shortly after their car was stopped for speeding. Their lifeless bodies were found weeks later.

The very week of the murders, a 75-day filibuster in the U.S. Senate was broken, and on July 2 the Civil Rights Act of 1964, the most comprehensive such legislation in U.S. history (see p.315), became law. The federal government now stood squarely behind the fight to end racial discrimination.

By early 1965 Rev. King decided the time was ripe to dramatize the push for black voter registration and to muster support for a voting rights bill. He chose Selma, Alabama, as the demonstration site. The Selma protesters were viciously attacked and several were killed. On March 15, President Johnson went before Congress to urge passage of a voting rights bill, saying that Selma exhibited "the effort of American Negroes to secure for themselves the full blessings of American life." "We shall overcome," he declared, invoking the battle cry of the civil rights movement. On March 21 some 3,000 protesters left Selma for an 87-kilometre march to the Alabama capital. Four days later they entered Montgomery, where 25,000 people joined them in a victory rally. That August, Congress passed the Voting Rights Act of 1965.

◀

Summer after hot summer, as Dr. King's dream remained unfulfilled, racially motivated violence erupted: New York in 1964, Watts in 1965, Chicago, Cleveland, and San Francisco in 1966, Newark and Detroit (left) in 1967. The flames were fanned by militants such as Stokely Carmichael (inset), who, after James Earl Ray shot King in April 1968, told followers, "Get your gun."

After three volunteers for the Freedom Summer black voter registration drive were killed, a new group of recruits signed up for the cause. Above, a student talks to a potential voter.

Days after the Act was signed into law, violence erupted again. Watts, a black neighborhood in Los Angeles, exploded in racial rioting after a black motorist resisted arrest and was shoved into a squad car. Within hours area residents took to the streets. As many as 80,000 rioters went on a spree, torching buildings and looting stores. Some 14,000 national guardsmen helped the Los Angeles police restore order. The violence exacted a heavy price: 34 people were killed, 891 injured, and 3,758 arrested.

As racial tensions shifted northward, many inner city blacks rejected the nonviolent strategies of Dr. King for more radical alternatives. Black Muslims exhorted blacks to found their own schools, businesses, and, ultimately, their own nation. Their most charismatic spokesman, Malcolm X, left the Nation of Islam in 1964 to form his own sect. Then, on February 21, 1965, Malcolm X was gunned down, and a more extreme group came to the fore. They were the Black Panthers, who armed themselves and provided black communities with "protection" from the police.

On April 4, 1968, the last hope of nonviolence as a tactic seemed all but lost when Dr. King himself was assassinated in Memphis. King, evidently foreseeing his own death, had told his followers: "I just want to do God's will. And He's allowed me to go to the mountain. And I've looked over, and I've seen the Promised Land. I may not get there with you. But I want you to know tonight that we as a people will get to the Promised Land."

Black Pride: Claiming an Afro-American Heritage

SING of our Race! SING out our Destiny / to your sons, to your warrior sons — in the ghettos, / on the tenant farms, / in the swelling cities by the Western Sea." So the American poet Rolland Snellings (who later adopted the Muslim name Askia Muhammad Touré) celebrated the reaffirmation of black society and culture that took place in the 1960's.

Prominent black leaders sought to establish the unique identity of their communities, apart from the context of white society. Alternatives to the word *Negro* were proposed: *black, Afro-American* — or just *African.* Malcolm X encouraged blacks to follow his example and drop their surnames, which he termed "slave names given by the slavemaster to our fathers during slavery time." And blacks reexamined their heritage and strove for a more vital connection to their African past.

Instead of straightening their hair to conform to white standards of beauty, blacks began to style their hair in Afros or braids and adorn it in African fashion. Many wore African jewellery, headwear, and garments, from *bubas* (scoop-necked dresses) and *djellabas* (flowing robes) to *dashiki* shirts and *gele* turbans. "Black is beautiful" became a theme of the times.

The new sense of pride influenced worship practices. Some blacks turned to African faiths, such as the religion of the Nigerian Yoruba, who recognize over 400 gods and spirits. And in 1966 a black American created *Kwanzaa* (Swahili for "first"), a Christmastime festival during which participants recite African tales, prepare traditional meals, and reflect on guiding principles by which to live.

"ONE GIANT LEAP FOR MANKIND"

"Before the first men tasted time, we thought of you. You were a wonder to us,

unattainable. . . . Now our hands have touched you in your depth of night."

— *Poet Archibald MacLeish, on the moon landing*

On April 12, 1961, Soviet cosmonaut Yuri Gagarin circled the earth once and landed safely 725 kilometres southeast of Moscow, the first human being to orbit the planet. Gagarin's astonishing flight, following on the heels of several Soviet space triumphs, dealt a hard blow to the pride of the United States. A month later Project Mercury astronaut Alan Shepard, Jr., rocketed into space for a 480-kilometre, 15-minute suborbital loop. It was a significant feat for the U.S. space program, but it was a poor second to the Russian's 40,000-kilometre flight.

Sensing the United States' mounting anxieties

Cosmonaut Yuri Gagarin strapped into Vostok I

Top: Astronaut Edward H. White II, tethered to the Gemini 4 capsule, takes his historic 22-minute walk in zero gravity as the craft orbits earth on its June 3–7, 1965, flight.

▶

A souvenir "medal," complete with space-suited figurine, commemorated the first moon landing.

FIRST
MICHAEL COLLINS
EDWIN E. ALDRIN
NEIL A. ARMSTRONG
ON THE MOON JULY 21st 1969

about the Soviet challenge in space, President John Kennedy made a bold promise. He vowed to land a man on the moon "before this decade is out. . . . No single space project in this period will be more impressive to mankind. . . ." Vice President Lyndon Johnson supported the president's goal and continued to do so throughout his own presidency.

Naysayers labelled the Apollo mission to the moon extravagant, even unattainable. It would cost $24 billion, use the labor of nearly half a million workers, and tie up much-needed scientific brainpower for several years. But Apollo's advocates argued that "whoever controls space may well control the earth," and the public raised few objections. Led by the National Aeronautics and Space Administration centre (NASA) in Houston, the massive program of research, development, and training sped forward.

In February 1962 John H. Glenn, Jr., orbited the earth three times. Three more Mercury flights followed, and the program was termed a success. "We are through the gates," exulted one Mercury team member.

The next step for the United States was the two-man space shots of the Gemini program. This time an on-board computer calculated many of the spacecraft's functions, from complex manoeuvres to reentries. In June 1965 Edward White became the first American to walk in space while James McDivitt took pictures from inside the capsule. White wore a 21-layered "moon suit." It shielded him from radiation, temperatures ranging from minus 101° to minus 157°C, and micrometeorites travelling hundreds of times faster than a bullet. A gold-coated "umbilical" cord anchored White to his craft as he moved by the propulsion of a jet gun. The astronaut, exhilarated by his encounter with the infinitude of space, called his return to the module "the saddest moment of my life."

Meanwhile, a Soviet cosmonaut had walked in space three months before White, and the Russians claimed the first woman in space and the first unmanned soft landing on the moon. But in the mid-1960's Soviet technology reached its limit, and the Russians began to recycle old craft. Still, they kept up a convincing propaganda campaign and, to all outward appearances, remained neck and neck with the United States in the space race.

Barely under way, the Apollo program suffered a terrible setback: in January 1967 astronauts Virgil (Gus)

▶

Despite an instrument failure, John Glenn (shown prior to suiting up for takeoff) successfully completed his mission.

Grissom, Ed White, and Roger Chaffee died in a flash fire that incinerated the interior of their module during a training exercise on the ground. The module design was altered substantially, and in December 1968 *Apollo 8* orbited the moon 10 times. In May the following year *Apollo 10* flew to within 15 kilometres of the lunar surface.

The true test came on July 16, 1969. Years of work and billions of dollars had led up to this one flight, *Apollo 11*. The rocket blasted off. Four days later, Michael Collins orbited the moon in the command ship *Columbia* as Neil Armstrong and Edwin (Buzz) Aldrin, Jr., dropped toward the lunar landscape in the landing vehicle *Eagle*. Pilot Armstrong, realizing the module's automatic navigation was steering them toward rough terrain, seized the controls and touched the craft down safely in the smooth Sea of Tranquillity. "The *Eagle* has landed," he reported back to NASA.

Buzz Aldrin makes his imprint on the moon while Neil Armstrong, reflected in Aldrin's visor, takes pictures. Bottom right: Quarantined to be checked for "space bugs," the Apollo 11 astronauts are greeted by President Richard Nixon.

Armstrong emerged from the craft as a television camera, mounted on the base of the lunar lander, beamed stunning images back to earth. When his foot touched the ground, he said, "That's one small step for a man, one giant leap for mankind." In their bulky space suits, Aldrin and Armstrong frolicked like bears, moving strangely in gravity a sixth that of the earth. They collected moon rocks, set up experiments for later research, and shed equipment to lighten the return trip. They spoke to President Richard Nixon and then lifted off to hook up with *Columbia*. The astronauts splashed down safely on July 24. Americans were euphoric: less than a decade after humanity's first fleeting moments beyond the safe blanket of the earth's atmosphere, President Kennedy's promise had been fulfilled.

Rᴵᴄʜ ʏɪᴇʟᴅs ꜰʀᴏᴍ sᴄɪᴇɴᴄᴇ

In many fields of knowledge — from astronomy to space technology, aeronautics to marine biology, computers to medicine — scientists made dazzling finds.

The launching of Alouette 1 *made Canada the third nation in space.*

The 120-kilogram Tiros 1 *enabled scientists to monitor cloud formations and track cyclones.*

Aʟᴍᴏsᴛ seven years before *Apollo 11* landed on the moon, Canada launched a satellite from the Vandenburg air base in California, and became the third nation in space. *Alouette 1,* sent up for research purposes to study the ionosphere, was the first of four research satellites Canada would launch over the period of 10 years.

Although these satellites provided data, they did not take photographs. But others did. The world got its first close-up look at the lunar landscape in 1964, when *Ranger 7,* an unmanned U.S. rocket, took 4,316 stunning photographs as it approached, and finally crash-landed on, the moon's Sea of Clouds. In 1965, another U.S. space wanderer, *Mariner 4,* gave a revealing look at Mars — and a disappointing one. *Mariner* pictures showed a terrain devoid of higher forms of life, and even of Martians. The existence of simpler forms of life, however, remained unknown.

As spacecraft probed the void, astrophysicists explored the cosmos by training their telescopes on distant phenomena. In 1963 astronomers discovered quasars, luminous energy sources at the centre of galaxies billions of light-years from earth. Quasars seemed to provide a tantalizing clue to the origin and destiny of our own universe. In 1967 Jocelyn Bell, a student at Cambridge University, made another crucial observation: she detected signals coming from pulsars, densely com-

Signals from Europe are bounced off Telstar *and* Early Bird *and reach the ear of "Big Horn," a 340-tonne antenna in Andover, Maine.*

These women of Project Tektite II leave their underwater dormitory to conduct experiments in the ocean surrounding St. John, Virgin Islands.

pacted stars that scientists theorized were formed in the aftermath of the collapse of supernovas.

In the 1960's NASA entered a partnership with industry to come up with practical uses for space technology. NASA launched the first weather satellite, *Tiros 1,* in 1960. With each 100 minute orbit of the earth, *Tiros* recorded shifting climate patterns in thousands of overlapping snapshots. The satellite *Telstar* transmitted television broadcasts across the Atlantic Ocean beginning in 1962, the first link in future worldwide communications. And the *Early Bird* satellite, introduced in 1965, greatly expanded the transatlantic telephone network.

Canada too expanded its interests in space. In 1964 it joined the global satellite communications system Intelsat, and five years later established Telesat Canada Corporation, run joint-

Before it began its test run, the X-15 plane was carried aloft under the wing of a B-52 bomber.

ly by the government and private telecommunications companies. In 1972 Canada became the first country to send a commercial domestic communications satellite into geostationary orbit (which keeps the communications antenna always pointing toward earth).

The Soviets sent aloft the world's first supersonic transport (SST), the Tupolev TU-144, in 1968. British and French companies teamed up to develop their own SST, the Concorde, which made its maiden voyage in 1969 and, within seven years, was shuttling jet-setters and business clients across the Atlantic in under four hours. Among experimental aircraft, the U.S.'s X-15, equipped with a liquid-fuelled rocket engine, achieved mind-boggling speeds of 8,000 kilometres per hour, seven to eight times the speed of sound.

While aeronautical engineers broke the sound barrier, marine biologists plumbed the depths of the underwater world. Astronaut Scott Carpenter joined the crew of *Sealab II* to help test human endurance in water pressures at 60 metres below sea level. And the *Tektite I* aquanauts lived for two months in a high-tech laboratory, studying marine life under the Caribbean Sea.

Medical Miracles and Health Warnings

In medicine, too, goals that had once seemed fanciful rapidly became realities. South African doctor Christiaan Barnard performed the first successful heart transplant in 1967. The recipient survived a mere 18 days, but a second transplant patient lived for more than 19 months. By decade's end, 148 patients, including an eight-day-old baby, had received healthy hearts. There was new hope too for victims of coronary artery disease, in the coronary artery bypass operation.

▼ *Dr. Christiaan N. Barnard performed the first heart transplant, at Groote Schuur Hospital in Cape Town, South Africa.*

The crippling disease polio has been almost eradicated, due in large part to an oral vaccine approved in 1961. Other vaccines first administered in the 1960's prevent the childhood diseases of measles, rubella (German measles), and spinal meningitis. In the field of obstetrics, doctors first used amniocentesis, in which amniotic fluid is drawn from the mother's uterus to diagnose inherited disorders before a child's birth. And surgeons found an invaluable tool in the laser, which could be used to perform delicate eye operations and destroy cancerous growths.

After two decades of emphasizing improved living standards as the path to public health, the Canadian government took a dramatic turn in 1968. It introduced a national health insurance scheme, popularly known as medicare, to provide treatment through hospitals and clinics. From that point, the main thrust of public health became the treatment of every individual.

From the computer silicon chip, patented in 1961, to the industrial robot, introduced in 1962, science and technology pervaded daily life. The relentless march of progress left some casualties in its path. Power generators produced toxic waste hazards. Residue from pesticides threatened animal life and the food supply. Oil tanker accidents and offshore drilling leaks contaminated beaches. Ordinary citizens were beginning to realize that modern technology had drawbacks as well as benefits.

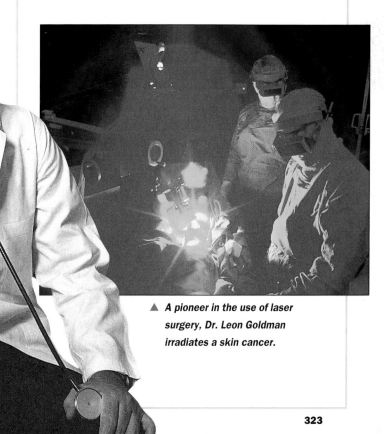
▲ *A pioneer in the use of laser surgery, Dr. Leon Goldman irradiates a skin cancer.*

LOOK, KIDS! CRAZY FUN AND GAMES

Before protests, alternative lifestyles, and general rebellion became popular pursuits, some teens spent their after-school hours doing little more than surfing, skateboarding, cruising, and dancing till dawn.

If youth culture took hold in the 1950's, in the early 1960's it took over. Teenagers looked at the workaday routine of their parents and, finding the older generation wanting, embarked on their own quest for pleasure.

One sign of the times was the surfing craze, with its worship of the deep suntan, the muscled male, the overexposed female ("Itsy Bitsy Teenie Weenie Yellow Polkadot Bikini" was a top song in 1960), and, most important, the cool attitude. Surfing bliss meant to "hang ten" (toes, that is) and "shoot the curl" (beneath the crest of a breaking wave) in Malibu, California; Waikiki, Hawaii; Queenscliffe, Australia — wherever the perfect wave rolled in. Teen idols Frankie Avalon and Annette Funicello starred in movies, including *Beach Party, Bikini Beach,* and *How to Stuff a Wild Bikini,* that glamorized the carefree lifestyle of the beach bum. And music groups such as the Surfaris, the Pyramids, and the Beach Boys — four clean-cut youths with a catchy

California sound — spread the gospel to the rest of the world in dozens of recordings. Ottawa's Paul Anka, whose "Diana" had already established him as an international figure, was joined in stardom by the Winnipeg rock group Guess Who. Then, as the decade ended, people began humming "Snowbird," a hit recorded by an alto from Nova Scotia. Canadians who had listened to her on CBC Halifax in the late 1960's already knew that Anne Murray's voice was something special.

When the sun went down, the partying began. Set up a phonograph, get out the record collection, dim the lights, and any teenager could turn the family rec room into a

▼ *Souped-up automobiles, such as this custom-painted 1933-vintage Ford, were the envy of every hot-rodder.*

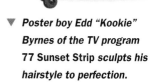

▼ *Poster boy Edd "Kookie" Byrnes of the TV program* 77 Sunset Strip *sculpts his hairstyle to perfection.*

The Beach Boys don Pendleton shirts in the photo shoot for the cover of their first album, Surfin' Safari.

The Barbie Phenomenon

Behind the invention of the first Barbie® doll is the story of a real little girl. Barbara Handler loved dressing paper dolls in cutout clothes. Her dolls weren't the baby-faced innocents usually associated with child's play. Instead, they resembled adults and had wardrobes to match.

Barbara's parents, Ruth and Elliot, started the toy company Mattel in 1945. In 1950 Ruth had an inspiration: to create a three-dimensional version of Barbara's paper doll and market it to girls her daughter's age.

Barbie hit the toy stores in March 1959. She was made of vinyl plastic with holes in her feet so she could be propped up on a stand. She came wearing a zebra-striped one-piece bathing suit, over her curvaceous 14 x 7.5 x 12 cm frame, and sported hoop earrings, shoes, and hepcat sunglasses. Her wardrobe boasted 22 outfits, from pedal pushers to a wedding gown.

Little girls adored Barbie and, by 1963, were sending her 500 letters a week. Mattel, Inc. became one of the largest toy manufacturers in North America.

1965, "probably also thinks that a girl is called a 'chick.'" Spin-off dances proliferated: the swim, monkey, pony, the shag, the dog, mashed potato, frug, wobble, watusi, and a dance whose only rule was to follow the beat, the jerk.

The beach and the dance floor were popular spots for meeting and pairing up, but adolescent life still centred around the automobile. The surfer's dream car was the modest woody, an old wood-panelled station wagon. "Revheads" (surfing lingo for people who preferred automobiles to surfboards) lavished attention on their "muscle cars" — Pontiac 409's, Barracudas, Stingrays, Dodge Chargers, Mustangs — the last of the great fuel-guzzlers. They also customized earlier cars, "chopped and channelled" them, "Frenched" the headlights, or "headers," and installed Hollywood mufflers, or "glasspacks," in the exhaust system to give their 400-horsepower engines a throaty roar. Singing groups intoned paeans to the automobile in tunes from "Little Deuce Coupe" to "Hey Little Cobra." In a hit song by Jan and Dean, "The Little Old Lady From Pasadena" drag races through town to a chorus of voices urging, "Go granny, Go granny, Go granny, Go!" In teen paradise the road and the surf beckoned, the sun always shone, and the party never ended.

◄ *"Grab your board and go sidewalk surfin' with me," sang surf music duo Jan and Dean. In 1965 manufacturers sold $30 million worth of skateboards to avid practitioners of the sport.*

▼ *Goldie Hawn, the dizzy blonde comedienne, lounges in little more than body paint, a fad made popular in discotheques beginning in the mid-1960's.*

dance floor. Everyone wanted to try out a sexy new step, the Twist, popularized in 1960 by singer Chubby Checker on Dick Clark's television show *American Bandstand*. Twisters didn't make contact. Instead, they gyrated in place as if drying their backs with a towel while rubbing out a cigarette with their feet.

Some "oldsters" expressed horror at the new development. "What has happened to our concept of beauty and decency and morality?" demanded former President Dwight D. Eisenhower. *Time* magazine advanced the theory that twisters might be reenacting "some ancient tribal puberty rite." But the dance quickly caught on with the trendy set. Before long, it seemed the entire over-30 crowd had joined the dance mania, co-opting the twist altogether. It was time for teens to take up some new steps. "Anyone who still believes the Twist is in," wrote reporter Gloria Steinem in

► *Dancers contort themselves in the Twist. Singer Chubby Checker instructed twisters to take a prizefighter's stance, swivel hips, twist feet, and move the body si de to side.*

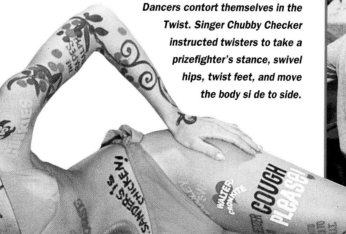

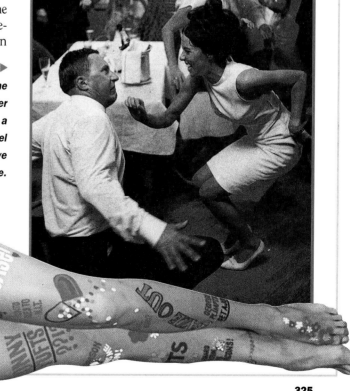

An Explosion of New Sounds

Rock music erupted in the soulful syncopations of the Motor City groups, in the potent voice of folk, and in the harmonies and discordances of the British bands.

With $700 in his pocket and a fervent desire to escape the Detroit ghetto, a young black song-writer named Berry Gordy, Jr., established his own production company, Motown Records. Motown signed on dozens of black artists drawn from the rich pool of talent found in Detroit at the time: The Four Tops, The Temptations, The Marvelettes, Smokey Robinson and The Miracles, Little Stevie Wonder — the list goes on. The Motown look and sound were perfected by The Supremes, three slinky female vocalists, including Diana Ross, whose smooth voices matched their choreographed moves.

Meanwhile, a white entrepreneur, Phil Spector, was at work developing his own unique music — a "Wall of Sound" — by throwing everything from Moog synthesizers to glockenspiels behind his singers. The recording technique would earn Spector a string of gold records and the nickname The First Tycoon of Teen before he hit age 25.

In smoke-filled coffee-houses, a countercultural sound evolved from the folk music earlier popularized by Pete Seeger and The Weavers. Three clean-cut college boys, The Kingston Trio, polished the genre with their hit "Tom Dooley." But to many, the pure sound of the solo voice accompanied by acoustic guitar, as performed by Joni Mitchell and Joan Baez, came to epitomize folk and the directness of its message. Alberta's Joni Mitchell sang of themes relevant to the 1960's, introducing a rich poetry into her lyrics. Joan Baez went still further, using folk music as a means of political protest. Baez performed old American songs as well as new tunes, many of them composed by a scruffy young man named Robert

The title song of this 1964 Supremes album topped the Billboard charts for two weeks.

▶ **Jimi Hendrix, who died of a drug overdose at 27, wailed out masterful guitar licks.**

▼ **Bob Dylan outraged folk-music purists when he "went electric" in 1964.**

▲ **Joni Mitchell charmed audiences with her poetic folk songs.**

▶ **Beatles Paul McCartney, Ringo Starr, George Harrison, and John Lennon**

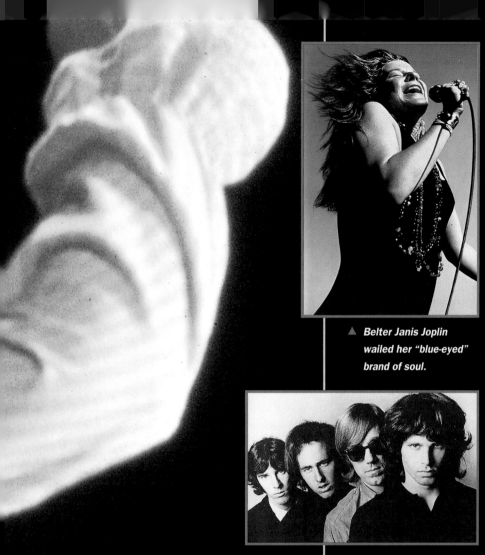

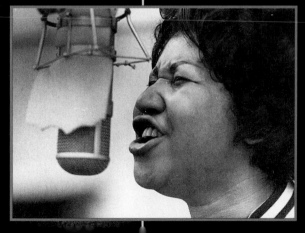

Belter Janis Joplin wailed her "blue-eyed" brand of soul.

Jim Morrison and The Doors evolved a hallucinatory rock style.

Supercharged vocalist James Brown came to be known as the Godfather of Soul.

Aretha Franklin earned the title First Lady of Soul.

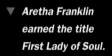

Zimmerman, or Bob Dylan, as he called himself. Dylan's lyrics bespoke a growing social consciousness among North America's youth: "Mothers and fathers throughout the land. . . . Your sons and your daughters are beyond your command." His "The Times They Are A-Changin' " and "Blowin' in the Wind" became anthems for participants in the 1960's protest movement.

The versatile group, The Mamas and the Papas, bridged the genres of rock and folk music.

Another 1960's rock revolution originated on the other side of the Atlantic, in Great Britain. Growing up in Liverpool, the foursome who would become the Beatles listened to gospel-based styles and the progenitors of rock and roll: singers such as Chuck Berry, Elvis Presley, Buddy Holly, and Little Richard. Then the group, known first as the Quarrymen, began to write their own distinctive music. Upbeat, tuneful recordings such as "Love Me Do" and "Please, Please Me" were early hits in England. With their North American tour in 1964, the Beatles, already an international phenomenon, launched a full-scale "British invasion" of the New World. On the heels of the winsome mop tops came the Dave Clark Five, the raw intensity of Britain's Rolling Stones, whose sexually charged performance on the *Ed Sullivan Show* caused the host to apologize for booking them, and then dozens of other English groups, including the Animals, Zombies, Yardbirds, and the Who.

A new generation of artists met the British challenge. Out of a fertile mix of protest, the folk scene, and the hippie movement arose a slew of groups who wore rock's anti-establishment uniform of long hair and weird clothing. They adopted colorful names, such as The Mamas and the Papas, The Lovin' Spoonful, The Mothers of Invention, The Grateful Dead, and Jefferson Airplane. Many of the groups used music as a weapon to assault conventional values or to shock. The Doors spun haunting, poetic images in "Light My Fire." Country Joe and the Fish mocked the wages of the Vietnam War with "Feel Like I'm Fixin' to Die Rag." Guitarist Jimi Hendrix twisted "The Star-Spangled Banner" into an electrified scream of protest. Simon and Garfunkel softened the message in "Sound of Silence": "The words of the prophets are written on the subway walls." Many of the rock artists would burn out, or die young, but not before they had forever changed popular music.

SUPER YEARS FOR SPORTS

Television, sponsors, team owners, and the athletes

themselves discovered to their delight that our

appetite for sports seemed to just grow and grow.

More teams, greater TV revenues, shiny new stadiums — all these fed the sports boom of the 1960's. Major league baseball expanded from 16 teams to 24. One of them, the Montreal Expos, was the first major league baseball team outside the United States. The lure of television revenue also brought a reverse expansion as the National Hockey League moved into six additional American cities, fattening revenues for owners and swelling scoring statistics as established teams romped over the expansion teams. Multiuse stadiums, suitable for more than one sport, sprang up in a dozen cities. The glitziest was the roofed, air-conditioned $32-million Houston Astrodome.

Such splendid trappings called for stellar performances, and the decade's athletes responded. In baseball the

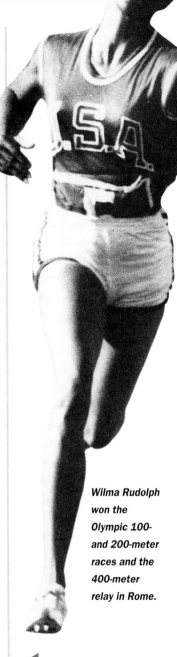

Wilma Rudolph won the Olympic 100- and 200-meter races and the 400-meter relay in Rome.

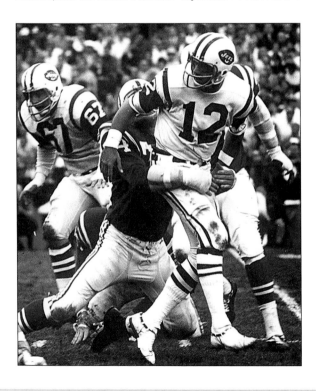

Cocky Joe Namath (No. 12) "guaranteed" his Jets would beat Baltimore in the 1969 Super Bowl, and they did.

▲ *Green Bay coach Vince Lombardi is credited with saying: "Winning isn't everything . . . it's the only thing."*

1961 season saw New York Yankee Roger Maris, in the last game of the regular season, best the record 60 home runs Babe Ruth had belted in 1927. The next year Los Angeles Dodger Maury Wills surpassed another immortal's record, stealing 104 bases to eclipse Ty Cobb's 1915 total of 96. Los Angeles Dodgers pitcher Sandy Koufax was a sensation in 1965. Worried before the season that arthritis in his left elbow would end his career, Koufax never missed a start, struck out a record 382 batters, and pitched a no-hitter. Two years later, Canadian Ferguson Jenkins, pitching for the Chicago Cubs, began the first of six consecutive seasons in which he won 20 or more games.

In football, Ottawa Rough Riders quarterback Russ Jackson dominated the game through the decade, passing for 23,341 yards and running for 5,045 yards more. He capped a remarkable career in 1969 by leading Ottawa to a Grey Cup championship. In 1979, an American survey would name him the best professional football player ever.

American football's Super Bowl I, in 1967, pitted the Green Bay Packers, winners of four NFL titles in the previous six years, against the Kansas City Chiefs of the upstart AFL. The Packers thrashed the Chiefs, 35–10. The result seemed to prove the superiority of the NFL, but two years later quarterback Joe Namath of the New York Jets, dubbed "Broadway Joe" for his showmanship on and off the field, gave the AFL its first Super Bowl win.

Maurice Richard's fiery hockey career ended in 1969, but fans found compensation in the equally intense Phil Esposito, in the remarkably offensive defenceman Bobby Orr, and in the muscular Bobby Hull whose thunderous slapshot tore past goalies a record 58 times in the 1968–69 season. Fans of the older ice sport of curling found their heroes in Alberta's Northcott Rink which began a series of Canadian world curling championships in 1968.

Arnold Palmer and Jack Nicklaus, as likable as fierce competitors can be, staged epic battles on the golf links. Arnie won the U.S. Open in 1960, the British Open twice, the Masters four times. The long-driving Nicklaus, then 22, became Palmer's chief rival in 1962, beating him in a play-off to win the U.S. Open.

In tennis, Billie Jean King captured the women's singles, doubles, and mixed-doubles titles in 1967, both in the U.S. and Britain. And Arthur Ashe, in 1968, won the first U.S. Open. Like many athletes of the 1960's, Ashe quickly learned about product endorsements. "The idea," he confided, "is to have a Coke in one hand, a Wilson racquet in the other . . . when they take my picture."

Dodging the poles, Nancy Greene slaloms downhill to become one of Canada's top female athletes. Boston Celtics John Havlicek (left) was a key player in 1966.

North Americans made their mark on the decade's three Olympics. Among the gold medallists in Rome in 1960 were the United States' Wilma Rudolph (photo, preceding page) and Canada's Anne Heggtveit, who won her country's first Olympic Gold in skiing. Heggtveit's fellow team member Nancy Greene won the 1967 World Cup, and in 1968 took the Olympic Gold in the giant slalom and the Silver in the slalom. She was named Canada's Athlete of the Year in 1968. Vancouver's Harry Jerome, who had won the Olympic Bronze for the 100 metres in 1960, went on to win the 100-yard dash at the Commonwealth Games in 1966 and the 100-metre dash at the Pan-American Games in 1967.

Increasing leisure time was spent not only in watching sports, but in participating. More attractive equipment such as buckle boots, stretch pants and metal skis drew Canadians to the winter slopes. So did the glamor of the winning performances of their athletes. Bicycles were improved, with multiple gears and ultralight frames. These enhancements, combined with growing environmental and fitness awareness, moved the bicycle up from child's toy to adult's status symbol. Canadian production of sporting goods soared from $31.6 million in 1960 to $81.7 million in just 10 years. For amateurs, as for professionals, sport had become big business.

"Float Like a Butterfly, Sting Like a Bee"

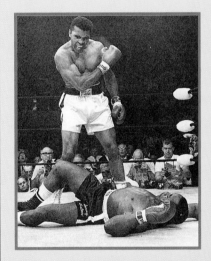

Not a few sportswriters and boxing fans have called Muhammad Ali the greatest heavyweight fighter of all time. Ali agreed, describing himself as "the greatest" and "a man/ With iron fists and a beautiful tan./ He talks a lot and he boasts indeed/ Of a powerful punch and blinding speed."

That kind of unabashed self-promotion got Ali a lot of press coverage and made him enemies as well as friends. From the time, as 18-year-old Cassius Clay, he won the light-heavyweight title at the 1960 Summer Olympics in Rome, there were people who saw him as a loudmouth (Gaseous Cassius) and wanted him humbled. But it would be years before any boxer would humble Ali. After he turned pro in 1960, he won 19 straight bouts, often predicting in what round he would finish off his opponent. He earned the chance to meet the heavyweight champion, the menacing ex-convict Sonny Liston. Before their fight in Miami Beach on February 25, 1964, just 3 of 46 ringside boxing writers picked Clay to win. Clay himself predicted that he would "float like a butterfly, sting like a bee," and knock out Liston in the eighth round. "Round eight to prove I'm great," Clay had announced at the prefight weigh-in. For once Ali had sold himself short. A hurting, bleeding Liston could not continue after the sixth round. Cassius Clay, at 22, was heavyweight champion of the world.

That same year, Clay made a momentous decision. Changing his name to Muhammad Ali, he became a follower of the Nation of Islam. He went on fighting superbly (defeating Liston again in a rematch, shown at left), but his chosen religion was leading him toward a confrontation that would cast a shadow over his name for many years. On April 28, 1967, in the middle of the Vietnam War, the champion refused to be drafted into the U.S. Army. Though he repeatedly explained (right) that his religion did not allow him to serve, a court convicted him of refusing induction, boxing authorities stripped him of his title, and he was effectively barred from boxing.

Three and a half years later the U.S. Supreme Court reversed Ali's conviction. It took him three more years, but he regained the heavyweight title. If Ali's judg-

ment was often questioned, his courage in the ring was not. In 1975, in the Philippines, he fought Joe Frazier in one of the most brutal bouts in history. Ali, with characteristic rhyming flair, had billed the bout as the "Thrilla in Manilla." He won, but after it was over, reporters asked him to describe the fight. Slowly and gravely Ali responded, "It was next to death."

NORTH AMERICAN FOOD & DRINK

Banana Split
This favorite dessert, with a three-scoop minimum and a reputation as a belly buster, made its appearance around 1920.

Milk
After pasteurization became commonplace around the turn of the century, people drank increasing amounts of milk.

Bacon and Eggs
Early risers across the continent hunker down to this rib-sticking breakfast.

Processed Cheese
Gourmets may scoff, but it's an institution in cheese steaks and grilled sandwiches.

Jell-O
Around 1900 a cook mixed powdered gelatin, fruit flavors, and sugar and dubbed the "dessert with a wiggle" Jell-O.

Kool-Aid
First available only through mail order in 1914, this number-one-selling powdered soft drink has wet whistles for decades — from thirsty youngsters to parched soldiers in Operation Desert Shield.

W hen an ice cream vendor at the 1904 St. Louis Purchase Exhibition ran out of serving dishes, a neighboring vendor reportedly gave him a paper-thin pastry rolled into a cone, and the rest is history. An all-time favorite, popcorn, was supposedly brought by a Wampanoag brave to the first Thanksgiving. Peanut butter was originally created by a Missouri doctor as a health food.

Whether stumbled upon by accident or born of entrepreneurial genius, some foods are known the world over as uniquely North American. But for every favorite local dish, there is one with a distinctly foreign origin. Pizza, bagels, and chow mein all arrived with immigrants, became westernized, and are now as familiar as barbecued chicken and corn on the cob. With the influx of newer immigrants from the Pacific Rim and former Soviet-bloc nations, North Americans continue to open their minds and palates and add new tastes to the cooking pot.

Dagwood Sandwich
Cartoon character Dagwood Bumstead first slapped together his famous snack on April 16, 1936.

Peanut Butter
More than half of America's peanut crop goes to producing the sticky stuff.

Home Canning
Every rural homemaker knew the secrets of preserving the garden's bounty — using a process developed by a French confectioner to save Napoleon Bonaparte's armies from starvation.

Apple Pie
Eaten plain, deep-dish, or à la mode, it has long been a favorite.

Turkey
Truly North American, turkey and cranberries continue to take centre stage at Thanksgiving dinners.

Coca-Cola

Concocted in 1886 by a pharmacist as a headache tonic, the carbonated, sugared soda won 20th-century popularity as "the pause that refreshes."

A Cavalcade of Confections

The Hershey Bar made its debut in 1894, followed by Cracker Jack (1896), Whitman's Sampler and Life Savers (1912), and M&M's (1941).

Potato Chips

This crispy snack was once called Saratoga Chips, after the resort where it was invented.

Ice Cream

North Americans consume some 27 litres of ice cream per person a year.

Frozen Foods

Scientist Clarence Birdseye learned to quick-freeze caribou steaks in Labrador in 1914, thus starting a new food industry.

The Best Spinach You've Ever Tasted

OR DOUBLE YOUR MONEY BACK!

Snow Crop

Guaranteed Top of the Frozen Food Crop

TV Dinner

The first — this one features chicken parmigiana —appeared in the early 1950's.

Popcorn

Once called "rice corn" or "parching corn," it reigns as the undisputed king of movie-time snacks.

Hot Dogs

Germans brought them over; Nathan's in Coney Island made them famous.

Breakfast Cereal

Born of a health movement begun in the late 19th century, and spearheaded by men like Dr. John H. Kellogg and C. W. Post, cereals like these have endured over the decades.

French Fries

Called chips in England, and *frites* in Quebec, these sizzly spuds are a North American staple.

READER'S DIGEST

LIVE LONGER COOKBOOK

500 DELICIOUS RECIPES FOR HEALTHY LIVING

PABLUM

PRECOOKED
mixed cereal
16 OZ NET

TWO EASY STEPS

Hamburger

Roadside stands helped to popularize this ground-meat sandwich. Give it the works!

Healthy Eating

The news that healthy eating means better living has people practicing in their kitchens what the nutrition experts preach.

Pablum

Babies around the world approved when Canadian doctors invented Pablum, a precooked cereal that is now the first step toward solid foods.

◄ This impish-looking mod sports an op-art miniskirt and matching cap.

Mod, mini, maxi, and more

A spirit of rebellion took hold of the fashion world as a crop of young, imaginative designers disassembled and reinvented the art of dressing.

Fashion started off conservatively enough. Young, demure Jacqueline Kennedy — who as the United States' First Lady reportedly spent $50,000 on clothes in 16 months — became the role model for style-conscious women. No rebel, she took her cues from the Parisian couturiers who had long led the fashion world. Her bouffant hairdos, pillbox hats, and sleeveless shifts sent thousands of women scurrying to shops and hairstylists in search of the Jackie look.

Meanwhile, strange things were afoot in London — in the boutiques along Carnaby Street, a little byway off the main shopping artery, and on the King's Road. A new generation of designers, most of them from working-class backgrounds and still in their twenties, was busily rewriting the book on taste.

Mod style turned the world of high fashion on its ear. For the boys, as exemplified by the rock group the Beatles, mod meant high pointy-toed boots, mop hair, lapelless jackets, and stovepipe pants. Mod girls wore high-rise hairdos, tiny leather skirts, and fishnet stockings. The queen of mod designs, Mary Quant, set the tone for the decade. "Good taste is death. Vulgarity is life," she proclaimed. What was the point of fashion? Quant summed it up: "Sex." In women's clothing, constraints of every kind were discarded. Bras and slips were out, and girdles disappeared. Ready-to-wear was in, along with synthetic materials, flashy colors and prints, and rising hemlines (Quant and French designer André Courrèges share credit for popularizing the miniskirt).

The first North American designers to enlist in the clothing revolution were a group of young turks operating on the fringe of New York's

A doe-eyed, 41-kilogram slip of a girl named Twiggy became the modelling sensation of the decade. Born Leslie Hornby in a working-class London suburb, Twiggy turned herself into an industry.

Seventh Avenue: Rudi Gernreich, Deanna Littell, Betsey Johnson, and others. The creative force behind the Paraphernalia boutique, Paul Young, heralded the North American fashion movement: "Personally, I've always thought anybody who takes fashion seriously is ridiculous. . . . nothing about wearing [clothes] should be taken seriously." Trendy shops offered op-art dresses that oscillated with

▲ **Diana Vreeland, editor in chief of** Vogue **magazine in the 1960's, readies model Marisa Berenson for a photo shoot.**

▶

The wearer of the bouffant applied liberal amounts of hair spray to keep her elegantly styled coif in place.

patterns and swirls; pop-art designs, which borrowed their motifs from the world of popular culture, such as consumer packaging; and outfits made of metal, vinyl, and other industrial and man-made materials. As a designer explained, "It was: 'Hey, your dress looks like my shower curtain!' The newer it was, the weirder — the better."

Men also experienced a fashion emancipation. They began to "do" their hair in expensive cuts, permanents, and blow-dried styles. The traditional tailored shirt underwent

radical change as designers worked in new silhouettes, a bolder palette — shocking pinks, cobalt blues — and wild prints. Jackets came in strange shapes and a wide variety of materials, from velvet to suede. In 1966 designer Pierre Cardin introduced close-fitting, standing-collared Nehru shirts and jackets. The same year, Cardin caused a sensation at his Paris showing when his "cosmonaut" male models walked the runway in helmets and zipped sleeveless jackets over matching turtlenecks. (Cardin had labelled neckties a "very bourgeois idea.") A spokesman for the venerable menswear store Brooks Brothers objected to the idea that the turtleneck might be donned as formal evening wear: "We will not go along with this evening business." But even Brooks Brothers couldn't stem the tide, and soon men's clothes were as outrageous as women's.

Rules remained to be broken. Elisa Stone's fashion workshop hit the cover of *Harper's Bazaar* in August 1967 with a dress composed of transparent theatrical lighting gel. "I loved the idea that my clothes were not going to last," she said. "I thought of them as toys." Giorgio Sant' Angelo created an outfit from corrugated cardboard. Spain's Paco Rabanne used contemporary chain mail. Betsey Johnson's wearable "happening" was a dress made of blotting paper planted with seeds: when watered, it sprouted blossoms. Diana Dew wired her designs with lights and supplied a portable battery pack. Paper and plastic dresses, skirts for men, the neo-Egyptian look, space-age garb — the fashion world had gone completely bonkers.

By the end of the decade, the flea market and second-hand clothing store had usurped the place of the boutique. Anything could be deemed fashionable as long as it made the wearer feel good. And high fashion, as Coco Chanel once knew it, lapsed into a series of fads that fizzled as fast as they flamed.

▶

Skirts reached near oblivion with the micro. Then hemlines fell briefly to midcalf and later dropped to the ground.

◀

Peggy Moffitt, model and muse for the "farthest out" of North American designers, Rudi Gernreich, strikes a theatrical pose.

LITTLE SCREEN, BIG SCREEN

Keir Dullea starred in the film 2001: A Space Odyssey **as part of a team of astronauts bound for Jupiter.**

Television won viewers with comedies and action-packed dramas. Moviemakers fought back with everything from mature themes to HAL, Julie Andrews, and wide-screen spectacles.

In *The Dick Van Dyke Show*, *My Three Sons*, and *Hazel*, the 1960's brought television viewers the standard situation comedy set in a loving home. But there was also a new crop of TV sitcoms characterized by far-fetched conceits and wild flights of fancy.

An array of wacky characters crowded the airwaves: *The Beverly Hillbillies*, with its family of unlikely hick millionaires living in a posh California neighborhood; *The Addams Family*, a clan of ghouls who can't understand why they don't fit in; and *The Munsters*, headed by a Frankenstein look-alike and his vampire wife. Witches, genies, and extraterrestrials populated *Bewitched*, *I Dream of Jeannie*, and *My Favorite Martian*.

TV heroes also took a variety of forms. The physicians on *Dr. Kildare* and *Ben Casey* solved new medical crises each week; on *The Man From U.N.C.L.E.*, spies Napoleon Solo and Ilya

◄

The Clampetts (Buddy Ebsen, Max Baer Jr., Donna Douglas, and Irene Ryan) struck oil on their Ozarks property and headed west in The Beverly Hillbillies.

Kuryakin fought James Bond style against the evil THRUSH. On *Batman*, the Caped Crusader and Robin protected Gotham City from a cluster of colorful criminals. "SPLATT!" "POW!" "CRUNCH!" flashed on the TV screen as the Dynamic Duo took out the Riddler, King Tut, the Penguin, and other cartoon villains.

Viewers across the continent enjoyed the old-fashioned fare served up in *Bonanza*, and the rugged philosophy of Lorne Greene as Ben Cartwright. But Greene had a special significance for Canadian television performers. Though long recognized as an outstanding talent in Canada, he had had to go to the United States for his success.

In Canada the CBC drew large audiences with the dramatic news program *This Hour Has Seven Days*. But nervous executives cancelled it as too controversial. The "down home" fiddling and dancing of *Don Messer's Jubilee* was equally popular — and without the controversy. In Quebec, the audience for the comedy series *Moi et l'autre* was said to be as much as a third of the province's population. As the decade ended, however, it was clear that it would always be cheaper for the Canadian networks to buy or copy American programs and that the future of Canadian television would lie in the field of news and public affairs broadcasting.

As television's small screen came to dominate entertainment, Hollywood mounted wide-screen spectacles — *El Cid* (1961), *Cleopatra* (1963), *The Bible . . . in the Beginning* (1966) — and brought audiences "adult" fare, such as *Butterfield 8* (1960), starring Elizabeth Taylor as a party girl, and *The Apartment* (1960), with Jack Lemmon as a junior executive who lends his apartment to his superiors for trysts.

At the same time, a younger generation of filmmakers was creating an eye-opening alternative to typical Hollywood fare. Stanley Kubrick directed *Lolita* (1962), based on the Vladimir Nabokov novel about a middle-aged man's obsession with a 12-year-old girl; *Dr. Strangelove* (1964), a send-up of nuclear war; and *2001: A Space Odyssey*, in which a leading character is HAL, a spaceship computer that develops a mind of its own.

HAL was only one of a vivid assortment of antiheroes who came to the screen: Dustin Hoffman played a success-bound young man who rejects the career track in *The Graduate* (1967); Peter Fonda

Two Julie Andrews vehicles served as lighthearted antidotes to other cinematic visions of the 1960's: Mary Poppins *and* The Sound of Music *(right). The latter broke box office records.*

and Dennis Hopper portrayed spaced-out bikers searching for America in *Easy Rider*; Faye Dunaway and Warren Beatty in *Bonnie and Clyde* (1967) made glamorous a pair of petty Depression-era bank robbers on a crime spree.

Canada's National Film Board continued to produce strong documentaries such as *Lonely Boy*, spotlighting the teen idol world of Paul Anka, and *Nobody Waved Goodbye*, a disturbing and challenging look at the problems of urban teenagers. Though severely hampered by the economic power of Hollywood, Canadian filmmakers were exploring the possibilities of their craft, laying the base for an explosion of outstanding films in the 1970's.

▲ *Adam West played Batman in the comic-book-for-TV classic, which premiered in January 1966. Adults and kids alike enjoyed the program's camp stylishness and its device of casting stars as "guest villains."*

◄

Star Trek, with William Shatner (Captain Kirk), DeForest Kelly (Bones), and Leonard Nimoy (Spock), lasted a scant three seasons, but the program made "trekkies" of legions of fans.

Hollywood's memorable treatment of the hippie counterculture in Easy Rider *(1969), made antiheroes and martyrs out of the asocial drifters played by Dennis Hopper (who also directed), Peter Fonda, and Jack Nicholson.*

ACTING OUT, ACTING UP

As Canadian theatre came of age, American theatre took a sharp left turn with audience participation and rowdy free-for-alls. Some folks were not amused.

After a long history of amateur productions in church basements, Canadian theatre at last moved into the spotlight. The Stratford Festival in 1953 was a commercial and artistic success, and following on from it, with the help of grants from Canada Council, professional theatre spread across the country. By the late 1950's, Toronto was producing plays at the Crest Theatre, and Winnipeg was mounting professional performances at the Manitoba Theatre Centre. By the end of the 1960's, theatre in every province except Newfoundland had turned professional.

Tourists came from as far as Japan to see the musical version of *Anne of Green Gables,* which toured across Canada in 1965. The Shaw Festival, the world's only festival devoted to the works of George Bernard Shaw, was founded in 1962 at Niagara-on-the-Lake. A flood of Canadian

▲ The cast of Hair, the tribal-love-rock musical that stunned the world, celebrates the joys of youthful rebellion.

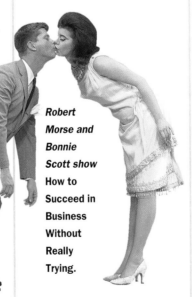

Robert Morse and Bonnie Scott show How to Succeed in Business Without Really Trying.

plays, from George Ryga's *The Ecstasy of Rita Joe* to Robert Gurik's satiric *Hamlet, prince du Québec,* to the musical spoof *My Fur Lady* and the revue *Clap Hands*, created new devotees of Canadian theatre. A genuinely Canadian theatre was on the rise.

In the United States, much of the excitement came from imported productions. English playwright Harold Pinter made his American debut in 1961 with *The Caretaker*, a work of ambiguous dialogue and menacing silences. Eugène Ionesco's comic *Rhinoceros* had nothing to do with animals. Instead, it was the dark absurdity of human existence that obsessed the author. Samuel Beckett, who in the 1950's had produced *Waiting for Godot* and *Endgame*, in which life's meaninglessness is discussed at length by the characters, went on to create *Krapp's Last Tape* and *Happy Days*. Another import, *Marat-Sade,* was set inside an insane asylum. As directed by Britain's Peter Brook, it shattered theatrical decorum with two hours of angry, anarchic, and uninhibited mayhem.

At the same time, the United States spawned a bumper crop of outspoken new talents. Edward Albee's *Who's Afraid of Virginia Woolf?,* an acid-etched portrait of family strife, opened to rave notices in 1962 and helped save an otherwise disastrous Broadway season. A new Albee play or adaptation appeared almost every year thereafter. Bitter send-ups, like *MacBird*, a blank-verse parody that heaped ridicule on President Lyndon Johnson, fed a growing appetite for political satire. Black voices began making themselves heard following Lorraine Hansberry's 1959 success with *A Raisin in the Sun.* Poet LeRoi Jones won an Obie award for *The Dutchman.* Actor James Earl Jones gained national acclaim for his

One of Canada's greatest Shakespearean actors, Christopher Plummer performs in Anthony and Cleopatra *at Stratford, Ontario. He went on to play lead roles in several movies and was made a Companion of the Order of Canada.*

Glenn and His Magic Piano

The piano recording was brilliant, so much so that listeners forgave the sounds of humming and grunting that overlay it. Canadian pianist Glenn Gould just could not suppress his love for music.

A soloist with the symphony orchestra of his hometown of Toronto when he was only 14, Gould won international fame in 1955 while still in his early 20s. Audiences around the world idolized the magnificent pianist who brought to them the mathematically precise music of Bach, the romanticism of Beethoven, and the atonality of Schoenberg played with deep intensity, his head bent close to the keys. Then, abruptly in 1964, he quit the concert stage. It was, he said, too much like a sports arena, and outdated in this age of electronic recording. From then till his death in 1982, he performed only in recording studios where he had more freedom to perfect his art.

Gould also composed and performed for movies and television, while his talent for writing found an outlet in radio scripts and reviews. His love of music was equally wide, ranging from the 16th century to the most modern composers and pop stars.

portrayal of black heavyweight boxing champion Jack Johnson in *The Great White Hope,* which opened in Washington, D.C., before moving to Broadway.

The most daring productions mixed radical politics with a heady dose of sexual revolution. Spontaneity became the cry as alternative venues pushed the limits of theatrical expression. The actors in Julian Beck's Living Theater took part in sit-ins and antibomb rallies, then romped onstage to shed clothes, shout ritual slogans, protest drug laws, and generally outrage the Establishment. At the Performance Group's *Dionysus in '69,* ticket holders sat on the floor or perched on wooden scaffolding while the cast cavorted about in the nude — a dramatic technique critic John Simon dismissed as "group therapy for actors."

▶

In The Caretaker *by Harold Pinter, Alan Bates and Robert Shaw give shelter to a tramp, played by Donald Pleasance. Everyone suffered in the end.*

▼ *The nightclub routines of comedian Lenny Bruce sizzled with angry wit and four-letter rhetoric. Commentator Walter Winchell called him the "man from outer taste."*

Nightclub comedy grew steadily darker. Early in the decade, a gifted pair of Chicago improvisers, Mike Nichols and Elaine May, delighted viewers with ad-lib routines based on audience suggestions. Then came the bitter racial monologues of Dick Gregory, which gave a new sting to "black humor." A TV gag writer named Woody Allen, launching out on his own, dredged up laughs from the murky tides of urban neurosis. Nothing was sacred to Lenny Bruce, who mocked religion, motherhood, the law, and the American flag. Arrested repeatedly for obscenity and drug use, he died of an overdose in 1966.

One bright spot continued to illuminate conventional musical comedy on Broadway. Perky acting and an inspired story line reaped a 1961 Tony award for Frank Loesser's *How to Succeed in Business Without Really Trying.* Zero Mostel made a hilarious hit of *A Funny Thing Happened on the Way to the Forum.* Carol Channing started belting out the upbeat songs of *Hello, Dolly!,* which opened in 1964 and ran for 2,844 performances. Next came Barbra Streisand as *Funny Girl,* followed by the *Man of La Mancha* galloping in pursuit of "The Impossible Dream." Even when the counterculture invaded, as in *Hair,* the promise of a brighter future, an "age of Aquarius" free from the torments of war and racial strife, shone through. Meanwhile, boy continued to meet girl in *The Fantasticks,* a bit of lyrical whimsy that opened in 1960 at a tiny 152-seat theatre. It played through the decade and every decade since — North America's longest-running show ever.

Members of the Road Hog Commune rollick on their psychedelic bus.

Artist Peter Max created a vibrant style, as shown in the "Love" poster below, that perfectly expressed the 1960's youth culture.

Dr. Timothy Leary extols the virtues of his mind-bending drug experiences at the Human Be-In in San Francisco's Golden Gate Park in 1967.

FLOWER POWER EXPLODES

Suddenly they were everywhere, those woolly-maned, strangely outfitted, acid-tripping, peace-and-love-spouting hippies — and their numbers appeared to just keep growing.

The gradual creeping of men's hair over the forehead and ears and down the shoulders was perhaps the first sign that the Age of Aquarius had arrived. It started during the presidency of tousled John Kennedy, and before long, moustaches, beards, and long sideburns flourished everywhere. *Life* magazine spotted the culprits: "The Beatles did it!"

The principal of a Nova Scotia school sent long-haired boys home. A father bought his mop-topped son a dog licence. In Connecticut a businessman rented a billboard: "Students of Norwalk: Beautify America, Get a Haircut." But what was the use? Even former President Lyndon Johnson grew his hair long once he retired.

By that time, city streets and college campuses were swarming with a new breed of alienated youth called hippies. But hippies were a gentle lot. They pieced together bizarre outfits from clothing found in secondhand stores, attic trunks, and funky shops: bowler hats, fringed jackets, western boots, bell-bottoms, tie-dyed shirts, Victorian shawls, and army fatigues. And they donned headbands, love beads, peace symbols, and flowers, lots of flowers, tucked behind ears, woven into their hair, crowning their heads.

To some, the blissful, or spaced-out, look typical of the hippie seemed drug induced, and often it was. The future high priest of the drug world, psychologist Timothy Leary, taught at Harvard University in the early 1960's. Then he began to experiment with, and promote the use of, the hallucinogen LSD (lysergic acid diethylamide), and Harvard dismissed him. Leary felt LSD had led to his spiritual awakening, and he sought converts.

Hippies adhered to Leary's creed: "Turn On, Tune In, Drop Out," or in other words, take drugs, raise your con-

Buddhist monk Suzuki-roshi taught meditation and founded San Francisco's Soto Zen Center.

Flower child and clothes designer Eileen Levy gathers a hatful of blossoms.

sciousness, and drop out of school, work, society. They drifted, joined communes, and scraped up just enough money and food to survive. They said, "make love, not war," staged "be-ins," "love-ins," and "happenings," and hung out in city parks and on mystical retreats strumming beat-up guitars and intoning yogic chants.

There was a hippie newspaper, *Georgia Straight*, in Vancouver. Toronto had Rochdale, a hippie college that was supposed to point to a new way of education, but that soon dissolved in drugs and disorganization. Public reaction to the hippies varied. The old guard tended to agree with *Li'l Abner* cartoonist, Al Capp, who called them a "herd of semi-domesticated animals . . . uttering their mating cries and scratching their pelts." A kinder observer, Bishop James Pike, likened the flower children to the early Christians.

The hippie scene culminated in 1967 with the "Summer of Love" in San Francisco. During the previous decade, the Haight-Ashbury district of the city had become a countercultural mecca for the Beat Generation. Then, in the 1960's, the Haight attracted a huge influx of flower children. The streets teemed with rootless, jobless young people in search of a peaceful, free-form existence. Poets recited their works on street corners. Self-appointed prophets spoke to all who would listen.

As word of the Haight phenomenon spread, the media and tourists descended on the district. Buses ran the "Hippie Hop," taking gawking passengers on "a safari through Psychedelphia, the only foreign tour within the continental limits of the United States." The summer wore on. Strange organizations sprang up, such as the True Light Beavers, who built shrines out of garbage. Souvenir stores and head shops selling drug paraphernalia multiplied.

The situation degenerated further. Squalor set in and crime became rampant. The food supply dwindled, and growing numbers of sick, tired, hungry flower children began an exodus. A feeling of doom befell Haight-Ashbury as "weather prophets" predicted that the Great California Earthquake was coming. The higher hippie ideals of love, peace, and the rejection of materialism had been undermined. It seemed they could escape the real world for only a brief moment.

The Grateful Dead (below) became a musical voice of the peace-and-love generation. The band's house was a major attraction on bus tours of Haight-Ashbury.

Dr. Leary's Harvard colleague Gunther Weil cavorts in the Berkshire Hills, Massachusetts.

In the summer of 1969, some 400,000 rock-music fans flocked to a dairy farm in upstate New York for the Woodstock Festival. The first day the sun shone, then the sky opened up; but the audience stuck it out together through the mud and grime.

Vietnam becomes America's battle

Out of the small nation of South Vietnam, prized as

a bulwark against communism in Southeast Asia,

grew a war that would torture consciences.

In the early 1960's few Americans questioned their nation's involvement in Vietnam. Ho Chi Minh, the formidable Communist leader of North Vietnam, had to be contained. From his capital city of Hanoi, Ho was supporting guerrilla actions in South Vietnam in an effort to reunite the two countries under his Communist rule. Reflecting the United States' view that anything was better than the spread of communism in the region, Vice President Johnson lauded Ngo Dinh Diem, the South Vietnamese president, as "the Winston Churchill of south Asia."

The New York Times warned that the struggle in Vietnam was one "this country cannot shirk." Chairman of the U.S. Joint Chiefs of Staff, Gen. Lyman L. Lemnitzer, predicted that if South Vietnam were to fall, "We would lose Asia all the way to Singapore."

By 1959 the terrorist activities of the Vietcong, a Hanoi-backed guerrilla force composed of Communists, peasants, and opponents of Diem, had escalated into open warfare in some sectors of the South. The United States threw its support behind the South Vietnamese government in Saigon, sending it billions of dollars in aid, military advisers — by 1961 there were 700, by 1962, 3,000, and by the end of 1963, 16,000 — and providing nonmilitary expertise. In 1961 President Kennedy committed the first U.S. troops there,

◀

Vice President Johnson and his South Vietnamese counterpart, Nguyen Ngoc Tho, wave each other's national flag during Johnson's May 1961 visit to the Asian country.

◄ The first U.S. helicopters used in Vietnam were CH-21's, here shown landing to pick up South Vietnamese troops in 1962. Inset: Johnson meets his top military advisers in mid-1964 at the LBJ Ranch to discuss the deepening commitment of the United States to the conflict in Vietnam.

400 men from the Special Forces group, or Green Berets. But Diem, aware of his pivotal role in U.S. Cold War policy, became "a puppet who pulled his own strings." He and his brothers, including head of the secret police Nhu, along with Nhu's beautiful and imperious wife, ran South Vietnam as a private fiefdom. They jailed opponents, censored the press, discriminated against the Buddhist majority, and handed out patronage appointments to loyal, often incompetent followers.

In 1963, just as Diem had gained the upper hand, Buddhist monks began to stage dramatic protests that included acts of self-immolation. Diem grew increasingly reclusive, and Nhu expanded his influence. Kennedy concluded that America could no longer afford to prop up Diem's doomed administration. With the support of the U.S. government, a junta overthrew the South Vietnamese president that November. He was executed by his captors.

Just a few weeks later, Kennedy himself fell to an assassin's bullet, and Lyndon Johnson became president. At first Johnson took a cautious position on Vietnam. "We don't want to . . . get tied down in a land war in Asia," he assured a crowd during a 1964 presidential campaign stop. But the situation in South Vietnam rapidly deteriorated: the junta that had toppled Diem itself collapsed and was succeeded by a series of short-lived military governments. The Vietcong exploited the disarray in Saigon and extended their control to encompass almost half of South Vietnam.

Then, on August 2, 1964, North Vietnamese patrol boats fired on the U.S. destroyer *Maddox* as it plied the Gulf of Tonkin. Two days later sonar technicians aboard the *C. Turner Joy* reported signals indicating that the ships were again under attack, and a battle with nearby North Vietnamese boats ensued. Those signals were probably false and, as it later became known, Johnson himself may have been told they were false. But he ordered immediate retaliatory strikes against naval bases and oil depots.

On August 4 he took to the airwaves: "Aggression by terror against the peaceful villages of South Vietnam has now been joined by open aggression on the seas against the United States," he declared, and asked Congress to grant him extraordinary powers to take "all necessary measures"

▲ U.S. marines of the 9th Expeditionary Brigade land on Red Beach Two at Da Nang in northern South Vietnam.

▼ Along one thread in the web of ancient trade pathways called the Ho Chi Minh Trail, North Vietnamese trucks transport military supplies south.

in repelling armed attacks against United States forces and to "prevent any further aggression." With only two nay votes, Congress passed the Tonkin Gulf Resolution. The resolution, Johnson exulted, was like "grandma's nightshirt — it covered everything." The military made plans to accelerate the bombing of North Vietnam. Soon tens of thousands of U.S. troops, together with South Vietnamese units, would begin a series of joint operations against the Vietcong.

By the spring of 1965, the Joint Chiefs were convinced that drastic steps had to be taken if the United States was to win the war. They called for U.S. combat forces, currently numbering 80,000, to be doubled. Johnson summoned his advisers for a conference. Only one, Under Secretary of State George W. Ball, opposed the plan for military escalation. Ball foresaw a possibly disastrous end to the war, in which "the mightiest power on earth is unable to defeat a handful of guerrillas." But Johnson yielded to those who sought to expand the U.S. military role.

Hawks, Doves, and the Tet Offensive

Over the next few years, U.S. aircraft would rain down 800 tonnes of explosives a day on North Vietnam's bridges, ammunition dumps, and oil refineries. By December 1967,

485,000 American soldiers were fighting in Vietnam and some 1.5 million tonnes of bombs had been dropped on the North, more than the total tonnage used on the enemy during all of World War II. Beginning with the first major battle, in the Ia Drang Valley in 1965, U.S. forces would win every major engagement of the war, causing heavy casualties among the North Vietnamese and Vietcong. But the Communists displayed remarkable resilience. Ho Chi Minh continually replenished the flow of arms and soldiers south by way of the Ho Chi Minh Trail, a network of pathways twisting through the jungles of Laos and Cambodia. By 1967 some 20,000 North Vietnamese regulars made their way to South Vietnam monthly.

As the United States sank deeper into the Vietnam conflict, the debate at home grew acrimonious. Senator J. William Fulbright of Arkansas charged that the nation's warmaking was "not living up to [America's] capacity and promise as a civilized example for the world." Johnson shot back, labelling Fulbright and other dissenters "nervous Nellies." Within the Johnson administration, the consensus was breaking down. Defense Secretary Robert McNamara had come to consider the war "dangerous, costly, and unsatisfactory." He would announce his resignation in November 1967 and leave office at the end of the following February.

Moreover, public antagonism toward the war mounted. Americans splintered into "hawks," who favored

escalation of the conflict, and "doves," who pressed for a negotiated settlement. Then something happened that forever changed public perception of the war. On January 31, 1968, during the Vietnamese New Year, called Tet, the Communists seized the initiative. Some 70,000 Vietcong and North Vietnamese regulars lunged at dozens of South Vietnamese cities, up to then spared the onslaught of combat. Just before 3 A.M. in Saigon, a suicide squad blew its way into the U.S. embassy compound, killing some guards. Four hours later U.S. troops secured the area.

From a military standpoint, the Tet offensive could have been counted a failure. American and South Vietnamese forces swiftly restored order in most cities. But Tet galvanized the war's critics. "The terrible quality of the war in Vietnam came home to people," explained Johnson aide Harry McPherson. "It appeared that these guys . . . were never going to quit." On March 31 a distraught Johnson appeared on television to announce he had ordered a partial halt to the bombing of North Vietnam and would offer to initiate peace talks with Hanoi. He would not seek reelection. But the war was far from over. It would take its toll on thousands more American fighting men and countless Vietnamese soldiers and civilians.

Throughout the war, the Canadian government played the part of a neutral observer, supplying humanitarian aid and serving on two international truce commissions as

▲ *Scenes from a war: The incandescent glow of machine-gun fire streaks the air during a "mad minute" in the Iron Triangle. Insets, left to right: Their village under attack by U.S. marines, a Vietnamese mother and her children flee across a river. Wounded medic Thomas Cole comes to the aid of a fallen comrade. Vietnamese troops take Communists captive in the Mekong Delta, a Vietcong stronghold.*

U.S. marines hurl grenades from Mutter's Ridge during close combat near the demilitarized zone bordering North Vietnam. ▶

negotiators working for peace. Few Canadians knew the truth about their country's involvement.

All Canadian humanitarian aid was routed through the American government, and so reached only American allies. Canadian observers and negotiators used their positions behind North Vietnamese lines to act as informers for the Central Intelligence Agency and as spotters for American bombers. They routinely issued reports supporting American moves and suppressed those that questioned them.

Canada also supplied $12.5 billion of war material to the Americans, including explosives and napalm. Chemicals, including the defoliant "agent orange", were tested at Gagetown, the Canadian Armed Forces base in New Brunswick. American air crews trained for Vietnam over Alberta and Saskatchewan. And 10,000 Canadians served with American forces in Vietnam.

But Canadians were told only that Canada was working impartially for peace, and providing refuge for 32,000 Americans who refused to serve in Vietnam. It was a myth that Canada was a peacemaker. The reality was that it was America's powder monkey.

Lyndon Johnson breaks down after listening to a recording taped by his son-in-law Capt. Charles Robb, describing the horrors he experienced during his tour of duty in Vietnam.

▼ *Anti-Vietnam protesters march through Toronto, on March 26, 1966, calling for Canada to end its arms sales to the U.S.*

A wounded 12-year-old girl and her neighbor leave their homes behind as they cross a littered battle site toward a waiting evacuation helicopter.

South Vietnamese soldiers look on as an area on the outskirts of Saigon goes up in flames following the Vietcong attack known as the Tet Offensive.

FERMENT IN THE ARTS

Canadians both shaped and rebelled against an American culture that sometimes delved into the lives of the underclasses, and sometimes made playful art of soup cans, junk food, and movie stars.

Canadians, flooded with American culture even in their universities where American-born professors downgraded Canadian literature, reacted through the 1960's and into the 1970's with demands that Canadian culture be given breathing space. In 1969, *The Struggle for Canadian Universities*, by Robin Mathews and J. Steele, set off a storm of demands that Canadian universities pay more attention to their own culture.

Ironically, the demand rose at a time when Canadians were winning unprecedented international attention. Margaret Atwood was publishing poetry (*The Circle Game*, 1966, which won the Governor General's Award) and novels (*The Edible Woman*, 1969), which explored the alienation of women. Leonard Cohen, poet, songwriter and novelist, painted a black view of the world, made even more sombre in his songs by the sonorous bass of his voice. Mordecai Richler, already internationally known for *The Apprenticeship of Duddy Kravitz* (1959), published a wickedly funny novel of Canadian nationalist fervor with *The Incomparable Atuk* in 1963. Marshall McLuhan became an international guru for his writings on communications, notably *The Medium is the Message* in 1961.

Leonard Cohen

Though McLuhan predicted its demise, the printed word thrived during the 1960's. Absurdity and black humor were the hallmarks of a new literature. Joseph Heller's *Catch-22,* whose very title has come to connote a no-win situation, mocked

◄

Pop-art guru Andy Warhol and two stars of his cult films, Edie Sedgwick and Chuck Klein, emerge from the underground. Above, one of Warhol's many tributes to the Campbell's soup can.

World War II and all war: The anti-hero wants to plead insanity to get out of the military, then learns that, by doing so, he would prove his sanity.

The Jewish literary hero, battling angst and his own conscience, gained his voice in the novels of Saul Bellow (*Herzog*) and Philip Roth, whose *Portnoy's Complaint* is a hilarious extended monologue delivered from the psychiatrist's couch. And black writers delineated their experience in autobiographical works, among them James Baldwin's *The Fire Next Time*, about the author's Harlem youth; *Soul on Ice,* a collection of essays written by Eldridge Cleaver from his jail cell; and *The Autobiography of Malcolm X*, a collaborative effort of Malcolm X and Alex Haley, author of the 1976 bestseller about his African ancestry, *Roots*.

Author Susan Sontag

The "new journalism," a hybrid of reportage and fiction, bristled with energy. It was exemplified in Truman Capote's "nonfiction novel" *In Cold Blood* (1966), which recounted the tale of two real-life murderers, and in Tom Wolfe's chronicle of the antics of a band of hippie nomads, *The Electric Kool-Aid Acid Test*.

While several writers took an active role in the events of the day, a group of artists strove to regard their subjects from a remove — the "sublime neutrality" of essayist Susan

▲ *Taking his inspiration from the pages of action-packed comic books, Roy Lichtenstein painted "Whaam!", now in the Tate Gallery, London.*

▼ *Claes Oldenburg crafted oversized soft sculptures of everyday items, such as restaurant food. Here he props up his giant ice-cream cone, part of a "triptych of edibles."*

Sontag. They rejected abstract expressionism and mined popular culture — television, advertising, the consumer market — for new topics. The result was pop art: Andy Warhol's kaleidoscopic images of Coca-Cola bottles, Roy Lichtenstein's magnified comic books, and multimedia works such as Robert Rauschenberg's "Monogram," Jim Dine's "5 Toothbrushes on Black Ground," Claes Oldenburg's "Two Cheeseburgers with Everything," and Jasper Johns's "Painted Bronze (Beer Cans)." Pop art enticed the art-buying public, and the market boomed. Money flowed into the building and expansion of museums.

Art had become big business, and its human subjects and creators, a kind of commodity. Andy Warhol's workshop, The Factory, churned out personalities as well as silk screens. As Warhol, the darling of the "beautiful people," said: "In the future, everybody will be famous for 15 minutes." The fame of Warhol and most of his contemporaries proved somewhat longer lasting.

The vocabulary of pop art was first used in the 1950's to describe artworks such as Jasper Johns's "Three Flags."

This 14-year-old was among tens of thousands of anti-Vietnam demonstrators on April 15, 1967.

On "Anti-Bra Day," women were called on to send in their bras for a great bra-burning, in the name of women's liberation.

▼ Folksinger Joan Baez sang her support for many causes at hundreds of protests throughout the 1960's and 1970's.

CHALLENGING THE ESTABLISHMENT

The renewed struggle for black civil rights seemed to have a ripple effect. Whether students or pacifists, women or migrant workers, many were ready for a fight against established authority and the status quo.

The 1960's were barely a month old when black college students sat down and waited to be served at a segregated lunch counter in Greensboro, North Carolina (see p.316). Nobody could have guessed it at the time, but the lunch counter sit-ins set the tone for the decade. Established authority was in for some hard knocks, and not surprisingly, young people would do most of the knocking.

By the mid-1960's, dozens of U.S. colleges, including Yale, Notre Dame, and the University of Kansas, had been hit by demonstrations. Students demanded action on everything from curfew hours and cafeteria food to open admissions policies and revisions in academic programs. Anti-Vietnam War demonstrations, and protests over attendant issues, such as defence-related university research and the presence of military recruiters on campus, escalated along with the war and spilled over into the streets.

Then, in August 1968, television viewers witnessed what *Life* magazine called "the most widely observed riot in history," at the Democratic National Convention in Chicago. Youth International Party members, or "yippies," a crowd made up of drug culture supporters and hippie activists, protested in the streets. Facing them in a series of running battles before the TV cameras were Mayor Richard Daley's Chicago police, a force that needed no excuse for brutality and simply waded in with clubs and boots.

Feminists, Friedan, and Women's Rights

Just two weeks after the tumultuous Democratic National Convention of 1968, at the annual Miss America contest in Atlantic City, feminists crowned a sheep and tossed steno pads, false eyelashes, and brassieres into "freedom trash cans." By then feminists were beginning to describe insensitive men as "male chauvinist pigs." Like the civil rights activists, student protesters, and antiwar marchers of the 1960's, a lot of women were fed up. They felt they were suffering injustices due to their gender and no longer intended to keep quiet about it.

Feminism, of course, was not new, but as the 1960's opened, there were few signs that women's roles would become a heated issue. A 1962 Gallup poll found that three out of five women were at least "fairly satisfied" with their lives. Then, the next year, came Betty Friedan's book *The Feminine Mys-*

Yippie cofounder Abbie Hoffman

tique, an explosion of frustration at women's lives. In 1966, Friedan and others founded the National Organization for Women (NOW), the preeminent force for women's rights in the United States for years to come.

A female reporter helped women attain one important legislative breakthrough, the inclusion of women in the 1964 Civil Rights Act. TV journalist May Craig was interviewing Representative Howard W. Smith of Virginia on *Meet the Press* when the civil rights bill was in congressional committee. Would he, she asked, consider revising the bill to include women? Yes, Smith replied, he might do just that.

In fact, Smith hoped to defeat the civil rights bill by adding women to the list of minorities it covered. When Smith proposed the inclusion of women in the bill before the House, laughter broke out on the floor. The Civil Rights Act of 1964 did pass, and Title VII prohibited discrimination in employment on the basis of sex. The Equal Employment Opportunity Commission was set up to enforce the law, but it would be another eight years of legal manoeuvring before the Equal Employment Opportunity Act was passed and the EEOC had any real power.

Betty Friedan

▼ **At San Francisco State College, President S. I. Hayakawa called in 600 police to keep it open in 1968, then faced a more violent strike the next year. Antiwar protesters (inset) burn their draft cards at a 1965 rally.**

A RIGHT FOR ALL

When Saskatchewan's government introduced a medical insurance plan in 1962, the province erupted in bitter protests. But by the end of the decade, even the doubters were cheering and the rest of the country had followed Saskatchewan's lead.

On July 1, 1962, the sound of doctors closing their offices in angry protest could be heard right across Saskatchewan. In an unheard-of action, doctors went on strike. Some even left the province forever. The issue was the right of every Saskatchewan resident to medical care regardless of ability to pay. The Saskatchewan government had just passed medicare, a universal, government-administered, medical insurance program.

Doctors fumed that relieving the patient of financial responsibility would destroy the sacred doctor-patient relationship. Premier Woodrow Lloyd shot back that, however sacred it might be, too many of Saskatchewan's people could not afford any doctor-patient relationship at all, and many of those who needed care faced bankruptcy as a result. Passions ran high as Keep Our Doctors' committees (KOD) held demonstrations and advertised in the media in support of the doctors. It was a quarrel made all the more passionate because 19th-century values were clashing with 20th-century realities.

A century earlier, Canada had been a place where people were expected to look after themselves. Those who couldn't were considered either lazy or incompetent and were sent off to charities, to poorhouses, and in New Brunswick, even auctioned off to neighbors to work for their keep. In the first half of the 20th century a new class of wealthy Canadians had developed. But at the same time, by 1940 one-third of urban Canada and half of rural Canada were living below the poverty line, and nowhere was the cost to the nation more evident than in health. In 1942, 44 percent of young men called up for military service were rejected because of poor health. And the social programs of Mackenzie King's Liberals barely touched on the inadequacies of old age pensions and child allowances. That was when Saskatchewan took over to set the pace for change.

In the early 1960's, medical care in Canada was enjoyed only by the wealthy. But political pressure forced the federal government to improve things, and by 1967 a medicare plan had been instituted nationwide.

Douglas Puts Up His Dukes

Tommy Douglas was a small man, a bantamweight, but one with all the scrappiness of the boxer he had once been. And his temper had been raised to battle pitch by the experiences of friends and neighbors who had lost all their savings and even been driven to bankruptcy by medical costs in their old age. In 1946, as premier of Saskatchewan (and a member of

The fiery rhetoric and dogged determination of Tommy Douglas won full medical insurance for every citizen of Saskatchewan.

the socialist Cooperative Commonwealth Federation, C.C.F.), he introduced a government hospital insurance program that provided coverage at a cost of $5 per person or $30 per family per year.

The program was immediately popular, and federal parties, always watchful for any growth of C.C.F. support among voters, began considering a national plan in 1957. But Saskatchewan was already forcing a faster pace. Hospital insurance still left enormous medical costs to be paid by patients and did nothing to help those who needed care to prevent hospitalization. So Douglas announced in 1959 that his government would move to full medical insurance. In 1961, when he became leader of the federal New Democratic Party, Douglas handed the battle flag to his successor, Woodrow Lloyd.

And what a battle it was! Enraged doctors stormed that bureaucracy would destroy the quality of care. Business leaders, private health insurance companies, and many newspapers, never comfortable with the socialist leanings of the C.C.F., happily took up the cry. But Premier Lloyd dug in. On the day medicare came into effect and doctors went on strike Lloyd filled their places with doctors from other parts of Canada, the United States, and even Britain. Local citizens' groups pitched in by organizing clinics. Within weeks, as the people of Saskatchewan showed their support for medicare, the doctors' strike collapsed. Eventually, the doctors were won over. By 1965, most of them supported the new system.

Medicare For The Rest Of Canada

Justice Emmett Hall of the Supreme Court was won over, too. Appointed to study the implications of Saskatchewan's new health insurance program, Hall recommended medicare for all of Canada. Lester Pearson, who became prime minister in 1963, promised that it would be implemented by centennial year, 1967.

Despite opposition from provincial premiers and even within his own party, Pearson knew that public opinion was

Lester Pearson, PM

for the insurance program. By 1965, when the Canadian Medical Association voiced its approval, he knew he had the support of the medical profession. The fear that the New Democratic Party was growing in popularity brought the remaining necessary converts. By the end of 1966, the federal government offered the provinces a shared-cost medicare plan.

Within six years, all the provinces and territories had joined the program and Justice Hall, reviewing the system once again, pronounced it one of the best in the world. When Quebec medical specialists went on strike to protest against medicare in 1970, the strike sputtered out in days. When Ontario doctors went on strike in 1986 to protest medicare's ban on extra billing, in a pale imitation of the

Saskatchewan strike, many doctors and virtually all Ontarians opposed them, and the strike soon collapsed.

Medicare was the success story of the decade. For the first time in Canadian history, medical care had become a right for all — not merely a privilege for the rich and a charity for the poor.

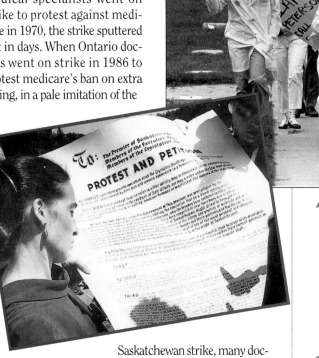

▲ In June 1986, striking Ontario doctors marched in their white coats through downtown Toronto. The placards they carried protested against the government's plan to ban extra billing.

◄ Supporters of the Keep Our Doctors movement in Saskatchewan present a protest and petition to the provincial government in July 1962.

 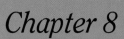
Chapter 8

THE SEESAW 1970's

Watergate stuns, Canada falls in love with

a prime minister from Quebec — then faces the threat

of separation from Quebec, and the Me Generation finds

time to disco and watch Archie Bunker, M*A*S*H,

Jaws, Star Wars, and two Godfathers.

Fireworks explode over three famous symbols of democracy on America's 200th birthday, July 4, 1976.

THE OCTOBER CRISIS

FLQ

Years of terrorist bombings climax in kidnappings and a murder. Prime Minister Trudeau intervenes to save the government of Quebec from collapse, but disturbing questions remain.

On the morning of Monday, October 5, 1970, three armed and hooded men entered a Montreal home. Minutes later, they came out with a British diplomat in handcuffs, and Quebec was pushed to the edge of an abyss. The hooded men were from the Front de Libération du Québec (FLQ), a tiny organization numbering no more than a few dozen people, devoted to the idea of an independent Quebec. Influenced by Pierre Vallières, a member of their organization and, later, author of *Nègres Blancs d'Amérique* (*White Niggers of America*), the FLQ saw French-speaking Quebeckers as a people held in virtual slavery by capitalists who were largely English and Jewish. Appointing themselves to remedy the situation, they launched a series of 200 terrorist bombings and uncounted fires, beginning in 1963. Most of the bombs were placed in federal buildings and in mailboxes in English-speaking districts of Montreal. In 1964, the FLQ robbed a firearms company, murdering the vice-president. And in 1968 they exploded a bomb in the Montreal Stock Exchange, injuring 27 people.

Then, in October of 1970, they kidnapped the British trade commissioner, James Cross. The FLQ issued their demands to newspapers and radio and television stations in a communiqué. The document deplored the plight of "French-speaking Quebeckers, a majority that has been belittled and downtrodden on its own territory," and demanded the release of 23 people who had been imprisoned for terrorism. Jérome Choquette, Quebec minister of justice, refused the demands, offering only safe conduct for the kidnappers in exchange for the release of James Cross.

Trudeau the Titan, as drawn by cartoonist Aislin for the Montreal Gazette, after his show of force to save the Quebec government from collapse.

But there was uneasiness in government offices in both Quebec and Ottawa. Some French-speaking Quebeckers seemed sympathetic toward the kidnappers. Even though such powerful positions as Prime Minister of Canada and most of the posts in the Quebec civil service at all levels were held by francophone Quebeckers, and though they had controlled the provincial government for almost two centuries, there was a school of thought that preached that francophones were a colonized people whose culture was suppressed by "the English," and who suffered under them. The FLQ diatribe against the "English and American bosses" was just an extension of this point of view, and found sympathetic listeners.

Five days after the FLQ abducted Cross, they kidnapped Quebec labor minister Pierre Laporte, who sent a pleading note to the provincial government, "Decide whether I live or die." Premier Robert Bourassa's government, now close to collapse in fear and confusion, agreed to open negotiations with the FLQ. In Ottawa, Prime Minister Pierre Trudeau was becoming alarmed at the weakness of the Quebec government, and particularly by rumors that a group of prominent Quebeckers was preparing to take over the provincial government and cave in to the demands of the FLQ. Trudeau leaped to take control and restore leadership.

Trudeau Gets Tough

At 1.07 p.m. on October 15, troops of the Canadian Armed Forces took up posts to guard public buildings and officials, mostly in Montreal. Their helicopters thudded overhead.

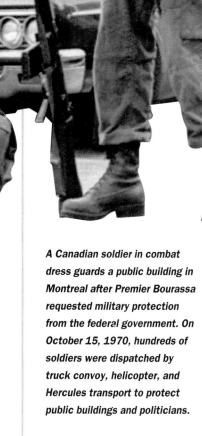

A Canadian soldier in combat dress guards a public building in Montreal after Premier Bourassa requested military protection from the federal government. On October 15, 1970, hundreds of soldiers were dispatched by truck convoy, helicopter, and Hercules transport to protect public buildings and politicians.

Frightened officials had asked for the troops so that the police could be freed to search for Cross and Laporte. When Trudeau was asked how far he was prepared to go, all he said was "Watch me."

The next day, Canadians watched Trudeau explain on national television just how far he would go. Unruffled and firm, he told the nation that he had advised the governor-general at 4 a.m. to proclaim the War Measures Act. It was a stunning display of authority. A piece of legislation passed at the beginning of the First World War, the act gave federal authorities unusual powers in case of "war, invasion or insurrection, real or apprehended." Suspects could be held incommunicado for up to 20 days without charge. Armed with these powers, police promptly rounded up more than 450 suspects.

Much criticized then and since, the act was certainly abused as police arrested many people whose connection to terrorism was at least doubtful. The act was even used by Montreal's Drapeau in the October 25 mayoralty election to brand his opponents as terrorist sympathizers. But Trudeau's firm action had filled a dangerous vacuum of power created by the weakness of the Quebec government.

Crisis Defused

Pierre Laporte's body was found on October 17, in the trunk of a car near St. Hubert airport south of Montreal. His kidnappers had strangled him. Even those who had sympathized with the FLQ drew back in horror. But Laporte's death, dreadful though it was, brought a positive result. Combined with Trudeau's tough stance and his refusal to allow Canada to be run by a bunch of "self-selected dictators," it defused the crisis. Events now settled into a long, plodding search for the kidnappers.

After 59 days as a hostage, Cross was freed. And in early December, Canadian television screens showed a procession of cars with a police escort heading to Dorval Airport with his captors. Jacques Lanctôt, Marc Carbonneau and his sister Louise, Yves Langlois, and Jacques Cossette Trudel were on their way to Cuba and then to France.

At the end of December, Laporte's killers were arrested at a farm south of Montreal. Jacques Rose, his brother Paul, Francis Simard, and Bernard Lortie refused to say who had killed Laporte. All received prison terms — though none would serve the full time. The crisis was over.

Or was it? As Canadians at last learned who the FLQ terrorists were and how few they numbered, many wondered that such a small and nondescript group could have shaken the government of a province and, but for Trudeau, might have brought Canada to the brink of fragmentation. It was nine people — only nine! — who had created the cri-

▲ *British diplomat James Cross, abducted by the FLQ, plays solitaire in captivity as police continue their search for him and his abductors. Cross's kidnappers sent four photos of him to Quebec's provincial police a few days after the abduction.*

sis. And despite their lofty pretensions at analyzing the economic and social ills of Quebec, none had much education. In fact only one, Nigel Hamer (a student at McGill whose involvement did not become known until the late 1970's), had any university education at all. Their analysis, like Pierre Vallières' book, was little more than a blend of folk myth, half-understood marxism, and garbled liberationism.

Yet these nine, as much by their ideas as by their violence, had struck a sympathetic chord in Quebec and so paralyzed Bourassa's Liberals that they lost the power to lead. Without Trudeau's decisive intervention, the FLQ might well have succeeded in bringing down the Quebec government — with catastrophic results for both Quebec and Canada.

▶

Pierre Laporte, martyred to the cause of Quebec's independence, was found dead in the trunk of a car on October 17, 1970. He was buried with full honors, below.

NIXON'S HARD ROAD TO PEACE

President Nixon entered the White House with one overriding mandate: to get the United States out of Vietnam. It took years and cost another 20,000 U.S. lives, but he scored some notable Cold War breakthroughs along the way.

The greatest honor history can bestow is the title of peacemaker. This honor now beckons America." With these solemn phrases, Richard Nixon, upon his inauguration, declared his ambitions as president. Almost immediately he began withdrawing U.S. combat troops from South Vietnam. But while talking peace was easy, achieving it was another matter entirely.

More than 1 million Americans so far had fought in the jungles of Southeast Asia. Some 30,000 had already given their lives. It was the longest armed conflict in the history of the United States. In June of 1969, Nixon announced a troop reduction of 25,000 men, the first step in a policy of "Vietnamization," whereby the burden of fighting would gradually shift to the armies of South Vietnam. The United States would supply arms, advisers, and an air shield of bombers and fighter planes; native Vietnamese soldiers would slog through the rice paddies and fire the bullets. The troop withdrawals would continue throughout Nixon's first term. By the end of 1970 total U.S. military strength in Vietnam was down to 334,600 men, from approximately 540,000 when Nixon took office.

Yet every move Nixon made seemed to pull the United States deeper into the war. Even as his national security adviser, Henry Kissinger, was meeting in Paris with representatives from North Vietnam, attempting to hammer out a ceasefire, the president was secretly stepping up the pres-

▲ *At a press conference on May 9, 1970, Nixon describes the Cambodian incursions. Five days earlier, on the final day of the Kent State confrontation, a student demonstrator tosses back a tear gas canister at a national guardsman.*

▶ *Tankers of the U.S. 25th Infantry Division roll into Cambodia. The attack, aimed at Vietcong bases, began on April 30, 1970, and was over by late summer.*

sure on the enemy. Clandestine flights of B-52 bombers began roaring over Cambodia to drop their payloads. The strategically vital Ho Chi Minh Trail, the main Communist supply route through Cambodia and Laos, had grown from a jungle footpath into a vast network, hidden by foliage, protected by antiaircraft batteries, and dotted with Vietcong rest-and-resupply camps, arms depots, and field hospitals. Unless these sites were wiped out, Nixon reasoned, South Vietnam could never be defended.

Then, on April 30, 1970, Nixon dropped a bombshell on the American public. Appearing on national television, the president announced he was sending U.S. ground troops into Cambodia. Even as he spoke, a joint U.S. and South Vietnamese assault force, 20,000 strong, was sweeping across the border. The Vietcong sanctuaries had to be cleared, Nixon explained, before the United States could quit Vietnam. Furthermore, Hanoi's delegates in Paris were digging in their heels at the negotiating table, and U.S. credibility was at stake. "When the chips are down," the president declared, "the world's most powerful nation" cannot afford to act "like a pitiful, helpless giant."

The nation was stunned. Shorten the war by escalating it? "This is madness," exclaimed Senator Edward Kennedy, and many of his congressional colleagues agreed. The Senate repealed the six-year-old Gulf of Tonkin Resolution, which had given legislative sanction to the country's involvement in Southeast Asia.

▷

Home from the battlefront, Green Berets get a joyous family welcome.

▽ *Even as students protested, construction workers marched in favor of Nixon's war policy.*

Just days after Nixon's announcement, a second shock sent the United States reeling. At Kent State University in Ohio, a group of student activists had met to protest the Cambodian invasion. The meeting was peaceful, but that evening several hundred other students, fuelled by cold beer and warm spring weather, started throwing bottles and smashing windows in downtown Kent. The next night campus demonstrators attacked a building, burning it to the ground. The authorities called in the National Guard. The final confrontation occurred on May 4, shortly after noon. The guardsmen moved to break up an antiwar rally on the university commons. A melee erupted, with students hurling rocks and insults, and guardsmen responding with tear gas. A salvo of rifle shots rang out. When the smoke cleared, four students lay dead. Ten others were left seriously wounded. In a way that seemed unimaginable, the Vietnam War had come home to the United States.

Nationwide Protest, No End in Sight

In the wake of Kent State, student strikes shut down more than 400 other colleges and universities across the land, and two more students were killed. More than 100,000 student demonstrators gathered in Washington to stand vigil before the White House and other government buildings. Nixon, who had earlier branded antiwar activists "bums," was left shaken by the events. He made a 5 A.M. visit to the Lincoln Memorial to reason with protesters there. Still, opposition to the war continued to build.

The president was determined to wind down the conflict at his own pace, leaving a pro-Western government in control of South Vietnam. "I will not be the first president

▲ *Savoring a Cold War triumph, the president and First Lady Pat Nixon tour the Great Wall of China in February 1972. Then, in Moscow, Nixon celebrates détente with Soviet party boss Leonid Brezhnev (left) and Premier Alexei Kosygin.*

▶ *A B-52 Stratofortress, principal arm of the United States' strategic air might, drops its 24,500-kilogram payload over enemy territory.*

Papers, secret Defense Department documents that further eroded the public's confidence in the way the war was being conducted. As *Time* magazine put it: "Vietnam is the wound in American life that will not heal."

Diplomatic Breakthroughs

Even as Nixon's Vietnam policies were dividing the United States, his skill as a statesman was reshaping world politics. One July day in 1971, while vacationing at his home in San Clemente, California, the president delivered yet another TV blockbuster. An invitation had arrived from the People's Republic of China, the United States's archenemy in Asia, and the president was delighted to accept. Again, the nation was stunned. Richard Nixon, who had battled left-wingers all his political life, traipsing off to shake hands with Party Chairman Mao Tse-tung? Astute observers might have detected the early signs: an end to State Department travel restrictions, the U.S. table tennis team playing exhibition matches in Peking. But the thaw in relations, engineered by Nixon and Kissinger, caught most of the world by surprise.

A few months later Nixon did it again. This time the invitation came from the Soviet Union, and soon Nixon was in Moscow tossing back vodka with Soviet leader Leonid Brezhnev. A new spirit of détente emerged, accompanied by much fanfare and some genuine achievement: cultural exchanges, trade agreements, and a $1-billion sale of U.S. wheat to Russia. Delegates at the Strategic Arms Limitation Talks (SALT), already in progress, drew up their first agreements. With any luck, the lurking terror of nuclear mass destruction might soon be banished from earth.

But nothing would make Vietnam go away. On March 30, 1972, Communist forces launched a massive offensive. Three waves of North Vietnamese troops and guerrillas, armed with Soviet tanks and artillery, stormed into South Vietnam. A drive out of Cambodia reached to within 100 kilometres of Saigon before being turned back. Nixon responded with an equally massive escalation of U.S. armed might: heavy bombing of North Vietnam, mining of Haiphong Harbor, and a U.S. naval blockade. North Vietnam lost 100,000 men and most of its tanks. Still, the stalemate persisted.

In July, the peace negotiations between Henry Kissinger and Le Duc Tho of North Vietnam resumed after a temporary suspension. Into autumn, Kissinger jetted between Paris, Washington, and Saigon to hammer out an accord. Then, in October, the talks broke down again, and Nixon, in an effort to force Tho back to the negotiating table, ordered a final outpouring of aerial destruction. Starting the week before Christmas, for 12 days straight, U.S. B-52's and

of the United States to lose a war," he declared. Yet each day victory seemed more elusive. The Cambodian offensive had failed to end the flow of Vietcong troops and supplies. In February 1971 a South Vietnamese assault into Laos backed by U.S. air strikes ended in headlong retreat. And each night on television, the American public found new reasons to dislike the war. In March a military court convicted Lt. William L. Calley of war crimes, reminding viewers that Calley's platoon had massacred more than 100 South Vietnamese villagers at My Lai in 1968. Three months later *The New York Times* began publishing the Pentagon

If politics is the national soap opera, the plot twists of the Nixon years deserve a special Emmy award. By his second year in office, the president's popularity had tumbled to 50 percent, and support for his conduct of the Vietnam War, to 34. Police barricaded the White House gates with transit buses as antiwar protesters took to the streets of the capital. Then in 1972 Nixon was reelected by one of the largest victory margins on record.

Others' misfortunes had a part in Nixon's triumph. Well before the election, his most dangerous opponent,

Senator Edward Kennedy, drove off a bridge late one night in Chappaquiddick, Massachusetts, causing the death of a young woman passenger. That temporarily ended Teddy's presidential aspirations. A rifle shot by a would-be assassin crippled Alabama Gov. George Wallace, thus removing a formidable contender from the political far right. Senator Edmund Muskie started strong for the Democrats, then bombed in the New Hampshire primary when false rumors about his wife reduced him to tears of outrage. That left South Dakota's Senator George McGovern (shown above with wife, Eleanor) as the Democratic Party candidate.

Nixon ran a smoothly disciplined campaign and managed to project a skilled, statesmanly image to voters. McGovern came across as a naive prairie populist who promised a quick end to the Vietnam War and who attracted a new breed of political idealist. His campaign was doomed from the start by inexperienced management and the radical image of many of his followers. Republican detractors liked to call him the candidate of "acid, amnesty, and abortion."

The results for McGovern were devastating. Nixon won just under 61 percent of the popular vote and lost only Massachusetts and the District of Columbia. Yet, in defeat, McGovern kept his sense of proportion, telling journalists: "For years I wanted to run for president in the worst possible way—and I'm sure I did."

other aircraft droned over Hanoi and Haiphong to drop more than 36,000 tonnes of explosives in one of the most savage air attacks in history. The Paris talks reopened, and on January 27, 1973, the negotiators signed a cease-fire.

At last the war seemed over. The last of the U.S. ground troops began arriving home. Hanoi released some 600 American POW's. Secretary of Defense Melvin Laird ended the draft. The U.S.-backed government of Gen. Nguyen Van Thieu remained in power in Saigon. "We have finally achieved peace with honor," Nixon announced. Few agreed. No one could guess how long the Thieu regime would survive. Many thousands of North Vietnamese troops remained in South Vietnam, controlling wide areas of the countryside, poised to resume the battle. Said one returning U.S. veteran: "It isn't peace. And there is no honor."

In the jungles of Southeast Asia, the gunfire never entirely stopped. A civil war was ravaging Cambodia, genocidal in its intensity. In April 1975 rebel forces of the Communist Khmer Rouge took over most of the country, including the capital of Phnom Penh. Meanwhile, fighting broke out again in South Vietnam, with the Communist armies closing steadily southward. Though Nixon had promised Thieu that if the North were to attack, the United States would support him, Congress had prohibited further military involvement in Vietnam. On April 25 Thieu fled the country.

Four days later, as enemy tanks roared into Saigon, U.S. helicopters lifted 1,373 Americans from the roof of the Saigon embassy to the safety of nearby warships. During 18 years of intervention in Vietnam, the United States had lost 57,000 men. Vietnam's dead have been estimated at more than 1 million to as high as 2.5 million. The numbers of its people maimed and orphaned are beyond any estimate.

▲ Negotiators Henry Kissinger (right) and Le Duc Tho shake hands as they near the signing of the Paris peace accord.

▼ In the wake of South Vietnam's surrender, a North Vietnamese tank crashes the gates of the Presidential Palace in Saigon.

An ADMINISTRATION ON TRIAL

It began as a back-page news item: five men caught breaking into Democratic Party headquarters in Washington. Two years later it ended with a slew of indictments and a president's resignation.

In Washington in the early 1970's, the Watergate complex on the Potomac River was the place to be. Half a dozen members of Congress lived there, several agency heads, and Attorney General John N. Mitchell. It was also where the Democratic National Committee maintained its headquarters. In the wee hours of June 17, 1972, five men broke into the committee offices to bug its phones and rifle its files. A night watchman detected them and called the police. Hardly anyone took notice. "A third-rate burglary attempt" is how White House Press Secretary Ron Ziegler described it. But the Watergate break-in just would not go away.

The five men were no ordinary burglars. James W. McCord, a former agent of the CIA, was security coordinator for the Committee to Reelect the President (later called CREEP). The other four were anti-Castro Cubans who thought their assignment was to look for a connection between the Cuban premier and the Democrats. The break-in had been planned, police learned, by a pistol-packing former FBI agent named

White House Chief of Staff H. R. Haldeman gets ready to testify before the Senate Watergate committee. Later convicted of perjury and conspiracy, he spent 18 months in federal prison.

A Capital Collection of Convicted Cover-uppers

John D. Ehrlichman
Domestic adviser. Convicted of conspiracy, obstruction of justice, perjury: 18 months in prison.

John N. Mitchell
Former attorney general and director of CREEP. Convicted in Watergate cover-up: 19 months in prison.

Jeb Stuart Magruder
Deputy campaign director of CREEP. Pleaded guilty in cover-up: seven months in federal prison.

G. Gordon Liddy
CREEP finance counsellor. Masterminded Watergate burglary and other illegal acts: 52 months in prison.

E. Howard Hunt
White House consultant. Pleaded guilty to burglary, wiretapping, conspiracy: 33 months in prison.

Charles Colson
Special counsel to the president. Pleaded guilty to obstruction of justice: seven months in prison.

John W. Dean III
Presidential counsel. Implicated Nixon in cover-up. Served four months in prison for obstructing justice.

The soul of integrity, Special Prosecutor Archibald Cox lost his post when he tried to make Nixon hand over the White House tapes. But the tapes became public anyway when the Supreme Court voted 8 to 0 that they be released.

"I'm a plain old country lawyer," Senator Sam Ervin would say in his North Carolina drawl as he craftily pried the truth from reluctant witnesses. In six months of testimony, Ervin's Select Committee on Campaign Practices blew apart the Watergate cover-up.

G. Gordon Liddy, who now worked for CREEP and was assisted by former CIA operative E. Howard Hunt. Could it be that Republican strategists, gearing up for the 1972 election campaign, had broken the law just to snoop on the Democrats?

With Richard Nixon's landslide victory, Watergate faded momentarily from view. But not for long. Liddy, Hunt, and the five burglars were brought to trial. Most of the defendants revealed little about the burglary. But, at sentencing, Judge John J. Sirica read a letter by McCord indicating that pressure had been exerted on the defendants to keep silent, and that some had committed perjury, and it implicated others in the break-in. Meanwhile, two reporters for *The Washington Post*, Carl Bernstein and Bob Woodward, conducted their own investigation. Citing a source known only as Deep Throat, they found out that the burglary had been financed by money from CREEP. John Mitchell, they also reported, maintained a slush fund for sabotaging the Democrats.

Just how far did the circle of involvement reach? Televised hearings began in May 1973 in the Senate, with the deceptively folksy Sam Ervin presiding. They revealed a White House steeped in wiretapping, forgery, and other shady dealings. Viewers learned about the Plumbers, charged with plugging press leaks, and Nixon's "enemies list" of real and imagined foes.

Even more shocking, the hearings showed that Nixon himself may have ordered a cover-up of the break-in. Aides had been instructed to stonewall. Presidential counsel John W. Dean testified that he had been told to "deep-six" a briefcase full of evidence. It seemed apparent that the White House was engaged in a conspiracy to obstruct justice, a criminal offence. But little of this could be corroborated. Then, on July 16, Alexander Butterfield, a Nixon aide, disclosed that since 1971 the president had taped all conversations in the Oval Office. Now almost every charge could be checked.

Even before the hearings had opened, presidential aides John D. Ehrlichman and H. R. (Bob) Haldeman resigned. Then came the Saturday Night Massacre. Nixon, under heavy public pressure, had authorized a Justice Department investigation. But when the special prosecutor, Harvard law professor Archibald Cox, probed too close to Nixon himself, the president ordered him fired. The new attorney general, Elliot Richardson, resigned in protest, as did his deputy, William Ruckelshaus.

At issue were the tapes of White House conversations. Nixon refused to turn them over, citing "national security" and "executive privilege." Instead, he would provide the committee synopses of their contents. Nixon's offer was rejected. Investigators suspected that somewhere in that avalanche of words lay clear evidence of executive complicity: a "smoking gun" proving beyond doubt that Nixon had attempted to block the Watergate investigation. But when the courts finally forced Nixon to give up some of the tapes, a key 18 ½-minute segment had been erased.

By now Nixon's innocence was in grave doubt. In May 1974 the House Judiciary Committee began impeachment proceedings. The hearings continued through July. Then on August 5 the smoking gun was found: a tape of Nixon ordering the cover-up. The Judiciary Committee voted to recommend impeachment, and on August 9 Richard Nixon became the first American president in history to resign from office.

That same afternoon Gerald R. Ford took over as president. Earlier, Ford had replaced Vice President Spiro Agnew, who had resigned amid charges of taking bribes and cheating on his income tax. Ford was loyal, hardworking, and as plain as a Michigan corn patch. He seemed just the man to heal a scandal-riven nation. "Our long national nightmare is over," he announced, and all the United States was ready to believe him.

On August 9, 1974, President Richard M. Nixon, surrounded by his family, bids a tearful good-bye to White House aides and Cabinet members.

MINDING OUR PLANET

Faced with the effects of oil spills, smog, strip-mining, pesticide use, and other assaults on nature, North Americans faced up to the damage they had done.

Looking every inch the authentic, unspoiled Canadian Indian, a fringe-jacketed, long-haired Grey Owl impressed listeners and readers of the 1930's with the importance of saving the environment from exploitation and pollution. They were fascinated by tales of his time spent with beavers as part of a conservation program. But in the 1940's they dismissed his message in outrage when it was revealed that Grey Owl, man of nature, was really English-born Archibald Belaney. Only a generation later, though, Canadians woke up to the realization that Grey Owl had been right. Remote forests were suffering from ruthless cutting, distant streams were polluted with mercury, and species of animals and plants were being wiped out.

The alarm over the effects of human activity on the environment had been sounded back in 1962 by a crusading book, *Silent Spring*, in which biologist Rachel Carson warned that unrestricted use of chemical pesticides was destroying much of the wildlife. The newspapers took up the cry, and over their morning coffee, people learned that Illinois's drinking water was tainted with nitrates from farmers' fertilizers, that fish suffocated by sewage were piling up on Lake Erie's shores, that bass and salmon had been wiped out downstream from power plants, that Antarctic penguins carried traces of DDT.

The bulletins grew steadily more worrisome. The world was in danger of losing to extinction the beluga whale, and also the bighorn sheep, the Pacific sea otter, the whooping crane, the spotted owl, even the bald eagle, the very symbol of the United States. Land and resources were being gobbled up as if they were snack food: millions of hectares ravaged by strip-mining, broad swaths of forest laid bare by the clear-cutting of timber, more than 400,000 hectares paved over each year. Even more alarming, the world's population had nearly doubled since the century's start, to more than 3 billion souls. By the year 2000 it would double again. In the crush of bodies, how could the planet survive?

In Canada, groups like Pollution Probe, formed in the 1960's, mounted pressure on governments to act. By the

▲ **As early as the 1930's Grey Owl was alerting Canadians to the environmental damage in our wildernesses.**

▼ **Hikers enjoy unblemished nature along a backcountry mountain trail .**

▼ **In a national park, young environmentalists examine local fauna under the expert eye of a park ranger.**

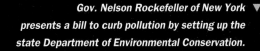

1970's they were followed by a growing number of environmental organizations, including Greenpeace. Formed in Vancouver in 1970, Greenpeace was originally a small group that protested against nuclear testing in the Pacific. It was to grow into one of the largest international movements, active on a large range of local and international issues. Established conservation groups, like the Sierra Club and the Audubon Society, took on a new militancy and swelled with a deluge of new members. In 1968 protests by nature lovers blocked construction of two dams that would have flooded sections of the Grand Canyon. Yet the assaults upon nature continued. In January of 1969 an oil rig in the Santa Barbara Channel blew its top, turning kilometres of pristine California beachfront into a gooey graveyard for pelicans, porpoises, and fish. An oil slick on the Cuyahoga River in Cleveland, Ohio, caught fire and burned two railway bridges. But each disaster only sharpened public awareness that things had to change and that no amount of industrial wealth or material progress was worth the price of a permanently damaged world.

By the early 1970's, most North Americans thought the environment was one of the most pressing domestic problems. Canada established a federal department of the environment for the first time. It set into motion wide-ranging legislation covering the fisheries, pollution of streams and Arctic waters, a ban on detergents containing high levels of phosphates, and transportation of dangerous materials. In 1971, Ontario enacted endangered species regulations that set an example for the world, since they protected not only animals and plants, but also recognized the importance of even the smallest life forms, insects.

In the United States, the Clean Air Act was amended, giving the government authority to set new air-purity standards. Congress set up the Environmental Protection Agency. Then came the Clean Water Act, the Endangered Species Act, and statutes to limit factory pollution, protect seacoasts, and remove the scars left by strip-mining. Some 35 environmental laws took effect during the decade, addressing every aspect of conservation and cleanup, from saving redwoods and protecting songbirds to regulating auto emissions and the disposal of toxic chemicals. And despite several sharp setbacks — the accidental escape of radioactive gas from a nuclear power plant at Three Mile Island in Pennsylvania (see box, p.363), leaks from a toxic dump that forced the evacuation of more than 1,000 families from New York's Love Canal, the derailment of a tanker containing chlorine and other toxic chemicals in Mississauga, Ontario, forcing the evacuation of 220,000 people — by the decade's end, large sections of the battered environment seemed to be on the road to recovery.

▲ **Biologist Rachel Carson alerted the world to the high risks of using chemical pesticides and herbicides.**

▼ **Tree lovers improve the environment by planting a large sapling in a city square.**

Gov. Nelson Rockefeller of New York ▼ **presents a bill to curb pollution by setting up the state Department of Environmental Conservation.**

361

Oil Shock, Stagflation

First OPEC cut off oil exports to the United States, then gas prices shot up. "Things Will Get Worse Before They Get Worse," predicted one newspaper in 1973. For a moment afterward, things actually seemed to improve. Then inflation struck.

Bumper stickers on some Alberta cars sprouted an ugly message: "Let the eastern bastards freeze in the dark." World oil prices quadrupled in 1973–74, but to protect Canadian industry the Canadian federal government intervened at the provincial level, holding down the price of domestic crude across the nation. Albertans reacted with anger at this threat to windfall oil profits.

Across the continent, homeowners were turning down thermostats and stocking up on sweaters. But it was worse in the United States, where motorists waited long hours at gas stations, in lines of cars that sometimes stretched for blocks. In New York angry drivers took out their frustration in fistfights. The price tag at the pump delivered another strong punch. Gas in Miami ran as high as $1 a gallon; months earlier it had been 35 cents. Gas prices rose in Canada, too, but thanks to ample domestic oil supplies, gas prices were well below world levels.

The root of the crisis was an embargo on oil shipments to the United States imposed by the Arab-dominated Organization of Petroleum Exporting Countries. The embargo arose from Middle East political strife: the United States had sent an emergency arms shipment to Israel, then at war with its Arab neighbors, and the Arabs struck back in the best way they knew. The embargo hurt Canada too, since its oil from the Middle East had to be piped from the United States, which now was receiving none.

Canada, however, was able to boost domestic oil production by exploiting oil fields that had been previously too expensive for development. This meant that throughout the crisis Canada was able to export more oil than it imported. It also used the period to challenge foreign dominance of the oil industry by encouraging exploration by Canadian companies. Then, in 1975, Canada challenged foreign control of domestic oil all the way to the gas pumps when it established its own Petro-Canada service stations.

As fuel supplies slowed to a trickle, homemade signs like this one began appearing at gas stations across the United States. Even fuel-efficient Volkswagens were sometimes left stranded.

To help save fuel, many people bicycled to work. Even mayors were not exempted from doing their bit.

The 55-mile-per-hour (80 kph) speed limit saved lives as well as gasoline. After it was imposed, it cut highway fatalities by 1,000 a month.

U.S. motorists cut their speed to 80 kilometres an hour, following a new limit set first by individual states and then by federal decree. Gas stations closed on Sundays, and some states introduced rationing. Commuters took to carpooling and mass transit. To conserve electricity, the nation went on year-round daylight saving time. Factories shortened their hours; some colleges cancelled midwinter sessions. Airline traffic was cut by 10 percent. No statutes were imposed on Canadians, but they, too, were urged to reduce their oil consumption.

Other Sources — But No Real Relief

A search began for alternative energy sources and for ways to make appliances, engines, and turbines run more efficiently. In Canada, proposals were put forward to build more pipelines, and to extract oil from Alberta's oil sands. Planners rolled out schemes for using coal oil, wind power, solar power, and gasohol (90 percent gasoline, 10 percent alcohol).

Then, as swiftly as it had struck, the oil shortage abated. In March 1974, OPEC lifted its embargo, though its prices remained high. Still apprehensive, the Americans built a 1,300-kilometre pipeline from their Alaska fields at Prudhoe Bay to the ice-free port of Valdez. Canada, too, extended a pipeline that ran south from Norman Wells in the Northwest Territories to Yellowknife, in 1985.

The energy pinch had exacted a painful toll, however. Prices for gas and heating oil remained high, and food costs had soared following the rising costs of transportation. Out on the highways, newer cars tended to be small, cheap, fuel-

The Nuclear Alternative Gets A Black Eye

In the quest for new energy sources, no area seemed as promising as the mighty atom. Nuclear plants had been generating power since 1957, and experts predicted that they might soon supply up to 50 percent of North America's energy needs. To concerns about nuclear waste and, worse yet, a possible accident, the experts said not to worry: only once in a million years would a major disaster occur. Then came March 28, 1979. Some 3 million litres of radioactive water leaked from Unit Two of the reactor at Three Mile Island, Pennsylvania, threatening a meltdown of the reactor core. About 100,000 citizens fled their homes, and Unit Two was shut down. Since then, not a single nuclear power construction permit has been approved in the United States.

▼ A Syncrude dragline hauls tonnes of earth from the Athabasca tar sands in Alberta. Oil is extracted from the sands for use as an industrial fuel.

efficient imports from Germany and Japan. Meanwhile, automakers across the continent, hit by plunging sales, cut production and laid off workers. The cuts spread quickly to other industries — rubber, steel, glass, machine tools.

The stock market tumbled, interest rates climbed, unemployment soared, and the economy shifted into reverse. By 1975 North America had fallen into a severe recession. At the same time, prices continued to go up. To the bewilderment of economists, an unlikely combination of spiralling inflation and stagnant growth set in — stagflation, as the ailment came to be called. Unlike the 1930's, however, this economic trough was softened by social programs.

Inflation became the economic norm of the 1970's. In the United States, Nixon attacked it early in the decade with a 90-day freeze on wage and price increases. In a dramatic bid to boost production and promote exports, he devalued the currency. For the first time in memory, the U.S. dollar was no longer pegged to a fixed price of gold. Canada raised interest rates to discourage consumer borrowing. The prime rate reached an unheard-of 22.75 percent as the 1980's began. Still inflation galloped ahead, reaching a high of 12.5 percent by 1981. Inflation was even higher in the United States in 1979, at 13.3 percent.

Then the worst happened. A harsh winter, followed by an unexpected slump in Middle East oil production and a stiff price hike by OPEC, plunged North America into yet another oil crisis. Gas lines, plant closings, rationing schemes — to everyone's horror, it was *déjà vu*.

ALL FOR ME, BODY AND SOUL

Tired of the oil crisis, turned off by politics, people focused on the best topic of all: themselves.

They sought fulfillment in everything from hot tubs and singles' bars to macrobiotic diets,

encounter groups, pop psychology, and a widening spectrum of religious cults.

In the summer of 1976, *New York* magazine, always quick to spot new trends, ran an inspired article by social critic Tom Wolfe. A cosmic shift had occurred in the way people looked at life, Wolfe suggested, in which the public crusades of recent years were being replaced by more personal goals.

To some people this meant adopting the creed of self-improvement. They threw their energies into study groups, exercise schedules, and bizarre new forms of psychotherapy. Others headed for the seductive joys of sexual revolution. Many turned to religion. Whatever their choice, the key word was *self*. The 1970's, Wolfe concluded, were the Me Decade.

If any single spot marked the era's birthplace, it was Big Sur, California, where well-heeled self-seekers gathered at the Esalen Institute for what Wolfe called "lube jobs for the personality." Lodged above the Pacific Ocean in a setting of Eden-like splendor, they shed clothes, plunged into hot tubs, and bared their inner selves in brutally intense encounter sessions. Dozens of similar groups spread across the land as part of the so-called Human Potential Movement, all striving to achieve an ideal of perfect selfhood. Arica, bioenergetics, Gestalt therapy, primal scream, Synanon, Zen meditation — the list of programs and disciplines went on and on.

New techniques of psychotherapy helped propel the movement. *Games People Play,* a self-help guide by psychiatrist Eric Berne, launched a fashion for transactional analysis (TA), which emphasized encounter groups and interpersonal relations.

An exhilarating "lift toss" helps a disciple at the Esalen Institute get in touch with her psyche during a sensitivity training session.

The book sold more than 5 million copies and spent years on best-seller lists until finally edged out by another TA volume, Thomas Harris's upbeat *I'm OK — You're OK.* Equally popular, est (Erhard Seminars Training) drew thousands of participants to weekend encounter sessions. By helping people "get in touch with themselves," former used-car salesman Werner Erhard was soon grossing $10 million a year.

Werner Erhard, est creator

Hand in hand with psychic self-expression, the era's fitness devotees sweated and groaned in search of bodily perfection. Health spas, tennis clubs, exercise centres, and diet clinics boomed. Thousands of otherwise ordinary people began eating brown rice, seaweed, and tofu and

Soaking away all inhibition, eight West Coast sybarites luxuriate in the effervescent comfort of a hot-tub party. The 40-degree water was considered to be therapeutic.

Some 40 million North Americans took up running, both to stay fit and to experience a promised aerobic euphoria known as runner's high. Here, a massed field of 11,553 swarms into Brooklyn at the start of the 1979 New York City Marathon.

growing alfalfa sprouts on windowsills. Sales of running shoes took off like startled rabbits. And when the sun went down, the same thousands of ordinary people flocked to disco singles' bars in quest of approval of their "new improved" selves, and a "relationship." Self-help volumes like *The Joy of Sex: A Gourmet Guide to Love Making* appeared on night tables. A soft-porn aesthetic seeped into Hollywood, where movies like *Last Tango in Paris*, starring a nude Marlon Brando, soon became acceptable.

Often the search for self led into exotic byways of religious experience. The 15-year-old Hindu guru Maharaj Ji, head of the Divine Light Mission, boasted 60,000 disciples, two large estates, and a string of fancy cars. Another Hindu leader, Maharishi Mahesh Yogi, preached a yogic discipline he called transcendental meditation (TM) and drew 350,000 followers. Major corporations such as General Foods and AT&T endorsed TM, and *Time* pronounced it "the turn-on of the 70's — a drugless high even the narc squad might enjoy." Meanwhile, young people flocked to the Unification Church of Sun Myung Moon, a religious leader from South Korea; or they shaved their heads and danced in the streets with the Hare Krishna sect. And in one of the decade's grimmer footnotes, more than 900 members of the People's Temple followed their deranged messiah, Californian Jim Jones, to the jungles of Guyana and an apocalyptic mass suicide by gunshot and a poisoned Kool-Aid brew.

At the same time, an older form of religious commitment was on the rise. The decade's charismatic Protestantism rivalled the religious awakenings of the 19th century, with mass baptisms, torrid confessionals, and joyous revival meetings. The list of notables who took Jesus Christ as their personal savior included singers Pat Boone and Johnny Cash, and Watergate felons Charles Colson and Jeb Stuart Magruder.

Television brought the movement into Canadian homes, where evangelistic churches gained at the expense of declining traditional denominations. In turn, these responded with their own charismatic movements. Canada's own evangelists included Leighton Ford, Billy Graham's Canadian brother-in-law. But the most prominent was David Mainse, whose *100 Huntley Street* was broadcast daily. By decade's end, evangelical fervor was bringing some businessmen very nice profits — the Virginia-based Christian Broadcast Network, for example, was making $60 million a year.

Drumming and chanting, youthful devotees of Krishna, the Hindu god, add a new noise and rhythm to city streets.

Celebrants at a March for Jesus lift index fingers in a gesture that meant "one way to salvation." Thousands of young people "turned on to Jesus" as an escape from drugs and sex.

Platform shoes, worn by many women and even some men, marched onstage in 1970, then quickly left.

Film star Diane Keaton launched the Annie Hall look — man's shirt, baggy pants, floppy hat — with her laid-back attire in Woody Allen's 1977 movie.

▼ Hot pants seized the world's attention in the early 1970's; these, with matching jacket, are made of snakeskin.

Hot pants, platforms, and polyester

Never had fashions changed so rapidly or reached such eccentric and bewildering extremes. People seemed determined to express themselves in what they wore.

here are no rules," announced the fashion magazine *Vogue* in 1970, and the parade was on: hot pants, leisure suits, lycra stretch pants, fake fur, ultrasuede and Naugahyde, floppy bow ties, outsize lapels, elephant bell-bottoms, peasant blouses, Mao Tse-tung caps, slogan-printed T-shirts, ripped jeans, designer jeans, Frye boots, clogs, sandals, platform shoes, plaid shirts, and cowboy hats — all adding up to an exuberant chaos of sartorial self-expression. Some people detected a certain tackiness: "The decade that taste forgot," as one observer put it. Others gloried in the sheer outrageousness of it all. But whatever one's sensibility, the decade offered something for everyone.

The rebellion started in the late 1960's, when fashion designers in Paris and New York, hoping to wean clients away from miniskirts, announced the calf-length midi. The response was all but universal outrage. "If the midi becomes the style, I'll commit suicide or murder," declared one Chicago woman. Groups like GAMS (Girls Against More

Rock star David Bowie helped spawn a gender-bending glitter look with costumes inspired by Japan's Kabuki theatre.

Skirt) and SMACK (Society of Men who Appreciate Cute Knees) sprang up to protest what seemed like a descent into terminal dowdiness. In 1971 the midis enjoyed a brief flurry, but for every woman who bought one, thousands more kept their chequebooks in their handbags.

As the designers retreated to their cutting rooms, women turned to the shock value of a mode originated by European streetwalkers: hot pants. Skintight, brief as an impulse, they came in satin, velvet, denim, leather, vinyl, and mink, and they could be dyed in one or more Day-Glo colors. Jane Fonda squeezed into them in the movie *Klute*, Liberace played his piano in them, brides took their vows in white lace versions of them.

The favored footwear for hot pants was the platform shoe. Popularized by rock stars like Elton John — who touched up his platforms with glitter and sequins — the shoes sent wearers clomping and teetering precariously on soles up to 18 centimetres thick. One custom-made pair featured hollow, transparent plastic heels with live goldfish swimming inside.

This was the golden age of polyester, a synthetic fibre that many people hoped would wear out, but didn't. Almost anything could be constructed from it: drip-dry shirts, double-knit blazers, stretch blue jeans, gaucho pants, and the glittery fantasy costumes that people wore to discos. It was also the fabric of choice for that ultimate 1970's statement, the leisure suit. Golfers in Miami and Palm Springs had worn these garments for years, but now they were everywhere, multiplying across the land in every sickly shade of pastel. So offensive did leisure suits become to certain viewers that many of the more elegant restaurants posted signs forbidding them.

Some of the decade's styles took inspiration from earlier times or more exotic places. When Robert Redford and Mia Farrow appeared in *The Great Gatsby*, a Hollywood costume drama based on F. Scott Fitzgerald's novel of the 1920's, fans decked themselves out in pleated skirts, rope necklaces, white suits, and baggy flannels. The Slavic Peasant Look, featuring high boots, large earrings, and flowered print skirts, was briefly popular. President Nixon's visit to Peking, China, revived a 1960's leftist fascination for Mao jackets and workers' caps.

A Retreat to the 1950's — or Nothing

The decade's biggest nostalgia trip led directly back to the Nifty Fifties. What helped kick it off was a rock-and-roll musical, *Grease*, which was about the 1950's hot-rod youth culture and ran for eight years after it opened in 1972. Then came the TV show *Happy Days*, starring Henry Winkler as Arthur Fonzarelli. A tough-guy 1950's biker with a tender heart, The Fonz won over the nation. There were Fonzie posters, Fonzie knee socks, Fonzie pillowcases. Not every young male plastered his hair into a ducktail, nor did every girl wear saddle shoes, but the black leather jacket became a standard wardrobe item.

One form of rebellion was to affect no style at all, which led, of course, to its own distinctive look. In the spring of 1970, a Danish yoga instructor introduced Earth Shoes, which allowed the wearer to walk as if barefoot, "the way nature intended." The trudge back to nature could also be taken in Birkenstock sandals or Vibram-soled hiking boots, in an ensemble that often included faded jeans, a plaid flannel shirt, and a down vest. The most extreme natural look was to wear no clothes at all, and a momentary fad for "streaking" erupted. At a Canadian Football League game in Toronto, fans saw an unorthodox play as a man ran naked across the field. Another young man treated TV viewers to his body in the buff by streaking into the 1974 Academy Awards.

Toward the middle of the decade, a newfound soberness began to infect the fashion world. Men took to wearing three-piece business suits, and a "dress-for-success" ethic

The leisure suit, a 1970's classic, proliferated through mid decade and included this double-knit, flare-legged model.

Pet Rocks and Lava Lamps

No novelty appeared too outlandish to avoid attracting at least 15 minutes of fleeting fame. Consider the Pet Rock. Little more than a beach stone nested in a fancy box, it came with a manual explaining that it required neither feeding nor paper training. Who would pay $5 for such silliness? At least 5 million people in the autumn of 1975. And how about the Mood Ring, which shifted color according to the wearer's state of mind? In point of fact, the color change occurred when liquid crystals in the ring's clear plastic "stone" responded to changes in skin temperature. That did not discourage as many as 20 million customers from shelling out anywhere from $2.98 (at trinket shops) to $250 (the 14-karat-gold model) for the fun of owning one. Joe Namath, Muhammad Ali, and Sophia Loren all succumbed.

Another decade totem was the Lava Lamp, a cone-shaped fixture that, when plugged in, seethed with molten, multihued excitement. It fitted just perfectly on a Parson's table in the archetypal 1970's setting: acrylic shag carpet, exposed brick wall, perhaps a water bed, and a hanging jungle of ferns, spider plants, and begonias, all strung up by a cat's cradle of knotted macramé cords.

MOOD RING

BLACK — Anxious · Excited
AMBER — Nervous · Tense
AMBER-GREEN — Troubled · Uneasy
GREEN — Sensitive
BLUE-GREEN — Relaxed · Calm
DARK BLUE — Happy · Love

ADJUSTABLE

put women into tailored jackets and conservative-length skirts. Not everyone went along, to be sure. For every Dorothy Hamill hairdo — an austere wedge-shaped cut named for the Olympic figure skater — there was a blow-dried Farrah Fawcett "big-hair" extravaganza, worn by someone hoping to emulate the sex appeal of the *Charlie's Angels* TV star. But the rebirth of design was evident, and by the end of the decade, the fashion moguls returned with a vengeance. Every jacket, every polo shirt, every pair of jeans, seemed to be stamped with a designer logo. It became clear that the no-style revolt was over.

HAPPY 200TH, AMERICA!

BUNKER HILL, BOSTON
In British uniforms, Revolutionary War buffs attack the rebels' hilltop positions in a replay of the famous battle.

July 4, 1976, fell on a Sunday. That weekend, right up to the moments when the celebrating reached a crescendo, the skeptics were saying that the birthday party would be all glitz and no soul, a tasteless mixture of jingoism and commercialism. But when the party was over, even most of the naysayers had to admit that something rare and wonderful had happened. As they had at the end of two world wars or when Neil Armstrong and Buzz Aldrin stepped out onto the surface of the Moon, Americans all over their vast country smiled the same smile, cheered the same cheer. In the end it was not the parades, the fireworks, the speeches, the costumes, the reenactments of glorious events, or even the magnificent tall ships (shown here off Newport, Rhode Island, on their way to New York) that most moved them. It was the feeling that, despite their differences, they were all Americans, and that being an American was something to be very happy and proud about.

BALTIMORE
Grade schoolers show their true colors by creating the Grand Old Flag in chalk.

DALLAS
A fifth-generation Texan decks her hair with American flags, under a wide Bicentennial bonnet.

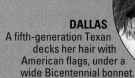

SEATTLE
For this enthusiastic well-wisher, it was not enough to make a cake for the nation's birthday; he found a way to wear it, too.

CROSS-COUNTRY WAGON TRAIN
Creaking through South Carolina on a Bicentennial journey, these latter-day covered wagons evoked the days of westward expansion.

WASHINGTON, D.C.
A wildly patriotic float joins a Bicentennial parade in the nation's capital. Even in the city of big bureaucracies, it was hard to be blasé about America's 200th birthday party.

PHILADELPHIA
The city where the Second Continental Congress adopted the Declaration of Independence on July 4, 1776, hosted a yearlong party. "Texas Day" (above), was one of 50 celebrations honoring the states.

VERMONT
Standing very tall, Uncle Sam on stilts leads the Bread and Puppet Theater's Independence Day parade in Plainfield, Vermont.

PHILADELPHIA
Red, white, and blue fireworks explode over Independence Hall, or Old State House, where John Hancock signed the Declaration exactly 200 years before.

CANADA STRAINS AT ITS SEAMS

Prosperous as never before, Canadians were also testy with each other as never before.

They cheered together as Pierre Trudeau brought a new flair to federal government,

but they trusted their provincial governments more than Ottawa.

Until 1982, when the Canadian Charter of Rights and Freedoms *was drawn up, Canadian rights were protected by various disparate laws and the 1960 Bill of Rights, whose illustration is shown left.*

In 1968, Canada elected as prime minister a trim bachelor who sported a flower in his lapel. Pierre Elliott Trudeau's popularity was so great that the press dubbed it "Trudeaumania." Dedicated to maintaining Ottawa's power, he was determined to govern as prime minister of all Canadians rather than as a broker for the provincial premiers. So Trudeau set out on a program of national measures.

In 1969 he established the Department of Regional Economic Expansion (DREE) to provide loans and tax incentives for industry in depressed regions. Despite the general prosperity of Canada, some provinces were struggling. In Atlantic Canada, for example, the unemployment rate was 11 percent and rising, and incomes were 20 to 35 percent below the national average. Life would have been even worse if it were not for federal unemployment insurance and welfare programs.

In 1969, too, Trudeau passed the Official Languages Act, ensuring that francophones and anglophones in all parts of Canada could be served by federal government agencies in both languages.

By that time, however, the devolution of power to the provinces was clear to every Canadian, even in the routine of daily life. When the alarm clock went off in the morning, it was usually powered by electricity from a provincial utility. When children were sent off to school, they were going to a provincial institution. Parents went to work by car or public transport on roads built by provincial or local governments. Old age pensions, medical care, and welfare came from provincial funds or from federal funds administered by the provinces. Federal spending, dominant in the early postwar years, had fallen to barely 42 percent of all government spending in Canada by the 1970's.

So, accustomed now to thinking of provincial governments as representing their interests, many Canadians rebelled at Trudeau's national programs. Some westerners fumed against the Official Languages Act, saying that French was being "forced down our throats." Francophone Quebeckers feared that language protection would encourage growth of the anglophone community. Federal moves to control pollution in air and water alarmed industrialists who urged provincial premiers to resist intrusions from Ottawa. As a result, Trudeau's Liberals barely salvaged a minority government in the 1972 elections.

Regional Resentments

Regional tensions were almost as old as Canada. Prairie resentment of "eastern interests" went back to the days when Ottawa's tariff rates had forced prairie farmers to "buy dear"

Pierre Trudeau, famed for his sartorial style, was one of Canada's most charismatic leaders.

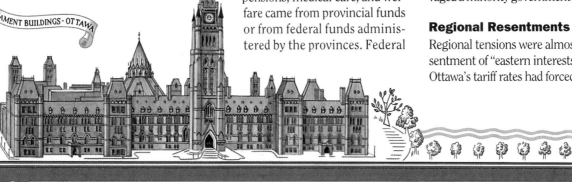

PARLIAMENT BUILDINGS · OTTAWA

from Ontario and Quebec manufacturers while "selling cheap" on the world grain market. Frustrations built up on the Prairies as people there realized that the large populations of Ontario and Quebec guaranteed Ottawa's eternal domination of the central provinces.

Though western Canada saw Quebec's position as one of power, there was resentment in Quebec, too. Its francophone majority had long felt vulnerable to anglophone dominance of the federal government. In 1973 the Parti Québécois, which had pledged to take the province out of Canada, became the province's official opposition. In 1976 the PQ formed a government.

What brought the tensions to a head in the 1970's was a boom in natural resources for a few provinces. In Alberta, it was oil and gas. In Quebec, it was the water power that made provincially owned Hydro-Quebec one of the world's leading resource industries. Conscious of their new strength, resource-rich provinces like Alberta, British Columbia, and Quebec became openly contemptuous of Ottawa, demanding a bigger share of constitutional power.

Then came the oil crisis and rising energy prices. Alberta flourished. Unemployment dropped to 4 percent, and personal incomes were above the national average. But the crisis threatened Canadian industries, and to protect them Trudeau responded with the National Energy Act of 1973. The act kept domestic oil prices below world levels, and fixed the rate Alberta could charge for its oil. Quebec and Ontario,

whose industries consumed oil, were delighted. Alberta, which produced it, was furious. In 1979, Trudeau's Liberals were narrowly defeated by Joe Clark and his Conservatives.

The first western-born prime minister, Joe Clark pledged to restore good relations between Ottawa and the provinces. But his first budget, taking aim at a Petro-Canada hated in the West, was defeated and Pierre Trudeau returned to power in 1980. Trudeau promptly scored a clear success against regionalism with the defeat of the Quebec referendum on separation in that year. His second move, however, was flawed.

With the Constitution Act of 1982, which contained the *Canadian Charter of Rights and Freedoms,* Trudeau brought to Canada for the first time a constitution made in Canada, which could be changed without reference to the British parliament. But there was a price. The premiers insisted that the charter have a "notwithstanding" clause that would enable the provinces to ignore rights when they interfered with provincial powers. Then, spearheaded by Premier Lougheed of Alberta who at last got his revenge for the National Energy Act, the provinces secured the right to opt out of any future constitutional amendment that might reduce provincial powers. Regionalism was still a powerful force that threatened to pull Canada apart.

Three national leaders — Israeli Prime Minister Menachem Begin, Jimmy Carter, and Egyptian President Anwar el-Sadat — stand proudly at attention during a White House ceremony to mark the signing of the Camp David peace accord.

CAMP DAVID HOPE, HOSTAGE HORROR

Deeply earnest, with an engineer's mind for absorbing facts and figures, President Carter strove mightily to do good. But despite some important reforms, and a historic peace accord, Carter's presidency ended in frustration.

Some presidents — John Kennedy, for example — liked to read spy stories. Harry Truman preferred history books. For Jimmy Carter, bedside reading was the neo-Calvinist theologian Reinhold Niebuhr, who taught that a politician's highest duty is "to bring justice to a sinful world." No one can say that Carter did not aim high or give his utmost.

Carter moved to Washington resolved to cut costs, relieve poverty, promote civil rights, banish corruption, protect the environment, pursue détente with China and the Soviet Union, and generally encourage good behavior in domestic and world affairs. Right after his inauguration on Capitol Hill, he and First Lady Rosalynn waved aside the government limousine and walked up Pennsylvania Avenue to the White House, demonstrating their sense of the com-

mon touch. Once inside, he trimmed the White House staff, sold the presidential yacht, and ordered subordinates to drive their own cars. More substantial measures soon followed, including civil service reforms and a strict new code of government ethics. The president also moved to deregulate the airline, railway, and trucking industries and to ease federal control of banks.

Washington is a hazardous city for newcomers, however, and Carter soon ran into trouble. By vetoing a fistful of expensive water projects, he ruffled the feathers of important congressmen. Then, launching an oil conservation program designed to relieve the decade's persistent energy worries, Carter declared "the moral equivalent of war." Critics shortened the phrase to MEOW, thereby transforming a lion's roar into a kitten's whine. Other lapses in political etiquette eroded his support even further. His budget director, Atlanta banker Bert Lance, was charged with sloppy financial dealings and forced to resign. A longtime aide from Georgia, Hamilton Jordan, was reportedly seen sniffing illegal substances at a trendy discotheque.

A Triumph of Statesmanship

One area in which the president from Plains came to show surprisingly strong leadership was foreign affairs. Taking his usual high-minded approach, he launched a global campaign for human rights, vowing that "fairness, not force" would guide American policy. This approach struck some people as hopelessly naive, but Carter persisted. He signed an agreement giving control of the Panama Canal to the Panamanians by the year 2000, raising howls of protest from conservatives. No one could fault the president's next initiative, however.

The story began in Jerusalem, the world's holiest city and the setting for some of its most savage hatreds. Here, to everyone's utter astonishment, a strange diplomatic courtship was taking place between those ancient enemies Israel and Egypt. The two nations had been at war for 30 years, with major eruptions in 1948, 1956, 1967, and in the Yom Kippur War of 1973. No peace treaty had ever been signed. Then, almost on impulse, Egyptian President Anwar el-Sadat decided to fly to Jerusalem and meet with Israel's hard-line prime minister, Menachem Begin.

As the two men attempted to talk peace, the old enmities resurfaced. So in stepped Jimmy Carter. Determined to

Iranian militants in the U.S. Embassy show off 1 of the 53 American hostages, most of them embassy staffers, who would spend the next 444 days in Iranian captivity. Freedom came January 20, 1981, just as Carter was leaving the White House.

Canadian Ambassador to Iran, Kenneth Taylor, details how he and his wife smuggled six Americans out of Iran to safety.

"Tie a yellow ribbon round the old oak tree," sang Tony Orlando and Dawn. And to honor the hostages, Americans did just that.

Month after month Iranian students paraded through the streets of Tehran denouncing the United States. A death's-head tops this Uncle Sam effigy, and the flags bear slogans reading "Down With U.S. Imperialism" in both English and Farsi.

restore harmony, Carter invited Begin and Sadat to Camp David, the presidential retreat in the Maryland hills. Here, in early September of 1978, they forged the framework for a peace agreement. It was not easy. "The atmosphere is really relaxed," said an Israeli aide, "but when it comes to ideas and positions, that's another story." At one point Sadat, enraged over some point of policy, fled to his cabin and started packing; Carter talked him into staying. After 13 days of intense negotiation, an agreement was reached.

It was Carter's greatest triumph. Then came 1979.

A Disaster in the Middle East

In February the president's brother, Billy — whose worst sin so far had been a genial, good-ole-boy oafishness — was found to be lobbying for Libya, a terrorist state. Then between March and June, the OPEC oil cartel raised the price of petroleum by 65 percent, bringing on the second oil crisis of the decade. The economy stumbled to a halt. The

mighty Chrysler Corporation, the United States's 10th largest business, ran out of money and needed $1.5 billion in government loan guarantees to stay afloat.

The bottom was hit on November 4. Some 12,800 kilometres to the east, in dusty, petroleum-rich Iran, a vengeful mob stormed the United States Embassy compound in Tehran and took everyone prisoner. A fundamentalist Islamic revolution, led by the stern Ayatollah Khomeini, had recently overthrown the pro-American shah, who escaped into exile. The Americans were beaten and humiliated during more than a year of imprisonment. Six others, however, found refuge with Canadian ambassador Kenneth Taylor and immigration officer John Sheardown. For two, harrowing months, these Canadian officials and their wives hid the prisoners, then got them to freedom using Canadian passports.

The Taylors and the Sheardowns got out, too, to a wave of gratitude in the United States. It was the only bright spot in the whole affair for that country. A helicopter attempt to rescue the prisoners turned to farce as the helicopters crashed in the desert. Americans were reduced to helplessly watching Iranian television clips of mobs parading the prisoners and chanting, "Death to America! Death to the Great Satan!" Never, it seemed, had America's star sunk so low.

373

Rock meets disco

After the Beatles split up, listeners wondered where rock music would go. Every which way, as it turned out, from soft to hard, funk to punk, glitter to disco.

Their fans were horrified. In the very first year of the 1970's, the Beatles, rock music's reigning superstars, announced they were parting company. John Lennon underwent primal scream therapy, recorded some major hits, including "Imagine," and settled into countercultural married life with Yoko Ono. George Harrison, deep into Hindu philosophy, released the mystical *All Things Must Pass* and other albums. Ringo made numerous recordings and pursued an acting career. But only Paul McCartney, with his new group, Wings, remained consistently on the charts. By 1979 he was the richest musician in the world. Even so, an era had clearly ended.

It seemed inconceivable that anyone could take their place. But no sooner had the Fab Four's shadow lifted than talented performers sprouted up by the hundreds. The mellow lilt of soft rock drifted in early. James Taylor and Joni Mitchell crooned confessional lyrics in muted tones, as though asking listeners for absolution. Carole King's moody 1971 *Tapestry* sold more than 14 million copies, making it the best-selling album up to that time. At the opposite extreme, hard rock bands like the Allman Brothers and Led Zeppelin radiated waves of cranked-up volume. And the hard-edged voice of black funk groups, such as Sly and the Family Stone and George Clinton and Funkadelic, boomed across the land. Ottawa's Bruce Cockburn blended folk, rock, and reggae with political and social convictions, and Gordon Lightfoot charmed his audiences with gentle folk and pop ballads, such as *Early Morning Rain*, *If You Could Read my Mind*, and *Sundown*.

Many musicians attempted to recapture the Beatles' chameleon charm, borrowing from a range of musical idioms. Flaxen-haired Peter Frampton poured out a cleaned-up rock that some critics termed bland but that teenage girls adored. The mainstream sound of Fleetwood Mac propelled the group to

Disco's hottest tickets included, clockwise on this page from left: Donna Summer, shown on the cover of her hit album **Bad Girls**; the Bee Gees in concert; the Village People, in macho guise as cowboy, Indian, soldier, biker, cop, and construction worker; and John Travolta, in his signature white suit, making a slick disco move on the set of **Saturday Night Fever**.

megahit stardom, and its 1977 album *Rumours* won a Grammy award. Others donned costumes and struck poses that would have shocked Oscar Wilde. For the purveyors of glitter rock — Elton John, David Bowie, and Alice Cooper among them — outrageousness was all.

And some just presented their own natural selves. When Bruce Springsteen's *Born to Run* exploded off the charts in 1975, it seemed to usher in a virile, blue-collar reality: fanfare for the common man.

Dance! Dance! Dance!

Then disco entered the mainstream, offering a fast express to fantasyland. Gays, blacks, and Hispanics in underground after-hours clubs were already gyrating to a pounding, metronomic dance beat that — combined with simple, repetitive lyrics — eventually set the entire country in motion. "Dance! Dance! Dance! — Yowsah! Yowsah! Yowsah!" urged the black disco group Chic, and just about everyone jumped in. "The Hustle," by Van McCoy and the Soul City Symphony, sold 10 million copies in 1975. The next year "Love to Love You, Baby" established Donna Summer as the Queen of Disco. (During the song's 17-minute run, she moaned the title 28 times: "Ooooh, Aaaah . . . Love to Love You, Bay-Bee . . .") Then *Saturday Night Fever*, starring John Travolta as a flashy club dancer, added Hollywood's seal of approval. The sound track album, featuring the Bee Gees, who revived their careers by mastering the disco sound, sold 25 million copies.

A camp sexual irony was part of the fun. Grace Jones, in a wedding dress and holding a whip, belted out "I Need a Man" on *The Merv Griffin Show*. A game Rod Stewart asked the public "Do Ya Think I'm Sexy?" and came up with a career best-seller. And The Village People, six hulking males, offered straight audiences such gay anthems as "Macho Man," "In the Navy," and "Y.M.C.A." The lyrics offended some listeners, but most people just kept dancing.

Before the rage subsided, some 20,000 glittering discotheques were amplifying the noise. The most famous electronic temple was New York's celebrity-studded Studio 54, whose owners (before they went to jail for income tax evasion) insisted on "good-looking waiters and abusive doormen." Jackie Onassis, Truman Capote, and Bianca Jagger made the scene. Dance floors pulsated as DJ's blended their "mixes," adapting songs and volume to the mood of the crowd.

Toward the decade's end, a new kind of rock called punk began elbowing its way into the music arena. Groups like the Ramones and the Sex Pistols preached a defiant message of raucous anarchy. The fresh, innocent sound of the Beatles was rapidly fading into memory.

Swelling the chorus of musical styles, Fleetwood Mac (top left) served up a melodic rock with wide appeal, and James Taylor (top right) was even gentler on the mind. Not so the ear-splitting dissonance of Led Zeppelin (above) or even the "watch-me" antics of Elton John, shown below in outsize shades and a feather boa. But Bruce Springsteen was just the working stiff next door.

BLOCKBUSTERS HIT MOVIELAND

A crew of bright young directors brought new sparkle to the silver screen, rolling out lavish studio extravaganzas that reaped millions at the box office.

Some came from film school; others started out in television. Martin Scorsese, whose *Mean Streets* gave a tough new edge to the genre of the "gangster picture," had studied to be a priest. Whatever their background, the decade's *wunderkind* directors set out to redefine films and make a few bucks along the way. They succeeded beyond anyone's wildest expectations.

Francis Ford Coppola had been working in Hollywood nearly a decade when, at age 31, he won an Academy Award in 1970 for the script to *Patton*. Still, Paramount was taking a long shot when it chose him to film *The Godfather* (1972), from a best-selling novel chronicling the rise of the Corleone crime family. ("He knew the grit," an insider explained.) Against studio objections, Coppola cast Marlon Brando as the family patriarch Don Corleone; insisted on Al Pacino, a little-

Dark interiors and powerful acting added to the impact of Francis Ford Coppola's The Godfather. *The film won an Oscar for Marlon Brando (left) and another for the director (above).*

The real stars of George Lucas's Star Wars *were two robots, C-3PO and R2D2, who some thought upstaged the human leads, Carrie Fisher, Mark Hamill, and Harrison Ford.*

known stage actor, as Corleone's youngest son; and demanded total period authenticity.

The Godfather grossed $43 million and earned Coppola another Oscar. He followed up with *The Godfather, Part II* (1974), a look at Don Corleone's youth. The picture earned him three more Oscars, for best screenplay, picture, and directing. His masterstroke was casting Robert de Niro, until then best known for his tough-guy lead in *Mean Streets,* as the young Don Corleone. (De Niro went on to play a psychopathic killer in Scorsese's 1976 *Taxi Driver,* making him a specialist in nastiness.) Nor was Coppola finished. In 1979 he released the decade's most ambitious film, *Apocalypse Now,* a Vietnam War saga that cost more than $30 million and took years to make.

The next newcomer to hit it big was Steven Spielberg, who got his start by walking onto the Universal lot. Spielberg was assigned low-budget chase movies at first, then, in 1975, at age 28, he was asked to direct *Jaws,* about a killer shark with an appetite for swimmers. To fill the title role, the producers devised a mechanical sea monster, which, unhappily, still had a few kinks when filming began. The studio was frantic. Spielberg rescued the film with inspired cinematic zoom-ins and zoom-outs for blood-chilling effects. No more snickers, just screams. *Jaws* became one of the top grossers ever.

Then Spielberg hit pay dirt again. *Close Encounters of the Third Kind* (1977) took a man and a woman to remote Wyoming for a rendezvous with UFO's and extraterrestrials. The movie was riddled with plot holes and awash in false premises. No matter. Spielberg performed his sleight of hand with the camera, and — presto — people in droves left the theatres feeling wonderful.

George Lucas went straight from USC's film school to Warner Brothers. In 1973, still in his mid-20's, he made the low-budget, highly acclaimed *American Graffiti*. His next move was a 180° swerve into science fiction. *Star Wars* took the best elements of Hollywood's past — the western's stark locales, World War II's aerial dogfights, *The Wizard of Oz*'s Tin Man camaraderie — and transformed them into desert planets, laser-beam spacecraft, and talking robots. Critics likened the result to a cinematic comic strip, but audiences loved it. The movie's gross went ballistic: nearly $300 million by the decade's end.

No movieland event had more critics shaking their heads than the remarkable success story of Sylvester Stallone, creator of *Rocky* and its socko sequels. In 1975 the 29-year-old Stallone — broke, his wife pregnant — penned a screenplay about a down-on-his-luck boxer

Sylvester Stallone poses as the dogged prizefighter Rocky Balboa in the first of many Rocky movies.

▶ *Steven Spielberg's* **Close Encounters of the Third Kind** *featured dazzling special effects created by electronics wizard Douglas Trumbull.*

▼ *Director Spielberg enjoys a friendly moment with the star of Jaws.*

who miraculously gets to fight the world heavyweight champion. Offered $360,000 for the script, Stallone refused the money unless he could play the lead. People hemmed, people hawed, but he got his way. The Italian Stallion trotted into the ring, and there he stayed year after year.

Hollywood still made all manner of films, of course. Director Bob Fosse had a musical hit with *Cabaret* and followed up with *All That Jazz*. Stars like Jack Nicholson *(Five Easy Pieces, One Flew Over the Cuckoo's Nest, Chinatown)*, Robert Redford *(The Sting, Three Days of the Condor, All the President's Men)*, and Donald Sutherland *(Klute, Don't Look Now, Invasion of the Body Snatchers)* attracted ticket buyers and demanded upward-spiralling multimillion-dollar fees. Sex continued to sell: Jane Fonda played a prostitute stalked by a psychotic murderer in *Klute* and won an Oscar; ex-footballer Burt Reynolds, cavorting bare-chested, became the decade's hottest cinematic stud as well as *Cosmopolitan* magazine's first-ever nude male centrefold.

Other movies bucked the trend and still did magnificently. Ted Kotcheff's *The Apprenticeship of Duddy Kravitz*, the debut of Richard Dreyfuss, amused and enraged audiences with the antics of a young Jewish hustler in 1940's Canada. And who would have thought that Woody Allen, not everyone's idea of a suave leading man, would win over viewers in his sly urban romance *Annie Hall*?

ROOTS: A MEGAHIT

For eight consecutive nights in January 1977, North America sat mesmerized. Businessmen cancelled meetings, movie houses remained half empty, and even Congress went home early. No one wanted to miss a single episode of *Roots,* a brutal and riveting 12-hour epic of slavery in the United States, based on Alex Haley's best-selling family history and starring newcomer LeVar Burton (above). Viewers had seen other multipart dramas but *Roots* was the first true megahit. More than 130 million people watched at least part of it, giving ABC its highest one-week rating ever. And a new TV staple, the miniseries, came into being.

At home with All in the Family: *Carroll O'Connor and Jean Stapleton as Archie and Edith, with Rob Reiner and Sally Struthers*

ARCHIE, MARY, HAWKEYE, AND FRIENDS

Accustomed to a diet of silly comedies, conventional drama, and wacky variety shows, TV viewers were about to get the shock of their lives.

By the mid-1970's, it cost Canadian broadcasters $30,000 to produce a half-hour sitcom. Or they could import an American program for $2,000. As a result, some two-thirds of the television programs Canadians watched originated in the United States. CTV usually chose the cheaper American product. CBC, however, responded with excellent public affairs programs like *Man Alive*. It also scored with vignettes of an immigrant district in Toronto, *The King of Kensington*. Another hit was Bruno Gerussi who played Nick Adonidas, a scavenger for logs on the B.C. coast in *The Beachcombers*. His competitor in the scramble for logs was a grimy but lovable scoundrel appropriately named "Wreck."

Some American sitcoms tackled serious questions, as with Archie Bunker, the blue-collar hero of *All in the Family,* carrying a satchel of blustery quirks and stubborn ethnic prejudices that made people's hair stand on end. "Archie Bunker ain't no bigot," TV's new everyman told a black neighbor, "it ain't your fault you're colored." Viewers did a double take and burst out laughing. Enter the real-life sitcom, which served up brash humor along with social relevance. Television would never be the same again.

All in the Family brought a gritty, tell-it-like-it-is immediacy to the tube. Archie, played by Carroll O'Connor, shared his Queens, New York, home with "dingbat" wife Edith (Jean Stapleton), good-natured daughter Gloria (Sally Struthers), and long-haired son-in-law Mike (Rob Reiner), whom he referred to as meathead. The show dealt regularly with hitherto taboo subjects, such as racism, rape, impotence, and menopause. Mike got a vasectomy. Gloria made friends with a transvestite. ("She's a nice fella," Archie grudgingly admitted.)

Audiences could not get enough. *All in the Family* continued for 12 years, one of the longest runs in television. Several of its characters moved on to shows of their own, establishing *Maude* and *The Jeffersons* as decade hits.

Another sitcom with a social conscience, *The Mary Tyler Moore Show,* struck a particularly resonant chord with career women. *MTM* depicted the weekly comic travails of Mary Richards, an aspiring TV executive (played by Mary Tyler Moore) who works as associate producer for a Minneapolis news program. Mary was over 30, still single, and spunky. When her boss, Lou Grant (Ed Asner), asked personal questions during a job interview, she at first protested. Then, like many other job seekers in the 1970's, she swallowed her pride. Lou: "What religion are you?" Mary: "Mr. Grant, you're not allowed to ask that. . . . It's against the law." Lou, persisting: "Are you married?" Mary, in a tiny voice: "Presbyterian."

Over seven seasons, *The Mary Tyler Moore Show* won 27 Emmys, including 3 for best comedy, 5 for writing, and 14 for acting. And it spun off three successful series: *Rhoda, Phyllis,* and *Lou Grant.*

For a country deeply divided by the Vietnam conflict, *M*A*S*H,* a black comedy about a Mobile Army Surgical Hospital unit in the Korean War, tugged hard on raw emotions. Amid the bloodshed and the boredom of life at the front, a grim, sardonic humor bubbled up. Here was Capt. Hawkeye Pierce (Alan Alda) making surgical rounds in a gorilla suit; performing a phony appendectomy in order to sideline an inept general; eavesdropping on the sexual exploits of Maj. Hot Lips Houlihan (Loretta Swit), a supposedly prim head nurse. Hawkeye and his pals, confronting death daily, used wisecracks like morphine. "I loathe you," rasped one nonadmirer, exasperated at Hawkeye's antics. "I call your loathe and raise two despises," came the retort. *M*A*S*H,* with its powerful antiwar message, ran 11 seasons. Some 125 million viewers watched the final episode, a 2½-hour special called "Good-bye, Farewell, and Amen."

Stars of the 1970's, clockwise from top left: the cast of M*A*S*H, *Alan Alda sitting; Mary Tyler Moore; Mike Wallace and Harry Reasoner from* 60 Minutes; *John Belushi and Garret Morris as Coneheads on* Saturday Night Live; *and at centre,* Sesame Street's *feathery, friendly Big Bird*

In 1975 the TV news-magazine *60 Minutes,* which had been limping along for years, received a face-lift. CBS added a third correspondent, Dan Rather, to the Morley Safer–Mike Wallace duo and moved the show to prime time.

It proceeded to take off. Sharply different reportorial styles gave balance and pace: Safer was polished; Wallace, confrontational; Rather, reasonable. The trademark technique of putting the reporters before the camera, on location, lent immediacy and controversy. Safer went to Arizona to uncover a real estate scam, and federal indictments followed; Wallace journeyed to the Middle East to interview Jews in Syria; Rather spent time in Florida exposing the finances of a congressman, and a formal House reprimand ensued.

Canada's own Robert MacNeil became co-anchor on the MacNeil/Lehrer Report, first aired on New York's WNET-TV in 1975. In 1983 this popular news show was to become the MacNeil/Lehrer Newshour.

Some shows still mined tried-and-true nuggets of formula comedy and drama. Teenagers saw their idealized selves in *The Partridge Family* and *The Brady Bunch.* The heartwarming courage of *The Waltons,* a rural family facing Depression-era hardship, gave inspiration to millions. *Charlie's Angels* and *Happy Days,* both sheer escapism, zoomed to the top in the ratings. Meanwhile, the newly established Public Broadcasting System was treating North America to a stream of upscale British imports, including *The Forsyte Saga, Elizabeth R,* and *Upstairs, Downstairs.* Public television also gave children a year-round Christmas present: with Big Bird and Kermit the Frog, *Sesame Street* made it really fun to learn your ABC's.

WOMEN ON THE MOVE

They had come far, but full equality for women remained a long, frustrating march ahead. A cry went up for day-care centres, equal employment opportunity, equal pay, and an Equal Rights Amendment.

Demanding full equality, demonstrators parade to celebrate 50 years of say-so at the ballot box.

Barbara Jordan (top) addresses the 1976 Democratic Convention; Congresswoman Millicent Fenwick (middle) represents a New Jersey district; and Shirley Chisholm (above) runs for president in 1972.

Canadian universities learned a new word in the 1970's. It was "Herstory," and that simple word was a challenge to the "His-story" of the male-dominated academic world. A new field called Women's Studies emerged to counter the male view of the world all the way from graduate school down to kindergarten. The development was strongest in academia, but it expanded well beyond the universities. In 1971, 30 women's groups formed the National Action Committee on the Status of Women to pressure governments to ensure that women had equal opportunities and equal pay with men. The committee had a daunting task.

Canadian women had won the right to vote in 1919, so political equality was no longer the issue. What women wanted now was full equality over the whole range of public life. Most especially, they wanted equality in the workplace. By 1973, women were rivalling men in education by winning 40 percent of all bachelor's degrees, and half of all women were in the labor force. But they were still relegated to lower-level jobs and, if they gained "men's" jobs, were usually paid less for the same work.

Both the situation and the protest were much the same in the United States, though there they found a more political focus. Congress, responding to the liberated mood of the moment, dusted off an equal rights amendment (ERA) to the Constitution, which had been languishing in committee since 1923. "Equality of rights under the law shall not be denied or abridged by the United States or by any State on account of sex," the proposal read, and in 1972 Congress passed it overwhelmingly. All that was needed for ERA to become law was formal approval by three-fourths of the states. Other measures sped through Congress: a Child Development Act, an extension of the Equal Employment Opportunity Act of 1972 (to give the Equal Employment Opportunity Commission some muscle), and an Equal Credit Opportunity Act. "This is not a bedroom war," noted

Editor Gloria Steinem, showing a gleefully pregnant President Carter on her latest cover of Ms. magazine, expresses disappointment over his first year in office.

First Ladies Lady Bird Johnson, Rosalynn Carter, and Betty Ford join Bella Abzug to raise a torch at the National Women's Conference in Houston, Texas.

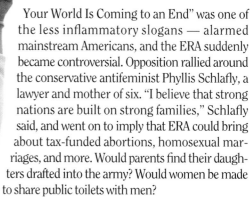

Betty Friedan, author of *The Feminine Mystique* (1963) and a founder of the National Organization for Women (NOW), "this is a political movement." And politics seemed to be winning.

Fast Start, Slow Death, for ERA

Then came the cold realities. President Nixon vetoed the Child Development Act, claiming that the day-care centres it authorized might undermine America's family-centred traditions. A hodgepodge of legal decisions supported the Equal Employment Opportunity Act, but their effect was hard to discern. Even though more than half of all adult females would join the work force by 1980, most found themselves restricted to a "pink-collar ghetto" (as Gloria Steinem's *Ms.* magazine put it) of low-wage "women's" jobs, such as typing, cleaning house, waiting tables, selling perfume, and teaching school. For every dollar men earned in 1973, women made only 57 cents, a significant drop from the 63-cents-to-the-dollar ratio recorded 10 years earlier. "We are triumphantly galloping toward tokenism," remarked Steinem of the statistics.

Perhaps the biggest disappointment in the women's rights movement was the roller-coaster course of ERA. On its way to what seemed like certain ratification, the amendment passed quickly through 35 state legislatures. Then, with just three states needed for ratification, progress screeched to a halt. The strident tone of much feminist rhetoric — "Repent Male Chauvinists,

From an apron full of buttons to a samplerlike poster (right, above), by 1977 the campaign for women's rights reached fever pitch.

Your World Is Coming to an End" was one of the less inflammatory slogans — alarmed mainstream Americans, and the ERA suddenly became controversial. Opposition rallied around the conservative antifeminist Phyllis Schlafly, a lawyer and mother of six. "I believe that strong nations are built on strong families," Schlafly said, and went on to imply that ERA could bring about tax-funded abortions, homosexual marriages, and more. Would parents find their daughters drafted into the army? Would women be made to share public toilets with men?

The answer was no on all counts, but the damage had already been done. The time limit for ratifying the ERA expired, and it went down in defeat.

Despite such setbacks, women across North America increasingly entered the work force. But they paid a price. Most two-career families required a "superwoman," who, after eight hours of wage-earning toil, was expected to come home, cook dinner, do the laundry, and tuck in the children. "There's a socioeconomic jet lag," declared one California professional woman. "Now we get the jobs all right, all the jobs — at home, with the kids, and at work." Or as Archie Bunker, the never-to-be-reconstructed male chauvinist in TV's *All in the Family,* declared: "All right, Edith, you go right ahead and do your thing . . . but just remember that your thing is eggs over easy and crisp bacon."

In November 1977 women rallied again, some 20,000 strong, at the National Women's Conference in Houston, Texas. Bella Abzug, head of President Carter's National Advisory Committee for Women, gave a speech, and in an interview with *Time* magazine after the conference, said it all: "The issues aren't going to go away and neither are we."

TEARS OF JOY, TEARS OF SORROW

Quebec votes to stay in Canada. And Canada gets

a new Constitution.

O n the night of November 15, 1976, Canadians were mesmerized by the images on their television screens — jubilant crowds in Montreal waving blue-and-white fleur-de-lys flags; Rene Lévesque waving to supporters who wept for joy. Quebec had elected a government pledged to withdraw the province from Canada.

Canadians in other provinces were shocked, but they should not have been since most had been drifting into their own provincial enclaves for decades. It began in 1920 when the emergence of hydro power and road-building shifted power from Ottawa to the provinces. Ottawa regained some power during World War II and after it, when it developed social programs. But by 1976, those programs, too, had been handed over to the provinces. The provincial premiers, especially those from wealthier provinces like Quebec, On-

tario, Alberta, and British Columbia, grew louder in their demand for ever more powers. In effect, they were asking for greater independence from the rest of Canada. Quebec was simply going one more step.

Quebec Tries to Stand Alone

Although "separation" was part of their agenda, Quebec's governing party, the Parti Québécois (PQ), rarely used the word. The preferred term was sovereignty because PQ leaders knew that separation was opposed by the majority of Quebeckers. The voters would have to be coaxed to break their ties with Canada, by a step-by-step strategy known by its French term *étapisme*. First, the PQ would concentrate on updating and reforming several laws. Then it would offer voters a referendum on sovereignty before the party actually pushed for a break with Canada.

But if the PQ was soft in its nationalism, it was hard on language. In 1977 it passed a charter of rights for the French language, Bill 101. This document made French the official language of Quebec, required most businesses to operate in French, and even banned outdoor advertising in any language but French. For many in French Quebec, Bill 101 was a powerful symbol of their dominance. For English Quebeckers, it was a sign that they were no longer welcome. Hundreds of thousands left the province in a migration that still continues.

The sovereignty referendum was announced for May of 1980 with as gentle a question as could be found: whether Quebeckers would allow their government simply to negotiate something vaguely referred to as "a new agreement." The forces of the "Yes" were headed by the popular PQ leader René Lévesque, those of the "No" by the patrician Liberal leader Claude Ryan. But there was also a powerful voice from Ottawa — that of the returning Prime Minister, Pierre Trudeau. A long-time foe of Quebec nationalism, he pledged that he would never negotiate separation — but would be willing to discuss constitutional change if Quebec voted no.

The Kitchen Cabinet

In 1981, three old friends — Roy Romanow (Saskatchewan's Attorney General), Jean Chrétien (Federal Justice Minister) and Roy Mc-Murtry (Ontario's Attorney General), above — met often in the kitchen of Chretien's home to discuss the proposed new Constitution. The premiers and their aides had debated the issue at a series of first minister's conferences. But the premiers each took a tough line and no sooner was a measure of agreement accomplished by some than it collapsed under refusal by others. On November 4, a basic proposal was worked out, without René Lévesque. Meanwhile, the trio above met in the kitchen of the conference centre and crystallized their plan. Newfoundland Premier Brian Peckford presented it to Trudeau the next morning. The deal was signed a few hours later, by all except Lévesque who felt that the premiers had gone behind his back during what came to be known as the "night of long knives." For the rest of Canada it was the final act of independence.

Weeks of rallies and flag-waving ensued, with emotionally moving speeches by Lévesque, and pugnacious responses from Trudeau. But, for all the excitement, few minds were changed. As the results came in on that spring evening on May 20, the mood at PQ headquarters sagged from high anticipation to tears, not of joy this time but of sorrow. They had lost, 60 percent to 40 percent.

Canada Writes its Own Constitution

Now was the time for Trudeau to honor his promise of constitutional change. Trudeau's legal advisors warned him that it would be wise to proceed with the consent of the premiers. The search for that consent turned into a raw struggle for expanded powers by the premiers, led by Peter Lougheed of Alberta.

Trudeau insisted on incorporating a charter of rights in the new Constitution. But the premiers, fearful that it might weaken their own powers, added an opt-out clause (the so-called "notwithstanding clause"), which allowed them to suspend rights at will. It was agreed that future changes would require the consent of Ottawa and at least seven provinces containing 50 percent of Canada's population.

The new Constitution was signed into law on April 17, 1982, and marked Canada's final break with Britain. The "notwithstanding clause," as many had feared, was used by some provinces to break strikes. And even though Quebec had not signed the constitution compromise, its government used the clause to overturn a Supreme Court ruling that part of Bill 101 was unconstitutional. However, the charter did prove useful for protests against U.S. missile testing in Canada, and for storeowners contesting Sunday laws. Moreover, simply by existing, the charter gives pause to those who might discriminate against minorities.

Perhaps the most troublesome feature of the Constitution, though, is the process required to alter it. That it is necessary to seek the consent of the federal government and seven provincial governments representing half the Canadian people makes this Constitution a difficult one to change ever again.

... MAUDITS ANGLAIS ...
.... MAUDITS FRANÇAIS ...

PROBING THE SECRETS OF LIFE

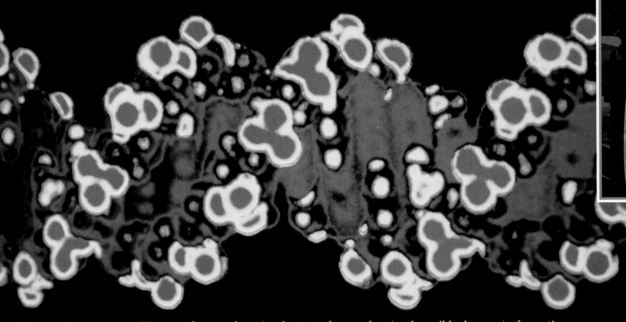

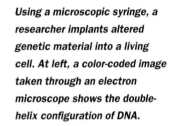

From arthroscopes to CT scans, from embryo implants to the wonders (and possible dangers) of genetic manipulation, an arsenal of new techniques propelled medical science headlong toward the future.

Using a microscopic syringe, a researcher implants altered genetic material into a living cell. At left, a color-coded image taken through an electron microscope shows the double-helix configuration of DNA.

▼ At age two, test-tube baby Louise Brown was as normal as any other healthy child.

She has a set of lungs like a glassblower," marvelled a hospital staffer in Oldham, England, on July 25, 1978. Even if the 5-pound 12-ounce blonde, blue-eyed Louise Brown had been delivered without opening her mouth, her birth would have been one of the most resounding in history. She was the world's first test-tube baby.

Blocked fallopian tubes had prevented Louise's mother, Lesley, from conceiving. So surgeons removed an egg from one of Lesley's ovaries, fertilized it in a glass dish with her husband's sperm, and then implanted it in her uterus. Nine months later Louise came squalling into the world. This first in vitro fertilization to result in a full-term pregnancy, after 80 previous failures, gave new hope to infertile women everywhere.

The 1971 invention of the silicon chip microprocessor foretold another revolution in medicine. Computers invaded hospitals to serve as electronic nurses in critical care units. Patients found themselves hooked to an array of electronic monitoring devices, which kept tabs on blood pressure, heartbeat, respiration, kidney function, and the like. A computer could sound an alert for help, or recommend a treatment, or even direct the automatic pumping of needed substances into the patient's body.

The computer was central to another invention, the CT (computerized axial tomography) scanner. This remarkable machine, for which inventors Allan Cormack and Godfrey Hounsfield won a Nobel Prize, allows doctors a close look at a patient's internal organs without surgery. It takes a series of X rays, which the computer integrates into a minutely detailed portrait. Abnormalities as small as one or two millimetres show up clearly. Other internal viewing techniques soon followed: positron-emission tomography (PET), in which the patient receives an injection of radioactive glucose that helps generate an image; and sonarlike ultrasound, which is used in viewing fetuses in pregnancy and to detect problems such as kidney stones.

One medical advance was prompted not by disease but by a health craze, jogging. Many

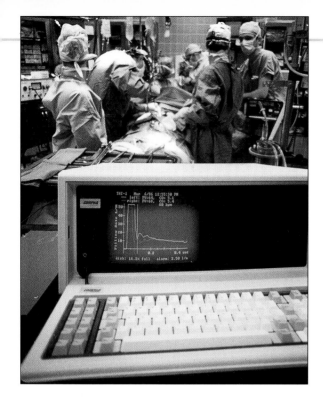

Microelectronic receptors in this artificial forearm will amplify signals from an amputee's remaining muscles, causing motion in the computerized hand.

In a balloon angioplasty, surgeons thread a catheter up a patient's leg toward a clogged artery in his or her heart. When the catheter reaches the damaged section, a tiny balloon will inflate to dislodge the blockage. A computer in the foreground monitors the procedure.

runners, pounding out their daily kilometres, found that their knees gave way under the strain. Traditional operations to repair damaged knees required large incisions and could mean months of painful recovery time.

Enter the arthroscope, a new instrument thin enough to slip through a small incision in the knee. Its optical fibres allowed doctors to see right into the joint, and its tiny instruments could perform many types of surgical repair. Patients often returned to work within three to five days.

Other microsurgical techniques were bringing dramatic improvements to patients' lives. Surgeons learned to stitch tiny nerves and blood vessels, to reconnect severed limbs, to probe the eye with diamond-bladed scalpels. A procedure called balloon angioplasty allowed surgeons to ream out clogged coronary arteries without opening the chest.

The surpassing technological achievement of the decade, as important in its way as splitting the atom, was the splicing of genes. With genetic engineering, first accomplished in 1973, scientists could alter a cell's behavior by manipulating its DNA — the hereditary material that controls it. Each strand of DNA contains genes, heredity's building blocks, and by snipping out a particular gene or transplanting a gene from another organism, researchers undertook to custom-tailor life's basic elements. Simple *E. coli* bacteria were transformed into factories for the low-cost manufacture of human insulin (to treat diabetics) and of growth hormone (to overcome hormonal dwarfism).

Bacteria were altered to gobble up oil spills. Plants were engineered to resist disease, drought, frost, and insects. Other research led to tests to determine who might be predisposed to genetic disorders such as Huntington's disease.

Scientists' newfound ability to alter life raised shudders of alarm among many people who worried that researchers, in manipulating DNA, might unwittingly create a virulent killer bacterium that, escaping the laboratory, would sweep the planet. Strict controls were set, but the concerns persisted. "Biologists have become, without wanting it, custodians of great and terrible power," admitted one biologist. "It is idle to pretend otherwise."

Most medical wonders aroused less anxiety. When residents of Old Lyme, Connecticut, developed mysterious arthritic and neurological problems, researchers found the cause to be a bacterium carried by the deer tick. Antibiotics lessened the symptoms of Lyme disease. Antibiotics also provided treatment for Legionnaires' disease, a hitherto unknown strain of pneumonia that killed 29 celebrants at an American Legion convention in Philadelphia. And in 1977 a native of Somalia suffered the last-known case of smallpox, a scourge that is now thought to have been eradicated.

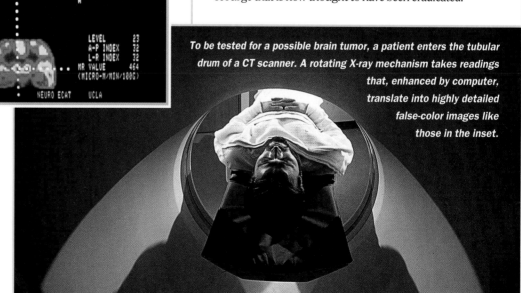

To be tested for a possible brain tumor, a patient enters the tubular drum of a CT scanner. A rotating X-ray mechanism takes readings that, enhanced by computer, translate into highly detailed false-color images like those in the inset.

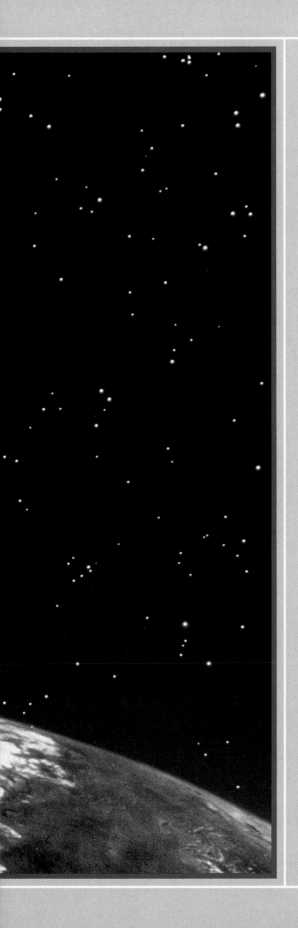

Chapter 9

THE CLOSING YEARS

The Soviet Union dissolves, leaving the United

States as the lone superpower. Canada repatriates

its constitution, and swings to the right. Quebec

decides not to separate — but only just.

The tools of the Information Age, like this International Maritime Satellite, draw us ever closer together.

OUT OF THE WEST COMES RONALD REAGAN

More than Reagan's robustness and movie-star charm, it was his deep-seated belief in the old-fashioned traditions of patriotism, optimism, and self-sufficiency that stirred many Americans.

◄
Reagan poses with one of the horses at his California ranch in 1979, before launching his bid for the presidency. He presented an image of youthful vigor even though, at age 69, he would be the oldest American ever elected to the presidency.

▲ *Standing proud even though he is the smallest, young Ronnie steals the show in this family portrait taken around 1915. Though his family was poor, he was a leader: high school football star, student council president, and summer life-guard credited with saving 78 people from drowning.*

American President Ronald Reagan looked embarrassed — as well he might have been. In March 1985, he stood on a stage in Quebec City in a foursome with his wife Nancy and Canadian Prime Minister Brian Mulroney and his wife Mila. They were singing "When Irish Eyes Are Smiling" for an international television audience. To some viewers, there was more than a touch of vaudeville about the performance. Though both Reagan and Mulroney were of Irish descent, they were gen-

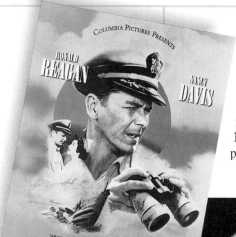

Lovers on-screen and married off, Ron and Nancy share a tender moment in Hellcats of the Navy, *their only film together.*

◀

In his first adult job, Reagan mans the microphone at an Iowa radio station in 1932.

▲ *A future president plays opposite Pat O'Brien in Knute Rockne — All American in 1940.*

erations removed from Ireland. The song was even further removed; it was American.

The Shamrock Summit, as their meeting was called, was intended to signal easier relations between Canada and the United States. But Canada paid a price for it, by abandoning its restrictions on foreign investment and removing the protection of its oil and gas resources that had been accomplished in the National Energy Program of 1980. Reagan and Mulroney also agreed to move immediately on establishing free trade between their countries.

But the meeting had an added importance for Mulroney. Reagan was a popular president, and the joining of hands for their song was intended to show they were close friends in the hope that some of that popularity would rub off on Mulroney.

A President of the People

Reagan established his popularity in the United States from the start. After delivering his address on Inauguration Day, 1981, he made an electrifying statement. Iran, he announced, was releasing all the hostages it had taken prisoner in 1979. The long-awaited news won the American people's optimism in the Reagan presidency.

As Reagan and his wife of almost 30 years,

Nancy, swept into the White House, Americans watched with fascination. Gone was the down-home frugality of the Carter administration. The new president and his First Lady were a combination of elegance, graciousness, and easy-going style not seen since the Kennedy administration. Yet Reagan projected the image of a man of the people. He was a self-proclaimed citizen politician.

Ronald Reagan was born in Tampico, Illinois. Dutch, as his father had nicknamed him, played football, acted, and became involved in college politics. After graduation he pursued a career as a radio sports announcer, which ultimately led him to Hollywood. Along the way Reagan honed his rhetorical skills, which one day would earn him the moniker the Great Communicator. As host of the *General Electric Theater* television series and one of the company's

The Quebec Quartet — Brian and Mila Mulroney, and Ronald and Nancy Reagan join in song in a show of Canadian-U.S. friendship.

Running against Reagan in 1984, Walter Mondale and Geraldine Ferraro (right), the first female vice presidential candidate of a major party, work a Columbus Day crowd. Jesse Jackson (below) campaigns during the Democratic primary.

spokesmen, Reagan had ample opportunity to further fine-tune his talent for persuasive public speaking.

Though still a New Deal Democrat through the 1950's, Reagan grew increasingly conservative. By 1962 he was a registered Republican; two years later he supported the ultraconservative Arizonan Barry Goldwater's presidential campaign. Reagan thrilled TV audiences with a powerful speech at the 1964 Republican National Convention, prompting a group of California Republicans to ask him to run for governor. He did so and won easily. The year was 1966, and almost immediately talk of a bid for the presidency began. He would first run for the highest office in 1976, after two terms as governor.

President at last in 1981, Reagan had served only 70 days in office when a would-be assassin's bullet lodged in his chest. His reaction to the brush with death displayed a fortitude rarely seen outside the movies. "Honey, I forgot to duck," he told his wife, quoting boxer Jack Dempsey after his loss to Gene Tunney. Within days Reagan was back in the presidential saddle.

Over his two terms, Reagan became a hero to many Americans. He seemed sincerely concerned with the questions that kept them up at night, and comfortably familiar, right down to his corny jokes and jelly-bean habit. At the

same time, he was tough enough to fire illegally striking air traffic controllers, sending a message that labor unions should henceforth stay in line. As likable on television as he was in person, Reagan was welcome in U.S. living rooms. He used TV to sell his administration's supply-side economic plan (later called Reaganomics), which proposed to slash federal spending and cut income taxes dramatically. The money freed by this plan, he said, would encourage investments, stimulating economic growth. As a result, profits from the ensuing prosperity would "trickle down" from the upper to the middle and even to the lower classes.

After a short, virulent recession in Reagan's first term, his economic program seemed to work. From late 1982 to 1988, the United States enjoyed the longest peacetime economic expansion in its history. The economy added more than 17 million new jobs, inflation dropped to single digits, and the gross national product showed the biggest percentage increase in 33 years. But other figures seemed less reassuring. Despite big cuts in social programs, federal spending continued to escalate as the Pentagon's budget soared to offset the perceived Soviet threat. Because of Reagan's massive tax cuts, the government took in less money, and it had to borrow heavily to pay its bills. Once the world's biggest lender, the United States became its largest debtor.

Many Americans also admired Reagan's firm hand in dealing with the Soviets, who were not only beefing up their nuclear arsenal but expanding their influence in countries

Chief Justice Warren Burger escorts Reagan appointee Sandra Day O'Connor, the first female Supreme Court justice.

The Iran-Contra Affair

The worst crisis of the Reagan presidency, as intricate as the plot of a James Bond thriller, erupted in the autumn of 1986. That November reports surfaced that the United States, despite a strict long-standing embargo and a pledge never to pay tribute to terrorists, was secretly selling military equipment to Iran. In return, Iran was supposed to obtain release of American hostages held in Lebanon.

Revelations came thick and fast. Money from the arms sales, it turned out, was being diverted to help Contra rebels battle the leftist Sandinista government in Nicaragua. Back in 1982 Congress had prohibited the use of federal funds for this purpose. Both operations — the Iran arms deal and the Contra aid — were being masterminded by Oliver North, an aide to National Security Adviser Robert C. McFarlane and his successor John M. Poindexter. Was Reagan himself involved? A seven-year investigation cleared him of wrongdoing.

such as Afghanistan and Angola. Reagan convinced Americans that Soviet expansionism could be stemmed through negotiations combined with a revitalization of the U.S. military. Pouring more than $2 trillion into the Pentagon, the largest peacetime arms buildup in history, the president boosted the size of the armed forces and modernized equipment. And he championed a program to develop weapons that, from their orbit in outer space, would destroy nuclear warheads before they fell to earth: the Star Wars program, opponents dubbed it.

The pressure seemed to slow Communist expansion. The Soviets removed themselves from Afghanistan. Their allies, the Cubans, did the same in Angola. But curbing Communist influence wasn't easy. No amount of discreet intervention seemed sufficient to dislodge the leftist Sandinista government from Nicaragua (top of column). In addition, throughout the 1980's, Islamic militants carried out hijackings and terrorist attacks against Westerners. Dozens of foreign nationals were taken hostage, tortured, and imprisoned in Lebanon. (The last U.S. captive, journalist Terry Anderson, won release only in 1993.) Despite these distractions, Reagan successfully concluded negotiations with Gorbachev on the Intermediate-Range Nuclear Forces (INF) Treaty in December 1987. The INF Treaty had been 10

▼ *Reagan loved the ceremonies of office, from signing autographs for visiting Girl Scouts to giving foreign dignitaries personal tours around Washington, D.C. Here he reviews the White House Honor Guard with Britain's Prime Minister Margaret Thatcher in 1988.*

Reagan confers with National Security Adviser Robert McFarlane (left) and Secretary of State George Shultz aboard Air Force One.

years in the making and represented a warming of relations on both sides of the Iron Curtain.

Reagan also had his detractors. Some saw him as a lightweight. "You could walk through Ronald Reagan's deepest thoughts," one critic said, "and not get your ankles wet." Others considered his ideological leanings too far to the right. Poor people and their advocates denounced as a sham the "trickle down" principle implied by Reaganomics: the wealth created at the top never did trickle down, they said. Indeed, each day more Americans fell below the poverty line. Some farmers, confronted with shrinking federal subsidies, faced bankruptcy. "This administration doesn't give a cocklebur for rural America," raged one farm-state senator. Meanwhile, opponents of Reagan's allies on the new religious right began to turn on the president. And civil rights supporters became alienated as Reagan criticized affirmative action and school integration and only reluctantly agreed to renew the Voting Rights Act of 1965.

But many of his adversaries' criticisms seemed not to stick to this popular president, whom Colorado Congresswoman Pat Shroeder had called "Teflon coated." His supporters felt the United States was in many respects "back," just as the Republican campaign ads had promised. Most Americans were happy with a leader who could lick the bad guys, get his programs through Congress with bipartisan approval, and at the end of the day go home to his wife and watch a movie in the White House screening room. When Ronald Reagan left office in 1989, he enjoyed one of the highest presidential approval ratings ever.

FROM GLITZ TO GRUNGE

A lot of people in the 1980's wanted to look like they were rich and powerful, and clever designers were glad to oblige. Then came a crash and a slump and an astonishing inner-city style called hip-hop.

"You ought to do jeans," said a licencing company owner to designer Calvin Klein one night at Studio 54, the late-1970's disco hot spot in New York City. Klein took the advice and created a snug-fitting version of the tradition-al blue jeans. He got Brooke Shields (then, in 1980, a mere 15 years old) to slip them on for a commercial. Many objected to the sexy ads, but before long, a lot of people were paying extravagantly for denims that displayed Calvin Klein's, Glorida Vanderbilt's, and oth-er designers' names on the derrière.

Glamor, wealth, and power — from the elegant First Couple to glitzy nighttime soap operas — were back in style. Business was booming. The rich were out in full force, not only organizing lavish, highly publicized charity functions, but also throwing extravagant parties for themselves (billionaire Malcolm Forbes flew some 1,000 of his closest friends to Morocco for his 70th birthday party to the tune of a few million dollars). Fas-cinated viewers were shown a world where "champagne wishes and caviar dreams" came true in television shows like *Lifestyles of the Rich and Famous,* and got a

glimpse of *haute couture* and the latest in fashion trends from pro-grams like CNN's *Style,* with Elsa Klensch, and MTV's *House of Style.* High-gloss fashion magazines, such as *Vogue* and *Harper's Bazaar,* continued to devote effusive columns to gleaming socialites swathed in sequinned couture. Many not-so-wealthy people got caught up in a fever of materialism that found them spending their disposable income on anything that smacked of having it all. Young upwardly mobile couples with large incomes defined themselves by owning luxury cars and expensive watches. Anything by fashion de-signer Ralph Lauren, whether it was his knit sport shirts or his bed linens, was *de rigueur* in many house-holds. Those who couldn't afford Lauren settled for im-itations of his "country club" effect, a tailored casual look that many associated with the rich at ease.

At the office "power dressing" became an important part of climbing the corporate ladder, and businesswomen, armed with expensive briefcases, went to work in designer suits by Donna Karan. Though her suit jackets were more modestly tailored, some suits by other designers had shoulder pads that ri-valled a football linebacker's.

Ralph Lauren remade what men once bought as work and outdoor clothes into fashion statements.

▲ *Fashion designer Donna Karan (top) models her own "body-friendly" ensemble. A Giorgio Armani suit (above) was a staple of the corporate climber's power wardrobe.*

◄ *Exaggerated shoulders, a short jacket, and an above-the-knee skirt added up to a 1980's look.*

With city dwellers snapping up hiking boots and shoes (right) and sturdy jackets (right, below) as if they really needed them, the rugged outdoor look spread like wildfire. Another phenomenon (below) was the sneaker descendant: the high-tech athletic shoe.

Grunge, or lumberjack chic (left), made its way into magazines and onto runways despite its antifashion aura.

Businessmen purchased suits and ties by Giorgio Armani, Perry Ellis, and Calvin Klein.

Looking sexy was in, spurring a demand for body-revealing clothing made of clingy stretch fabrics. Formfitting bodysuits and leggings and miniskirts (which had gone underground for some 10 years) motivated the figure-conscious to join health clubs. But even the gym itself was not safe from the reach of fashion: the exercise togs one wore became a matter of style. Everyone from arbitrageurs to inner-city kids fell for athletic shoes, snapping them up at what some felt were exorbitant prices. The passion for upscale casual footwear was matched by a passion for athletic clothes. Between 1979 and 1982 activewear grew from a $2.5-billion to a $4.5-billion annual business. Sweat suits and bicycle shorts became perfectly acceptable street clothes, though many of the "athletes" wearing them were nonexercisers trying to look chic.

The Plain, Simple, Rugged Look

Inevitably, the spendthrift ostentation of the 1980's ran its course. One image consultant, when questioned about the 1990's, said that people had become more interested in the quality of life. "We were very flashy in the 1980's. And I think we're seeing the pendulum swing back the other way." The October 1987 stock market crash rattled more than a few who had been caught in the web of "godless consumerism." Some cut up their credit cards; others traded in expensive cars for cheaper models. "The strength of fashion now is in its almost total plainness and simplicity," stated one fashion magazine. Shoulder pads disappeared. Party dresses lost their poufs. Designers trotted out moderately priced lines of ready-to-wear clothes. A poll of 500 adults reported only 7 percent believing that status-symbol products were worth their price. In what some observers have called the We Decade, people seemed to want to slow down. After all the fast-paced scrambling for more, more, more, they were just plain pooped. And there was something else: as baby boomers grew older, settled down, and started families, their priorities began to shift from spending money and time on themselves to spending it on their

families. With a new agenda of simpler living, shoppers began responding to sales pitches that stressed value and practicality. Sportswear stores and mail-order houses fed a growing demand for a rugged, outdoor look. "For a lot of people trapped in the urban environment, who can't really get to the woods or the mountains, wearing the clothes is a kick," observed one fashion editor.

The outdoor look hit urban streets in a surprising way: inner-city teens appropriated the clothing as part of hip-hop style. Hiking boots and hooded sweatshirts worn with oversized jeans and T-shirts became a uniform that then moved out of urban centres, such as Toronto and New York, and into middle-class suburbs and even onto the high-fashion runway. Because of its associations with gang attire, this hip-hop look made some people nervous, but the style took off anyway. "When you see Giorgio Armani doing pants with the crotch almost down to the knee," said a vice president of a major department store, "it shows you how important it is."

Boots and flannel shirts or long shapeless dresses and cardigans were the basic elements of the "grunge" look, which was adopted by the twenty-something crowd that some demographers dubbed "baby busters" (in contrast to the older baby boomers). Long, limp hair, torn sweaters, and on the grunge extreme, body piercing comprised what a December 1992 issue of *Business Week* called "slovenly, asexual, antifashion fashion." Grunge nevertheless soon made its way into the style-setting pages of *Vogue* magazine, thus receiving a kind of blessing from fashion moguls. Once again, as had happened so often before, the establishment had absorbed the antiestablishment by imitation.

◄

Rap group TLC models the hip-hop look that was popular among young people in the cities and suburbs in the 1990's.

◀ On Black Monday, October 19, 1987, the stock market dropped 22.6 percent, almost double the record set on October 28, 1929.

▶ In 1989 financier Henry Kravis engineered one of the largest corporate takeovers in world history, $25 billion for RJR Nabisco, and became a hero to the decade's deal makers.

WHEELERS, DEALERS, AND YUPPIES

"Greed is all right.... You can be greedy and still feel good about yourself," Ivan Boesky

assured business-school graduates at a college commencement.

It was one of the most expensive cars that money could buy, not counting the machines that were legal only on the racetrack. The shiny red Ferrari Testarossa (sticker price $90,000) belonged to a young financier who had made $12 million trading in stocks. But the trader was so busy making money that he hardly had time to drive.

The Ferrari was typical of the trophies that hotshot traders bought to congratulate themselves on their immense success during the great bull market of the 1980's. In August 1982, stock prices began a long and seemingly endless rise. But oddly enough, the best of times for corporations were also the worst of times. Financial raiders realized that huge profits could often be made by acquiring companies, breaking them apart, and selling the pieces one at a time. The people who engineered such deals were investment bankers, enthusiastically aided by high-priced law firms. A single deal involving a large corporation could yield multimillion-dollar fees for the banking and law firms and fancy bonuses for the individuals most responsible. In the wings were the specialists in arbitrage, who made money on the sudden fluctuations in stock prices that accompanied a takeover. Investing in the stock market had always been a

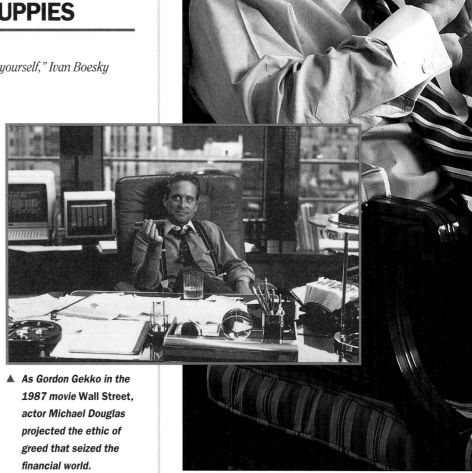

▲ As Gordon Gekko in the 1987 movie Wall Street, actor Michael Douglas projected the ethic of greed that seized the financial world.

Tom Wolfe's scathing novel of 1980's morality, The Bonfire of the Vanities, became a film with (left to right) Tom Hanks, Melanie Griffith, and Bruce Willis.

Traders gape at the latest prices as the stock market plummets in a free fall in October 1987.

gamble, but in the 1980's it became one gigantic casino. As long as the market kept going up, it seemed everyone could win, except the workers who lost their jobs when corporations were broken up or restructured.

A horde of aspiring young financial wizards fresh from business school took the wisdom of such idols as Ivan Boesky and Michael Milken (see box, p. 396) to heart and flocked to Wall Street, Toronto, and other financial centres across the continent. With profits flowing freely, investment firms offered starting salaries of $80,000 to $110,000, plus signing bonuses. The boom, which spilled into many other professions, came as history's blessing for the baby boomers. The generation born after World War II was going to work in an atmosphere of splendid prosperity. In 1984 it was estimated that the 25- to 35-year-old group, which represented 25 percent of the North American population, controlled 25 percent of the continent's disposable income, an astonishing achievement for men and women at the outset of their careers. Their elders looked in awe and envy at the advent of a new social phenomenon: the Young Urban Professional, or yuppie.

Yuppies poured into the cities, and, in a process known as gentrification, mom-and-pop businesses were driven out to make way for gourmet shops and upscale restaurants. Opportunistic landlords seized the chance to convert rental apartments into condominiums that sold for six-figure sums. Though many observers and social activists decried gentrification, yuppies brought new life to decaying residential and industrial neighborhoods that the political establishment had written off. The young professionals wanted the best quality money could buy — in houses, food, clothes, and high-tech gadgets of all kinds. But it was with their cars that they really expressed themselves: BMW's, Mercedeses, and other costly, high-performance automobiles became the badges of success.

Polls showed that the yuppies' economic beliefs were close to those of President Reagan and Prime Minister Mulroney: first they wanted to cut government spending (and taxes) and sometime later perhaps do more for the welfare of the poor and the needy. They felt that they deserved their

High Fliers and Crashers

High rollers in the 1980's games of chance, from left to right: Ivan Boesky, Michael Milken, Albert Reichman, and Donald Trump.

The Reichman brothers, Albert, Paul and Ralph, moved to Canada in 1956 after migrating from Austria to France, Spain and Morocco. Starting with a tile company, they moved into real estate with a company called Olympia and York which, by 1980, held property in some 30 North American cities and was reputedly the largest real-estate company in the world. In the 1980's, they spent more than $500 million for Abitibi-Price, the world's largest paper producer, and bought control of Gulf-Canada Resources. Then, in 1987, the Reichmans announced their most ambitious plan yet — a $6.5 billion dollar real-estate development in London, England. It was called Canary Wharf.

Donald Trump was a more flamboyant success. A New York real-estate developer who created a vast empire of high-rises and gambling casinos, he was legendary for sweet-talking bankers and crushing competitors as he built up his fortune to $3 billion. He was also very generous in aiding worthy causes. One friend, attempting to explain Trump in the psychological jargon of the era, commented: "No achievement can satisfy what he wants.... He is playing out his insecurities on an incredibly large canvas."

Another big player was Ivan Boesky, the master of arbitrage, who had uncanny luck in guessing before anyone else that a company would be up for grabs. Boesky's forays were often bankrolled by the firm of Drexel Burnham Lambert, whose Beverly Hills office was the domain of Michael Milken. Milken specialized in junk bonds: high-yield lending to finance high-risk ventures. So great was the demand for his financial advice that the limousines of corporate executives clogged the driveway of his home at 6:00 A.M. on Sundays.

As the rich continued to get richer, federal and state authorities began to get wind of abuses in the financial industry. Ivan Boesky turned out to be not as clairvoyant as he had seemed: he had been paying cash for corporate secrets. Boesky was hit with the high-est fine in U.S. history: $100 million. In an attempt to avoid a long jail term, Boesky fed regulators information about the activities of the king of all traders, Michael Milken, who was himself eventually jailed for fraud.

Trump and the Reichmans, having made their money on the right side of the law, had no cause to worry about legal problems. However, the stock market crash of 1987 was another matter. The Canary Wharf project was axed, Olympia and York went under, and Donald Trump's holdings suffered a severe blow. Trump and the Reichmans would survive (though much of the Reichman empire was broken up), but the summer of growth was over.

▼ *The hero in Jay McInerney's Bright Lights, Big City regains his sense of self after burning out on the good life.*

success; after all, they drove themselves to exhaustion to get it, working 100 hours a week if the job demanded it. Leisure time was just an extension of work: eating at posh restaurants, vacationing at exclusive spas, and exercising at swank health clubs provided opportunities to make business contacts (an activity more commonly known as networking). All of this took its toll, however, and one of the expenses that came along with the yuppie lifestyle was the cost of psychotherapy to answer the question "Why am I doing this?"

Despite the size of yuppie salaries, enough never seemed to be enough. The yuppie dream was built on a precarious mountain of debt. Asked why he continued to work at a killing pace, one man replied, "The wife expects a new Jaguar every year, and the three houses aren't paid for yet." In his novel about New York in the 1980's, *The Bonfire of the Vanities*, Tom Wolfe described an investment banker going broke on $1 million a year. Another novel, *Bright Lights, Big City,* by Jay McInerney, captured the spirit of the era with its depiction of the frenetic nightlife of fast-living Manhattanites: a dizzying round of partying and nightclub hopping, fuelled by generous doses of cocaine and alcohol. Many readers took the novel as a guide to the "good life," missing its strong undertone of disillusion over the morally bankrupt hedonism of such a lifestyle.

By mid-decade many voices were beginning to question prevailing ethics, finding a pervasive attitude of "rules are for fools." One observer wrote of "the affluent society and the impoverished soul." And there were disquieting signs that many of the era's gains may have been ill-gotten. Even the bible of big business, *Fortune* magazine, declared: "Almost everywhere you look in the business world today ... you glimpse something loathsome."

In the second half of 1987, the glittering towers of new wealth were beginning to look as if they rested on shaky foundations. The stock market, which had reached great heights in August thanks to frenzied speculation, was start-

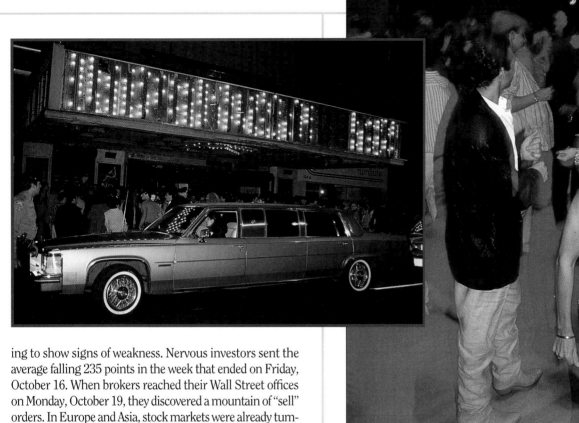

ing to show signs of weakness. Nervous investors sent the average falling 235 points in the week that ended on Friday, October 16. When brokers reached their Wall Street offices on Monday, October 19, they discovered a mountain of "sell" orders. In Europe and Asia, stock markets were already tumbling. When the trading bells at the New York and Toronto stock exchanges sounded the start of the day, they unleashed a wave of panic. By the day's end, the Dow Jones average had plunged 508 points, with 604 million shares traded, ending the five-year bull market. October 19, 1987, was "the nearest thing to a meltdown that I ever want to see," said a financier.

▲ One of the hot spots among the limousine-riding, designer-clothes-wearing set was New York City's Palladium, where patrons mingled with like-minded souls on the dance floor.

◄

The CEO of Chrysler, Lee Iacocca (now retired), was a strong critic of the trend toward mergers and short-term profits.

Soon the very magazines that had trumpeted the achievements of the yuppies were running headlines such as "Where Have All the Yuppies Gone?" "Is Greed Dead?" "The New Volunteerism," and "The Simple Life" and opining that "upscale is out; downscale is in."

Though in the coming years Canadians would share the pain of downsizing, and though some Canadian firms like Olympia and York were among the spectacular collapses of the period, Canada was spared most of the excesses that the United States experienced. For once, the legendary caution of Canadian investors and financial houses had erred on the right side.

By the early 1990's the market had rebounded, and the Dow Jones average resumed a mainly upward course. But the high-flying era of the 1980's was gone, and with it went the wilder antics of the yuppies. The spirit of the 1990's had arrived, and the stock market's hotshots came to the sobering realization that, at least for a while, the party was over.

President Bush works the White House phone to rally support for the 1991 Gulf War against Saddam Hussein. As a young U.S. Navy bomber pilot in World War II (inset, shown with members of his flight crew), Bush flew 58 missions, was shot down over the Pacific, and won the Distinguished Flying Cross.

▼ Almost everyone loved Barbara Bush, a gracious and unpretentious First Lady who wrote the "memoirs" of Millie, the adored White House spaniel.

TWO LEADERS COME TO THE END OF THE ROAD

Mulroney and Bush come to power with high expectations. Both flounder with their national economies, but they succeed in creating the most wide-ranging trade agreement in the history of either country.

George H. W. Bush, the Republican choice for U.S. president in 1988, embodied the old-fashioned virtues of loyalty and devotion to duty. The son of a wealthy family, Bush enlisted in the navy at 18, becoming one of its youngest pilots, and achieving a distinguished record. He then studied economics at Yale and, after graduating, went into the oil business. A seat in Congress came next, and then the position of vice president under Ronald Reagan.

The prospects for Bush's winning the presidency in 1988 looked promising: he had served alongside an enormously popular president, during which time the economy thrived. Playing to conservatives, he criticized big government and promised to hold down spending. "Read my lips: no new taxes!" he proclaimed. Bush won by a landslide, but his promise would come to haunt him after he was forced to break it as president.

In office, Bush vowed to uphold the Reagan legacy of laissez-faire government and a strong national defence. He was a master at foreign affairs and, when necessary, could act with lightning speed and decisiveness. He attended National Security Council briefings on a daily basis, travelled abroad at every opportunity, and developed close personal ties with heads of state the world over. His habit of writing hundreds of notes by hand, and of picking up the overseas phone to chat, enabled him to bring together 28 countries during the Persian Gulf crisis in 1991, assembling a broad-based military and political alliance that stopped dead the conquest of Kuwait by Iraqi dictator Saddam Hussein (see pp. 412–413).

Of humbler origins than George Bush, Brian Mulroney had to work his way up as a lawyer spe-

President Salinas, President Bush, and Prime Minister Mulroney share a joke after signing NAFTA, in October 1992.

Midway through his single term, not even a round of golf near the Bush family's summer house in Maine, could make the president forget the nation's mounting domestic troubles.

cializing in labor disputes, developing a reputation as a skillful bargainer. When Iron Ore Company was looking for a president who could close down its Quebec operations without creating political problems, it turned to the smooth-talking Brian Mulroney. Then, in 1983, he manoeuvred his way to the leadership of the Progressive Conservative Party. A deal maker rather than a man of social or political convictions, Mulroney had early decided that the only deals worth making were with the United States. From the day he became prime minister in 1984, no U.S. president ever had to worry about securing the cooperation of Brian Mulroney. He joined the coalition against Hussein with three warships, a squadron of CF-18 fighter planes, a tanker plane, and a field hospital.

Domestically, however, things went badly for both leaders. By 1990 both economies were in deep recession. Corporations, saddled with debt, were laying off workers — "downsizing" was the favored term — and unemployment

surged. One American in eight lived in poverty. In Canada, though perhaps due to different definitions of poverty, the figure was slightly higher. Real estate prices flattened, then slumped. Racial tensions exploded in the United States, with riots in Los Angeles bringing death to 52 people. In both countries, government debts were pushing into the ionosphere, destroying hopes of spending a way out of the recession. Brian Mulroney's popularity plunged even lower than that of Bush. Some Canadians muttered grimly that his percentage of approval was lower than the interest rate.

Only one important economic initiative remained for the two leaders. Both countries had long feared being left out of the massive trade agreements that were linking most of Europe and Asia. Their response was a proposal for a free-trade area that would join Canada, the United States, and Mexico. Eventually, the North American Free Trade Agreement, (or NAFTA, as it was called), would be open to other nations of the Americas.

Critics, like the Canadian Labour Congress, warned that a free-trade agreement would cost jobs for Canadians, and threaten Canadian control over such areas as social programs, the environment, and job creation. But against the critics were ranged the powerful voices of corporate Canada, especially those involved in transportation and banking. Having grown as large as they could within Canada, they looked longingly at the huge populations of the United States and Mexico.

Bush cooperated by "fast-tracking" the free-trade proposal, a process that set a deadline for reaching agreement. In 1992, as the Bush presidency was shuddering to a close, the North American Free Trade Agreement was signed. Canada, the United States, and Mexico pledged to eliminate most restrictions to trade and investment by the year 2003. Business was poised to reap huge benefits. It remained to be seen how widely those benefits would be shared, if at all.

An energetic diplomat, Bush spent much of his time in office conferring with other heads of state. Here (from left) he discusses trade problems with Japanese Prime Minister Kiichi Miyazawa, disarmament with Soviet Premier Mikhail Gorbachev, and the economy with French President François Mitterrand; and he swaps tips on leadership with Russian President Boris Yeltsin.

TELEVISION MAKES REALITY PAY

Peter Arnett
CNN
Baghdad, Iraq

Programs featuring clean-living folks with no secrets to hide became rarities on the home screen;

they were replaced by a constant stream of real or imaginary people confronting awful problems.

By the 1980's, the cosy world of three major television networks in the United States and two in Canada had come to an end. Part of the reason was cable television (more than 60 percent of homes with television had cable by the end of the 1980's) which encouraged a proliferation of networks, including commercial-free (or almost so) public television. Viewers could now access a huge and often bewildering variety of programs. Many areas had 30 or more channels, including those devoted to home shopping, weather, around-the-clock news, sports, rock music, and reruns. On a pay-per-view basis, recent films and major sporting events were also available.

Programmers discovered and tapped a seemingly insatiable appetite for news. CNN (Cable News Network) offered two channels of 24-hour TV news, as did the CBC with news channels in French and English. Communications satellites and the advent of portable video cameras gave new immediacy to "brought-to-you-live" coverage. News now arrived from practically anywhere in the world while it was happening; millions of people watched Operation Desert Storm in January 1991 as rockets lit up the Baghdad sky. The display of high-tech weaponry in action kept viewers glued to their TV sets.

Real-life dramas became a dominant theme of the decade, permeating all types of television fare. Out went the old taboos; in came more graphic sex and violence, private details of ordinary people's lives, and sensationalism. A supreme example was the trial, in 1995, of O. J. Simpson — film star, ex-football player, and black role model. Courtroom cameras relayed details of the bloody murder of his ex-wife and her lover to sitting rooms across the continent, and brought North America face to face with witnesses being cross-examined in the dock.

Gabfests and Tabloid Shows

No television genre benefitted more from the need to know the details of people's lives than the talk shows, with their intimate format. For years late-night talk had been dominated by a single host, Johnny Carson. But in the 1980's a bevy of rivals, from Joan Rivers to Arsenio Hall, arose to challenge the veteran. Carson, however, managed to beat them all and stay on top, attracting some 12 million viewers a night with guests such as Bob Hope (who appeared 121 times). After a 30-year stint, Carson made a much-ballyhooed exit in 1992 and was replaced by the affable Jay Leno.

Meanwhile, daytime talk shows thrived. Phil Donahue was their Carson.

Veteran journalist Peter Arnett won praise for staying in the enemy's capital to report on the Persian Gulf War, though he was accused by some of becoming the unwitting instrument of an Iraqi propaganda campaign.

▼ *Late-night TV host Arsenio Hall (right) yucks it up with actor-director Spike Lee (left) and blind singing legend Stevie Wonder.*

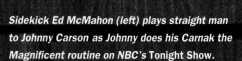

Sidekick Ed McMahon (left) plays straight man to Johnny Carson as Johnny does his Carnak the Magnificent routine on NBC's Tonight Show.

When NBC snubbed David Letterman, failing to offer him the Tonight Show, *Dave* jumped to CBS; but NBC retained rights to some comedic bits, calling them "intellectual property."

"Come on, help me out!" he pleaded, dragging studio audiences into debates on issues like incest and abortion. Many critics accused Donahue of sensationalism, but others hailed his candor. The first black talk-show star, Oprah Winfrey, was aired across the continent in 1986. Using a format similar to Donahue's, she quizzed guests on such sensitive topics as AIDS and battered wives. The most outrageous and combative host was Geraldo Rivera, who shocked and titillated huge audiences with investigations into such topics as sex rings, transsexuals, and the contents of Al Capone's secret vault (in which nothing of interest was found).

Fox Broadcasting, one of the new networks, was a pioneer in a type of television that freely mixed news with entertainment. *A Current Affair*, anchored by Maury Povitch, took its cue from tabloid newspapers like *The National Enquirer*. By paying handsome fees for appearances by people involved in real-life murders and sex scandals — and, even better, to broadcast their home movies — the program gave viewers the voyeuristic pleasure of looking through the peepholes of tightly closed doors.

▶ Rush Limbaugh (left) and Howard Stern (right) heat up the airwaves with their different styles of controversy and candor. Limbaugh specialized in conservative views and contempt for political liberals. Stern dealt in shock, vulgarity, and offensiveness to all.

▼ Along with her engaging style and easy rapport with audiences, gab guru Oprah Winfrey endeared herself to many viewers by shedding 30 kilograms, regaining the weight, then taking it off again.

Reality on a Roll

The reality craze spread. Other slice-of-life shows included *Cops, Rescue 911*, and *America's Most Wanted* (which helped law-enforcement officials track down hundreds of fugitive felons). And semibiographical TV movies proliferated, based on subjects torn from the headlines, sometimes before all the facts were known: *The People vs. Jean Harris* (1981); *The Billionaire Boys Club* (1987); *Baby M* (1988); the tale of the "Long Island Lolita," Amy Fisher, and her relationship with auto body mechanic Joey Buttafuoco, and *The Boys from St. Vincent* (1993).

Even fictional dramas became more realistic. Characters increased in complexity, and plots unfolded over several episodes rather than being neatly tied up in 30 or 60 minutes. The critically acclaimed *N.Y.P.D. Blue* told gritty stories about big-city cops fighting crime and waging personal

One of the first live-action shows, Cops sent camera crews along as police responded to emergency calls.

Bill Cosby played obstetrician Dr. Cliff Huxtable and Phylicia Rashad was his lawyer-wife, Clair, on The Cosby Show.

◀ As the compassionate Sgt. Phil Esterhaus on Hill Street Blues, Michael Conrad always ended morning roll calls with "Let's be careful out there."

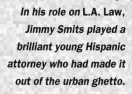

▶ In his role on L.A. Law, Jimmy Smits played a brilliant young Hispanic attorney who had made it out of the urban ghetto.

battles with alcoholism, graft, and racism. In *Due South* (winner of 1995 Gemini Award for best dramatic series) a Mountie joins the Chicago Police Department. *De Grassi High* showed Canadians a high school world in which problems of growing sexuality shared space with pep rallies. The medical drama *E.R.* found humor in healing without ignoring trauma and death. And in *North of 60* the life of native Indians trying to maintain traditional values while dealing with modern western life was played out.

▼ The **Cheers** gang in 1993 (clockwise from left): George Wendt, Rhea Perlman, Woody Harrelson, Kelsey Grammer, Bebe Neuwirth, John Ratzenberger, Ted Danson, Kirstie Alley

Family Sitcoms

One of the most popular programs of the 1980's, *The Cosby Show,* almost single-handedly revived family sitcoms. At its heart was an affectionate upper-middle-class black American family guided by intelligence, wit, and common sense. "I wanted to give the house back to the parents," said its star, Bill Cosby, who called the shots on every aspect of the show. Audience response was so strong that Cosby's earnings for a single year hit $92 million.

In the 1990's, the family sitcom *Home Improvements* won popularity with its lovable but bumbling father, an accident-prone toolshop instructor whose wife supplies common sense for the family.

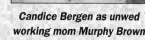

Candice Bergen as unwed working mom Murphy Brown

At the other end of the family comedy spectrum was *Roseanne,* featuring an overweight, harried, blue-collar mom who told it like it was. This was not TV's idealized version of family bliss but, as in *The Honeymooners* which had played more than 30 years before, Roseanne's tough talk and biting put-downs were softened by an underlying love for her spouse and offspring.

Married . . . With Children was a raunchy version of *The Adventures of Ozzie and Harriet.* One episode of the show offended a housewife so deeply that she attempted to organize an advertiser boycott in protest. But the program's Nielsen rating just shot up higher. Even animators came up with a hit antifamily sitcom. The bratty cartoon figure of Bart Simpson, who tells his father "Eat my shorts," delighted older and younger viewers alike.

At left, Dynasty stars (left to right) Linda Evans, John Forsythe, and Joan Collins pause in their machinations. At right, Larry Hagman flashes a J. R. Ewing grin.

Other sitcoms looked to the workplace for laughs and relevance. The regulars at Cheers, a Boston pub, won Emmys for more than a decade; as a natural extension of the show, Kelsey Grammer, who played the psychiatrist Frazier, went on to star in his own show *Frazier*, as an on-air psychiatrist working for a Seattle radio station; and *Murphy Brown* made the lifestyle of a feisty reporter a national issue when the character, played by Candice Bergen, and Vice President Dan Quayle traded gibes over the show's decision to make Murphy a single mother. The success of *Seinfeld*, *Friends*, and *Mad About You* produced a spate of imitations as the networks scrambled to add sitcoms featuring young urban professionals to their schedules.

▼ *That favorite dysfunctional family, the Simpsons, gazes in wonder as baby Maggie utters a word.*

Prime-Time Soaps

On November 21, 1980, the second largest audience in television history — an amazing 450 million fans in 57 countries around the world — tuned in to find out "Who Shot J.R.?" on the show *Dallas*. (It was a jilted mistress.) A weekly saga of lust, power, and betrayal in a wealthy Texas oil family, *Dallas* set the pace for prime-time TV soaps, which offered up an addictive array of plot twists, scandalous relationships, greed, and glamor.

Dallas enthralled viewers for 13 years; it was one of the longest-running prime-time series to date. Rapacious J. R. Ewing, played by Larry Hagman, was dubbed the Swine of the Decade by one TV critic. The *Dallas* craze soon begot *Dynasty*, about the lives of some rich and amoral residents of Denver. The cast, led by John Forsythe and Linda Evans, featured Joan Collins, whose character sleazed her way through orgies of conspicuous consumption and superheated lust. From 1982 to 1985 *Dynasty* ran neck and neck with *Dallas*, and it boasted cameo performances by former President Gerald Ford and Henry Kissinger.

Toward the end of the 1980's, viewers' interest in the lifestyles of the rich and neurotic seemed to level off. Audiences turned to the nostalgia of *The Wonder Years* and then to twin hits from Canada, *Anne of Green Gables* and *Return to Avonlea*. In Canada, humor bounced back too, with CBC's *This Hour Has 22 Minutes*, winner of the Gemini Award for best comedy show in 1995, *The Royal Canadian Air Farce*, and *The Kids in the Hall*.

Bruce McCulloch (left), Mark McKinney (centre), and Kevin McDonald camp it up in the offbeat comedy series created for the CBC, Kids in the Hall, winner of the 1993 Gemini Award for best comedy series.

▶

Fire fighters face an impenetrable wall of flame from wildfires that swept through 320,000 hectares of Yellowstone National Park in 1988.

▲ *Fisheries Canada officers check the nets from the Spanish fishing trawler Estai, seized for suspected illegal fishing in March 1995.*

Like the fabled phoenix, a fern rises from the ashes of Mount St. Helens.

▲ *Along with the collapse of sections of the Bay Bridge, the 1989 San Francisco earthquake left 62 dead, 3,258 injured, and $5 billion in property damage.*

Wake-up Calls from Mother Nature

While citizens of the earth debated among themselves about how to save the planet from further degradation, they learned anew that nature still has the final word.

It was a startling discovery. Scientists studying the stratosphere over the South Pole in 1983 were amazed to find sharp decreases in ozone, a gas that helps shield the earth from damaging ultraviolet radiation. It was a dramatic warning to humans that abuse of their environment could produce a lethal backlash. Faced with the prospect of an increase in deaths from skin cancer and of untold damage to crops, governments around the world took steps to limit the production of chlorofluorocarbons (CFC's), chemicals believed to hasten the depletion of ozone.

No one could predict if the banning of CFC's would save the ozone layer, and in any case this was just one item in a grim catalogue of humanity's sins against the planet. It was especially difficult to find solutions for pollution prob-

lems in developing countries, which could not afford to curb industries for the sake of cleaner air and water and of endangered species. At the first Earth Summit, officially called the United Nations Conference on Environment and Development, which was held in Rio de Janeiro in June 1992, Third World nations called on wealthier countries to pay for the preservation of biodiversity, arguing that poor nations could not be made to bear the cost of a cleaner environment, which would benefit all.

By the early 1990's almost half a hectare of tropical forest was being cut down every second, adding up to an annual loss of an area larger than Newfoundland. The loss of tropical forests was especially worrisome, since these immense concentrations of trees absorb carbon dioxide produced by

A sign of the times — the recycling symbol

humans and industry. Scientists monitoring climate patterns warned that increased levels of carbon dioxide and CFC's in the atmosphere could create a greenhouse effect, trapping heat and causing a global rise in temperature. Predictions of the polar ice caps melting and of sea levels rising to swamp coastal cities sparked a fierce debate in the environmental community. Some scientists, pointing to past fluctuations in the earth's temperature, scoffed at these doomsday scenarios. CFC's might actually cool the air, they said, and measurements showed that some glaciers were growing, not melting.

Natural Disasters, Natural Solutions

Doubts about the inevitability of the greenhouse effect did not diminish alarm over the environment. In British Columbia, where cutting machines were moving inexorably on the last stands of the province's once magnificent old-growth forests, protesters blocked roads. Crees in Quebec forced that government to abandon a power project that would have flooded much of the northern part of the province with incalculable environmental results. On the Grand Banks off Canada's east coast, nations shoved each other aside in the race to clean out the last stocks in what had been the world's richest fishery. In 1995, when Canada's tough-talking Brian Tobin, Minister for Agriculture and Fisheries, gave blunt warning to Spanish fishermen to stay within the law, a good many sabres were rattled in what became an international incident, before the lawbreakers backed off.

In the summer of 1993, rains fell almost unceasingly for two months in the central part of the United States, dropping as much as 10 times the normal rainfall. The Mississippi River rose in places to its highest recorded levels,

▲ *Some companies seemed to be learning that what is good for the earth's environment may turn out to be very good for business.*

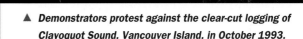

▲ *Demonstrators protest against the clear-cut logging of Clayoquot Sound, Vancouver Island, in October 1993.*

burst through levees, and spread over 5.5 million hectares of land. The flood led to 41 deaths, forced some 100,000 people from their homes, and wiped out crops across the Midwest.

The Los Angeles earthquake of 1994 and the Kobe earthquake in Japan the following year brought home the risks of living in quake-prone areas. By the 1990's most people were convinced that sensitivity to the environment was the way to survive into the future. Automobile manufacturers began discussing plans to build a zero-emission electric car. Many localities took steps to divert their flow of trash from landfills to recycling programs. New York City, faced with the necessity of building incinerators to get rid of its trash, embarked on an ambitious recycling program, with mixed results.

In many instances, young people led successful environmental crusades. They put pressure on companies to cease abuses: stopping a fast-food chain from using hard-to-recycle styrofoam packaging, for example, and persuading a tuna company to quit buying from fishermen who snared dolphins in their nets. A lot of these environmental foot soldiers were not even old enough to vote, but their sense of urgency was understandable: they realized all too well that if they remained passive, they would be the ones to inherit the consequences.

◄

The Mississippi River undid decades of flood-control efforts when it rampaged over farms and cities in 1993.

LOOKING FOR HEALTH AND HAPPINESS

As the breakneck pace and materialism of the 1980's took their toll, some people, from celebrities to stockbrokers, turned to New Age therapy as a means of relieving stress and attaining spiritual peace.

As the sun rose on August 16, 1987, hundreds of people who had gathered before the Great Pyramid in Egypt began to chant, beat drums, and raise an unearthly sound from conch shells. They were trying to stave off the end of the world as foretold in an ancient Mayan calendar by providing something they called harmonic convergence. As the new day dawned across the globe, thousands of like-minded souls joined in to create a huge outpouring of noise. If all went well, not only would the earth be saved from destruction but humankind would enter a New Age of peace and harmony.

The collective resonance that rose worldwide was also a cry from the heart. In the midst of the great wealth that piled up in the 1980's, many felt a yawning emptiness in their lives that money, professional achievement, fitness regimes, and conventional religion could not fill. Some people sought meaning and solace in a variety of unconventional ways, all of which came to be lumped under the term *New Age*. "They yearn to get in touch with the soul," explained one philosophy teacher, and to do so, New Agers took many paths, ranging from the serious to the silly: astrology, holistic medicine, crystal healing, meditation, and more.

Through "channelling," some believers claimed to contact the dead and tap the wisdom of the ancients. When a Seattle woman, J. Z. Knight, announced that she had reached Ramtha, a 35,000-year-old warrior and spiritual guide from the lost city of Atlantis, Knight reaped a fortune dispensing Ramtha's wisdom in books and personal appearances. Sedona, Arizona, became a centre of New Age spiritualism because it was thought to be a place where mystical magnetic energies emanate from the earth. The pyramids and other Egyptian monuments seemed to hold special allure for New Agers, who made pilgrimages there to chant and meditate, seek ancient truths, be healed of their ailments, and remember experiences from previous lives. "I have met over 130 Nefertitis and Cleopatras," remarked one Egyptian guide, "but I have trouble knowing which one is the real one."

Some New Age gurus offered men and women separate paths to wholeness. Robert Bly, a distinguished poet and author of the

New Age evangelist Shirley MacLaine displays a quartz crystal, used to focus her spiritual powers.

▼ *Devotees of New Age philosophy take part in harmonic convergence at the pyramids at Giza.*

bestseller *Iron John,* led men on a quest for "the primal, powerful, masculine qualities lost in the industrialized 20th century." On wilderness camp-outs Bly's followers beat drums, hunkered down in sweat lodges, revealed their personal problems, and in the process found their lost maleness. As for femaleness, Clarissa Pinkola Estes, a Jungian analyst from Denver, wrote a book to help women, who, she felt, had been cut off from their creative drive. Called *Women Who Run With the Wolves,* the book was a collection of folktales about Wild Woman mythology and, according to Estes, exposed the "ruins of the female underworld." Women also took up the drum. "Drumming is a powerful spiritual tool," said one woman. "It's a direct channel into the rhythms of your body."

One of the high priestesses of the New Age, the actress Shirley MacLaine, wrote a series of bestsellers about her wide-ranging New Age experiences. Her book *Going Within: A Guide for Inner Transformation* describes "techniques of meditation, visualization, color and sound therapy, how to work with crystals, how to work with colored jewelry, acupuncture, acupressure, things that have been helpful to me." Acolytes paid $300 each to hear her speak.

And stock market investors paid $360 a

Robert Bly took the title of his bestseller from a Brothers Grimm tale about a caged wild man who is freed by a boy. Marianne Williamson (below), author of A Return to Love, *taught "spiritual psychotherapy."*

#1 NATIONAL BESTSELLER

IRON JOHN

A Book About Men

"Important . . . timely . . . powerful."
—*The New York Times*

ROBERT BLY

Yoga in its many forms, among them hatha yoga, shown here, had won legions of adherents by the 1990's as a valuable physical and mental exercise regime and a means of seeking spiritual enlightenment.

year for a newsletter published by a New Age astrologist-stockbroker who consulted the stars for his market tips. Skeptics no doubt swallowed their derision when the broker warned his clients to get out of the market — fast! — just days before Wall Street crashed in October 1987.

In medicine some alternative therapies emerged alongside the quackery. New Agers stirred interest in acupuncture, Japanese shiatsu (finger pressure massage), reflexology, in which the feet are manipulated to treat other parts of the body, and aromatherapy, the therapeutic inhaling of plant and flower oils. They also promoted homeopathy, an alternative medicine based on the idea that the healing process is sped along by prescribing small amounts of substances that in larger doses would cause symptoms of the diagnosed illness. More dubious was the New Age faith in the medicinal properties of crystals.

Much energy was expended on merely soothing the soul. New Age music, minimalist but melodic, provided a sound track for the mind's meanderings. Accessories such as portable sound-and-light machines promised to induce meditation in the dentist's office and in other stressful surroundings. For a quick fix there were "mind salons" devoted to meditation. Disbelievers strolling through a New Age convention could find a great deal to chuckle at, such as a sign advertising "Brain Waves to Go," but it was hard to dismiss the movement entirely. After all, who could argue that the world lacked peace and harmony?

Using an instrument called a Synchro-Energizer and wearing goggles, a high-tech spiritualist seeks the ultimate in meditative tranquillity on a peaceful shore in Cardiff Beach, South Carolina.

▶
Country music took off in the 1980's. Styles ranged from the offbeat twang of Lyle Lovett to the reedy warble of veteran Willie Nelson (top inset) to the powerful clarity of k.d.lang (bottom inset).

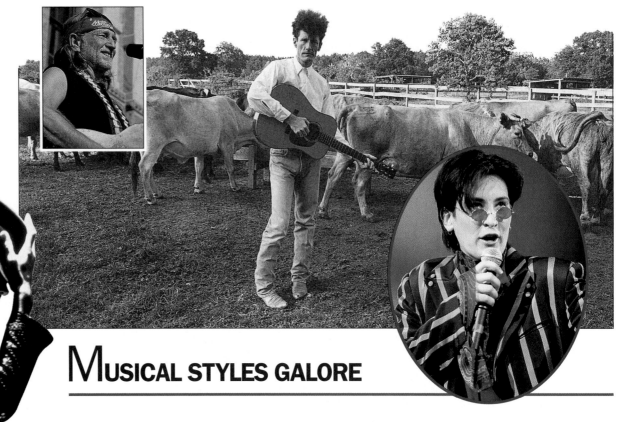

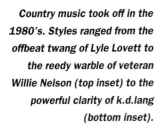

Musical Styles Galore

The variety of music competing for attention was bewildering, approaching the chaotic. And now it wasn't just sound that mattered. Music makers had to appeal to the eyes as well as to the ears.

Good old rock and roll still had power in the 1980's. Tina Turner, who had been perfecting her soulful style throughout the 1960's and 1970's, was still going strong performing her sexy gyrations. Mick Jagger, who once sneered that he "would rather be dead than sing 'Satisfaction' at 45," raked in some $80 million during the Rolling Stones 1989 Steel Wheels tour, and in 1994, at the age of 50, embarked on another gruelling worldwide tour.

While fans of all ages were enjoying the music of legends such as Pink Floyd, The Who, Paul Simon, and Eric Clapton, rock and roll itself was expanding to include new styles. On the fringes existed the short-lived punk rock, a music filled with anarchy and destruction that was imported from Great Britain in the late 1970's. Rebellion also infused the power chords and over-the-top antics of the heavy metal bands, from newer groups like Hole, Bon Jovi, Metallica, and Guns 'n' Roses, to

acts such as Aerosmith and Ozzy Osbourne, which had started up a decade earlier.

Other strains, collectively called alternative rock, surfaced in the music of the Pretenders, R.E.M., the Police, and U2, bands whose members were mostly kids when the Beatles and the Stones were getting started. All the while, rock kept evolving in unexpected directions, among them the highly synthesized, danceable sounds of the Cars, Talking Heads, and Duran Duran.

Canadian performers continued their assault on the North American market. Among the more prominent were Bryan Adams, a mainstream rock artist. In 1994, Céline Dion soared to the top of the U.S. charts with her album "The Colour of My Love" — though it made only second place in Canada. By then, Quebec's Roch Voisine was also becoming popular across Canada.

Though no more than an update of music films made for coin-operated machines in the 1940's, the music video

◀ *Even by superstar standards, Michael Jackson's fame in the 1980's reached extraordinary proportions.*

Rap Is in the House!

All at once it was everywhere: in suburban malls, in soft-drink commercials, in dictionaries. It was music called rap, full of cryptic chanting and teeth-rattling bass lines, which had sprung up from deep within the inner city to take its place in American culture.

Born in the 1960's of a Jamaican tradition called toasting, rap came to New York City in the early 1970's via DJ Cool Herc, who used two turntables to cut back and forth between songs, blending them into a sound later associated with hip-hop. It soon caught on and spread to the black population of other big cities. Initially the rapper's goal was to whip up the dance crowd, insult rivals, and brag (a tradition with roots in the African-American put-down game "playing the dozens"). The first rap hit, "Rapper's Delight" (1979), by the Sugarhill Gang, was full of playful hyperbole and one-upmanship.

As the 1980's unfolded, rap artists began to embrace serious social issues, such as drug abuse and racism. They also began to play to a wider audience, including many young whites who found the music spoke for them too (Music Television's program *Yo! MTV Raps* has a mostly young white male audience). In rap, white suburban teens seemed to find the rebellious mystique that rock and roll held for their parents a few decades earlier. Although critics, both black and white, charged that hard-core "gangsta" rappers were antisocial and, worse, advocated violence, obscenity, and misogyny, rap groups like Salt 'n' Pepa (above, top) and Arrested Development (above) have shown that rap music can also deliver a positive message of spirituality and nonviolence.

The sultry quartet En Vogue brought back the close harmony and soulful sound of such 1960's groups as the Supremes.

ing a million *Thriller* albums a week. The chameleon-like Madonna used MTV to grab attention with songs about issues such as teenage pregnancy and female sexuality. Alternately offending and charming her audiences, she succeeded in getting noticed to the tune of a multimillion-dollar annual income, and became a film star.

MTV rapidly became part of teen and subteen life, an essential exposure for the new performer who wanted a share of that market. Like other specialty channels, MTV also alienated people as they increasingly devoted their

created a revolution when it moved to television with its own television network (MTV) in 1981. Entertainers could no longer rely solely on musical talent: how an artist looked on video became as important as how he or she sounded. Pop stars sold themselves as dancers and actors, filming elaborate videos. By 1984, 97 of the top 100 albums, as reported in the music magazine *Billboard,* had promo videos, and artists were writing songs with video technology in mind.

Michael Jackson and videos hit it off splendidly after he broke through MTV's initial resistance to air videos by black artists. His album *Thriller* won a record eight Grammy awards in 1983 and became the biggest-selling album of all time in the world. The *Thriller* video, which cost more than $1 million to make, featured Jackson in monster makeup dancing with zombies. At one point Epic Records was sell-

▶

Mick Jagger and Tina Turner turn it loose for the 16-hour African relief benefit, Live Aid, *seen by millions via satellite.*

Pop idol Madonna arrived in New York City nearly penniless in 1978. A decade later the Material Girl was rich, famous, and not a little controversial.

Born to a tradition of music (her mother, Cissy Houston, is a gospel singer), Whitney Houston (inset) belts out a tune. Harry Connick, Jr., learned his craft as a teenager from blues and jazz greats James Booker and Ellis Marsalis.

like MC Hammer, Vanilla Ice, and L.L. Cool J, added the vitality of the streets to pop music.

Even classical music underwent a renaissance of sorts. Recording companies enthusiastically promoted classical musicians as pop stars (violinists posing in strapless gowns and pianists displaying perfect pectorals) and marketed them to audiences with titles like *A Carnegie Hall Christmas,* featuring opera soprano Kathleen Battle and jazz trumpeter Wynton Marsalis.

Country music — subjected to an urban cowboy makeover in the early 1980's that sometimes left it sounding syrupy and artificial compared to music from the earlier times of Hank Williams and Patsy Cline — boasted a bumper crop of new stars: Randy Travis, Clint Black, Reba McEntire, and Garth Brooks. On their heels came offbeat performers such as Lyle Lovett and k. d. lang, the "big-boned gal from southern Alberta," whose powerful voice switched effortlessly from raw country music to a raunchy celebration of her sexuality to sweet pop ballad. From the country line-

Celebrities from Gregory Peck to Cindy Crawford turned out on New Year's, 1993, for Barbra Streisand's first live commercial show in more than 20 years. Receipts for just two nights broke records.

watching time to programs that reflected a narrow range of interests.

With the music business getting more fiercely competitive and complex — as well as more lucrative for the winners and costly for the losers — marketing bigwigs hotly pursued "crossover entertainers" whose music spanned more than one segment of the vast market. In the United States, there was a further blurring of the line between "black" and "white" music. Black artists like Michael Jackson, The Artist that Used to be Called Prince, and Whitney Houston got airtime on stations that drew predominately white listeners. And white entertainers such as Sting, Madonna, Kenny G., and George Michael began turning up on stations aimed at the urban black audience. Reggae, country, Latino music (as performed by singers like Cuban-born Gloria Estefan), and jazz (for example, the big band orchestrations of Harry Connick, Jr.) also found crossover audiences. Joining them were the heirs and heiresses of earlier musical innovators. Anita Baker and Natalie Cole (daughter of the beloved Nat King Cole who died in his forties at the peak of his fame in 1965) sang in the tradition of the queen of soul, Aretha Franklin; and there were new male soul singers, too, like Michael Bolton. Soul's funky progeny, rap music (see box previous page), with artists

Luciano Pavarotti brought opera to a wider listening audience. His Christmas Eve concert recorded on video at Montreal's Notre Dame Church became an annual fixture on PBS from 1980.

Feline Grizabella sings wistfully of days gone past in the musical Cats.

"In looking back at the theatrical year — 1981 or any other — one must always begin by bemoaning the state of the art," said drama critic Frank Rich of *The New York Times*. "Leaden musicals," "star vehicles," and a lack of creativity off-Broadway were a few of the reasons Rich gave for his displeasure with the season of 1981. Nevertheless, Broadway was making money. Out-of-town theatregoers, half-price tickets, and telephone sales had brought the Great White Way its eighth straight profitable season. Musicals were one of the reasons people kept coming, and no one seemed to know how to turn them out better than British composer and wunderkind Andrew Lloyd Webber.

In 1982 Webber, with two hit musicals, *Evita* and *Joseph and the Amazing Technicolor Dreamcoat*, running on Broadway, brought a third to the New York stage: *Cats*. Based on T. S. Eliot's 1939 book *Old Possum's Book of Practical Cats*, it enchanted audiences with its fantastic sets and costumes and hummable theme song, "Memories." Webber's streak of hits continued with *Starlight Express* in 1987 and *The Phantom of the Opera* in 1988. Five years after *Phantom*, Webber turned to Hollywood and chose for his next musical Billy Wilder's legendary film *Sunset Boulevard*, an unsentimental probe into the psyche of an aging screen star as she descends into madness. It was to win several awards in 1995. The Los Angeles debut featured a real screen star, Glenn Close, in the lead role. Like Close, who was no stranger to the footlights, other Hollywood stars felt the need to turn,

or return, to the stage, among them Jessica Lange, Gene Hackman, and Al Pacino. Top screen stars had the power to draw audiences, and some fans felt they added a note of glamor.

There was more happening on Broadway, of course, than Andrew Lloyd Webber and Hollywood stars. Chicago playwright David Mamet won a Pulitzer Prize in 1984 for *Glengarry Glen Ross*, a sardonic tale of four hustling real estate agents. August Wilson explored the lives of African-Americans over six decades and five plays, including his Pulitzer Prize-winning *The Piano Lesson* (1989). Wendy Wasserstein won critical acclaim for her two largely autobiographical dramas, *The Heidi Chronicles* (1989) and *The Sisters Rosensweig* (1993). The creators of the 1987 megahit *Les Misérables*, based on the Victor Hugo novel, set their next musical in Vietnam just before the U.S. pulled out. *Miss Saigon* (1991), which opened on Broadway after a to-do over the casting of a white actor as a Eurasian, made a record $37 million in advance sales.

Miss Saigon and *Les Misérables* charmed Canadian audiences, too, as did *Kiss of the Spider Woman,* all three of them playing on stages in Toronto, which had become the dominant centre for Broadway-style theatre in Canada. More serious theatre also did well, thanks to the help of government subsidies. By 1990, Canada had 226 theatre companies offering an annual total of 39,000 performances. One of the highlights of that year was Canada's first native people's ballet, *In the Land of the Spirits*.

Angels in America *explored the spiritual landscape of America in the Reagan era.*

dancing craze to the country music programs, like *Billy Bob's Country Countdown*, that peppered network and cable television, country music was everywhere, its stars in demand as never before. No country singer made friends more quickly in the early 1980's than laid-back Willie Nelson, whose Farm Aid project, begun in 1985, helped relieve down-on-their-luck farmers and flooded-out Midwesterners.

Other performers, too, showed concern for the problems of humanity. "It feels good to be in a house full of people who care," remarked Madonna at an AIDS benefit in New York City in 1987, one of several in which she and other entertainers, including opera legend

Leontyne Price and rap star Queen Latifah, participated. Indeed, the quality that musicians and pop stars seemed to share most in an era of wildly different musical styles was a concern for the unfortunate. Many of them worked tirelessly to raise money and public consciousness by staging shows like Band Aid and Live Aid, rock telethons that reaped millions for African famine relief. Though sceptics charged that the real motive behind celebrity support for worthy causes was to attract more publicity, a great many people applauded the fact that, for a time at least, a social conscience was alive and well in music land.

POLICING THE WORLD

Neither the United States nor Canada wanted the job of policing the world. But, faced with the threat of international lawlessness, the world had few others to take on the job.

Canada had been involved in every United Nations peacekeeping effort since the first mission, in which they acted as observers, overseeing the partition of India and Pakistan in 1947. In others, Canada had supplied troops, logistic support, medical workers, and technical help. Among Canadian servicemen alone, 48,000 had seen duty on peacekeeping missions, and 88 had died.

It was not simply generosity on Canada's part that had led to the commitments; it was a hardheaded assessment of world affairs. No war could possibly be to Canada's advantage, so it made sense to snuff out potential conflicts before they could become wars. By the early 1990's, Canada's involvement showed no sign of diminishing. The 20 years of service keeping Greeks and Cypriots apart in Cyprus was winding down but Canadians were also doing United Nations duties in the former Yugoslavia, Somalia, Afghanistan, and Korea. In all of that service, there had been only one jarring note. Canadians were shocked as some of their troops

▲ *In Operation Restore Hope, U.S. marines arrive to distribute food in the Somalian interior in December 1992. Civil unrest hindered the humanitarian effort.*

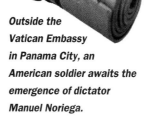

Outside the Vatican Embassy in Panama City, an American soldier awaits the emergence of dictator Manuel Noriega.

▼ *A Canadian soldier wearing the blue helmet of the U.N. Military Peacekeepers stands guard outside Sarajevo Airport in Bosnia-Herzegovina.*

in Somalia were charged in the death by torture of a civilian. Echoes of that incident would carry through the decade.

By the 1980's U.S. interests had expanded to include combatting terrorism and the drug trade. On April 28, 1986, U.S. warplanes bombed the compound of the Libyan leader, Muammar al-Qaddafi, the "mad dog of the Middle East," in retaliation for his backing of terrorist attacks, including the killing of marines in Beirut. In December 1989 President Bush sent armed forces to Panama to capture Gen. Manuel Noriega, the anti-American Panamanian dictator wanted in the United States for drug-trafficking. It was the biggest military operation since Vietnam. Hunted by 24,000 American troops, Noriega took refuge in the Vatican Embassy. U.S. forces surrounded the building and blasted the embassy with music, including the 1970's hit "You're No Good." Noriega gave up after 11 days.

Despite these successes, the Vietnam ordeal still weighed on the American spirit, creating a reluctance to use military force without clear goals and a good chance at victory. Then, on August 2, 1990, the Iraqi leader Saddam Hussein invaded Kuwait. His army, hardened from years of war against Iran, swept aside the small Kuwaiti defence forces. The invasion stunned the world, but even more ominous was the possibility that Saddam's war machine might roll south into Saudi Arabia, taking control of much of the world's oil supply.

Saddam's grab of Kuwait presented George Bush with the greatest crisis of his presidency. To do nothing would almost certainly inspire further conquest and other would-be conquerors. To dis-

▼ *In Grenada, U.S. troops guard members of the Cuban force sent by Fidel Castro to support the island's Communist regime.*

▲ An oil well fire, one of hundreds set by Iraqi troops fleeing the Desert Storm assault, frames an American and his personnel carrier.

Gen. Norman Schwarzkopf (right) and his boss, Gen. Colin Powell (left), chairman of the Joint Chiefs, made Desert Storm work.

lodge the Iraqis, however, would require a huge commitment of troops and risk American lives. Realizing that the United States could not and should not handle the task alone, Bush set about constructing a 28-nation alliance to take the field against Saddam. Canada promptly volunteered warships, aircraft, and medical personnel.

Troops, supplies, and an armada of aircraft poured into Saudi Arabia, and a massive fleet assembled in the Persian Gulf, all under the command of Gen. H. Norman Schwarzkopf, a Vietnam combat hero. Pentagon staffers readied plans for tight coordination between ground and air units. Despite the defence experts who talked of the unprecedented power of high-tech U.S. weaponry, there was gnawing fear that the United States would soon endure a bloodbath in a distant desert.

On the evening of January 16, 1991, the media flashed the news that Iraq was under air attack; Operation Desert Storm had begun. U.S. military sources reported that cruise missiles and "smart bombs" were hitting Iraqi targets with stunning accuracy, even blasting down ventilation shafts. Stealth bombers, virtually invisible on radar screens, destroyed Iraqi communications. Saddam remained defiant, so on February 23 General Schwarzkopf ordered his ground troops to invade Iraq and occupied Kuwait. As Allied forces

fell upon the Iraqis from the front and the flank, resistance crumbled.

After just 100 hours of ground fighting, the campaign ended with Iraqi forces effectively destroyed. Though some of the allies wanted to go on to occupy Baghdad and to arrest Saddam himself, Bush preferred to end the fighting, possibly fearing repercussions in the Middle East if Iraq were to be occupied. Limited though it was, the war was a military success, particularly for the Americans.

▼ Cable News Network (CNN) showed how pilots tracked smart bombs right down to impact with Iraqi targets.

Learning the hazards of desert warfare, a U.S. artillery unit sweats out a sudden dust storm in Saudi Arabia.

THE WAYS WE TRAVELLED

Bicycles 🌐 1900's
In ladylike garb, a biker takes a spin. Postmen of the era used bicycles to bring special delivery mail.

Steam Train 🌐 1905
Summer vacationers meet new arrivals to a mountain resort hotel.

As the century dawned, the locomotive represented the ultimate in power and speed, and the bicycle was the fastest machine most people could afford. Today's web of highways, bridges, and tunnels was not even a gleam in engineers' eyes. But once North America embraced the automobile, things changed. The days of depending on horses, bicycles, and ferries slipped into the past. Speed was one reason for the car's success, but it was more than that: having a personal car meant the freedom to go anyplace a road led, any time, at one's own pace. For many people that has always given cars an edge over buses and trains. Just as the automobile shrank distances, jet passenger service gave us an affordable magic carpet to the world. No longer is international travel the privilege of the leisured rich, sailing on luxury ships. Middle- and working-class families and students now roam the globe with the sangfroid of Jules Verne's Phileas Fogg in *Around the World in Eighty Days.*

Horse-Drawn Streetcar 🌐 1910
Horseless trolleys were just around the corner, but when they came, their style was a lot like this horsepowered model.

Ford "Woody" 🌐 1935
The great exodus to the suburbs came after World War II, but well-off city folk had set up country estates long before that. A fixture in their garages was a utility vehicle, or station car, like this classic Ford.

Double-Decker Bus 🌐 1920's
Packed with schoolboys gawking at the sights, a tandem double-decker makes its way on a city tour.

Steamer "Rapids King" 🌐 1901
In the early 20th century, thrill-seekers shot the Lachine Rapids using steam power. Today they use motorboats.

Nash Ambassador Six 🌐 1937
The company offered its bed feature in several sedan models during the Depression.

Yankee Clipper 🌐 1930's
When Pan American World Airways started the first transatlantic passenger service in 1939, it used this four-engine Boeing B-314, called the Yankee Clipper. Four years earlier Pan American had inaugurated regular transpacific flights.

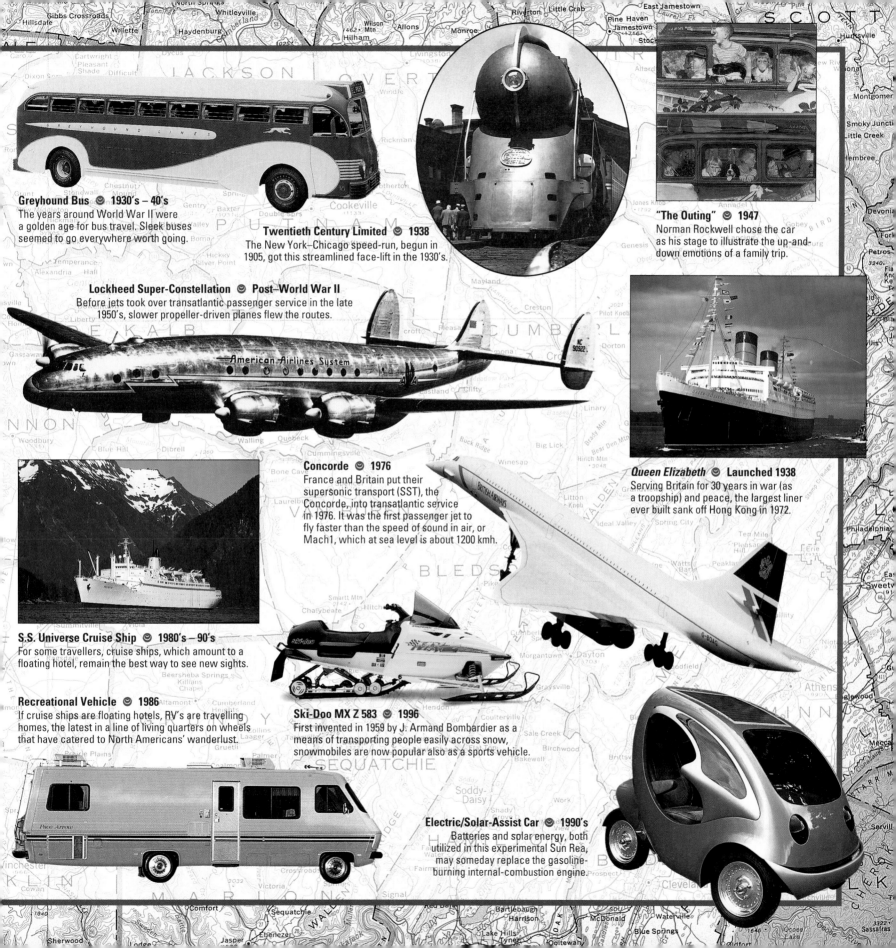

Greyhound Bus ⊛ 1930's – 40's
The years around World War II were a golden age for bus travel. Sleek buses seemed to go everywhere worth going.

Twentieth Century Limited ⊛ 1938
The New York–Chicago speed-run, begun in 1905, got this streamlined face-lift in the 1930's.

"The Outing" ⊛ 1947
Norman Rockwell chose the car as his stage to illustrate the up-and-down emotions of a family trip.

Lockheed Super-Constellation ⊛ Post–World War II
Before jets took over transatlantic passenger service in the late 1950's, slower propeller-driven planes flew the routes.

American Airlines System

Concorde ⊛ 1976
France and Britain put their supersonic transport (SST), the Concorde, into transatlantic service in 1976. It was the first passenger jet to fly faster than the speed of sound in air, or Mach1, which at sea level is about 1200 kmh.

Queen Elizabeth ⊛ Launched 1938
Serving Britain for 30 years in war (as a troopship) and peace, the largest liner ever built sank off Hong Kong in 1972.

S.S. Universe Cruise Ship ⊛ 1980's – 90's
For some travellers, cruise ships, which amount to a floating hotel, remain the best way to see new sights.

Recreational Vehicle ⊛ 1986
If cruise ships are floating hotels, RV's are travelling homes, the latest in a line of living quarters on wheels that have catered to North Americans' wanderlust.

Ski-Doo MX Z 583 ⊛ 1996
First invented in 1959 by J. Armand Bombardier as a means of transporting people easily across snow, snowmobiles are now popular also as a sports vehicle.

Electric/Solar-Assist Car ⊛ 1990's
Batteries and solar energy, both utilized in this experimental Sun Rea, may someday replace the gasoline-burning internal-combustion engine.

MILESTONES ON THE ROAD TO TOMORROW

Science marched ahead in double time, spewing out inventions along the way. Medicine, robotics, computers, communications, all staged breakthroughs. The space program, though hit by tragedy, reached new heights.

◀

This computerized robot hand, perfected by Japanese scientists in 1984, is deft enough to play a piano melody by Schumann.

One winter night in 1987, someone tried to break into the Bayside Exposition Center in Boston, but the intruder was soon detected by an exceptionally vigilant guard, whose calls for help brought quick reinforcement. The alert guard was neither man nor dog, but a robot. The high-tech world of computer-driven automation, so long imagined in film and fiction, was fast becoming a reality.

Perhaps the most familiar symbol of technological achievement in the 1980's was the space shuttle, the reusable spacecraft that takes off like a rocket and lands like a plane, on a runway. The first shuttle, *Columbia*, was launched in April 1981, and as it returned to Earth 54 hours later it penetrated the atmosphere at 24 times the speed of sound and endured temperatures of 1260°C caused by atmospheric friction. It touched down in California, according to one astronaut, "smoother than any airliner."

Since the shuttle had to carry satellites into space and retrieve damaged ones, a key to its success was a robot arm that could

Both wristwatch and beeper, this gadget takes messages from friends or associates who dial the owner's special phone number.

manipulate heavy satellites in the limited space of the shuttle's cargo area. It also had to be light, capable of placing satellites with great precision, and able to operate in the demanding conditions of frigid outer space. Canadian scientists met the challenge with Canadarm, a remote-controlled device using the latest technologies in titanium, graphite epoxy, and computer controls. First tested on the shuttle's maiden mission, it has become a mainstay of the space program. Canada has also contributed astronauts, among them Marc Garneau, Roberta Bondar, and Chris Hadfield, who used the Canadarm to repair a damaged part on the *Mir* space station in 1995.

Twenty-four shuttle flights took place from 1981 to 1986, and three new shuttles joined the fleet: *Challenger, Discovery,* and *Atlantis*. Space flight had become almost routine. Then, in one ghastly moment, catastrophe struck. In January 1986 *Challenger* rose into space carrying a seven-member crew. Just 73 seconds later, it burst into fire. A rubber seal on a booster rocket had given way, causing the fuel tank to explode. All the crew members died, including the first schoolteacher in space, Christa McAuliffe, selected from among 11,000 applicants. Millions of people, watching on TV, shuddered in horror.

But the space program moved forward. Thirty-two months after the disaster, a redesigned shuttle blasted into orbit. And for all its setbacks, the program was paying dividends in scientific progress. Shuttles launched and retrieved research satellites and enabled lab experiments in fields ranging from agriculture to computer-chip technology.

Riding piggyback on its huge external fuel tank with attached booster rockets, the space shuttle Columbia (lower right) blasts off from Cape Canaveral on its maiden voyage.

AIDS: Let There Be Hope

The crisis began as a medical oddity. Early in 1981 five young men entered Los Angeles hospitals with an illness caused by an extremely rare parasite, *pneumocystis carinii*. All five were homosexual; all five soon died. Other uncommon ailments began appearing, including a skin cancer, Kaposi's sarcoma, that normally afflicted the elderly. But these victims were young, sexually active gay males, all of whom had lost their natural resistance to a wide spectrum of exotic diseases. Scientists dubbed the condition Acquired Immune Deficiency Syndrome (AIDS), and began searching for a cause.

The circle of disaster widened to include heterosexual men and women, intravenous drug users, the children of AIDS victims, and hemophiliacs and other blood-transfusion recipients. Cases were reported in Europe, Latin America, Africa, Asia. Year by year the numbers escalated. By 1995 an estimated 13.5 million people worldwide had become infected and there were more than 12,000 reported cases of AIDS in Canada, of whom almost 9,000 had died.

The cause was a virus, HIV, that attacks the immune system. Several drugs proved effective in slowing the virus's assault; but a cure, or even a preventive vaccine, remained elusive. Meanwhile, the toll mounted. Screen star Rock Hudson died of AIDS; basketball whiz Magic Johnson tested HIV positive. As the disease touched more and more lives, millions of people wore AIDS Awareness Ribbons (above) and prayed for an end to one of the deadliest scourges in medical history.

tween 1973 and 1989, it declined by 37 percent, while the average workweek went up from 41 to 47 hours.

Other new devices, ranging from the serious to the silly, appeared. Compact discs, a laser-based sound-reproduction system, gave audio tapes stiff competition and rang the death knell for vinyl records. In the form of CD-Rom's, which could encapsulate encyclopedias, moving images, audio, and interactive games, many people thought they rang the death knell for books too. Microwave ovens had found a place in 83 percent of households in Canada by the early 1990's as people came to expect meals in minutes and then in seconds. Then there was the chair that played stereo music while giving a massage, and the hand-held computer that calculated the user's exact location within 30 metres.

In medicine, space exploration, communications, agriculture, business, education, and the home, science continued to revolutionize the way we lived. And the pace was accelerating.

▲ Biosphere 2, an enclosed ecosystem built in the Arizona desert for some $150 million in 1990, was home for two years to a volunteer team that grew its own food, drank recycled water, and breathed recirculated air.

Computers became steadily smaller, cheaper, and more powerful. This solar-powered laptop, weighing only a few pounds, makes a lengthy writing task an outdoor job.

They could do this at home, at work, in libraries, and even in cyber cafes, where as well as drinking a cup of coffee they could access the World Wide Web, try out the latest computer technology, or play action-adventure games in virtual reality. To experience virtual reality, a user dons a helmet equipped with a pair of small television screens that generate three-dimensional scenes of almost any kind. The user can walk through an imaginary building, skim over the bottom of the sea, or glide above the surface of a distant planet.

Instant communication exacted a price, however. People came to feel they were on duty all the time and leisure time shrank: be-

ND THE WALLS CAME TUMBLING DOWN

"It is possible to suppress, compel, bribe, break or blast — but only for a limited period," declared Soviet premier Mikhail Gorbachev. With that, decades of Communist oppression abruptly ended.

The most dramatic event in half a century of Cold War menace began without hype or fanfare. On November 9, 1989, three weeks after the forced resignation of Communist Party chief Erich Honecker, the new East German government held a press conference. Among the topics was a notice that all border restrictions on crossing into West Germany would be lifted, effective that midnight. No one anticipated what happened next. Tens of thousands of people began gathering by the Berlin Wall. At the stroke of midnight, a joyous, frenzied mob surged through the newly opened checkpoints. Horns honked, trumpets blared, and champagne bubbled over in the streets. "I don't feel like I'm in prison anymore!" shouted one East German. "I just can't believe it!" said another. Forty-five kilometres long and 28 years old, the Berlin Wall had stood since 1961 as the ultimate symbol of Communist oppression. In the blink of an eye, it became part of history's junk heap.

A great tide of freedom was sweeping over Eastern Europe and beyond. Satellite nations bordering the Soviet Union had begun to shake off Communist rule, and in Moscow itself the institutions of Soviet tyranny were lurching toward collapse. The forces of change even reached Communist China, where a free-market economy was tak-

In a frenzy of newly discovered freedom, jubilant Berliners smash away the wall that had divided their city for more than a generation. It happened after Soviet leader Mikhail Gorbachev (inset) launched his glasnost and perestroika policies, unwittingly writing the death warrant for European communism.

at age 54, the first in a new generation of Soviet leaders. Well educated and well travelled, he had seen firsthand the economic successes of the West; he was also painfully familiar with his own country's shortcomings. As secretary of agriculture from 1979 to 1982, he had witnessed four harvests so meagre that he did not dare release the production figures. Then, as deputy to two previous heads of state, Yuri Andropov and Konstantin Chernenko, he observed up close the decay and corruption that were eating away at Soviet society. Clearly the time had come for drastic change. Upon Chernenko's death in 1985, Gorbachev outmanoeuvred a clique of old-guard hard-liners and got himself elected general secretary. ("This man has a nice smile," said one compatriot, "but he has iron teeth.") Gorbachev then set to work.

His first major reform was to fling open the doors of government to public view, ending generations of official secrecy, an act he termed *glasnost.* Henceforth, the U.S.S.R. would enjoy a free press and open discussion of national issues. The second reform, *perestroika,* called for a cellar-to-attic restructuring of the 70-year-old apparatus of Soviet rule. Both initiatives horrified the old guard; *perestroika* was particularly distasteful, since it meant loosening the Communist Party's iron grip on all elements of Soviet society. To be sure, Gorbachev never meant to abolish communism entirely; he merely insisted that the old Marxist system of state ownership and control be brought up to date. Only by making it function more like a Western market-driven

ing hold and where a daring grassroots democracy movement rose up to confront the aging leadership. There was no question that years of pressure from the West had taken a toll on the Communist world. Back in 1983 U.S. President Ronald Reagan, fearing Soviet power, had called the U.S.S.R. "an evil empire" and ordered up a multibillion-dollar antimissile defence system to be based in space. But the empire mostly crumbled from within.

The person who made it happen was none other than the Soviet Union's top-ranking Communist. Mikhail S. Gorbachev had moved rapidly through party ranks to become,

▲ *In a supreme act of defiance, a lone Chinese demonstrator blocks a Red Army tank column as it nears Tiananmen Square in Beijing. Unlike most 1989 freedom movements, China's ended in tragedy, with the massacre of more than 5,000 civilians.*

▼ *Union leader Lech Walesa, father of Poland's Solidarity movement, addresses workers in Gdansk. Free elections in 1989 gave his party a sweeping parliamentary majority.*

▼ *Hungarian soldiers cut down barbed-wire fences along the border with Austria, ripping apart the Iron Curtain and opening the first free passage from East to West.*

economy, he reasoned, could the Soviet Union recover from its stagnation.

Determined to boost economic growth, Gorbachev granted a measure of autonomy to the 15 republics that made up the Union of Soviet Socialist Republics. In 1989 he oversaw the creation of a new legislature and the first free elections since 1917. A year later he won approval of a law to end the Communist Party's monopoly on power in the U.S.S.R. But events were running ahead of his control, and the very existence of the U.S.S.R. was coming into doubt.

By the end of 1990 all 15 Soviet republics had declared some form of autonomy. Gorbachev, alarmed that he had given away too much, proposed a Union Treaty that would cede certain powers to the republics while keeping them under the umbrella of the U.S.S.R. But if the pace of change in Gorbachev's view was breathtaking, there were some who wanted change to come even faster, notably Boris Yeltsin, the freely elected president of the Russian Republic. As Gorbachev struggled to mollify the hard-line Communists, Yeltsin publicly quit the Communist Party to dramatize his split with Gorbachev.

Meanwhile, the changes wrought by Gorbachev were noted with wonder in the long-suffering satellite countries of Eastern Europe, and with increasing nervousness by the satellites' old-guard dictators. Accustomed to relying on Moscow for military and economic aid, the Communist

Massed national flags proudly wave over a demonstration in Prague during Czechoslovakia's Velvet Revolution. And a young patriot (inset) bears a portrait of Vaclav Havel, the writer who became the new Czech head of state.

▶

Last of the hard-line dictators, Romania's Nicolae Ceausescu ordered elite troops to fire on demonstrators in December 1989. On Christmas Day he himself was executed.

leaders were gradually being cut loose to succeed or fail on their own. Declared Gorbachev: "Any nation has the right to decide its fate by itself." One by one, the countries of Eastern Europe began to do just that.

For some years Hungary, one of the more progressive satellites, had been experimenting with a consumer-oriented economy known as "goulash communism." The next move was political. In May 1989 Hungary dismantled the barbed wire along its Austrian border, thus becoming the first Communist nation to allow free travel to the West. Refugees poured into Austria by the tens of thousands, looking for a better life. In Poland severe economic troubles forced the nation's military dictator, Gen. Wojciech Jaruzelski, to seek help from the outlawed Solidarity labor union and its leader, Lech Walesa. A few years earlier Walesa, considered a threat to state security, had been thrown in prison. Now, after negotiations in early 1989, Poland became the first Iron Curtain country to form a non-Communist, multiparty parliament. The next year the unthinkable happened: Lech Walesa was elected president.

There was more. In Czechoslovakia thousands of demonstrators gathered in the fall of 1989 demanding freedom. Undaunted by attacks by riot police, the people chanted, "The game is over!" And so it was. A bloodless Velvet Revolution toppled the government, replacing it with one headed by playwright Vaclav Havel, a dissident who had been imprisoned many times for his beliefs. And in Romania, perhaps the most brutal of all the hard-line regimes, the 24-year reign of Nicolae Ceausescu abruptly came to an end, and the dictator and his wife were tried and convicted for commiting genocide. The sentence, death by firing squad, was immediately car-

ried out by soldiers who "could not restrain their hate," according to one witness. An interim president was named the next day. In 1991 the Baltic states of Lithuania, Latvia, and Estonia declared their independence from the Soviet Union.

The world barely had time to catch its breath when an even more astonishing drama began to unfold in Russia itself. In August 1991 Gorbachev was vacationing in his *dacha* by the Black Sea when an unexpected delegation showed up at his door. He grabbed one telephone, then another. No use: the lines were dead. In Moscow, tanks rolled through the streets as elements of the Red Army and the KGB took control. It was a classic coup d'état, launched by hard-line Communists intent on deposing Gorbachev.

Yeltsin put aside his differences with Gorbachev to throw his weight behind the embattled leader. He called on his own loyalists within the military, and they responded by sending troops and armored vehicles to back him up. The nation stood at the edge of civil war. In a show of courage that riveted the world, Yeltsin climbed atop a tank in Red Square and shouted his defiance. Thousands cheered him. The elite Alpha Force of KGB commandos was ordered to storm Yeltsin's residence and kill him, but it refused. Other units stationed outside Moscow refused to

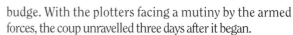

In the coup that fizzled, a crack Soviet tank unit, sent to occupy Moscow in 1991, decks out in flowers and fraternizes with civilians. A year later Russian president Boris Yeltsin (inset) earns a warm welcome during a visit to the United States.

budge. With the plotters facing a mutiny by the armed forces, the coup unravelled three days after it began.

After 72 hours under house arrest, Gorbachev emerged triumphant. But his victory was short-lived. His reforms were faltering, and the embryonic market economy was in shambles. In the first six months of 1991, the gross national product of the U.S.S.R. fell by 10 percent, prices went up by nearly 50 percent, and the military was still gobbling up half of all industrial production. On Christmas Day, 1991, Gorbachev resigned, turning power over to Yeltsin.

Yeltsin proclaimed his fervent hope of building a new society. "I want our people to live better," he said. It was a wish that both the newly liberated eastern nations and the staunchly capitalist West could heartily applaud.

◄ *As Soviet communism toppled, so did its icons, such as these statues of Joseph Stalin (foreground) and party leader Mikhail Kalinin, who died in 1946.*

▶ *Taking advantage of their newly won freedom, factory workers in Minsk, capital of Belarus, mob managers with a litany of grievances.*

Myriam Bédard skims over the snow to win gold in the women's 15-km biathlon at the 1994 winter Olympics in Lillehammer.

BIG BUCKS, BIG BANGS, IN SPORTS

As the 20th century neared the finish line, sports became associated with scandal and supermoney for superstars.

The Olympic scene opened badly for Canada in 1980. Without a single gold medal to show for the winter Olympics of that year, Canadian athletes could only assemble to cheer for a stunning David and Goliath hockey game between the United States and Russia. Barely considered contenders for any medal placing, the Americans shocked the sports world with a 4-3 win for the gold medal. Canada came back, though, in the winter Olympics of 1984 as speed skater Gaétan Boucher won two golds and a bronze. That same year, in the summer Olympics at Los Angeles, Canada had its best games ever with 10 gold medals. Half of them came in the pool, thanks to diver Sylvie Bernier and swimmers Anne Ottenbrite, Victor Davis, and Alex Baumann.

Rarely had sports seemed so pure and wholesome as they did in the early 1980's. But in the years that followed, it seemed to many that sports had lost every vestige of innocence (if sports ever had any, cynics chimed in) and had sunk into a world of acrimonious owner-player disputes, public tantrums, surly behavior, soaring salaries, multimillion-dollar commercial endorsements by athletes, scandals, and outright criminal behavior.

For Canadians, it began with the 1988 Olympics in Seoul, Korea. Millions watched as sprinter Ben Johnson set a world record for the 100-metre dash, cheered as cabinet minister Jean Charest telephoned his congratulations, then sank back in dismay as it was announced that Johnson had tested positive for forbidden drugs. In the United States, in January of 1994, figure skater Nancy Kerrigan had just finished a practice session in Detroit, Michigan, when a burly man materialized at the ice rink and swung a club at her leg, apparently intending to deal a crippling blow to her knee. Fortunately his aim was off, and a badly bruised Kerrigan resumed skating a few weeks later. The full horror of the incident soon emerged: it had been planned by people close to Kerrigan's figure-skating rival, Tonya Harding.

These and many more personal tragedies occurred at a time when athletes had never made more

The Toronto Blue Jays erupt with joy as they become the first Canadian team to win the World Series, in 1992.

Joe Montana, famous for come-from-behind heroics, won four Super Bowls for San Francisco (1982, 1985, 1989, and 1990).

Spunky 16-year-old Mary Lou Retton won the gold in the all-round gymnastics at the 1984 Los Angeles Olympics.

Wayne Gretzky is the greatest scorer in pro hockey history. In 1978, at age 17, he joined the Edmonton Oilers. He moved to the Los Angeles Kings in 1988.

money. In 1989 the average yearly pay for a National Basketball Association player reached $750,000 and kept climbing. Three years later, the average major-league baseball player's salary topped $1 million. At the end of 1993, Dallas Cowboys quarterback Troy Aikman signed an eight-year $50-million contract, which made him the highest-paid professional football player ever. Even so, Aikman's average yearly salary was exceeded by hockey's Wayne Gretzky of the Los Angeles Kings ($8.5 million), baseball's Barry Bonds of the San Francisco Giants ($7.29 million), and basketball's Larry Johnson of the Charlotte Hornets ($7 million).

Many fans resented their heroes making millions, a resentment that turned to anger and disgust in 1994. In that year, baseball players went out on strike against owners in a struggle over the enormous revenues flooding into the game. Hockey followed soon after when players were locked out by owners. Even basketball came close to a strike of its own.

The big money to be made in sports erased the national border between Canada and the United States. In hockey, which had been the most distinctively Canadian sport, only one of five expansion teams in the early 1990's, the Ottawa Senators, was Canadian. At the same time, American professional basketball came to Canada with the Toronto Raptors, soon followed by the Vancouver Grizzlies. But the most stunning developments were in baseball and football.

On October 24, 1992, the Atlanta Braves, playing at home, were at bat. The score was 4-3 for Toronto Blue Jays in the 11th inning. Two batters were out, but the tie run was on third base. The last Brave stepped up to the plate and bunted down the first base line. The pitcher scooped up the ball for the out and — it was unbelievable. For the first time in its history, the world series of baseball, the national sport of the United

States, had been won by a team from Canada. And, just to show it was no accident, Toronto won again in 1993.

The open border proved to be open in two directions. In 1993, the financially ailing Canadian Football League expanded into the United States, with the first franchise going to Sacramento. In just two years, the Grey Cup, traditionally the most Canadian of sports trophies, was on its way to Baltimore. In sport, as in commerce, it was becoming difficult to distinguish between Canada and the United States.

But if professional sport was blurring the Canada-U.S. border, amateurs were still making Canada's presence felt as the century moved through its final decade. In 1995, Elvis Stojko continued Canadian dominance of men's figure skating by winning his second straight world title. In the 1994 winter Olympics at Lillehammer, Norway, Myriam Bédard skied and shot her way to gold in both the 7.5- and 15-kilometre women's biathlons. Just two years earlier, at the Barcelona Olympics, Canada had won 18 medals — six gold, five silver, and seven bronze. If not quite as strong a showing as at the Los Angeles Olympics of 1984, it was Canada's best ever showing at a non-boycotted Olympics. And it left Canadians with two powerful images that summed up the frustration and the inspiration of the last ten years.

One was of synchronized swimmer Sylvie Fréchette, denied the gold medal by a judge's error in scoring, an error admitted by the judge but one which the committee refused to correct. She had to settle for a silver medal instead. The other image was of Silken Laumann, hobbling into her single-scull boat with one leg in a surgical brace, but still finding the strength and courage to row to a bronze medal against the best in the world.

Greg Louganis shows his gold-medal form. The diver won the springboard and platform events in both the 1984 and 1988 Olympics.

At the 1992 Olympics in France, Californian Kristi Yamaguchi performs her winning original program.

Chris Evert, still intense at 34, sets up at the 1989 U.S. Open. In earlier years she and Martina Navratilova had epic duels.

425

IN PURSUIT OF PHYSICAL PERFECTION

Whatever it took — sweating at the exercise machines, adopting the eating habits of a monk, going under the surgeon's knife — people were determined to realize their ideal bodies.

If there was one emblem of the 1980's, an object (aside from the dollar bill) that summed up the spirit of the age, it was the Nautilus machine — a maze of chrome, pulleys, and weights by which legions of exercisers pushed, pulled, sweated, and grunted their way to slimness, strength, and beauty. Some 400,000 Nautilus machines were sold between 1970 and 1984 as exercise became an obsession. Chanting the slogan "No pain, no gain," fitness addicts put themselves through endless hours of torture (and lightened their wallets in the process). Self-improvement has been a cherished tradition, but in the 1980's the goal was nothing less than physical perfection.

In 10 years, sales of exercise gear went from $5 million to $738 million. The actress Jane Fonda became a fitness maven and sold 1.2 million copies of her exercise videos in just three years.

The health club was the place to be seen. A far cry from the dank and smelly

TV personality Willard Scott with macho movie star Arnold Schwarzenegger, who presided over the opening ceremonies of the 1991 Great American Workout.

gymnasiums of the past, these temples of sweat were elaborately high-tech: they were fitted out with exercise bikes, treadmills, ballet barres, and skiing, stair-climbing, and rowing machines. Surrounded by mirrors and hooked up to pulse meters and gadgets to measure blood pressure and oxygen intake, patrons puffed to booming disco music. Those who could afford it built gyms at home to avoid the health-club crowds and beginner's embarrassment. "Who wants to be humiliated," said one well-heeled weakling, "trying to lift 35 pounds when the gorilla next to you is lifting a VW?" Small fortunes were poured into equipping these vest-pocket gyms. Along with the requisite hardware, there were extras like whirlpools and massage therapists. "The home gym threatens to replace the gourmet kitchen as a status symbol," observed one magazine. The ultimate accessory was a personal trainer to bark orders and encouragement.

The ideal of beauty underwent a radical change during the decade. "Today, health is

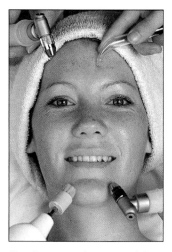

An exercise enthusiast gets a leg up on the competition with the aid of her personal trainer.

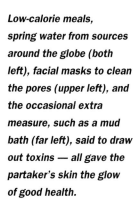

Beauty spas, using state-of-the-art equipment and techniques, offered the latest in facials.

Low-calorie meals, spring water from sources around the globe (both left), facial masks to clean the pores (upper left), and the occasional extra measure, such as a mud bath (far left), said to draw out toxins — all gave the partaker's skin the glow of good health.

A school class takes steps to reverse the results of a study that showed that the kids of North America are less fit than they were 20 years ago.

beauty," explained the head of a top modelling agency. Models who, in years past, did all they could to preserve the fragile look now sported the legs of boxers and a glint of "serene determination in the eyes." Advertisements featured sleek outlines and rippling muscles to link their products with health. People with waistline problems dived into diet foods, and by 1988 a third of the groceries bought in North America were low calorie. Those who wanted total immersion in a healthy regime took "vacations" at expensive spas, which offered exercise classes with names like Body Contouring and Positive Power. Some spas took the idea to its extreme and instituted "boot camp" programs. The toughest spa in America charged $1,300 per week for bare-bones accommodations and spartan meals. Guests shared rooms and started their days promptly at 6:30 A.M. with a meditation session. After a glass of orange juice, the sum total of breakfast, they headed off for a 2½-hour hike. One such fitness camp threatened to expel guests who sneaked extra pieces of bread at dinnertime.

To counteract the effects of aging, there was always the knife. In 1986 more than half a million North Americans underwent cosmetic surgery. Vanity was not the only reason: careers were at stake in a society that placed a premium on youthful vigor. "It's the competitive demand to look youthful," said one doctor explaining the boom in cosmetic surgery. One of the specialty's more popular innovations

was liposuction, a procedure in which fat was sucked out of the body. It was followed by lipofilling, in which the fat was redeposited elsewhere to form a perfect profile or create a comely curve. By the mid-1980's nearly a quarter of plastic-surgery patients were men. One salon offered male clients a three-day makeover, involving analysis of skin, nails, and hair, plus a shopping trip with a fashion expert. Retin-A, a drug derived from vitamin A, which stimulates the production of skin cells, was used by some in the belief that it helped correct the damage done by prolonged exposure to the sun. "It's the closest thing we have to a youth cream," said one doctor, although people who used the product sometimes suffered such side effects as skin irritation and scaling.

The benefits of the fitness craze were undeniable: the incidence of heart disease and stroke dropped in the 1980's, and life expectancy edged upward. However, it was only a small proportion of people that benefitted. On average, North Americans got heavier, and adults weigh today 3.5 kilograms more than they did 10 years ago. Sedentary lifestyles are partly responsible, but so too are high-fat foods — their taste is simply irresistible so we eat large amounts of them.

Jane Fonda (right) and Richard Simmons (upper right) became gurus of fitness when, like Raquel Welch, Arnold Schwarzenegger, Sandahl Bergman, Marie Osmond, and others, they marketed their expertise through videos (Jane Fonda's Workout and Every Day With Richard Simmons Family Fitness).

427

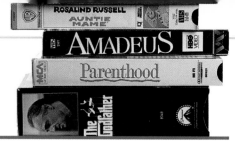

MOVIEGOING GETS A MAKEOVER

Certainly the film business has changed over the years, but our passion for movies burns as brightly as ever.

Though most of the old movie palaces are shut, the cineplex and the videocassette have filled the gap.

Listening to the gloomy predictions, many movie lovers in the late 1970's could be forgiven for thinking that the time-honored ritual of going out to the movies was on its last legs. One-screen movie houses, fixtures for generations, kept losing customers and shut down one by one. TV's drain on movie audiences seemed unrelenting, and there was a new threat in the early 1980's: videocassette recorders, user-friendly and increasingly affordable. A new industry was taking off, soon to make movie-video-rental stores as familiar as gas stations. It seemed all too obvious that the future of movies lay in the cozy confines of the home, where you could bring a favorite film selected from the video store and watch it at your leisure in comfort.

Clearly, going out to the movies, the movie date, and maybe the Hollywood film industry itself, had reached the exit door. That was what the pessimists were saying as the 1980's began, but it didn't happen.

Fast-forward to the mid-1990's. Some of the biggest movie hits of all time, and some of the best loved, had appeared over the past decade and a half. North America had a new crop of favorite stars, including a rubber-faced Canadian named Jim Carey who

delighted audiences as Ace Ventura, Pet Detective, the affable comic John Candy, and the new young heartthrob, Keanu Reeves. Arnold Schwarzenegger had taken action movies to new extremes in two *Terminators*. Through the efforts of actor-director Spike Lee and others, in films like *Malcolm X* (played by Denzel Washington), African-Americans attained greater influence in Hollywood; and Steven Spielberg turned Alice Walker's novel *The Color Purple,* about a black woman overcoming adversity, into a heart-wrenching film that made a star of Whoopi Goldberg. Director Oliver Stone put forth dark views of U.S. history in *Platoon,* about the Vietnam War, in *JFK,* dealing with the Kennedy assassination, and in *Nixon. Philadelphia* had versatile actor Tom Hanks as an AIDS victim fired by his law firm. In 1995 he would win an Oscar for his lead role as the lovable, mildly retarded hero in *Forrest Gump.*

Theatres were selling about a billion tickets a year, or almost 20 million a week. To be sure, ticket sales had hovered around a billion since the mid-1960's, indicating that the percentage of

▲ **Videocassettes of movies (above, right) created a smashing retail success story: video-rental stores.**

▼ **Akosua Busia (left) and Desreta Jackson (right) joined Whoopi Goldberg in the 1985 film The Color Purple.**

moviegoers had been declining slightly; but movies were obviously alive and well.

Part of the credit for saving the institution of moviegoing belongs to a Kansas movie house owner named Stanley H. Durwood, King of the Multiplex, who says he hit upon the idea of putting many screens in one theatre in 1963. The multiplex (or cineplex, to Canadians) took time to catch on, and many fans resented the switch from grand interior spaces to postage-stamp-size viewing rooms, but customers loved having a choice of films. And when cineplexes and malls teamed up, the lure of shopping, dinner, and a movie — all a short walk from free parking — made wonderful sense to millions of people.

While the cineplexes attracted substantial numbers of customers, sales of videocassette recorders were soaring. In 1982 sales of VCR's reached about 2 million. By the end of the decade, more than 60 million homes in North America had VCR's. By 1993 movies on videocassette were generating $12 billion in annual revenue. But instead of decimating the ranks of moviegoers, the video boom simply added a movie-watching option. Young people, the great majority of moviegoers, seemed to prefer getting out of the house and seeing a film when it opened, not months later when it showed up in the video store.

Competing for customers, theatre operators kept ticket prices low. Adjusted for inflation, a ticket cost about the same in 1993 as it had 10 years earlier. Theatres increasingly looked to their concession stands for profits. "Film exhibitors are mainly in the popcorn business," said a film industry analyst. (That's not surprising when a $2.50 bucket of popcorn typically contains 20 cents' worth of corn.)

Just like the theatre operators, Hollywood's big filmmakers also sought new ways to expand profits, and by and large the movie moguls were richly successful. Canada benefitted, as many Hollywood filmmakers came north to take advantage of tax benefits and lower production costs.

In the 1990's only about 20 percent of industry revenue came from the box office. Video income accounted for a good chunk of the rest. But two other big profit areas were the foreign market and licensed spin-off products. The whole world seemed to love American films. In fact, Hollywood's foreign sales were expected to account for half the industry's revenue by 1997. But sales really went through the roof when products were tied in to box office smashes like *The Lion King* and Steven Spielberg's *Jurassic Park*. In 1989 *Batman* grossed $250 million in its first six months, then made twice that much over the next two years from Batman toys, clothes, books, and other licensed merchandise.

Merchandising tie-ins work best for children's movies. A study conducted by a California research firm found that PG movies were three times more likely than R movies to surpass the magic $100 million mark at the box office. Family movies could be the wave of the future.

▲ Steven Spielberg began his 1980's string of hits with Harrison Ford and a cobra in Raiders of the Lost Ark.

▶

Canadian comedian Dan Aykroyd clowns around with the rest of the gang in The Last of the Ghostbusters.

Kevin Costner, as a U.S. Army officer, searches his soul and joins the Indians in Dances With Wolves.

After Raiders, Spielberg returned to space fantasy and again hit pay dirt with E.T., the Extra-Terrestrial in 1982.

Here TODAY, GONE TOMORROW

Recreational pursuits zigzagged wildly as the 20th century drew to a close. Cocooning at home was just fine for some, while others threw themselves into thin air and careened down roadless slopes.

I f I die, I die. I told everybody to bring a shovel and a mop, just in case." This intrepid soul was indulging in one of the hottest fads of the 1980's: jumping from a lofty tower with nothing below him but the cold, hard ground, his survival resting on a thick rubber cord, called a bungee, harnessed to his ankles. If all went well, he would zoom earthward at 95 kilometres an hour for about three seconds, come within one and a half metres of death, and then bounce skyward as the bungee took hold. "It's an indescribable feeling," exclaimed one enthusiast. "It's great. Oh, boy!"

Risk-taking came into vogue with a vengeance in the 1980's as thrill-seekers shot through rapids on rafts, flew into the air on skateboards, and hurtled down rocky trails on mountain bikes. Canadian skiers found a way to make their already risky sport even more daring. Hotdoggers, as they were called, soared off ramps, twisting in somersaults through the air until they landed in a swishing glide (usually) down the hill.

Other daredevils donned a new kind of roller skate — high-top shoes mounted on a line of rollers (better known under the brand name Rollerblades) — and whizzed along sidewalks and streets at 65 kilometres per hour. To give the idea a push, the Rollerblade company offered free samples to skate-rental shops along the beaches of Southern California, where the sport quickly caught on. Within three years Rollerblade sales zoomed from $3 million a year to $40 million.

In fads, as in physics, every action has a reaction: while some people were defying death for fun, others turned to gentler sports or curled up with parlor games. Trivial Pursuit migrated south from Canada to hit the living rooms of the United States in 1982 and kept players pinned to the couch for hours with its 6,000 trivia questions. Indeed, it was one of the favorite modes of "cocooning," the trend of sitting at home and enjoying quiet evenings with family and friends. In general, folks went nutty for games. Pool halls made a

A bungee jumper (top) launches himself from a hot-air balloon and plunges toward the ground; at Banff, Alberta, a hotdogger twists in midair in preparation for aerial acrobatics before gliding down the steep slope.

Marios, Ninjas, Cabbage Patch Kids, and Barney

Through a landscape beset by hideous creatures, two diminutive fellows, called the Super Mario Brothers, made their determined way, bouncing over dangers and leaping into the imaginations of millions of kids. Created by the Nintendo video game company, the Marios, who were somewhat lacking in conventional charm, became two of the most popular fantasy characters of the 1980's. Even more colorful were four creatures out of the comic books, slick-talking, ninja-kicking, pizza-gobbling crime fighters who, having fallen into radioactive sewage, were mutated from ordinary turtles into human-size talking turtles. The Teenage Mutant Ninja Turtles were featured on television and then starred in a movie that

became a monster hit, grossing $30 million in one week. Turtle products proliferated, accessories to every waking moment in a child's day: clothes, sheets, towels, lunch boxes, toothbrushes, and, of course, toys. By 1994 the mega-selling toys were the Mighty Morphin Power Rangers and their spin-off products, derived from a cult Japanese TV series.

Many parents disapproved of the violent ways of the Turtles and the Power Rangers and yearned for the days of the Cabbage Patch Kids, the homely "orphaned" dolls who had been all the rage only a few years before. Then came Barney — a gentle, cuddly purple dinosaur. Some adults found Barney cloying. But preschoolers adored the dinosaur and his TV

show, *Barney and Friends*, a half hour of relentless warmth and caring. The show's homey atmosphere, psychologists assured parents, helped compensate for the shrinking extended family. Barney so changed the image of the dinosaur that some children raised on him were no doubt shocked by the portrayal of man-eating Tyrannosaurus rexes and other vicious dinosaurs in the 1993 science fiction movie *Jurassic Park*. Through the world of make-believe, children, like their parents, confronted new challenges and risks.

Among recent children's favorites are a lovable, adoptable Cabbage Patch doll (above, left), Barney (above, right), and the Ninja Turtles (right). At top right, a Mario Brother gives the V sign.

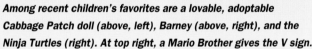

◄

A pair of mountain bikers (left, top) tear full tilt down a slope. A skateboarder (left) executes a difficult "lip slide" move off the top edge of a skateboard bowl.

comeback as an upscale yuppie pastime. Miniature golf, which had peaked in the 1930's, reappeared. Manhattanites could putt on a course with a tropical theme: fake flamingos and banana trees, and a 3.5-metre-tall mechanical alligator that snapped at the fluorescent golf balls aimed its way. Or they could try their skill at real-estate magnate Donald Trump's course in Central Park, which featured replicas of New York landmarks, such as the Statue of Liberty.

Of all the oddities to capture the public's fancy, not one was odder than the Wacky WallWalker, a gummy glob that, when flung onto a wall, slowly flip-flopped its way to the floor. It had all the excitement of watching plants grow; when interest waned, 75 million of them were packed into

cereal boxes and the marketer reaped a fortune. He knew exactly what to do next: he cocooned with his computer and wrote *How to Create a Fad and Make a Million Dollars*.

The most popular games of the 1980's were of the electronic video variety, especially those with extraterrestrial themes, such as Asteroids and Space Invaders. "It's a drug," said one 26-year-old addict, ruefully dropping in a quarter for another round. These games moved into the home in the 1990's, claiming addicts from all age-groups. Apart from Nintendo games, there were role-playing or real-life simulation games played with orchestral accompaniment on CD-Rom. The bestselling titles in 1994 reflected their escapist themes — *Myst*, and *Doom II*.

NORTH AMERICA STIRS THE MELTING POT

Canada and the United States remain the most attractive countries in the world for immigrants who continue to pour in — but with a difference.

So many undocumented aliens cross the U.S.-Mexican border by night that signs like this one have been posted warning motorists to be on the alert.

In Hong Kong, as the day of reunification with China comes closer, lines form for visas to Canada. Canadian officials scan the lists of their names, singling out those who bring money to invest. As it had for 40 years, Canada admitted enough immigrants in the 1990's to maintain them at about 16 percent of the total population. But there was a difference. In the 1950's, immigrants had come largely from Europe. Now, the majority come from Asia, the Middle East, and the Caribbean. Canadian cities, especially Toronto, Vancouver, and Calgary, the most popular magnets for the newcomers, blossom in the sights and sounds and smells of a dozen, exotic cultures. It is a migration that makes British Columbia and Alberta the fastest-growing provinces of Canada, with more than 21 percent of the nation's population by 1995.

The United States received 8.7 million immigrants between 1983 and 1992, the highest number in any 10-year period since 1910. And this was just the official count: an estimated 5 million more arrived without legal documentation. The newcomers flooded in from Korea and Vietnam, India and the Philippines, Ethiopia and Iran, Haiti and South America. Some were fleeing poverty, others were escaping political oppression or religious persecution. Huge numbers came from the Caribbean. Some 22 percent of immigrants to the United States travelled north across the border from Mexico. Immigrants who hailed from more progressive parts of the world hoped to achieve even greater prosperity for themselves and their children. By 1993 fully 20 million Americans and a proportionately greater 4.5 million Canadians had been born somewhere else.

A Japanese-American ranches cattle (left, above) in Kamuela on the big island of Hawaii. At an accredited Islamic primary school (left) in Illinois, pupils study Arabic culture along with more traditional subjects.

▶

Sikh Canadians, with their turbans and well-groomed moustaches and beards, bring an exotic touch to the scarlet cranberry fields of British Columbia.

Wherever the newcomers alighted, they transformed the landscape. Public schools in cities from Halifax to Los Angeles accommodated students from foreign lands whose native languages and dialects ranged from Tagalog (Philippines) to Lingala (Zaire), from Khmer (Cambodia) to Gujarati (India). Korean-owned grocery stores sprouted on street corners in Toronto and Vancouver as they did in Brooklyn and San Francisco. Haitians drove taxis in Mon-

treal. Chinese of all ages did tai chi chuan exercises in public parks. Clubs opened featuring salsa and other Latino-inspired music. An Islamic mosque rose resplendent in an Ohio cornfield. At Christmas Eve Mass in Lowell, Massachusetts — a 19th-century mill town settled by successive immigrant waves from Ireland, Portugal, Greece, and French-speaking Canada — "Silent Night" was regularly sung in Vietnamese.

Many of the recent arrivals, feeling the pressure to assimilate, did their best to fit in. They learned English or (in Canada) English and French, any way they could: reading newspapers, watching soap operas, listening to their

▲ **New Canadian citizens raise their hands as they are sworn in to their new nationality. In one day alone, more than 100 people from 20 different countries may become new Canadians.**

school-age children. For some, assimilation came through marriage, as both interethnic and interracial marriages became more common. Others clung to their heritage, speaking their native language and mixing little with people outside their own communities. For such groups, it seemed assimilation would come only gradually, if at all, through the course of generations.

Canada, on the whole, had long accepted cultural differences, even encouraging them under a government policy of multiculturalism. Attitudes were quite different in Quebec, however, where immigration was seen by many as a threat to Quebec culture, particularly since immigrants had shown a tendency to orient themselves to the English-speaking world. Accordingly, the melting-pot concept was introduced in the 1970's and all immigrant children were required to attend French schools. Even so, immigrants were blamed publicly for the narrow vote against Quebec's sovereignty in the 1995 referendum.

Multiculturalism was new to the United States where its advocates criticized the traditional ideal of the melting pot and favored words such as *mosaic, rainbow,* and *salad* to convey the diversity of contemporary American society. They called for modifications in the teaching of American history, giving greater emphasis to the roles of blacks, Hispanics, Asians, Native Americans, and others. Their demands challenged long-standing assumptions and raised troubling questions about the equity of the United States's social institutions. But some observers worried that multiculturalism threatened to tear apart the very matrix of American society.

Mexican-American girls celebrate Cinco de Mayo annually, wearing authentic native dress.

NEW LEADERS INHERIT OLD PROBLEMS

As both Bill Clinton and Jean Chrétien come to power, they find their power to move ahead limited by old roadblocks.

alk about long shots. Just 18 months earlier, back in mid 1991, few people had even heard of Bill (William J.) Clinton. Arkansas, where he served as governor, was hardly a bellwether state in U.S. politics. But Clinton was young, smart, and full of energy and ideas. Now, at 46, after one of the most riveting campaigns in years, he was president. Only his idol, John F. Kennedy, had been elected to the White House at a younger age. First he had to earn the party nomination. But just before the New Hampshire primary, a pair of sensational disclosures almost sent him crashing. A supermarket tabloid printed the lurid confessions of onetime torch singer Gennifer Flowers, who said she had been his mistress. Clinton denied it, then appeared with his wife, Hillary, on *60 Minutes* to express regret for causing "pain in my marriage." No sooner had he picked himself up than he blundered into a second land mine: a 23-year-old letter suggesting that years earlier, during the Vietnam War, he had cut ethical corners to avoid being drafted. Again Clinton waffled. But he managed to hang on.

Clinton seized upon the nation's money woes as a campaign issue. "The economy, stupid!" read a sign in the Little Rock campaign headquarters, and as a vote-winner it paid off. Voters picked Clinton over Bush by 43 to 38 percent. Clinton's inauguration, in January 1993, brought an ambitious set of plans to the White House. He would create jobs,

◀

President-elect Bill Clinton visits the Lincoln Memorial with Senator and Mrs. Al Gore and Hillary Rodham Clinton. Inset: Mrs. Clinton speaks on health care reform.

▶

Jean Chrétien, Prime Minister of Canada, argues for the unity of Canada, on October 6, 1995, just weeks before the referendum on Quebec's separation was due to be held.

◄

With Clinton as stage manager, Israeli Prime Minister Yitzhak Rabin shakes hands with Palestinian leader Yasir Arafat in 1993. Two years later, an Israeli right-wing extremist gunned down Rabin, but the quest for Israeli-Arab peace went on.

Reform Party, won 52. The Liberals, feeling pressure from the right with its demands for cutting the deficit, promptly began trimming the social programs it had done so much to create since 1945. As federal payments to provincial social programs were cut, many feared that all the gains of 50 years were about to be stripped away.

Bloc Québécois leader Lucien Bouchard played on fears of cuts in social programs as he toured Quebec in the fall of 1995, campaigning in a referendum to withdraw Quebec from Canada. The vote, held on October 30, 1995, was shockingly close. Those opposed to separation won by barely a percentage point.

By the middle of the 1990's, all the prophecies of those who had feared the development of regionalism since World War II seemed to be coming true. Ottawa, in order to reduce the deficit, was withdrawing from national leadership, particularly in the field of social programs. The provincial premiers had effectively become equal partners in national government, though they usually brought only provincial concerns to the national stage. Even within the federal Liberal party, there were many who acted as though they had been elected to defend provincial and regional interests rather than national ones. Fearful as they watched their social programs under attack, and stunned as they saw the growth of separatism in Quebec, ordinary Canadians could only look at the bickering of their regional politicians and wonder, "Who speaks for Canada?"

reduce the deficit, rebuild the infrastructure, revamp welfare. His top priority, a sweeping reform of the health care system, he delegated to Hillary; the First Lady would play a hands-on role in shaping policy. But the high hopes of the Clinton team ran head-on into the Republicans, who gained control of both houses of Congress in 1994. Clinton found himself fighting for programs that a few years before had seemed untouchable.

The economy was a major issue in Canada, too. Not only was it slumping but, as in the United States, the size of government deficits made it impossible to ease the effects of the slump with government spending. Late in 1992, Ralph Klein became premier of Alberta with a pledge to slash the government deficit by reducing spending, with much of the reduction aimed at social programs. In 1995, Conservative leader Michael Harris adopted Klein's proposals and swept into power in Ontario.

Similar thinking dominated the Conservative convention of 1993 that picked Kim Campbell as Conservative leader and first woman to be prime minister of Canada. But by then the national dislike for outgoing prime minister Brian Mulroney had spread like a virus to infect the party. In the federal election later that year, the Conservatives suffered the most humiliating defeat in their history, electing only two members to the House of Commons.

Jean Chrétien, who liked to think of himself as just "a guy from Shawinigan," led the Liberals to victory in that election. The Liberals were now the only national party left in Canada as a regional party from Quebec, the Bloc Québécois, won 54 seats and a regional party from the west, the

President Clinton encountered fierce congressional opposition from Republican senator Bob Dole (left) and House Speaker Newt Gingrich, who called their program of tax and spending cuts and reduced government regulation of big business a "contract with America."

▶

Former Bloc Québécois leader Lucien Bouchard, and Mario Dumont, leader of the Parti Action Démocratique, campaign for Quebec's independence in October 1995. In January 1996 Bouchard became Premier of Quebec.

EYES ON THE FUTURE

An oncologist (right) faces the 3-D interactive graphics he is developing to simulate brain surgery.

A headset and instrumented gloves take a NASA researcher into the computer-generated virtual reality of other planets.

Having embarked on the Information Superhighway, we can only guess where it will eventually lead us. Futurists extol the promise of nanotechnology, robotics, and virtual reality, but will such fields improve human life or yield merely toys and time wasters?

Predicting the future has always been a risky business. Back in the 1950's science writers were excited about a car-plane. The "Aerocar" was an idea whose time had come, they felt, and a prototype was actually built. What its backers overlooked was that not many motorists really wanted to learn to be pilots, and highway driving was stressful enough without adding takeoffs and landings. A similar lack of public demand met the two-way picture phone, which has been around since the 1960's.

Today many scientists are predicting that the Information Age will reach full bloom in the 21st century and dramatically change our lives. For that to happen, they say, the digitizing of information must simply continue at its present pace. Digitizing converts things that we are capable of sensing and knowing, such as sights, sounds, and printed text, into bits of energy that can be broadcast through the air on electromagnetic frequencies or sent over communications networks of wires or cables (especially fibre-optic cables, like the one shown at the top of the next page). On the receiving end of this

digitized information are devices such as TV sets, telephones, and computers — or in the not-too-distant future an all-in-one "box" combining the three, plus a fax machine, a VCR, and other gadgets. A fancy name for this electronic mishmash of communications networks and terminals is Information Superhighway.

Another name for it is *cyberspace*, a term originated by science fiction writer William Gibson. The amount of information in cyberspace is already vast and is growing exponentially as more people and services add to it. Sometime in the 21st century, the choice of movies for the home viewer may be limited only by the number of films that have *ever* been made. Writers may forgo magazines and books and simply publish on a computer network, and artists and composers may choose between introducing their work in cyberspace or in old-fashioned galleries and concert halls.

Tomorrow's homes, like Xanadu (below) in Orlando, Florida, could be built by inflating huge preshaped balloons, then spraying plastic foam over them. Computers maintain Xanadu's internal comfort. An insect-size robot (right) might do repairs and housework.

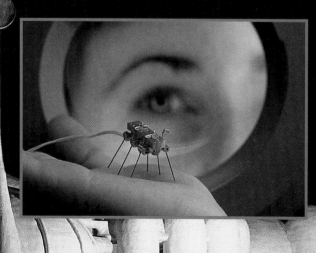

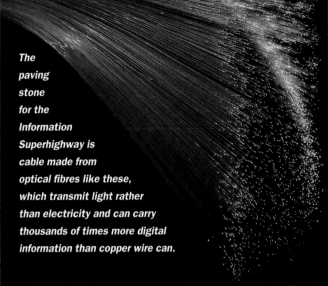

The paving stone for the Information Superhighway is cable made from optical fibres like these, which transmit light rather than electricity and can carry thousands of times more digital information than copper wire can.

People may send all their letters and other documents electronically, making the postal system simply a package delivery service.

Just because a high-tech service or futuristic product exists, however, is no guarantee that it will catch on in a big way. Virtual-reality games have made the leap from amusement arcade to home entertainment, but will they become a favorite pastime in the 21st century? Magazines and catalogues with interactive video animation and sound seem to pose a threat to print-on-paper publications. But do a lot of people really want multimedia magazines and catalogues, and do they really want to shop only by Internet?

Interactive media — TV programs, for example, that allow you to join the cast or win (or lose) money by placing bets — are touted as the wave of the future in home viewing. But how many couch potatoes will choose to interact?

Not too far in the future, "robotrucks" could be making streetside garbage pickups and cleaning up toxic-waste dumps. A "robocar" has been designed that uses a roof camera linked to an inside computer that scans what's ahead (and behind) and issues driving instructions to the car. But many people enjoy interacting with their cars (except in stop-and-go conditions), so will they really want a car that makes all the decisions for them?

Predictions for the 21st Century

Machines no bigger than molecules will become "assemblers," putting together atom by atom everything from new drugs and foods to skyscrapers and workstations on the moon and planets, writes K. Eric Drexler in his book *Engines of Creation: The Coming Era of Nanotechnology.* (*Nano*, a prefix meaning "one billionth," connotes extraordinarily small.)

Increasingly intelligent generations of tiny robots will be produced on "robot breeding farms," according to David H. Freedman, author of *Brainmakers.*

Early in the 21st century, inputting on computers will be done with thought waves, predicts Frank Ogden in *The Last Book You'll Ever Read,* and people will create artistic masterpieces without touching canvas, clay, or any other traditional surface or medium.

Clothes will be as comfortable as "second skins" — made of fabrics that keep you warm in winter, cool in summer, and dry in the rain. As reported in the cutting-edge publication *Mondo 2000,* some designers predict 4-D holographic "cyber-suits" and self-cleaning clothes, using built-in bacteria to eat stains and sweat.

Soon after 2001, antiaging treatments may extend our life span to 100 or more vigorous years, say Marvin Cetron and Owen Davies, authors of *Crystal Globe: The Haves and Have-nots of the New World Order.*

Neurologist Richard M. Restak, M.D., author of *Receptors,* believes that knowledge of the molecular structure of brain tissue and the chemicals that affect it will enable us to have exactly the minds we want.

Cars made of ultralight materials could run on hydrogen, the ultimate clean fuel, whose combustion emits only water and small amounts of nitrogen oxides, writes Marcia D. Lowe of the Worldwatch Institute in *State of the World.*

By 2500 a trillion people could have colonized the solar system, according to Los Alamos National Laboratory physicist Eric Jones and University of Hawaii anthropologist Ben Finney.

Beyond Saturn (above, in a color-enhanced photo from Voyager I *in 1980) lie Uranus, Neptune, and Pluto, and beyond them, the vast mysteries of space. Does space have an end? Is there life out there? Will such questions be answered in the next 100 or even the next 1,000 years?*

▼ *Michael Collins, who piloted the command module for the* Apollo 11 *moon landing, argues that the next goal of the U.S. space program should be to land astronauts on Mars (below, shown at sunset in a picture from the* Viking I *probe of 1976); but probably robots, like the Russian-built experimental Mars Rover (left), will roam the Red Planet first.*

FACTS AT YOUR FINGERTIPS

Here are dates, quotes, prices, pictures, charts, and hundreds more facts to help you relive

Our Glorious Century. The nine major sections amplify the book's chapters, and each section covers

seven topics: North American History & Politics, Everyday Life, Arts & Letters, Entertainment & Sports,

Business & Economics, Science & Medicine, and World Political Events.

Dawn of the 20th Century

NORTH AMERICAN HISTORY & POLITICS

1900

William McKinley, 25th president, reelected with Theodore Roosevelt as vice president

Sir Wilfrid Laurier's Liberals are reelected with 132 seats to Conservatives' 81

Hawaii becomes U.S. territory

Strathcona's Horse, a regiment raised and maintained by Lord Strathcona, leaves Canada for the Boer War

U.S. establishes civil government in Puerto Rico

U.S. population is 76 million; population of Canada is more than 5 million

1901

McKinley assassinated; Theodore Roosevelt becomes president

Prince Edward Island passes prohibition law

1902

Earthquake at Fernie, British Columbia, collapses coal mine, killing 128 men

Spooner Act authorizes building of Panama Canal

Maryland passes first state workmen's compensation law

African-American Matthew A. Henson reached the North Pole with Robert E. Peary in 1909.

1903

Panama Canal Treaty signed; U.S. recognizes Panama's independence

Muckraking journalists Lincoln Steffens, Ida Tarbell, and others assail big business and political bosses

Boundary commission decides against Canada in Canada/U.S. dispute over Alaska boundary

1904

Theodore Roosevelt, 26th president, wins reelection

Roosevelt Corollary to the Monroe Doctrine declares right of U.S. to intervene in the affairs of Western Hemisphere nations

Ottawa sets $500 head tax on immigrant Chinese

1905

Roosevelt organizes conference to end Russo-Japanese War

Canada creates provinces of Alberta and Saskatchewan. First premiers of Alberta and Saskatchewan are Alexander Cameron Rutherford and T. Walter Scott respectively

Sessional payment for members of parliament increased to $2,500

1906

Earthquake and fire devastate San Francisco

Canada assumes control of former British naval bases at Halifax, Nova Scotia, and Esquimault, British Columbia

U.S. troops occupy Cuba

Canada passes Lord's Day Act, severely limiting commercial activities on Sundays

1907

Ottawa offers payment for damages caused by anti-Oriental riots in Vancouver

Great White Fleet sails around the world

One million immigrants pass through Ellis Island

"The century upon which we have just entered must inevitably be one of tremendous triumph or tremendous failure for the whole human race."

— *Vice President Theodore Roosevelt at the 1901 Pan American Exposition*

Canada's first dial telephones installed in Sydney Mines, Nova Scotia

Sir Wilfrid Laurier leads Liberals to third consecutive victory with 139 seats against 75 for Conservatives

Roosevelt issues executive order prohibiting immigration by unskilled Japanese labor

1908

Sir Wilfrid Laurier leads Liberals to fourth consecutive victory with 133 seats against 85 for the Conservatives

William Howard Taft elected 27th president with James S. Sherman as vice president

Royal Mint opened at Ottawa

1909

Civil war in Honduras; U.S. sends troops

U.S. Adm. Robert E. Peary reaches North Pole with Matthew Henson and four Inuit

Geronimo, Apache Indian chief, dies

National Association for the Advancement of Colored People (NAACP) founded

Lord Strathcona creates fund to provide military training in Canada's public schools

1910

Royal Canadian Navy formed with its first major warships, H.M.S. *Rainbow* and *Niobe*

First Socialist elected to Congress

U.S. population is 92 million; Canada's is more than 7 million

1911

Conservatives, led by Robert Borden, defeat Liberals in federal election, 133 seats to 86

Senator Robert M. La Follette of Wisconsin founds National Progressive Republican League

U.S., Japan, Russia, and Britain sign treaty outlawing seal hunting

1912

Woodrow Wilson elected 28th president; he defeats the Progressive ("Bull Moose") ticket of Theodore Roosevelt and Hiram Johnson and the Republican ticket, led by William Howard Taft

Tornado in Regina kills 41 people, destroys 500 buildings

American statesman Elihu Root wins Nobel Peace Prize

IWW, or "Wobblies," organize strike of 10,000 textile workers in Massachusetts

Titanic hits iceberg and sinks on maiden voyage; more than 1,500 lives lost

U.S. marines sent to Nicaragua

1913

Ontario rules that French not be used as a language of instruction beyond grade 1

Storm on Great Lakes sinks 67 ships, 251 seamen die

Vancouver rioters protest Sikh immigration

EVERYDAY LIFE

1900

Work begins on rapid transit ("subway") system in New York City

First wall-mounted telephone with separate earpiece and mouthpiece

Photostatic copying machine invented

Kodak introduces the Brownie camera

Dance craze: the cakewalk

Connecticut restaurant serves first hamburgers; vendor sells first hot dogs

Paper clip patented

Architect Frank Lloyd Wright gains attention for his prairie-style design of homes

1901

Philadelphia department store installs first escalator

Ragtime becomes popular

Faddists take up Ping-Pong

1902

Spark plug invented

First electrical hearing aid

First animal crackers sold in U.S.

First teddy bear, named for Teddy Roosevelt

Disc brakes fitted to automobiles

First motor scooter

1903

First coast-to-coast crossing by auto, San Francisco to New York

Bottlemaking machine invented

Sanka introduced

1904

Tea bags go on sale

"Typhoid Mary," carrier of disease, identified

Tire chains give traction on icy roads

1905

First neon signs

First Rotary Club founded, in Chicago

Twentieth Century Limited makes express train trip from New York to Chicago in 18 hours

> *"Women are growing honester, braver, stronger, more healthful and skillful and able and free, more human in all ways."*
>
> — *Charlotte Perkins Gilman, in* Women and Economics, *1898*

Cullinan diamond found; weighs 3,000 carats

Vick's VapoRub introduced

Autos get bumpers

1906

Light bulbs use tungsten filaments

Stanley Steamer does more than 127 m.p.h. (203 kmh)

Jukeboxes

Public relations becomes an occupation

First permanent waves given by London hairdressers

The thermos invented

1907

Mother's Day proclaimed

First day-care centre opens in Rome, directed by physician and educator Maria Montessori

First electric clothes washer

Color photography pioneered

Head of U.S. Forest Service, Gifford Pinchot, begins to use the term *conservation*

Electric vacuum cleaner

Household detergents go on sale

First seaplane

1908

Gyroscopic compass

Silencer for guns invented

Women are wearing narrow sheath skirts and huge Merry Widow hats with dotted veils

First paper cups

Cellophane

Coffee filters

Boy Scout movement established in Canada

1909

Halley's Comet observed

J.A.D. McCurdy makes first airplane flight in Commonwealth at Baddeck, Nova Scotia

First hydrofoil

Jigsaw puzzles become popular

First electric toaster

Christmas blizzard (December 25–26) in eastern U.S.; 28 die, $20-million damage

Grand Falls Paper Mill opens at Grand Falls, Newfoundland

1910

Electric stoves

Tango sweeps Canada and the U.S.

1st St. Catharines Company becomes first group of Girl Guides in Canada

Pyjamas replace nightshirts in popularity

V-neck called unhealthy and immoral

First automatic transmissions in automobiles

Bathroom scales

First Father's Day celebration

1911

First transcontinental airplane flight, New York to Pasadena, California

Lincoln Memorial designed

Term *vitamin* coined

Electric self-starters for autos begin to replace cranks

Prototype air conditioners

First rotary eggbeater

Cold cream marketed

Electric frying pans

1912

First driver jailed for speeding

Immigrants to Canada: 1901–90

Immigrants' origins by continent were recorded from 1956 only.

SOS in Morse code adopted as international distress signal

1913

Sixty-story Woolworth Building, world's tallest to date, goes up in New York City

Brillo pads become available commercially

Red-mopped, button-eyed rag doll Ann became the heroine of the book Raggedy Ann Stories.

First home refrigerator

First modern bra, designed from handkerchiefs, ribbon, and cord

Kewpie dolls sell in the millions

First modern newspaper crossword puzzle

Zippers come into wide use

Couples dance the fox-trot

ARTS & LETTERS

1900

The Wonderful Wizard of Oz, by American author L. Frank Baum

French writer Colette publishes first of her *Claudine* novels

British writer and illustrator Beatrix Potter's *The Tale of Peter Rabbit*

American novelist Theodore Dreiser's *Sister Carrie*

Italian composer Giacomo

Puccini's opera *Tosca* premieres in Rome

Irish writer and wit Oscar Wilde dies

1901

English author Rudyard Kipling's *Kim*

German author Thomas Mann's first novel, *Buddenbrooks*

Spanish-born artist Pablo Picasso begins painting in the style of his Blue Period (1901–04)

Henri Toulouse-Lautrec, French painter of the Paris cabaret scene, dies

Russian composer and pianist Sergei Rachmaninoff's *Second Piano Concerto*

Russian writer Anton Chekhov's drama *The Three Sisters*

1902

Arthur Conan Doyle's *The Hound of the Baskervilles*

Joseph Conrad's *Heart of Darkness*

French composer Claude Debussy's only complete opera, *Pelléas et Mélisande*

Enrico Caruso makes first gramophone recording

1903

The Call of the Wild by American writer Jack London

Irish dramatist George Bernard Shaw's *Man and Superman*

Russian Wassily Kandinsky, considered by many the first abstract painter, shows the "Blue Rider"

Irish-born American composer and conductor Victor Herbert's operetta *Babes in Toyland*

First recording of an opera: Italian composer Giuseppe Verdi's *Ernani*

Three famous painters die: American James Whistler and Frenchmen Paul Gauguin and Camille Pissarro

1904

The Imperialist, by Sara Jeanette Duncan, examines the search for Canadian identity in an Ontario town

Hamilton McCarthy sculpture *Sieur de Monts* at Annapolis Royal

Controversial American dancer Isadora Duncan, a pioneer of modern dance, visits Russia, wows art critic and ballet producer Sergei Diaghilev

Italian composer Giacomo Puccini's opera *Madame Butterfly*

Irish poet and dramatist J. M. Synge's tragedy *Riders to the Sea*

Russian dramatist Anton Chekhov's *The Cherry Orchard*

1905

Canadian Duncan Campbell Scott's *New World Lyrics*

Les Fauves artists exhibit at Salon d'Automne in Paris; first major art movement of the 20th century

Pablo Picasso's Rose Period begins (to about 1906)

Hungarian composer Franz Lehár's operetta *The Merry Widow*

Russian-American Michel Fokine choreographs 3-minute crowd-pleasing solo "The Dying Swan" for legendary ballerina Anna Pavlova

German composer Richard Strauss's opera *Salome*

American photographer Alfred Stieglitz's 291 gallery begins to establish photography as an art form

1906

Albert Schweitzer's *The Quest of the Historical Jesus*

English novelist John Galsworthy publishes first book in his multivolume *The Forsyte Saga*

American author Upton Sinclair's *The Jungle*

O. Henry (William Sydney Porter) publishes his famous short story "The Gift of the Magi"

French painter Paul Cézanne dies

Children's book series — Bobbsey Twins, Hardy Boys — are launched

1907

Scottish-born Robert Service becomes Canada's first internationally famous poet with *Songs of a Sourdough*

Russian dancer Vaslav Nijinsky, still in his teens, makes debut at Maryinski Theatre in St. Petersburg

Irish dramatist J. M. Synge's *The Playboy of the Western World*

Cubism begins in France, marked by Pablo Picasso's *Demoiselles d'Avignon*

Russian author Maxim Gorki's *The Mother* supports revolutionary spirit

Austrian composer Gustav Mahler's *Symphony No. 8*

American philosopher William James's *Pragmatism*

1908

Lucy Maude Montgomery's *Anne of Green Gables,* set in Prince Edward Island, appears

Ashcan School, mostly realistic painters of city scenes, exhibit in New York City

Austrian-American composer Arnold Schoenberg vexes critics with his atonal *Second String Quartet*

Georges Braque, cofounder with Picasso of cubism, paints *Houses at l'Estaque* in France

French (Romanian-born) Constantin Brancusi, pioneer abstract sculptor, completes *The Kiss*

English novelist E. M. Forster's *A Room With a View*

French painter Maurice Utrillo's White Period (1908–14) explores use of many shades of white in Paris street scenes

English composer Sir Edward Elgar's *Symphony No. 1*

Hungarian composer Béla Bartók's *First String Quartet*

1909

Sowing Seeds in Danny, one of the first successful novels about the Canadian West, by Nellie McClung

French painter Henri Matisse's *The Dance*

Russian Sergei Diaghilev's

ballet company, Les Ballets Russes, perhaps the best ever assembled, debuts in Paris

Richard Strauss's *Elektra,* with libretto by Austrian poet Hugo von Hofmannsthal, gets mixed reviews because of its dissonant sections

1910

National Gallery of Canada pays $10,000 for Horatio Walker painting, *Oxen Drinking*

Giacomo Puccini's *La Fanciulla del West (The Girl of the Golden West)* premieres at the Metropolitan Opera House in New York City, with Arturo Toscanini conducting

Antonio Gaudí, Spanish architect much admired by the surrealists and abstract expressionists, designs one of his last major works, Casa Milá, in Barcelona

Igor Stravinsky writes the music for Sergei Diaghilev's Ballets Russes production of *The Firebird*

First Postimpressionist exhibit opens in London: Paul Cézanne, Vincent van Gogh, Henri Matisse, many others

1911

Petrouchka, produced in Paris by Diaghilev's Ballets Russes with music by Igor Stravinsky

Henri Matisse's *The Red Studio*

Richard Strauss's *Der Rosenkavalier,* his most popular opera

Leonardo da Vinci's *Mona Lisa* stolen from the Louvre in Paris; recovered in 1913

English author G. K. Chesterton's first book in a popular series about a mystery-solving priest: *The Innocence of Father Brown*

Georges Braque's *Man With a Guitar,* one of the best-known cubist paintings

American novelist Edith Wharton's *Ethan Frome*

1912

Stephen Leacock's *Sunshine Sketches of a Little Town* appears, establishing him as a Canadian humorist of international reputation

Robert Service's *Rhymes of a Rolling Stone* finds a wide audience with its vigorous themes and rhythms

German author Thomas Mann's short novel *Death in Venice*

Italian painter Amedeo Modigliani's *Stone Head*

French composer Maurice Ravel's *Daphnis et Chloë*

1913

O Pioneers! by American writer Willa Cather

American poet Robert Frost's first collection, *A Boy's Will*

First part of French author Marcel Proust's multivolume novel *A la Recherche du Temps Perdu (Remembrance of Things Past)* published

Irish-born British dramatist George Bernard Shaw's *Pygmalion*

English novelist D. H. Lawrence's first major work, *Sons and Lovers*

The Rite of Spring, a Diaghilev ballet with Igor Stravinsky's music, causes first-night audience to riot in Paris

New York Armory Show exposes many Americans to modern art; French maverick Marcel Duchamp's *Nude Descending a Staircase* is widely ridiculed; he introduces first mobile

ENTERTAINMENT & SPORTS

1900

Canadian George Orton, competing as a member of the U.S. team, wins gold medal for steeplechase at 1900 Olympics

Louis Armstrong born in New Orleans

First Davis Cup, international tennis tournament; U.S. beats Britain 3–0

Professional baseball's American League founded

Baseball cards, given away with cigarette packs, introduced

Baseball gets five-sided home plate

Canadian automobile record for 60 km between Toronto and Hamilton set at 3 hours 20 minutes

Ice hockey games now officially begin with a face-off

Dribbling introduced to basketball

1901

Walt Disney born

Baseball's National League now considers a foul ball a strike (except a foul ball after two strikes)

"A man who has a million dollars is as well off as if he were rich."

— *Multimillionaire John Jacob Astor (1864–1912)*

Boxing becomes legal in England

First openly professional hockey league formed with three U.S. teams and one (Sault Ste. Marie) Canadian team

1903

Thomas A. Edison produces the first western, *The Great Train Robbery*, filmed by E. S. Porter

First World Series between American and National leagues; Boston Red Sox defeat Pittsburgh Pirates 5 games to 3

1904

Ice hockey teams now have six players

Federation of International Football founded; establishes uniform rules for soccer

World Series not played, by decision of New York Giants manager John McGraw and owner John Brush, in midseason; Giants win National League pennant, Boston Red Sox are American League champs

1905

Dimple-faced golf ball patented

First nickelodeons open; admission, 5 cents

Public outcry over fatalities in college football will bring about stringent rule changes

Ontario Rugby Football Union introduces snap to put ball in play, adds rule that team must gain 10 yards within three downs to keep ball

Second World Series: New York Giants defeat Philadelphia Athletics 4 games to 1

1906

First French Grand Prix auto race

Thomas Edison's camera-phone synchronizes movie projector and phonograph

Forward pass introduced to football

Tommy Burns (Noah Brusso of Hanover, Ontario) wins world's heavyweight boxing title; he weighed only 77 kilograms

First film cartoon

Chicago White Sox defeat Chicago Cubs in World Series 4 games to 2

1907

First *Ziegfeld Follies*

First daily comic strip, H. C. (Bud) Fisher's *A. Mutt*, runs in *San Francisco Chronicle;* later becomes *Mutt and Jeff*

American actress Florence Lawrence is first movie celebrity, the Biograph Girl

Film titles replace commentators' running explanations

Chicago Cubs defeat Detroit Tigers in World Series 4 games to 0

1908

Jack Johnson first black heavyweight boxing champion

Limit of five personal fouls introduced in basketball to prevent rough play

U.S. wins 15 out of 28 track-and-field gold medals at London Olympic Games; Canada sends first official team to Olympics

Off the shoulder and décolleté, this gown may have turned turn-of-the-century heads.

Chicago Cubs defeat Detroit Tigers in World Series 4 games to 1

1909

Canada's governor-general Lord Grey donates cup for national football championship

First Grey Cup game won by University of Toronto over Parkdale before 3,807 fans

National Hockey Association (later National Hockey League) formed

Mary Pickford featured in *The Gibson Goddess* and other Biograph films

First newsreels

Clay tennis courts make their debut; most games still played on grass

Pittsburgh Pirates defeat Detroit Tigers in World Series 4 games to 3

1910

Hockey game length set at one hour played in three periods, a change from older rule that ended game as soon as any team had scored three goals

American driver Barney Oldfield breaks automobile speed record; drives a Benz 215 kmh (133 m.p.h.) at Daytona, Florida

William Howard Taft, on baseball's opening day, becomes first president to throw out the first ball

Enrico Caruso sings on an experimental radio broadcast from the Metropolitan Opera in New York City

Philadelphia Athletics defeat the Chicago Cubs in World Series 4 games to 1

1911

Irving Berlin's hit song "Alexander's Ragtime Band"

American composer W. C. Handy's "Memphis Blues"

Treemonisha, a folk opera, completed by black American ragtime composer Scott Joplin

Pitching legend Cy Young retires

Golfing legend-to-be Bobby Jones wins first title at age 9

Baseball adopts cork-centre ball

Philadelphia Athletics defeat New York Giants in World Series 4 games to 2

1912

Hollywood (and Canadian-born) producer-director Mack Sennett's slapstick Keystone Kops

International Lawn Tennis Association founded

Open net introduced in basketball; play no longer stopped to retrieve the ball

Jim Thorpe, outstanding athlete

WHAT IT COST

Prices: 1900

Montreal Gazette, daily, and Saturday, 2¢

Men's suits, overcoats, $15

Women's tailored suits, $15

Women's tailored skirts, $1.97

Corset, 50¢

Ladies' pumps, $1.50, $33.50; men's shoes, $2, $3.50; men's and ladies' boots, $2.95

Boys' Buster Brown suits, $4, $7

Sheets, pillowcases, 73¢, 15¢

Blankets, $3 a pair

Writing paper, 15¢ a lb.

Sheet music, 15¢

Upright piano, $205 to $305

Rolltop desks, $60; revolving office chairs, $6.50 to $17.50

Dickens's Complete Works, 15 vols.; Ruskin Complete Works, 15 vols.; Scott Complete Works, 12 vols., $13.50

97-piece dinner set, $11.98

Coffee and tea pots, 49¢; saucepan, 25¢

Scotch, $1.25 per bottle; Bols Liqueur Gin, $1.25 per bottle;

port wines, $2.50 per quart bottle; wine, $3.00 per case; champagne, $2.50 per quart bottle

Tea, 50¢ a lb.; can of sweet corn, 9¢; can of French peas, 10¢; can of asparagus, 15¢; can of peaches, 23¢; sardines, $1.00 a keg; strawberry jam, 60¢ a jar; Cornflakes and other cereals, 10¢ a packet

La Toscana cigar, 10¢ a case; cigarettes, package of 10, 15¢

Colgate's toothpaste, 20¢ a tube; hairbrushes, 25¢ to $2; pocket comb, 5¢ to 25¢; toilet soap, 25¢ a large tablet; Gillette safety razor, $5 to $7.50

Opera glasses, $10 to $14

Cruise to the Orient, 74 days, $350

Hockey tickets, Victoria vs. Montreal, 25¢ admission, $1 for box seats

10-room house in Westmount, $9,000; rented 6-room Montreal apartment, $16.50 a month

---

at Stockholm Olympics, is stripped of his medals for playing semipro baseball

Boston Red Sox defeat New York Giants in World Series 4 games to 3

1913

Husband-and-wife team Vernon and Irene Castle get North America dancing their castle walk, fox-trot, and other ballroom steps

Hollywood becomes centre of movie industry

College football players start to wear identifying numbers

World's first national squash organization, the Canadian Squash Rackets Association, is formed

Cecil B. DeMille's western *The Squaw Man,* one of first full-length films produced in Hollywood

---

Philadelphia Athletics defeat New York Giants in World Series 4 games to 3

BUSINESS & ECONOMICS

1900

Alphonse Desjardins founds first successful credit union in Canada at Lévis, Quebec

Canada establishes Department of Labour

International Ladies' Garment Workers' Union founded

High-speed steelmaking invented

Electric ignitions for internal-combustion engines

German aviation pioneer Count Ferdinand von Zeppelin tests his passenger dirigible

1901

Mercury-vapor arc lamp invented

Canadian Bankers' Association founded, resists efforts to charter regional banks

U.S. Steel Corporation, first billion-dollar company, organized

1903

North America's first high voltage transmission line from Shawinigan, Quebec, to Montreal

Ford Motor Co. founded

First cable under Pacific Ocean completed; President Roosevelt sends message around world on it

1904

Offset printing

Canadian company, Brazilian Traction Light and Power Company, is formed to develop transportation and natural resources in Brazil

1905

Caterpillar tractors developed

Compressed air used to excavate underwater rail tunnels

1906

American inventor Lee De Forest, "father of the radio," produces the triode: three-element vacuum tube

Canadian R.A. Fessenden makes world's first broadcast of voice and music

Haloid Co. founded; later becomes Xerox Corp.

Nitrogenous fertilizers increase crop yields

1907

Canada's Industrial Disputes Investigation Act limits power of unions

1908

Ford designs first Model T, priced at $850; more than 15 million will be sold over the next 20 years

Canadian R. S. McLaughlin begins manufacture of cars using Buick engines

General Motors founded

1909

Bakelite, the first plastic, is invented

1910

F.W. Woolworth Co. has in excess of 200 stores across North America

1911

Supreme Court orders dissolution of Standard Oil and American Tobacco companies

Frederick Taylor, efficiency expert, publishes *The Principles of Scientific Management*

1913

Removal of the U.S. tariff on newsprint spurs investment in Canadian pulp and paper industry

Ford sets up first moving assembly line, produces 1,000 Model T's daily

John D. Rockefeller starts Rockefeller Foundation with $100-million endowment

R. J. Reynolds pioneers the "American cigarette,"

William Frederick Cody, or Buffalo Bill, launched his Wild West Show in 1883. It was a hit in North America and Europe until Cody died in 1917.

a blend of mostly domestic tobaccos

SCIENCE & MEDICINE

1900

Palace of Knossos, centre of Minoan civilization, discovered by English archeologist Arthur Evans

---

Radon, a gaseous radioactive element formed when radium decays, discovered by German chemist F. G. Dorn

Quantum theory, dealing with energy transactions at the atomic and molecular level, formulated

First gamma rays observed

Austrian botanist Gregor Mendel's 19th-century work on genetics rediscovered

Austrian psychologist Sigmund Freud publishes *The Interpretation of Dreams*

Third law of thermodynamics postulated: heat flow from a higher to a lower temperature in solids stops at a temperature of absolute zero

1901

Code of Hammurabi, 18th-century B.C. Babylonian laws, found on tablets

U.S. army surgeon Walter Reed finds yellow fever virus is spread by mosquitoes

A, B, and O blood groups found

Adrenaline isolated

Guglielmo Marconi sends first transatlantic wireless message

White blood cells shown to fight disease

1902

AB blood group discovered

French husband-and-wife chemists Pierre and Marie Curie determine radium's properties

Ivan Pavlov, Russian physiologist, begins study of conditioned reflexes

Chromosomes seen to carry units of heredity

Layered structure of atmosphere observed

1903

The Curies share Nobel Prize in physics

Orville and Wilbur Wright make first flights at Kitty Hawk, North Carolina

Electrocardiograph invented

1904

General theory of radioactivity

Silicones, later widely used in lubricants and other commercial applications, discovered

First working photoelectric cell

1905

Albert Einstein formulates theory of relativity

First successful direct blood transfusion

First artificial joint restores hip movement

Sigmund Freud publishes *Three Essays on the Theory of Sexuality*

French psychologist Alfred Binet devises first intelligence tests

Female XX and male XY chromosomes identified

1906

German bacteriologist August von Wassermann develops syphilis test

Whooping cough bacterium isolated

Earth's interior determined to have a distinct core

1907

Existence of black holes in space postulated

Protozoans implicated in sleeping sickness and malaria

Radioactive decay of uranium used to find geologic age

TSE 300 Composite Index

Year End Values

(Bar chart showing values from 0 to 4500, with years along the x-axis: 1919, '21, '25, '28, '32, '36, '41, '45, '50, '55, '60, '65, '68, '70, '73, '75, '80, '82, '85, '90, '94. Values rise from near zero in the early years to approximately 4200 by '94.)

Cell culture outside the body introduced

1908

Ammonia synthesized

Barium meal technique indicates ulcers on X rays

Sunspots shown to be magnetic phenomenon

Helium liquefied

1909

Body louse found to transmit typhus

Word *gene* used to describe a factor of heredity

Sigmund Freud lectures in U.S.

1910

Lung disease diagnosed with X rays

Canadian government moves to protect bison (down from 60 million to 2,000) and begins to place them on reserves

1911

Norwegian polar explorer Roald Amundsen reaches South Pole

Atomic nucleus discovered

Superconductivity discovered

1912

First decompression chamber for underwater divers

Swiss psychologist Carl G. Jung's *The Theory of Psychoanalysis*

Gestalt psychology

Theory of continental drift

Cosmic radiation discovered

Nuclear transmutation, the conversion of one element into another, demonstrated

Protons and electrons detected within the atom

"A European war can only end in the ruin of the vanquished and the scarcely less fatal commercial dislocation and exhaustion of the conquerors."

— *Winston Churchill, 1901*

1913

Danish scientist Niels Bohr's theory of atomic structure

Diphtheria immunity test

Chlorophyll's composition discovered

Vitamins A and B isolated

Mammographs

Sigmund Freud publishes *Totem and Taboo*

WORLD POLITICAL EVENTS

1900

Boxer Rebellion begins in China

Umberto I of Italy assassinated; Victor Emmanuel III crowned

Boer War: British annex Orange Free State and Transvaal

1901

Queen Victoria dies; Edward VII crowned king of England

Commonwealth of Australia proclaimed

1902

Boer War ends

Aswan Dam on the Nile

1903

Anti-Jewish pogroms in Russia

1904

Russo-Japanese War begins

1905

"Bloody Sunday": Russian troops fire on workers in St. Petersburg; mutiny on battleship *Potemkin*

Sinn Fein, a nationalist political party, organized in Ireland

Sun Yat-sen, Chinese reformer, founds movement to overthrow Manchu dynasty

1906

French Army officer Alfred Dreyfus, a Jew, exonerated of cowardice in a case involving cover-up and bigotry

Zuider Zee drainage reclaims Netherlands land from the sea

1907

Triple Entente of Britain, France, and Russia formed to counter Triple Alliance of Germany, Italy, and Austria-Hungary

1908

Austria-Hungary annexes Bosnia and Herzegovina

"Young Turks" oust ruling sultan, but lose their dream of a resurgent Ottoman Empire

1910

Edward VII dies; George V crowned king of England

Portugal deposes King Manuel II, proclaims itself a republic

Union of South Africa proclaimed

Japan annexes Korea

Slavery abolished in China

1911

Airplanes deployed offensively in Turkish-Italian conflict

Francisco Madero becomes president of Mexico; executed by rebels two years later

1912

British coal miners, dockworkers, and transport workers go on general strike

Sun Yat-sen and Chiang Kai-shek establish republic in China; emperor abdicates

First Balkan War begins as Montenegro opens hostilities against Ottoman Empire

1913

King George I of Greece assassinated; Constantine I succeeds him

Suffragette Emmeline Pankhurst jailed in London and starts hunger strikes

Second Balkan War begins as Bulgaria attacks Greeks and Serbs

NORTH AMERICAN HISTORY & POLITICS

1914

War Measures Act gives Canadian government near-dictatorial powers

President Woodrow Wilson declares America's neutrality

Panama Canal opens; civil government established in Canal Zone

✠

"A war to end all wars."

— *English author H. G. Wells, 1914; phrase quoted by President Woodrow Wilson referring to World War I*

✠

Canada volunteers troops for service in Europe

C.P.R. liner *Empress of Ireland* sinks after collision in Gulf of St. Lawrence; over 900 drown

Pressed by anti-Oriental feeling, Vancouver authorities turn back immigrant ship *Komataga Maru* with 400 Indians aboard

Some 10.5 million immigrants from southern and eastern Europe have entered North America since 1905

1915

Ist Canadian Division lands in France

6,000 Canadians lost in Battle of Ypres, but line holds in face of first gas attack

Henry Ford charters "peace ship," sails to Norway in attempt to negotiate end to the fighting in Europe

Sir Robert Borden becomes first dominion prime minister to attend a British cabinet meeting

German sympathizer detonates bomb in U.S. Senate building, wounds American financier J. Pierpont Morgan, Jr.

U.S. marines sent to Haiti to protect American lives and property

U.S. Supreme Court rules employers may not deny employment on grounds of union membership

Ku Klux Klan revived in Georgia

Rocky Mountain National Park created

1916

Democrats Woodrow Wilson, 28th president, and Thomas R. Marshall, vice president, narrowly reelected

Canadian and Newfoundland troops participate in Battle of the Somme

---

WHAT IT COST

Prices: 1910

Safe deposit box, Royal Trust Company, $5 a year

Women's evening gowns, $27.50; women's suits, $17.50; women's coats, $4.95 to $25

Women's Hudson seal coats, $206.25

Men's shirts, 89¢; celluloid collars, 18¢ each

Men's suits, $16 to $27.50

Men's overcoats, $9.65 to $25

Campbell's soup, 12¢ a can

Can of baked beans, 10¢; clam chowder, 15¢; sugar corn, 20¢; spinach, 18¢

Jersey Cream (evaporated) Milk, 10¢

Coffee, 35¢ to 50¢ per lb.

Bottle of gin, $1 to $3.25 ; bourbon, $1.50; Labatt beer, 20¢; Concord wine, $5 a case

Russell-Knight "32" car, $2,650; Ford Touring Car, $530; Overland roadster coupe, $1,225; Dodge Winter Touring Car, $1,335

12-room bungalow overlooking Lake Ontario, $8,500

10-room brick and stucco house in York Mills vicinity, $8,500

3-storey house, Metcalfe Ave., Montreal, $9,500

9-room flat to let in Montreal, $32 per month

Denmark sells U.S. the Virgin Islands for $25 million

Mexican revolutionary Pancho Villa raids Columbus, New Mexico, then returns to Mexico; Gen. John J. Pershing pursues him across border

U.S. troops occupy the Dominican Republic to quell unrest caused by rival factions

Canadian troops discard the

Canadian-designed Ross rifle in favor of the British Lee-Enfield

17 schools close in Ottawa as teachers strike over bilingualism

Manitoba and Ontario temperance acts prohibit the retail sale of alcohol

Jeannette Rankin, a Montana Republican, elected first U.S. congresswoman

1917

Canadian Corps captures Vimy Ridge

U.S.S. *Housatonic* sunk; Wilson severs diplomatic relations with Germany

U.S. declares war on Germany; General Pershing commands American Expeditionary Forces; U.S. troops land in France

Sir Arthur Currie takes command of Canadian troops in Europe

Ottawa introduces income tax as a temporary war measure

Ottawa forbids use of grain to make alcohol for duration of war

Collision of two ships, *Mont Blanc* and *Imo*, causes

explosion that kills 1,630 people in Halifax-Dartmouth

Canada introduces conscription for military service

Puerto Rico becomes U.S. territory

1918

Arthur Roy Brown, of Stoufville, Ontario, is credited with shooting down Baron Manfred von Richtofen, Germany's greatest air ace

William Avery "Billy" Bishop makes last combat flight, claims five enemy aircraft downed

Conscription leads to rioting in Quebec, and angry demonstrations by prairie farmers

War ends with signing of armistice on Nov. 11

Canadian and British troops break Hindenburg Line in final push of war

✠

"It is a fearful thing to lead this great, peaceful people into war, into the most terrible and disastrous of all wars, civilization itself seeming to be in the balance. But the right is more precious than peace."

— *President Woodrow Wilson, April 2, 1917, asking Congress to declare war*

✠

Total Allied casualties: about 34 million

Canadian Pacific steamship *Sophia* sinks en route from Skagway to Vancouver; 343 die

---

Canadian Unemployment Rate: 1900–93

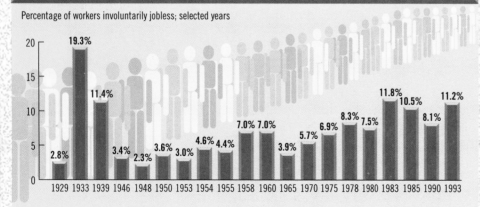

Percentage of workers involuntarily jobless; selected years

Year	Rate
1929	2.8%
1933	19.3%
1939	11.4%
1946	3.4%
1948	2.3%
1950	3.6%
1953	3.0%
1954	4.6%
1955	4.4%
1958	7.0%
1960	7.0%
1965	3.9%
1970	5.7%
1975	6.9%
1978	8.3%
1980	7.5%
1983	11.8%
1985	10.5%
1990	8.1%
1993	11.2%

President Wilson outlines 14 Points for world peace

U.S. socialist Eugene Debs sentenced to 10 years in prison for sedition

✠

"England, that nation of shopkeepers, cannot produce soldiers to equal ours."

— *Spokesman for Kaiser Wilhelm*

✠

1919

Versailles peace treaty signed

League of Nations founded; Woodrow Wilson presides over first meeting

Isolationists in U.S. Senate balk at ratifying Treaty of Versailles

President Wilson receives Nobel Peace Prize for advocating a just settlement of World War I and the creation of the League of Nations

Ottawa abolishes titles of peerage and knighthood for Canadians

General strike in Winnipeg highlights discontent over government management of wartime economy

E.C. Drury leads United Farmers of Ontario to victory in provincial general election

Sir Wilfrid Laurier dies, Liberals hold convention to rebuild party

Quebec Bridge is officially opened

18th amendment (Prohibition) ratified; Volstead Act passed

Workers at U.S. Steel strike, demanding union recognition

U.S. Attorney General A. Mitchell Palmer commences Red Scare arrests; seeks to control bombings and other violence

EVERYDAY LIFE

1914

First red and green traffic lights — in Cleveland

Self-service shopping introduced in California; items are arranged alphabetically

First major sewage system using bacteria to decompose waste opens in Manchester, England

Last passenger pigeon dies at Cincinnati Zoo

First live models in U.S. fashion shows

First successful heart surgery — on a dog

Pyrex glassware comes to market

Two-step becomes a popular ballroom dance

Mid-calf-length skirts with a fur stole and shapeless coat made a fashion statement in 1918.

1915

Taxicabs in major cities; fare is 5 cents

Lipstick marketed

Nevada establishes quickie-divorce law

1916

First public birth-control clinic opened, by Margaret Sanger in Brooklyn, New York; she is jailed for 30 days for creating a public nuisance

Jazz craze spreads

Electric clocks

First supermarket, with self-service and checkout, in Tennessee

U.S. and Canada act to protect migratory birds

Liquid nail polish

Automobile windshield wipers

Manitoba becomes first province to extend right to vote to women, a right limited to provincial elections

First women's Red Cross uniform

Prototype of agitator washing machines

British "summer time," with clocks pushed an hour ahead, mandated to save energy

French dress designer Coco Chanel makes jersey, a knit fabric hitherto used in underwear, chic for outerwear

Hetty Green — America's richest woman, worth $100 million — dies

1917

Food freezing introduced commercially

New York State amends its constitution to allow women the vote; women suffragists picketing the White House get jail sentences

Canadian government gives right to vote to women, but only to those with close relatives serving in the armed forces, and only for the election of 1917 in which conscription was the major issue

Financier Diamond Jim Brady dies

1918

Influenza epidemic will kill more than 25 million worldwide

before it runs its course; about 50,000 die in Canada and about 500,000 in the U.S..

Canada's first official air mail flight leaves Montreal field at Bois Franc for Toronto, flown by R.A.F. Capt. Brian Peck; he also carried liquor since it was legally available in Montreal but not in Toronto

Regular airmail service established from New York City to Washington and New York City to Chicago

Nova Scotia extends the vote in provincial elections to women

Canada gives women the right to vote in federal elections

U.S. divided into four time zones; daylight saving time introduced

Ouija boards go on sale

First pop-up toaster patented; not marketed until 1930

Raggedy Ann Stories, popularizing the doll, published by U.S. cartoonist Johnny Gruelle

The New York Times begins home delivery

1919

U.S. railroad lines total 426,000 kilometres of track

American Legion organized

ARTS & LETTERS

1914

Arcadian Adventures with the Idle Rich by Stephen Leacock; though seemingly set in a U.S. city, this best of his works is actually set in Montreal

Louis Hémon's novel of rural Quebec, *Maria Chapdelaine,* appears in serial form in a Paris newspaper

American poet Joyce Kilmer's *Trees and Other Poems*; he is killed in action in France, 1918

Irish writer James Joyce's *Dubliners* stories and parts of *A Portrait of the Artist as a Young Man* published in the English literary magazine *The Egoist*

French painter Georges Braque's *Music*

English composer Ralph

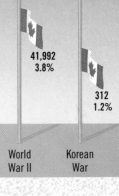

The Human Cost of War

Number Serving

	Boer War	World War I	World War II	Korean War
Number Serving	8,372	619,636	1,086,771	25,540
Casualties	244 (2.9%)	60,661 (9.8%)	41,992 (3.8%)	312 (1.2%)

Vaughan Williams's *A London Symphony*

American writer Edgar Rice Burroughs's *Tarzan of the Apes*

1915

English novelist Somerset Maugham's *Of Human Bondage*

Dadaist group forms in Zurich, Switzerland, led by, among others, French artist Jean Arp, German poet Hugo Ball, and French poet Tristan Tzara

Ezra Pound begins his poems *The Cantos*

The Prairie Wife by Arthur Stringer, first of a trilogy of Alberta life

Czech-born Austrian writer Franz Kafka publishes his long story *The Metamorphosis*

English novelist D. H. Lawrence's *The Rainbow* banned for obscenity

Scottish writer John Buchan's thriller *The Thirty-nine Steps* is published Marc Chagall, Russian painter living in France, paints *The Birthday*

1916

Lundy's Lane, a volume of poetry by Canadian Duncan Campbell Scott

American writer Carl Sandburg's *Chicago Poems* celebrates working-class America

Norman Rockwell begins painting covers for *The Saturday Evening Post*

Austrian-born philosopher Martin Buber's *The Spirit of Judaism*

American novelist Theodore Dreiser's *The "Genius"* suppressed by censors

1917

Tom Thomson, Canadian landscape painter whose style

dominates Canadian painting in the 1920's dies

✠

"Time is a great legalizer, even in the field of morals."

— *Journalist H. L. Mencken, A Book of Prefaces (1917)*

✠

First Pulitzer prizes: for biography, *Julia Ward Howe*, by Laura E. Richards, Maude H. Elliot, and Florence H. Hall; for history, *With Americans of Past and Present Days*, by J. J. Jusserand

French poet Guillaume Apollinaire coins term *surrealism;* Picasso designs surrealistic sets and costumes for ballet *Parade*

American-born English poet T. S. Eliot's *Prufrock and Other Observations*

Italian sculptor and painter Amedeo Modigliani's *Crouching Female Nude*

Russian composer Sergei Prokofiev's *Classical Symphony*

Hungarian-born American composer Sigmund Romberg's operetta *Maytime*

1918

First Pulitzer prizes: for fiction, *His Family*, by Ernest Poole; for drama, *Why Marry?* by Jesse L. Williams; for poetry, *Love Songs*, by Sara Teasdale

Albert Laberge's *La Scouine*, the story of the hard life of a Quebec farmer, appears in only 60 copies; it is published in translation in 1977 as *Bitter Bread*

American novelist Willa Cather's *My Ántonia*

U.S. Post Office burns issues of the American magazine *Little Review* containing installments of James Joyce's *Ulysses*, judged obscene

English biographer and critic Lytton Strachey's *Eminent Victorians*

German philosopher Oswald Spengler's *Decline of the West*

Spanish painter Juan Gris's cubist *Scottish Girl*

Swiss painter Paul Klee's abstract *Gartenplan*

Norwegian painter Edvard Munch's *Bathing Man*

With publication of his *Poems*, English poet Gerard Manley Hopkins achieves measure of fame almost 30 years after his death

New York Philharmonic Society bans works of living German composers; Karl Muck, German conductor of Boston Symphony Orchestra, arrested as enemy alien

1919

American editor and critic H. L. Mencken's *The American Language*

English writer Thomas Hardy's *Collected Poems*

Already famous, draftee Irving Berlin wrote and sang this tune for a show at his army camp.

Austrian-born British expressionist artist and writer Oskar Kokoschka's *The Power of Music*

Bauhaus school of architecture founded by Walter Gropius in Weimar, Germany

✠

"I think that I shall never see A poem lovely as a tree. . . . A tree that may in summer wear A nest of robins in her hair; . . . Poems are made by fools like me, But only God can make a tree."

— *"Trees" (1913), by American poet Joyce Kilmer, killed in action in France, 1918*

✠

French painter Claude Monet's *Nymphéas*

English composer Edward Elgar's *Concerto in E Minor for Cello*

German composer Richard Strauss's opera *Die Frau*

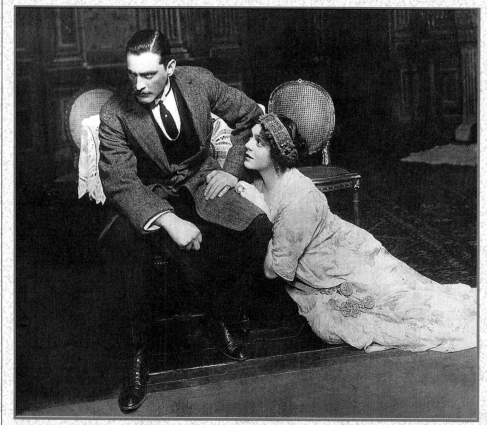

John Barrymore and his older sister, Ethel, do an emotional scene in the prewar Broadway drama Slice of Life. *With their older brother, Lionel, the Barrymores entertained stage and screen audiences for more than 50 years.*

Ohne Schatten, with the Austrian poet Hugo von Hofmannsthal as librettist

German film *The Cabinet of Dr. Caligari,* directed by Robert Wiene and script by Carl Mayer, landmark in expressionist cinema

U.S. philanthropist A. D. Juilliard dies, leaving $20-million endowment to the music institute that will become the Juilliard School of Music

French-born American composer Edgard Varèse conducts the New York Symphony Orchestra in its first concert of modern music

The Magnificent Ambersons, by Booth Tarkington, wins Pulitzer Prize for fiction

American man of letters Henry Adams's autobiography, *The Education of Henry Adams* (printed privately, 1906), wins Pulitzer Prize for biography

ENTERTAINMENT & SPORTS

1914

Vancouver Millionaires win Stanley Cup

American Society of Composers, Authors, and Publishers (ASCAP) founded by John Philip Sousa, Victor Herbert, and others to protect musical copyrights

Charlie Chaplin introduces his tramp outfit in *Kid Auto Races at Venice*

Mack Sennett's *Tillie's Punctured Romance,* with Charlie Chaplin and Canadian-born Marie Dressler

U.S. black composer W. C. Handy's "St. Louis Blues"

Yale Bowl, first of college football super stadiums, opens, seating 80,000

Jack Dempsey starts his boxing career under the name Kid Blackey

American golfer Walter Hagen, at 21, wins U.S. Open, the first of his 11 major championships (1914–29)

Boston Braves defeat Philadelphia Athletics in World Series, 4 games to 0

1915

78-r.p.m. records

American film director D. W. Griffith's *The Birth of a Nation*

Movie serials: *The Perils of Pauline, Ruth of the Rockies, What Happened to Mary?*

Chaplin's *The Tramp*

Douglas Fairbanks stars in *The Lamb*

Welsh composer Ivor Novello writes "Keep the Home Fires Burning," popular wartime song

Jess Willard becomes heavyweight boxing champion, knocking out Jack Johnson in the 26th round

Wimbledon tennis suspended for duration of the war

Edmonton Grads begin 25-year domination of international women's basketball

James Edward "Tip" O'Neill, Canadian who was most admired U.S. baseball player of 1880's, dies in Montreal; he had all-time highest batting average at .492

Boston Red Sox defeat Philadelphia Athletics in World Series 4 games to 1

1916

Annual Rose Bowl game begins; Washington State beats Brown 14–0

Professional Golfers' Association (PGA) founded in U.S.

D. W. Griffith's film *Intolerance*

Boston Red Sox defeat Brooklyn Dodgers in World Series 4 games to 1

1917

French actress Sarah Bernhardt, 73, makes her last U.S. tour

Canadian-born actress Mary Pickford ("America's Sweetheart") stars in the movie *The Little Princess*

American musical comedy dynamo George M. Cohan writes "Over There"

Charlie Chaplin signs a contract worth $1 million annually

First jazz recordings, by the

Original Dixieland Jazz Band, a group of white musicians, include "Tiger Rag," "Clarinet Marmalade," and "Ostrich Walk"

Keds makes the first tennis footwear

Boston Red Sox pitcher Ernie Shore throws a perfect game against the Washington Senators

First Sunday baseball game is played in New York's Polo Grounds; managers are arrested for breaking the blue law

National Hockey Association is disbanded. National Hockey League is formed, with three teams: Montreal Canadiens, Ottawa Senators, and Toronto Arenas

Seattle Metropolitans defeat the Montreal Canadiens, to become first U.S. team to win hockey's Stanley Cup

Chicago White Sox defeat New York Giants in World Series 4 games to 2

1918

Robert LeRoy Ripley begins *Believe It or Not* newspaper cartoon series

Knute Rockne named Notre Dame football coach

Irving Berlin's song "Oh! How I Hate to Get Up in the Morning" is released

George Gershwin's "Swanee"

John L. Sullivan, former heavyweight boxing champion, dies

Jerome Kern's "Rock-a-Bye, Baby"

Six-a-side game accepted for Stanley Cup playoffs

Joe Malone of Montreal Canadiens scores 44 goals in 20 games in 1917-18 season

Boston Red Sox defeat Chicago Cubs in World Series 4 games to 2

Dumbells, Canadian army performers drawn from front-line troops, stage shows in London, England

Hockey rules drop ban on forward pass between blue lines

✠

"It was I who invented the telephone and it was invented wherever I happened to be at the time. Of this you may be sure, the telephone was invented in Canada. It was made in the United States."

— Inventor Alexander G. Bell, 1909

✠

1919

Movie giants Charlie Chaplin, Mary Pickford, Douglas Fairbanks, and D. W. Griffith form United Artists to produce and distribute films

Hollywood agrees to submit films to censorship

Jack Dempsey wins world heavyweight boxing crown from Jess Willard

Babe Ruth hits 537-foot home run

Sir Barton is first horse to win the Triple Crown: Kentucky Derby, Preakness, and Belmont Stakes; J. Loftus rides him in all three triumphs

American bandleader Paul Whiteman forms orchestra to play "symphonic jazz"

Mechanical rabbit launches modern greyhound racing

Cincinnati Reds defeat Chicago White Sox in World Series 5 games to 3; in "Black Sox" scandal several Chicago players accused of trying to lose World Series

BUSINESS & ECONOMICS

1914

Cadillac develops V-8 engine

Teletypewriter invented

U.S. Circuit Court of Appeals decides airplane patent suit in favor of Wright brothers

1915

First transcontinental telephone

call, between Alexander Graham Bell in New York City and Thomas A. Watson in San Francisco

Ford produces its millionth Model T; price is $440

First airport in Canada at Long Branch, Toronto

U.S. bankers, led by J. Pierpont Morgan, Jr., float $500-million loan to Britain and France to help their war effort

1916

Trans-Siberian Railroad between Moscow and Vladivostok completed

Dodge introduces first all-steel auto body

✠

"History is more or less bunk."

— Industrialist Henry Ford, 1916

✠

1917

Union Carbide founded

Radios used for ground-to-air and air-to-air communication

World's largest electrical steel plant opens in Toronto

Canadian Press news agency founded

1918

Canada prepares to amalgamate failing private railways into government-owned Canadian National Railways

1919

Postwar labor unrest in Canada reaches peak with General Strike in Winnipeg

SCIENCE & MEDICINE

1914

Thyroxine, an amino-acid hormone produced by the thyroid gland, identified

U.S physicist and inventor Robert Goddard's first rocket experiments; liquid-fuel rockets patented

Interstellar matter, clouds of gas and dust, observed, indicating that space between the stars is not as empty as had been supposed

Guttenberg discontinuity announced: it marks boundary between Earth's core and mantle

1915

Niacin deficiency in diet associated with pellagra

Dysentery bacillus isolated

Albert Einstein completes theory of relativity; his ideas remake physics and astronomy

First carcinogen identified

Disposable scalpel patented

1916

Plastic surgery advances through treatment of war injuries

Blood for transfusion is first refrigerated

F.W. Mott puts forward the theory of shell shock, or war neurosis

Vitamins A and B declared essential for growth

National Research Council of Canada established

American physical chemist Gilbert N. Lewis proposes theory of atomic structure that is later (1919) developed, with colleague Irving Langmuir, into Lewis-Langmuir theory of atomic structure and valence

1917

Vitamin D produced from cod-liver oil

100-inch telescope erected at Mount Wilson, California

Swiss psychologist Carl G. Jung publishes his ground-breaking Psychology of the Unconscious

Sigmund Freud completes Introductory Lectures on Psychoanalysis

Existence of "black holes" in far space predicted

Rearrangement of chromosomes during meiosis, or cell division, is demonstrated

Rocky Mountain Spotted Fever vaccine

1918

German physicist Max Planck, father of quantum theory, wins Nobel Prize

Development of alkyd resins, used extensively in paints for durability, color stability, uniform drying

✠

"Before I built a wall I'd ask to know What I was walling in or walling out."

—"Mending Wall" (1914), by American poet Robert Frost

✠

American astronomer Harlow Shapley determines the size of the Milky Way; places our solar system near the outer edge of the galaxy

1919

Bees found to communicate through body action

British physicist Ernest

Rutherford investigates the structure of the atom

English philosopher and mathematician Bertrand Russell's Introduction to the Philosophy of Mathematics

American geneticist Thomas Hunt Morgan's The Physical Basis of Heredity summarizes his genetics research on fruit flies; it influences future genetics research and fruit flies remain an important source for experiments in genetics

WORLD POLITICAL & WAR EVENTS

1914

Archduke Francis Ferdinand, heir to the Austrian throne, and wife assassinated at Sarajevo

Austria-Hungary declares war on Serbia

European conflicts widen into world war: Germany, Austria-Hungary, and Turkey (Central Powers) oppose Britain, France, and Russia (Allies)

Britain lands troops in France

Battle of the Marne; 1st Battle of Ypres

Trench warfare along entire western front

Pope Pius X dies; Pope Benedict XV elected

Egypt becomes British protectorate

Run on European banks

1915

First German submarine attacks at Le Havre

Italy declares war on Germany

First use of poison gas by Germans, in 2nd Battle of Ypres

German zeppelins raid England

Tetanus in the trenches

German sea-blockade of Britain

Allied landings at Gallipoli, Turkey

Czar Nicholas II takes personal control of Russian army

Douglas Haig becomes British commander in France; Joseph Joffre is French commander

English nurse Edith Cavell executed by Germans, outraging British

Germany builds the Fokker, first plane with interrupter mechanism allowing machine-gun fire between propeller-blade rotations

Britain produces first armored vehicle with tracks, called Little Willie

German aeronautical designer

Children of families laid low by influenza bring food pots to be filled by volunteers. The epidemic peaked in 1918–19. While the flu virus alone seldom killed, it resulted in deadly bacterial infections.

Hugo Junkers makes first all-metal fighter plane

Germans sink *Lusitania*

Reflecting concern that alcohol consumption weakens war effort, France outlaws sale of absinthe; England's George V and the royal household announce they are abstaining from alcohol

✠

*"Was it for this
the clay grew tall? —
Oh, what made
fatuous sunbeams toil
To break earth's
sleep at all?"*

—"Futility," by English poet Wilfred Owen, killed in action in France, 1918

✠

1916

First zeppelin attack on Paris

Battle of Jutland, between fleets of Britain and Germany, ends in a costly draw

Battles between Italian and Austrian forces along the

Isonzo River in northern Italy rage on

David Lloyd George is British prime minister; Paul von Hindenburg becomes German chief of staff

Battle of Verdun

Allied offensive on the Somme begins

British merchant ship losses during year total 1.5 million tons; ultrasonic machine developed to detect submarines

"Mad monk" Rasputin assassinated in Russia

1917

Revolution in Russia; Czar Nicholas II abdicates

Russian Black Sea fleet mutinies; October Revolution in Petrograd; Bolsheviks V. I. Lenin and Leon Trotsky assume leadership; Russia sues for peace with Germany

U.S. declares war on Germany

Britain's George V orders members of royal family to drop their German titles

First use of massed tanks in battle, by British at Cambrai, France

Mata Hari, charged with spying for the Central Powers, executed by Allies

The streets of St. Petersburg (above), the capital of Russia from 1712 to 1917, were the scene of riot after riot in the 50 turbulent years that culminated in Czar Nicholas II's giving up his throne on March 15, 1917.

Passchendaele (3rd Battle of Ypres) continues slaughter on western front

King Constantine of Greece abdicates; Greece severs relations with Central Powers

Pact of Corfu: Serbia, Montenegro, Slovenia, and Croatia agree to form Yugoslavia

Balfour Declaration calls for Jewish state in Palestine

Sinn Fein, Irish nationalist organization, holds convention in Dublin

Reform in Mexico: universal suffrage, 8-hour workday, minimum wage

1918

Former Russian Czar Nicholas II and family secretly executed by Lenin's agents

Germany's Kaiser Wilhelm abdicates

As war ends, Hungary declares independence from Austria; Baltic states of Estonia, Latvia, Lithuania assert independence from Russia; Czechoslovakia created

Bolsheviks form Communist Party under Lenin, move Russian capital to Moscow from Petrograd (called St. Petersburg 1703–1914 and 1991–, Leningrad 1924–91)

Women get suffrage in Britain

1919

Hapsburg dynasty expelled from Austria

Weimar Republic begins in Germany

Eamon de Valera heads

Ireland's Sinn Fein; rebellion breaks out

Benito Mussolini founds Fascist Party in Italy

✠

*"I felt like a man
standing on a planet
that had been
suddenly wrenched
from its orbit
by a demonic hand
and that was
spinning wildly into
the unknown."*

— David Lloyd George, then Chancellor of the Exchequer, recalling Britain's entering the war

✠

Mohandas K. Gandhi begins passive resistance movement in India

Turks exterminate 1.5 million Armenians

Famine in Germany and central Europe

Canadian Population: 1900–90

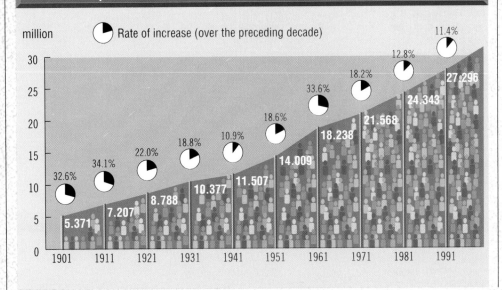

million

◐ Rate of increase (over the preceding decade)

Year	Population	Rate of increase
1901	5.371	32.6%
1911	7.207	34.1%
1921	8.788	22.0%
1931	10.377	18.8%
1941	11.507	10.9%
1951	14.009	18.6%
1961	18.238	33.6%
1971	21.568	18.2%
1981	24.343	12.8%
1991	27.296	11.4%

NORTH AMERICAN HISTORY & POLITICS

1920

U.S. Senate fails to ratify Treaty of Versailles, containing the commitment to League of Nations desired by President Wilson

Canada becomes founding member of the League of Nations

19th Amendment (woman suffrage) ratified in the United States

Royal Northwest Mounted Police amalgamated with Dominion Police to form new, federal police force, Royal Canadian Mounted Police

Red Scare in the United States; federal government arrests Communists, anarchists, labor agitators

British Columbia abandons Prohibition, adopts a form of government sale of liquor called "government control"

Anarchists Nicola Sacco and Bartolomeo Vanzetti indicted for murder

Warren G. Harding elected 29th president; Calvin Coolidge, vice president; their Republican ticket defeats Democrats James M. Cox and Franklin D. Roosevelt

U.S. population: some 106 million; Canada's population nears 9 million

1921

Roaring Twenties beget rapid social change

Sacco and Vanzetti found guilty, later executed

Following victory of United Farmers of Ontario, United Farmers of Alberta win election to form provincial government

After general election, Liberals can form only minority government as new party, Progressive, captures 65 seats; Mackenzie King becomes prime minister for first time

Montreal leads Canadian cities with population of 618,566; next

are Toronto (521,893), Winnipeg (179,087), and Vancouver (163,220)

Armistice Day (Nov. 11) declared national holiday in the United States; Tomb of the Unknown Soldier established at Arlington Cemetery.

Ku Klux Klan violence grows in the southern United States

Gen. "Billy" Mitchell demonstrates bombing capabilities of military aircraft

Four-Power Pacific Treaty: U.S., Britain, France, and Japan recognize spheres of influence

1922

Hurricane and forest fire kill 41 at Haileybury, Ontario

U.S.-British-Japanese treaty limits warships

Britain asks Canada to send troops to support British against Turks at Chanak; Canada refuses

Bonar Law, born at Rexford, New Brunswick, becomes British prime minister

1923

Warren Harding dies in office (Aug. 2); Calvin Coolidge becomes president

◆

"If you don't say anything, you won't be called on to repeat it."

— *President Calvin Coolidge*

◆

KKK membership in the United States estimated at 2 million; conclave in Indiana draws 200,000 members; attacks grow on blacks, Jews, Catholics, immigrants; KKK terrorism in Oklahoma brings about martial law

U.S. troops begin final withdrawal from Germany

Coolidge addresses U.S.

On June 13, 1927, Charles A. Lindbergh gets a ticker tape parade in New York City, 24 days after he took off on his solo transatlantic flight.

Congress; radio carries presidential message for first time

Chinese Immigration Act passed in Canada places severe limitations on Chinese immigration to Canada, effectively ending it

Canadian government takes over Grand Trunk Railway, merged with Canadian Northern and other railways to form Canadian National Railways; forms world's largest railway with 35,300 kilometres of track in Canada and 3,200 kilometres in U.S.; Sir Henry Thornton is first president

1924

Financier Charles Dawes puts forth plan to reduce German reparations and stabilize German currency; Dawes's plan accepted by Germany and the Allies

Calvin Coolidge elected 30th president; his vice president is Charles Dawes

J. Edgar Hoover named director of the Bureau of Investigation, later renamed Federal Bureau of Investigation

Pan-American Treaty signed; provides for arbitration to settle Western Hemisphere disputes

British merchant marine ensign (red flag with union jack in upper left) adopted as

Canadian flag with addition of Canada's coat of arms

Royal Canadian Air Force established (Canadian fliers in World War I had served with Britain's Royal Flying Corps)

1925

John Scopes "monkey trial" tests Tennessee law prohibiting the teaching of evolution; matches Clarence Darrow for defence vs. William Jennings Bryan for the prosecution; teacher Scopes is convicted, then acquitted on technicality

Canada's Conservatives, led by Arthur Meighen, form minority government

North American stock prices rise as speculators enter market

1926

Gold Rush at Red Bank, Ontario

Mackenzie King Liberals return to power in general election as Governor General's power to choose governments is effectively limited

Canada's first Old Age Pension legislation is passed

Vincent Massey appointed first Canadian ambassador to Washington

Mackenzie King's Liberal government resigns to avoid parliamentary questions about scandal in customs department

U.S. Marines sent to Nicaragua

1927

Charles Lindbergh makes first solo transatlantic nonstop flight; pilots his monoplane, *The Spirit of St. Louis*, from New York to Paris in 33 hours 29 minutes; "Lucky Lindy" becomes national hero

Judicial Committee of Britain's Privy Council rules that Labrador is part of Newfoundland

Ontario abandons prohibition in favor of government sale of liquor

Prince of Wales opens Peace Bridge joining Fort Erie, Ontario, to Buffalo, New York

1928

U.S. joins 64 countries in signing Kellogg-Briand Pact, outlawing war

Eileen Vollick of Ontario becomes first woman in Canada to receive pilot's licence

Herbert C. Hoover elected 31st president; Charles Curtis, vice president; their Republican ticket defeats Democrats Alfred E. Smith, first Catholic nominated for presidency, and Joseph T. Robinson

1929

"Black Thursday" (October 24) in North America; stock prices fall; market then steadies briefly before plummeting on October 29, signalling start of worldwide Great Depression

St. Valentine's Day Massacre in Chicago; six mobsters machine-gunned by rival gang

Canadian schooner *I'm Alone* sunk by U.S. coast guard in Gulf of Mexico while smuggling liquor

Tidal wave strikes Newfoundland, killing 27

EVERYDAY LIFE

1920

First transcontinental airmail route: New York to San Francisco

First commercial radio station:

KDKA in Pittsburgh; an experimental station, XWA, had been licenced in Montreal a year earlier

Canned horse meat for dog food introduced

Jantzen makes one-piece elasticized swimsuit

"The victor belongs to the spoils."

— *F. Scott Fitzgerald,* in The Beautiful and Damned *(1922)*

U.S.S.R. first country to legalize abortion

Band-Aid adhesive strips

1921

French fashion-setter Coco Chanel introduces Chanel No. 5

Polygraph (lie detector) test invented

Knee-length skirts turn heads

Eskimo Pie ice-cream bars

Betty Crocker character introduced

Movie actor Fatty Arbuckle sex-and-sadism scandal rocks Hollywood

First Miss America Pageant, Atlantic City, New Jersey

Cultured pearls perfected

First public lending library for recordings opens in Detroit

1922

British Columbia changes to driving on right side of road

First mechanized telephone switchboard, in New York City

Self-winding watch invented

Reader's Digest is founded by Lila and DeWitt Wallace in basement apartment in Greenwich Village section of New York City

Ship-to-shore radio service

A 21-tonne meteorite lands near Blackstone, Virginia; creates 122-metre-wide crater

Scripps-Howard becomes first U.S. newspaper chain

First transcontinental flight in less than 24 hours: Lt. James Doolittle flies from California to Florida in 23 hours 35 minutes

Prince Edward Island and Newfoundland extend the provincial franchise to women

First shopping mall with unified architecture and management appears in the U.S. — Country Club Plaza, Kansas City, Missouri

Emily Post's *Etiquette,* the first of her books on proper social behavior and good manners

1923

The treasures of Egyptian pharaoh Tutankhamen's tomb, discovered the year before, give rise to a King Tut craze

First antiknock gasoline

Sedans become more popular than open cars

Mah-jong becomes a fad

Milky Way candy bar

Dance marathons

Henry R. Luce and Briton Hadden start *Time* magazine

1924

First North American gay rights organization formed, in the United States

First around-the-world flight; U.S. Army pilots make the trip in 175 days

First disposable handkerchiefs, Celluwipes; later renamed Kleenex

First Popsicles

Flagpole sitting

First crossword puzzle books

Women's "knickers" are shortened, become "panties"

1925

The New Yorker magazine begins publication

First international radio broadcast: London to Maine

First electric phonograph

Flashbulb prototype introduced

Dry ice (solidified carbon dioxide) used for refrigeration

Electric coffee percolators

Spelling bees begin

The Charleston becomes a dance rage

Flapper fashions are in vogue: cloche hats, waistlessness, above-the-knee dresses

1926

Increase in air traffic results in U.S. Congress passing first law to regulate aviation, the Air Commerce Act

First public demonstration of TV

Book of the Month Club starts

Magician Harry Houdini dies

Miniature golf craze

1927

Wall-mounted can openers

First underwater color photographs, published in *National Geographic*

Couples dance the fox-trot

Commercial transatlantic telephone service begins, between New York and London

Al Capone's fortune estimated at $105 million

Holland Tunnel, first underwater vehicular tunnel, opens; creates auto link between New York and New Jersey under the Hudson River

1928

Adhesive tape

Rolleiflex, double-lens reflex camera, introduced

First transatlantic television transmission

1929

FM radio

Birdseye company markets frozen food

Foam rubber

Jimmy Doolittle makes first "blind" (by-instruments-only) plane flight

First air-conditioned rail passenger car

ARTS & LETTERS

1920

First Dada Fair, in Berlin; at dadaist exhibit in Cologne, visitors are allowed to smash paintings

Canadian Forum launched in Toronto to promote newer forms of literary expression

Canadian Group of Seven artists hold first exhibition; their style, with that of Thomson, would dominate Canadian painting into the 1950's

F. Scott Fitzgerald publishes his first novel, *This Side of Paradise*

American novelist Sinclair Lewis's *Main Street*

French writer Colette's novel *Chéri* explores an affair between a woman and a younger man

The Outline of History, an account of humankind's development, by Englishman H. G. Wells

English abstract painter Ben Nicholson's *Sunflowers*

Spanish painter Juan Gris's *Book and Newspaper*

French composer Maurice Ravel's ballet music *La Valse*

American novelist Edith Wharton's *The Age of Innocence*

American dramatist Eugene O'Neill's *The Emperor Jones*

1921

American novelist John Dos Passos's *Three Soldiers*

English writer D. H. Lawrence's novel *Women in Love*

English biographer and critic Lytton Strachey's *Queen Victoria*

Italian-born English writer Rafael Sabatini's historical novel *Scaramouche*

French painter Fernand Léger's *Three Women*

French painter Georges Braque's *Still Life With Guitar*

Two masterpieces by 18th-century English painters, Thomas Gainsborough's *Blue Boy* and Sir Joshua Reynold's *Portrait of Mrs. Siddons,* sold for total of 200,000 pounds

Italian tenor Enrico Caruso dies in Naples

Russian composer Sergei Prokofiev's opera *The Love for Three Oranges* debuts in Chicago

Russian-born American composer Igor Stravinsky's *Symphony for Wind Instruments*

Hungarian-born American composer Sigmund Romberg's operetta *Blossom Time,* based on the music of Franz Schubert

1922

American-born English poet T. S. Eliot's *The Waste Land*

American novelist Sinclair Lewis's *Babbitt*

Lionel Groulx novel *L'Appel de la Race* stresses incompatibility of French- and English-speaking peoples

American dramatist Eugene O'Neill produces *Anna Christie*

1923

American poet Robert Frost's collection *New Hampshire*

Ernest (later Sir Ernest) Macmillan of Toronto directs the first of his annual Bach's *St. Matthew's Passion*

Merill Denison, first important Canadian playwright of 20th century, produces *Marsh Hay*

Irish writer James Joyce's *Ulysses*

French writer Marcel Proust dies

English poet A. E. Housman's *Last Poems*

German expressionist Max Beckmann's woodcut *Charnel House*

Italian composer Ottorino Respighi's *Concerto Gregoriano*

German-born American composer Paul Hindemith's song cycle *Das Marienleben*

Russian Marc Chagall, living in France, paints *Love Idyll*

British painter Augustus John's portrait of English novelist and poet Thomas Hardy

French painter Maurice de Vlaminck's *Village in Northern France*

Finnish composer Jean Sibelius's *Symphony No. 6*

Austrian-born American composer Arnold Schoenberg's *Piano Suite,*

451

first work based solely on 12-tone system

1924

German writer Thomas Mann's novel *The Magic Mountain*

English novelist E. M. Forster's *A Passage to India*

Surrealism in art and poetry: Salvador Dali, Max Ernst, and Guillaume Apollinaire

Irish dramatist Sean O'Casey's *Juno and the Paycock*

English writer P. G. Wodehouse's comic character Jeeves, the quintessential English butler, achieves fame on both sides of the Atlantic

Spanish painter Joan Miro's *Catalan Landscape*

American composer Rudolf Friml's *Rose Marie*

German composer Richard Strauss's *Intermezzo*

Robert Frost wins the first of his four Pulitzer prizes for poetry (1924, 1931, 1937, 1943)

A.J.M. Smith, A. M. Klein, Leon Edel, F. R. Scott and others launch *McGill Daily Literary Supplement* for new poetry

"[Flapper] Jane isn't wearing much this summer: one dress, one step-in, two stockings, two shoes. No petticoat; no brassiere; of course, no corset."

— *Journalist Bruce Bliven*

1925

American novelist Theodore Dreiser's *An American Tragedy*

American writer F. Scott Fitzgerald's *The Great Gatsby*

U.S. poet Ezra Pound publishes *A Draft of XVI Cantos*

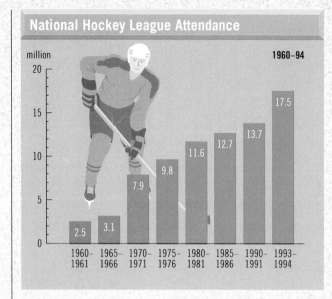

National Hockey League Attendance

1960–94

Year	million
1960–1961	2.5
1965–1966	3.1
1970–1971	7.9
1975–1976	9.8
1980–1981	11.6
1985–1986	12.7
1990–1991	13.7
1993–1994	17.5

Czech-born Franz Kafka's novel *The Trial,* written in German, published posthumously

Spanish painter and sculptor Pablo Picasso's *Three Dancers*

French painter Georges Rouault's *The Apprentice*

Russian composer Dmitri Shostakovich's *Symphony No. 1*

U.S. novelist Sinclair Lewis's *Arrowsmith*

1926

U.S. writer Ernest Hemingway's novel *The Sun Also Rises*

British archaeologist, soldier, and writer T. E. Lawrence's *The Seven Pillars of Wisdom*

English poet and dramatist A. A. Milne's children's book *Winnie-the-Pooh*

English historian G. M. Trevelyan's *History of England*

British sculptor Henry Moore's *Draped, Reclining Figure*

Norwegian painter Edvard Munch's *The Red House*

Italian composer Giacomo Puccini's unfinished opera *Turandot* debuts posthumously at La Scala in Milan, under Italian conductor Arturo Toscanini

Hungarian-born American

composer Sigmund Romberg's operetta *The Desert Song*

1927

U.S. novelist Willa Cather's *Death Comes for the Archbishop*

Sinclair Lewis's novel *Elmer Gantry*

English author Virginia Woolf's novel *To the Lighthouse*

Canadian writer Mazo de la Roche publishes first of 16 novels in *Jalna* series

Canadian National Railways' CNRV Players (Vancouver) begin first regular drama series for Canadian radio

U.S. artist Edward Hopper's *Manhattan Bridge*

U.S. dancer Isadora Duncan's autobiography *My Life;* she dies in accident

1928

Morley Callaghan's *Strange Fugitive* establishes the realistic urban novel in Canadian writing

Our Daily Bread by Frederick Philip Grove concerns prairie life

Chatelaine magazine is launched in Canada

U.S. painter Georgia O'Keeffe's *Nightwave*

English novelist and critic Aldous Huxley's *Point Counterpoint*

D. H. Lawrence's *Lady Chatterley's Lover*

English writer Evelyn Waugh's *Decline and Fall*

French painter Georges Braque's *Still Life With Jug*

English composer William Walton's *Viola Concerto*

U.S. dramatists Ben Hecht and Charles MacArthur's *The Front Page* opens on Broadway

1929

English author and critic Virginia Woolf's long essay *"A Room of One's Own,"* about obstacles facing a woman writer

U.S. novelist Thomas Wolfe's *Look Homeward, Angel*

German writer Erich Maria Remarque's pacifist novel of World War I, *All Quiet on the Western Front*

U.S. novelist William Faulkner writes *The Sound and the Fury*

Ernest Hemingway's *A Farewell to Arms*

U.S. dramatist Elmer Rice's *Street Scene*

Raymond Knister's *White Narcissus* is first realistic novel of rural Ontario

U.S. painter Lyonel Feininger's *Sailing Boats*

U.S. painter Grant Wood's *Woman With Plants*

Museum of Modern Art opens in New York City

ENTERTAINMENT & SPORTS

1920

Winnipeg Falcons win first world hockey championship at Antwerp Olympics

Bill Tilden becomes first American to win men's tennis singles title at Wimbledon

Boston Red Sox sell Babe Ruth to New York Yankees for $125,000

Super horse Man o' War retires after winning 20 of 21 races

Waterskiing becomes popular

American composer Jerome

Kern writes the music for the hit Broadway show *Sally*

Swashbuckling American actor Douglas Fairbanks in Hollywood film *The Mark of Zorro*

"Four be the things I am wiser to know: Idleness, sorrow, a friend, and a foe. Four be the things I'd been better without: Love, curiosity, freckles, and doubt."

— *Dorothy Parker, in Enough Rope (1926)*

American dancer and choreographer Martha Graham makes her professional debut as a lead dancer in the modern ballet *Xochitl* after studying at the Denishawn School of Dancing under Ruth St. Denis and Ted Shawn

Cleveland Indians batter Roy Chapman killed by spitball; pitch outlawed in major-league baseball the next year

American bandleader Paul Whiteman's "Whispering" and (flip side) "The Japanese Sandman" first record to sell a million copies

After 1919 Stanley Cup series cancelled due to influenza epidemic, Ottawa Senators win hockey championship in 1920

Joe Malone scores 7 goals in one hockey game, the N.H.L. record; in his professional career, he scored 338 goals in 271 games

1921

Graham McNamee makes the first broadcast of a baseball game, from the New York Giants stadium, the Polo Grounds

Rin Tin Tin in Hollywood debut

The Kid, with Charlie Chaplin as star, writer, and director

U.S. film director D. W. Griffith's *Dream Street*

Edmonton Eskimos are first western team to challenge for Grey Cup, but lose

Football teams are reduced to 12 players

Ottawa Senators win Stanley Cup for second consecutive year

1922

Irving Berlin's "April Showers"

Brother-sister song-and-dance team of Fred and Adele Astaire appear on Broadway in *For Goodness Sake*

Musician Louis Armstrong leaves New Orleans, joins King Oliver's band in Chicago

U.S. explorer and filmmaker Robert Flaherty's *Nanook of the North,* documentary on Inuit life

French director Maurice Tourneur's American film *Last*

of the Mohicans, based on American writer James Fenimore Cooper's 1826 novel

Comedian Will Rogers begins writing a weekly column for *The New York Times;* his homespun, wry humor will make him one of the most popular journalists in the United States

Toronto St. Pats win Stanley Cup

Canadian press critical of violence in lacrosse as game begins to fall in popularity, partly due to lack of player development system

First National Basketball Championships held; first Canadian Women's Basketball Championships held — winners are Edmonton Grads

1923

U.S. film director and producer Cecil B. DeMille's *The Ten Commandments*

King Oliver and Jelly Roll Morton make jazz recordings

U.S. actor Lon Chaney appears as Quasimodo in *The*

Hunchback of Notre Dame, continues playing monsters in *The Phantom of the Opera* (1925) and other movies

Popular tunes: "Tea for Two," "Yes, We Have No Bananas," "I Want to Be Happy"

Jack Dempsey, knocked out of the ring by Luis Firpo, climbs back in and retains his world heavyweight title

Ottawa Senators win Stanley Cup

N. Albert gives first radio broadcast of ice hockey, in Toronto

Foster Hewitt broadcasts his first hockey play-by-play

1924

U.S. composer George Gershwin's pioneering symphonic jazz composition *Rhapsody in Blue* premieres, played by Paul Whiteman's orchestra with Gershwin at piano

Fred and Adele Astaire dance in George Gershwin's Broadway musical *Lady Be Good*

St. Louis Cardinal Rogers Hornsby has batting average of .424, still highest in modern baseball era

Bandleader Guy Lombardo of London, Ontario, forms band called Royal Canadians

U.S. heartthrob Douglas Fairbanks stars in *The Thief of Bagdad*

Hollywood film comedian Buster Keaton's *The Navigator*

Brothers George and Ira Gershwin write songs "Lady Be Good," "Fascinating Rhythm," "The Man I Love"

Montreal Canadiens win Stanley Cup

Montreal Forum opens

Canadian Basketball Association formed; later changes name to Canadian Amateur Basketball Association

1925

Hollywood film director King Vidor's *The Big Parade*

Hit song: "Show Me the Way to Go Home"

Charlie Chaplin's *The Gold Rush*

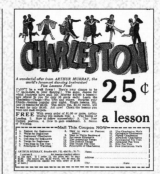

First air-conditioned theatres, in New York City

Grantland Rice starts picking All-American college football players in *Collier's Weekly* magazine

Jazz pianist Oscar Emmanuel Peterson born in Montreal

Victoria Cougars win Stanley Cup

1926

Gene Tunney takes the heavyweight boxing title from Jack Dempsey

Film idol Rudolph Valentino dies; in the crush of 100,000 mourners at his New York City funeral, many are injured and get first aid in the funeral home

John Barrymore stars in the film *Don Juan*

Jazz great Duke Ellington begins recording

Songs: "One Alone," "I Found a Million-Dollar Baby in the Five-and-Ten-Cent Store," "Bye, Bye, Blackbird"

Montreal Maroons win Stanley Cup

1927

H.O.D. Segrave drives automobile some 328 kmh (204 m.p.h.) at Daytona Beach, Florida; first time a motor vehicle exceeds 320 kmh (200 m.p.h.)

Babe Ruth hits 60 home runs

Harlem Globetrotters professional basketball team organized

Johnny Weissmuller, U.S. swimmer who later stars in

Tarzan movies, sets 100-yard-freestyle world record

U.S. performer Al Jolson stars in *The Jazz Singer,* first movie talkie

Swedish actress Greta Garbo's Hollywood film *Flesh and the Devil*

Broadway musical *Funny Face:* music and lyrics by George and Ira Gershwin, starring Fred and Adele Astaire

Jerome Kern and Oscar Hammerstein's innovative musical drama *Show Boat*

Richard Rodgers and Lorenz Hart's Broadway musical *A Connecticut Yankee*

Canadian Rugby Union accepts limited use of forward pass

Macdonald Brier trophy presented for Canadian curling championship

◆

"Honey, I just forgot to duck."

— Jack Dempsey to his wife after losing the heavyweight title to Gene Tunney, September 1926

Ottawa Senators win Stanley Cup

Electric timing device first used in ice hockey rinks

1928

Canadian Percy Williams wins gold in 100-meter and 200-meter sprints; Canadian women's relay team of Florence Bell, Myrtle Cook, Fanny Rosenfeld and Ethel Smith win women's first 4 x 100 meters; Ethel Catherwood, the Saskatoon Lily, wins Olympic gold for Canada in the high jump; University of Toronto Grads win ice hockey gold

Baseball's Ty Cobb retires with lifetime .367 batting average

Walt Disney's Mickey Mouse film shorts gain wide popularity

Eddie Cantor stars in Broadway musical *Whoopee*

When Rudolph Valentino died at age 31 in 1926 in New York City, fans backed up 11 blocks to view "The Sheik's" body at the undertaker's.

Hit songs: "Bill," "Makin' Whoopee," "You're the Cream in My Coffee"

New York Rangers win Stanley Cup

Grey Cup game first broadcast on radio

1929

Hollywood sees its future in talkies; slow fade-out of silent films begins

"Kissing your hand may make you feel very very good but a diamond and sapphire bracelet lasts forever."

— *Anita Loos, in* Gentlemen Prefer Blondes *(1925)*

U.S. comedians the Marx Brothers' first movie, *Cocoanuts,* is based on their 1925 Broadway show of the same name

Gypsy Rose Lee attracts notice with her burlesque act

American singer, actor, and composer Hoagy Carmichael's song "Star Dust"

First Academy Awards (Oscars): for acting to Janet Gaynor and Emil Jannings, for best picture to *Wings*

First of Hollywood's lavish musicals is produced: *The Broadway Melody*

Cole Porter's musical *Fifty Million Frenchmen* is performed on Broadway

Hit songs: "Tiptoe through the Tulips," "Singin' in the Rain"

Boston Bruins win Stanley Cup

Forward pass accepted in football; thrown for first time in Grey Cup game

Football game played between University of Western Ontario and McGill first in Canada to be broadcast in French

BUSINESS & ECONOMICS

1920

Post-war recession spreads from U.S. to Canada

1921

Canadian government stops wheat purchasing policy, leaving prairie farmers to find markets themselves

1922

U.S. puts high protectionist tariffs on goods from abroad

Shell Oil Company incorporates

Labor unrest across United States: strikes by coal miners, rail workers

1923

Post-war recovery spreads from U.S. to Canada

Cape Breton steelworkers try to form a union and meet violent police opposition

Bulldozer invented; prototype of future earthmoving machines

Oklahoma regulates oil fields to discourage excess production; regulations become model for other oil-producing states

Begun in 1926, the Chrysler Building in New York City was not finished until after the Crash.

Continuous hot-strip rolling for steel developed

1924

Ford's 10-millionth auto comes off the assembly line

First regular air-mail service in Canada between Haileybury, Ontario, and Rouyn, Quebec

Leica produces first 35mm camera, prototype for many others

U.S. leads industrialized countries in working days lost because of strikes

1925

First analog computer

Chrysler Corporation's Caterpillar tractor unit established

1926

Scottish inventor John Logie Baird transmits recognizable TV images

Continuous casting method for nonferrous metals developed

Aerial crop dusting with insecticides improves harvests

1927

Prototype color motion pictures

First teleprinters

Joseph-Armand Bombardier invents the prototype of the snowmobile

1928

General Mills founded

Boeing Corporation, North American Aviation established

First working robot

Record day of trading on the New York Stock Exchange: 6.6 million shares

U.S. short-term interest rates hit record high: 10 percent

De Havilland Aircraft established in Canada

1929

German dirigible *Graf Zeppelin* flies around world in 20 days 4 hours 14 minutes; future of lighter-than-air travel seems bright

Empire State Building construction begins

Toronto's Royal York Hotel is completed, largest in the Commonwealth

Brylcreem, a nongummy hair cream, marketed in Britain

October 29th stock market crash in the United States and Canada; signals beginning of Depression

SCIENCE & MEDICINE

1920

Structure of the Milky Way defined

Sigmund Freud publishes his ground-breaking *General Introduction to Psychoanalysis*

Existence of neutrons within atoms postulated

1921

Nobel Prize for Chemistry to Canadian Frederick Soddy for work on radioactivity

German psychiatrist Hermann Rorschach introduces inkblot test for investigating mental illness

Vitamin E discovered

Vitamin D found to prevent rickets

White corpuscles isolated from the blood

1922

Canadians Frederick Banting, Charles Best and J.J.R. McLeod discover insulin

Romanian-born German scientist Hermann Oberth, the "father of space travel," presents his dissertation on long-range liquid-propelled rockets; his "The Rocket Into Interplanetary Space" is rejected as foolishness

King Tut's tomb discovered

1923

Bacterium that causes scarlet fever isolated

Sigmund Freud publishes *The Ego and the Id*

Vladimir Zworykin develops the iconoscope, prototype of later TV tubes

Earth's magnetism studied

Relationship of a star's radiance to its mass calibrated

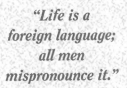

"Life is a foreign language; all men mispronounce it."

— *American journalist and literary critic Christopher Morley, in* Thunder on the Left, *1925*

1925

Dog teams deliver antidiphtheria serum to Nome, Alaska, during epidemic

Height of ionosphere measured

Quantum mechanics, dealing with the structure of the atom and the movement of sub-atomic particles, advances with the work of French physicist Louis de Broglie, German physicist Werner Heisenberg, and Austrian physicist Erwin Schrodinger

First successful experiments with hydroponics

1926

Vitamin B isolated

New method of capturing atmospheric nitrogen results in cheaper agricultural fertilizers

Americans Richard Byrd and Floyd Bennett fly to the

North Pole and back from Spitsbergen Island, northern Norway

X rays found to cause genetic mutations

Speed of light measured by German-born American physicist A. A. Michelson

1927

First tetanus shots for humans

1928

Coming of Age in Samoa, by anthropologist Margaret Mead, published

Improved tests for pregnancy, involving injecting women's urine into experimental animals, such as mice, rabbits, and rats

Geiger counter, for detecting radioactivity, invented

Iron lung invented

Vitamin C discovered

British bacteriologist Alexander Fleming discovers penicillin

U.S. physiologist and physician George Papanicolaou develops Pap smear to detect uterine cancer

1929

Relationship of high blood pressure to heart disease explored

Sex hormone estrone identified

Nerve impulses measured

WORLD POLITICAL EVENTS

1920

The Hague becomes the seat of the International Court of Justice

Civil war ends in Russia

Adolph Hitler reorganizes German Workers' Party under his leadership

Government of Ireland Act: Southern and Northern Ireland to have separate parliaments

Free City of Danzig, mandated by Treaty of Versailles, established under League of Nations

Poland, with France's help,

invades Communist Russia and occupies the Ukraine and western Belorussia

Treaty of Sèvres recognizes Armenian independence after years of war with Turkey, but Communist Russia then takes over eastern Armenia, and Russia and the Turks eventually divide up Armenia between them

Mohandas K. Gandhi leads campaign for Indian independence from Britain

Japan is given former German colonies in Pacific

British East Africa renamed Kenya; becomes crown colony

French heroine Joan of Arc canonized

Famine in China

Alvaro Obregon elected president of Mexico

1921

Germany assessed for some $32 billion in reparations for World War I; German mark plunges in value, inflation soars; Hitler organizes Nazi Party

Takashi Hara, Japanese premier, assassinated; Crown Prince Hirohito becomes prince regent

Sweden abolishes capital punishment

1922

Germany cedes Upper Silesia to Poland

Mussolini marches on Rome; forms Fascist government

Pope Pius XI elected by College of Cardinals

Britain gives Egypt independence

Irish Free State established

Turkey proclaimed a republic by its first president, Kemal Ataturk

British-controlled Indian government gives Gandhi 6-year prison sentence for civil disobedience

Communist Russia reorganizes itself into the Union of Soviet Socialist Republics

1923

Hitler leads Nazi storm troopers in Beer Hall Putsch (revolt), an attempt to overthrow the Bavarian state government in Munich; it fails; Hitler jailed for 9 months and there writes his famous *Mein Kampf (My Struggle)*

Russian-born Jewish scientist and statesman Chaim Weizmann becomes president of Zionist World Organization

Tokyo-Yokohama earthquake kills 120,000

1924

Lenin, U.S.S.R. premier, dies; Stalin emerges as Soviet strongman; Leon Trotsky's influence wanes

Stanley Baldwin becomes British prime minister; Winston Churchill is made Chancellor of the Exchequer

1925

Locarno Pact: in which Germany agrees not to maintain or build fortifications in the Rhineland

Hitler reorganizes Nazi Party; publishes first volume of *Mein Kampf*

Boundaries between Irish Free State and Northern Ireland defined

Pahlavi dynasty founded in Iran, ending the 131-year Kajar dynasty; new leader is former army officer Reza Khan, who becomes Reza Shah Pahlavi

Sun Yat-sen, head of China's Nationalist Party, dies

Britain passes Unemployment Insurance Act, aimed at giving jobless some relief

Japan grants general men's suffrage in a move toward greater democratization

1926

Hitler Youth organization established; Joseph Göbbels becomes Nazi Party leader in Berlin, signalling Hitler's expansion from his power base in Bavaria

Stalin exiles Trotsky from the Soviet Union

General strike cripples Britain

Republic of Lebanon founded

French-Spanish forces subdue the fiercely independent Berber tribes, known as the Riffs, in Morocco

Ibn Saud declared king of Saudi Arabia

Hirohito is emperor of Japan

Mexico nationalizes Catholic Church property

1927

"Black Friday" in Germany; economy in ruins

Rioting in Austria

Civil war in China

1928

President Obregon of Mexico assassinated

First five-year economic plan begins in U.S.S.R.; many more will follow

Chiang Kai-shek becomes president of China

1929

Hitler appoints Heinrich Himmler Reichsführer SS, head of the black-uniformed elite security forces called the Schutzstaffel

Arabs and Jews clash in Palestine

"The Italian proletariat needs a blood bath for its force to be renewed."

— *Benito Mussolini in 1920*

Lateran Treaty, signed in Rome by Cardinal Gasparri for Pius XI and by Mussolini for King Victor Emmanuel III, creates independent Vatican City and recognizes Roman Catholicism as Italy's only state religion

NORTH AMERICAN HISTORY & POLITICS

1930

Depression deepens as almost 5 million are unemployed in Canada and U.S.; 1,300 bank failures in U.S.

Smoot-Hawley Act raises tariffs, restricts trade; worldwide depression under way

"I am convinced we have seen the worst."

— *President Herbert Hoover, 1930*

Richard Bedford Bennett becomes prime minister, leading Conservatives to majority over Mackenzie King Liberals; Progressives are reduced to 12

U.S., Britain, and Japan continue limitation on naval armaments

British airship R-100 docks at St. Hubert near Montreal after crossing Atlantic in 78 hours 52 minutes

U.S. population reaches 123 million; Canada goes over 10 million

1931

Canada becomes independent nation with passage of Statute of Westminster in Britain

U.S. unemployment at 9 million, bank closings total 2,300

Hoover, acknowledging world economic crisis, suggests one-year moratorium on war reparations

"The Star-Spangled Banner" becomes the official U.S. national anthem

U.S. social worker Jane Addams and educator Nicholas Murray Butler share the Nobel Peace Prize

1932

Franklin Delano Roosevelt elected 32nd president; John Nance Garner, vice president; they defeat Republicans Herbert Hoover and Charles Curtis

FDR coins the term New Deal

Socialist party, the Cooperative Commonwealth Federation (CCF), founded at Calgary

Ottawa establishes a federally owned broadcasting system as a counter to U.S. dominance of broadcasting through commercial radio

U.S. and Canada agree to build the St. Lawrence Seaway

Lindbergh baby kidnapped; later found dead

1933

FDR temporarily shuts down all U.S. banks; gives first "fireside chats"

Both 20th Amendment, setting presidential inauguration on Jan. 20, and 21st Amendment, repealing Prohibition, ratified

U.S. drops gold standard

Cooperative Commonwealth Federation, meeting at Regina, issues Regina Manifesto calling for wide range of government ownership and control of business

Ranger, first U.S. aircraft carrier to be originally designed for that purpose, is launched

1934

FDR initiates Good Neighbor Policy in Latin America

1935

Mackenzie King Liberals win national power from Conservatives as CCF elects 7 and Social Credit 17

World's first Social Credit government elected in Alberta under Premier W. B. "Bible Bill" Aberhart

1936

FDR and Garner reelected with huge majority; Democrats dominate Congress

Memorial to Canadian troops unveiled at Vimy Ridge

Newspaper *Toronto Globe* buys Toronto *Mail and Empire* to form *Globe and Mail*

Bruno Hauptmann, convicted of Lindbergh baby kidnapping and murder, executed

1937

Mackenzie King supports British prime minister Chamberlain's policy of "appeasing" Nazi Germany

1938

Reflecting U.S.-German tensions, both nations recall their ambassadors

U.S. House of Representatives establishes Committee on Un-American Activities

U.S. Supreme Court upholds "equality" of education for blacks and black petitioner's right to be admitted to University of Missouri Law School

1939

Canada declares war on Germany

Commonwealth Air Training Plan established in Canada to provide training for Commonwealth pilots at bases across Canada

U.S. Supreme Court rules sit-down strikes illegal

FDR appoints William O. Douglas and Felix Frankfurter to the Supreme Court

EVERYDAY LIFE

1930

Apple sellers set up stands on city street corners

Hydraulic brakes, balloon tires, and self-starters now common on cars

Pundits proclaim that technological advances will transform Canada and U.S. into technocracies, or government by technical wizards

Coin-operated jukeboxes

Homemaking listed by U.S. government as an occupation

Al Capone arrested for income tax evasion

Betty Boop makes her debut in

Max Fleischer's cartoon "Dizzy Dishes"

1931

Nevada legalizes gambling; casinos in Reno and Las Vegas hope to attract respectable tourists

In New York City, Empire State Building, world's tallest, opens; George Washington Bridge completed; Rockefeller Center construction begins

Dick Tracy comic strip debuts

Alka-Seltzer

Episcopal Church decides formally to permit remarriage after divorce

"Better the occasional faults of a government that lives in a spirit of charity than the constant omissions of a government frozen in the ice of its own indifference."

— *President Franklin D. Roosevelt, accepting renomination in June 1936*

1932

Amelia Earhart becomes first woman to fly solo across the Atlantic

Canadian government sets up relief camps under military control for single young men

Bennett buggies, breadlines and soup kitchens multiply

RCA demonstrates TV picture

3 Musketeers candy bars

1933

René Lacoste's cotton tennis shirt, *Le Crocodile*

Depth of Depression in U.S. and Canada

Organized Labor's Ups and Downs

Canadian Union Membership As a percentage of civilian labor force

1925	1930	1940
7.6%	7.9%	7.9%

1951	1955	1960
19.7%	23.6%	23.5%

1970	1980	1992
27.2%	30.5%	29.7%

First solo around-the-world flight; Wiley Post does it in 7 days 18 hours

Ritz crackers, 7-Up, Spam introduced

Alcatraz, maximum-security prison on island in San Francisco Bay, opens

Violence erupts as coal miners strike in Pennsylvania; governor calls out the National Guard

Earthquakes in Los Angeles

1934

Nylon developed

Dionne quintuplets, first known to have lived past earliest infancy, born in Ontario, to Elzire and Oliva Dionne; Annette, Émilie (the first to die, of an epileptic seizure, at age 20), Yvonne, Marie, and Cécile all lived into adulthood

John Dillinger, Public Enemy No. 1, killed by FBI agents

Congress establishes death penalty for kidnapping across state lines

Diesel locomotives in passenger-train service

Drought worsens on the Prairies, wind storms cause black blizzards of topsoil

Union Pacific train goes from New York City to Los Angeles in 57 hours

1935

Prime Minister R. B. Bennett shocks Canadians with series of radio broadcasts outlining proposals known as "Bennett New Deal"

U.S. agriculture officials seek to control Great Plains "Dust Bowl" erosion; Soil Conservation Service set up

First acrylics are marketed: Lucite, Plexiglas

Pan Am World Airways begins transPacific service: San Francisco to Manila in the Philippines

Will Rogers dies in Alaska plane crash with his friend, aviator Wiley Post

Rumba latest dance craze

Alcoholics Anonymous organized

European cars offer front-wheel drive

By the 1930's drive-up, carryout establishments like this teapot-topped ice cream parlor in Hollywood were sprouting up everywhere in America.

First canned beer
Fluorescent lighting

1936

Dale Carnegie's self-help book, How to Win Friends and Influence People

Exodus from Dust Bowl region reaches peak

Life magazine begins publication

Two luxury ocean liners go into service: France's Normandie and Britain's Queen Mary

Waring blender, early electric food blender, promoted by popular bandleader Fred Waring

17-year locusts appear in the Northeast U.S.

Boulder (later renamed Hoover) Dam, on Colorado River between Arizona and Nevada, provides Southwestern U.S. with hydroelectric power; forms Lake Mead

First U.S. low-income government housing units, in Greenbelt, Maryland; Public Works Administration constructs two-story apartment building

1937

San Francisco's Golden Gate Bridge opens

German dirigible Hindenburg explodes in Lakehurst, New Jersey; disaster reported live on national radio

Howard Hughes sets new transcontinental flying record: 7 hours 28 minutes

Aviatrix Amelia Earhart disappears while flying over the Pacific in an attempt to circle the globe

Xerography invented

Polyurethane, polystyrene

First cellophane tape on sale

First grocery carts

1938

General Motors strike at Oshawa represents peak of labor unrest in Canada

Teflon

Some 20,000 TV sets in use in New York City area

British ocean liner Queen Elizabeth launched

Howard Hughes circumnavigates world in 3 days 9 hours 17 minutes

Hurricane devastates New England

Orson Welles's radio version of H. G. Wells's War of the Worlds terrifies listeners, who believe Martians have actually invaded the U.S.

Ballpoint pen patented

First commercial use of nylon: toothbrush bristles

1939

World's Fair opens in New York City

Goldfish swallowing

Roller-skate dancing the rage; women skaters popularize full skirts with matching bloomers

U.S. cigarette manufacturers, fearful war will cut European paper supplies, develop domestic substitute

ARTS & LETTERS

1930

U.S. writer Sinclair Lewis becomes first American to win Nobel Prize for literature

English actor and dramatist Noël Coward's comedy Private Lives

U.S. writer William Faulkner's As I Lay Dying

German expressionist painter Max Beckmann's Self Portrait With Saxophone

Hungarian composer Béla Bartók's vocal work Cantata Profana: The Nine Enchanted Stags

U.S. writer Dashiell Hammett's The Maltese Falcon, with hard-boiled detective character Sam Spade

Vancouver Symphony founded

U.S. painter Grant Wood's American Gothic

German-born U.S. composer and violist Paul Hindemith's Concerto for Viola and Chamber Orchestra

1931

U.S. novelist Pearl Buck's The Good Earth

French painter Pierre Bonnard's The Breakfast Room

Spanish surrealistic painter Salvador Dalí's The Persistence of Memory

French painter Henri Matisse's The Dance murals

Australian soprano Nellie Melba and Russian ballerina Anna Pavlova die

English composer William Walton's oratorio Belshazzar's Feast

U.S. writer William Faulkner's novel Sanctuary

German philosopher Oswald Spengler's Mankind and Technology

U.S. philosopher and educator John Dewey's Philosophy and Civilization

RCA-Victor releases first LP recording: Beethoven's Fifth Symphony

"There are three things which I shall never forget about America — the Rocky Mountains, the Statue of Liberty, and Amos 'n' Andy."

— George Bernard Shaw, 1933

1932

U.S. writer Ernest Hemingway's Death in the Afternoon, on bullfighting

U.S. popular historian and philosopher Will Durant starts writing his multivolume The Story of Civilization

U.S. writer William Faulkner's Light in August

Lithuanian-born American painter Ben Shahn's Sacco and Vanzetti

U.S. composer Samuel Barber's Overture to School for Scandal

English writer Aldous Huxley's novel Brave New World

Sir Thomas Beecham establishes London Philharmonic Orchestra

U.S. sculptor Alexander Calder shows his stabiles (stationary

works) and mobiles (moving sculptures)

English painter Ben Nicholson's *Black Swans*

U.S. architect Frank Lloyd Wright publishes both *An Autobiography* and *The Disappearing City;* founds the Taliesin Fellowship, a training program for architects and artists in Wisconsin and Arizona

U.S. poet Archibald MacLeish's *Conquistador*

1933

U.S. writer Gertrude Stein's *The Autobiography of Alice B. Toklas*

U.S. writer Erskine Caldwell's novel *God's Little Acre*

U.S. historical novelist Hervey Allen's *Anthony Adverse*

Exiled Russian Communist leader Leon Trotsky's three-volume *The History of the Russian Revolution*

French writer and art historian André Malraux's *La Condition Humaine* (*Man's Fate,* 1934 English translation)

English novelist James Hilton's *Lost Horizon;* a Hollywood film version made in 1937

●

"Mellon pulled the whistle /
Hoover rang the bell /
Wall Street gave the signal/
And the country went to hell."

— *Depression doggerel*

●

Tobacco Road, a play by Jack Kirkland based on Erskine Caldwell's 1932 novel, opens on Broadway

U.S. composer Aaron Copland's *The Short Symphony*

Robert Choquette, most important francophone

WHAT IT COST

Prices: 1930

Men's suits, $35; two-piece white linen suit, $12.50; overcoats, $35; striped cotton pyjamas, $1.79

Men's sport shoes, $3.95 to $4.85

Boy's 2-pant suit, $10

Women's shoes and pumps, $10 and $12.50; patent leather bag, $7.50

Women's suits, $65 to $150; silk frocks, $39.50; blouses, $7.95 to $15; jacket frock, $19.50 to $125

Bath towels, 25¢ to 49¢

Quebec maple syrup, 35¢ a bottle

Red Rose tea, 49¢ a lb

Heinz Tomato Ketchup, 19¢ a bottle; strained food for babies, 3 tins for 25¢; tomato soup, 12¢ a tin

Cigars, 5¢ each

Radios, $115; Marconi radio models, $72.95 to $156.50

General Electric refrigerator, $132

Electric washers, $59.89

9½-day Bermuda cruise from New York, $70

Hand electric vacuum cleaner, $18.50 to $19.75

Chevrolet Standard Roadster, $610; Sport Coupe, $745; Standard Sedan, $820

North Toronto apartments: 4 rooms, $28 per month

Toronto apartment hotel, $2.50

Canadian poet of his day, publishes *Poésies Nouvelles*

Russian-born U.S. choreographer George Balanchine and patron Lincoln Kirstein establish the School of American Ballet

1934

U.S. writer F. Scott Fitzgerald's *Tender Is the Night*

English composer Benjamin Britten's *Fantasy Quartet*

British author Robert Graves's historical novel *I, Claudius*

English novelist James Hilton's *Goodbye, Mr. Chips*

Russian composer, pianist, and conductor Sergei Rachmaninoff's *Rhapsody on a Theme of Paganini*

Canadian author Morley Callaghan publishes *Such is My Beloved,* to be followed in 1935 and 1937 by *They Shall Inherit the Earth* and *More Joy in Heaven*

Montreal Symphony is founded with Wilfrid Pelletier as first director; name changed to Orchestre Symphonique de Montreal in 1979

Orchestral version of German composer Paul Hindemith's

Mathis der Maler causes uproar in Berlin; Nazis ban it, denounce Hindemith as a "spiritual non-Aryan"

1935

Canadian Frederick Niven's *The Flying Years* appears as first of a trilogy whose theme is historical development of the prairies

U.S. writer Clarence Day's *Life With Father;* in 1939 a successful Broadway play

U.S.-born British poet and critic T. S. Eliot's verse drama *Murder in the Cathedral*

Swedish theologian Karl Barth's *Credo*

Russian composer Sergei Prokofiev's ballet music *Romeo and Juliet*

John Steinbeck's novel *Tortilla Flat*

English firm Penguin Books' paperbound books catch on, presage the paperback revolution in book publishing

U.S. dramatist Clifford Odets's *Waiting for Lefty*

1936

Margaret Mitchell's *Gone With the Wind*

U.S. dramatist Eugene O'Neill wins Nobel Prize for literature

Final book in writer John Dos Passos' *U.S.A.* trilogy published

Dutch painter Piet Mondrian's *Composition in Red and Blue*

U.S. composer Samuel Barber's *Symphony No. 1*

Welsh poet Dylan Thomas's *Twenty-Five Poems*

Canadian Authors' Association launches *Canadian Poetry Magazine,* a bulwark of artistic conservatism

Establishment of Canadian Broadcasting Corporation creates a major market for Canadian writers, composers, and performers

Eric Harris drama *Twenty-Five Cents* deals with depression years in Toronto

U.S. poet Robert Frost's collection *A Further Range*

1937

Compagnons de Saint-Laurent formed as theatrical group to stimulate Quebec interest in theatre

Ernest Hemingway's novel *To Have and Have Not*

Spanish painter and sculptor Pablo Picasso's *Guernica*

Spanish painter Joan Miro's *Still Life With Old Shoe*

French painter Georges Braque's *Woman With a Mandolin*

Russian composer Dmitri Shostakovich's *Symphony No. 5*

John Steinbeck's novel *Of Mice and Men*

1938

U.S. composer Aaron Copland's ballet score *Billy the Kid*

Spanish-born U.S. philosopher George Santayana's *The Realm of Truth*

U.S. writer Carl Van Doren's biography *Benjamin Franklin*

British novelist Graham Greene's *Brighton Rock*

French painter Raoul Dufy's *Regatta*

Italian-born U.S. composer Gian Carlo Menotti's first

---

performed opera, *Amelia Goes to the Ball*

German composer Richard Strauss's opera *Daphne*

U.S writer Marjorie Kinnan Rawlings's *The Yearling*

George S. Kaufman and Moss Hart's *The Man Who Came to Dinner* opens on Broadway

"Leaping lizards!
Who said
business is bad?"

— *Cartoon figure Little Orphan Annie*

●

U.S. writer Pearl S. Buck wins Nobel Prize

Trente Arpents by "Ringuet" Philipe Paneton appears, portraying tragic life of Quebec farmers; English translation, *Thirty Acres,* wins Governor General's Award in 1940

1939

John Steinbeck's *The Grapes of Wrath*

Welsh writer Richard Llewellyn's novel *How Green Was My Valley*

Waste Heritage, a documentary novel by Canadian Irene Baird, chronicles Depression in Vancouver and Victoria

Irish poet and dramatist W. B. Yeats dies

British sculptor Henry Moore's *Reclining Figure*

French painter Maurice Utrillo's *La Tour Saint Jacques*

U.S. primitive painter Anna Mary Robertson Moses ("Grandma Moses") wins acclaim

ENTERTAINMENT & SPORTS

1930

Hamilton, Ontario, is host to Empire (later Commonwealth) Games

Nelson (Nels "Old Poison" Stewart) wins N.H.L.'s Hart

Trophy as most valuable player; he reputedly spat tobacco juice in opposing goaltenders' eyes

Hell's Angels, produced by Howard Hughes, makes Jean Harlow a star

Radio detective program *The Shadow* premieres

Marx Brothers' film *Animal Crackers*

Hit songs: "I Got Rhythm," "Embraceable You," "Walkin' My Baby Back Home"

Germany's Max Schmeling wins world heavyweight boxing title

German-born U.S. actress Marlene Dietrich stars in the film *Blue Angel*

Bobby Jones becomes first golfer to achieve a Grand Slam by winning all four major titles: U.S. Amateur and Open, British Amateur and Open

Montreal Canadiens win Stanley Cup

1931

Film *The Viking* made in Newfoundland as docudrama of the seal fishery, filmed by American Varick Frissell

---

"When women go wrong, men go right after them."

— Mae West, in
She Done Him Wrong *(1933)*

Charlie Chaplin writes, directs, and stars in *City Lights*

James Cagney and Jean Harlow in *Public Enemy*

Radio program *Little Orphan Annie* premieres

Boris Karloff in the movie *Frankenstein* plays his specialty, a monster

The first movie in full technicolor: Walt Disney's cartoon *Flowers and Trees*

George S. Kaufman and Morris Ryskind's satirical Broadway show *Of Thee I Sing,* with songs by George Gershwin

---

Notre Dame football coach Knute Rockne dies in plane crash

Hit songs: "Goodnight, Sweetheart," "When the Moon Comes Over the Mountain"

Montreal Canadiens repeat as winners of Stanley Cup

1932

Associated Screen News of Montreal begins Canadian Cameo film series, virtually only Canadian filmmaker active as industry is overwhelmed by Hollywood

Dominion Drama Festival founded at Ottawa, national competition for theatre groups in both French and English

U.S. movie director and producer Cecil B. DeMille's *Sign of the Cross* continues his line of religious spectaculars

Greta Garbo, John and Lionel Barrymore, Joan Crawford, and Wallace Beery in Hollywood's *Grand Hotel*

Cole Porter's Broadway musical *The Gay Divorce* with Fred Astaire

Katharine Hepburn's first movie, *A Bill of Divorcement,* makes her a Hollywood star after successful Broadway roles

Jack Sharkey takes world heavyweight boxing title from Max Schmeling

Olympic Games in Los Angeles draw 1,400 athletes from 37 countries

Toronto Maple Leafs win Stanley Cup

1933

Miniature golf courses become a fad in Canada and U.S.

Greta Garbo in the movie *Queen Christina*

King Kong, with Fay Wray in the hands of the big special-effects gorilla

Radio program *The Lone Ranger* premieres

Ruby Keeler, Dick Powell, and Ginger Rogers in the movie musical *42nd Street,* with dances choreographed by Busby Berkeley

---

Italian boxer Primo Carnera wins world heavyweight title

Busby Berkeley's innovative Hollywood musical *Gold Diggers of 1933*

Mae West stars with Cary Grant in *She Done Him Wrong;* speaks the famous line "Come up and see me sometime"

Jimmy and Tommy Dorsey form one of the swing era's most popular orchestras

Radio City Music Hall opens in New York City; boasts world's largest movie screen: 21 metres wide by 12 metres high

Katharine Hepburn in the movie *Little Women*

Hit songs: "Easter Parade," "Stormy Weather"

First baseball All-Star game

New York Rangers win Stanley Cup

1934

Movie director Frank Capra's *It Happened One Night*, with Clark Gable and Claudette Colbert, wins five major Academy Awards

Shirley Temple sings "On the Good Ship Lollipop" in the film *Bright Eyes*

Fred Astaire and Ginger Rogers dance in the movie musical *The Gay Divorcée*

"I zigged when I should have zagged."

— Jack Roper after being knocked out by Joe Louis, 1939

William Powell and Myrna Loy in *The Thin Man,* first in their lighthearted detective series

Cole Porter's Broadway musical *Anything Goes* debuts with Ethel Merman

Benny Goodman organizes his swing band

Joe Louis wins his first professional fight

New York's Madison Square Garden pioneers college basketball doubleheaders

Chicago Black Hawks win Stanley Cup

1935

George Gershwin's Broadway musical drama *Porgy and Bess*

Greta Garbo stars in the film *Anna Karenina*

British film director Alfred Hitchcock's suspense thriller *The Thirty-Nine Steps,* based on novel by John Buchan (Baron Tweedsmuir), governor general of Canada 1935-40

U.S. film director John Ford's *The Informer* wins him his first Academy Award

Marx Brothers' *A Night at the Opera*

Fred Astaire and Ginger Rogers in Hollywood musical *Top Hat*

Jeanette MacDonald and Nelson Eddy in Hollywood version of Victor Herbert's 1910 operetta *Naughty Marietta*

Clark Gable, Charles Laughton in the film *Mutiny on the Bounty*

Hit songs: "Begin the Beguine," "I Got Plenty o' Nuthin'," "It Ain't Necessarily So"

Radio program *Fibber McGee and Molly* premieres

Two of the most popular film comedians of the 1930's, Mae West and W. C. Fields (born William Claude Dukenfield), finally get together in their first and only joint movie, My Little Chickadee, released in 1940.

Sex symbol Jean Harlow (born Harlean Carpentier) was just 26 when she died of uremic poisoning in 1937 after making more than 20 movies.

First night baseball game, in Cincinnati

Winnipeg Blue Bombers sign 9 players imported from U.S. and become first western team to win Grey Cup

Montreal Maroons win Stanley Cup

1936

U.S. black athlete Jesse Owens wins four gold medals at Olympic Games in Berlin

Charlie Chaplin's film *Modern Times*

Broadway musical *On Your Toes;* music and lyrics by Richard Rodgers and Lorenz Hart

Canadian Rugby Union establishes residency rule to limit importation of U.S. players

Canoeist Frank Amyot wins Canada's only gold at Berlin Olympics

Detroit Red Wings win Stanley Cup

1937

Walt Disney's first full-length animated film is produced, *Snow White and the Seven Dwarfs*

Ventriloquist Edgar Bergen with his dummy Charlie McCarthy quickly rises to become the country's top-rated radio program

Richard Rodgers and Lorenz Hart's Broadway musical *Babes in Arms*

Harold Rome's Broadway musical revue *Pins and Needles,* performed by ILGWU workers, starts run of more than 1,100 consecutive performances

French director and writer Jean Renoir's film *Grand Illusion*

Hit songs: "A Foggy Day in London Town," "I've Got My Love to Keep Me Warm," "Bei Mir Bist Du Schön"

Joe Louis beats James J. Braddock, becomes world heavyweight boxing champion

U.S. beats Britain in Davis Cup tennis

Detroit Red Wings repeat as Stanley Cup winners

1938

Swing innovator Glenn Miller forms his band

Benny Goodman and his orchestra play jazz concert at New York City's Carnegie Hall

Ella Fitzgerald writes (with bandleader Chick Webb) and sings "A-Tisket, A-Tasket," which becomes a hit

Spencer Tracy and Mickey Rooney star in *Boys' Town*

Errol Flynn and Olivia de Havilland in the movie *The Adventures of Robin Hood*

Henry Fonda and Bette Davis in the film drama *Jezebel*

●

"You're the Nile,
You're the
tower of Pisa,
You're the smile
On the
Mona Lisa. . . ."

— *Cole Porter,*
Anything Goes (1934)

●

Leslie Howard in the British film version of *Pygmalion,* George Bernard Shaw's 1913 play

British suspense-film master Alfred Hitchcock directs *The Lady Vanishes*

Spread of movie theatre chain, Odeon, challenges near-monopoly of Famous Players in Canada

U.S. athlete Don Budge becomes first to achieve tennis Grand Slam, winning all four major titles in one year: Australian, French, British, and U.S.

Chicago Black Hawks win Stanley Cup

1939

David O. Selznick's film version of Margaret Mitchell's novel *Gone With the Wind;* Clark Gable and Vivien Leigh star

Swedish actress Ingrid Bergman's first U.S. film, a remake of *Intermezzo*

Judy Garland stars in *The Wizard of Oz*

John Ford's film *Stagecoach,* starring John Wayne

Greta Garbo stars in the film *Ninotchka*

James Stewart in Frank Capra's film *Mr. Smith Goes to Washington*

Gary Cooper stars in the film *Beau Geste*

Hit songs: "Roll Out the Barrel," "The Last Time I Saw Paris," and in Germany, "Lili Marlene"

First televised major-league baseball game: W2XBS telecasts Cincinnati Reds vs. Brooklyn Dodgers at Ebbets Field in Brooklyn

Little League baseball founded

Baseball player Lou Gehrig sets record for consecutive games played: 2,130; retires suffering from fatal disease

Boston Bruins win Stanley Cup

BUSINESS & ECONOMICS

1930

Stock market doldrums continue

Great Atlantic and Pacific Tea Co. (A&P) becomes world's largest retailer

1931

Synthetic rubber

U.S. inventor Thomas A. Edison dies

1932

Canada sets up "relief camps" to get unemployed young men out of cities

British Commonwealth Conference leads to Ottawa Agreement for freer trade, but has little effect

Glass-Steagall Act authorizes easing credit, selling off gold reserves as Depression-fighting measures

1933

Worst year of Depression for Canada and the U.S.

●

"Bankers are
just like
anybody else,
except richer."

— *Ogden Nash,*
I'm a Stranger Here Myself (1938)

●

1934

Muzak Company supplies background music in the workplace

Radar demonstrated

1935

Canadian prime minister R. B Bennett promises wide range of economic reforms in his "Bennett New Deal" radio broadcasts

Royal Commission on price spreads reveals some Canadian companies were making largest profits in history during Depression

Bank of Canada created to set bank rate and formulate monetary policy; also replaces chartered banks as issuer of Canadian currency

1936

Douglas DC-3 goes into service; becomes aviation's workhorse

Sit-down strike at General Motors plant in Flint, Michigan, forces management to recognize United Automobile Workers

Oil discovered in Saudi Arabia

1937

Government-owned Trans-Canada Airlines begins operating passenger and mail service between Vancouver and Seattle

1939

War contracts bring revival of business in Canada and U.S.

First jet airplane flight, in Germany

Russian-born American aeronautical engineer Igor Sikorsky builds and flies a direct-lift helicopter

Two U.S. aircraft builders, Northrop Aircraft and McDonnell-Douglas, founded

SCIENCE & MEDICINE

1930

Planet Pluto discovered

Antityphus serum

Yellow-fever vaccine

Electromechanical analog computer

Bathysphere used to explore ocean floor

Sigmund Freud's *Civilization and Its Discontents* published

Adler Planetarium, first in the U.S., opens in Chicago

1931

Vitamin A isolated

Cyclotron invented

Heavy water, with a heavy isotope of hydrogen called deuterium, separated from ordinary water; later used in regulating nuclear chain reactions

First electron microscope

First clinical use of penicillin

Sex hormone androsterone isolated

1932

Auguste Piccard ascends to altitude of 28 kilometres in a balloon

First example of antimatter is found: positrons (positive electrons)

1933

Insulin shock therapy developed for psychoses

Sodium pentathol used for anesthesia

Swiss psychologist Carl Jung's book *Psychology and Religion* is published

Vitamin B$_2$ isolated

Cosmic rays thought to be evidence of massive explosion creating the universe 10 billion years before

1934

Sex hormone progesterone identified

Canadian Dr. Wilder Penfield founds Montreal Neurological Institute

1935

Lobotomy, surgical cutting of brain's frontal lobe, used to treat mental illness

U-235, isotope of uranium, discovered; later used as a nuclear fuel

Sulfa drugs for streptococcal infections

1936

Oxygen tents for severe breathing difficulties

Austrian psychologist Sigmund Freud publishes his *Autobiography*

Earth's inner core confirmed

1937

Insulin to control diabetes

First blood bank

National Cancer Institute founded in the U.S.

"The most beautiful thing we can experience is the mysterious. It is the source of all true art and science."

— Albert Einstein, What I Believe (1930)

Electroshock therapy first used as a treatment for schizophrenia

1938

Swiss chemists first manufacture LSD

Living coelacanth caught off the coast of Africa; primitive fish thought to have become extinct 60 million years ago

Uranium atom split

Vitamins E and B$_6$ discovered

1939

Rh factor identified in human blood

Vitamin K isolated

Nuclear fission: uranium bombarded by neutrons

WORLD POLITICAL EVENTS

1930

Nazi Party scores heavy gains in German elections

Mahatma Gandhi, continuing to preach nonviolence, leads 320-kilometre march demanding Indian independence from Britain

Revolutions in Argentina and Brazil

Emperor Haile Selassie begins reign in Ethiopia

Osachi Hamaguchi, Japanese prime minister, shot by right-wing assassin, later dies of wounds

1931

Oswald Mosley forms a fascist party in Britain

Japan occupies Manchuria

1932

Nazis win majority in German Reichstag elections; Adolph Hitler, Austrian-born, becomes German citizen

Famine in U.S.S.R.; second five-year plan begins

Japan accused of pricing goods under cost to gain market share

1933

Adolph Hitler appointed German chancellor; Reichstag fire in Berlin further bolsters Nazis; Hitler given dictatorial authority

Germany begins to rearm; Joseph Göbbels named minister of propaganda,

Hermann Göring, Prussian prime minister

Germany and Japan quit the League of Nations

Stalin purges opposition in U.S.S.R.; restores diplomatic relations with the U.S.

1934

Hitler takes title of Führer, meets Mussolini in Venice, solidifies power in "Night of the Long Knives"

Japan renounces naval arms treaties that limit size of its navy and ships

Mao Tse-tung starts "Long March," a retreat to Shanghai, which saves his Red Chinese Army

U.S.S.R. joins the League of Nations

1935

Germany absorbs the Saar; adopts compulsory military service

Italy invades Ethiopia

Stalin stages "show trials," effectively purging Soviet Union of Communist leaders he did not trust

1936

Civil war erupts in Spain

Britain's George V dies; Edward VIII succeeds him, despite rumors of his relationship with U.S. divorcée Wallis Simpson; Edward abdicates in order to marry Mrs. Simpson and is succeeded by his brother George VI

Germany occupies Rhineland; German elections give Hitler 99 percent of vote

Creation of the Axis: Hitler and Mussolini pledge a joint foreign policy for Germany and Italy; Germany signs anti-Communist agreement with Japan

1937

Neville Chamberlain becomes British prime minister; pursues appeasement of Hitler

Japan invades China; Chiang Kai-shek's Nationalists join

with Mao's Communists to meet the threat

1938

Germany annexes Austria

Winston Churchill leads anti-appeasement movement in Britain; France calls up reservists

Spanish Nationalists bomb Barcelona

"I have found it impossible to carry the heavy burden of responsibility and to discharge my duties as King as I would wish to do without the help and support of the woman I love."

— Edward, duke of Windsor, in December 1936 after his abdication

Chinese Nationalists retreat to Chungking, new capital

1939

German invasion of Poland triggers World War II; Britain and France declare war; FDR declares U.S. neutral

Germany annexes Danzig, absorbs Czechoslovakia; Hitler signs alliance with Italy, nonaggression pact with U.S.S.R.

Britain evacuates women and children from London for their safety; issues gas masks to Londoners

British Expeditionary Force arrives in France to fight German invasion

U.S.S.R. invades Finland and eastern Poland

Spanish Civil War ends as Franco captures Madrid

Pope Pius XII elected by College of Cardinals

NORTH AMERICAN HISTORY & POLITICS

1940

Canada introduces unemployment insurance

U.S. authorizes sale of surplus war matériel to Britain

U.S. trades overage destroyers to Britain in exchange for leases on military bases; some destroyers go to Canada for convoy duties

U.S. 1940 political campaign: limited television coverage of Democratic and Republican conventions and election returns

Hepburn has challenged federal policies; King wins with 178 Liberal seats to 39 Conservative

Canadian population over 11 million; U.S. population some 132 million; for both countries, increase over decade is lowest of century

1941

Mackenzie King and FDR sign Hyde Park Agreement for shared production of military equipment

U.S. makes lend-lease agreement with Britain; freezes Germany's assets in the U.S.

Canada sends Winnipeg Grenadiers and Royal Rifles of Canada to reinforce British garrison at Hong Kong

FDR and British prime minister Winston Churchill confer at sea off Newfoundland coast; sign Atlantic Charter, joint statement of peace aims

Japanese-U.S. relations reach impasse; at end of November U.S. War and Navy departments warn Pacific commanders of possibility of Japanese attacks

December 7: Japanese bomb Pearl Harbor; U.S. fleet suffers major losses, carriers escape

living on west coast, imprison them in internment camps for duration of war, and confiscate all property; in Canada, RCMP protests it has no evidence that Japanese-Canadians are a security threat

Gen. Douglas MacArthur named commander in chief of Allied forces in the Far East

RCMP patrol vessel *St. Roch* arrives in Halifax, having circled North America by Panama Canal and Northwest Passage

Alaska Highway opened

1943

First Gallup poll taken in Canada shows CCF the most popular national party

The Marsh Report (Report on Social Security for Canada) reveals high levels of poverty across the country, recommends wide range of social programs

Winston Churchill and FDR confer in Casablanca on conduct of war

FDR and Churchill meet Chiang Kai-shek in Cairo and Stalin in Tehran

Enrico Fermi and Robert Oppenheimer are among the scientists on the atom bomb (Manhattan Project) research and development team at Los Alamos, New Mexico, under the command of Brig.-Gen. Leslie R. Groves

Construction begins in Washington State of two reactors to produce plutonium for atom bombs

1944

U.S. Congress establishes rank of five-star General of the Army

Dumbarton Oaks, a mansion in the Georgetown section of Washington, D.C., hosts conference of Chinese, Soviet, British, and U.S. officials that lays plans for United Nations

General H.D.G. Crerar appointed commander of First Canadian Army in Europe

CCF wins provincial general election in Saskatchewan, forms first CCF government in Canada

Liberal government of Mackenzie King introduces Family Allowances Act

FDR, with running mate, Harry S. Truman, wins fourth term

1945

First Family Allowance cheques mailed to Canadian mothers

Mackenzie King federal Liberals win general election with 125 seats, staving off threat of CCF in the polls; CCF wins 28 seats and Conservatives 67

Japanese balloons carrying incendiary bombs found in British Columbia

Victory riot in Halifax paralyzes city

Igor Gouzenko defects from Soviet embassy in Ottawa, reveals Soviet spy network in Canada and U.S.

United Nations charter signed at ceremonies in San Francisco

Big Three Conference: FDR, Churchill, and Stalin confer at Yalta, a resort town on the Black Sea in the Crimean region of the Ukraine, Soviet Union

Franklin Roosevelt dies; Vice President Harry S. Truman succeeds him

Truman, Churchill (replaced midway by new British prime minister, Clement Attlee), and Stalin meet at Potsdam,

Echoing the verdigris on the mansard roofs of the Houses of Parliament in Ottawa is the National War Memorial, designed by Vernon French, and unveiled in 1939 by King George VI and Queen Elizabeth.

FDR reelected for third term; first and only U.S. president elected for more than two terms; vice president is Henry A. Wallace

Mackenzie King calls election on pretext that Ontario premier

U.S. Office of Scientific Research and Development set up; oversees work on atom bomb and other projects

Sir Frederick Banting, co-discoverer of insulin, killed in airplane crash

Britain and U.S. declare war on Japan, one day after Canada had done so; Axis powers declare war on U.S.

1942

Both Canada and U.S. round up citizens of Japanese ancestry

The zany antics of Portuguese-born "Brazilian bombshell" Carmen Miranda delighted audiences in wartime Hollywood musicals.

Germany, to discuss policies after the war

MAJOR MILITARY ACTIONS OF WORLD WAR II

1940

Germany invades France, Belgium, Holland, Luxembourg, Denmark, Norway

"Sighted sub, sank same."

— U.S. Navy pilot Donald F. Mason, reporting sinking of German submarine with depth charges, January 28, 1942

Some 380,000 British and other Allied troops are evacuated from Dunkirk

Germans enter Paris

Blitz of London — night bombing by planes of the Luftwaffe (German Air Force) — begins, continues into 1941

RAF (Royal Air Force of Britain) counters Blitz with night bombing of Germany

Battle of Britain: RAF sweeps the skies over England; prevents a German invasion

Germany steps up U-boat attacks

British 8th Army goes on offensive in North Africa

1941

German general Rommel assumes command of Axis forces in North Africa

Germans land in Crete

German super battleship *Bismarck* sunk in North Atlantic after repeated torpedoing and bombardment by British ships

Germany invades U.S.S.R., making huge gains; enters the Ukraine; reaches outskirts of Leningrad and Moscow

Soviets launch counter-offensive against German invaders

Pearl Harbor

British battleship *Prince of Wales* and battle cruiser *Repulse* sunk by Japanese torpedo planes near Singapore

Japanese invade Philippines

Hong Kong falls to Japanese on Christmas Day; surviving Canadian, British, and Indian troops enter prison camps

1942

Japan invades Dutch East Indies, Burma, Singapore; destroys combined British, U.S., Dutch fleet; Churchill records fall of Singapore as worst news he received during war

Canadian raid on Dieppe ends in disaster as 3,367 killed, wounded or captured in force of 5,000

Jimmy Doolittle bombs Tokyo

In Battle of the Coral Sea, U.S. naval and air forces halt Japanese drive to Port Moresby, New Guinea; both sides suffer severe losses

U.S. wins Battle of Midway, first major engagement fought entirely by carrier-based forces

Rommel battles with British field marshal Montgomery at El Alamein; U.S. troops land in North Africa; Rommel pushed back

British-led troops in Burma take the offensive against Japanese, with mixed results

Britain steps up bombing attacks on Germany

French fleet scuttled in Toulon

German U-boats begin Operation Drumbeat, a strategic assault on Canadian and U.S. coasts

1943

Island-hopping in the Pacific: U.S. takes Guadalcanal in the Solomons, lands in New Guinea, captures Tarawa in the Gilberts

German forces defeated with huge losses at Stalingrad

Dwight Eisenhower assumes command of Allied North

African forces; U.S. and British troops unify; Tunis and Bizerte fall; Germany's African army surrenders

Canadian, British and U.S. forces take Sicily, then invade Italian mainland; Canadians are involved in heavy fighting at Ortona

Patrol ship HMCS *Raccoon* torpedoed in St. Lawrence River; ferry S.S. *Caribou* torpedoed with loss of 137 lives

Nonstop Allied bombing of Germany begins; Canada forms No. 6 (RCAF) Bomber Group of RAF Bomber Command

1944

Canadians play leading role in breaking Hitler Line in Italy

Allied landings at Anzio, 53 kilometres south of Rome; Allies take Rome, June 4

D-Day in Normandy; Allies land greatest invasion force in history; Canadian force turns east to clear English Channel coast

British capture Florence, Italy

British airborne assault on Arnhem, Netherlands, fails

Germans now retreating on two fronts: from U.S. and Allied forces in the west, from Soviet forces in the east

Allies liberate Paris at end of August, cross German frontier

Battle of the Bulge, last major German offensive on the western front, begins in December, ends in January 1945 with German defeat

"Wars are not 'acts of God.' They are made by man. . . . What man has made, man can change."

— Frederick M. Vinson, future chief justice of the Supreme Court, at Arlington Cemetery, Memorial Day, 1945

Russians attack in the Ukraine, rout Germans at Minsk, enter Brest Litovsk

Soviet forces occupy Hungary and Yugoslavia

Commonwealth forces inflict heavy losses on Japanese in Burma

Canadian University Enrollment: 1901–90

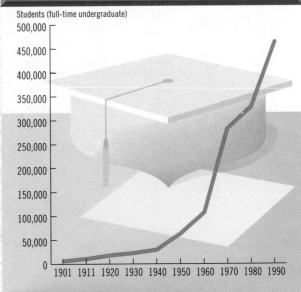

Students (full-time undergraduate)

U.S. naval and air forces win Battle of Leyte Gulf; American troops under Douglas MacArthur land in Philippines

1945

U.S. and British troops cross the Rhine River at Remagen, move deeper into Germany

Canadian troops clear area between Maas and Rhine rivers in Battle of the Rhineland

Canadian troops liberate Holland; link up with U.S. troops in northern Germany; war ends with Canadian army in Oldenburg, Germany

U.S. forces capture Manila, capital of the Philippines, occupied by the Japanese since 1942

Soviet forces take Warsaw, Krakow, Budapest; reach Oder River

Allies triumphant in Burma

U.S. drops atom bombs on two Japanese cities, Hiroshima and Nagasaki

"Comin' In on a Wing and a Prayer."

— Title of a song written by Harold Adamson in 1943

EVERYDAY LIFE

1940

War in Europe results in mass migration of artists, composers, writers, and scientists to North America

Women in Quebec given right to vote in provincial elections

Oglethorpe University in Georgia puts bottle of beer, encyclopedia, movie fan magazine, and hundreds of similar everyday artifacts in "Crypt of Civilization" time capsule, to be opened in the year 8113

Simplicity prevailed in wartime fashions, as in this 1942 dress worn by actress Brenda Marshall.

Electronic flash for camera marketed

Dances: the jitterbug, conga line, lindy hop, kangaroo jump

Life expectancy is 64; it was 49 in 1900

Nylon stockings in; silk stockings on the way out

Tacoma (Washington) Narrows Bridge collapses in high winds; design flaw blamed

Earl Tupper invents Tupperware

1941

Canada's Wartime Prices and Trade Board given expanded control over wages and prices, and introduces rationing

M&M candies introduced in U.S., but not in Canada due to wartime restrictions

Rationing of car tires starts

Canadian women enlisted for non-combat duties in Royal Canadian Women's Army Corps and Royal Canadian Air Force (Women's Division); thousands already serving as nursing sisters in all services

Dacron, a synthetic polyester textile fibre, introduced

Greta Garbo chooses seclusion

"Look at an infantryman's eyes, and you can tell how much war he has seen."

— Bill Mauldin, cartoon caption in Up Front (1944)

Mt. Rushmore National Monument completed: faces more than 15 metres high of Washington, Jefferson, Lincoln, and Teddy Roosevelt carved out of granite cliff in Black Hills of South Dakota

Grand Coulee Dam in Washington completed

Cheerios on sale

Slumber parties popular with teenage girls

Aerosol can invented

Lincoln Continental, American luxury car, makes debut

1942

Canada's Lorne Greene, "Voice of Doom" as CBC newscaster, leaves CBC Toronto for war service

Canada's National Selective Service lists all working age Canadians according to skills, assigns them to jobs

Canadian women are enlisted for non-combat roles in Royal Canadian Naval Women's Service

Employment shortage; more women go to work

1943

FDR orders 48-hour workweek in areas of labor shortage; time-and-a-half pay for hours over 40

Income tax withholding on wages introduced

Baggy, pleated, double-breasted zoot suits become antiestablishment symbols

Rationing continues to tighten on many kinds of food

Salvage drives collect scrap for the war effort

Polio epidemic kills hundreds, cripples thousands

Scrabble

1944

First eye bank

Ringling Brothers and Barnum & Bailey Circus fire kills 163 persons in Hartford, Connecticut

Black markets grow; estimated illegal annual gross is $1 billion

Inflation rampant

1945

B-25 bomber crashes into the Empire State Building at the 78th and 79th floors; 13 die

Silly Putty developed

Water fluoridation introduced

ARTS & LETTERS

1940

U.S. writer and journalist Ernest Hemingway's novel *For Whom the Bell Tolls*, about the Spanish Civil War

British novelist Graham Greene's *The Power and the Glory*

Hungarian-born British writer Arthur Koestler's novel *Darkness at Noon*

German expressionist painter and printmaker Max Beckmann's *Circus Caravan*

U.S. writer Carl Sandburg wins Pulitzer Prize for *Abraham Lincoln: The War Years*, his biography of Lincoln, which Sandburg began writing in1920

U.S. writer Carson McCullers's novel *The Heart Is a Lonely Hunter*

English writer Eric Ambler's *Journey Into Fear*, dealing with international espionage and crime

U.S. writers Elliott Nugent and James Thurber's Broadway comedy *The Male Animal*

European composers now in the U.S. include Béla Bartók (Hungarian), Paul Hindemith (German), Arnold Schoenberg (Austrian), Igor Stravinsky (Russian), Kurt Weill (German)

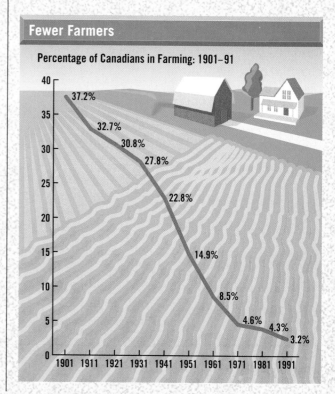

Fewer Farmers

Percentage of Canadians in Farming: 1901–91

37.2% (1901), 32.7% (1911), 30.8% (1921), 27.8% (1931), 22.8% (1941), 14.9% (1961), 8.5% (1971), 4.6% (1981), 4.3%, 3.2% (1991)

WHAT IT COST

Prices: 1940

Daily newspapers, 5¢
Men's suits and overcoats, $27.50; all-wool gabardine coats, $36.90
Men's shoes, $5 to $8.50; shirts, $2; men's fall hats, $1.39
Women's cocktail dresses, $23.95 to $34.95; print dresses, $10.95 to $13.95; women's fur felt hats, $2.49; women's shoes, $5 to $8.50
Women's suits, $19.95; coats, $39.50
Mink coats, $1,265 to $2,399; Persian lamb coats, $245 to $350
2-piece Lawson suite (sofa and chair), $169; 4-piece walnut bedroom suite, $199
Seagram's Canadian Whiskies, $2.55 to $3.40 a bottle; G & W Old Rye

Whisky, 25 oz, $2.55; Gilbey's Gin, 12 oz., $1.20
Jell-o puddings, 7¢ a pkt
Kraft Dinner, 18¢ a pkt
Coca-Cola and Pepsi Cola, 5¢ a bottle
Kleenex tissues, 200's, 25¢
Lifebuoy soap, 7¢
Max Factor lipstick, 65¢ and $1.15; powder, $1.15; rouge, 65¢
Turf cigarettes, 10¢ and 25¢
Automatic record player, $59.50
Vacation fares, Winnipeg to the Pacific Coast, 30 days: Coach, $40.60; Tourist, $47.95; Standard, $55.15
North Toronto, 5-roomed house, brick with stone front, air conditioned, $11,000
Spadina Hotel, Toronto, $2.50 and up per day

French painter Édouard Vuillard and Swiss painter Paul Klee die

1941

As For Me and My House, by Sinclair Ross, appears as best fictional account of life on Canadian prairies in Depression years

Canadian Hugh MacLennan's *Barometer Rising* recounts Halifax explosion

Scottish physician and novelist A. J. Cronin's *The Keys of the Kingdom*

U.S. author James Agee and photographer Walker Evans's text-and-picture book about Alabama sharecroppers, *Let Us Now Praise Famous Men*

National Gallery of Art opens in Washington, D.C.

German dramatist Bertolt Brecht's *Mother Courage and Her Children*, with music by Paul Dessau, performed in Zurich, Switzerland

English actor and dramatist Noël Coward's *Blithe Spirit*

U.S. painter Edward Hopper's *Nighthawks*

1942

Canadian Thomas Raddall's *His Majesty's Yankees* appears, bearing Raddall's mark of historical accuracy

Ralph Gustafson's *Anthology of Canadian Poetry* brings Canadian poets to an international audience

Canadian poets John Sutherland, Irving Layton, Louis Dudek and others begin publication of periodical *First Statement*, encourage interest in poetry

U.S. writer William Faulkner's novel *Go Down, Moses*

U.S. journalist William Shirer's *Berlin Diary: The Journal of a Foreign Correspondent*

English poet laureate John Masefield's tribute to the successful evacuation of Dunkirk, *The Nine Days of Wonder*

British sculptor Henry Moore's drawings of Londoners during the Blitz

English composer Benjamin Britten's *Violin Concerto*

Russian composer Dmitri Shostakovich's *Symphony No. 7*, composed during the Germans' siege of Leningrad

U.S. author Thornton Wilder's Broadway play *The Skin of Our Teeth*

U.S. journalist William L. White's bestseller *They Were Expendable*, about PT-boat action against the Japanese in the Pacific

U.S.-born English poet T. S. Eliot's *Four Quartets*

French novelist Albert Camus's *The Stranger*

English novelist C. S. Lewis's *The Screwtape Letters*

U.S. writer Philip Wylie's wide-ranging attack on American values and institutions, *Generation of Vipers*

U.S. composer Aaron Copland and choreographer Agnes de Mille team up on the ballet *Rodeo*

1943

U.S. writer William Saroyan's *The Human Comedy*

U.S. novelist Betty Smith's *A Tree Grows in Brooklyn*

"Books cannot be killed by fire. People die, but books never die. No man and no force can abolish memory. . . . In this war, we know, books are weapons."

— Franklin D. Roosevelt, to the American Booksellers Association, 1942

U.S. poet Robert Frost's collection *A Witness Tree*

French dramatist, novelist, and philosopher Jean-Paul

Sartre's *Being and Nothingness* sets out his basic views on existentialism

Dutch painter Piet Mondrian's *Broadway Boogie Woogie*

English sculptor Henry Moore's large stone piece, *Madonna and Child*

Russian-born French painter Marc Chagall's *The Juggler*

U.S. war correspondent Richard Tregaskis's fighter's-eye view of the first major U.S. landing in the Pacific, *Guadalcanal Diary;* becomes a Hollywood movie the same year

U.S. war correspondent Ernie Pyle's *Here Is Your War*, a collection of his frontline dispatches that were popular with soldiers and civilians alike

U.S. flying ace and writer Robert L. Scott, Jr.'s, *God Is My Co-Pilot*, a firsthand account of the China-Burma air war

U.S. abstract expressionist painter Jackson Pollock's first one-man exhibit, at a New York City gallery

U.S. regionalist painter Thomas Hart Benton's *July Hay*

U.S. poet Stephen Vincent Benét's unfinished verse epic *Western Star*, published posthumously

1944

English novelist W. Somerset Maugham's *The Razor's Edge*

U.S. novelist John Hersey's *A Bell for Adano*

Canadian author Roger Lemelin, *Au pied de la pente douce* (appeared in English in 1948 as *The Town Below*); satire on life in working-class urban district; presages popular TV series *La Famille Plouffe*

Russian composer Sergei Prokofiev's vocal work *War and Peace*

British novelist Joyce Cary's *The Horse's Mouth*

Canadian novelist Hugh MacLennan's *Two Solitudes;* becomes influential for its analysis of French-English relations

Danish author Isak (Karen Christence) Dinesen's *Winter Tales*

U.S. author and social critic Lewis Mumford's *The Condition of Man*

1945

U.S. dramatist Tennessee Williams's *The Glass Menagerie* opens on Broadway

English author George Orwell's novel *Animal Farm*

Austrian-born Israeli philosopher Martin Buber's *For the Sake of Heaven*

U.S.-born British sculptor Jacob Epstein's *Lucifer*

Broadway stars ran the Stage Door Canteen for GI's, and in 1943 this movie told the story.

Russian-born U.S. abstract painter Max Weber's *Brass-band*

German composer Richard Strauss's instrumental work *Metamorphoses*

Russian composer Sergei Prokofiev's ballet score *Cinderella*

English writer Evelyn Waugh's novel *Brideshead Revisited* is published

U.S. novelist Sinclair Lewis's *Cass Timberlane*

ENTERTAINMENT & SPORTS

1940

Charlie Chaplin plays both the Tramp and a Hitler figure in Chaplin's first talking picture, *The Great Dictator*

Welsh playwright Emlyn Williams's *The Corn Is Green* opens on Broadway

U.S. director John Ford's film *The Grapes of Wrath*, starring Henry Fonda

Walt Disney's animated film *Fantasia* uses a sound track by the Philadelphia Orchestra, conducted by Leopold Stokowski

Katharine Hepburn, Cary Grant, and James Stewart star in the movie *The Philadelphia Story*

Bing Crosby, Bob Hope, and Dorothy Lamour make the first of seven "Road" films, *Road to Singapore*

British film director Alfred Hitchcock produces *Rebecca*

Gaslight, Hollywood remake of a British film, stars Swedish-born Ingrid Bergman and French actor Charles Boyer

Jazz musician Duke Ellington's reputation as a serious composer grows

Richard Rodgers and Lorenz Hart's Broadway musical *Pal Joey*

Hit songs: "The Last Time I Saw Paris," "Oh, Johnny," "When You Wish Upon a Star," "Blueberry Hill"

Popular radio shows: *The Shadow, Fibber McGee and Molly, The Jack Benny Show, Gangbusters*

U.S. tennis men's singles title won by W. Donald McNeill; women's singles title, by Alice Marble

World's first ice hockey telecast, Montreal Canadiens vs. New York Rangers, at Madison Square Gardens; New York Rangers win Stanley Cup

1941

Popular singer and songwriter Paul Anka born in Ottawa

Orson Welles in the title role of the movie masterpiece *Citizen Kane*, which he also directed and produced

U.S. film director John Ford makes *How Green Was My Valley*

Humphrey Bogart plays hard-boiled private eye Sam Spade in Hollywood's *The Maltese Falcon*, directed by John Huston

Walt Disney's *Dumbo*

Hit songs: "Deep in the Heart of Texas," "Chattanooga Choo Choo," "White Cliffs of Dover," "Boogie Woogie Bugle Boy"

Long-running radio show *Duffy's Tavern* premieres

First baseball helmets, to protect against pitched balls, tested by Brooklyn Dodgers

Lou (Iron Horse) Gehrig dies; New York Yankee played in 2,130 consecutive games, 1925–39

"There are no atheists in the foxholes."

— Sermon by Father William T. Cummings, serving as a chaplain on Bataan, the Philippines, 1942

New York Yankees Joe DiMaggio sets long-standing record of hitting safely in 56 consecutive games

Kenny Lindsay of Vancouver wins world professional bantamweight title

Boston Bruins win Stanley Cup

1942

Walt Disney's *Bambi*

Humphrey Bogart and Ingrid Bergman in *Casablanca*

Bing Crosby and Fred Astaire in Hollywood musical *Holiday Inn*

Hit songs: "White Christmas," "Praise the Lord and Pass the Ammunition," "That Old Black Magic," "I Left My Heart at the Stage Door Canteen," "Paper Doll"

Joseph-Henri-Maurice ("The Rocket") Richard plays first season as major-leaguer with Montreal Canadiens, scores 32 goals in 50 games

Toronto Maple Leafs win Stanley Cup

1943

Richard Rodgers and Oscar Hammerstein's music and lyrics for Broadway musical *Oklahoma!*, their first collaboration, with choreography by Agnes de Mille

Alfred Hitchcock's *Shadow of a Doubt*

Broadway musical *One Touch of Venus*, with music by Kurt Weill and lyrics by Ogden Nash, stars Mary Martin

Hit songs: "Oh, What a Beautiful Morning," "I'll Be Seeing You (in All the Old Familiar Places)," "Mairzy Doats"

Detroit Red Wings win Stanley Cup

1944

Lawrence Olivier is director and star of British film version of Shakespeare's *Henry V*

Alfred Hitchcock's *Lifeboat*

Bing Crosby and Barry Fitzgerald in *Going My Way*

Otto Preminger directs Gene Tierney and Dana Andrews in suspenseful Hollywood mystery *Laura*

Hit songs: "Don't Fence Me In," "Rum and Coca-Cola," "Accentuate the Positive"

Montreal Canadiens win Stanley Cup

1945

Five-year-old Tommy Ambrose begins singing career at Toronto Youth for Christ Rally; later stars on CBC television in 1960's and 70's

John Wayne stars in film version of William L. White's 1942 book *They Were Expendable*

Ray Milland and Jane Wyman star in *The Lost Weekend*, based on Charles Jackson's novel published the year before

U.S. musicians Dizzy Gillespie, Charlie Parker, and Thelonious Monk establish bebop as new direction for jazz

Richard Rodgers and Oscar Hammerstein produce *Carousel*

Open City — an Italian semidocumentary directed by Roberto Rossellini, script

Pvt. Joe Louis says_

"We're going to do our part ...and we'll win because we're on God's side"

Heavyweight champ from 1937 to 1949, Louis donated his money, time, and name to the war effort.

by Sergei Amidei and Federico Fellini, and featuring Anna Magnani — films suffering in wake of war as Germans retreat

Popular radio shows: *The Green Hornet, Superman, The Red Skelton Show, Inner Sanctum, Allen's Alley*

Calgary football team changes names from Bronks to Stampeders

National Hockey League gets monopoly control of future hockey careers of all players 15 and over

Maurice Richard scores 50 goals in 50 games for Montreal Canadiens

Toronto Maple Leafs win Stanley Cup

BUSINESS & ECONOMICS

1940

Canada expands civil service to centralize planning of war economy

Canadian federal government imposes excess profits tax to ease inflationary pressures

1941

U.S. embargoes oil shipments to Japan

Hasselblad develops first single-lens reflex camera with interchangeable lenses

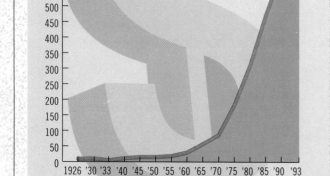

Gross Domestic Product: 1926–93

At market prices, in millions of dollars

| $750 |
| 700 |
| 650 |
| 600 |
| 550 |
| 500 |
| 450 |
| 400 |
| 350 |
| 300 |
| 250 |
| 200 |
| 150 |
| 100 |
| 50 |
| 0 |

1926 '30 '33 '40 '45 '50 '55 '60 '65 '70 '75 '80 '85 '90 '93

Union Pacific puts world's largest steam locomotive in service: the 6,000-horsepower Big Boy

Quality Inns, a motel chain, founded

1942

Canadian Pacific Airlines formed

1943

First Liberty cargo ships launched in U.S.; Canada has already built many Park type, a similar class

Striking miners cut off coal production: U.S. takes over the mines

World's longest oil pipeline opens; the "Big Inch" stretches from Texas to Pennsylvania

1944

International Monetary Fund established

1945

World Bank founded

Throughout war, Canadian industry has produced 15,000 aircraft

SCIENCE & MEDICINE

1940

Penicillin developed as antibiotic

Cyclotron for atomic research goes into operation at the University of California

Freeze-drying of food

First vaccine against leprosy

1941

Element plutonium discovered by a team of U.S. scientists led by Glenn Seaborg; it will be used in atomic reactors and weapons

Sulfadiazine becomes most widely used sulfa drug, effective against many types of infections

1942

First U.S. jet plane, Bell XP-59, flown

Italian-born U.S. physicist Enrico Fermi achieves the first nuclear chain reaction, in an

atomic pile at the University of Chicago

German scientists develop V-2 rocket

First electronic digital calculator

DDT, considered a miracle pesticide, is marketed

Aqua-Lung designed

Dexedrine, central nervous system stimulant, produced

1943

ACTH, a naturally occurring hormone produced by the pituitary gland, isolated

Streptomycin, an antibiotic that fights bacterial infection, developed

Army doctors prevent venereal disease with sulfathiazole

Silicones

1944

Quinine, important in fighting malaria and previously obtainable only from the bark of cinchona trees, is synthesized

DNA, building block of heredity in living things, isolated

First atom bomb, equivalent to 20,000 tonnes of TNT, tested in desert at Alamogordo, New Mexico; its explosive power comes from the element plutonium

Scarlet fever successfully treated with penicillin

Science: The Endless Frontier

— Title of a book by Vannevar Bush, chairman of the U.S. Office of Scientific Research and Development, 1945

1945

Rocket-testing range established at White Sands, New Mexico

Dr. Benjamin Spock's groundbreaking book *The Common Sense Book of Baby and Child Care* is published

WORLD POLITICAL EVENTS

1940

Italy declares war on Britain and France

Winston Churchill becomes British prime minister; gives his famous "blood, toil, tears, and sweat" speech

Slacks fit women's wartime can-do spirit; and Broadway's Natalie Schafer showed them off in style.

France's premier, Marshal Henri Philippe Pétain, signs armistice with Germany, overruling many of his countrymen; Pétain then heads collaborationist Vichy government

Britain allies herself with Polish government-in-exile and with Free French under Charles de Gaulle

Rationing begins in Britain

Japan joins with Germany and Italy in a military and economic pact

Exiled Soviet leader Leon

Trotsky assassinated by Stalin's agents in Mexico

1941

Rudolf Hess, a trusted lieutenant of Hitler's, flies to Scotland, apparently intending to negotiate peace; he is jailed by British, later sentenced to life imprisonment for war crimes

1942

Gestapo head Reinhard Heydrich assassinated by British-trained Czech partisans; in reprisal, Nazis kill thousands

Nazis begin mass murder of Jews in gas chambers

1943

Italy surrenders to Allies, later declares war on Germany

1944

German army officers fail in attempt to assassinate Hitler

Germany's "desert fox," Field Marshal Erwin Rommel, commits suicide

Civil war in Greece, after Germans withdraw, between Communists and royalists

1945

V-2 rocket attacks on Britain cease

German army in Italy surrenders

Concentration camps liberated

Hitler commits suicide; Mussolini murdered by Italian partisans

Germany capitulates; V-E Day: May 8

Japan gives up (August 14); surrender signed on U.S. battleship *Missouri* in Tokyo Bay (September 2, V-J Day)

Douglas MacArthur heads Allied occupation of Japan; his administration lasts until 1951

Vietnam, led by Ho Chi Minh, unilaterally declares independence from France

Germany cut into four zones of military occupation, with Great Britain, France, the Soviet Union, and the United States each controlling a

sector; Berlin similarly divided into four zones

Churchill overwhelmingly rejected by British voters; Clement Attlee succeeds him as prime minister

Vidkun Quisling, Norwegian wartime leader who collaborated with the Nazis, executed for high treason

World War II dead: some 50 million, including 10 million victims of Nazi concentration camps

Nationalists and Communists fight to control China

"We shall fight on the beaches . . . we shall fight in the fields and in the streets . . . we shall never surrender."

— British Prime Minister Winston Churchill, after the evacuation from Dunkirk, June 4, 1940

Arab League, a loose alliance of Arab nations, founded to advance Arab unity; its original members are Egypt, Iraq, Lebanon, Saudi Arabia, Syria, Transjordan, and Yemen

Nuremberg trials of Nazi war criminals begin

Marshal Tito heads Communist regime in Yugoslavia

Charles de Gaulle, Free French leader, elected president of liberated France's provisional government

Europe impoverished; black markets flourish

War in Indochina looms as French seek to reassert control of their former colonial holdings in Southeast Asia (Vietnam, Laos, and Cambodia)

NORTH AMERICAN HISTORY & POLITICS

1946

U.N. General Assembly holds first meeting in London; Norway's Trygve Lie elected secretary-general; John D. Rockefeller, Jr., gives $8.5 million for U.N. centre in New York City

Atomic Energy Commission of Canada established

Fred Rose, Labour Progressive Party member of parliament for Montreal-Cartier, charged with communicating secrets to the U.S.S.R.; it was the first of the cold war spy trials

U.S. wartime spy agency OSS (Office of Strategic Services) becomes CIA (Central Intelligence Agency)

U.S. conducts nuclear weapons tests in the Pacific

1947

U.S. Congress approves aid to Greece and Turkey; policy to resist Communist aggression becomes the Truman Doctrine

"Our policy is directed not against any country or doctrine but against hunger, poverty, desperation, and chaos."

— *George C. Marshall, address at Harvard University on the European Recovery Program, June 5, 1947*

Gen. George Marshall named U.S. secretary of state; calls for European Recovery Program

Canadians become Canadian citizens rather than British subjects

Canadian Supreme Court replaces British Privy Council as court of final appeal for Canadian trials

House Un-American Activities Committee (HUAC) charges "Hollywood Ten" with contempt; they are sentenced to jail terms

Canada elected to United Nations Security Council

Philippines gives U.S. 99-year leases on military bases

John F. Kennedy married socialite Jacqueline Bouvier in 1953 in as glamorous a ceremony as patrician Newport, Rhode Island, had ever seen.

1948

Alger Hiss indicted for perjury after denying he passed secret State Department documents through Whittaker Chambers to the Soviets

Congress approves European Recovery Program, known as Marshall Plan: $17 billion to Europe

William Lyon Mackenzie King steps down as prime minister after longest service in that position in history of British Empire and Commonwealth; succeeded by Louis St. Laurent

Democrat incumbent Harry S. Truman becomes 33rd president; running mate is Alben W. Barkley

1949

NATO (North Atlantic Treaty Organization) formed by U.S., Canada, and 10 Western European countries

U.S. withdraws troops from Korea

Quebec Airways DC-3 explodes with 23 killed over St.-Joachim, Quebec, from bomb stowed by J. Albert Guay; Guay and two accomplices later hanged

Newfoundland joins Canada as 9th province; in first provincial election, Joseph Smallwood is elected as premier

Japanese-Canadians granted full civil rights

Louis St. Laurent takes federal Liberals to election victory with 190 seats to 41 for Conservatives

1950

Two Puerto Rican nationalists make unsuccessful attempt to assassinate Truman

North Korean troops invade South Korea; U.N. sends forces to repel aggression under Gen. Douglas MacArthur; Chinese troops join conflict

First Canadian troops for U.N. service in Korea arrive at Pusan; Canada also sends destroyers for naval support

Canada supports Colombo Plan, providing economic assistance for needy Commonwealth countries

National railway strike paralyzes Canada

Red River floods, causing $24 million damage to Winnipeg; fire destroys much of Rimouski, Quebec

Truman orders development of the hydrogen bomb

Alger Hiss convicted of perjury

Senator Joseph McCarthy warns of Communists in the State Department; begins his committee hearings

U.S. diplomat Ralph Bunche wins the Nobel Peace Prize for negotiating an end to the Arab-Israeli war; he is the first black to win the award

Canadian population, pushed by immigration, moves close to 14 million; U.S. population is 151 million as California becomes second most populous state; New York City called world's most densely packed area, with some 230,000 persons per square kilometre

1951

Canada makes NATO commitment of troops and aircraft to be based in Europe

First election held in Northwest Territories

Japanese peace treaty formally ends World War II

Fighting continues in Korea; General MacArthur relieved of command

22nd Amendment goes into effect, limiting a president to two terms in office

Korean War cease-fire talks commence

1952

W. A.C. Bennett leads Social Credit party to victory in British Columbia

Lester B. Pearson of Canada elected president of U.N. General Assembly

Vincent Massey is named governor general, the first Canadian-born to hold that post

Puerto Rico becomes a U.S. commonwealth

Republican vice presidential nominee, Richard M. Nixon, makes his "Checkers" speech

U.S. explodes first hydrogen bomb on atoll in the Marshall Islands

Japan agrees to U.S. military bases on its territory

Dwight David Eisenhower elected 34th president with running mate, Richard Milhous Nixon; the first Republican ticket to win since 1928

1953

Louis St. Laurent Liberals win federal election with 171 seats to 94 for all other parties

U.N. headquarters building in New York receives gift of main doors from Canada

"We must not confuse dissent with disloyalty."

— *Edward R. Murrow, on his See It Now broadcast about Senator Joseph McCarthy, March 7, 1954*

Julius and Ethel Rosenberg, found guilty of atomic espionage two years before, executed at Sing Sing prison in Ossining, New York

George Marshall wins Nobel Peace Prize for his European Recovery Program

Korean War ends; armistice signed at Panmunjom

Eisenhower orders the dismissal of any federal employee who takes the Fifth Amendment during congressional hearings

U.S. Refugee Relief Act increases immigration quotas for refugees from Communist countries

1954

Senator McCarthy, in televised hearings, seeks to prove Communist infiltration of the U.S. military

Canada and the U.S. agree to build St. Lawrence Seaway

Hurricane Hazel strikes Toronto area, dumping over 100 mm of rain, causing $24 million damage, and killing 82

U.S. and Canada agree to build DEW radar line: early-warning system against aircraft and missile attacks

Supreme Court, in *Brown* v. *Board of Education of Topeka*, calls for an end to "separate but equal" public schools

Nautilus, first atomic-powered submarine, launched

U.S. backs coup to overthrow the government in Guatemala

Eisenhower signs legislation to permit the sharing of atomic knowledge and fuel with friendly nations

1955

Ngo Dinh Diem, premier of South Vietnam, rejects unification elections, claiming North Vietnam would not conduct fair elections; U.S. supports him and sends military advisers to train South Vietnamese army

U.S. president Eisenhower suffers heart attack; stock market suffers $14-billion paper loss

Senator Joseph McCarthy (above) squared off against special army counsel Joseph N. Welch In the Army-McCarthy hearings.

Laying of first transatlantic telephone cable begins from Newfoundland

Canada Dam, a gift from Canada, officially goes into operation at West Bengal, India

Rosa Parks refuses to give up seat in "whites only" bus

"Get together a half-dozen like-minded Americans and pretty soon you'll have an association . . . and a fund-raising campaign."

— Frederick Lewis Allen, Big Change *(1952)*

---

section in Montgomery, Alabama; Dr. Martin Luther King, Jr., leads bus boycott

1956

Southern U.S. congressmen urge resisting desegregation of schools "by all lawful means"

Canadian troops arrive in Egypt as part of a United Nations peacekeeping force

Canadian general E.L.M. Burns named commander of U.N. international force

Mrs. Ann Shipley moves the address in reply to the speech from the throne; first woman in the history of Canada's parliament to do so

U.S. Supreme Court rules that firing a public employee for taking the Fifth Amendment is unconstitutional

Dwight David Eisenhower, 34th president, and Richard Milhous Nixon win reelection; first Republicans reelected since William McKinley ticket in 1900

1957

John George Diefenbaker leads Conservatives to upset victory over Liberals in Canadian general election; result is Conservative minority government with 112 of 265 seats

Eisenhower Doctrine proposes broad-based aid to nations in the Middle East resisting Soviet aggression

---

Arkansas governor Orval Faubus calls up National Guard to keep black students out of Central High in Little Rock; Eisenhower sends federal troops to enforce desegregation

Ottawa establishes Canada Council to fund creative projects, and study and enjoyment of arts, humanities and social sciences with an endowment fund of $50 million

Lester B. Pearson wins Nobel Prize for peace

1958

Diefenbaker calls snap election, wins largest majority (208 seats) to that time

World's largest non-nuclear blast set off at Seymour Narrows, British Columbia, to remove navigation hazard known as Ripple Rock

Maurice Duplessis, Union Nationale premier of Quebec, dies

Coal Mine explosion at Springhill, Nova Scotia, kills 74

Lester B. Pearson succeeds Louis St. Laurent as leader of the Liberal Party of Canada

Second Narrows Bridge at Vancouver collapses under construction, killing 18

Blanche Margaret Meagher appointed Canadian ambassador to Israel, first Canadian woman to receive such a posting

National Aeronautics and Space Administration (NASA) established

Arkansas governor Faubus blocks desegregation by closing some public schools, reopening them as private facilities

1959

Alaska, Hawaii become 49th, 50th states

Vice President Richard Nixon and Soviet premier Nikita Khrushchev stage "Kitchen Debate" in Moscow

St. Lawrence Seaway is officially opened, connecting all St. Lawrence River and Great Lakes ports directly with ocean shipping

---

Canada creates Emergency Measures Organization to deal with nuclear attack; Canadians are urged to build their own nuclear bomb shelters

U.S. launches first ballistic-missile submarine

Supreme Court rules Little Rock school closings unlawful

Soviet premier Nikita Khrushchev makes unprecedented U.S. tour

---

EVERYDAY LIFE

1946

Wartime price controls lifted in U.S. on most consumer goods, but remain in Canada for more orderly transition

European immigrants, many displaced by war, flood to Canada and U.S.

Canadian veterans qualify for wide range of benefits including education, hospital care, loans and civil service job preference

A-bomb tests at Bikini atoll in the Pacific inspire creation of the bikini swimsuit

Fulbright Scholarship program set up

"A good gulp of hot whiskey at bedtime — it's not very scientific, but it helps."

— Alexander Fleming, discoverer of penicillin, on treating the common cold, March 1954

1947

Parisian designer Christian Dior's "New Look": V-shaped necklines, ruffles, tiny waists, flouncy skirts to mid-calf

Young Canadian boys swept by fad for air force surplus flying boots in winter, always worn open with tongue hanging over toes

---

Temperature in Snag, Yukon, dips to record -63°C

Appearance of war surplus stores across Canada, selling used military gear

Flying saucer sightings reported

Slinky toy introduced

Florida Everglades designated a national park

1948

Food rationing ends in Canada

Trumpeter Miles Davis introduces cool jazz

First electronically controlled elevators

CBS begins nightly TV newscast

1949

Cost of living drops; GM workers accept pay cut, car prices are down

Levittown, Long Island, New York, the first prefab suburban community, is completed

1950

Brink's robbery: 7 men in Halloween masks steal $1.5 million in cash and cheques

Estimated number of television sets: 3.1 million

Prefab fallout shelters for sale

Prepackaged meat in supermarkets becomes common

1951

Massive flooding of Mississippi River valley causes over $1 billion in losses

Fluoridated water shown to reduce tooth decay

First transcontinental TV broadcast: Edward R. Murrow's *See It Now*

Direct long-distance dialling

Saddle shoes, poodle skirts, and crinolines the rage

1952

Revised Standard Version of the Bible

U.S. clergyman Norman Vincent Peale's inspirational and self-help book *The Power of Positive Thinking*

Pocket-size transistor radios

Bwana Devil, first 3-D movie, draws big crowds

Panty raids

WHAT IT COST

Prices: 1950

Daily newspapers, 5¢

Men's classic "Palm Beach" cord suit, $55; **men's "Rub-a-Dub" suit,** $69.50

Men's "Manhattan" terry robes, $20 and $22.50

Men's classic silk cravat, $3.50

Men's slim Bermuda shorts, $12.95

Women's "little boy" blouse, $12

Ogilvy's women's suit-dress, $39.95; **contour jacket suit,** $75; **bloused and belted suit,** $69.75

Women's pumps, $16.95, $14.95

Nylons, 19¢ a pair

Elizabeth Arden products: eyelash pomade, $2.75, **eye shadow,** $2, **mascara,** $3;

lipstick, $1.50, **nail lacquer,** $1; **rouge,** $2.25

General Electric appliances: refrigerator, $398; **vacuum cleaner,** $49.50; **washers,** $149.50 to $199.50; **table radio,** $19.95

Zenith portable transistor radio, $59.95

RCA Victor 17-inch portable TV, Model One, $249.95

Smith-Corona electric typewriter, $199.50

8 mm movie camera, $54.95

Mercury 4-door sedan, $2,659

Morris Oxford, $2,075

Town of Mount Royal, Montreal, 8-room house, $30,000

Frontenac Arms Hotel, Toronto, business men's lunches, 85¢

1953

Sir Edmund Hillary and Tenzing Norkay make the first ascent of Mt. Everest

Hugh Hefner launches *Playboy* magazine

First noncommercial television station begins broadcasting from Houston, Texas

1954

The Reverend Billy Graham holds revival meetings in U.S., England, and Germany

Plastic contact lenses available

Canada's first subway opens in Toronto

Hurricanes Carol, Edna, and Hazel cause millions of dollars in damage in U.S.

TV dinners gain popularity

Comic book publishers, enjoying record sales, respond to complaints about violence and vulgarity by promising self-censorship

Davy Crockett TV show sets off craze for coonskin caps

Pianist Liberace a TV sensation

1955

Kermit the Frog debuts on TV show *Sam and Friends*

Eisenhower gives first televised presidential news conference

College fashions: straight skirts, matching pastel sweaters, circle pins, for women; the button-down Ivy League look for men

World Boy Scout Jamboree at Niagara-on-the-Lake

Disneyland opens in Anaheim, California

Ray Kroc opens his first McDonald's in Des Plaines, Illinois

Kentucky Fried Chicken opens

1956

Ringling Brothers and Barnum & Bailey presents last show under the Big Top tent

Best-selling book *The Search for Bridey Murphy* sets off reincarnation craze

Bermuda shorts popular with men and women

Stainless-steel razor blades

Battery-powered wristwatches

The Huntley-Brinkley Report, nightly TV news show with Chet Huntley and David Brinkley, debuts on NBC

1957

Montreal *Herald* daily newspaper folds after 146 years

Mayflower II re-creates original voyage from Plymouth, England

Frisbee fad

Drive-in movie theatres peak in popularity

1958

Hula Hoops: 100 million sold

"Beat" clothes: sandals, baggy sweaters, khaki pants

1959

Collegians stuffing themselves into phone booths is a fad

First Barbie dolls marketed

House of Representatives investigates rigged TV quiz shows

Average family watches television 5 hours a day

U.S. postmaster general bans English novelist D. H. Lawrence's 1928 book *Lady Chatterley's Lover* from the mails

TV cowboy shows spur sales of kids' boots, ten-gallon hats, and lassos

ARTS & LETTERS

1946

U.S. novelist John Hersey's *Hiroshima*

U.S. playwright Eugene O'Neill's *The Iceman Cometh*

●

> *"An atheist is a man who has no invisible means of support."*
>
> — Fulton Sheen, auxiliary bishop of New York, December 1955

●

Russian-born U.S. choreographer George Balanchine's ballet *Nightshadow*

U.S. poet and novelist Robert Penn Warren's *All the King's Men*

1947

U.S. playwright Arthur Miller's *All My Sons*

Holocaust victim Anne Frank's *The Diary of a Young Girl* published in German, five years later in English

U.S. playwright Tennessee Williams's *A Streetcar Named Desire*

French novelist Albert Camus's *The Plague*

Austrian painter Oskar Kokoschka's *Das Matterhorn*

English sculptor Henry Moore's *Three Standing Figures*

U.S. novelist William Faulkner wins Nobel Prize

1948

South African novelist Alan Paton's *Cry, the Beloved Country*

U.S. novelist James Michener's *Tales of the South Pacific*

U.S. novelist Norman Mailer publishes his *The Naked and the Dead*

English novelist Graham Greene's *The Heart of the Matter*

U.S. painter Andrew Wyeth's *Christina's World*

U.S. abstract expressionist artist Jackson Pollock's *Composition No. 1*

English composer Benjamin Britten's *Beggar's Opera*

1949

German-born U.S. theologian Paul Tillich's *Shaking the Foundations*

English poet and dramatist T. S. Eliot's verse play *The Cocktail Party*

Canadian Earle Birney's humorous novel of army life, *Turvey*

U.S. playwright Arthur Miller's *Death of a Salesman*

English novelist George Orwell's satiric *1984*

Russian-born French painter Marc Chagall creates *The Red Sun*

1950

U.S. novelist John Hersey's *The Wall*

Swiss sculptor Alberto Giacometti's *Seven Figures and a Head*

1951

Canadian W.O. Mitchell's radio play, *The Black Bonspiel of Wullie MacCrimmon*

The sleek, angular styles of some 1950's fashions were softened with long bows and gloves.

U.S. novelist J. D. Salinger's *The Catcher in the Rye*

Canadian Robertson Davies' *Tempest-Tost* appears, first of the Salterton trilogy

Canadian A.M. Klein's novel *The Second Scroll*, about Jews' return to Israel after World War II

U.S. marine biologist and writer Rachel Carson's *The Sea Around Us*

U.S. novelist William Faulkner's *Requiem for a Nun*

U.S. novelist Herman Wouk's *The Caine Mutiny*

Spanish Surrealist painter Salvador Dali's *Christ of St. John of the Cross*

Russian-born U.S. composer Igor Stravinsky's opera *The Rake's Progress*

English composer Benjamin Britten's opera *Billy Budd*

Dutch-born U.S. painter Willem de Kooning's *Woman*

1952

Irish-born French dramatist Samuel Beckett's *Waiting for Godot*

Black American novelist Ralph Ellison's *Invisible Man*

U.S. novelist Ernest Hemingway's *The Old Man and the Sea*

U.S. novelist John Steinbeck's *East of Eden*

U.S. novelist Bernard Malamud's *The Natural*

French painter Georges Rouault's *End of Autumn*

French painter Raoul Dufy's *The Pink Violin*

French painter Fernand Léger completes murals for U.N. building in New York City

1953

Black American novelist James Baldwin's *Go Tell It on the Mountain*

Canadian-born U.S. novelist Saul Bellow's *The Adventures of Augie March*

Stratford Festival opens first season with Alec Guinness in Shakespeare's *Richard III*

Canadian Patricia Joudry's *Teach Me How to Cry* appears as radio and television play, as New York stage play in 1955, and winner of Dominion Drama Festival Best Play award in 1956

U.S. playwright Arthur Miller's *The Crucible*

U.S. playwright William Inge's *Picnic*

Russian-born French painter Marc Chagall's *Eiffel Tower*

1954

Canadian Fred Cogswell launches Fiddlehead Books to encourage young poets

Canadian Robertson Davies' play, *A Jig for the Gypsies*, presented at Toronto's Crest Theatre

●

"From birth to age 18, a girl needs good parents. From 18 to 35, she needs good looks. From 35 to 55, she needs a good personality. From 55 on, she needs good cash."

— Sophie Tucker, in 1953 at age 69

●

U.S. historian Bruce Catton writes *A Stillness at Appomattox*

French modernist painter Jean Dubuffet's *Les Vagabonds*

English composer Benjamin Britten's opera *Turn of the Screw*

Austrian-born U.S. composer Arnold Schoenberg's opera *Moses and Aaron*

Purchasing Power of the Canadian Dollar: 1950–93

(1986 = $1)

1950	$5.26
'55	$4.65
'60	$4.22
'65	$3.89
'70	$3.23
'75	$2.26
'80	$1.49
'85	$1.04
'86	$1
'90	$0.84
'93	$0.77

1955

American Shakespeare Festival opens

English novelist William Golding's *Lord of the Flies*

U.S. playwright Tennessee Williams's *Cat on a Hot Tin Roof*

U.S. playwright William Inge's *Bus Stop*

U.S. novelist Sloan Wilson's *The Man in the Gray Flannel Suit*

U.S. Patrick Dennis's Broadway comedy *Auntie Mame*

Marian Anderson becomes first black American to sing at the Metropolitan Opera

Russian-born U.S. novelist Vladimir Nabokov's *Lolita* published in France, three years later in America

English novelist Graham Greene's *The Quiet American*

1956

Beat poet Allen Ginsberg's *Howl and Other Poems*

U.S. novelist Grace Metalious's *Peyton Place*

Canadian Leonard Cohen's first book of poetry, *Let us Compare Mythologies*

Canadian Adele Wiseman's novel, *The Sacrifice*, deals with the immigrant experience

U.S. composer Lejaren Hiller produces *Illiac Suite*, the first major piece of computer-generated music

Greek-born U.S. singer Maria Callas makes her debut at the Metropolitan Opera in Vincenzo Bellini's *Norma*

British prime minister Winston Churchill's first of four volumes of *A History of the English-Speaking Peoples*

U.S. sociologist William H. Whyte's *The Organization Man*

1957

Russian Boris Pasternak's *Dr. Zhivago*, denied publication in the Soviet Union, published in Italy

English playwright John Osborne's *Look Back in Anger*

U.S. playwright Eugene O'Neill creates *Long Day's Journey Into Night*

Beat novelist Jack Kerouac's *On the Road*

English novelist John Braine's *Room at the Top*

U.S. writer John Cheever produces his novel *The Wapshot Chronicle*

Some of the prefab houses built in Levittown, such as this model priced at under $8,000, were reserved for returning veterans and their families.

U.S. novelist Leon Uris creates *Exodus*

U.S. sociologist Vance Packard's *The Hidden Persuaders*

English composer William Walton's *Concerto for Cello and Orchestra*

1958

U.S. novelist Truman Capote's *Breakfast at Tiffany's*

U.S. poet Archibald MacLeish's verse drama *J.B.*

Canadian-born U.S. economist John Kenneth Galbraith's *The Affluent Society*

Guggenheim Museum, designed by Frank Lloyd Wright, opens in New York City

Soviets force writer Boris Pasternak to refuse the Nobel Prize

English playwright Harold Pinter's *The Birthday Party*

English sculptor Henry Moore's *Reclining Figure*

1959

U.S. novelist Philip Roth's *Good-bye Columbus*

U.S. novelist William Faulkner completes trilogy that includes *The Hamlet* (1940), *The Town* (1957), and *The Mansion* (1959)

U.S. novelist James Michener's *Hawaii*

Canadian Mordecai Richler's *The Apprenticeship of Duddy Kravitz*

Canadian Irving Layton wins Governor General's Award for Poetry

Canadian Hugh MacLennan's *The Watch that Ends the Night*, his most critically acclaimed novel

ENTERTAINMENT & SPORTS

1946

U.S. film director William Wyler's *The Best Years of Our Lives*, about homecoming GI's

U.S. film director Frank Capra's *It's a Wonderful Life*, with James Stewart

Humphrey Bogart and Lauren Bacall in director Howard Hawks's screen version of mystery writer Raymond Chandler's *The Big Sleep*

English director Alfred

Hitchcock's *Notorious,* with Ingrid Bergman and Cary Grant

Americans Alan Jay Lerner and Frederick Loewe's Broadway musical *Brigadoon*

U.S. songwriter Irving Berlin's Broadway musical *Annie Get Your Gun*

Hit songs: "Chiquita Banana," "To Each His Own," "Come Rain or Come Shine," "Doin' What Comes Natur'lly," "Full Moon and Empty Arms"

A new football team, the Montreal Alouettes, joins Canadian Football League

Montreal Canadiens win Stanley Cup

Toronto Argonauts win Grey Cup

A "nuclear" family made up of mannequins is posed around the dinner table inside a frame house about two miles away from ground zero just before an atom bomb test conducted in Nevada on March 17, 1953.

1947

Turkish-born U.S. director Elia Kazan's *Gentleman's Agreement*

Hit songs: "Almost Like Being in Love," "Open the Door, Richard," "Woody Woodpecker," "How Are Things in Glocca Morra?"

Jackie Robinson, first black in major league baseball, plays for the Brooklyn Dodgers; named Rookie of the Year

On TV: *Kraft Theater, Howdy Doody, Meet the Press*

Thor Heyerdahl sails *Kon-Tiki* raft from Peru to Polynesia in 101 days

Toronto Argonauts win Grey Cup

Toronto Maple Leafs win Stanley Cup

1948

British film director Michael Powell's *The Red Shoes*

U.S. film director Jules Dassin's *Naked City*

U.S. songwriter Cole Porter's Broadway musical *Kiss Me, Kate*

On TV: Ed Sullivan's *The Toast of the Town,* Milton Berle's *Texaco Star Theater, Philco Playhouse, Ford Theater, Ted Mack's Amateur Hour*

Hit songs: "Buttons and Bows," "It's a Most Unusual Day," "A — You're Adorable,"

"So in Love," "Enjoy Yourself — It's Later Than You Think"

Olympic Games are held in London

Calgary Stampeders win Grey Cup at game played in Toronto; Calgary fans set tone of future Grey Cup weekends with exuberant celebration

Toronto Maple Leafs win Stanley Cup

1949

Italian director Vittorio de Sica's *The Bicycle Thief*

Americans Richard Rodgers and Oscar Hammerstein's Broadway musical *South Pacific*

British film director Carol Reed's classic thriller *The Third Man*

On TV: *The Lone Ranger, The Perry Como Show, Arthur Godfrey and His Friends, Hopalong Cassidy*

Hit songs: "Some Enchanted Evening," "Let's Take an Old-Fashioned Walk," "My Foolish Heart," "Dear Hearts and Gentle People"

Joe Louis retires; Ezzard Charles captures heavyweight boxing crown

Toronto Tip Tops win world softball championship

Montreal Alouettes win Grey Cup

Toronto Maple Leafs win Stanley Cup

1950

Hollywood film director Joseph Mankiewicz's *All About Eve,* with Bette Davis and Anne Baxter

U.S. film director Billy Wilder's *Sunset Boulevard* is produced, with Gloria Swanson and William Holden

On TV: *The George Burns and Gracie Allen Show, Your Hit Parade, The Jack Benny Show, What's My Line?*

Composers Frank Loesser and Abe Burrows's Broadway musical *Guys and Dolls*

Hit songs: "Good Night, Irene," "Third Man Theme," "Mule Train," "Mona Lisa"

U.S. cartoonist Charles Schultz creates the comic strip *Peanuts*

Toronto Argonauts win Grey Cup

Detroit Red Wings win Stanley Cup

1951

Film director Elia Kazan's version of *A Streetcar Named Desire,* with Marlon Brando

Humphrey Bogart and Katharine Hepburn in director John Huston's *The African Queen*

A Place in the Sun, with Elizabeth Taylor and Montgomery Clift

An American in Paris, with Gene Kelly and Leslie Caron

Japanese film director Akira Kurosawa's *Rashomon*

Americans Richard Rodgers and Oscar Hammerstein's Broadway musical *The King and I*

Hit songs: "Tennessee Waltz," "How High the Moon," "Too Young," "Because of You"

●

"I refuse to endanger the health of my children in a house with less than three bathrooms."

— *Film actress Myrna Loy,* Mr. Blandings Builds His Dream House *(1947)*

●

On TV: *I Love Lucy, The Red Skelton Show*

Jersey Joe Walcott wins heavyweight boxing title

Ottawa Rough Riders win Grey Cup; the team name comes not, as is often thought, from Teddy Roosevelt's cavalry regiment but from the name given to lumberjacks who rode logs down Ontario rivers

Toronto Maple Leafs win Stanley Cup

1952

Fredric March in screen version of Arthur Miller's *Death of a Salesman*

Grace Kelly and Gary Cooper in *High Noon,* directed by Fred Zinnemann

Gene Kelly, Debbie Reynolds, and Donald O'Connor in *Singin' in the Rain*

On TV: *The Today Show, Dragnet, This Is Your Life, The Adventures of Ozzie and Harriet*

Hit songs: "Cry," "Blue Tango," "Any Time," "Kiss of Fire"

Olympic Games held in Helsinki

Rocky Marciano KO's Jersey Joe Walcott to win heavyweight boxing title

N.H.L. hockey is televised for first time, and "Hockey Night in

Canada" goes from sound to pictures

Toronto Argonauts win first Grey Cup game to be shown live on television

Detroit Red Wings win Stanley Cup

1953

Roman Holiday, with Audrey Hepburn and Gregory Peck

From Here to Eternity, directed by Fred Zinnemann, starring Burt Lancaster, Deborah Kerr, Frank Sinatra, and Montgomery Clift

On TV: *My Little Margie, Our Miss Brooks, Person to Person, Captain Kangaroo*

La Famille Plouffe debuts on Radio-Canada television

Hit songs: "Song From the Moulin Rouge," "Till I Waltz Again With You," "April in Portugal," "Vaya con Dios"

U.S. tennis star Maureen (Little Mo) Connolly wins women's Grand Slam

Hamilton Tiger-Cats win Grey Cup

Montreal Canadiens win Stanley Cup

1954

English director Alfred Hitchcock's *Rear Window,* with James Stewart and Grace Kelly

U.S. director Elia Kazan's film *On the Waterfront,* with Marlon Brando

Japanese director Akira Kurosawa's *Seven Samurai*

Italian director Federico Fellini's *La Strada*

On TV: *Disneyland, Make Room for Daddy,* Groucho Marx's *You Bet Your Life*

Canadian singer Juliette Augustina Sysak gets her own CBC television show

Hit songs: "Little Things Mean a Lot," "Hey There," "Young at Heart," "Sh–Boom"

Roger Bannister breaks the 4-minute barrier for the mile: 3 minutes 59.4 seconds

U.S.S.R. wins gold medal in hockey at Cortina Olympics, shattering Canadian dominance of international, amateur game

Edmonton Eskimos win Grey Cup

Detroit Red Wings win Stanley Cup

1955

Hollywood's film version of *Mister Roberts*, with Henry Fonda and Jack Lemmon

U.S. actor James Dean stars in *East of Eden* and *Rebel Without a Cause*

The Blackboard Jungle, with Glenn Ford and Sidney Poitier, has Bill Haley and the Comets' hit song "Rock Around the Clock" on its sound track

French director Henri Georges Clouzot's *Diabolique*

Hit songs: "Maybellene," "Ballad of Davy Crockett," "Cherry Pink and Apple Blossom White," "Yellow Rose of Texas," "Ain't That a Shame"

On TV: *Gunsmoke, Beat the Clock, The Mickey Mouse Club, The Honeymooners*

Edmonton Eskimos repeat as Grey Cup champions

Detroit Red Wings win Stanley Cup for second consecutive year

1956

Elvis Presley performs on Ed Sullivan's television program

Hollywood epic *Giant*; James Dean's last film

Producer Mike Todd's *Around the World in 80 Days*

Americans Alan Jay Lerner and Frederick Loewe's Broadway musical *My Fair Lady*

On TV: *The $64,000 Challenge, Wyatt Earp*

Hit songs: "Heartbreak Hotel," "Don't Be Cruel," "Great Pretender," "My Prayer," "Wayward Wind," "Love Me Tender," "Whatever Will Be, Will Be"

Rocky Marciano retires unbeaten; Floyd Patterson KO's Archie Moore to win heavyweight boxing championship

Edmonton Eskimos win Grey Cup for third year in a row

Movie actor James Dean became a heartthrob to legions of teenage girls in movies like East of Eden.

Montreal Canadiens win Stanley Cup

1957

English director David Lean's *The Bridge on the River Kwai*, with Alec Guinness and William Holden

U.S. director Sidney Lumet's *Twelve Angry Men*

Swedish director Ingmar Bergman's *The Seventh Seal*

U.S. composer Leonard Bernstein's enormously successful Broadway musical *West Side Story*

On TV: *The Jack Parr Show, Leave It to Beaver, American Bandstand, Alfred Hitchcock Presents*

CBC television begins two highly successful series with *Front Page Challenge* and *Close-Up*

Hit songs: "Tammy," "Love Letters in the Sand," "It's Not for Me to Say," "Young Love," "Chances Are," "That'll Be the Day," "Whole Lotta Shakin' Goin' On" "Wake Up, Little Susie"

Bobby Fischer, age 13, hailed as chess genius

Hamilton Tiger-Cats win Grey Cup

Montreal Canadiens win Stanley Cup for second time in a row

1958

Screen version of Tennessee Williams's play *Cat on a Hot Tin Roof*, with Elizabeth Taylor and Paul Newman

On TV: *Lawrence Welk, Playhouse 90, Maverick, The Pat Boone Show*

Hit songs: "Volare," "It's All in the Game," "All I Have to Do Is Dream," "Bird Dog," "At the Hop," "Peggy Sue"

Golfer Arnold Palmer wins his first Masters Tournament

U.S. beats England for yachting's America's Cup

Winnipeg Blue Bombers win Grey Cup

Montreal Canadiens win third straight Stanley Cup

1959

Marilyn Monroe, Tony Curtis, and Jack Lemmon in *Some Like It Hot*

Ben Hur, with Charlton Heston and Stephen Boyd; wins 11 Oscar awards, highest number ever

French director Jean-Luc Godard's *Breathless*

French director François Truffaut produces *The 400 Blows*

Hit songs: "Mack the Knife," "Battle of New Orleans," "Venus," "Lonely Boy," "There Goes My Baby," "Sixteen Candles"

On TV: *Bonanza, Rawhide, General Electric Theater, Perry Mason*

Pale Horse, Pale Rider, an example of excellent CBC television drama production of the period

Boston Celtics win first of eight straight NBA championships

Winnipeg Blue Bombers win Grey Cup

Montreal Canadiens win fourth straight Stanley Cup, tying record set by Montreal Victorias in 1898

BUSINESS & ECONOMICS

1946

Wave of strikes in Canada and U.S.; Canadian arbitrator Ivan Rand agrees to payment of union dues by non-union members (Rand Formula)

1947

Canadian Pacific Air Lines begins developing international routes

1948

United Auto Workers (UAW) wins first escalator clause from management, basing wages on cost of living

Canadian Broadcasting Corporation is largest employer of musicians in North America

Oil discovered at Leduc, Alberta

1949

Canada's Avro C-102 jetliner is second in world

Norgate Shopping Centre in St. Laurent, Quebec, is first suburban mall in Canada

Cost of living drops; UAW takes pay cut; car prices fall

First Volkswagen sold in U.S.

1950

Canada-wide railway strike paralyzes transport, begins 16 years of labor strife for railways

Diner's Club introduces the first multiuse credit card, accepted in lieu of cash in 27 restaurants

U.S. produces two-thirds of world's cars and trucks

General Motors' earnings top $600 million, largest ever for a U.S. corporation

1951

Trading stamps catch on as a sales incentive

Atomic Energy Commission (AEC) builds first nuclear reactor

UNIVAC, first commercially practical computer, debuts

AT&T has a record 1 million stockholders

1952

George Meany heads American Federation of Labor (AFL); Walter Reuther becomes president of the Congress of Industrial Organizations (CIO)

●

"What is good for the country is good for General Motors, and what's good for General Motors is good for the country."

— *Charles E. Wilson, testifying before Senate Armed Forces Committee, 1952*

●

1953

Tidelands Oil Act: U.S. gets offshore oil rights

CF-100 Canuck is only fighter plane to be designed, built, and put into service in Canada

IBM's first commercial computers are produced and marketed

1954

Premium gasoline introduced

Atomic-generated electricity will one day be "too cheap to meter," says Lewis Strauss, chairman of the U.S. Atomic Energy Commission

World's largest crude oil pipeline (1,882 kilometres) is completed in Canada, running from Alberta to Sarnia

1955

Container ships revolutionize cargo shipping

AFL and CIO unions, with a total of 15 million members, merge under George Meany

1956

Canadian Labour Congress represents 80 percent of organized labour in Canada

Canadian armored vehicles of "C" Squadron, Lord Strathcona Horse, cross a pontoon bridge over the Han River in Korea, May 1951.

TV videocassette recorder demonstrated by Ampex

1957

Royal commission on Canada's economic prospects draws attention to Canada's heavy reliance on U.S. trade and U.S. ownership of much of Canadian business

AFL-CIO expels Teamsters Union, whose leader, Jimmy Hoffa, faces corruption charges

Ford introduces the Edsel

1958

Aluminum car engine developed

Pan Am begins transatlantic jet service

American Express launches credit card

1959

St. Lawrence Seaway opens

Canada's Avro Arrow jet fighter cancelled, ending hopes of market for Canada in advanced, military aircraft

Computers with transistors instead of vacuum tubes are marketed

COBOL: first computer programming language for business use

SCIENCE & MEDICINE

1946

ENIAC, often called the first computer, unveiled

Mayo Clinic reports that the antibiotic streptomycin checks tuberculosis

Sun found to emit radio waves

1947

Dead Sea Scrolls discovered by goatherd near Qumran, in region of Jordan later occupied by Israel

Edwin Land invents Polaroid instant-picture camera

Mumps vaccine developed

Polio virus is isolated

1948

Peter Goldmark perfects long-playing record: 33⅓ r.p.m.

U.N. establishes World Health Organization

Cesium atomic clocks: accurate to 1 second in 1,000 years

Dr. Alfred Kinsey's *Sexual Behavior in the Human Male*

200-inch mirror telescope dedicated on Mount Palomar, California

Britain adopts national health plan

William Shockley and associates at Bell Labs invent the transistor

1949

American Cancer Society takes stand against cigarette smoking

Cortisone, believed effective in treating rheumatoid arthritis, is manufactured

1950

Antihistamines available to alleviate colds and allergies

First embryo transplants in cattle

New elements created by the Berkeley cyclotron: Berkelium 97 and Californium 98

1951

Researchers generate electricity from nuclear fuel

1952

Atomic Energy Commission of Canada founded as crown corporation

Polio epidemic strikes over 50,000 in the U.S., and more than 8,000 in Canada where it kills 481 people

In Denmark first sex-change operation: George Jorgenson becomes Christine Jorgenson

Amniocentesis introduced

First artificial heart-valve implant; electric shock first used to restart human heart

Galaxies found to be twice as far away as previously thought

New element: Einsteinium 99

1953

Heart-lung machine used for the first time during surgery

Breeder reactors, which make their own fuel as they run

U.S. pilot Chuck Yeager, in rocket-powered Bell X-1A, hits a record Mach 2.5, or 2.5 times the speed of sound

U.S. scientist James D. Watson and English scientist Francis

H. C. Crick build model of double-helix deoxyribonucleic acid (DNA)

New element: Fermium 100

Dr. Alfred Kinsey's *Sexual Behavior in the Human Female*

1954

Virologist Jonas Salk's polio vaccine tested on public

Astronomers, observing blue-green area on Mars, postulate theory of extraterrestrial life

FORTRAN: first computer programming language

First images of atoms produced by newly invented ion microscope

First successful kidney transplant

1955

First widespread testing of a birth control pill

First optical fibres

New element: Mendelevium 101

▬

"Science is the search for truth — it is not a game in which one tries to beat his opponent, to do harm to others."

— Linus C. Pauling,
No More War! *(1958)*

▬

1956

Kidney machines

Human growth hormone isolated

Neutrinos, particles without mass or charge, discovered

1957

Interferon, a family of virus-fighting proteins, discovered

First nuclear power plant, in Shippingport, Pennsylvania

Soviets launch first man-made satellites: *Sputniks I* and *II*

DNA synthesized

Soviet nuclear-waste facility explodes, contaminating 259 square kilometres in southern Urals

1958

Measles vaccine developed

Explorer I, first U.S. earth satellite, detects Van Allen radiation belt

Ultrasound for examining fetuses in the womb

Pacemaker to regulate heartbeats invented

New element: Nobelium 102

1959

Explorer VI, U.S. satellite, transmits first TV pictures of Earth from space

British paleontologist Louis Leakey discovers the remains of a human who lived 1.75 million years ago

Soviet *Lunik II* is first man-made object to strike the Moon

WORLD POLITICAL EVENTS

1946

Civil war in China between Nationalists and Communists

Italy votes to become republic; Umberto II abdicates

Churchill makes his "Iron Curtain" speech in Fulton, Missouri; Cold War begins

Top Nazis put on trial in Nuremberg, Germany; tribunal sentences Goering and 11 others to death

Japanese war criminals go on trial; 7 are sentenced to hang, 16 to life imprisonment

1947

Princess Elizabeth, heiress to British throne, marries Philip, duke of Edinburgh

Britain nationalizes coal mines, communications, and electrical industry

Both Arabs and Jews reject British proposal to divide

Palestine; U.N. suggests alternate partition plan

India gains independence from Britain; Jawaharlal Nehru prime minister

1948

U.S.S.R. sets up European satellite nations; stages coup d'état in Czechoslovakia and forms another satellite

Berlin Airlift by Allies begins after Soviet Union blockades roads and railways from the West

Israel becomes a nation with David Ben-Gurion as prime minister and Chaim Weizmann as president; war erupts with the Arab League; 400,000 Palestinian refugees flee from Israel to nearby Arab countries, creating the long-standing Palestinian homeland problem

Korea is divided into North and South

Mohandas K. Gandhi assassinated in India

1949

Germany is divided into East and West

Berlin blockade lifted by Soviets

Republic of Ireland cuts ties

Actress Grace Kelly, star of 10 films between 1951 and 1956, weds Prince Rainier III of Monaco in a lavish royal ceremony.

---

with Great Britain and declares independence

Communists under Mao Tse-tung win mainland China; Nationalists under Chiang Kai-shek flee to Taiwan

Israel admitted to U.N.; capital moved to Jerusalem

U.S.S.R. tests atom bomb

"Whether you like it or not, history is on our side. We will bury you!"

— *Nikita Khrushchev, referring to capitalist nations, at a reception held in the Polish Embassy, Moscow, 1956*

1950

China invades Tibet; claims sovereignty

U.S.S.R. and China begin aiding Communist leader Ho Chi Minh's Democratic Republic of Vietnam

German-born British scientist Klaus Fuchs jailed for giving

---

atomic secrets to Soviet Union.

1951

Conservative Party wins British election; Churchill once again prime minister

Eamon De Valera prime minister of Ireland

1952

Anti-British riots in Egypt; King Farouk abdicates

Britain's George VI dies; his daughter Elizabeth II's reign begins

Mau Mau terrorism in Kenya against British

1953

Joseph Stalin dies, succeeded by Georgy Malenkov; Nikita Khrushchev becomes head of the Communist Party Central Committee in U.S.S.R.

Norway's Dag Hammarskjold elected U.N. secretary-general

Coronation of Elizabeth II

U.S.S.R. explodes hydrogen bomb

1954

Ho Chi Minh defeats French at Dien Bien Phu; conference in Geneva grants independence to Laos and Cambodia, and approves a temporary split of Vietnam into North and South Vietnam

Col. Gamal Abdel Nasser comes to power in Egypt

1955

First summit conference since World War II convenes in Geneva; Eisenhower's "open skies" proposal rejected by Soviets

European Communist countries join Warsaw Pact; West Germany joins NATO

Anthony Eden is elected British prime minister, replacing Churchill

Nikolai Bulganin succeeds Georgy Malenkov as Soviet premier

Argentine dictator Juan Domingo Perón deposed

1956

Israel invades Sinai Peninsula; Anglo-French forces occupy the Suez Canal, then withdraw; all parties agree to cease-fire; U.N. force takes over the canal

Khrushchev denounces Stalin's policies at 20th Soviet Communist Party Conference

Ghana gains independence

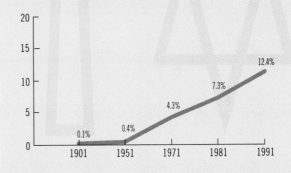

Canadian Church Membership: 1901–91

Percentage of people who consider themselves of Christian or Jewish faith

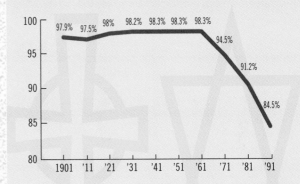

Percentage of people who claim no religious affiliation

Anti-Communist Hungarian revolution suppressed by Soviet troops

Fidel Castro begins guerrilla campaign to oust Cuban dictator Fulgencio Batista

Golda Meir becomes prime minister of Israel

1957

Israel withdraws from Sinai

Britain's prime minister Anthony Eden resigns; Harold Macmillan succeeds him

---

Soviets test intercontinental ballistic missile (ICBM)

European Common Market founded

1958

Nikita Khrushchev becomes Soviet premier

Algerians revolt against French rule; Charles de Gaulle becomes president of France

Chinese Communists shell Quemoy and Matsu, offshore islands held by Nationalist Chinese

Pope John XXIII elected

1959

Pope John XXIII calls Vatican Council II, first since 1870

China suppresses Tibetan revolt; Dalai Lama flees

Fidel Castro overthrows Batista in "freedom coup", becomes Cuban premier

NORTH AMERICAN HISTORY & POLITICS

1960

Northwest Territories Council meets at Resolute Bay, becoming the most northerly legislative body in the world

U-2 spy plane shot down over U.S.S.R.; U.S. pilot Francis Gary Powers imprisoned, later exchanged for convicted Soviet spy Rudolf Abel

U.S. flag adds stars for Alaska and Hawaii, making 50 stars

Lunch-counter sit-ins begin in Greensboro, North Carolina, to protest local practice of not serving black customers

Canada's population reaches 18 million, for the first time exceeding 10 percent of U.S. population which stands at 179,323,000

John F. Kennedy and Texas senator Lyndon Johnson defeat Republicans Richard M. Nixon and U.N. ambassador Henry Cabot Lodge, Jr., to win 35th presidency and vice presidency

1961

New Democratic Party replaces Co-operative Commonwealth Federation (CCF) in Canada

U.S. severs ties with Cuba

Bay of Pigs invasion: U.S.-backed attempt to foment an uprising against Cuba's Fidel Castro fails

JFK proposes 10-year space program with goal of "landing a man on the Moon in this decade"

John Diefenbaker meets in Washington with John F. Kennedy; the dislike is mutual as Kennedy treats both countries as one while Diefenbaker insists on Canadian integrity

T. C. Douglas leaves premiership of Saskatchewan to become national leader of the newly formed New Democratic Party

Montreal authorizes the building of a subway

1962

In Canadian general election, Conservatives drop to minority government with only 116 seats against 99 Liberal, 30 Social Credit, and 19 New Democratic Party

For a week in October 1962, the world held its breath wondering if the Cuban missile crisis meant nuclear war.

James Meredith becomes first black student at University of Mississippi after federal troops quell rioting

Medicare introduced in Saskatchewan, the first in North America

Claire Kirkland-Casgrain becomes the first woman cabinet minister in Quebec

Sioux Rock, depicting Indian petroglyphs, discovered near Port Arthur, Ontario; age unknown and could range from 8000 B.C. to A.D. 1200 .

Cuban missile crisis: JFK imposes a naval blockade on Cuba and demands removal of Soviet ballistic missiles from Cuban bases; Khrushchev refuses, then backs down in exchange for U.S. pledge not to attack Cuba

Canada's Conservative government delays placing armed forces on high alert at start of Cuban missile crisis; relations between Diefenbaker and Kennedy deteriorate further

Canada's last execution: hanging of Ronald Turpin and Arthur Lucas at Don Jail, Toronto

Work begins on Red River Floodway, largest earth-moving project in Canadian history, covering 47.3 km of Red and Assiniboine rivers

1963

Liberals, led by Lester Pearson, win federal election over Diefenbaker Conservatives in another minority government; 129 Liberals face 136 opposition members

Quebec takes over 11 private power companies to form publicly owned Hydro-Québec

After a wave of terrorism in Quebec, 11 members of the Front de Libération du Québec (FLQ) plead guilty to charges of bombing and arson

Canadian government old-age pension reaches $75 per month

JFK visits Berlin Wall; makes "Ich bin ein Berliner" speech before West German crowd

Black activist Medgar Evers of the National Association for the Advancement of Colored People (NAACP) slain in Mississippi

More than 200,000 people gather in Washington, D.C., for civil rights march; Martin Luther King, Jr., gives his "I have a dream" oration

Nov. 22: JFK assassinated in Dallas; Vice President Lyndon Johnson assumes the presidency; Lee Harvey Oswald, arrested as the gunman, shot by Dallas nightclub owner Jack Ruby two days later

Warren Commission set up to investigate JFK assassination

1964

Canadian peacekeeping troops join UN in Cyprus, and remain there for almost 30 years

Liberals introduce proposal to parliament for new Canadian flag to replace modified British merchant marine flag

Jack Ruby convicted for murdering Lee Harvey Oswald, alleged assassin of JFK

Three civil rights volunteers for the black voter registration drive found murdered in Mississippi

North Vietnam attacks U.S. Navy ships in Gulf of Tonkin; LBJ orders bombing of North Vietnam; first U.S. antiwar demonstrations

Warren Commission finds no evidence of conspiracy in JFK assassination; 888-page report cites Oswald as the sole triggerman

Martin Luther King, Jr., wins Nobel Peace Prize

Lyndon Johnson, incumbent 36th president, elected with Minnesota senator Hubert Humphrey as vice president

1965

First U.S. ground combat troops land in Vietnam; U.S. forces grow to 184,300

Malcolm X, Black Muslim leader, fatally shot in Harlem

Liberals win Canadian federal election, again with minority government; Liberals have 131 seats to 97 for Conservatives

"Let us never negotiate out of fear, but never fear to negotiate."

— President John F. Kennedy, in his Inaugural Address, January 20, 1961

Canada's new maple leaf flag raised in Ottawa

U.S. consulate in Montreal is bombed, possiby by FLQ

Ottawa announces pensionable age to be dropped from 70 to 65

Abraham Ookpik elected first

Inuit member of Northwest Territories Council

Canadian Wheat Board sells over 5.7 million tonnes of wheat to Soviet Union

Martin Luther King, Jr., leads more than 3,000 people on 87-km march from Selma to Montgomery

Race rioting devastates Los Angeles's Watts district

Quebec premier Daniel Johnson insists that Quebec must have more powers, making it equal to Canada as a whole rather than to other provinces, or should consider separation

1966

Vietnam: U.S. bombs Hanoi and Haiphong, supports South Vietnamese government of Gen. Nguyen Cao Ky; U.S. defence secretary Robert McNamara reports that neither air war nor "pacification program" is succeeding; U.S. forces grow to some 400,000

Roman Catholic churches in Canada abandon tradition of Latin to celebrate mass in French or English

Opposition to Vietnam war spreads from U.S. to Canada which receives Americans evading draft; few Canadians realize extent of Canadian involvement in the war

U.S. B-52 bomber collides in midair with a fuel-resupply plane over Spain; unarmed H-bomb dislodged and falls into Atlantic but is later recovered by midget sub

National Organization for Women (NOW) founded by Betty Friedan and others

1967

On official visit to Canada, President de Gaulle is greeted as a hero in Quebec, raises cheer in Montreal for "Vive Québec Libre" speech, and is told by Canadian government that he is no longer welcome in Canada

Expo 67 opens in Montreal as Canada's first world fair

Thurgood Marshall becomes first black Supreme Court justice in the U.S.

Canadian army, navy, and air forces merged to become Canadian Armed Forces

"The Negro says 'Now.' Others say 'Never.' The voice of responsible Americans says ... 'Together.' There is no other way."

— *Vice President Lyndon Johnson, May 1963*

Race riots erupt in Detroit; death toll reaches 40, with 2,000 injured

Canadian Department of Manpower and Immigration establishes "points system" for immigrants

Anti-Vietnam war protests grow; some 75,000 protesters march on the Pentagon

1968

Pierre Trudeau succeeds Lester Pearson as Liberal leader; Liberals win majority in general election with 155 seats to 72 for Conservatives, 22 for New

Democratic Party, and 14 for Créditistes

René Lévesque becomes leader of newly formed Parti Québécois (PQ)

Vietnam: U.S. forces total some 500,000; Vietcong stage Tet Offensive

North Koreans seize U.S. intelligence ship *Pueblo* and its crew in Sea of Japan, claiming violation of territorial waters

LBJ announces he will not seek reelection; proposes peace talks with North Vietnam and partial halt to bombing

Martin Luther King, Jr., assassinated by James Earl Ray in Memphis; riots break out in over 100 cities; Ray pleads guilty, sentenced to 99 years in prison

Senator Robert F. Kennedy, Jr., assassinated by Sirhan Sirhan in Los Angeles after celebrating victory in California presidential primary

Shirley Chisholm becomes first black woman elected to U.S. Congress

American Indian Movement (AIM) founded in Minneapolis, quickly spreads to Canada

Feminists crash Miss America contest, tossing false eyelashes, bras, and steno pads into "freedom trash cans" and proclaiming "Women's Liberation"

Richard Nixon elected 37th president, with Maryland

governor Spiro Agnew as his vice president

1969

Vietnam War: U.S. forces peak at 543,000 in April; My Lai massacre raises issue of U.S. atrocities; Nixon announces troop withdrawal: by year's end 75,000 Americans return home; U.S. looks to South Vietnam to play greater role in the fighting; bombing of Cambodia continues; North Vietnamese leader, Ho Chi Minh, dies; 250,000 antiwar demonstrators march on Washington

Senator Edward Kennedy drives his car off bridge on Chappaquiddick Island; he escapes injury but companion, Mary Jo Kopechne, drowns

Official Languages Act provides that all federal services will be available across Canada in either French or English

Trudeau government's White Paper on Indian Policy advocates doing away with reserve system, causes confrontation between federal government and native peoples

EVERYDAY LIFE

1960

National Gallery of Canada opens in Ottawa

Restaurateur Roy Kroc owns and operates 228 McDonald's restaurants; plans to open 100 new ones every year

Oral contraceptives available

High rate of heart fatalities among middle-aged men attributed to cigarette smoking

Aluminum cans for beverages and food begin to appear

85 million TV sets in use

1961

Upper Canada Village (Morrisburg, Ontario) opens; takes advantage of flooding caused by St. Lawrence Seaway to preserve 19th-century buildings

First electric toothbrushes, named Broxodents, introduced by Squibb

Jackie Kennedy look: bouffant hairdos, pillbox hats, and gloves; also two-piece suits by Oleg Cassini

1962

Seattle World's Fair, with 185-metre Space Needle, opens

Diet colas Tab and Diet Rite appear in supermarkets

Walter Cronkite becomes anchor of *CBS Evening News*; remains for 20 years

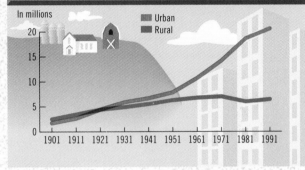

Canadian Population, Urban and Rural: 1901–91

In millions

- Urban
- Rural

1963

Kodak introduces Instamatic camera with film cartridge; Polaroid color camera goes on sale

Tranquillizer Valium produced by Roche Labs

First Trimline push-button telephones

Pentel invents and markets felt-tip pens

British Columbia establishes Simon Fraser University at Burnaby, B.C.

Trans-Canada Airlines DC-8 crashes at Ste. Thérèse de Blainville shortly after takeoff from Dorval Airport; 118 killed

Place des Arts concert hall at Montreal opens

1964

Canadians get social insurance cards

New York World's Fair: visitors see Michelangelo's *Pietà*, on loan from the Vatican; General Motors' Futurama is most popular attraction

Spectacular jewel heist from New York's American Museum of Natural History; perpetrators, led by Murph the Surf, return most of loot in exchange for lenient sentences

U.S. psychologist Eric Berne's book *Games People Play* encourages many to analyze their own and others' social interactions

Austrian fashion designer Rudi Gernreich rocks the fashion

world with his topless bathing suit, the "monokini"; French designer André Courrèges favors short white boots, short skirts, and trapezoidal lines, topped off with dark sunglasses; British designer Mary Quant takes everything to new mod heights

1965

Young men's hair getting shaggier while young women sport the Sassoon look: short, smooth, swingy bobs with bangs

Miniskirt introduced

Failure of Ontario Hydro relay device at Queenston plunges eastern North America into darkness

1966

Winston becomes bestselling cigarette; for first time filter brands surpass nonfilters

Canada Pension Plan is set up

1967

British model Twiggy comes to

At the Lincoln Memorial on August 28, 1963, Martin Luther King, Jr., began his famous speech: "I say to you today . . . I still have a dream."

New York City and wows Americans in her short skirts, jumpsuits, and boots

1968

Jacqueline Kennedy marries Greek shipping magnate Aristotle Onassis

U.S. social scientist Paul Ehrlich, in *The Population Bomb,* predicts famine will cause the death of billions of people between 1970 and 1985

Afro hairdos and loose-fitting robes in colorful fabrics become popular among black people

First quartz watches cost $1,000

1969

Saturday postal deliveries end in Canada

Breathalizer comes into use

Granny dresses, floor-length maxicoats, clogs, tie-dyed fabrics

Pesticide DDT banned in residential areas

Commune leader Charles Manson and followers murder pregnant actress Sharon Tate and four others in Los Angeles

ARTS & LETTERS

1960

U.S. author John Updike's *Rabbit, Run*

U.S. artist Jasper Johns produces *Painted Bronze (Beer Cans)*

U.S. writer Harper Lee's novel *To Kill a Mockingbird*

Russian-born violinist Isaac Stern begins campaign to save Carnegie Hall in New York City from the wrecking ball

American Ballet Theatre tours the U.S.S.R.; first North American. dance company ever to do so

1961

U.S. journalist Theodore H. White's *The Making of the President: 1960*

U.S. novelist Joseph Heller's *Catch-22*

Jazz pianist Oscar Peterson, born in Montreal in 1925, became an influential performer in the jazz world and has won scores of awards.

Black American author James Baldwin's *Nobody Knows My Name*

Canadian Leonard Cohen's *The Spice Box* establishes him as most widely read Canadian poet of his day

U.S. playwright Tennessee Williams's *The Night of the Iguana*

British playwright Robert Bolt creates tribute to Sir Thomas More, *A Man for All Seasons*

"Today nothing is out because everything is in. Every costume from every era. . . . Nowadays the doorman doesn't know who to let in."

— Marshall McLuhan, 1968

World-renowned Spanish cellist Pablo Casals, 84, plays at a White House state dinner

Ballet dancer Rudolf Nureyev defects from the U.S.S.R.

1962

U.S. novelist William Faulkner's *The Reivers*

U.S. author John Steinbeck's *Travels With Charley: In Search of America*

Russian-born U.S. author Vladimir Nabokov's *Pale Fire*

U.S. writer Ken Kesey's novel *One Flew Over the Cuckoo's Nest*

German writer Günter Grass's *The Tin Drum* is published in North America

U.S. playwright Edward Albee's *Who's Afraid of Virginia Woolf?*

U.S. artist Andy Warhol's *Marilyn Monroe* and *Green Coca-Cola Bottles*

Montreal Symphony Orchestra becomes first Canadian symphony to tour Europe

1963

German-born U.S. political theorist Hannah Arendt's *Eichmann in Jerusalem: A Report on the Banality of Evil*

U.S. composer Samuel Barber wins Pulitzer Prize for *Piano Concerto No. 1*

Russian writer Alexander Solzhenitsyn creates his novel *One Day in the Life of Ivan Denisovitch*

U.S. feminist Betty Friedan criticizes the myth of the happy homemaker in her book *The Feminine Mystique*

British novelist John Le Carré's *The Spy Who Came In From the Cold*

U.S. poet Sylvia Plath's novel *The Bell Jar*

U.S. playwright Neil Simon's *Barefoot in the Park*

Pop art — in which everyday objects are used as subject matter or in the work itself — is given a major showing in New York City's Guggenheim Museum; works by Andy Warhol, Jasper Johns, Robert Rauschenberg, and Roy Lichtenstein exhibited

Russian-born dancer Rudolf Nureyev and British dancer Margot Fonteyn electrify audiences as ballet partners at the Royal Ballet in London

War Requiem, by English composer Benjamin Britten, is widely lauded

1964

U.S. writer Saul Bellow's novel *Herzog*

Canadian Marshall McLuhan's *Understanding the Media* establishes him as an international authority on communications

Canadian novelist Margaret Laurence's *Stone Angel*

Los Angeles County Museum of Art opens

U.S. writer Ernest Hemingway's *A Moveable Feast* published posthumously

U.S. artist Helen Frankenthaler's *Interior Landscape*

Russian-born French artist Marc Chagall finishes stained-glass panel for U.N. building in New York City in memory of Nobel Peace Prize winner and U.N. secretary-general Dag Hammarskjold

Los Angeles Music Center for the Performing Arts opens; 28-year-old Indian-born conductor Zubin Mehta leads the Los Angeles Philharmonic

1965

U.S. historian Arthur Schlesinger, Jr.'s, *The Thousand Days: John F. Kennedy in the White House*

Canadian Hubert Aquin's novel *Prochaine épisode* expresses revolutionary sympathies

U.S. sculptor Louise Nevelson's *An American Tribute to the British People*

U.S. playwright Neil Simon's *The Odd Couple*

Canadian poet Al Purdy's *The Cariboo Horses* wins Governor General's Award for Poetry

Canadian poet Jacques Brault's *Mémoire* is one of better volumes of poetry of Quebec nationalism

Canadian Phyliss Webb restores the long poem to Canadian attention with her collection, *Naked Poems*

U.S. artist George Segal's *The Diner*

Bestsellers: British spy novelist Ian Fleming's *Thunderball,* Robin Moore's *The Green Berets,* Arthur Hailey's *Hotel*

Op Art tours the U.S. in The Museum of Modern Art show, "The Responsive Eye"

Canadian singers Maureen Forester and Lois Marshall join Bach Aria Group

U.S. composer and conductor Leonard Bernstein and the New York Philharmonic begin a two-year retrospective program of 20th-century music

Canadian Orford String Quartet formed

1966

Canadian Margaret Atwood wins Governor General's Award for Poetry for *The Circle Game*

Canadian Leonard Cohen publishes novel *Beautiful Losers;* later translated into Danish, Dutch, French, German, Italian, Japanese, Norwegian, and Spanish

New Metropolitan Opera House, adorned with immense Marc Chagall murals, opens at New York's Lincoln Center with an all-star cast and top ticket price of $250; Samuel Barber's opera *Antony and Cleopatra* performed

Whitney Museum opens in New York City

U.S. writer Bernard Malamud's novel *The Fixer*

U.S. writer Jacqueline Susann's *Valley of the Dolls*

British playwright James Goldman completes *The Lion in Winter*

Canada and U.S. join efforts to save temples and statues in Abu Simbel, Egypt, from rising waters of Lake Nasser

Floods in northern Italy damage priceless Venetian and Florentine art treasures

1967

British ethnologist Desmond Morris's popular account of human evolution and behavior, *The Naked Ape*

Canadian Marshall McLuhan's *The Medium is the Message*

U.S. playwright Eugene O'Neill's *More Stately Mansions* opens on Broadway

U.S. avant-garde composers John Cage and Lejaren Hiller collaborate on *HPSCHD*, scored for 59 amplified channels and 7 harpsichords

Indian-born conductor Zubin Mehta begins world tour with Los Angeles Philharmonic

1968

U.S. playwright Neil Simon's *Plaza Suite*

Black American activist Eldridge Cleaver's *Soul on Ice*

U.S. writer Tom Wolfe's novel *The Electric Kool-Aid Acid Test*

Canadian novelist Roch Carrier's *La guerre, Yes Sir!*

Spermatogenesis II by Canadian sculptor Walter Redinger

The Temple of Dendur arrives from Egypt in 661 pieces to be reconstructed in The Metropolitan Museum of Art in New York

U.S. composer Philip Glass's *Piece in the Shape of a Square* is performed for first time in New York City

1969

U.S. writer Philip Roth's novel *Portnoy's Complaint*

U.S. writer Kurt Vonnegut's novel *Slaughterhouse Five*

U.S. writer Mario Puzo's bestselling *The Godfather*

Canadian poet and novelist Margaret Atwood's *The Edible Woman*

ENTERTAINMENT & SPORTS

1960

Camelot — with songs by lyricist Alan Jay Lerner and composer Frederick Loewe and starring Richard Burton, Julie Andrews, and Robert Goulet — opens on Broadway

British film director Alfred Hitchcock's *Psycho*

French film director François Truffaut's *Shoot the Piano Player*

Hit songs: "Theme From *A Summer Place*," "Never on Sunday," "Itsy Bitsy Teenie Weenie Yellow Polkadot Bikini"

Italian director Federico Fellini's *La Dolce Vita*, with Marcello Mastroianni

"Liberty without learning is always in peril and learning without liberty is always in vain."

— John F. Kennedy, Vanderbilt University, 1963

U.S. rock-and-roll star Chubby Checker popularizes hit dance the twist on Dick Clark's *American Bandstand*

The Fantasticks, starring Jerry Orbach, opens; becomes longest-running musical to date

Twenty-year-old folksinger and composer Bob Dylan ("Blowin' in the Wind," "The Times They Are A-Changin'," "Like a Rolling Stone") comes to New York, sings in Greenwich Village clubs

Black American entrepreneur Berry Gordy establishes Motown Records

On TV: *Route 66, My Three Sons, The Andy Griffith Show,* and first prime-time cartoon, *The Flintstones*

Black American sprinter Wilma Rudolph wins three gold medals at Rome Olympics

Ottawa Rough Riders win Grey Cup

Montreal Canadiens win Stanley Cup for record-breaking fifth straight year; Canadiens also hold best lifetime win record of any team in professional sport

1961

U.S. composer and lyricist Frank Loesser's musical *How to Succeed in Business Without Really Trying*

Audrey Hepburn and George Peppard star in film version of Truman Capote's *Breakfast at Tiffany's*

Clark Gable, Marilyn Monroe in *The Misfits,* the last film for both of them

On TV: *Dr. Kildare, Bonanza, The Dick Van Dyke Show, Wide World of Sports*

Roger Maris of New York Yankees hits 61 homers in 162 games; tops Babe Ruth's total of 60 homers in 154 games

Reacting to declining showings in international sport, Canada passes National Fitness and Amateur Sport Act to offer federal support to sports

Grey Cup won by Winnipeg Blue Bombers

Stanley Cup won by Chicago Black Hawks, interrupting domination by Montreal Canadiens

1962

"Four Strong Winds" by Canadians Ian and Sylvia (Ian Tyson and Sylvia Fricker) becomes international hit song; it was written by Ian

U.S. film director John Frankenheimer's political suspense thriller *The Manchurian Candidate*

U.S. actresses Bette Davis and Joan Crawford star in Robert Aldrich's *Whatever Happened to Baby Jane?*

U.S. movie actress Marilyn

Monroe dies; death ruled suicide

British director David Lean's *Lawrence of Arabia*

British actor Sean Connery plays first James Bond role in *Dr. No,* U.S. director Stanley Kubrick's film of Vladimir Nabokov's novel *Lolita*

Hit songs: "Blowin' in the Wind," "Walk On By," "Locomotion"

The Tonight Show with Johnny Carson premieres

Musical *Stop the World — I Want to Get Off,* with British actor Anthony Newley, opens on Broadway

Jackie Robinson is first black American inducted into the Baseball Hall of Fame

Basketball centre Wilt Chamberlain scores a record 100 points in a single game for the Philadelphia Warriors

Grey Cup game, held in Toronto, played over two days as dense fog covered field; Winnipeg Blue Bombers emerge from fog as winners

Stanley Cup won by Toronto Maple Leafs

1963

U.S. cartoonist Charles M. Schulz's Peanuts book *Happiness Is a Warm Puppy* is a bestseller

British-born film director Alfred Hitchcock's thriller *The Birds*

U.S. film director Stanley Kubrick's *Dr. Strangelove*

Rock-and-roll sensations the Beatles top the charts in Britain

Hit songs: "Puff (The Magic Dragon)," "If I Had a Hammer," "The Times They Are a-Changin'"

U.S. chef Julia Child makes *boeuf bourguignon* on TV; her cooking demonstrations give French cuisine a boost in North American kitchens

Stan "the Man" Musial retires after 22 seasons of baseball as a St. Louis Cardinal; his lifetime batting average is .331

Grey Cup won by Hamilton Tiger-Cats

WHAT IT COST

Prices: 1960

Daily newspapers, 5¢

Men's two-piece suits, luxury-tailored-to-measure, $74.50; overcoats, $55.60 to $100; cardigans, $13.88; pullover, $11.88; nylon hooded parka, $19.99; windbreakers with Borg lining, $16.99

Men's shoes, $15.95 to $18.95

Women's suit, $135 to $225; navy silk shirt-waist dress, $39.95; other dresses, $16.95 to $28.99; nylons, $1.39 to $1.65; girdles, $4.99 to $18.50

Women's shoes, $18.95

Philishave Speedflex for men, $19.88

Hemsley's diamond rings, ¼ carat, $82.25; ½ carat, $229.50; 1 carat, $689

Broccoli, 29¢ a large bunch; 10 lbs onions, turnips, beets, carrots, 69¢; 10 lbs potatoes, 49¢

All-purpose white flour, 25-lb paper bag, $1.79; Betty Crocker Angel Cake Mix, 59¢

Blueberry, mince, or raisin pies, 2 for $1

Blue Bonnet Margarine, 2 lbs for 55¢

LP records, $2.99

Tickets for movie *The Sound of Music*, $1.50 to $2.50

N.H.L., Toronto vs Canadiens, terrace seats $1.75; general admission, $1.50 and $1.75; tickets on the day, $1.25

Hillman cars, from $1,795

Vancouver, 3-bedroom post-and-beam house, $22,500

Toronto Maple Leafs win second consecutive Stanley Cup

1964

Hit songs: The Beatles' "I Want to Hold Your Hand," Roy Orbison's "Oh, Pretty Woman," Supremes' "Baby Love"

Gilles Vigneault composes "Mon Pays" which becomes immensely popular in Quebec; later sells well in U.S. as "From L.A. to New York, From New York to L.A."

Roger Maris connects at Yankee Stadium for his 61st home run of the season on October 1, 1961.

Hit musicals: *Hello, Dolly; Fiddler on the Roof; Funny Girl*

In discotheques, go-go girls dance the frug, monkey, watusi, funky chicken

On TV: *Peyton Place, The Munsters, Gilligan's Island, The Man From U.N.C.L.E., Flipper*

CBC's *This Hour Has Seven Days* dramatizes news, generates controversy

The Beatles tour the U.S., appear on the Ed Sullivan show; make their acting debut in *A Hard Day's Night;* their second film, *Help!,* appears a year later, and the animated feature *Yellow Submarine* appears in 1968

Anthony Quinn stars in *Zorba the Greek*

Elizabeth Taylor divorces singer Eddie Fisher; 10 days later marries Richard Burton, her costar in *Cleopatra*

Julie Andrews and Dick Van Dyke star in movie musical *Mary Poppins*

Northern Dancer becomes first Canadian-bred horse to win Kentucky Derby; its time of two minutes flat had been bettered only by Secretariat

Cassius Clay (later Muhammad Ali) knocks out Sonny Liston to win heavyweight boxing title

British Columbia Lions win Grey Cup

Stanley Cup won by Toronto Maple Leafs for third consecutive year

1965

Black American jazz singer Nat King Cole dies

British rock group the Rolling Stones come on strong with hit single "(I Can't Get No) Satisfaction"; mod husband-and-wife duo Sonny and Cher strike it big with a cover of Bob Dylan's "I Got You, Babe"; Beach Boys' "Help Me, Rhonda" is a hit

CBC begins long-running *Tommy Hunter Show,* featuring country singer Tommy Hunter of London, Ontario

Canadian singer Gordon Lightfoot composes "Early Morning Rain" for Ian and Sylvia; by early 1970's, Lightfoot is Canada's most popular male vocalist

The Sound of Music, movie musical starring Julie Andrews and Christopher Plummer

Man of La Mancha opens on Broadway

On TV: *Get Smart, Green Acres, I Spy, I Dream of Jeannie*

U.S. film director Sidney Lumet's *The Pawnbroker,* with Rod Steiger

Governor General Georges Vanier donates Vanier Cup for Canadian university football championship

Houston Astrodome, first roofed stadium, opens

Grey Cup won by Hamilton Tiger-Cats

Stanley Cup won by Montreal Canadiens

"This is the greatest week in the history of the world since the Creation."

— *President Richard M. Nixon, after the Moon landing, July 1969*

1966

Elizabeth Taylor and Richard Burton star in *Who's Afraid of Virginia Woolf?*

British actor Michael Caine plays title role in *Alfie*

French film director Jean-Luc Godard's masterpiece *Masculin-Féminin*

Hit songs: "Born Free," Simon and Garfunkel's "The Sounds of Silence," "Winchester Cathedral," the Beach Boys' "Good Vibrations"

Canadian Neil Young joins folk-rock group Buffalo Springfield; later teams up with Crosby, Stills and Nash

Walt Disney dies

America's Jim Ryun sets world record for the mile: 3 minutes 50 seconds

Cabaret opens on Broadway with Joel Grey and German actress Lotte Lenya; *Mame* opens with Angela Lansbury and Beatrice Arthur

First black coach of a professional sports team: Bill Russell of basketball's Boston Celtics

On TV: *Star Trek, The Dating Game, The Smothers Brothers' Comedy Hour, Mission Impossible, Batman*

CBC begins color television broadcasting; cancels popular *This Hour Has Seven Days*

Radio-Canada TV sit-com *Moi et l'autre* begins, draws 2,000,000 viewers by 1970

Grey Cup won by Saskatchewan Roughriders

Montreal Canadiens repeat as Stanley Cup winners

1967

Bonnie and Clyde, with Warren Beatty and Faye Dunaway

Mike Nichols's *The Graduate,* with music by Simon and Garfunkel, stars Dustin Hoffman and Anne Bancroft

Aretha Franklin tops the charts with "You Make Me Feel (Like a Natural Woman)"; other hit songs: Petula Clark's "To Sir With Love," "Windy," The Beatles' "Penny Lane," The Doors' "Light My Fire"

You're a Good Man, Charlie Brown opens on Broadway

The Phil Donahue Show premieres on TV

First Super Bowl: Green Bay Packers defeat Kansas City Chiefs 35–10

U.S. tennis player Billie Jean King reigns as top women's player

Grey Cup won by Hamilton Tiger-Cats

Miniskirts were barely a year old when this Paris model displayed her silvery kidskin outfit in 1966.

Stanley Cup won by Toronto Maple Leafs

1968

Motion Picture Association establishes voluntary G, M, R, and X rating system

Stanley Kubrick's *2001: A Space Odyssey*

French-born Polish director Roman Polanski's witchcraft film *Rosemary's Baby,* with Mia Farrow

U.S. director Mel Brooks's *The Producers*

Hit songs: Simon and Garfunkel's "Mrs. Robinson," Otis Redding's "Sittin' on the Dock of the Bay," O. C. Smith's "Little Green Apples"

Robert Charlebois brings "joual" (Quebec street slang mixing French and English forms) to popular music

Canadian rock band Guess Who launched in Winnipeg, changing name from earlier Chad Allen and the Expressions

On TV: *60 Minutes, Julia, Rowan and Martin's Laugh-In, The Mod Squad, The Dick Cavett Show*

Soap operas start expanding from 15 minutes to half-hour formats

The musical *Hair,* nudity and all, moves from Joseph Papp's Public Theater to Broadway

Ron Northcott from Alberta wins first "Silver Broom" world curling championship at Montreal

Ottawa Rough Riders win Grey Cup

Stanley Cup won by Montreal Canadiens

1969

Paul Newman and Robert Redford in *Butch Cassidy and the Sundance Kid*

Easy Rider, with Peter Fonda, Jack Nicholson, and Dennis Hopper

Oh! Calcutta! nude musical, opens on Broadway

Premiere of *Sesame Street* on public television

Hit songs: "Raindrops Keep Fallin' on My Head," "A Boy Named Sue," "Aquarius/Let

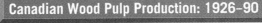

the Sunshine In," "Sugar, Sugar"

Canadian singer-songwriter Joni Mitchell's album "Clouds" wins Grammy award

Some 400,000 people gather on a 240-hectare dairy farm in Bethel, New York, for the Woodstock Music Festival

> *"Can't grown-ups understand? This music makes us go. It's what's happening!"*
>
> — Teenager, on rock and roll, 1965

Baseball's two major leagues are split into east and west divisions; division winners at end of season meet each other in play-offs for league pennant; winners of play-offs meet in World Series

Major league baseball comes to Montreal with Expos, first major league team to be formed outside the U.S.

Ottawa Rough Riders win second consecutive Grey Cup

Montreal Canadiens win second consecutive Stanley Cup

BUSINESS & ECONOMICS

1960

Canadian mineral production, less than $500 million in 1945, reaches $2.5 billion

Skyway Bridge opens, joining Prescott, Ontario, to Ogdensburg, New York; span is 2,235 metres

Halifax International Airport opens

Canadian National Railways redesigns logo; critics charge it is "tapeworm rampant"

54 percent of Canadian energy comes from petroleum, up from 33 percent in 1950

Chrysler's De Soto line is discontinued after 32 years

1961

Completion of 1,200-km Mackenzie Highway to Yellowknife, as Canada turns attention to northern development

Imperial Bank of Canada and Canadian Bank of Commerce merge

Texas Instruments patents silicon chip

Maraging steel, an alloy 10 times stronger than normal steel, introduced; finds use in making rockets and missiles

1962

American Airlines introduces computerized reservations

Trans-Canada Highway officially opened, the longest highway in North America, stretching for 7,307 kilometres

1963

Provincially owned Hydro-Quebec, formed in 1944, expands by taking over all private power companies in the province

Canada sells $500 million worth of wheat to the U.S.S.R.; it is the largest wheat sale in history

1964

Canada Student Loans Act provides government subsidies for chartered banks lending money to students

Boeing's 727 airliner debuts

First fully automated factory: Sara Lee plant in Deerfield, Illinois

Chesapeake Bay Bridge-Tunnel, 37 kilometres long, completed; Verrazano-Narrows Bridge, world's longest single-span suspension bridge (1,300 metres) to date, opens

Jimmy Hoffa, Teamsters Union president, convicted on corruption charges; is fined $10,000 and sentenced to eight years in prison; beginning in 1967

Strike against Toronto newspapers over their use of computers in typesetting

---

Canadian Wood Pulp Production: 1926–90

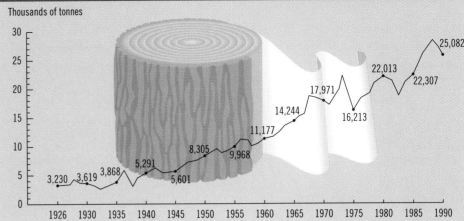

Thousands of tonnes

3,230 · 3,619 · 3,868 · 5,291 · 5,601 · 8,305 · 9,968 · 11,177 · 14,244 · 17,971 · 16,213 · 22,013 · 22,307 · 25,082

(1926 1930 1935 1940 1945 1950 1955 1960 1965 1970 1975 1980 1985 1990)

1965

Use of pure oxygen to reduce impurities in steelmaking is developed; open-hearth method declines

International Telephone and Telegraph (ITT) acquires the American Broadcasting Company (ABC) in major communications merger

Stock tickers are connected to computers for instant printout of transactions

Trans-Canada Airlines becomes Air Canada

U.S. labor leader Cesar Chavez organizes strikes and nationwide boycotts to win contracts from California grape growers

1967

Muriel Siebert is first woman to buy a seat on New York Stock Exchange

Public Broadcasting Service created to provide financial support for educational and noncommercial television and radio broadcasting

Major oil deposits are discovered in Alaska

Giant-screen IMAX cinema developed in Canada and first shown at Expo 67

Purse-seining of herring banned on Canada's west coast to avert depletion of fish stocks

Montreal's Expo 67 generates $480 million in tourist revenue

1968

N.Y. Stock Exchange trades over 16.4 million shares for first time since 1929

John Hancock Building completed in Chicago; at 343 metres, tallest multiuse structure in world

1969

The Peter Principle, a book by Laurence J. Peter and Raymond Hull, proposes that company employees rise to the level of their incompetence

Chevron Corporation offshore oil-well spill near Santa Barbara fouls California's coast, triggers public outrage

Full-time enrolment at Canadian postsecondary educational institutions more than doubles since 1960

British-French Concorde supersonic airliner (SST) makes maiden flight

Canadian rate of employment at record high levels as U.S. contracts for Vietnam war fuel Canadian industry

SCIENCE & MEDICINE

1960

First laser, high-intensity light beam, developed by U.S. scientist Theodore Maimen; first laser eye surgery performed two years later

---

Term *bionics* used by U.S. scientist J. E. Steel to describe creating devices and machines modelled on living organisms and their parts

Nuclear submarine *Triton* cruises underwater around the world

Pioneer 5 orbits sun, sends back radio signals

Team led by anthropologists Mary and Louis Leakey finds first *Homo habilis* fossils at Olduvai Gorge, Tanzania; human ancestor estimated to be 1.6 to 1.9 million years old

First underwater firing of Polaris, an intermediate range ballistic missile (IRBM) with nuclear warhead

Bathyscaphe *Trieste*, a navigable underwater ship for deep-sea exploration, descends 11,580 metres to the bottom of the Mariana Trench in the Pacific

1961

Yuri Gagarin, Russian cosmonaut, is first man in space

Astronaut Alan Shepard, Jr., America's first man in space, takes 15-minute suborbital flight

Earth found to be not a perfect sphere but a slightly irregular ellipsoid, based on information from Vanguard satellites

Oral polio vaccine, developed by Russian-born U.S.

Top-Rated Shows of TV's Golden Age (listed by average rating over the decade)

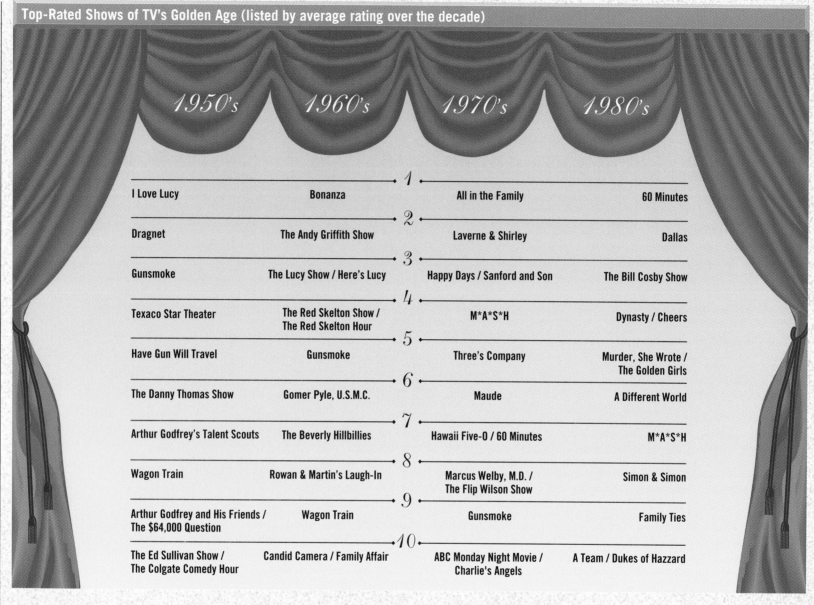

	1950's	1960's	1970's	1980's
1	I Love Lucy	Bonanza	All in the Family	60 Minutes
2	Dragnet	The Andy Griffith Show	Laverne & Shirley	Dallas
3	Gunsmoke	The Lucy Show / Here's Lucy	Happy Days / Sanford and Son	The Bill Cosby Show
4	Texaco Star Theater	The Red Skelton Show / The Red Skelton Hour	M*A*S*H	Dynasty / Cheers
5	Have Gun Will Travel	Gunsmoke	Three's Company	Murder, She Wrote / The Golden Girls
6	The Danny Thomas Show	Gomer Pyle, U.S.M.C.	Maude	A Different World
7	Arthur Godfrey's Talent Scouts	The Beverly Hillbillies	Hawaii Five-O / 60 Minutes	M*A*S*H
8	Wagon Train	Rowan & Martin's Laugh-In	Marcus Welby, M.D. / The Flip Wilson Show	Simon & Simon
9	Arthur Godfrey and His Friends / The $64,000 Question	Wagon Train	Gunsmoke	Family Ties
10	The Ed Sullivan Show / The Colgate Comedy Hour	Candid Camera / Family Affair	ABC Monday Night Movie / Charlie's Angels	A Team / Dukes of Hazzard

immunologist Albert Sabin, becomes available

Chimpanzee is transported 250 kilometres into space in successful Project Mercury suborbital test flight

The element Lawrencium is discovered by scientist Albert Ghiorso and his team

First intercontinental ballistic missile (ICBM) fired; travels 6,750 kilometres

Canadian nuclear research reactor, a gift to India, is officially opened near Bombay.

1962

Canadian spacecraft *Alouette* launched

John H. Glenn, Jr., first American in orbit, circles Earth three times; Scott Carpenter and Wally Schirra follow with orbital flights

U.S. scientist James Watson and British scientists Francis Crick and Maurice Wilkins share Nobel Prize for physiology or medicine

Dr. Frances O. Kelsey leads successful effort to ban thalidomide after babies with deformities are born to mothers who used the sedative

Satellite *Telstar 1* carries out communications tests

IBM introduces disk storage system for computers

Savannah, first nuclear-power surface ship, puts to sea

Mariner II launched to probe Venus

U.S. marine biologist and conservationist Rachel Carson publishes *Silent Spring*, a warning about the damage pesticides cause to the environment

1963

Russia's Valentina Tereshkova is first woman in space

Astronaut L. Gordon Cooper completes 22 orbits around Earth, first American to stay in space over 24 hours

Nobel Peace Prize awarded to U.S. chemist Dr. Linus C. Pauling; first person to hold two unshared prizes (Nobel Prize for chemistry in 1954 was his first)

First successful microcomputer, the PDP-8, is introduced by Digital Equipment Corporation

First quasar (quasi-stellar radiation source) identified; at that time it was the most distant object known

A home video recorder is demonstrated in London

1964

U.S. physicists Murray Gell-Mann and George Zweig propose quark theory positing that subatomic particles, including neutrons and protons, are made up of even smaller particles

IBM word processor that corrects and stores typing

Ranger VII produces close-up photos of Moon

Home kidney dialysis for diabetics

Green Revolution: new rice strain bolsters food supply in underdeveloped countries

TV transmission via stationary satellite used to relay Tokyo Olympic Games to North America

1965

U.S. astronaut Edward White takes "space walks"

Mariner IV transmits close-up pictures of Mars

Measles vaccine

World's first working commercial communications satellite, *Early Bird*

1966

First successful artificial heart pump implanted in a patient at Methodist Hospital, Houston, Texas

First direct-dial transatlantic phone call

Surveyor I soft-lands on Moon; sends back more than 11,000 photos of lunar surface

U.S. physician William Masters and his research associate, Virginia Johnson, publish *Human Sexual Response*

Boreholes cut into Greenland glacier date ice layers; bottom layer is more than 150,000 years old

1967

Launch pad fire at Cape Kennedy, Florida, kills Apollo astronauts Virgil I. (Gus) Grissom, Edward H. White II, and Roger B. Chaffee

Dolby device invented; filters out background noise in audio recordings

U.S. surgeon René Favalero introduces coronary artery bypass operation

Cholesterol named a factor in heart disease

South African surgeon Dr. Christiaan Barnard performs first human heart transplant operation

1968

Medicare (universal medical and hospital insurance) goes into effect in Canada

Nobel Prize for Medicine to Gobind Khorana for work begun at British Columbia Research Centre

Apollo 8: first manned flight around Moon

Geneticist James Watson's *The Double Helix*, about the discovery of the structure of DNA, is a bestseller

Theory of plate tectonics introduced by U.S. scientists; explains origin of mountain chains, distribution of earthquakes and volcanoes, development of ocean basins

Vaccine against meningitis

1969

Composition of hemoglobin in human blood determined

Cyclamates, used in artificial sweeteners, banned because of possible harmful effects

U.S. engineer invents first microprocessor, the Intel 4004

"We have always said that in our war with the Arabs we had a secret weapon — no alternative."

— *Golda Meir, prime minister of Israel, October 3, 1969*

Bubble memory invented: computers now can retain data when turned off

The element Hahnium discovered by scientist Albert Ghiorso and his team

Astronaut Neil A. Armstrong becomes first man to walk on the Moon; his *Apollo 11* crewmates are Edwin E. (Buzz) Aldrin, Jr., and Michael Collins; 100 million viewers

The Apollo 11 lunar landing, on July 20, 1969, was followed by five more landings, ending with the Apollo 17 mission in December 1972.

worldwide watch live TV broadcast from Moon

WORLD POLITICAL EVENTS

1960

Soviet premier Nikita Khrushchev visits U.N. General Assembly in New York

Belgian Congo gains independence, followed by nearly 20 other European colonies in the 1960's

Israelis capture Nazi Adolf Eichmann in Argentina; he is convicted of war crimes in 1961 and hanged in 1962

Organization of Petroleum Exporting Countries (OPEC) is founded by third-world oil-producing countries to oversee production and prices

South Vietnam established

1961

East German authorities erect Berlin Wall

U.S.S.R. resumes nuclear testing

U.N. secretary-general Dag Hammarskjold killed in air crash in the Congo

U Thant of Burma is named third U.N. secretary-general

1962

East and West Pakistan established

Pope John XXIII convenes Vatican Council II to renew Roman Catholic doctrine and religious life

Rebel French Army officers, opposed to a free Algeria, fire on President Charles de Gaulle's car near Paris; Algeria gains independence

1963

South Vietnamese government overthrown in coup; Ngo Dinh Diem assassinated

Pope John XXIII dies; Pope Paul VI succeeds him

Profumo crisis in Britain: cabinet officer John Profumo forced to resign in sex scandal involving call girls Christine Keeler and Mandy Rice-Davies; Profumo's friend, Stephen Ward, called a procurer, commits suicide

1964

Khrushchev ousted as Soviet premier; replaced by Alexei Kosygin, who shares power with Leonid Brezhnev

Yasir Arafat leads Arab Al Fatah guerrillas against Israelis

Jawaharlal Nehru, India's first prime minister, dies

Emerging African nations: Kenya, Tanzania, Zambia

1965

Winston Churchill dies

Pope Paul VI visits United States

Civil war erupts in Dominican Republic; LBJ sends U.S. troops

Rhodesia declares independence from Britain

1966

Cultural Revolution in China; Red Guards formed

France withdraws almost completely from NATO military affairs; NATO headquarters moved from Paris to Brussels the next year

Prime Minister Hendrik Verwoerd of South Africa assassinated; John Vorster succeeds him

Indira Gandhi, Nehru's daughter, becomes prime minister of India

Svetlana Alliluyeva, Soviet dictator Joseph Stalin's daughter, defects to West

1967

Arab-Israeli Six-Day War: responding to attacks by its Arab neighbors, Israel occupies territories within Egypt, Jordan, and Syria; occupies all of Jerusalem

Ché Guevara, Cuban revolutionary leader, killed in Bolivia

French president de Gaulle calls for a "free Quebec"

1968

Clashes between Catholics and Protestants in Northern Ireland escalate

Alexander Dubcek's democratic reforms in Czechoslovakia culminate in Prague Spring; Soviet and Warsaw Pact troops crush dissent; Dubcek arrested

1969

Strategic Arms Limitation Talks (SALT) held in Helsinki, Finland; U.S. and U.S.S.R. have preliminary discussions about limiting nuclear arms

France's President de Gaulle resigns; Georges Pompidou succeeds him

Soviets and Chinese clash in Manchuria

Yasir Arafat heads Palestine Liberation Organization; Golda Meir is prime minister in Israel

Willy Brandt becomes West German chancellor

NORTH AMERICAN HISTORY & POLITICS

1970

Prime Minister Pierre Trudeau proclaims War Measures Act, giving government emergency powers to deal with FLQ terrorism in Quebec; British trade commissioner James Cross is kidnapped and detained; Quebec cabinet minister Pierre Laporte is murdered, James Cross is later freed

Bearing the seals of the 13 original states under a 50-star flag, a float glides past the Library of Congress on America's 200th, July 4, 1976.

U.S. and South Vietnamese forces attack North Vietnamese military bases in Cambodia

National Security Adviser Henry Kissinger begins secret peace talks with Hanoi

National Guard troops, called out to quell student demonstrations, panic and open fire, killing four antiwar protesters at Kent State University in Ohio; hundreds of colleges close in sympathy

Report of the Royal Commission on the Status of Women released in Canada

As concern for environment increases, The Sierra Club is established in Canada

U.S. population 203 million, Canada's population over 21 million, 724,000 of them are immigrants of the 1960's

1971

Vietnam: Lt. William Calley, Jr., found guilty of murder for My Lai massacre; U.S. forces fight in Cambodia and Laos, bomb and mine North Vietnamese targets; U.S. troops down to 140,000

Prime Minister Pierre Trudeau marries Margaret Sinclair

Canada Development Corporation established to encourage investment in Canadian-controlled companies; major investments are in petroleum, petro-chemicals and mining

Canadian Senate publishes report on poverty

1972

National Action Committee on the Status of Women established, umbrella organization for women's groups across Canada; to lobby for recommendations of Royal Commission on the Status of Women

Pierre Trudeau's federal Liberals come second in federal general election at 107 seats to Conservatives' 109, but maintain power through alliance with 31 NDP

Nixon visits China; U.S.-China joint communiqué pledges normalization of relations; Nixon becomes first U.S. president to visit Moscow

Watergate break-in: police arrest five men inside Democratic National Committee headquarters in Washington, D.C.; cover-up by members of Nixon's staff begins

President Richard Nixon and Vice President Spiro Agnew reelected, winning 60.7 percent of the popular vote and 520 electoral votes

1973

Vietnam cease-fire signed in Paris; last U.S. troops leave Vietnam; prisoners of war released in Hanoi; sporadic fighting continues between North and South Vietnam

OPEC oil embargo creates energy crisis in Canada and U.S.

Canadian peacekeeping troops sent to Middle East to serve with U.N. Emergency Task Force; observers sent to Golan Heights

Supreme Court of Canada gives limited recognition to aboriginal rights in Nishga case claiming land in Nass Valley, northern British Columbia

Parti Québécois becomes official Opposition party in Quebec

American Indian Movement (AIM) protesters occupy village of Wounded Knee, South Dakota, where in 1890 U.S. Cavalry killed more than 150 Sioux

Watergate scandal: Senate committee holds TV hearings; former White House counsel John Dean implicates Nixon and others; presidential advisers John Ehrlichman and H. R. Haldeman and former Attorney General John Mitchell eventually indicted and go to jail; White House releases tapes of discussions between Nixon and staff after Watergate break-in; tapes have gaps

1974

Watergate: House Judiciary Committee votes to impeach Nixon, who then resigns; Gerald Ford becomes 38th president; Nelson Rockefeller, vice president

Canada creates Foreign Investment Review Agency to establish some control over foreign investment in Canada

Trudeau Liberals win majority with 141 seats in federal general election; Conservatives win 95, NDP 16, Social Credit 11

Pauline McGibbon becomes first woman lieutenant-governor (for Ontario) in Commonwealth

1975

Vietcong and North Vietnamese triumph in South Vietnam, take Saigon; last Americans evacuated

Province of Alberta creates Alberta Heritage Fund with government oil revenues

Land settlement reached with native Cree of James Bay region

❤

> *"What did the president know and when did he know it?"*
>
> — *Senator Howard Baker, at the Watergate hearings, June 1973*

❤

Ottawa creates Petro-Canada to monitor practices of petroleum industry

CN Tower is completed; tallest free-standing structure in world at 553 metres high

Federal government imposes wage and price controls in effort to stop inflation

America's *Apollo 18* links up with Soviets' *Soyuz 19*; astronauts and cosmonauts hold joint news conference from space

1976

Berger commission recommends delay in building Canada's Mackenzie Valley pipeline until native land claims are discussed

Parti Québécois wins Quebec general election, forms government with René Lévesque as premier and promises referendum on separation

U.S. celebrates Bicentennial; millions watch "tall ships" enter New York Harbor

Jimmy Carter elected 39th president with Walter Mondale as vice president; they defeat Gerald Ford and Robert Dole

1977

Bill 101 makes French official language of Quebec, severely restricts access to English-language schools as well as limiting use of English in public and in work-place

Canadian Human Rights Act extends rights guarantees

Ottawa passes Established Programmes Financing Act to improve quality of public services in poorer provinces

Human rights becomes cornerstone of Carter's foreign policy

Carter declares a national energy crisis; Congress adopts Carter's proposal to establish a Department of Energy

1978

Carter arranges Camp David talks on Mideast peace between Egypt's Anwar Sadat and Israel's Menachem Begin

U.S. agrees to give up Panama Canal by year 2000

Soviet nuclear-powered satellite crashes in northern Canada

1979

Joe Clark leads Conservatives to form minority government with 136 seats; Liberals have 114, NDP win 26, and Social Credit 6

Beginning of dramatic increase of Asian immigration to Canada, from less than 25,000 people in 1978–79 to more than 62,000 ten years later, in 1979-80

Carter administration reels under *stagflation* (stagnant economic growth, high inflation), caused in part by surge in oil prices

Three Mile Island nuclear reactor in Pennsylvania suffers near meltdown; accident casts doubt on future of nuclear energy as an alternative to fossil fuels

Worst air disaster to date in U.S. history: 275 die in Chicago DC-10 crash; all DC-10's are grounded to check for possible accident-causing design flaws

EVERYDAY LIFE

1970

U.S. chemist and two-time Nobel Prize winner Linus Pauling advocates huge doses of vitamin C to combat colds and flu

Health foods gain favor with health-conscious North Americans

Price of gold drops below official standard of $35 an ounce

The Beatles break up

1971

76.1 percent of Canadians live in cities

"It occurred to me when I was 13 and wearing white gloves and Mary Janes and going to dancing school, that no one should have to dance backwards all their lives."

— Feminist Jill Ruckelshaus, 1973

Cigarette advertisements are banned from U.S. television

Ontario adopts advanced legislation to protect endangered species

In Canada's larger cities, proportion of those living in poverty is increasing

California is first in U.S. to adopt standards reducing lead emissions in gasoline

Hot pants, shag haircuts, and midi skirts arrive on the scene

1972

Canada plays prominent role in United Nations Conference on the Human Environment

Ms. magazine, focusing on changing aspirations of women, founded; *Life* magazine suspends regular publication

Hurricane Agnes hits eastern U.S. killing 118

First woman rabbi ordained

Pocket calculators hit the market with hefty price tags starting at $100; prices to be driven down in following years by calculator glut

1973

Gasoline shortages precipitate energy crisis

Airline passengers screened in an effort to halt rash of skyjackings

Sears Tower is completed in Chicago; at 443 metres it is tallest building in the world to date

"Gatsby" look is popular, inspired by new film version of *The Great Gatsby*

1974

Heiress Patricia Hearst kidnapped; later joins radical

Symbionese Liberation Army; captured by FBI agents in 1975 and convicted for robbery in 1976; released in 1979, after President Carter commuted her sentence, having served 22 months in prison

Mikhail Baryshnikov, Soviet ballet star, defects to Canada

Running naked at public events (streaking) becomes a fad

Speed limit on U.S. roads set at 55 m.p.h. (88 kph) to conserve fuel

Smog effects: up to 4,000 deaths and 1 million lost workdays annually attributed to tailpipe exhaust, according to EPA

1975

Mirabel International Airport, world's largest at the time, opens near Montreal

Unemployment rate in Canada reaches 7 percent

Four women are ordained Episcopal priests in Washington

Teamster leader Jimmy Hoffa disappears

Energy crisis continues due to oil embargo

Pet rocks and mood rings are popular fads

Van McCoy's number one single, "The Hustle," starts dance craze of the same name

WHAT IT COST

Prices: 1970

Men's blazers, $110; business shirts, $13.50

Mink coats, $1,295

Adidas running shoes, $15.88

Sheets & pillowcases, $2.99 to $6.59

5-piece teak dining-room suite, $288

Convertible couches, $298 to $398

Stereo system, $595

Sanyo Super 8 movie camera, $219.95

Sony digital clock-radio, $59.95

Hertz rental car, free mileage, $11.95 a day

Datsun 1200 Sedan, $1,975

Mississauga, 4-bedroomed condo, $91,900

West Vancouver, 3-bedroomed house, $54,900

Five Most Inflationary Years Since 1960

Canadian Consumer Price Index, Annual Percentage Changes (1986 = 100)

ALL ITEMS

1974	1975	1980	1981	1982
10.8%	10.8	10.2	12.4	10.9

FOOD

1974	1975	1980	1981	1982
16.4%	12.8	10.7	11.4	7.2

HOUSING

1974	1975	1980	1981	1982
8.9%	9.9	8.1	12.4	12.5

TRANSPORT

1974	1975	1980	1981	1982
10.0%	11.6	12.8	18.4	14.0

MEDICAL

1974	1975	1980	1981	1982
8.5%	11.5	9.9	10.9	10.6

CLOTHING

1974	1975	1980	1981	1982
9.5%	6.0	11.8	7.1	5.6

1976

Women get Rhodes Scholarships for the first time

Barbara Walters becomes first woman news anchor, makes $1-million deal

Rev. Sun Myung Moon's Unification Church accused of brainwashing its members by parents of "Moonies"

Canadian-born British newspaper publisher Roy Thomson dies

Billionaire Howard Hughes dies a recluse

Swine flu is cited as a danger by the Center for Disease Control

Shere Hite's *The Hite Report: A Nationwide Study of Female Sexuality* is a bestseller

Fashion notes: designer Diane von Furstenberg's jersey wrap dresses; ethnic chic; wedge haircuts inspired by Olympic gold medallist Dorothy Hamill are popular

Concorde supersonic transport begins commercial run between Washington, D.C., and Europe

1977

Blackout in New York City leaves 9 million without electricity for up to 25 hours; looting results in 3,700 arrests

Exodus of business and English-speaking people from Montreal begins in wake of Bill 101

Elvis Presley dies in Memphis, Tennessee, at age 42

Convicted murderer Gary Gilmore refuses to appeal his death sentence; executed by firing squad in Utah; first capital punishment in U.S. since 1967

Screen legend, Charlie Chaplin ("The Little Tramp") dies

Disco nightclub, Studio 54, opens in Manhattan

Transcendental meditation, yoga, Eastern religious movements captivate many across Canada and U.S.

Ottawa ends program, begun in 1950, to lend money for home-building to veterans

Pierre Trudeau, Margaret Sinclair separate

Highway signs throughout most of Canada become metric

Diane Keaton character in movie *Annie Hall* inspires new look: floppy hats, long skirts, large glasses, clunky boots

1978

Mass suicide in Guyana: some 900 Americans kill themselves on orders of their cult leader, Jim Jones, who also dies

Love Canal area, near Niagara Falls, New York, evacuated because of toxic waste contamination

Mississauga, Ontario, evacuated because of derailed tanker containing chlorine and other chemicals

Jim Fixx's *The Complete Book of Running* is a bestseller

The last Volkswagen Beetle is made in Germany

1979

Sony Walkman introduced

The Complete Scarsdale Medical Diet and *The Pritikin Program for Diet and Exercise* become bestsellers

Soaring inflation, worst since 1946, creates great anxiety; investors flee to gold, driving price above $500 an ounce

Roller disco skating becomes popular pastime

ARTS & LETTERS

1970

Canadian Robertson Davies' novel, *Fifth Business*

Canadian Pierre Berton's best-seller, *The National Dream*

Canadian Brass Quintet is formed

Canadian John Glassco's *Memoirs of Montparnasse* appears as a masterpiece of autobiography

U.S. writer Saul Bellow's novel *Mr. Sammler's Planet*

U.S. writer James Dickey's *Deliverance*, later made into a film starring Jon Voight and Burt Reynolds

British playwright Anthony Shaffer's thriller *Sleuth* opens on Broadway; later (1972) a Hollywood movie

U.S. playwright Neil Simon's *Last of the Red-Hot Lovers* opens on Broadway

U.S. painter Alice Neel's *Andy Warhol*

♥

"Dare to be naive."

— Buckminster Fuller, 1975

♥

U.S. designer Buckminster Fuller receives award from American Institute of Architects for his geodesic domes — large, lightweight, prefabricated structures

1971

English novelist and essayist E. M. Forster's *Maurice*, written in 1914, published after author's death in 1970

U.S. writer Erich Segal's bestselling tale of young lovers facing fatal illness, *Love Story*

U.S. novelist Herman Wouk's *The Winds of War*

Russian novelist Alexander Solzhenitsyn's *August 1914*, about the Russian defeat by the Germans at Tannenberg early in World War I

Pierre Berton's *The Last Spike* completes story of the construction of the C.P.R.

Canadian Alice Munro's *Lives of Girls and Women*, a collection of connected short stories

U.S. artist Nancy Graves's *Pacific Ocean Floor, 150 Miles Out*

U.S. composer Leonard Bernstein's *Mass*, specially commissioned for the occasion, is performed at the opening of the John F. Kennedy Center for the Performing Arts in Washington, D.C.

1972

Treemonisha, a ragtime opera written by Scott Joplin (1868–1917) in 1911 and performed just once in New York City's Harlem, is revived in Atlanta, Georgia

First volume of Lester B. Pearson's autobiography, *Mike*, appears; completed by 1975

James Gray's *Booze*, a history of alcohol in the Canadian West

U.S. composer Aaron Copland's *Three Latin-American. Sketches*

U.S. painter Andrew Wyeth's *Bale*

U.S. regionalist painter Thomas Hart Benton's *Turn of the Century Joplin*

Michelangelo's *Pietà*, in St. Peter's basilica in Rome, is damaged by a maniac with a hammer

1973

Canadian Richard Rohmer's *Ultimatum*, a novel of disaster based on current events in politics and business

Canadian Rudy Wiebe's novel, *The Temptations of Big Bear*, draws on native oral history

Canadian Alden Nowlan's *Various Persons Named Kevin O'Brien*

Halfbreed, autobiography of Canadian Maria Campbell

U.S. novelist Thomas Pynchon's *Gravity's Rainbow*

U.S. journalist David Halberstam's *The Best and the Brightest*

U.S. poet Robert Lowell's collection *The Dolphin*

Russian novelist Alexander Solzhenitsyn publishes the first of his three-volume (1973–76) *The Gulag Archipelago*; Soviet authorities strip him of his citizenship, and he settles in U.S. in 1976

U.S. sculptor Duane Hanson's *Janitor* and other hypernaturalistic pieces

U.S. painter Alfred Leslie's *A View of Sunderland From Mt. Sugarloaf*

U.S. painter Helen Frankenthaler's *Nature Abhors a Vacuum*

Canadian-born Robert MacNeil, co-anchor of the MacNeil/Lehrer Report on U.S. television in 1975.

English composer Benjamin Britten's opera *Death in Venice*

U.S. composer Walter Piston's orchestral work *Fantasia* performed

1974

Tinker, Tailor, Soldier, Spy, newest spy novel by English writer John Le Carré (pen name of David John Moore Cornwell) is best-seller

U.S. novelist Erica Jong's *Fear of Flying*

U.S. author Robert Pirsig's *Zen and the Art of Motorcycle Maintenance*

Canadian Doris Anderson's novel, *Two Women*, is published

Ralph Gustafson wins Governor General's Award for *Fire and Stone*, a collection of poetry

Canadian Margaret Laurence's *A Jest of God*, one of her 'Manawaka' novels; later a film as *Rachel, Rachel*

U.S. journalists Carl Bernstein and Bob Woodward's *All the President's Men*, an account of the Watergate scandal

English-born U.S. poet W. H. Auden's collection *Thank You, Fog: Last Poems*, published the year after Auden's death

British playwright Peter Shaffer's *Equus* opens on Broadway

U.S. painter Chuck Close's *Robert/104,072*

U.S. sculptor Alexander Calder's *Universe* mounted in Chicago's Sears Tower

1975

U.S. writer E. L. Doctorow's novel *Ragtime*

British novelist Richard Adams's *Watership Down*, about a community of humanlike rabbits that faces crisis and tragedy

U.S. novelist Robert Stone's *Dog Soldiers*, mixing drugs and the Vietnam War

British playwright Tom Stoppard's *Travesties* opens on Broadway

Peter C. Newman's *The Canadian Establishment*

William Stevenson's true spy story, *A Man Called Intrepid*, is Canadian best-seller

French composer Hector Berlioz's nearly 140-year-old opera *Benvenuto Cellini* is performed for the first time in the U.S.

1976

U.S. writer Alex Haley combines fact and fiction in his book *Roots: The Saga of an American Family* to tell of his search for his African forebears

British novelist Paul Scott's *The Raj Quartet*, about India under British rule

U.S. painter Audrey Flack's still life *Queen*, combining, like many other notable works of the period, traditional painting and photography

U.S. painter Jennifer Bartlett completes her 48-metre-long work, *Rhapsody*, which contains 988 30-cm-square metal units depicting variations on themes such as trees, mountains, oceans, and houses

U.S. composer Philip Glass and artist Robert Wilson's collaborative opera *Einstein on the Beach*

1977

Australian novelist Colleen McCullogh's *The Thorn Birds*

U.S. writer Joan Didion's *A Book of Common Prayer*

U.S. playwright David Mamet's *American Buffalo*

Radio Canada International

begins recording its *Anthology* series, works by Canadian composers for international distribution

U.S. artist Nicholas Africano's *The Cruel Discussion*

U.S. poet James Merrill's complex, intellectually far-ranging verse work *Divine Comedies*

English author and scholar J.R.R. Tolkien's *The Silmarillion* is published; a story begun in 1917 of his fantasy world called Middle-Earth and finished, after Tolkien's death in 1973 by his son Christopher

Polish composer Henryk Gòrecki's *Symphony No. 3*, completed the year before, premieres at Royan, France; dealing with the suffering of World War II, the symphony achieves worldwide fame in the early 1990's

1978

U.S. writer William Manchester's *American Caesar: Douglas MacArthur 1880–1964*

♥

"Future shock . . . the shattering stress and disorientation that we induce in individuals by subjecting them to too much change in too short a time."

— *Alvin Toffler in* Future Shock *(1970)*

♥

U.S. author James Michener's *Chesapeake;* like many of his books, a study of a region's history and people

John Howard Gray's two-man drama, *Billy Bishop Goes to War*, based on the war career of Canada's most famous fighter pilot

1979

Peter Desbarats and Terry Mosher (Aislin), *The Hecklers*, a history of political cartooning in Canada

Antonine Maillet, *Pélagie-la-Charette*, first Canadian novel to win Prix Goncourt in France

U.S. writer Tom Wolfe's *The Right Stuff*, about America's first group of astronauts

U.S. historian and social critic Christopher Lasch's *The Culture of Narcissism* portrays Americans as self-absorbed, celebrity dazzled, and guilt ridden

English writer John Le Carré's *Smiley's People*

Paule Saint-Onge's *La Vie défigurée*, autobiography from feminist perspective

ENTERTAINMENT & SPORTS

1970

The Bootmakers of Toronto form for serious study of the life of Sherlock Holmes

Company opens on Broadway, first of several collaborations by composer-lyricist Stephen Sondheim and producer-director Harold Prince

U.S. cartoonist Garry Trudeau's comic strip *Doonesbury* debuts

The Mary Tyler Moore Show, The Partridge Family, The Odd Couple, and *The Flip Wilson Show* are among the premieres on TV

Canadian film *Goin' Down the Road* is commercial and artistic success

Number one singles: Jackson 5's "I Want You Back," "ABC"; Simon and Garfunkel's "Bridge Over Troubled Waters"; Carpenters' "Close to You"

Canadian singer Anne Murray records *Snowbird*

Kansas City Chiefs (AFL) defeat Minnesota Vikings (NFL) 23 to 7 in Super Bowl IV at Tulane Stadium, New Orleans, Louisiana

Monday Night Football, featuring games between professional teams, premieres; announcers are Howard Cosell and Don Meredith

Merger of National Football League (NFL) and American Football League (AFL), negotiated in 1966, takes effect; National Football League now has two divisions: National Football Conference (NFC) and American Football Conference (AFC)

Arthur Ashe lifts the victory cup after defeating Jimmy Connors to win Wimbledon's singles in 1975.

U.S. yacht *Intrepid* wins the America's Cup

Grey Cup won by Montreal Alouettes

Stanley Cup won by Boston Bruins

1971

Canadian musical *Anne of Green Gables* opens on Broadway and has highly successful run

Claude Jutras' *Mon Oncle Antoine* is hailed as one of finest Canadian films ever made

Barbara Frum brings listeners back to CBC radio with *As it Happens*

Broadway musical *Follies*, music and lyrics by Stephen Sondheim, produced and directed by Harold Prince

U.S. movie director Stanley Kubrick's *A Clockwork Orange*, based on the 1962 novel by English author Anthony Burgess

George C. Scott's performance in *Patton* wins him an Oscar

New on TV: *All in the Family, Columbo, The Sonny and Cher Comedy Hour;* and from the British Broadcasting Corporation: *Masterpiece Theatre*

Bestselling album: Carol King's *Tapestry;* hit singles: "One Bad Apple," "Joy to the World," "Maggie May," "Theme From Shaft"

Baltimore Colts (AFC) defeat Dallas Cowboys (NFC) 16 to 13 in Super Bowl V at Orange Bowl Stadium, Miami, Florida

Billie Jean King, tennis star, becomes first woman athlete to capture $100,000 a year in prize money for competition

Returning to boxing after being stripped of his heavyweight title in 1967 for refusing military service, Muhammad Ali loses to Joe Frazier, who keeps the world heavyweight title

World Hockey Association is formed; breaks N.H.L. monopoly of major league hockey and leads to increase in players' salaries

Calgary Stampeders win Grey Cup

Montreal Canadiens win Stanley Cup

1972

Liza Minnelli and Joel Grey star in Hollywood musical *Cabaret*, set in 1930's Berlin

U.S. director Francis Ford Coppola's movie *The Godfather*

Marlon Brando in the steamy, controversial *Last Tango in Paris*

Broadway musical *Jesus Christ*

487

Superstar; later becomes a Hollywood movie (1973)

Swedish film director Ingmar Bergman's *Cries and Whispers*

*M*A*S*H* premieres on TV

Canadian Bruno Gerussi appears as Nick Adonidas on CBC television's *The Beachcombers*

Hit singles: "I Am Woman," "American Pie," "Let's Stay Together," "Candy Man"

Dallas Cowboys (NFC) defeat Miami Dolphins (AFC) 24 to 3 in Super Bowl VI at Tulane Stadium, New Orleans, Louisiana

Professional baseball players strike; start of season delayed 13 days

U.S. swimmer Mark Spitz wins 7 gold medals at the 1972 Olympics in Munich

Bobby Fischer captures world chess title from Boris Spassky of the Soviet Union

Canadian Football Hall of Fame opens at Hamilton, Ontario

Canadian professional hockey players edge Soviet team in Canada-Russia series, 4–3–1; first hockey series between Canada and U.S.S.R.

Hamilton Tiger-Cats win Grey Cup

Boston Bruins win Stanley Cup

1973

Composer-lyricist Stephen Sondheim and producer-director Harold Prince's *A Little Night Music* opens on Broadway

New York City judge rules pornographic film *Deep Throat* obscene and bans it; film goes on to make $30 million

French director François Truffaut's *Day for Night*

Paul Newman and Robert Redford star as 1940's cardsharps in *The Sting*

U.S. film director George Lucas produces *American Graffiti*

Top songs: "Tie a Yellow Ribbon," "You're So Vain," "Killing Me Softly With His Song," "Rocky Mountain High"

American League introduces Designated Hitter (DH) to bat for pitcher: DH only hits, does not play a field position; pitcher only pitches, does not bat

Ottawa Rough Riders win Grey Cup

Montreal Canadiens win Stanley Cup

1974

Polish director Roman Polanski's Hollywood movie *Chinatown,* starring Jack Nicholson and Faye Dunaway

Movie, *The Apprenticeship of Duddy Kravitz,* made from book by Mordecai Richler, successfully combines Canadian and U.S. talent; debut of Richard Dreyfuss

British import *Upstairs, Downstairs* debuts on TV; *The Autobiography of Miss Jane Pittman* wins an Emmy

Barbra Streisand's "The Way We Were," Hues Corporation's "Rock the Boat" are number-one hits

Muhammad Ali regains world heavyweight boxing title by knocking out George Foreman

Hank Aaron tops Babe Ruth's lifetime mark of 714 home runs; he will reach 755 before retiring after the 1976 season

Frank Robinson of the Cleveland Indians becomes first black to manage a major league team, the Cleveland Indians

Montreal Alouettes win Grey Cup

Philadelphia Flyers, capitalizing on physical style of play, win Stanley Cup

1975

U.S. movie director Steven Spielberg's *Jaws*

Robert Altman's film *Nashville*

One Flew Over the Cuckoo's Nest wins Academy Awards for best picture; best director, Milos Forman; best actor, Jack Nicholson; and best actress, Louise Fletcher

Canadian film, *Lies My Father Told Me,* is released

A Chorus Line opens on Broadway

British-made film *The Rocky Horror Picture Show* lampoons old monster movies, wins cult following

On TV: *Saturday Night Live*

CBC television's *King of Kensington* starring Al Waxman, appears

Golfer Jack Nicklaus wins fifth Masters title

Arthur Ashe, the first black man to attain number one ranking in tennis (1968), defeats heavily favored fellow American Jimmy Connors to win the Wimbledon singles tennis championship

Casey Stengel dies at 85, former player (1912–25) and manager (Brooklyn Dodgers, Boston Braves, New York Yankees, New York Mets) whose clowning, colorful double-talk, and winning teams made him a baseball legend

Team Canada wins first Canada Cup hockey series

Edmonton Eskimos win Grey Cup

Philadelphia Flyers win Stanley Cup

1976

Canadian rock group *The Band* holds farewell concert which becomes basis for film, *The Last Waltz*

Sylvester Stallone in the first of the *Rocky* movies

Taxi Driver, with Robert de Niro as a bitter Vietnam veteran

Dustin Hoffman and Robert Redford in the film version of Woodward and Bernstein's book *All the President's Men*

John Wayne's last film, *The Shootist;* he dies at 72 three years later

British rock star Peter Frampton's album *Frampton Comes Alive* goes gold

Jimmy Connors wins U.S. Open men's tennis singles title; Chris Evert wins women's singles

Summer Olympics held in Montreal; Canada wins only 11 medals (no gold); Romanian gymnast Nadia Comaneci wins 3 gold medals, has 7 perfect scores for the first

occasions on which perfect scores are awarded at Olympics

Kathy Kreiner wins giant slalom gold medal for Canada at Innsbruck winter Olympics

Ottawa Rough Riders win Grey Cup

♥

"I'm as mad as hell, and I'm not going to take it anymore."

— From the movie Network *(1976)*

♥

Montreal Canadiens win Stanley Cup

1977

Star Wars, U.S. director George Lucas's hit sci-fi film starring Harrison Ford

Close Encounters of the Third Kind, a Hollywood sci-fi fantasy, directed by Steven Spielberg

Annie Hall, with Woody Allen as director, actor, and coauthor, also stars Diane Keaton

Saturday Night Fever, with John Travolta, lifts disco dancing to a new level of popularity

Canadian film, *Who Has Seen the Wind?,* with Gordon Pinsent

Canada's National Film Board wins Oscar for animation with John Weldon and Eunice MacAulay's *Special Delivery*

Broadway musical *Annie,* based on Harold Gray's comic strip *Little Orphan Annie,* which debuted in 1924

Fleetwood Mac releases hit album *Rumors;* first million-selling album in Canada

Punk rock, typified by loud, simplistic music and anarchic themes, finds a niche

On TV: *Roots* miniseries, based on Alex Haley's 1976 book, captures huge audience, estimated at more than 100 million viewers

Toronto Blue Jays become second major league baseball team (after Montreal Expos) to be located outside U.S.

Canadian Cindy Nicholas becomes first woman to swim English Channel both ways non-stop

Brazilian superstar Pelé (Edson Arantes do Nascimento), the greatest soccer player of his era, retires after playing his last three years with the New York Cosmos

Canadian ice hockey great Gordie Howe, at age 49 playing for the New England Whalers, scores his 1,000th professional goal; he retires at 52 in 1980

Baseball speedster Lou Brock of the St. Louis Cardinals passes Ty Cobb's nearly 50-year-old record of 892 career steals; Brock reaches 938 before retiring after 1979 season

Grey Cup won by Montreal Alouettes

Stanley Cup won by Montreal Canadiens

1978

Vietnam films: *The Deer Hunter* with Robert de Niro and *Coming Home* with Jon Voight and Jane Fonda

Hollywood musical *Grease,* with John Travolta and Olivia Newton-John

Swedish film director Ingmar Bergman's *Autumn Sonata,* with Swedish-born U.S. actress Ingrid Bergman and Liv Ullmann

Ain't Misbehavin', a musical tribute to jazz pianist, entertainer, and composer Fats Waller (1904–43), opens on Broadway

Canadian pianist Oscar Peterson named to Juno Hall of Fame

On TV, a banner year for prime-time premieres: *Dallas, Fantasy Island, The Incredible Hulk, Mork and Mindy, Taxi;* also the TV news magazine *20/20*

Hit songs: Billy Joel's "Just the Way You Are"; Bee Gees'

"Stayin' Alive," "Night Fever"; Rolling Stones' "Miss You"

Canadian Gilles Villeneuve wins Canadian Grand Prix for Formula One cars at Montreal

Muhammad Ali beats Leon Spinks; becomes first boxer to capture the heavyweight crown three times

Chris Evert wins fourth straight U.S. Open tennis singles title

Edmonton Eskimos win Grey Cup

Montreal Canadiens repeat win of Stanley Cup

1979

Director Francis Ford Coppola's dark vision of the Vietnam War, *Apocalypse Now,* starring Charlie Sheen and Marlon Brando

China Syndrome, Hollywood drama about an accident and cover-up at a nuclear power plant, stars Jane Fonda and Jack Lemmon

Hollywood's *Kramer vs. Kramer,* with Meryl Streep and Dustin Hoffman, dramatizes a bitter child-custody battle

Edmonton Eskimos win Grey Cup for second consecutive year

Montreal Canadiens win Stanley Cup for fourth consecutive year

BUSINESS & ECONOMICS

1970

Foreign control of Canadian manufacturing nears 60 percent; in petroleum industry, it is 80 percent

First jumbo jet: Boeing 747

One of world's most sought-after stamps, 1856 British Guiana one penny, fetches $280,000 at auction; the same stamp will sell for $935,000 10 years later

1971

Women make up less than 10 percent of undergraduate enrolment in Canadian university business programs

Amtrak, a semipublic corporation created by the U.S. Congress in 1970, takes over intercity passenger trains

Rolls-Royce, Britain's prestigious carmaker, files for bankruptcy while continuing to make luxury cars

1972

Gray Report (after chairman Herb Gray) recommends regulation of foreign investment in Canada

Dow Jones stock index tops 1,000 for first time

Standard Oil changes name to Exxon

1973

New York City's World Trade Center opens; taller of nearly identical twin towers is 416 metres high

Congress approves trans-Alaska pipeline, linking Alaska's North Slope oil fields and Valdez tanker terminal; set to open in 1977

Nuclear power: orders are placed for 41 reactors; eventually 32 will be cancelled

U.S. devalues dollar for second time in three years

"There's no such thing as a free lunch."

— attributed to American economist Milton Friedman, 1974

1974

U.S. wage and price freezes end

AT&T establishes a homosexual antidiscrimination policy

Worldwide inflation, Canadian and U.S. stock markets sink

Canadian government creates Foreign Investment Review Agency to regulate foreign investment in Canada

1975

Canadian government establishes anti-inflation board to limit wage and price increases

Canadian unemployment rate at 7 percent, while U.S. reaches 8.75 percent; both figures understate real levels of unemployment

A year after the oil crisis of 1973, this gas station was up-front with its customers: they could fill their tanks, but it would not be cheap.

1976

Canada suffers record time lost due to strikes

Canada announces 200-nautical-mile coastal fishing zone

U.S.-born oil tycoon J. Paul Getty dies at 84

Tanker disaster off Massachusetts coast spills million of gallons of oil

Genentech founded; first biotechnology company to develop new products through genetic engineering

1977

Laker Airlines, British carrier owned by entrepreneur Freddy Laker, offers bargain-basement fares between New York and London, starts trend toward low-cost, no-frills air travel

1978

Canada's official unemployment figure climbs to over 8 percent as job creation fails to match

growing numbers seeking to enter work force

Canadian dollar hits 45-year low against U.S. dollar as it, too, tumbles against major currencies

Conrad Black wins control of Argus Corporation

Strikes shut down New York City newspapers

Minimum wage in the U.S. rises from $2.65 to $2.90 an hour; average women's wages are 59 percent of men's

Five American Cyanamid women employees agree to voluntary sterilization; normally company bars women of reproductive age from working in jobs exposing them to lead

U.S. GNP (gross national product) reaches $2 trillion, having doubled in six years

1979

U.S. Steel closes 15 plants, lays off 13,000 workers

Minnesota Mining and Manufacturing Company (3M) introduces Post-it notes, which soon become ubiquitous in home and office

Fresh round of OPEC crude-oil price hikes; spot fuel shortages; meanwhile, U.S. automakers resist downsizing cars

SCIENCE & MEDICINE

1970

Lasers find increasing use in communications, industry, military devices, medicine, and science

First nerve transplant

Artificial gene synthesized

L-dopa approved for treating Parkinson's disease

Floppy disks for storage of computer data are introduced

1971

Vitamin B_{12} synthesized

Phosphates in detergents found to cause water pollution

Gerhard Herzberg of Canada's National Research Council wins Nobel Prize for Chemistry, for studies of chemical reactions that help produce smog

Canada's first commercial CANDU (nuclear) reactor in operation at Pickering, Ontario

U.S. Food and Drug Administration (FDA) warns use of DES (diethylstilbestrol) by pregnant women can cause cancer and birth defects in offspring

Astronomers discover two previously undetected galaxies next to Milky Way

1972

Canada severely restricts use of amphetamines for diet pills as test show dangerous side effects

CAT (computerized axial tomography) scan introduced, giving 3-D images of internal body

Artificial satellites begin photographing Earth's surface

Brain pacemaker for epileptics

1973

Nuclear magnetic resonance (NMR) helps scientists explore molecular structure and aids doctors in studying and diagnosing abnormalities and diseases

U.S. space station program: astronauts of *Skylab 2* return

489

to Earth after 28-day mission involving rendezvous with previously launched, unmanned *Skylab 1*

DNA molecules cut and joined by using enzymes; recombinant DNA produces chimera, or hybrid tissues

1974

Freon, a fluorocarbon propellant released into atmosphere from aerosol sprays, suspected of depleting Earth's ozone layer

Mariner 10, unmanned U.S. spacecraft launched in 1973, sends data and photos from flybys of Venus and Mercury

1975

620-million-year-old marine worm is oldest fossil yet found within U.S.

Astronomers detect galaxy 10 times larger than Milky Way

1976

Lyme disease, transmitted by tick bites, first identified in Old Lyme, Connecticut

Artificial gene, implanted in human cell, functions normally

Oil-eating microbes and algae developed as possible aid in fighting pollution

1977

Voyager 1 and *Voyager 2* unmanned spacecraft launched, will later transmit discoveries about Jupiter and Saturn, including newly discovered moons of both planets; *Voyager 2* eventually travels on past Uranus and Neptune

Balloon angioplasty allows repair of obstructed arteries

Brains of schizophrenics found to have chemical imbalances

Austrian-born American psychologist Bruno Bettelheim's *The Uses of Enchantment: The Meaning and Importance of Fairy Tales*

1978

First test-tube baby, Louise Joy Brown, conceived outside the mother's body, born in England to Lesley and John Brown

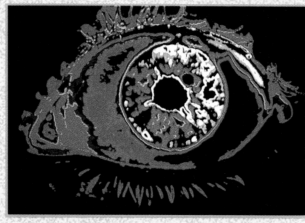

Scientists and doctors in the 1970's pioneered new ways of seeing without visible light. Here infrared light reveals hemorrhages in the eye.

Scientists discover a moon orbiting Pluto

1979

Black hole found in centre of Milky Way

U.S. surgeon general affirms that cigarettes cause heart disease, cancer, and other illnesses

WORLD POLITICAL EVENTS

1970

Anwar Sadat becomes president of Egypt

Edward Heath is elected British prime minister

Chileans elect Marxist Salvador Allende Gossens president

General, and former president of France, Charles de Gaulle, dies at age 79

Assassination attempts: on Pope Paul VI and on Jordan's King Hussein

1971

People's Republic of China (mainland China, under Communist rule) admitted to U.N.; Taiwan ousted

East Pakistan becomes the independent nation of Bangladesh

Maj. Gen. Idi Amin takes control of East African republic of Uganda

1972

"Bloody Sunday" Derry massacre in Northern Ireland; Britain imposes direct rule

Arab terrorists kill 2 Israelis and take 9 others hostage at Munich Olympics; all 9 Israeli hostages, a West German policeman, and 5 terrorists later killed in shoot-out

1973

Chile's President Salvador Allende Gossens dies during military takeover; allegedly a suicide

After 18-year exile, Juan Perón elected president of Argentina

Yom Kippur War: Egypt and Syria attack Israel in October; cease-fire in November

Under the banner of OPEC (Organization of Petroleum Exporting Countries), Arab nations, protesting support for Israel, embargo oil shipments to U.S., Western Europe, Japan; Canada is indirectly affected; crude-oil prices soar from $2 to as high as $34 a barrel by decade's end

1974

Generalissimo Francisco Franco, dictator of Spain for 35 years, steps down at 81, turning nation over to Prince Juan Carlos de Borbón

Emperor Haile Selassie of Ethiopia deposed after 58 years

Mexico announces discovery of vast oil reserve

1975

Khmer Rouge take power in Cambodia; accelerate reign of terror

Communist Pathet Lao rule in Laos

Civil war in Lebanon involves Christians, Muslims, and PLO (Palestine Liberation Organization) guerrillas

Suez Canal, closed since 1967 Arab-Israeli war, reopens

Portugal grants Angola independence after years of civil war

Chiang Kai-shek, president of Taiwan and longtime leader of Chinese Nationalists, dies

Eamon de Valera, a former prime minister and president of Ireland, dies

1976

Israeli commandos rescue hostages held by pro-Palestinian skyjackers at Entebbe, Uganda

China's Mao Tse-tung and Chou En-lai die; "Gang of Four," including Mao's widow, attempt unsuccessful coup

Military junta takes over in Argentina

Blacks in South Africa riot against apartheid

Venezuela nationalizes its oil industry, kicking out American and other foreign companies

North and South Vietnam become one country

1977

Nicaragua's Roman Catholic bishops charge President Anastasio Somoza with atrocities against civilians in Somoza's escalating conflict with left-wing Sandinista Front of National Liberation

Menachem Begin becomes Israel's new premier when his Likud Party bests the Labor Party of Shimon Peres

1978

Rioting in Iran against rule of shah (Mohammad Reza

Pahlavi); Muslim religious leader, Ayatollah Ruholla Khomeini, unites opposition to shah

Italian Red Brigades kidnap and kill former Italian premier Aldo Moro

Pope Paul VI dies; his successor, John Paul I, dies within the year and is succeeded by John Paul II, formerly Poland's Cardinal (Karol) Wojtyla, who is the first non-Italian elected pope in 456 years

1979

U.S.S.R. invades Afghanistan

Shah of Iran ousted after 28 years of rule by followers of Ayatollah Khomeini; Iranian mob storms American Embassy in Tehran, holds 66 Americans hostage

❦

"Human rights is the soul of our foreign policy, because human rights is the very soul of our sense of nationhood."

— *President Jimmy Carter, December 6, 1978, commemorating the 30th anniversary of the U.N. Declaration of Human Rights*

❦

Sandinistas take control in Nicaragua; Somoza flees

Margaret Thatcher is Britain's first woman prime minister

Irish Republican Army (IRA), a terrorist group dedicated to ending British rule of Northern Ireland, assassinates Britain's revered Earl Mountbatten by blowing up his yacht in the Irish Sea

Anthony Blunt, former curator of the queen's art collection, admits spying for the Soviet Union against Britain and its allies

NORTH AMERICAN HISTORY & POLITICS

1980

Pierre Trudeau returns from retirement to defeat Joe Clark's conservative government in general election; 147 Liberal seats to 103 Conservative and 32 NDP

Jeanne Sauvé is first female speaker of House of Commons

O Canada becomes Canada's national anthem

Ottawa announces National Energy Policy to regulate supply and prices of energy and to conserve oil; anger in oil-producing Alberta

Quebec referendum on Sovereignty-Association defeated as "No"side wins 59.5 percent of vote

U.S. breaks diplomatic relations with Iran; attempt to rescue 53 American hostages in Iran fails; Canadian diplomats shelter 6 Americans in Tehran, then take them to safety

Mount St. Helens erupts in southwestern Washington; some 57 people are killed, and ash spreads 193 km

Canada's population passes 24 million; U.S. population is more than 226 million

---

Ronald Reagan elected 40th president as he and running mate George Bush win 489 of 538 electoral votes; defeat Democrat incumbents Jimmy Carter and Walter Mondale with almost 51 percent of the popular vote

"I really can't express with words what it's like to be back in America again. I just wish there were 52 more with me."

— *Richard Queen, hostage, upon being released for health reasons after 250 days of captivity in Iran in July 1980*

1981

Iran frees American hostages after 444 days in captivity

President Reagan wounded in assassination attempt; John

Hinckley, Jr., later charged with attempted murder, found not guilty by reason of insanity

Prime Minister Trudeau is co-chair of North-South Summit meeting in Mexico

Canadian government reports charges that some major oil companies are guilty of price-fixing

Ocean Ranger, an oil platform off the Newfoundland coast, sinks; 84 men die

Premier Lougheed of Alberta forces Ottawa to accept Energy Pricing Agreement, giving provinces a role in setting oil and gas prices

Bertha Wilson is first woman to be appointed justice of Canada's Supreme Court

1982

Canada's Constitution Act proclaimed, though Quebec refuses to agree; amending formula gives substantial powers to provinces; Charter of Rights and Freedoms is added, provoking anger among Quebec nationalists

The Vietnam War Memorial in Washington, D.C., is dedicated; designed by architecture student Maya Lin and inscribed with more than 57,000 names of Americans killed or missing in Vietnam

---

Dominion Day is renamed Canada Day

Quebec's claim of right to a constitutional veto rejected by Quebec Court of Appeal and Supreme Court of Canada

1983

Martin Luther King, Jr.'s birthday declared a national holiday in the U.S.

Canadian parliament sits through its longest session in history; over 591 days, starting April 14, 1980, it passed more than 150 bills into law

Terrorist bombs blow up U.S. Embassy in Beirut; extremist drives explosives-laden truck into U.S. barracks in suicide mission, kills 241 U.S. troops

Prime Minister Maurice Bishop of Grenada is ousted in left-wing coup; U.S. sends troops to restore order

Canada's Roman Catholic bishops criticize government and business as charges fly over responsibility for high unemployment

Representatives of aboriginal peoples meet in Ottawa to discuss aboriginal rights

Jeanne Sauvé named governor general of Canada, the first woman in that post

---

The U.S. Naval Academy class of 1980 made history: it included 55 proud young women like this one.

1984

Canadian Security Service (federal intelligence agency) created

Pierre Trudeau retires; John Turner succeeds as leader of federal Liberal Party and prime minister

Brian Mulroney leads federal Conservative Party to record majority, 211 Conservatives to 40 Liberals, 30 NDP and 1 independent

Reagan and Bush reelected, routing Democrats Walter Mondale and New York congresswoman Geraldine Ferraro, first female vice-presidential candidate of a major party

1985

Report of Royal Commission *Economic Union and Development Prospects for Canada* (Macdonald Commission report) advocates free trade

Supreme Court of Canada rules that Manitoba's laws must be written in both French and English

Sabotage causes Air India passenger jet crash, killing 329; 280 are Canadians

U.S. icebreaker *Polar Sea* cruises Arctic through waters claimed by Canada; Canadian government, with no choice, gives permission

---

How Canadians Eat

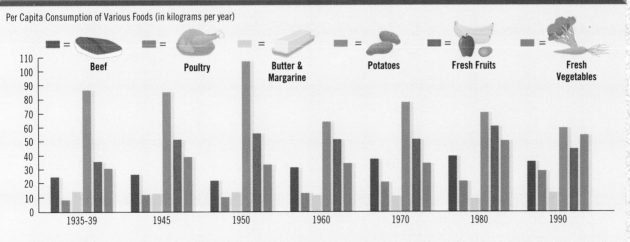

Per Capita Consumption of Various Foods (in kilograms per year)

Legend: Beef, Poultry, Butter & Margarine, Potatoes, Fresh Fruits, Fresh Vegetables

Years: 1935-39, 1945, 1950, 1960, 1970, 1980, 1990

WHAT IT COST

Prices: 1990

Daily newspapers, 50¢

Ports International cotton shirts for men, $70; men's wool coat, $450; men's shoes, $69.95 and $71.95

Women's suede skirt, $150; women's suits, $250; pure wool coats, $349

Reebok: men's, $54.88 and $69.88; ladies', $39.88 and $74.88

Levi's Red Tabs, men's, $33.88

Flannel sheet set, 100 percent cotton: twin, $24.99; double, $33.99; Queen, $37.99

Grapes, 69¢ a lb; bananas, 25¢ a lb; P.E.I. potatoes, 50-lb bag, $4.99; McIntosh apples,

98¢ a 3 lb bag

Green Giant Niblets corn, 39¢

Life cereal, $1.39 a box

Dad's Cookies, $1.39

Planters peanuts, 99¢

Sprite, or Coca-Cola, 29¢

Motorola cellular phone, $29.95

Sanyo microwave oven, $799.99

Hitachi VHS Video Recorder, $598

Apple Macintosh computer, $1,999.99

Toronto, Yonge-Ellington, 2-bedroom condo, $395,000

Oakville, Ontario, 3-bedroom brick home, $71,900

1986

Iran-Contra scandal: National Security Adviser John Poindexter, his aide Oliver North, and others implicated in secret plan to sell arms to Iran in exchange for help in freeing U.S. hostages in Lebanon; profits from arms sales are used to supply arms to Contras fighting Sandinista regime in Nicaragua

Scandals continue to plague Mulroney government as industry minister Sinclair Stevens resigns over controversial $2.6 million loan to save one of his companies

Libya fires on U.S. planes; in retaliation for Libyan attack on disco frequented by GI's in West Germany, U.S. bombs Qaddafi headquarters in Tripoli, killing 15 civilians

U.S. Congress approves $100 million military and humanitarian aid to Contras

Holocaust survivor and author Elie Wiesel wins Nobel Peace Prize

Bill Vander Zalm becomes Social Credit Premier of B.C.

Economic Council of Canada comes out in support of free trade with U.S.

1987

Prime Minister Mulroney and premiers adopt Meech Lake Accord, proposing changes to constitution; referred to provincial legislatures for approval

Reform Party founded to press for reduction of government deficits

Ontario passes pay equity law, first in North America

Iran-Contra update: Oliver North tells Congress his covert actions were justified for national security and authorized by his superiors; Poindexter backs up North; congressional committee states that president bears "ultimate responsibility"

Earthquake measuring 6.1 on the Richter scale hits Los Angeles; 6 killed, 100 injured

Tornado in Edmonton kills 26, injures 250

1988

Gallup poll shows Canadian support for free trade stands at only 26 percent

Preston Manning is leader of Reform Party of Canada

Panamanian leader Gen. Manuel Noriega indicted by

U.S. grand jury on international drug trafficking charges; U.S. imposes sanctions on Panama, civil disorder ensues

U.S. cruiser *Vincennes* downs Iranian airliner, mistaking it for a warplane, 290 die; U.S. offers reparations to survivors

All Canadian premiers endorse Meech Lake Constitutional Accord

Quebec government invokes "notwithstanding" clause to override Supreme Court decision that its ban on bilingual signs is unconstitutional

Conservative Party wins re-election with 169 seats to 83 for Liberals and 43 for NDP

George H. W. Bush, with Indiana Sen. J. Danforth Quayle as his running mate, elected 41st president, with 53.9 percent of popular vote

Terrorist bomb blows up Pan American flight 103 over Lockerbie, Scotland, killing 70

1989

Free Trade Agreement between Canada and U.S. comes into effect

NDP chooses Audrey McLaughlin as federal leader; first woman to lead a federal party in Canada

Earthquake measuring 7.1 on the Richter scale hits San Francisco Bay area; highways and sections of the Bay Bridge collapse; some 62 people are killed

Marc Lepine, driven by hatred of women, kills 14 young women at Ecole Polytechnique in Montreal using semi-automatic rifle; 10th worst gun massacre in the world

Gen. Colin Powell becomes first black chairman of U.S. Joint Chiefs of Staff

U.S. invades Panama; Manuel Noriega surrenders; tried and convicted of drug trafficking, money laundering, racketeering

Iran-Contra update: Oliver North convicted on three charges, acquitted on nine; his convictions are later overturned on appeal

Exxon Valdez oil tanker spill in Alaska is largest in history: 35,600 tonnes of crude oil foul coast

1990

Iraq's Saddam Hussein invades Kuwait; U.N. imposes sanctions and U.S. organizes allies for Operation Desert Shield; Canada pledges three warships and a squadron of fighter planes

Meech Lake Accord fails to meet deadline for approval by provincial legislatures

At Oka, Quebec, town council rejects Ottawa bid to settle Mohawk land claim; Mohawks blockade road and police officer is killed; Mohawks at nearby Kanawake stage sympathy blockade; Canada ends standoff with troops

Iran-Contra update: John Poindexter convicted on five felony counts; sentenced to six-month prison term for lying to Congress

Canada's population tops 26 million; U.S. population tops 248 million

"Government is not the solution, it's the problem."

— *President Ronald Reagan, inaugural address, 1981*

1991

The Gulf War: high-tech bombs and missiles hit Iraqi targets; later U.S. and U.N. tank forces rout enemy on ground; 100,000 Iraqi troops surrender, some 100,000 are killed; Saddam Hussein remains in power

Last U.S. hostage in Lebanon, Terry A. Anderson, freed by Islamic terrorists after six years in captivity

Ovide Mercredi becomes leader of Canada's Assembly of First Nations

Ontario's NDP government brings down its first budget; increases spending, projecting record deficit, to boost economy out of recession

Supreme Court Justice Thurgood Marshall retires; Bush's nominee Clarence Thomas accused by University of Oklahoma Law School professor Anita Hill of having sexually harassed her 10 years earlier; after hearing before Senate Judiciary Committee, Thomas wins Senate confirmation

1992

Prime Minister Mulroney and provincial premiers reach agreement on constitutional change in Charlottetown Accord, but it is defeated in national referendum

Canada signs North American Free Trade Agreement (NAFTA) with U.S. and Mexico

Gwich'in Indians are given title to nearly 24,000 sq km of land in NWT and Yukon

Iran-Contra update: President Bush pardons Reagan administration officials involved in Iran-Contra affair

Riots in Los Angeles after four white police officers are acquitted of 1991 beating of black motorist Rodney King; 58 people are killed, $1 billion worth of damage; two officers are later found guilty of violating King's civil rights

Explosion at Westray coal mine in Nova Scotia kills 26

Canada pledges up to 1,200 peacekeeping troops for UN service in former Yugoslavia

Arkansas Gov. Bill Clinton elected 42nd president, with Tennessee Sen. Albert Gore as his running mate

Operation Restore Hope, U.N. effort to relieve famine, meets resistance from hostile Somali warlords; more than a dozen Americans are killed; U.S. gives U.N. control of operation in May 1993

1993

Brian Mulroney retires as federal Conservative leader;

succeeded by Kim Campbell, first woman to become prime minister of Canada

Conservatives are crushed in federal general election, winning only 2 seats; Liberals led by Jean Chrétien win majority with 176; Bloc Québécois leads opposition with 54; Reform Party has 49, and NDP 9

President Bush and Russian President Boris Yeltsin sign Strategic Arms Reduction Treaty II to cut U.S. and Russian arsenals by two-thirds

Canadian Supreme Court rules against right to doctor-assisted suicide, in Sue Rodriguez case

Explosion rocks World Trade Center in New York City, killing five; 15 suspects are indicted, including Islamic Sheikh Omar Abdel Rahman

Four U.S. federal agents are killed and more than a dozen wounded in raid on religious cult compound in Waco, Texas; 51-day standoff ends when compound is burned to the ground; more than 80 cult members, including leader, David Koresh, die

Four members of Canada's Airborne Regiment, serving as peacekeepers in Somalia, charged in beating death of Somali civilian

Ontario NDP government approves Social Contract Act, freezing salaries in public sector for three years

Canada announces withdrawal of its peacekeepers from Cyprus after 29 years

Holocaust Memorial Museum opens in Washington, D.C., to honor the 6 million Jews and millions of others killed by Nazis in World War II

Floods hit the Midwest U.S. as Mississippi River and its tributaries break through levees; many die, 100,000 are left homeless

1994

Earthquake measuring 6.7 on the Richter scale hits Los Angeles, killing 67, causing $20 billion in damage

CIA official Aldrich Hazen Ames and his wife accused of spying for eight years for Soviet Union and betraying U.S. double agents

U.S. Congressional elections see Republicans win control of U.S. House and Senate for first time since early 1950's; Newt Gingrich of Georgia becomes Speaker of the House

"I have come to the definite conclusion that if the United States is indeed the great melting pot, the Negro either didn't get in the pot or he didn't get melted down."

— Supreme Court Justice Thurgood Marshall in 1987

Ontario court rejects libel suit by veterans of Canadian Bomber Command against McKenna brothers, makers of World War II documentary, *The Valour and the Horror*

Parti Québécois wins Quebec election with 77 seats to 47 for Liberals and 1 Parti Action Démocratique; new premier, Jacques Parizeau, pledges referendum on separation

Supreme Court of Canada rules that extreme drunkenness can be used as defence against rape accusation

1995

Quebec referendum on separation narrowly defeated; charges of voting irregularities

Canada seizes Spanish fishing vessel *Estai*, enforcing conservation laws in international waters; the E.C. protests, but Canadian view prevails

Terrorist bomb in Oklahoma City kills 168, injures more than 500

Mike Harris becomes premier of Ontario on promise of cuts in social programs; begins with cuts in welfare cheques

Chrétien government introduces severe austerity plan; includes privatization of Petro-Canada and CNR, 14 percent reduction of federal civil service, and cuts in transfer payments to provinces

EVERYDAY LIFE

1980

Game of the year: Rubick's Cube, with 43.2 quintillion possible combinations

Low-calorie, low-cholesterol foods begin to be marketed

Designer jeans by Calvin Klein, Gloria Vanderbilt, and others are fashion craze; preppy look, including blazers, kilts, cardigans, and buttoned-down shirts, are popular among college crowd

Ted Turner's Cable News Network (CNN) offers round-the-clock news coverage

1981

Storybook wedding: Britain's Prince Charles marries Lady Diana Spencer; 700 million watch ceremony on TV around the world

Nutrasweet, a sugar substitute, is introduced

Nintendo markets Pac-Man video game, which becomes an arcade craze

1982

A new U.S. daily newspaper, *USA Today*, debuts

Sun Myung Moon's Unification Church marries more than 2,000 couples in mass ceremony; separately, jury convicts Moon of income tax evasion

Tylenol terror: tamperer puts cyanide in over-the-counter medication; seven people die

EPCOT Center, $800-million Disney futuristic theme park, opens in Orlando, Florida

Dedicated in 1993, the Vietnam Women's Memorial in Washington, D.C., pays special tribute to the women who served in the Vietnam war.

Jane Fonda's workout videos become huge success

Campaign against fur-trapping and other exploitation of animals gathers force as European Economic Community moves to ban imports of seal products

1983

First compact discs (CD's) marketed

Dr. Henry Morgentaler opens abortion clinics in Winnipeg and Toronto

Cabbage Patch dolls

Cajun cuisine, sushi bars, and homemade pasta become eating trends

"Flashdance" look, inspired by actress Jennifer Beals in movie of that name, makes off-the-shoulder sweatshirts, headbands, leg warmers popular among young people

The word *yuppie*, meaning young urban professional, comes into use

1984

New York passes the U.S.'s first mandatory seat belt law

Gunman kills 21 at McDonald's in San Ysidro, California

New York real estate magnate Donald Trump builds 39-storey, 614-room casino in Atlantic City, New Jersey

Motion Picture Association of America introduces new movie rating: PG-13, film off-limits to children under 13 unless accompanied by an adult

Hugely successful board game Trivial Pursuit introduced, invented by two Canadians

1985

Wreckage of the *Titanic* is discovered on ocean floor after 73 years

Live Aid concert raises more than $450 million for African famine relief

The Lord's Day Act, limit to commercial activity in Canada for most of 20th century, is ruled unconstitutional by the Supreme Court of Canada

Steve Fonyo completes run across Canada to raise funds for cancer research

Crack, smokable crystallized cocaine, creates a new drug menace

The shoulder pad makes a comeback in women's wear

New Coke is marketed; consumer complaints cause Coca-Cola Company to bring back original product under the name Coca-Cola Classic

Pop star Madonna wears undergarments as outerwear and sets a new style

1986

Vancouver, British Columbia, hosts Expo 86

Britain's Prince Andrew and Sarah (Fergie) Ferguson wed

A fourth major U.S. television network, Fox, begins telecasts

1987

"Baby M" case: surrogate mother Mary Beth Whitehead denied custody of child to which she gave birth

Pope John Paul II visits Fort Simpson in Canada's NWT

Eighteen-month-old Jessica McClure falls down abandoned well in Midland, Texas; millions watch rescue broadcast live on TV

Miniskirts make a comeback

Fuji markets the Quicksnap disposable camera; Acuvue disposable contact lenses are introduced

The term *couch potato* enters the vocabulary: a person who spends a lot of time lounging around, often in front of the TV

1988

Quintuplets born to the Colliers of Holland Landing, Ontario; birth is the result of *in vitro* fertilization

Fax machine sales hit 1 million

McDonald's switches from nonbiodegradable to recyclable packaging

Increasing concern for environmental health in Canada leads to federal anti-smoking legislation; Canadians also want their government to take a stronger stand against U.S. on question of acid rain

The United Church of Canada agrees to accept gays and lesbians as clergy

Latest rage: Nintendo home video games

Prince Charles, heir to the British throne, married kindergarten teacher Lady Diana Spencer on July 29, 1981, at St. Paul's Cathedral, London.

Teens favor ragged jeans ripped open at knees

Retin-A, an acne medicine, becomes a hot commodity when it is found to help repair damaged skin

1989

Digital audiotape recorders appear on the market

Oat bran becomes popular when studies show it may reduce cholesterol

Teenage Mutant Ninja Turtles are big hit among young audiences

Aunt Jemima is slimmed down, her bandanna is gone, and she wears earrings and modern clothes

1990

200 million celebrate 20th anniversary of Earth Day

Most popular baby names in Canada are Jessica and Michael

Canadian university enrollments continue to rise with over 0.5 million students registered

Jeffrey Dahmer arrested in Milwaukee, Wisconsin, and charged with multiple murders

Job equity for Canadian women, visible minorities, native peoples, and the handicapped improves slightly in 10 years

1991

Crisis of confidence in Roman Catholic clergy across Canada as supervisor of Mount Cashel church orphanage is sentenced to 12 years for sexual abuse of boys

Grunge chic and hip-hop styles become popular with teens

1992

UN report ranks Canada as best country in the world to live in

Ontario retailers get permission to open on Sunday

Environment Canada warns sunbathers that thinning ozone layer makes sun's radiation dangerous

Baseball caps, usually worn backward or sideways, become a fad.

1993

Environmental protests rise in BC as government gives loggers permission to cut one of last stands of old-growth trees at Clayoquot Sound

New guidelines for food labels require that amounts of fat, sodium, cholesterol, protein, and carbohydrate be printed on packaging; terms such as "light" and "low fat" must meet certain criteria

Britain's Prince Charles and Princess Diana separate

1994

Victoria Matthews is first woman in Canada to be named an Anglican bishop

Tobacco continues to draw attacks as Ontario bans sale of tobacco to anyone under age 19

1995

Prince Charles and Princess Diana admit on television to adultery; Queen Elizabeth orders Prince Charles to divorce

"They're like — whooah! — bigger than any man!"

— A 10-year-old Michigan boy, explaining why he likes dinosaurs, 1993

The Internet goes mainstream; more than 10 million North Americans subscribe to various on-line computer services

O.J. Simpson murder trial; eight and a half months later Simpson is found not guilty

Following spread of gambling casinos in Canada, Nova Scotia opens one in Halifax and one in Sydney

Canadian veterans mark 50 years since end of World War II with visits to Holland

ARTS & LETTERS

1980

Retrospective of works by Spanish artist Pablo Picasso at the Museum of Modern Art, New York; some 1,000 works displayed

Canadian Hugh MacLennan's *Voices in Time* appears

Novel *General Ludd* by Canadian John Metcalf is satiric attack on aspects of university life

Canadian Madeleine Gagnon draws attention to feminist view with *La vie en prose*

Study of Pierre Trudeau, *The Northern Magus,* by Richard Gwyn, appears

U.S. novelist James Michener's *The Covenant*

1981

Indian novelist and critic Salman Rushdie's *Midnight's Children*

South African novelist Nadine Gordimer's *July's People*

U.S. writer John Updike's novel *Rabbit Is Rich*

Radio-Canada wins International Emmy for dance film, *L'Oiseau de feu*

1982

Black American novelist Alice Walker's *The Color Purple*

U.S. dramatist Harvey Fierstein's *Torch Song Trilogy* opens on Broadway

Canadian Christopher Pratt screenprint *Memorial Window* continues style of simplicity and realism

1983

Environmental artist Javacheff Christo wraps 11 islands in Biscayne Bay, Florida, with pink polypropylene at a cost of $3 million

British novelist John le Carré writes *The Little Drummer Girl*

Magazine *Vanity Fair* is reintroduced after 47 years

Canadian Morley Callaghan releases novel, *A Time for Judas*

Publication of the first *The Oxford Guide to Canadian Literature*

1984

Canadian Alex Colville has highly successful exhibit in Japan; it is the first exhibit in that country for any Canadian artist

In the 1980's this hand-held TV set reflected the rapid pace of electronic miniaturization.

Swift Current, a new Canadian literary magazine, appears as an electronic publication to be received by computer only

U.S. novelist Norman Mailer's *Tough Guys Don't Dance*

U.S. dramatist David Mamet's *Glengarry Glen Ross*

1985

Record auction price for a painting: $10.5 million for Mantegna's *Adoration of the Magi*

Canadian writer Margaret Atwood's futuristic novel *The Handmaid's Tale*

U.S. novelist Anne Tyler's *Accidental Tourist*

U.S. novelist Tom Clancy's *The*

Hunt for Red October; later made into a movie

1986

Major retrospective of paintings by Canadian Christopher Pratt tours Canada

U.S. painter Andrew Wyeth's *Helga* series of paintings is shown

 U.S. novelist Tom Clancy's *Red Storm Rising*

1987

$53.9 million paid for *Irises* painted by Dutch artist Vincent van Gogh

U.S. writer Tom Wolfe's novel *The Bonfire of the Vanities*

Black American novelist Toni Morrison's *Beloved*

U.S. lawyer and novelist Scott Turow's *Presumed Innocent*

Black American dramatist August Wilson's *Fences* opens on Broadway

1988

Colombian novelist Gabriel García Márquez's *Love in the Time of Cholera*

U.S. writer Don DeLillo's novel *Libra*

Canada's Frederick Back (Radio-Canada) wins Oscar for animated film, *The Man Who Planted Trees*

U.S. playwright David Henry Hwang's *M. Butterfly* opens on Broadway

1989

Record price for 20th-century painting: $47.8 million for a self-portrait by Pablo Picasso

Record price for work by a living artist: $20.68 million for *Interchange* by Dutch-born U.S. painter Willem de Kooning

British writer John le Carré's spy novel *The Russia House*

Indian novelist and critic Salman Rushdie's *Satanic Verses* creates furor in Islamic world, where many consider the book blasphemous; the Ayatollah Khomeini of Iran offers a

> *"It may be that the deep necessity of art is the examination of self-deception."*
>
> — Artist Robert Motherwell, 1985

$1-million bounty for the killing of Rushdie, who goes into hiding

U.S. novelist E. L. Doctorow's *Billy Bathgate*

U.S. novelist Amy Tan's *The Joy Luck Club*

U.S. dramatist Wendy Wasserstein's *The Heidi Chronicles* opens

Canadian Louis Lortie records *Twentieth Century Original Piano Transcriptions*

1990

$82.5 million paid for Vincent van Gogh's *Portrait of Dr. Gachet*

Canadian Mordecai Richler wins Commonwealth Writers Award for *Solomon Gursky Was Here*

U.S. writer John Updike's *Rabbit at Rest,* in which protagonist of previous novels, Rabbit Angstrom, dies

U.S. lawyer and novelist Scott Turow's *Burden of Proof*

1991

Rohinton Mistry wins Governor General's Award for Fiction with *Such a Long Journey*

1992

Black American novelist Toni Morrison's *Jazz*

U.S. novelist Michael Crichton's thriller *Rising Sun*

Black American novelist Alice Walker's *Possessing the Secret of Joy*

Canadian Michael Ondaatje shares Booker Prize for *The English Patient*

1993

Black American writer Toni

Morrison wins Nobel Prize for Literature

The Bridges of Madison County by Robert James Waller

1994

The cleaning of Michelango's *Last Judgment* is finally completed

Andrew Lloyd Webber's *Sunset Boulevard* opens on Broadway

Canadian Michael Ignatieff wins Gelber Prize for *Blood and Belonging*

1995

Canadian Carol Shields wins Pulitzer Prize for *The Stone Diaries;* it was earlier awarded the Governor General's prize, in 1993

Robertson Davies, Canadian writer, critic, and teacher, dies

For the first time since World War II, 74 long-hidden masterpieces are displayed at the Hermitage Museum in St.. Petersburg, Russia

ENTERTAINMENT & SPORTS

1980

U.S. director Martin Scorsese's *Raging Bull,* with Robert DeNiro

Ordinary People, directed by Robert Redford

Coal Miner's Daughter, with Sissy Spacek

Former Beatle John Lennon is shot and killed by fan outside his apartment

Canadian Consumer Price Index: 1914–92

(1986 = 100)

Year	Index
1914	9.2
1920	17.3
1925	13.9
1930	13.9
1933	10.9
1935	11.1
1940	12.2
1945	13.9
1950	19.0
1955	21.5
1960	23.7
1965	25.7
1970	31.0
1975	44.2
1980	67.2
1985	96.0
1990	119.5
1992	128.1

First album, *Loverboy*, by Vancouver rock group Loverboy

83 million watch *Dallas* to find out "who shot J.R."

On TV: CBS news anchor Walter Cronkite retires, Dan Rather replaces him; Ted Koppel's *Nightline* debuts on ABC

Canada, U.S. and 52 other nations boycott Moscow summer Olympics to protest Soviet invasion of Afghanistan

U.S. hockey team upsets U.S.S.R., defeats Finnish team to win gold at winter Olympics in Lake Placid, New York; speed skater Eric Heiden wins five golds

Sweden's Bjorn Borg wins fifth straight men's singles tennis title at Wimbledon

"Somewhere out in this audience may even be someone who will one day follow in my footsteps, and preside over the White House as the President's spouse. I wish him well!"

— *Barbara Bush, Wellesley College commencement, 1990*

Edmonton Eskimos with third consecutive Grey Cup

New York Islanders win Stanley Cup

1981

On Golden Pond, with Katharine Hepburn, Henry Fonda, and Jane Fonda

Director Steven Spielberg's *Raiders of the Lost Ark*, starring Harrison Ford

British director Hugh Hudson's *Chariots of Fire*

Heavy Metal, Canada's most expensive animated film, does well at box office

Canadian film, *Not a Love Story*, is a critical success for National Film Board

Musical *Cats* opens on Broadway

On TV: *Hill Street Blues, Dynasty, Falcon Crest*

Britain's Sebastian Coe sets world record for the mile: 3 minutes 48.4 seconds

Edmonton Eskimos win fourth Grey Cup in four years

New York Islanders repeat win of Stanley Cup

1982

Director Steven Spielberg's *E.T. The Extra-Terrestrial*

British director Richard Attenborough's *Gandhi*, with Ben Kingsley

Tootsie, with Dustin Hoffman and Jessica Lange

Sophie's Choice, with Meryl Streep and Kevin Kline

Canadian film, *The Grey Fox*, released, starring Jackie Burroughs; wins three Genies

On TV: *Cagney & Lacey, Cheers, St. Elsewhere, Family Ties*

Barbara Frum moves from radio to become host of CBC television's *The Journal*

Paul Cowan's television docudrama on Billy Bishop, *The Kid Who Couldn't Miss*

Michael Jackson's hit album *Thriller*

Canadian Ginette Reno releases best-selling album *Je ne suis qu'une chanson*

Canada's Steve Podborski wins world cup for downhill skiing

Edmonton Eskimos win record fifth straight Grey Cup

New York Islanders win third consecutive Stanley Cup

1983

The Big Chill, with Glenn Close, William Hurt, and Kevin Kline

The Year of Living Dangerously, with Mel Gibson, Linda Hunt, and Sigourney Weaver

In his 1988 book A Brief History of Time, British physicist Stephen Hawking elucidated cosmology.

Director James Brooks's *Terms of Endearment*, with Shirley MacLaine and Jack Nicholson

On TV: Epic series make it big with *The Thorn Birds* and *The Winds of War*

Final regular *M*A*S*H* episode watched by over 120 million viewers, largest audience for any nonsports TV program

Toronto Argonauts win Grey Cup

New York Islanders win fourth consecutive Stanley Cup

1984

Czech-born film director Milos Forman's *Amadeus*

U.S. director Steven Spielberg's *Indiana Jones and the Temple of Doom*

British film director David Lean's *A Passage to India*, based on E. M. Forster's novel, with Peggy Ashcroft and Alec Guinness

Arnold Schwarzenegger in *The Terminator*

On TV: *The Bill Cosby Show, Murder, She Wrote*

Michael Jackson wins record eight Grammys; *Thriller* album sells 37 million copies

Summer Olympic Games held in Los Angeles; Canada had best performance ever with 44 medals, including two gold

Winter Olympics in Sarajevo, Yugoslavia; Canada's Gaetan

Boucher wins two gold medals and one bronze in speed-skating for best ever Olympic performance by a Canadian; later wins world sprint speed-skating championship

Martina Navratilova wins Grand Slam in women's tennis; takes fifth Wimbledon singles title

Winnipeg Blue Bombers win Grey Cup

Edmonton Oilers win Stanley Cup

1985

Sydney Pollack's *Out of Africa*, with Robert Redford and Meryl Streep

Japanese film director Akira Kurosawa's *Ran*

Radio host Garrison Keillor's *Lake Wobegon Days*

On TV: *The Golden Girls*

On TV, docudrama *Canada's Sweetheart: The Saga of Hal C. Banks*

Canadian film from British Columbia, *My American Cousin;* wins four Genies

"We Are the World," top-selling single record, wins Grammy

55 Canadian popular music artists organized as *Northern Lights* produce *Tears are not Enough* to raise money for African Famine Relief

Bruce Springsteen's *Born in the U.S.A.* is top-selling album: 15 million

British Columbia Lions win Grey Cup

Edmonton Oilers win Stanley Cup

1986

Writer-director Woody Allen's *Hannah and Her Sisters*, with Michael Caine and Mia Farrow

British film director James Ivory's *A Room With a View*

U.S. director Oliver Stone's *Platoon*

Top Gun, with Tom Cruise

Children of a Lesser God, with Marlee Matlin

Denys Arcand's comedy of sexual attitudes, *The Decline of the American Empire*, wins many awards, including four Genies

Canadian film *Dancing in the Dark* premieres at Cannes, wins critical praise

Canada's CBC announces severe budget reductions and layoffs

On TV: *L.A. Law, Matlock, A Current Affair; The Oprah Winfrey Show*

Hamilton Tiger-Cats win Grey Cup

Montreal Canadiens win Stanley Cup

1987

Italian director Bernardo Bertolucci's *The Last Emperor*

Broadcast News, written and directed by James L. Brooks

Fatal Attraction, with Michael Douglas and Glenn Close

Wall Street, with Michael Douglas and Charlie Sheen

Award-winning Canadian film *I've Heard the Mermaids Singing*

On TV: *A Different World, Beauty and the Beast, Jake and the Fat Man*

Les Misérables opens on Broadway

Madonna has 10 straight top-10 singles

Michael Jackson's album *Bad* sells 25 million copies

Montreal Alouettes football team folds

Canada defeats Soviet Union 6-5 to win Canada Cup

Canada has 238,305 registered amateur baseball players

Edmonton Eskimos win Grey Cup

Edmonton Oilers win Stanley Cup

1988

Dustin Hoffman in *Rain Man*

Dangerous Liaisons, with Glenn Close and John Malkovich

The Accused, with Jodie Foster

Canadian director David Cronenberg's *Dead Ringers*, starring Jeremy Irons

Phantom of the Opera opens on Broadway

On TV: *thirtysomething, Murphy Brown, Roseanne*

Summer Olympics at Seoul, Canada wins 3 gold, 2 silver, 5 bronze; Canadian sprinter Ben Johnson wins gold for 100 metres, then loses it after failing steroid drug test

Winter Olympics at Calgary, Canada wins 2 silver, 3 bronze

Winnipeg Blue Bombers win Grey Cup

Edmonton Oilers win Stanley Cup for second consecutive year

1989

Oliver Stone's *Born on the Fourth of July*, with Tom Cruise

Driving Miss Daisy, with Jessica Tandy and Morgan Freeman

Black American actor and director Spike Lee's *Do the Right Thing*

Batman, with Michael Keaton and Jack Nicholson

My Left Foot, with Daniel Day-Lewis

Denys Arcand's award-winning *Jesus of Montreal*

On TV: *Life Goes On, Coach*; Special: *Lonesome Dove*

Saskatchewan Rough Riders win Grey Cup

Calgary Flames win Stanley Cup

1990

Comedian Johnny Wayne, of Wayne and Shuster, dies

U.S. film director Martin Scorsese's *Goodfellas*

Kevin Costner stars in and directs *Dances with Wolves*

Reversal of Fortune, with Jeremy Irons and Glenn Close

Misery, with James Caan and Kathy Bates

Ghost, with Whoopi Goldberg, Demi Moore, and Patrick Swayze

On TV: *The Simpsons, Hard Copy, Cops, Seinfeld, Northern Exposure*; Special: *Twin Peaks*

CBC television's *Road to Avonlea* wins its fifth Gemini award

Rita MacNeil is named Canada's top female vocalist of the year

Winnipeg Blue Bombers win Grey Cup

Edmonton Oilers win Stanley Cup

1991

U.S. film director Jonathan Demme's *The Silence of the Lambs*, with Anthony Hopkins and Jodie Foster

U.S. director Oliver Stone's *J.F.K.*

"Ninety feet between bases is perhaps as close as man has ever gotten to perfection."

— Red Smith on baseball, 1981

Disney animated feature *Beauty and the Beast*

Film *Black Robe*, a Canadian-Australian co-production, wins three Genie awards

On TV: *Homefront, Home Improvement*

Ferguson Jenkins, formerly pitcher for Chicago Cubs, becomes first Canadian to be inducted into Baseball Hall of Fame

Los Angeles Lakers basketball star "Magic" Johnson announces he is HIV positive and retires from regular play

Canada's Kurt Browning wins fourth world figure skating title

Toronto Argonauts win Grey Cup

Pittsburgh Penguins win Stanley Cup

1992

Director-actor Clint Eastwood's western *Unforgiven*

Aladdin, Disney's animated tale from the Arabian Nights

Canadian director David Cronenberg's *Naked Lunch* wins three Genie awards, including best director

Johnny Carson retires from *The Tonight Show*; comedian Jay Leno replaces him

---

On TV: *Melrose Place, Martin, Picket Fences*

Canada's Manon Rhéaume becomes first woman to play NHL hockey when she appears in goal for an exhibition game

Canada wins 7 gold, 5 silver, and 7 bronze medals in the summer Olympics at Barcelona

Ottawa Senators reborn to play hockey in the NHL

Calgary Stampeders win Grey Cup

Pittsburgh Penguins win Stanley Cup for second consecutive year

Toronto Blue Jays win World Series; first time title leaves U.S.

1993

U.S. film director Martin Scorsese's *The Age of Innocence*, based on Edith Wharton's novel

Steven Spielberg's *Jurassic Park* and *Schindler's List*

The Piano with Holly Hunter and Harvey Keitel; *The Fugitive*, with Harrison Ford

Documentary film directed by François Girard, *Thirty-Two Short Films about Glenn Gould*, wins four Genie awards

On TV: *NYPD Blue, Lois and Clark, Frasier*

Chicago Bulls basketball superstar Michael Jordan announces his retirement

Tennis star Monica Seles stabbed and seriously injured by spectator at a tournament in Hamburg, Germany

Tennis great Arthur Ashe dies of complications from AIDS contracted through a transfusion of tainted blood

In world curling championships at Geneva, Canada wins both men's and women's titles

Canadian Football League announces expansion to San Antonio and Sacramento

Canadian Kate Pace wins world's downhill skiing title

Edmonton Eskimos win Grey Cup

Montreal Canadiens win Stanley Cup; crowd riots in downtown Montreal

Toronto Blue Jays win World Series for second consecutive year

1994

On TV: *Mad About You, Grace Under Fire, E.R.*

Forrest Gump with Tom Hanks; *The Lion King, Pulp Fiction* with John Travolta and Bruce Willis, directed by Quentin Tarantino

At Lillehammer, Norway, Canada wins 3 gold, 7 silver, and 3 bronze medals for its best showing at a winter Olympics

Manon Rhéaume, first woman to play in the NHL, played goalie in an exhibition game in 1992.

National Basketball Association announces that Vancouver is second Canadian city to receive an NBA franchise; team will be called Vancouver Grizzlies

Winnipeg Blue Bombers win Grey Cup

New York Rangers win Stanley Cup

Baseball's two major leagues split into three divisions; each league's three division winners, plus a runner-up, to

---

Canadian Longevity, Years of Life Expected at Birth

Years of Life Expected at Birth: 1921–2011

■ Female ■ Male

Year	♀ Female	♂ Male
2011	84.0	77.2
2001	82.1	75.5
1991	80.9	74.6
1981	79.2	72.1
1971	76.6	69.6
1961	74.2	68.4
1951	70.8	66.3
1941	66.3	63.0
1931	62.1	60.0
1921	49.2	49.1

vie in post-season playoffs, and the two winners to meet; in World Series; August strike ends play

1995

Only 3 percent of films in Canadian theatres are Canadian films

On T.V: *Friends*

O.J. Simpson trial dominates television

Apollo 13 with Tom Hanks; Disney's *Pocahontas; Bridges of Madison County* with Meryl Streep and Clint Eastwood

Toronto Raptors have first season as first NBA team outside U.S.

Canadian Elvis Stojko wins second world figure skating title

Jacques Villeneuve becomes first Canadian to win Indianapolis 500 automobile race; is named Canada's Athlete of the Year

"If, in fact, the great ride is over, I don't know how the skills of investment manipulation will translate to anything else."

— Tom Wolfe, author of The Bonfire of the Vanities, 1987

Baltimore Stallions win Grey Cup; first time trophy leaves Canada; Baltimore officials expect franchise to move, however, as fan interest is low

New Jersey Devils win Stanley Cup

BUSINESS & ECONOMICS

1980

Chrysler reports largest loss ever by a U.S. carmaker;

Big screen televisions, with VCR's and stereo hookups, turn homes into private screening rooms to watch the latest release or a favorite classic.

Chrysler Canada receives $200 million in loan guarantees from Ottawa

Dow Jones ends year at 960.58

Ottawa introduces National Energy Programme to encourage Canadian ownership of energy resources

1981

Canada has 23 million credit cards in circulation

Canada's bank rate soars to over 20 percent

Canada's Bombardier reports $100 million sale of subway cars to Mexico

HDTV (High Definition Television) developed

General Motors reports worst loss in 60 years; Chrysler loses $1.7 billion

First computerized trading on stock exchange

IBM personal computer (PC) goes on sale

Dow Jones ends year at 875.00

1982

Canada and U.S. have highest unemployment figures since Depression years; Canada's gross domestic product drops 6½ percent

General Motors Canada receives $625 million contract to build armored vehicles for U.S. armed forces

First decline in Consumer Price Index in nearly 17 years

Coca-Cola agrees to buy Columbia Pictures

Compaq markets IBM PC clones

Dow Jones ends year at 1046.54

1983

Unemployment in Canada climbs to almost 12 percent

Ottawa ends preferential rates for grain shipments in Crow's Nest Pass agreement

OPEC countries drop oil prices to $29 per barrel, a $5 cut

Popular cable channel MTV helps to revive record industry

Dow Jones ends year at 1258.64

1984

Canadian Jobs Strategy reorganizes labor programs

Dow Jones ends year at 1211.57

1985

Australian entrepreneur Rupert Murdoch buys seven TV stations and 20th Century-Fox; plans to start Fox TV network

R. J. Reynolds buys Nabisco for $4.9 billion

General Electric buys RCA for $6.2 billion

Record fatalities in civilian air travel: over 2,000 die worldwide in crashes

Prime Minister Mulroney replaces Foreign Investment

Review Act with Investment Canada, conceding to U.S. demands to relax regulation of foreign investment

1986

In Canada, Northland Bank and Canadian Commercial Bank collapse

Robert ("Bob") White leads Canadian members out of U.S. United Automobile Workers union to form Canadian Automobile Workers Union

Hyundai announces plan to build car assembly plant at Bromont, Quebec

Canadians own over 24,000 private airplanes and over 1,200 helicopters

Hydro-Québec completes LG-2, LG-3 and LG-4 dam projects

Arbitrageur Ivan Boesky caught in insider trading scandal; agrees to pay $100 million fine and name other lawbreakers

$39 billion in merger deals as "merger mania" continues

Dow Jones ends year at 1546.67

1987

Canadian government begins privatization of some federal airports

Stock markets crash around world

Ottawa sells Teleglobe Canada to Memotec Data for $488 million

Canada and U.S. in trade dispute as U.S. imposes tax on Canadian softwood lumber

Dow Jones ends year at 1938.83

1988

Canada sells $28-million nuclear reactor to South Korea

Kohlberg Kravis Roberts buys RJR-Nabisco for $25 billion

Honda plant in Allison, Ontario, produces first Honda Civic to be built in North America

Canadian government approves sale of government-owned Air Canada; two days later, Air Canada announces plans to purchase European Airbus A-320

Dow Jones ends year at 2168.57

1989

Junk-bond broker Michael Milken charged with fraud; later Milken pays $600 million fine, is sentenced to jail term

Warner Communications and Time-Life merge in $11.7-billion deal, making Time Warner

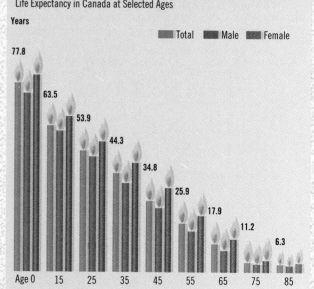

Still Years to Go at 85

Life Expectancy in Canada at Selected Ages

Years

■ Total ■ Male ■ Female

77.8 (Age 0)
63.5 (15)
53.9 (25)
44.3 (35)
34.8 (45)
25.9 (55)
17.9 (65)
11.2 (75)
6.3 (85)

largest communications company in North America.

Dow Jones ends year at 2753.20

1990

Canadian government announces cod fishery quota to be cut by 16 percent

McDonald's opens in Moscow

Canadian government enacts GST (Goods and Services Tax)

Dow Jones ends year at 2633.66

1991

Pan Am files for bankruptcy

BCCI (Bank of Credit and Commerce International) scandal: fraud charged in seven countries

General Motors announces closing of 21 North American plants and loss of 74,000 jobs over four years

IBM's first loss ever: $1.73 billion in first quarter

Algoma Steel Corporation narrowly avoids bankruptcy with loans of $60 million from Bank of Canada and $15 million from Dofasco and governments of Canada and Ontario

British publishing magnate Robert Maxwell found dead in waters off Canary Islands; his empire collapses because of financial irregularities

Dow Jones ends year at 3168.83

1992

Newfoundland cod fishery closed for at least two years as fish stocks severely threatened due to overfishing

Canada real estate company, Olympia and York, announces loss of $2.05 billion for year

76,139 Canadian companies go bankrupt in a single year; a record

Russia agrees to purchase $200 million of Canadian wheat

Dow Jones ends year at 3301.11

1993

Tioxide Canada announces plan to close plant at Tracy, Quebec, after company is prosecuted for severe industrial pollution of St. Lawrence River

---

Bell Canada announces plans to cut work force by 10 percent

IBM announces $8.9-billion downsizing charge

Dow Jones ends year at 3754.09

1994

Exxon Corp. ordered to pay $5 million in punitive damages as compensation for the 1989 *Exxon Valdez* oil spill

Windsor Casino in Ontario makes $100 million in first 10 weeks of operation

"A few years ago, there was only a handful of people who could bid $1 million. Today you have unlimited billions . . ."

— *Dealer Richard Feigen on the art auction boom, 1986*

U.S.-based Walmart Stores buys 120 Woolco stores in Canada in preparation for expansion

NAFTA becomes effective January 1, 1994, creating largest free trade zone in world

Dow Jones ends year at 3834.44

1995

Canada's chartered banks report largest profits in history

At rumors of a factory opening in Pickering, Ontario, 26,000 line up to apply for work

Microsoft's Windows 95 goes on sale after one of history's most lavish advertising campaigns

One of Britain's oldest banks, Barings PLC, declares bankruptcy after Nicholas Leeson, the firm's chief trader in Singapore, gambles with and loses more than $1 billion of bank's assets

---

Walt Disney Co. buys Capital Cities/ABC for $19 billion, creating world's largest media and entertainment organization

Dow Jones breaks 5000 points in November

SCIENCE & MEDICINE

1980

Nuclear reactors produce 38 percent of Ontario's electrical power

Hepatitis B vaccine

Sonar device breaks up kidney stones, supplants surgery for kidney stones in many cases

Aegyptopithecus, thought to be oldest primate fossil, found in Egypt

Voyager I completes first successful flyby of Saturn; discovers a 15th moon of Saturn

1981

Autoimmune deficiency syndrome (AIDS), newly named disease

Largest known star discovered; R136A's mass is 2,500 times greater than that of sun

First commercial MRI (magnetic resonance imaging) unit; it produces detailed images of internal body tissues

Auto, factory, and power plant emissions said to be culprits in the formation of acid rain

First flight of *Columbia*, a reusable spacecraft called the space shuttle

1982

First artificial heart implant; patient Barney Clark survives 112 days

Halley's Comet observed by astronomers, first time since 1909–11; makes closest approach to sun in 1986 as it continues on its orbit that will bring it back in view in about 77 years

1983

First successful human embryo transplant

First synthetic chromosome created

1984

Marc Garneau is first Canadian in space, on board shuttle *Challenger*

First successful fetus surgery

Genetic fingerprinting based on DNA code discovered

Two more rings found around Saturn

First baby born from frozen embryo

Baboon heart is transplanted to 15-day-old baby; she survives for 20 days

1985

Fuel consumption of new cars produced in Canada and the U.S. reduced by half since 1975

Blood test to detect AIDS becomes available

Single optical fibre carries 300,000 phone calls

Laser used to clear arteries

Scientists confirm progressive depletion of ozone layer above Antarctica

1986

Experts forecast AIDS cases and deaths will increase tenfold in next five years

Chernobyl nuclear-reactor disaster in U.S.S.R.: hundreds of square kilometres affected by fallout

First triple transplant (heart, lung, liver)

First growth-inhibiting gene discovered

Space shuttle *Challenger* explodes just after liftoff; schoolteacher Christa McAuliffe and the other six crew members are killed

Canadian scientist Dr. John Polanyi shares Nobel Prize for Chemistry

1987

Hydro-Québec generators at James Bay produce 735,000 volts, highest electricity transmission voltage in world

Canada spends $7.1 billion on scientific research and development

---

Coelacanths, so-called living fossil fish, observed in depths of Indian Ocean

1988

International treaty to reduce chlorofluorocarbon (CFC) emissions

Homo sapiens fossils found in Israel dating back 92,000 years

British theoretical physicist Stephen Hawking produces his book *A Brief History of Time: From the Big Bang to Black Holes;* is a surprise bestseller

The personal computer, with nearly infinite uses, becomes the workhorse of busy offices.

1989

Canadian Space Agency created

Genetic indicator for cystic fibrosis discovered

Voyager 2 makes first flyby of Neptune and discovers a third moon of Neptune

Deer ticks found to carry Lyme disease

1990

Cancer therapy using genetically altered cells

A tiny golden calf sculpture dating from second millennium B.C. found in Israel

Powerful Hubble telescope put into orbit; fails to operate successfully but is repaired in late 1993 by space-walking

499

astronauts aboard the space shuttle *Endeavor*

1991

Cholera reappears in U.S. after 100-year absence

Taxol, drug derived from yew tree, approved for trials in treatment of ovarian and breast cancer

Biosphere 2 begins; scientists live in artificial ecosystem

1992

Tuberculosis reappears in Canadian cities; new strain is resistant to treatment

Twelve million people worldwide dead of AIDS

1993

Department of Energy Secretary Hazel R. O'Leary declassifies documents relating to effects of radiation on human subjects tested during the Cold War by U.S. agencies and military services

Dr. Michael Smith, biochemist at University of British Columbia, is co-winner of Nobel Prize for Chemistry

"The more we tried to build humanlike machines, the more we admired what a human is."

— David Nitzan of SRI International
on the development of robots, 1988

Lou Gehrig's disease gene found

Princeton University's Dr. Andrew Wiles claims to have found proof for French mathematician Pierre de Fermat's "last theorem," sought for more than 350 years

1994

Heterosexual transmission accounts for 9 percent of new

AIDS cases, up from less than 2 percent in 1985

A Utah microbiologist isolates DNA from bone fragments of dinosaurs that lived 80 million years ago

1995

Scientists add "leap second" to end of 1995 as compensation for gradually slowing of earth's rotation

Astronomers detect two new planets outside our solar system

Canadian Dr. David Williams, specialist in emergency medicine, begins training for U.S. space mission; astronaut Chris Hadfield uses Canadarm in space to repair *Mir* space station

A network of caves containing hundreds of undisturbed cave paintings said to be 20,000 years old discovered in southern France; there are doubts about its authenticity

WORLD POLITICAL EVENTS

1980

Rhodesia wins independence; is renamed Zimbabwe

Yugoslav leader Marshal Tito dies at age 87 after 35 years in power

Deposed shah of Iran, Mohammad Reza Pahlavi, 60, dies in exile in an Egyptian military hospital

Shipyard workers in Gdansk, Poland, strike to protest rising price of meat; electrician Lech Walesa emerges as leader of labor movement that becomes known as Solidarity, first independent labor union allowed in a Soviet satellite

Assassins kill exiled Nicaraguan dictator Anastasio Somoza in Paraguay

Christian Democrat José Napoléon Duarte is elected president of El Salvador; first civilian president in 49 years

1981

Pope John Paul II is shot and wounded; would-be assassin

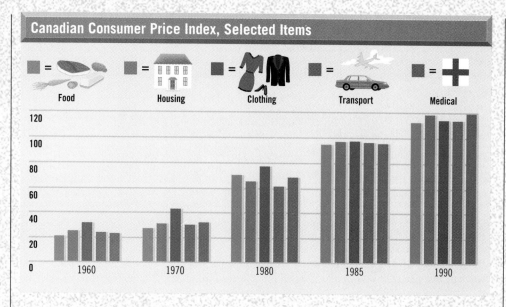

Canadian Consumer Price Index, Selected Items

■ = Food
■ = Housing
■ = Clothing
■ = Transport
■ = Medical

Mehmet Ali Agca arrested, tried, and sentenced to life imprisonment; Pope later hears Agca's confession and absolves him

François Mitterrand is first Socialist to be elected president of France

Irish Republican Army (IRA) member Robert (Bobby) Sands, 27, dies after a 66-day hunger strike in prison in Belfast, Ireland

Egypt's President Anwar Sadat, 62, assassinated in Cairo by Islamic extremists; Vice President Hosni Mubarak succeeds him; Sadat's peace treaty with Israel stands

Israeli statesman and war hero Moshe Dayan dies at age 66

China's Communist Party denounces former leader Mao Tse-tung's policies; Mao's widow, Jiang Qing, given suspended death sentence and imprisoned

1982

Argentina invades British Falklands Islands; Britain blockades Argentina and sinks its sole cruiser, killing 320; in final assault, 9,000 British soldiers accept surrender of 11,000 Argentinians; dead (not counting those killed on cruiser), 652 Argentinians and 255 British

Israel withdraws from Sinai and returns it to Egypt, abiding by 1978 Camp David accord

Poland outlaws Solidarity labor union

Leonid Brezhnev, Communist Party secretary for 17 years, dies at 75; KGB head Yuri Andropov, 68, succeeds him

Israeli land, sea, and air forces invade southern Lebanon in effort to wipe out PLO strongholds; PLO is evacuated as multinational peacekeeping force moves in

1983

Klaus Barbie, Nazi Gestapo "Butcher of Lyons," is extradited from Bolivia to France; found guilty of war crimes and sentenced in 1987 to life imprisonment

NATO ministers affirm decision to deploy intermediate range nuclear forces (INF) if U.S.-Soviet arms talks fail; Green Movement mounts protests in Western Europe

Korean Airlines Boeing 747 en route from New York to Seoul shot down by Soviet missile for violating Soviet air space in North Pacific; all 269 passengers and crew are killed

Conservative Margaret Thatcher becomes British prime minister

Israeli Prime Minister Menachem Begin resigns; Foreign Minister Yitzhak Shamir succeeds him

Syria shoots down U.S. plane, captures navy pilot; Rev. Jesse Jackson wins pilot's release in 1984

Poland's Solidarity leader Lech Walesa wins Nobel Peace Prize

Benigno Aquino, returning from exile to Philippines to continue opposing Ferdinand Marcos, is murdered; 1 million mourners attend his funeral

1984

Soviet leader Yuri Andropov, 69, dies; Politburo member Konstantin Chernenko, 72, becomes General Secretary of Communist Party Central Committee

U.S.S.R. and 14 other nations, professing fear of anti-Soviet actions, boycott summer Olympics in Los Angeles

British agree to leave Hong Kong in 1997

Bishop Desmond Tutu of South Africa wins Nobel Peace Prize for antiapartheid efforts

Indian troops retake Golden Temple in Amritsar after Sikh extremists seize it; 800 Sikhs, 200 soldiers die; Indira Gandhi, 66, assassinated by her Sikh bodyguards; 1,000 are killed in anti-Sikh riots; Gandhi's son Rajiv becomes prime minister

1985

Israel begins pullout from Lebanon

Shiite terrorists hijack TWA jet, kill American sailor, hold other American passengers hostage in Beirut; terrorists release hostages after Israelis free Arab prisoners

Remains of Nazi war criminal Dr. Joseph Mengele, buried in Brazil, are identified

Earthquake measuring 7.8 on Richter scale hits Mexico City; more than 5,000 perish

Members of the Palestinian Liberation Front seize cruise ship *Achille Lauro*, murder Leon Klinghoffer, wheelchair-confined American

Colombian volcano erupts, 25,000 are killed or missing

Soviet General Secretary Chernenko dies; Mikhail Sergeyevich Gorbachev comes to power in U.S.S.R. and asks for economic reforms

Terrorists attack El Al Airlines counters in Rome and Vienna, killing and wounding dozens; Israel retaliates against PLO headquarters in Tunis, kills leaders and bodyguards

1986

Austrian presidential candidate and former U.N. head Kurt Waldheim is accused of hiding his Nazi past

President Ferdinand Marcos of the Philippines is deposed; he and his family are given refuge in Hawaii; Corazon Aquino, widow of slain opposition leader Benigno Aquino, becomes president

120 nations call for antiapartheid trade sanctions against South Africa

Haitian dictator Jean-Claude "Baby Doc" Duvalier deposed, flees to France

1987

Soviet leader Gorbachev initiates policy of *glasnost,* or openness

West German Mathias Rust, 19,

flies small plane undetected into Moscow; Soviet defence minister is fired

Margaret Thatcher voted into office as British prime minister for third time

Costa Rican President Oscar Arias's Central American Peace Plan is signed; Arias receives Nobel Peace Prize

"[This is] the clearest opportunity to reduce the risk of war since the dawn of the nuclear age."

— *Secretary of State James Baker speaking of Gorbachev's reforms, 1989*

South Korea holds first direct presidential election; ruling party is reelected

1988

Vietnam sets withdrawal from Cambodia; 50,000 troops to leave by end of year, remainder by end of 1990

Voters remove Chilean dictator Augusto Pinochet Ugarte from office

Earthquake strikes Armenia; over 55,000 are killed

Cease-fire between Nicaraguan Sandinistas and Contras

Benazir Bhutto is prime minister of Pakistan, first woman to head any Moslem state

Iran and Iraq declare peace, both sides claiming victory

1989

Communist regimes crumble in Eastern Europe: Solidarity wins first free Polish elections in 40 years; the next year Lech Walesa becomes president of Poland; Berlin Wall comes down; Romanians overthrow and execute Nicolae Ceausescu; Velvet Revolution in Czechoslovakia ends with

playwright Vaclav Havel elected president

Tiananmen Square reform protests in China bring government crackdown; some 5,000 die

Japan's Emperor Hirohito dies after 62-year reign

1990

West and East Germany reunite after 45 years

Soviet republics, led by Lithuania, Armenia, and Georgia, agitate for independence

Elections in Nicaragua: Sandinistas ousted in free elections; Violeta Chamorro becomes president

South Africa, in conciliatory move, frees antiapartheid leader Nelson Mandela after decades of imprisonment

Margaret Thatcher resigns as British prime minister; John Major succeeds her

South African President F.W. de Klerk and African National Congress (ANC) leader Nelson Mandela shake hands at a luncheon in Philadelphia.

Charter of Paris signed by 34 nations; brings formal end to Cold War

Hungary ends Communist rule by electing a centrist coalition government; Yugoslav republics of Croatia and Slovenia declare independence; non-Communist regimes take hold in Albania, Bulgaria, Romania

1991

Hard-line Communists attempt coup against Gorbachev; Russian Republic President Boris Yeltsin calls for general strike; coup defeated; Soviet Union breaks up as republics declare independence; Gorbachev resigns

Rajiv Gandhi assassinated while campaigning for prime ministership of India

South African President F. W. de Klerk proposes dismantling apartheid

Arab-Israeli peace talks commence in Madrid, Spain

Haiti's Jean-Bertrand Aristide, first democratically elected president, is deposed; Haitians seek asylum in U.S.

Mt. Pinatubo erupts in the Philippines

1992

British Prime Minister John Major narrowly reelected

Earth Summit in Rio de Janeiro: largest gathering of world leaders to date; agreements signed on endangered species, environmental law, and global warming

White South Africans vote to end white rule by 1994

Bloody civil war erupts between the Serbs, Croats, and Moslems in Bosnia

1993

President F. W. de Klerk and African National Congress leader Nelson Mandela jointly win Nobel Peace Prize

Czechoslovakia peacefully splits into two states: the Czech Republic and Slovakia

In Russia, power struggle between President Boris Yeltsin and parliament; Yeltsin survives vote on impeachment, dissolves parliament; former parliament members revolt and are put down by troops loyal to Yeltsin

Israel and the PLO sign peace accords; Yitzhak Rabin and Yasir Arafat shake hands at White House

1994

Jewish settler slaughters more than 36 Muslims inside a shrine in Israeli town of Hebron

First fully free elections in post-apartheid South Africa bring Nelson Mandela to power as head of the African National Congress

Civil war erupts in Rwanda; 500,000 people are killed and 2 million flee the country as a result of the conflict

Russia invades Chechnya, a former Soviet republic

Jean-Bertrand Aristide is reinstated as Haiti's president after U.S. threatens an invasion to oust the military government

1995

U.S. normalizes relations with Vietnam

Earthquake kills 4,000 in Kobe, Japan

Jacques Chirac wins French presidential election; former President François Mitterand dies

Japanese doomsday cult launches nerve-gas attack in Tokyo subway system; kills 10, injures more than 5,000

Israeli prime minister Yitzhak Rabin assassinated in Tel Aviv

Nigerian government executes poet and playwright Ken Saro-Wiwa

Credits

2 *middle left (flagship)* Lake County (IL) Museum/Curt Teich Postcard Archives; *"Peace" and "Pearl Harbor" buttons* Hake's Americana & Collectibles; *remainder* Private Collection. **3** *top (5&10¢ store) and middle (amusement park)* Lake County (IL) Museum/Curt Teich Postcard Archives; *remainder* Private Collection. **7** *top* Library of Congress; *bottom* FPG International. **8** ©Equitable Life Assurance of the USA; *bottom* Library of Congress. **9** *top* National Archives; *bottom* Archive Photos/Camerique. **10** *top* James H. Karales/Peter Arnold, Inc.; *bottom* Wally McNamee/Woodfin Camp & Associates. **11** Rob Matheson/The Stock Market. **12-13** National Archives of Canada C68842. **14** *left* Brown Brothers; *right* The Lewis W. Hine Collection, The New York Public Library. **14-15** Library of Congress. **15** *left* National Archives of Canada PA34014; *right* Glenbow NA-3241-11. **16** *top* Chicago Historical Society; *bottom (l. to r.)* Library of Congress; National Archives; The Bettmann Archive; Culver Pictures. **17** *top left* National Archives of Canada C1971; *top right* The Bettmann Archive; *bottom (l. to r.)* Laurier House; The Bettmann Archive; UPI/Bettmann. **18** *left* Library of Congress; *right* Culver Pictures. **19** *top right* Geological Survey of Canada GSC25255; *middle right* Hulton Deutsch Collection; *remainder* The Bettmann Archive. **20** *left* The Bettmann Archive; *middle* Culver Pictures; *right* Brown Brothers. **21** *top left* Culver Pictures; *bottom right* The Bettmann Archive; *remainder* Library of Congress. **22** *top* Culver Pictures; *bottom* The Bettmann Archive. **23** *top left* National Archives of Canada C9062; *top right* Culver Pictures; *bottom* B.C. Archives & Records Service. **24** *background* Library of Congress; *left* National Archives of Canada C7673; *right* Knight Library, University of Oregon. **24-25** From the collection of David R. Phillips. **25** *top* Library of Congress; *remainder* The Bettmann Archive. **26** *box: left* Brown Brothers; *top right* Culver Pictures; *middle right* C.N. Visual Communications; *bottom right* Pach/Bettmann; *far right* Library of Congress; *bottom* Culver Pictures. **27** *left* California Museum of Photography/Keystone-Mast Collection/University of California, Riverside; *right* The Texas Collection, Baylor University, Waco, Texas; *bottom* From the collection of the Minnesota Historical Society. **28** *top* General Motors of Canada Ltd.; *bottom left* Courtesy National Automotive History Collection, Detroit Public Library; *bottom right* Brown Brothers. **28-29** *background* The Bettmann Archive. **29** *both* Brown Brothers. **30** *top* The Bettmann Archive; *center (both)* Library of Congress. **30-31** *bottom (l. to r.)* Culver Pictures; The Bettmann Archive; Brown Brothers. **31** *upper left* National Film Board of Canada; *upper right* Culver Pictures; *middle right* Seaver Center for Western History Research, Natural History Museum of Los Angeles County. **32** *left* Bell Canada Historical Collection; *middle* The Bettmann Archive; *right* Frank Driggs Collection. **32-33** *top* The Bettmann Archive. **33** *right* New York Public Library Picture Collection; *remainder* Library of Congress/Photographed by M. Rudolf Vetter. **34** *top* The Bettmann Archive; *middle* From the Eaton Collection at the Archives of Ontario; *bottom* From the collection of David R. Phillips. **35** *left (top to bottom)* The Bettmann Archive; Private Collection; The International Museum of Photography at George Eastman House; *remainder* Library of Congress. **36** *clockwise from top left:* "His Master's Voice" is a registered trademark of the General Electric Company/Culver Pictures; Morton International, Inc.; Courtesy of the Dial Corp.; Courtesy Springs Canada Inc.; The "Sailor Jack & Bingo" logo is a registered trademark and is reproduced with the permission of Borden, Inc.; Advertisement courtesy of the Faultless Starch-Bon Ami Company/The Bettmann Archive; Uniroyal Goodrich Licensing Services, Inc./Collection of Ruth Kravette, Authentic Old Ads, Jericho, NY; Used with permission of General Mills, Inc.; Flexible Flyer is the trademark of the Roadmaster Corporation, Olney, IL. **37** *clockwise from top left:* "Simple Simon and Pieman" logo courtesy of Franchise Associates, Inc.; Courtesy of Motorola Museum of Electronics; Coca-Cola is a registered trademark of The Coca-Cola Company; A registered trademark of Schering-Plough HealthCare Products, Inc., USA/Reproduced with permission of Schering-Plough HealthCare Products, Inc., the trademark owner; Courtesy Air Canada; ©Revlon, Inc.; Eveready Battery Company, Inc.; The USDA Forest Service, the State Foresters, the Ad Council and Foote, Cone & Belding; Fruit of The Loom, Inc.; Courtesy of Clairol, Inc.; *center* Peter Max, 1972/Courtesy ViaMax, New York. **38** *top right* Brown Brothers; *bottom left* Courtesy of The Adirondack Museum; *remainder* Culver Pictures. **39** *top left* National Archives of Canada PA127246; *top right* Culver Pictures; *bottom* Brown Brothers. **40** *left* Culver Pictures; *top right* Collection on the History of Canadian Psychiatry and Mental Health Care; *middle right* from the book "Ernest Jones: Freud's Alter Ego," courtesy Caliban Books. **41** *"Heidelberg Belt"* Original poster from the Lindan Historical Collection of Electrotherapy and Unusual Healing Devices, Cleveland, OH; Published by the Museum of Questionable Medical Devices, Minneapolis, MN; *"Iron Bitters"* From the collection of Romy Charlesworth; *"Warburg's Tincture" and "Dr. Shoop's Tablets"* Smithsonian Institution; *bottom left* The Bettmann Archive; *bottom right* The Granger Collection, New York. **42** *left (top to bottom)* Culver Pictures; Collection of Theodore Robinson, Richboro, PA; Brown Brothers; *top right* The Granger Collection, New York; **42-43** *bottom* Brown Brothers. **43** *clockwise from top:* The Bettmann Archive; The Granger Collection, New York; Library of Congress; Culver Pictures. **44** *upper left and upper right* Culver Pictures; inset Courtesy Department Library Services, American Museum of Natural History; *bottom right* The Bettmann Archive. **44-45** *background* Courtesy Department Library Services, American Museum of Natural History. **45** *left* UPI/Bettmann; *right (ship)* National Archives of Canada C24942; *(figure)* National Archives of Canada C6674. **46** *center top* Private Collection/Photographed by Steven Mays; *center bottom* Brown Brothers; *top right* National Archives of Canada C-034443; *bottom right* Library of Congress. **47** *top* National Archives; *circle* Brown Brothers; *remainder* The Bettmann Archive. **48** *left* The Bettmann Archive; *bottom middle* Library of Congress; *buttons* Sophia Smith Collection/Photographed by Mark Sexton. **49** *left* City of Toronto Archives; *right* courtesy Graeme Decarie. **50** *top left* J. Messerschmidt/Bruce Coleman Inc.; *middle left* Canadian Pacific Ltd.; *top right* The Bettmann Archive; *bottom right* Culver Pictures. **51** *left* Theodore Roosevelt Collection, Harvard College Library; *top right* The Bettmann Archive; *bottom right* Culver Pictures. **52** *top left* The Bettmann Archive; *middle left and bottom left* Culver Pictures; *bottom middle* Canada's Sports Hall of Fame; *bottom right* The Bettmann Archive. **53** *left* UPI/Bettmann; *middle top and bottom* The Bettmann Archive; *right* Club de Hockey Canadien, Inc. **54** *top grouping* Culver Pictures; *bottom* The Bettmann Archive; *remainder* US Department of the Interior, National Park Service, Edison National Historic Site. **55** *top* Brown Brothers; *bottom* Culver Pictures. **56** *left* Philadelphia Museum of Art/Louise and Walter Arensberg Collection; *center* Yale Collection of American Literature, Beinecke Rare Book and Manuscript Library, Yale University; *right* Art Gallery of Ontario, gift of Mr. and Mrs. R.W. Finlayson, 1957. **57** *bottom right* Brown Brothers; *remainder* Culver Pictures. **58** *left (grouping)* Collection of William L. Simon; *center* Brown Brothers. **59** *top left* The Bettmann Archive; *top middle* Frank Driggs Collection; *top right* Collection of William L. Simon; *bottom* Museum of The City of New York, The Theater Collection. **60** *top left* Culver Pictures; *top right* Courtesy P.E.I. National Park; *bottom left* Henry W. and Albert A. Berg Collection, The New York Public Library; *bottom right* The Bettmann Archive. **61** *top grouping (Collier's)* The Bettmann Archive; *(Saturday Night)* Metropolitan Toronto Reference Library; *(remainder)* Culver Pictures. **62-63** National Archives of Canada PA1020. **64** *inset* The Granger Collection, New York; *bottom left* The Hulton-Deutsch Collection, London; *right* National Archives of Canada C2082. **65** *top* The Granger Collection, New York; *bottom left* Brown Brothers; *bottom right* National Archives. **66** *top middle* Süddeutscher Verlag; *bottom* UPI/Bettmann; *remainder* Imperial War Museum, London. **67** *top* New York Public Library Picture Collection; *bottom* Imperial War Museum, London. **68** *top (l. to r.)* Imperial War Museum, London; Culver Pictures; Edward Vebell Collection/Photographed by Steven Mays; *bottom* Musée d'Histoire Contemporaine. **68-69** *bottom* Bayerisches Armeemuseum, Germany. **69** *top* Culver Pictures; *middle left* Brown Brothers; *top right* National Archives of Canada; *remainder* Imperial War Museum, London. **70** *all* Imperial War Museum, London. **70-71** *bottom (background)* Imperial War Museum, London. **71** *bottom left* National Archives; *top right* Bruce Bairnsfather Estate, Courtesy of A.E. Johnson Artists' Agents; *remainder* Imperial War Museum, London. **72** *top to bottom:* Culver Pictures; National Archives; Ullstein Bilderdienst, Germany; Popperfoto, London. **72-73** *background* Imperial War Museum, London. **73** *both* Imperial War Museum, London. **74** *top left* Canadian War Museum; *top middle* Musée du Royal 22e Régiment; *top right* National Archives of Canada C33344; *top far right* National Archives of Canada C9271; *bottom middle* National Archives of Canada PA1027; *bottom* National Archives of Canada PA40138. **75** *top* National Archives of Canada PA3587; *inset* National Archives of Canada PA1370; *bottom* National Archives of Canada PA2853. **76** *top (all)* Sovfoto; *bottom* Imperial War Museum. **76-77** *bottom* Robert Hunt Library. **77** *top right* UPI/Bettmann; *center* Edward Vebell Collection; *remainder* Novosti from Sovfoto. **78** *left* Imperial War Museum, London; *right* Hulton Picture Company. **79** *top left* Illustrated London News; *medal* Edward Vebell Collection/Photographed by Steven Mays; *top right* Private Collection; *bottom* UPI/Bettmann. **80** *clockwise from top left:* The Cousley Historical Collections/Photographed by Richard Levy; The Cousley Historical Collections/Photographed by Richard Levy; The Nancy Drew Game™ photograph is used with permission from Hasbro, Inc.; David Galt/Games & Names, New York, NY; Steven Mays/"The Encyclopedia of Collectibles" for Time-Life Books, courtesy Rebus, Inc., NY; David Galt/Games & Names, New York, NY; Derik Murray Photography Inc.; center Monopoly® is a registered trademark of Tonka Corporation ©1936, 1992 Parker Brothers, a subsidiary of Tonka Corporation. All rights reserved. Used with permission. **81** *clockwise from top left:* The Cousley Historical Collections/Photographed by Richard Levy; Milton Bradley Company, a division of Hasbro, Inc., all rights reserved; The Cousley Historical Collections/Photographed by Richard Levy; Milton Bradley Company, a division of Hasbro, Inc.; Nintendo of America, Inc.; Nintendo of America, Inc.; Milton Bradley Company, a division of Hasbro, Inc.; Milton Bradley Company, a division of Hasbro, Inc., all rights reserved. Used with permission; The Cousley Historical Collections/Photographed by Richard Levy; Milton Bradley Company, a division of Hasbro, Inc., all rights reserved; *center* The Cousley Historical Collections/Photographed by Richard Levy. **82** *(l. to r.)* National Archives; The Granger Collection, New York; *remainder* Stock Montage, Inc. **83** *top left* Culver Pictures; *top right* State Archives of Michigan; *bottom* National Archives; *poster grouping (center)* Smithsonian Institution; *(top left)* The Granger Collection, New York; *(top right)* Imperial War Museum, London/Photographed by Angelo Hornak, London; *(bottom left)* Culver Pictures; *(bottom right)* Library of Congress. **84** *top right* Collection of William L. Simon; *remainder* Edward Vebell Collection. **85** *top* Collection of William L. Simon; *remainder* National Archives. **88** *top* Courtesy Graeme Decarie; *middle left* National Archives of Canada C694; *middle right* National Archives of Canada PA24436; *bottom* National Archives of Canada PA170462. **89** *top* City of Toronto Archives (James 873); *middle* National Archives of Canada C95278; *bottom* National Archives of Canada C97753. **90** *top* The Gazette; *top right* National Archives of Canada C33388; *middle* National Archives of Canada C29484; *bottom* Archives of Ontario S-13458. **91** *top* National Archives of Canada C19948; *middle* National Archives of Canada C3624A; *bottom* Concordia University Archives. **92** *top left* Movie Still Archives; *bottom left* Frank Driggs Collection; *bottom right* National Archives of Canada PA5735; *sheet music* Collection of William L. Simon. **93** *top* Brown Brothers; *remainder* Culver Pictures. **94** *helmets* Edward Vebell Collection/Photographed by Steven Mays; *top* National Archives; *bottom right* National Archives of Canada PA1168. **95** *top left* National Archives; *top middle* Harry S. Truman Library; *top right* Imperial War Museum, London; *bottom middle* National Archives of Canada PA1654; *bottom right* National Archives. **96** *left* Col. John McCrae Birthplace Society/photo Jerome Knap; *top* National Archives; *bottom left* Robert Hunt Library; *bottom right* Imperial War Museum, London. **97** *top* Brown Brothers; *bottom* National Archives; inset Popperfoto. **98** *top right* National Archives of Canada PA1613; *remainder* National Archives. **99** *top left* National Archives; *top right* Brown Brothers; *bottom* National Museum of Man/National Museums of Canada. **100-101** ©Equitable Life Assurance of the USA. **102** *top* National Archives; *bottom* ©L'illustration/Sygma. **103** *left* E.T. Archive; *top right* National Archives; *bottom right* Globe Photos. **104** *left* The Bettmann Archive; *top right* National Archives of Canada PA72524. **105** *top* Museum of The City of New York, L1226.3G/Permanent deposit of the Public Works Art Project, through the Whitney Museum of American Art; *bottom middle* The Cousley Historical Collections/Photographed by Steven Mays; *remainder* The Bettmann Archive. **106** *top* UPI/Bettmann; *bottom* Photography Collection, Harry Ransom Humanities Research Center, The University of Texas at Austin. **107** *bottom* Museum of The City of New York, L1226.3G/Permanent deposit of the Public Works Art Project, through the Whitney Museum of American Art; *remainder* UPI/Bettmann. **108** *top left* Memphis Commercial Appeal; *bottom left* Smithsonian Institution; *bottom middle* Steven Laschever; *top right and middle right* UPI/Bettmann; *bottom right* Stock Montage, Inc. **109** *top* Glenbow A626; *bottom* Ohio Historical Society. **110** *left* Provincial Archives of Manitoba N12296; *middle* University of Hartford, Museum of American Political Life; *right* Culver Pictures. **111** *top left* Ontario Archives ACC9912; *top right* Brown Brothers; *bottom* UPI/Bettmann. **112** *clockwise from top* Library of Congress; Brown Brothers; Library of Congress; Rudolph Vetter; Rudolph Vetter; Museum of American Political Life/Photographed by Sally Andersen-Bruce; Culver Pictures. **113** *top left* AP/Wide World Photos; *top right* National Archives of Canada C24304; *middle* National Archives of Canada C75053; *bottom* National Archives of Canada C9064. **114** *top* UPI/Bettmann; *middle* National Archives; *bottom* courtesy Canada Post Corporation. **115** *bottom left* Department of National Defence, Ottawa; *center (stickers)* Smithsonian Institution; *top right* Culver Pictures; *bottom right* Collection of William L. Simon. **116** *top* Brown Brothers; *bottom middle* The Cousley Historical Collections/Photographed by Steven Mays; *bottom right* Canada's Sports Hall of Fame; *remainder* National Baseball Library, Cooperstown, NY. **117** *top left* Hockey Hall of Fame, Toronto; *top middle* Culver Pictures; *top right & bottom left* Brown Brothers; *center* UPI/Bettmann. **118** *top left* Culver Pictures; *top right* Cover-drawing by Rea Irvin ©1925, 1953 The New Yorker Magazine, Inc.; *middle* The Bettmann Archive; *bottom* McCord Museum of Canadian History, Notman Photographic Archives. **119** *top left* courtesy Chatelaine Magazine ©Maclean Hunter Publishing Ltd.; *top right* UPI/Bettmann; *bottom left* Reader's Digest; *bottom middle* Brown Brothers; *Scopes Trial page (left)* Brown Brothers; *(middle)* The Bettmann Archive; *(right)* UPI/Bettmann. **120** *both* Brown Brothers. **121** *top left* ® & ©1994 Tribune Media Services, Inc., All rights reserved; *bottom left and bottom right* The Cousley Historical Collections/Photographed by Steven Mays; *remainder* Piggly Wiggly Corporation. **122** *center* Culver Pictures; *bottom right* UPI/Bettmann; *remainder* The Bettmann Archive. **123** *top left* Culver Pictures; *bottom left* Courtesy of Illustration House, Inc., New York City; *top middle* Brown Brothers; *top right* The Bettman Archive; *bottom right* Library of Congress. **124** *top left* The Bettmann Archive; *middle left* Private Collection; *bottom left* Culver Pictures; *right* Brown Brothers. **125** *top left* UPI/Bettmann; *top middle* The Cousley Historical Collections/Photographed by Steven Mays; *top right* City of Toronto Archives; *bottom* The Bettmann Archive. **126** *top left (Sheik)* Sy Seidman Collection/Culver Pictures; *(Nellie)* Private Collection; *center* Brown Brothers; *top right* Frank Driggs Collection; *bottom left* Private Collection and Collection of William L. Simon/Photographed by Richard Levy. **127** *top to bottom* Frank Driggs Collection; Michael

Ochs Archives/Venice, CA; The Bettmann Archive; UPI/Bettmann Newsphotos. **128** *top left and top right* Culver Pictures; *stars* The Bettmann Archive; *remainder* Brown Brothers. **129** *top left* Movie Still Archives; *top right* Edwin Bower Hesser/The Kobal Collection; *remainder* Culver Pictures. **130** *left* The Bettmann Archive; *middle* Henry Ford Museum & Greenfield Village, Dearborn, Michigan/Photographed by Ted Spiegel; *right* Springer/Bettmann Film Archive. **131** *top* National Archives of Canada PA98735; *bottom left* Brown Brothers; *bottom right* Culver Pictures. **132** *left* Brown Brothers; *inset* National Automobile Museum Library. **133** *top left* National Archives of Canada PA48757; *top right* Automobile Quarterly/Photographed by Nicky Wright; *middle* Musée J. Armand Bombardier; *bottom* Culver Pictures. **134** *left (top to bottom)* SuperStock; ©1988 Cindy Lewis, All rights reserved; Richard Spiegelman. *right (top to bottom)* SuperStock; Richard Spiegelman; ©1989 Cindy Lewis, All rights reserved; ©1992 Cindy Lewis, All rights reserved. **135** *clockwise from top left* ©1986 Cindy Lewis, All rights reserved; ©1982 Cindy Lewis, All rights reserved; ©1991 Cindy Lewis, All rights reserved; Automobile Quarterly; Ford Motor Company; ©1992 Cindy Lewis, All rights reserved; ©1990 Cindy Lewis, All rights reserved; Automobile Quarterly; *center (top)* ©1986 Cindy Lewis, All rights reserved; *(bottom)* ©1991 Cindy Lewis, All rights reserved. **136** *top left* The Granger Collection, New York; *top right* courtesy Barry Callaghan; *bottom left* Brown Brothers; *middle* The Bettmann Archive. **137** *top* Culver Pictures; *bottom left* The Bettmann Archive; *bottom right* ©Al Hirschfeld. Drawing reproduced by special arrangement with Hirschfeld's exclusive representative, The Margo Feiden Galleries Ltd., New York. **138** *top middle* The Bettmann Archive; *top right* Brown Brothers; *bottom left* Banting Museum and Education Centre/Canadian Diabetes Association; *bottom middle* The Bettmann Archive. **139** *top left grouping: (top)* ©1928 by Simon & Schuster Inc., Reprinted by permission of Pocket Books, a division of Simon & Schuster Inc.; *(left)* The Bettmann Archive; *(right)* UPI/Bettmann Newsphotos; *top right* NASA; *bottom* Lee Boltin Picture Library. **140** *background* The Bettmann Archive; *top right* International Museum of Photography at George Eastman House; *bottom left* The Bettmann Archive; *bottom right* B.C. Archives and Records Service. **141** *top left* The Bettmann Archive; *top right* National Archives of Canada C026108; *middle left* Culver Pictures; *bottom* The Bettmann Archive. **142** Brown Brothers; *inset* Culver Pictures. **143** *top right* Notman Photographic Archive; *remainder* Brown Brothers; **144** *top* Museum of American Political Life/University of Hartford; *middle* Culver Pictures; *bottom* The Bettmann Archive. **145** *top left* Dale/Winnipeg Free Press, January 19, 1931; *top right* UPI/Bettmann; *center* Culver Pictures; *bottom right* Brown Brothers. **146-147** Library of Congress. **148** *left* UPI/Bettmann; *right* Glenbow Alberta Institute, Calgary, NB-16-180. **149** *left* Culver Pictures; *right* Collection of William L. Simon. **150** *bottom right* Museum of The City of New York; *remainder* The Bettmann Archive. **151** *top left* Brown Brothers; *box (clockwise from top)* Reprinted with permission Macmillan Publishing Company from "Gone With The Wind" by Margaret Mitchell ©1936 by Macmillan Publishing Company; UPI/Bettmann; Culver Pictures; From "The Grapes of Wrath" by John Steinbeck, ©1939, renewed ©1967 by John Steinbeck, Used by permission of Viking Penguin, a division of Penguin Books USA Inc./Photography courtesy of the Henry W. and Albert A. Berg Collection, The New York Public Library; UPI/Bettmann; Culver Pictures. **152** Culver Pictures. **153** National Archives; *insets top* Glenbow Alberta Institute, Calgary, McD6742; *middle* Library of Congress. **154** *top left* Museum of American Political Life, University of Hartford/Photographed by Steven Laschever; *grouping (top)* The Cousley Historical Collections; *(middle)* Culver Pictures; *(bottom)* Franklin D. Roosevelt Library/©1933, 1961 Peter Arno. **155** *left* courtesy of the New Brunswick Museum 2652; *right* UPI/Bettmann. **156** *bottom* Brown Brothers. **157** *left* Sherman Grinberg Film Library, Inc./Courtesy of the Franklin D. Roosevelt Library; *center* UPI/Bettmann; *right* The Bettmann Archive. **158** *top left* Library of Congress; *bottom left* UPI/Bettmann; *right* National Museum of American Art, Washington, DC/Art Resource, NY. **159** *top* Saskatchewan Archives photograph; *center* Culver Pictures; *bottom right* National Archives of Canada PA36697. **160** *background* Culver Pictures; *clockwise from top* The Kobal Collection; The Kobal Collection; Culver Pictures; Smithsonian Institution; Lester Glassner Collection/Neal Peters. **161** *background* Culver Pictures; *clockwise from top (Astaire & Rogers)* The Kobal Collection; Photofest; Lester Glassner Collection/Neal Peters; Culver Pictures; ©The Walt Disney Company. **162** *top left* Fred Cook Collection; *bottom left* UPI/Bettmann; *bottom middle* The Bettmann Archive; *bottom right* Culver Pictures. **162-163** *background* Frank Driggs Collection. **163** *box (left)* Culver Pictures; *(right)* Fred Cook Collection; *(Ellington)* The Bettmann Archive; *(Goodman)* Culver Pictures; *remainder* Frank Driggs Collection. **164** *top* Canada Wide; *bottom left* Chicago Playing Card Collector, Inc.; *bottom right* UPI/Bettmann. **165** *top left* Provincial Archives of Alberta B1 2636/3; *top right and bottom right* UPI/Bettmann; *middle left* private collection; *oval* UPI/Bettmann Newsphotos; *remainder* AP/Wide World Photos. **166** *top right (poster)* New York Public Library; *(actors)* Culver Pictures; *remainder* Museum of The City of New York/The Theater Collection. **167** *top left* New York Public Library; *top right* Culver Pictures; *remainder* Museum of The City of New York/The Theater Collection. **168** *top left* Brown Brothers; *top right* The Cousley Historical Collections; *bottom* UPI/Bettmann. **169** *top left* AP/Wide World Photos; *grouping (top)* UPI/Bettmann Newsphotos; *(bottom left)* ©1935 Oklahoma Publishing Company, reprinted with permission; *(bottom right)* UPI/Bettmann; *remainder* The Bettmann Archive. **170** *top left* The Bettmann Archive; *bottom left* UPI/Bettmann; *remainder* Brown Brothers. **171** *top* Hake's Americana & Collectibles; *bottom left* UPI/Bettmann; *bottom middle* Brown Brothers; *bottom right* Hake's Americana & Collectibles/Photographed by Richard Levy. **172** *background & lower right* Archives of Labor and Urban Affairs/Wayne State University; *both insets* UPI/Bettmann. **173** *top* Culver Pictures; *bottom* UPI/Bettmann. **174** *bottom left* Museum of American Political Life, University of Hartford/Photographed by Steven Laschever; *remainder* UPI/Bettmann. **175** *top left* Library of Congress; *bottom* National Archives of Canada C19518. **176** *top* The Bettmann Archive; *bottom left* AP/Wide World Photos; *bottom right* Brown Brothers. **177** *both* UPI/Bettmann. **178** *background* Brown Brothers; *car* UPI/Bettmann; *box (top)* Brown Brothers; *(bottom)* UPI/Bettmann. **179** *top left* Brown Brothers; *top right* Smithsonian Institution; *center (top to bottom)* Hake's Americana & Collectibles; Archives Unit, University of Liverpool; Brown Brothers. **180** *middle left* Courtesy of Edith Bel Geddes; *middle right* Brown Brothers; *remainder* UPI/Bettmann. **181** *clockwise from top right* Culver Pictures; City of Vancouver Archives; Courtesy of Western Pennsylvania Conservancy; The Frank Lloyd Wright Archives; Angelo Hornak, London; The Brooklyn Museum/Gift of The Walter Foundation. **182** *clockwise from top right* Library of Congress; Moulin Studio Archives, San Francisco; The Bettmann Archive; Culver Pictures; *circle* H. Armstrong Roberts. **183** *clockwise from top left* Moulin Studio Archives, San Francisco; New York Public Library Picture Collection; Collection of The Queens Museum of Art, New York/Gift of Bob Golby; ©Warren Gofdon/Comstock; Private Collection (3). **184** *top* UPI/Bettmann; *bottom left* AP/Wide World Photos; *bottom middle* UPI/Bettmann; *bottom right* Brown Brothers. **185** *top* UPI/Bettmann; *middle* Paul Dorsey/Life Magazine ©1938 Time Warner Inc.; *bottom* Library of Congress. **186** *left* AP/Wide World Photos; *center (both)* Library of Congress; *right* FPG International. **187** *top* Bundesarchiv; *bottom* UPI/Bettmann; *inset* National Archives. **188-189** Department of National Defence, Ottawa. **190** *left* Roger Schall; *inset* National Archives. **191** *bottom right* Novosti Photo Library; *remainder* Imperial War Museum, London. **192** *top left* National Archives; *top right* Joe Lyndhurst; *bottom* UPI/Bettmann. **193** *top left* ©Canadian War Museum "We Flew With the Heroic Few" by R. Thistle; *inset* Bettmann/Hulton; *bottom left* Robert Hunt Library; *bottom right* Robert Capa/Magnum. **194** *top left* UPI/Bettmann Newsphotos. **194-195** *bottom* National Archives. **195** *left* Department of National Defence, Ottawa, RCN L5524; *right* Department of National Defence, Ottawa. **196** *left* UPI/Bettmann; *right* AP/Wide World Photos. **197** *top* The Cousley Historical Collections/Photographed by James McInnis; *bottom* National Archives. **198** UPI/Bettmann. **199** *top left* Department of National Defence, Ottawa, WRC2428; *top right (roof)* Marc Riboud/Magnum; *middle right* from The Lords of Japan, pg. 10 by Henry Wiencek, Tree Communications, Stonehenge Press; *bottom right* National Archives; *bottom center* Joe Lyndhurst. **200** *left* National Archives; *right* Imperial War Museum, London. **200-201** *background* SuperStock. **201** *box (both)* National Archives; *bottom left* Roger Viollet; *bottom right* Imperial War Museum, London. **202** *top* Royal Canadian Military Institute, Toronto; *bottom* Sovfoto. **202-203** *background* Smithsonian Institution. **203** *left* Sovfoto; *right* ITAR-TASS/Sovfoto. **204** *top left* National Archives; *top right* Jack Novak/Photri; *inset* Smithsonian Institution. **204-205** *bottom* AP/Wide World Photos. **205** *top* US Marine Corps; *bottom* National Archives. **206** *top to bottom* National Archives; National Archives; Roger Schall; AP/Wide World Photos; National Archives. **207** *top* Imperial War Museum, London; *middle* Sovfoto; *bottom* Imperial War Museum, London. **208** *top to bottom* National Archives; National Archives; US Marine Corps. **209** *all* National Archives. **210** *top left* National Archives; *bottom left* Ewing Krainin; *bottom middle* Culver Pictures; *bottom right* Joe Lyndhurst. **211** *top left* John Phillips/Photo Researchers, Inc.; *top middle* ©1944 Bill Mauldin, reprinted with permission of Bill Mauldin; *top right* The Maple Leaf; *middle right* Culver Pictures; *bottom* ©1944 George Baker. **212** *left* National Archives of Canada PA174268; *right* US Army. **213** *top & bottom left* UPI/Bettmann Newsphotos; *top middle & right* Library of Congress. **214** *top* National Archives Trust Fund Board; *bottom* Library of Congress. **215** *top left* Bildarchiv Preussischer Kulturbesitz, Berlin; *top right* Eddie Adams/Sygma; *bottom* UPI/Bettmann. **216** *left grouping* Erich Lessing/Art Resource, N.Y.; *center* UPI/Bettmann; *top right* National Archives; *bottom* UPI/Bettmann. **217** *top left* UPI/Bettmann; *top right* Royal Canadian Navy; *bottom* National Archives. **218** *top left* National Archives of Canada PA24437; *top right* Norman Rockwell Trust; *center* National Archives; *bottom* US Naval Historical Center. **219** *top left* AP/Wide World Photos; *center* National Archives of Canada C33442; *bottom* UPI/Bettmann Newsphotos. **220** *left* National Archives; *middle* AP/Wide World Photos; *right* Canadian War Museum. **221** *page* AP/Wide World Photos; *inset* courtesy Ruth Irwin. **222** National Archives; *inset* Department of National Defence, Ottawa. **223** *top* Bundesarchiv; *bottom* National Archives. **224** *all* National Archives. **225** *top left* AP/Wide World Photos; *bottom center grouping* Submarine Force Library and Museum, Groton, CT; *remainder* National Archives. **226-227** *all* National Archives. **228** *top left* James McInnis; *remainder* Charles Silliman. **228-229** *background* US Army. **229** *top* National Archives; *bottom* National Archives of Canada PA145490. **230** *bottom right* Photri; *remainder* National Archives. **231** *left* UPI/Bettmann Newsphotos; *top middle* Smithsonian Institution; *right* National Archives; *bottom middle* Department of National Defence, Ottawa. **232** *top left* National Archives of Canada PA116139; *bottom left* AP/Wide World Photos; *remainder* Library of Congress. **233** *top left* Frank Driggs Collection; *top right* Lester Glassner Collection/Neal Peters; *bottom left and middle* Courtesy of Carol Nehring; *bottom right* AP/Wide World Photos. **234** *top left* National Archives of Canada PA169339; *bottom* Printed by permission of the Norman Rockwell Family Trust ©1942 The Norman Rockwell Family Trust. **234-235** Brown Brothers. **235** *top* Frank Driggs Collection; *bottom left* Performing Arts Research Center/New York Public Library At Lincoln Center; *bottom middle* The Bettmann Archive; *bottom right* ©Hulton Deutsch Collection Ltd. **236** *top left* National Archives Collection; *top right* National Archives of Canada C19516; *bottom left* National Archives of Canada C29452. **237** *middle left* The Gazette; *top* Canadian War Museum; *center* National Archives of Canada PA107909; *bottom* Archives nationales du Québec, Direction de l'ouest du Québec. **238** *top middle* The Kobal Collection; *top right & center right* Photofest; *bottom left* Culver Pictures; *bottom right* Springer/Bettmann Archive; *remainder* Movie Still Archives. **239** *top (circle & sailors)* Culver Pictures; *(Patton)* Photofest; *center left (Canada Carries On)* National Archives of Canada C115723; *center middle (oval)* Neal Peters Collection; *center right* courtesy Gala Productions; *bottom right* Photofest; *bottom left* Culver Pictures; *remainder* Movie Still Archives. **240** *top* UPI/Bettmann; *center* Keystone Press. **241** *top left (oval)* Ed Clark, Life Magazine ©Time Warner, Inc.; *top right* The Bettmann Archive; *bottom left* Smithsonian Institution; *bottom right* Department of National Defence, Ottawa. **242** *left* AP/Wide World Photos; *bottom* National Archives. **243** *left* The Bettmann Archive; *right* Alfred Eisenstaedt, Life Magazine ©Time Warner, Inc. **244-245** Archive Photos/Camerique. **246** *both* UPI/Bettmann. **246-247** *background* United Nations; *bottom* Brown Brothers. **247** *left* National Archives; *right* National Archives of Canada C020129. **248** *left* UPI/Bettmann; *center* Jack Novak/Photri; *right* Brown Brothers. **249** *top left* National Archives of Canada PA093664; *top right* H. Cartier-Bresson/Magnum; *bottom right* Culver Pictures; *inset* State Historical Society of Missouri, Columbia. **250** *top left* Tim Street-Porter; *top right* FPG International; *bottom right* H. Armstrong Roberts; *inset* UPI/Bettmann. **251** *top left* Ernst Haas/Magnum; *top middle* AP/Wide World Photos; *top right* The Bettmann Archive; *bottom left* UPI/Bettmann Newsphotos; *bottom right* Brown Brothers. **252** *left* The Kansas City Star; *right* David Harris. **253** *left* Culver Pictures; *right* UPI/Bettmann. **254** *top left* Nova Scotia Public Archives PANS N820. **254-255** National Archives of Canada C45079. **255** *top right* courtesy Bata Ltd.; *center right* "Hot Day in Kensington Market" (Toronto), 24" x 30" 1972, William Kurelek, courtesy The Isaacs Gallery, Toronto, and the estate of William Kurelek. **256** *left* Culver Pictures; *right* UPI/Bettmann. **257** *both* UPI/Bettmann. **258** *left* Culver Pictures; *middle* The Bettmann Archive; *right* UPI/Bettmann. **259** *top left* George Rodger/Magnum; *remainder* The Bettmann Archive. **260** *left* Archive Photos; *right* Eve Arnold/Magnum. **260-261** Archive Photos. **261** *top* Photofest; *bottom* ©Ken Bell. **262** *bottom* Photofest; *right* Howard Frank. **263** *top left* Motion Picture and TV Photo Archive; *top right* courtesy Société Radio-Canada; *bottom right* Photofest; *bottom left and middle* Movie Still Archives. **264** *top left* Neal Peters Collection; *top right* Canadian Broadcasting Corporation; *remainder* Movie Still Archives. **265** *top left* Photofest/©Walt Disney Productions; *top middle* Movie Still Archives; *bottom right* Globe Photos; *remainder* Photofest. **266** *left* Magnum; *inset* Brown Brothers. **267** *top left* The Bettmann Archive; *top middle* UPI/Bettmann; *top right* Brown Brothers; *bottom* Movie Still Archives. **268** UPI/Bettmann Newsphotos. **269** *top left* UPI/Bettmann; *top right* National Archives; *bottom* The Bettmann Archive. **270** *top and middle left* The Cousley Historical Collections/Photographed by Steven Mays; *right* UPI/Bettmann; *bottom left* The Cousley Historical Collections. **271** *top left* National Archives of Canada C94168; *remainder* AP/Wide World Photos. **272** *background* Dennis Stock/Magnum; *top* UPI/Bettmann; *bottom left* Elliot Erwin/Magnum; *bottom right* The Bettmann Archive. **273** *top right* ©1953 Marvin Koner/Black Star; *bottom left and right* UPI/Bettmann. **274** *bottom right (Wood)* Cincinnati Art Museum, The Edwin and Virginia Irwin Memorial, ©1994 Estate of Grant Wood/VAGA, New York; *remainder (clockwise from top)* The Cleveland Museum of Art; Columbus Museum of Art, Ohio; Art Resource, N.Y.; The University of Arizona Museum of Art; Emily Carr, "Big Raven" 1931, VAG42.3.11 oil on canvas 87.3 x 114.4 cm, courtesy Vancouver Art Gallery, Emily Carr Trust, photo Trevor Mills. **275** *center* Collection of the Brandywine River Museum, gift of Harry G. Haskell ©Andrew Wyeth; *remainder from top center* The Phillips Collection, Washington, D.C.; The Lavalin Collection of the Musée d'art contemporain de Montréal photo: Richard-Max Tremblay; Collection of the Montreal Museum of Fine Arts, Purchase, Horsely and Annie Townsend Bequest and Anonymous Donor, photo MMFA; Janet Fish; National Gallery of Art, Washington; Krannert Art Museum and Kinkead Pavilion, University of Illinois, Champaign/Photographed by Wilmer Zehr, ©1994 Estate of Stuart Davis/VAGA, New York; "Composition," 1955 by Willem de Kooning, Solomon R. Guggenheim Museum, New York/Photographed by David Heald ©The Solomon R. Guggenheim Foundation, New York. **276** US Air Force Photo; *inset left* Cornell Capa/Magnum; *inset right* Francis Laping/Black Star. **277** *top left* AT & T Archives; *top center and left* UPI/Bettmann; *bottom* The Bettmann Archive. **278** *top both* UPI/Bettmann; *bottom* AP/Wide World Photos. **279** *top middle* Dan Weiner, Courtesy of Sandra Weiner; *bottom* Bob Henriques/Magnum; *right* Karsh/Woodfin Camp & Associates. **280** *left* National Archives of Canada PA112691; *middle top* UPI/Bettmann Newsphotos; *middle bottom* Brown Brothers; *right* UPI/Bettmann. **281** *top left* UPI/Bettmann Newsphotos; *top middle and right* UPI/Bettmann; *bottom* The Bettmann Archive. **282** *left* The Bettmann Archive; *top right* Hake's Americana & Collectibles/Photographed by Steven Mays; *bottom right* Burt Glinn/Magnum. **283** *left* FPG International; *top right* Private Collection/Photographed by Steven Mays, by permission of Little, Brown and Company; *middle right* Private Collection/Photographed by James McInnis, by permission of Simon and Schuster; *bottom right* ©Dennis Hallinan/FPG International. **284** *bottom left* BMI/Michael Ochs Archives, Venice, CA; *middle* Charles Trainor/Globe Photos; *top right* By permission of MCA Records/Photographed by Richard Levy; *middle* Kevin Jordan Collection/Photographed by Richard Levy, by permission of MCA Records; *bottom right* Michael Ochs Archives/Venice, CA. **285** *top left* Kevin Jordan Collection/Photographed by Richard Levy, by permission of Ace Records, Ltd.; *bottom left* Frank Driggs Collection; *middle* Bob Martin/Globe Photos; *inset* By permission of MCA Records/Photographed by Richard Levy; *bottom right* Michael Ochs Archives/Venice, CA. **286** *top left and right* Photofest; *bottom left* Movie Still Archives. **287** *bottom left* Photofest; *remainder* Archive Photos. **288** *left (top three)* Museum of The City of New York/The Theater Collection; *left bottom* Frank Driggs Collection/Photographed by James McInnis;

top right New York Public Library; *bottom right* Museum of The City of New York/The Theater Collection. **289** *inset* Archive Photos; *remainder* Museum of The City of New York//The Theater Collection. **290** *top right* By permission of The Detroit Free Press; *top left* TASS/Sovfoto; *bottom* RIA-Novosti/Sovfoto. **291** *left* Denis Gifford Collection; *right* National Archives; *top inset* Brown Brothers; *bottom inset* NASA. **292** *top left* Eastfoto; *bottom left* UPI/Bettmann; *right* Culver Pictures. **293** *left* Gillhausen/Black Star; *top right* UPI/Bettmann; *bottom right* MTI/Eastfoto. **294** Department of National Defence, Ottawa. **295** *middle* Photri; *remainder* Sovfoto. **296** *left* UPI/Bettmann; *top right* Motorola; *bottom right* Dan McCoy/Rainbow. **297** *top left and center* March of Dimes Birth Defects Foundation; *bottom left* From "The Double Helix" by James D. Watson, Atheneum Press, New York, 1968, pg. 215; *bottom right* AP/Wide World Photos. **298** *top* Elliot Erwitt/Magnum; *bottom* National Archives. **298-299** *top* Chrysler Corporation; background *(highway cloverleaf)* The Bettmann Archive. **299** *top* Volkswagen of America, Inc.; *bottom* The Bettmann Archive. **300** *top left* Eve Arnold/Magnum; *top right* Movie Still Archives; *bottom* UPI/Bettmann Newsphotos. **301** *top left* UPI/Bettmann; *top right* Michael Ochs Archives/Venice, CA; *bottom* Burt Glinn/Magnum. **302-303** James H. Karales/Peter Arnold, Inc. **304** UPI/Bettmann. **305** *top right both* J. Scherachel/Life Magazine ©Time Warner, Inc.; *middle* Duncan Macpherson/Toronto Star; *bottom* Canada Wide. **306** *top* UPI/Bettmann; *bottom* Paul Conklin. **307** *top left* UPI/Bettmann Newsphotos; *top right* Fred Ward/Black Star; *bottom* The Mark Shaw Collection/Photo Researchers, Inc. **308** *right* Fotokhronika/Tass/Sovfoto; *remainder* UPI/Bettmann. **309** *left* New China Pictures/Eastfoto; *right* Volker Krämer/Stern/Black Star. **310** Bob Henriques/Magnum; *inset* Semyon Raskin/Magnum. **311** *top* Rene Burri/Magnum; *bottom* UPI/Bettmann. **312** *left* The Cousley Historical Collections/Photographed by James McInnis; *right* UPI/Bettmann; *bottom* Fred Ward/Black Star. **313** *left* Bettmann Newsphotos; *top right* Gene Daniels/Black Star; *bottom right* UPI/Bettmann. **314** *top* Canada Wide; *bottom* La Presse. **314-315** Centre d'archives Hydro Québec. **315** *top right* George Hunter/Comstock; *bottom middle* National Archives of Canada PA137682; *bottom right* National Archives of Canada PA137864. **316** *left* Flip Schulke/Black Star; *right* Bob Adelman/Magnum. **317** *top left* UPI/Bettmann; *top right* Flip Schulke/Martin Luther King, Jr. Picture Collection/Black Star; *bottom left* Canada Wide; *bottom right* ©1963 Charles Moore/Black Star. **318** *top left* ©1969 John Launois/Black Star; *top right* Bob Fitch/Black Star; *bottom inset* Hicks/FPG International; *bottom* Charles Moore/Black Star. **318-319** Deelan Haun/Black Star. **319** *top* Bob Adelman/Magnum; *bottom* Leonard Freed/Magnum. **320** *top* Photri; *bottom left* ITAR-TASS/Sovfoto; *bottom right* Hake's Americana & Collectibles/Photographed by James McInnis. **321** *all* Photri. **322** *top left* Telesat Canada; *middle right* Fred Ward/Black Star; *remainder* NASA. **323** *top* Photri; *bottom left* Karsh/Woodfin Camp & Associates; *bottom right* Howard Sochurek. **324** *center* ©1993 Cindy Lewis, All rights reserved; *bottom right* Photofest; *remainder* Michael Ochs Archives/Venice, CA. **325** *top* Photos courtesy of Mattel, Inc.; *bottom left* Laufer/Globe Photos; *bottom right* Scheler/Black Star. **326** *left* Kevin Jordan Collection/Photographed by Richard Levy, by permission of Motown Records; *middle right* Canada Wide; *remainder* Lester Glassner Collection/Neal Peters. **326-327** *background* Photofest. **327** *left* Photofest; *top middle* Photofest; *center* Frederic Lewis/Archive Photos; *bottom middle* Steve Paley/Michael Ochs Archives, Venice, CA; *right* Kevin Jordan Collection/Photographed by Richard Levy, by permission of MCA Records. **328** *left* AP/Wide World Photos; *middle* UPI/Bettmann; *right* AP/Wide World Photos. **329** *top middle* Canada Wide; *bottom right* Michael Sullivan/Black Star; *remainder* AP/Wide World Photos. **330** *banana split and turkey* L. Fritz/H. Armstrong Roberts; *Jell-O* H. Armstrong Roberts; *Dagwood* Karen Leeds/The Stock Market; *remainder* James McInnis. **331** *pablum* Museum of Civilization, Ottawa; *coke* The Coca-Cola Company; *ice cream cone* L. Fritz/H. Armstrong Roberts; *spinach ad* The Granger Collection, New York; *TV dinner* Victor Scocozza/FPG International; *fries* Rick Osentowski/Envision; *hot dogs* Brent Bear/H. Armstrong Roberts; *hamburger* R. Kord/H. Armstrong Roberts; *remainder* James McInnis. **332** *left* Roy Cummings/Camera 5; *middle* David Steen/Camera Press, London; *right* Camera 5. **333** *top left* James H. Karales; *top right* William Claxton/Visages; *bottom left* Carl Shiraishi; *bottom right* Archive Photos. **334** *top* Movie Still Archives; *bottom left* CBS, Inc.; *bottom right* Photofest. **335** *top left* Photofest; *remainder* Lester Glassner Collection/Neal Peters. **336** *top left* Museum of The City of New York/The Theater Collection; *inset* Collection of Richard Seidel/Photographed by James McInnis; *bottom left* Photofest; *right* Canada Wide. **337** *top left* Karsh/Comstock; *top right* Sam Siegel; *bottom* Dennis Stock/Magnum. **338** *top right* Peter Max; *remainder* Lisa Law. **339** *top left and bottom left* From *Aquarian Odyssey* ©Don Snyder; *middle left and bottom background* Lisa Law; *buttons* Hake's Americana & Collectibles/Photographed by James McInnis; *bottom right* Herb Green/Michael Ochs Archives/Venice, CA. **340** *top* Larry Burrows/Life Magazine ©Time Warner, Inc.; *inset* Yoichi R. Okamoto; *bottom* AP/Wide World Photos. **341** *top* Larry Burrows/Life Magazine ©Time Warner, Inc.; *bottom* Vietnam News Agency. **342** *top* Co Rentmeester/Time Warner, Inc.; *left inset* UPI/Bettmann; *middle inset* AP/Wide World Photos; *right inset* Larry Burrows/Life Magazine ©Time Warner, Inc; *bottom* National Archives. **343** *top* Jack Kightlinger/LBJ Library Collection; *center* Canada Wide; *right* AP/Wide World Photos; *bottom* AP/Wide World Photos. **344** *top left* The Andy Warhol Foundation for the Visual Arts, Inc./Art Resource, N.Y.; *bottom left* Burt Glinn/Magnum; *middle* courtesy Sony Music Canada; *bottom right* Collection of Richard Fox/Photographed by James McInnis. **345** *top left* Collection of Richard Fox/Photographed by James McInnis; *middle left* Fred W. McDarrah; *bottom left* Scala/Art Resource, N.Y.; *top right* Roy Lichtenstein; *bottom right* Charles Moore/Black Star. **346** *top left* UPI/Bettmann; *top right* UPI/Bettmann; *bottom* John Launois/Black Star. **347** *top left* Bernard Gotfryd/Woodfin Camp & Associates; *bottom right* Hiroji Kubota/Magnum; *top right* UPI/Bettmann; *bottom* Nacio Jan Brown/Black Star. **348** *left* Saskatchewan Archives Board; *right* Comstock. **349** *top right* Canada Wide; *remainder* Canapress. **350-351** Wally McNamee/Woodfin Camp & Associates. **352** *left* Aislin, The Gazette; *right* Canada Wide. **353** *middle* Canada Wide; *remainder* Canapress. **354** UPI/Bettmann; *inset* Fred Ward/Black Star. **355** *left* AP/Wide World Photos; *center* Michael Abramson/Liaison Agency; *right* UPI/Bettmann Newsphotos. **356** *top* Bettmann; *middle* AP/Wide World Photos; *bottom* US Air Force. **357** *left* UPI/Bettmann; *top right* Reuters/Bettmann; *bottom right* Demylder/Gamma Liaison. **358** *right* J.P. Laffont/Sygma; *crooks (l. to r.)* UPI/Bettmann Newsphotos; J.P. Laffont/Sygma; UPI/Bettmann; UPI/Bettmann; UPI/Bettmann; UPI/Bettmann; Fred Ward/Black Star. **359** *top left* J.P. Laffont/Sygma; *bottom left* David Burnett/Contact Press Images; *bottom middle* AP/Wide World Photos; *bottom right* David Burnett/Contact Press Images. **360** *top left* Parks Canada; *top right* Canadian Museum of Civilization; *bottom left* Keith Gunner/Bruce Coleman Inc.; *bottom right* Jeff Foott. **360-361** *background* NASA. **361** *top left* Hake's Americana & Collectibles/Photographed by James McInnis; *top right* Camilla Smith/Rainbow; *bottom left* UPI/Bettmann; *bottom right* Bernard Gotfryd/Woodfin Camp & Associates. **362** *top* Dennis Brack/Black Star; *bottom left* Coco McCoy/Rainbow; *bottom right* Associated Press/Time Picture Syndication. **363** *top* courtesy Syncrude; *bottom* George Herben/Woodfin Camp & Associates. **364** *top left* Harold Krieger/New York Magazine; *top right* Sandy Solmon/Globe Photos; *remainder* Paul Fusco/Magnum. **365** *top* Andy Levin; *bottom left* Bill Stanton/Magnum; *bottom right* Globe Photos. **366** *top left* James McInnis; *top right* Photofest; *bottom left* Lee Childers/Neal Peters; *bottom right* Ormond Gigli/Time Magazine. **367** *left* Montgomery Ward; *top middle* Al Freni; *remainder* James McInnis. **368** *clockwise from top left* The Cousley Historical Collections/Photographed by James McInnis; Ellis Herwig/Stock, Boston; Philip Gould; Doug Wilson/Black Star; Costa Manos/Magnum. **368-369** *(ships)* Kenneth Garrett/Woodfin Camp & Associates. **369** *clockwise from top* Wally McNamee/Woodfin Camp & Associates; Wally McNamee/Woodfin Camp & Associates; Salvatore C. DiMarco, Jr.; Richard Howard; Wally McNamee/Woodfin Camp & Associates. **370** Canapress. **371** *top* Canapress; *middle right* Canada Wide; *bottom* Peter Bregg/Canapress. **372** Black Star. **373** *left* O. Franken/Sygma; *top inset* Ledru/Sygma; *bottom inset* C. Spengler/Sygma; *right* Canapress. **374** *top and bottom left* Photofest; *bottom right* Frank Driggs Collection. **374-375** Michael Ochs Archives/Venice, CA. **375** *top left and bottom left* Photofest; *top right* Kevin Jordan Collection/Photographed by James McInnis; *middle right* Brian D. McLaughlin/Michael Ochs Archives/Venice, CA.; *bottom right* Michael Ochs Archives/Venice, CA. **376** *top left and bottom left* Movie Still Archives; *top right* Stefani Kong/Sygma; *bottom right* Lester Glassner Collection/Neal Peters. **376-377** *background* James McInnis. **377** *both* Movie Still Archives. **378** *both* Movie Still Archives. **379** *top left* Photofest; *top right* Thomas Arma/Photofest; *bottom right* Howard Frank/Personality Photos, Inc.; *remainder* Movie Still Archives. **380** *left (top to bottom)* Library of Congress; Robert McElroy/Woodfin Camp & Associates; Paul Fusco/Magnum; *right* Werner Wolff/Black Star; *pendant* The Cousley Historical Collections/Photographed by James McInnis. **381** *top left* UPI/Bettmann; *top right* Diana Mara Henry; *top center* Library of Congress; *bottom center* Abigail Heyman. **382** *top* Luc Simon Perrault/La Presse; *bottom* Canapress. **382-383** Canapress. **383** *top* Canada Wide; *bottom* M. Graston/Windsor Star. **384** *top left* Howard Sochurek; *top right* John Marmaras/Woodfin Camp & Associates; *bottom* Lester Sloan/Woodfin Camp & Associates. **385** *top left* Jim Olive/Peter Arnold, Inc.; *top right* Dan McCoy/Black Star; *bottom left* Gould/DeAnza/Peter Arnold, Inc.; *bottom right* Howard Sochurek/John Hillelson Agency. **386-387** Rob Matheson/The Stock Market. **388** *left* Ronald Reagan Library/National Archives; *right* The Bettmann Archive. **389** *top* Ronald Reagan Library/National Archives; *bottom* Photofest; *left* The Bettmann Archive; *right* Movie Still Archives. **390** *top* Canapress; *bottom left* D. Goldberg/Sygma; *bottom middle* Gianfranco Gorgoni/Contact Press Images; *bottom right* Fred Ward/Black Star. **391** *both* Ronald Reagan Library/National Archives. **392** *top left* Erica Lansner/Photoreporters; *bottom left* Dan Lecca/GQ Magazine; *magazines* Courtesy of Harper's Bazaar, Photography by Patrick Demarchelier, and GQ Magazine, Photography by Wayne Maser; *center* Karl Lagerfeld; *bottom right* Theo Westenberger/Gamma Liaison. **393** *left* Luigi Cazzaniga; *center top & middle* Courtesy of Timberland, Inc.; *bottom* Karl Lagerfeld; *top left* L. Norovitch/Gamma Liaison. **394** *left* Susan Meiselas/Magnum; *right* ©1987 Twentieth Century Fox Film Corp. **394-395** Jonathan Levine/Onyx. **395** *left* DPA Photoreporters; *right* Andrew Popper. **396** *top (l. to r.)* Joyce Ravid/Onyx; UPI/Bettmann; Canapress; Rick Maiman/Sygma; *bottom* Random House Inc. **397** *top left* James Colburn/Photoreporters; *top right* John Roca/LGI; *bottom* Enrico Ferorelli. **398** *top left* John Ficara/Sygma; *top right* The White House; *bottom* Courtesy of the Bush Presidential Materials Project. **399** *top left* Canapress; *top right* Larry Downing/Woodfin Camp & Associates; *bottom (l. to r.)* Jeffrey Markowitz/Sygma; P. LeSegretian/Sygma; D. Aubert/Sygma; Jeffrey Markowitz/Sygma. **400** *top* Turner Broadcasting; *bottom left* Paramount Pictures/EC; *bottom right* Chris Haston, NBC/Globe Photos. **401** *top left* NBC/Globe Photos; *top middle* Kimberly Butler/LGI; *top right* Paul Morse/LGI; *bottom left* Karen Kuehn/Matrix; *bottom right* Barry Slobin/Motion Picture & TV Photo Archive. **402** *top left* NBC/Globe Photos; *top middle* Motion Picture & TV Photo Archive; *top right* Courtesy of NBC, Inc.; *bottom right* Courtesy of CBS, Inc.; *bottom left* Everett Collection/Paramount Pictures. **403** *top left* Neal Peters Collection; *bottom left* Motion Picture & TV Photo Archive; *center* ©CBS Inc.; *bottom right* Canapress. **404** *top left* Canapress; *top right* Craig Fujii/The Seattle Times; *bottom left* George Nikitin/Sygma; *bottom right* Harald Sund. **405** *top right* Canapress; *center* Martha Stanitz; *bottom* Les Stone/Sygma. **406** Ken Regan/Camera 5; *bottom* Elkoussy/Sygma. **407** *top left* Vintage Books, a division of Random House; *top right* Alon Reininger/Contact Press Images; *bottom left* Lynn Goldsmith/LGI; *bottom right* Peter Menzel. **408** *left* Ken Regan/Camera 5; *top* ©David Gahr; *inset* Neal Peters Collection; *oval* Richard Young/Rex/Ponopresse. **409** *top left* Michael Benabib/Retna Pictures; *middle left* Alice Arnold/LGI Photo Agency; *bottom left* J.L. Atlan/Sygma; *top right* Bruce Malone/Retna Pictures; *bottom right* Herb Ritts/Warner Brothers Records. **410** *top left* ©David Gahr; *top right* Ross-Marino/Sygma; *bottom left* Globe Photos; *bottom right* Paul Valesco/Wide World Photos. **411** *top left* Martha Swope; *top right* Marc Thibodeau/Merle Frimark; *bottom right* Playbill, Inc.; *bottom center* Boneau/Bryan-Brown. **412** *top left* A. Tannenbaum/Sygma; *top right* Betty Press/Woodfin Camp & Associates; *bottom left* Peter Jordan/Network Matrix; *bottom right* Luc Delahaye/Sipa/Ponopresse. **413** *top left* J. Langevin/Sygma; *bottom left* Sygma; *top right* Kenneth Jarecke/Contact Press Images; *bottom right* ©1991 Cable News Network, Inc., All Rights Reserved. **414** *top right and center* The Bettmann Archive; remainder (*clockwise from top left*) The Bettmann Archive; Culver Pictures; M. Theriot/H. Armstrong Roberts; Pan American World Airways; FPG International; Notman Photographic Archives/McCord Museum. **415** *Ski-Doo* Bombardier; *remainder* (*clockwise from top left*) FPG International; UPI/Bettmann; Norman Rockwell Paintings Trust; Dick Davis/Photo Researchers, Inc.; Tony Stone Worldwide; Bob Abraham/The Stock Market; Bill Varie/The Image Bank; Renee Lynn/Photo Researchers; Renee Lynn/Photo Researchers, Inc.; Library of Congress. **416** *top* Gregory Heisler/The Image Bank; *bottom* Lizzie Himmel. **417** Schneeberger, Johnson & Peritore/National Geographic Society; *left inset* Michelle McDonald Picture Group; *right inset* Canapress. **418** *top left* Panasonic Company/Division of Matsushita Electric Corporation of America; *bottom left* Craig Blankenhorn/Black Star; *right* Peter Menzel. **419** *top left* Richard Pan/The Image Bank; *top right* Peter Menzel; *bottom* Jeffrey Aaronson/Network Aspen. **420** *top* Alexandra Avakian/Woodfin Camp & Associates; *bottom* Francis Apesteguy/Gamma-Liaison. **421** *top* S. Franklin/Magnum; *bottom left* Wesolowski/Sygma; *bottom right* Eric Bouvet/Gamma-Liaison. **422** *left* Peter Turnley/Black Star; *center* J. Groch/Sygma; *right* B. Bisson /Sygma. **423** *top left* Peter Turnley/Black Star; *top right* Deborah Copaken/Contact Press Images; *bottom left* Alexandra Avakian/Contact Press Images; *bottom right* Yuri Ivanon/Time Picture Syndication. **424** *left* Gilbert Iundt/Temp Sport/Ponopresse; *top right* Canada Wide; *bottom right* David Madison/Duomo. **425** *top left* Steve Powell/Allsport; *top right* Michael Layton/Duomo; *center* Rick Steart/Allsport; *bottom left* Tony Duffy/Allsport; *bottom right* Focus On Sports. **426** *top left* Tony Stone Worldwide; *oval* James Colburn/Photoreporters, Inc.; *bottom (l. to r.)* Mark Sennet/Visages; Steven Mark Needham/Envision; *(bottles)* Michael A. Keller/The Stock Market; *top right* Thomas Del Brase; *bottom right* Al Satterwhite/The Image Bank. **427** *top* Tobey Sanford; *middle right* Ray Fairall/Photoreporters; *bottom right* Douglas Dubler/LGI. **428** *top left* Robert McElroy/Woodfin Camp & Associates; *top right* James McInnis; *bottom* Everett Collection/Warner Brothers, Inc. **429** *bottom* Globe Photos; *top right* James McInnis; *middle right* Ponopresse; *bottom inset* The Kobal Collection. **430** *top left* Tim Davis/David Madison Photography; *middle left* Alec Pytlowany/Masterfile; *top right* Mike Powell/Allsport; *bottom* William R. Sallaz/Duomo. **431** *top right* Nintendo of America, Inc.; *bottom left* Jacques Chenet/Woodfin Camp & Associates; *bottom middle* Lisa Rose/Globe Photos; *bottom right* Photoreporters, Inc. **432** *top left* Mike Yamashita/Woodfin Camp & Associates; *bottom left* Steve Liss/Time Magazine; *top right* Steven Rubin/J.B. Pictures for Time. **432-433** Kaj Svensson/Viewpoints West Photofile Ltd. **433** *top left* Canapress; *bottom right* James Balog/Black Star. **434** *left* John Ficara/Sygma; *top right* Robert F. Kusel/Sygma; *bottom right* P.P. Poulin/Ponopresse. **435** *left* Carlos Humberto/Contact Press Images; *center* Houghton Mifflin Company; *right* P.P. Poulin/Ponopresse. **436** *top left and bottom right* Peter Menzel; *top right* NASA/Photo Researchers, Inc.; *bottom left* Kevin Fleming. **437** *top left* Adam Hart-Davis/Science Photo Library; *top right* SuperStock; *bottom left* Peter Menzel; *bottom right* Photri. **438** The Bettmann Archive. **440** Collection of the Museum of American Folk Art, New York, Gift of Anne Baxter Klee. **441** Culver Pictures. **442** Culver Pictures. **445** The Bettmann Archive. **446** *both* Culver Pictures. **448** The Bettmann Archive. **449** Library of Congress. **450** The Granger Collection, New York. **453** *left* UPI/Bettmann Newsphotos; *right* Culver Pictures. **454** Pete Saloutos/The Stock Market. **457** UPI/Bettmann. **459** Movie Still Archives. **460** Photofest. **462** Bill Brooks/Masterfile. **463** Lester Glasner Collection/Neal Peters. **464** UPI/Bettmann Newsphotos. **465** New York Public Library/Theater Collection. **466** George C. Marshall Research Foundation. **467** UPI/Bettmann Newsphotos. **468** The Bettmann Archive. **469** AP/Wide World Photos. **470** The Bettmann Archive. **471** ©1949 New York Newsday. **472** UPI/Bettmann. **473** Movie Still Archives. **474** National Archives of Canada PA128819. **475** UPI/Bettmann. **476** New York Daily News. **477** AP/Wide World Photos. **478** Canapress. **480** *left* UPI/Bettmann; *right* UPI/Bettmann Newsphotos. **483** NASA. **484** Wally McNamee/Woodfin Camp & Associates. **486** Canapress. **487** Focus On Sports, Inc. **489** Ellen Pines Sheffield/Woodfin Camp & Associates. **490** Howard Sochurek/Woodfin Camp & Associates. **491** US Naval Academy. **493** Dirck Halstead/Gamma Liaison. **494** Sygma Paris. **495** Geltzer & Company; *inset (ballgame)* David Madison/Duomo. **496** David Gamble/Sygma. **497** Ponopresse. **498** Mitsubishi; Movie Still Archives. **499** Camerique/H. Armstrong Roberts. **501** AP/Wide World Photos.

Efforts have been made to reach the holder of the copyright for each picture. In several cases, these sources have been untraceable, for which we offer our apologies.

INDEX

*Page numbers in **bold** type refer to illustrations and captions; those in brackets [ ], to charts.*